Casebook and Study Guide

Abnormal Psychology
Third Edition

David L. Rosenhan and E. P. Seligman

Casebook and Study Guide

Abnormal Psychology
Third Edition

David L. Rosenhan and Martin E. P. Seligman

STEVEN L. DUBOVSKY
University of Colorado

LISA D. BUTLER
Stanford University

W. W. NORTON & COMPANY • **NEW YORK / LONDON**

Grateful acknowledgment is extended to the holders of copyright for granting permission to reprint excerpts on the following pages: *p. 17*, Steinmann, A. The psychopharmacological treatment of Anna O. In M. Rosenbaum & M. Muroff (Eds.), *Anna O.: Fourteen contemporary reinterpretations.* Copyright ©1984 Free Press. Reprinted by permission; *pp. 111, 112, 113*, Plath, Sylvia, *The Bell Jar,* New York: Bantam Books, 1963.

Cover illustration: Will Barnet, *Nightfall,* 1979, oil on canvas, 40½ × 70½", private collection. Courtesy of the artist.

ISBN 0-393-96658-5

W. W. Norton & Company, Inc., 500 Fifth Avenue, New York, N.Y. 10110
W. W. Norton & Company Ltd., 10 Coptic Street, London WC1A 1PU

1 2 3 4 5 6 7 8 9 0

CONTENTS FOR THE CASEBOOK

INTRODUCTION   xiii

CASE 1 [CHAPTER 1]   The Damm Family: Homeless in America   1

Discussion of a family made homeless by economic adversity raises questions about how to differentiate normal from abnormal adaptations to stress.

CASE 2 [CHAPTER 2]   Wolf Madness   6

Lycanthropy (werewolfism) illustrates the influence of culture and religious factors on psychological diagnosis.

CASE 3 [CHAPTER 2]   What Goes Around Comes Around: Witchcraft in America   9

A review of some of the clinical ramifications of "recovery" of memories of having been victims of ritual, bizarre, or satanic abuse during childhood.

CASE 4 [CHAPTERS 3–5]   Anna O. from Different Perspectives   13

A discussion of ways in which the first case described by Sigmund Freud and Josef Breuer, the founders of psychoanalysis, would be understood by theoreticians of different persuasions. Psychological, biological and behavioral perspectives on the case are discussed.

CASE 5 [CHAPTER 6]   The Office as Laboratory: Clinical Applications of the Experimental Method   19

How to interpret psychotherapy outcome research in choosing a treatment for depression.

CASE 6 [CHAPTER 7]   Projective Test Protocols   25

Results from two types of projective tests, the Rorschach and the Thematic Apperception Tests, illustrate what these kinds of tests tell us about the person who completes them.

CASE 7 [CHAPTER 8]   Dread of Church Steeples: Specific Phobia   31

A classical report of a patient with a phobia of church steeples demonstrates the psychology of phobias of

uncommon situations and discusses the significance of
common specific phobias such as fears of snakes and spiders.

**CASE 8 [CHAPTER 8]   The Hidden Crisis: Masked Post-
Traumatic Stress Disorder   35**

How to recognize post-traumatic stress disorder when the
symptoms are not obvious.

**CASE 9 [CHAPTER 9]   The Insistent Ideas of Miss M.: Obsessive-
Compulsive Disorder   39**

A classical case of obsessive-compulsive disorder described in
the psychological literature illustrates typical symptoms and describes older and modern treatment approaches.

**CASE 10 [CHAPTER 9]   George's Magic Bullet: Obsessive-
Compulsive Disorder   44**

An unusual case of a man whose obsessive-compulsive disorder
seems to have been cured by a self-inflicted gunshot wound to
the head.

CASE 11 [CHAPTER 9]   Mr. P.'s Travels: Dissociative Fugue   46

The case of a man described around the turn of the century
teaches us why people dissociate large segments of mental experience, sometimes forgetting who they are.

**CASE 12 [CHAPTER 9]   The Two Faces of Eve: Genuine and
Pseudo Multiple Personality Disorder   50**

Two patients with similar symptoms illustrate the difference
between multiple personality disorder developing spontaneously
and a condition that mimics multiple personality but actually is
an entirely different condition.

**CASE 13 [CHAPTER 10]   Psychosomatic Medicine: The Mirsky
Ulcer Study   55**

A discussion of the strengths and weaknesses of one of the first
formal studies to show that the mind can directly harm the body.

**CASE 14 [CHAPTER 10]   Hopelessness: The Interface between
Research and Practice   58**

The real-life complexities of research show how to decide
whether hopelessness can make physical illness more dangerous.

**CASE 15 [CHAPTER 11]   Comprehensive Treatment of Unipolar
Depression   62**

A demonstration of cognitive and interpersonal therapies for depression.

CASE 16 [CHAPTER 11]   Moods and Great Men: Bipolar Disorder   66

Descriptions of famous people who may have had bipolar (manic-depressive) disorder show us some of the ways in which mood influences public behavior.

CASE 17 [CHAPTER 12]   Causative Factors and Outcome in Schizophrenia   71

A demonstration of the additive effects of psychotherapy, family therapy, and antipsychotic drugs in the treatment of schizophrenia.

CASE 18 [CHAPTER 12]   The Genain Quadruplets: Schizophrenia   75

The interaction between genetic, environmental, and learned factors explains why four children who were genetically identical had drastically different forms of schizophrenia.

CASE 19 [CHAPTER 12]   Does a Diagnosis of Schizophrenia Tell the Whole Story?   81

The strengths and weaknesses of the modern diagnostic system are illustrated by the contrast between the diagnosis of the disorder based on signs and symptoms with an understanding of the person with the disorder.

CASE 20 [CHAPTER 13]   Please Tread on Me: Paraphilia   87

The description of a classical paraphila (misdirected sexual desire) provides insight into the psychology and treatment of a group of disorders that impair sexual adaptation.

CASE 21 [CHAPTER 13]   What's the Real Illness?   90

Just because homosexual patients consult therapists for emotional problems does not mean that being homosexual is the emotional problem. This case demonstrates that we should not attribute the cause of every symptom in a homosexual patient to the person's sexual orientation.

CASE 22 [CHAPTER 14]   Famous Substance Abusers   94

What to do about substance-related disorders in famous people, colleagues, and friends.

CASE 23 [CHAPTER 14]   Does Treating Stress Cure Alcoholism?   99

Does treating a second disorder in an alcoholic make the person stop drinking?

CASE 24 [CHAPTER 15]   The Mask of Sanity: Antisocial Personality Disorder   104

A practical guide to the treatment of patients whose personality is organized around lack of loyalty to society, law, and other people.

CASE 25 [CHAPTER 15]   The Agony and the Ecstasy: Borderline Personality Disorder   109

The life and death of poet Sylvia Plath illustrate the agony and self-hatred that reside at the core of a common personality disorder.

CASE 26 [CHAPTER 16]   Predicting the Unpredictable: Childhood Emotional Disorders   115

A glimpse at the range of childhood disorders and their treatment illustrated by cases of childhood depression and childhood bipolar disorders.

CASE 27 [CHAPTER 16]   The Hollow Idol: Anorexia Nervosa   122

A case of anorexia nervosa described 300 years ago illustrates the timelessness of what has been considered a modern disorder.

CASE 28 [CHAPTER 16]   Nate G.: Down's Syndrome   126

Down's syndrome, a common cause of mental retardation, does not preclude living a rewarding and productive life. What are the clinical and ethical roadblocks to achieving this goal?

CASE 29 [CHAPTER 17]   Mind and Brain: Alzheimer's Disease   130

Alzheimer's disease, a progressive neurological illness, is untreatable, but this does not mean that psychologists cannot make a substantial contribution to the quality of life of Alzheimer's patients.

CASE 30 [CHAPTER 17]   Witty Ray: Tourette's Syndrome   135

Mind-body interactions in Tourette's disorder, a malfunction of movement centers in the brain with profound effects on the personality.

CASE 31 [CHAPTER 18]   Give Me Liberty and Give Me Death: Involuntary Treatment   139

Philosophical debates about involuntary treatment become much more complex when dealing with patients who will die if they do not receive proper treatment. This case illustrates the legal and moral dimensions of the debate applied to a real patient.

CASE 32 [CHAPTER 18]   Sale of the Century: Adversarial Psychology   145

How reliable is an expert opinion when the expert is paid by proponents of one side of a complex clinical issue?

CASE 33 [CHAPTER 19]   So Many Psychotherapies, So Little Time   150

There is no single best treatment for most mental disorders and most of the time treatments are combined. This case illustrates a number of psychological, social, and biological approaches that could be used to cure anxiety.

CONTENTS FOR THE STUDY GUIDE

INTRODUCTION   xxv

PART 1   The Nature and History of Abnormality

CHAPTER 1   The Meanings of Abnormality   157
CHAPTER 2   Abnormality across Time and Place   166

PART 2   Models and Treatments of Abnormality

CHAPTER 3   The Biomedical Model   177
CHAPTER 4   Psychodynamic and Existential Approaches   189
CHAPTER 5   The Learning Models: Behavioral and Cognitive Approaches   209

PART 3   Investigating and Diagnosing Abnormality

CHAPTER 6   Investigating Abnormality   225
CHAPTER 7   Psychological Assessment and Classification   239

PART 4   Anxiety and Psychosomatic Disorders

CHAPTER 8   Phobia, Panic, and the Anxiety Disorders   253
CHAPTER 9   Obsession, Hysteria, and Dissociation: Anxiety Inferred   269
CHAPTER 10   Health Psychology   283

PART 5   Depression and the Schizophrenias

CHAPTER 11   Depression and Suicide   296
CHAPTER 12   The Schizophrenias   316

PART 6   Social and Interpersonal Disorders

CHAPTER 13   Sexual Dysfunction and Sexual Disorder   334
CHAPTER 14   Psychoactive Substance Use Disorders   349
CHAPTER 15   Personality Disorders   364

PART 7   Abnormality across the Lifespan

CHAPTER 16   Childhood Disorders and Mental Retardation   376
CHAPTER 17   Disorders of the Nervous System and Psychopathology   389

PART 8   Abnormality, the Law, and Choosing a Psychotherapy

CHAPTER 18   The Law and Politics of Abnormality   404
CHAPTER 19   A Consumer's Guide to Psychological Treatment   414

Introduction to the Casebook

Abnormal psychology is one of the most interesting, but also one of the most challenging, courses offered in an undergraduate curriculum. The field deals with everyday concepts, but it uses a unique jargon. We are supposed to learn how to differentiate the pathological from the normal, but at first glance it seems as if the line between the two is very thin and most of us are not always on the safe side of that line. We read about problems that seem dramatic, but we cannot imagine what they would look like in real life. Without actually seeing people who have the conditions describe in the course, it is even more difficult to imagine how they are helped. Yet abnormal psychology provides a foundation for treatment as well as description.

The third edition of *Abnormal Psychology* by David Rosenhan and Martin Seligman is a comprehensive description of the field. To help you to master the material in the textbook, this casebook provides more detailed descriptions of some of the ways the conditions described in the textbook translate into clinical psychopathology. The cases correspond to each of the chapters in *Abnormal Psychology* and are designed to amplify the concepts presented in those chapters. Each case is accompanied by questions that are designed to stimulate further thought on the topic presented, but better questions undoubtedly will occur to you as you proceed through the course. The cases presented here are not theoretical. Each one is drawn from actual clinical practice or from the published literature on clinical practice. In a few instances, biographies of public figures are used to illustrate clinical points. There is also a description of the treatment that was utilized in each case. Much of the time, the outcome of treatment was positive, but sometimes it was not. At times, a global cure was achieved, and at other times the goals were more circumscribed. You may find yourself satisfied with the results in some cases and not in others. This is just what happens in real life, and discussing how you feel about the way the case turned out may help to further amplify your understanding of the topic. Your instructor will be in a good position to help you with this task.

The last edition of this casebook was written by Christopher Peterson of the University of Michigan. I have revised Cases 1, 2, 4, 6, 7, 9, 10, 11, 16, 18, 19, 20, 22, 27, 28, and 30 from Professor Peterson's work. These cases, which are drawn from writings in the field and in one case from a description of psychological test findings, contain classic descriptions of pathological states and their therapies. While they are timeless, I have updated most of them and added my own perspective, so that readers of a previous edition may not recognize them. Cases 22, 29, and 34 in the last edition of this casebook have been omitted because circumstances have rendered them somewhat less timely.

Cases 3, 5, 8, 12, 13, 14, 15, 17, 21, 23, 24, 25, 26, 29, 31, 32, and 33 are entirely new to this edition. One of these cases is based on the writings and a brief autobiography of the poet Sylvia Plath. The rest of the cases come from my own practice. I have disguised them sufficiently to prevent anyone from recognizing them as individuals, but the problems, the treatments, and the outcomes, all reflect what actually happened. You will therefore have an opportunity to see just how theory translates into practice. Toward the end of the casebook, I have included a few cases that illustrate social, economic, and political pressures, in addition to clinical complexities, that make the real-life practice of treating psychological ills so challenging. I hope that your enjoyment, as well as your understanding, of the field of abnormal psychology will be enriched by your experience with my patients.

I am grateful to Don Fusting for his encouragement and help with this and other projects, and to my family for putting up with me as I added this casebook to my labors. I would also like to acknowledge the influence of Jack Wasinger, D.D.S., M.A., Ph.D., a psychologist for all seasons.

Steven L. Dubovsky
Denver, CO
January 1995

Introduction to the
Study Guide

This study guide is intended to help you understand the material presented in the third edition of *Abnormal Psychology* by David Rosenhan and Martin Seligman. The material here is a substitute neither for the textbook nor for your time and energy. However, it should help make *Abnormal Psychology* familiar and comfortable. The study guide sections correspond to chapters in the textbook, and you should read and study them in conjunction with the relevant material in *Abnormal Psychology*. The bulk of this third edition was adapted from the excellent second edition *Study Guide* developed by Chris Peterson. I wish to thank David Rosenhan for offering me this wonderful opportunity, Donald Fusting for his encouragement and patience, and Robert W. Garlan for his considerable help in preparing the "Central Concepts" sections as well as his creative suggestions for, and assistance with, other sections.

Each chapter in the study guide has several sections: "Chapter Overview," "Essential Terms," "Central Concepts," "Sample Exam," (multiple-choice questions), "Self-Test (fill-in questions), "Matching Items," "Short Answer Questions," "Tying It Together," "Further Readings," "Term-Paper Topics," and "Exercises." These sections serve several purposes: (a) aiding you in acquiring the important ideas in each chapter; (b) preparing you for course examinations; (c) helping you to see the big picture presented in *Abnormal Psychology*; and (d) directing you toward further activity: reading, writing, and doing. Let me comment briefly on the sections contained in each chapter of this study guide.

Chapter Overview

The chapter overviews describe the purpose of the chapter and its major topics so that you will know what to expect as you read the textbook. You may find it useful to read the chapter overview before you read the chapter itself. The study guide's overviews have been written independently of the textbook's summaries, so that you will have two points of view about each chapter's important ideas.

Essential Terms

Students are often overwhelmed by the vocabulary of psychology. Some of these terms seem familiar; we use them in everyday conversation. Other terms seem esoteric; we must write them down to remember their meanings and even how to spell them. And yet other terms may seem downright contrary. But the terminology of abnormal psychology is not just jargon. It is the way in which the understanding provided by psychology is expressed; in a sense, it *is* the understanding. Imagine watching a baseball game and not knowing what strikes or balls are, or what an infield fly, a balk, or a designated hitter is. You are not watching the same game as an individual who has mastered baseball terminology. The same is true of psychology. When its terminology is mastered, psychology looks different—richer, more coherent, and more interesting.

For this reason I have extracted from each chapter the important terms and provided a brief definition and page reference for each. In most cases, I have tried to use the phrasing of the textbook in explaining a term. However, the best way for you to learn terms is to express them, in your own words. As you read the textbook, you may wish to compile your own list of definitions. Another good way to master terms is to think of your own example for each one. If you think of *positive reinforcement* as an environmental event that increases the frequency of an operant, you understand this term on an abstract level. If you also think of *positive reinforcement* as exemplified by the Hershey bar (with almonds) you buy after studying in the library for three hours, you will have an additional understanding of this term.

Central Concepts

This section expands upon and clarifies some of the central conceptual issues and difficult material raised in each chapter. Students usually study text material with a very narrow focus, rarely taking the time (they rarely have the time!) to step back and think deeply about the issues at hand, and how they may relate to larger real world concerns and their own experience. However, many of the issues raised in abnormal psychology, especially those covered in the historical, theoretical, and legal chapters of the text, are philosophical in nature, complex in meaning, and significant in their implications. The Central Concept sections examine a number of these issues and, hopefully, facilitate your understanding and appreciation of them.

Sample Exam (Multiple-Choice Questions)

For each chapter there are multiple-choice questions that cover the textbook material. They follow the order of the textbook chapter. In almost all cases there is one best answer, but for a handful of questions there are several "best" answers.

Multiple-choice questions like these are often used in examinations because they employ a common format with which to assess several different aspects of what you have learned: (a) factual information; (b) distinction among concepts; (c) similarity among concepts; (d) application of concepts; and (e) integration of concepts. Most of the questions cover material presented in the textbook, but some of the questions deal with material that was not presented. Abnormal psychology is a growing and changing field, and in some areas, knowledge is incomplete. The textbook authors have been careful to distinguish what is known from what is not known, and I have tried to help you make the same distinction by asking you in some questions about what is *not* the case.

How should you make use of these multiple-choice questions? Read the chapter carefully. Then answer the questions. They touch upon most of the important concepts in a chapter, so you should try to see the point of each. If possible, try to answer a question before you look at the alternatives. When you do look at the choices, do more than select the best answer. Reflect on why your answer strikes you as being the best, and, just as important, reflect on why the other alternatives do not seem as good. When you take a multiple-choice examination in a course, you will probably employ strategies of answering, such as eliminating obviously wrong alternatives and making educated "guesses" from among those left. You can practice such strategies here, but I urge you also to understand why any given strategy does or does not work.

Correct answers and the page numbers on which the answer can be found in the text are provided at the end of each sample exam. Don't peek!

Self-Test (Fill-In Questions)

There are fill-in questions for each chapter. Like multiple-choice questions, they are also frequently used in examinations, where they do a good job of assessing your knowledge of terminology and your understanding of concepts. Unlike multiple-choice questions, fill-ins ask you to produce answers rather than just recognize them. The questions, which follow the order of the textbook chapter, ask you to provide the missing word or phrase. Use these questions as you use the multiple-choice questions: answer them correctly, but also know why your answers are good ones.

Correct answers are provided at the end of each self-test.

Matching Items

The Matching Items section offers another opportunity to test your memory and understanding of the text material. For each chapter there are 10–22 key terms which must be matched with equivalent terms, definitions, or related information such as the name of the associated researcher or theory. Each term has one best match among the choices offered, although others may look right on your first pass. Again, an answer key is provided for this section.

Short-Answer Questions

Clearly constructed answers convey organized thinking and understanding, and they help instructors to grade your answers. They are also more time and space efficient. Short-answer questions are often used in examinations, and so learning the discipline of answering them in a succinct heading and point form format, rather than rambling sentences, is an *extremely* important skill to develop and practice. This skill can also be applied to structuring study notes and generating outlines for constructing longer essay answers. Even if your instructor requires answers in full sentences, you can use the heading and point-form structure as your outline for these. This format should be the backbone of your studying and answer-writing. The questions in this section are amenable to either short answer or essay answer format; I encourage you to try answering them in either or both styles depending on the type of test questions your instructor favors, or the kind of practice you desire. Answers are not provided for these questions.

Tying It Together

In this section I briefly describe some of the ways in which the chapter pertains to other chapters—those already read as well as those yet to be read. Abnormal psychology is a coherent discipline, but students encountering the field for the first time may see it as more fragmented than it really is. The textbook covers topics ranging from brain chemistry to historical change, from unconscious desires to political persecution. In particular, the disorders described in the textbook are extremely varied, representing the range of human experience.

What I have tried to do is to direct you toward the forest that may be hidden by the trees of abnormal psychology. The "big picture" that emerges will be your own, but I hope that this aspect of the study guide starts you on your way toward seeing it.

It may be a good idea to read "Tying It Together" before as well as after studying each chapter. There is nothing in these sections to memorize. Rather, they contain food for thought. Psychologists have long investigated learning and memory, and what has emerged from this research is that individuals usually do not learn material verbatim. Rather, they learn the gist of material; they abstract its major points. Details are not "stored" in memory so much as they are "reconstructed" from the structure created by the individual when material is learned. To the degree that you are successful in creating your own "big picture" to serve as this structure, the material in *Abnormal Psychology* will be yours long after your psychology course is completed.

Further Readings

Almost all topics in abnormal psychology are interesting, but the textbook cannot go into as much detail as you may like for all topics. What I have tried to do in this section of the study guide is to suggest some readings pertinent to the textbook chapter. Some of these are from classical and technical sources, while others are from popular sources. You should be able to find most of them in your college library or in your campus bookstore.

Term-Paper Topics

Your instructor may ask you to write a paper as part of the course. This section contains possible topics for such papers. Each suggestion asks you to take a stance on some issue and then to defend it as best you can. In my opinion the key to a good paper is knowing, before you start, just what you are trying to convey to the reader. Once you have this knowledge, you also have answers to question that may otherwise seem quite puzzling to you: "How should it start?" "How should it end?" "How many pages should it be?" "How many references should it have?"

P.S. Type your papers! Please believe me, typed papers are better for all concerned.

Exercises

Abnormal psychology is not a discipline that lends itself to an undergraduate laboratory course. Unlike the classic studies in physics, chemistry, or general psychology, the classic investigations of abnormal psychology are not easily replicated. Considerations of time, money, and ethics preclude replication attempts. However, learning is well served by active doing, and for this reason I have tried to come up with exercises that take off from the chapter material. These are not the same thing as laboratory experiments, but they serve the same purpose: providing you with hands-on experience with concepts important to the field.

In each case the exercises bring important ideas down to earth. Some pose thought problems for you to solve. Others ask you to see a movie or read a book. And still others ask you to talk to people. These latter exercises must be approached carefully because they may infringe on people's right not to be talked to about certain matters. It would be wise to follow the ethical guidelines employed by psychologists in their research. Prior to the exercise, (a) tell the persons what you will require of them and obtain their permission to conduct the exercise (informed consent); (b) inform the persons that they can cease their interaction with you at any time (right to withdraw); and (c) let them know that you will answer any questions about the exercise to the best of your ability when it is finished (debriefing). If you have any doubts or questions about the appropriateness of an exercise, please consult with your instructor!

Lisa D. Butler
Stanford, CA
January 1995

Casebook

The Damm Family:
Homeless in America

What is abnormal? Rosenhan and Seligman argue that there is no unalterable line separating the normal from the abnormal. If we tried to draw such a line, many of us would be straddling it. As arbitrary as they may be in everyday life, however, decisions about abnormality are the bread and butter of clinical psychology.

There are two obvious reasons why such judgments must be made. First, it is necessary to minimize the number of people who receive psychological treatments but do not have a psychological illness (i.e., "false positives"). In addition to wasting a good deal of time, effort, and money in an era of cost containment in health care, data about treatment efficacy would not be reliable if subjects who did not need treatment were included in outcome studies. In some studies people who were already well might seem not to benefit from therapy, whereas in others normal fluctuations in mood might seem like either dramatic improvements in response to treatment or placebo responses that no active treatments could beat.

Another issue, which is addressed in Chapter 18 of the text, is that it is more important, at least in the United States, to protect individual liberty than to make everyone conform to the norms of the majority, norms that change over time anyway. Wearing a beard, for example, was a sign of a professional during the last century, the hallmark of a hippie during the 1960s, and something that we hardly notice these days. We force people to conform to certain standards only when their actions involve the safety of society of the individual or when their abilities to make rational choices about how to behave are severely impaired: We can allow someone to be uncommunicative or eccentric, but not to burn down the house next door. If they do not break the law, people are free to live on the street, to join cults, or to act in any manner they chose, so long as the choice is based on free will and not psychotic reasoning. It is our interest in protecting personal liberty that makes us not want to label something as pathological just because it is different.

Does this mean that it is impossible to say when psychological functioning is abnormal, as opposed to unpopular? Not under many circumstances of clinical reality. A woman who chose to live on the street even though housing was available might not be making a choice that most people would make, but her choice might not be based on psychotic logic or delusional premises. A man who lived on the street because every time he went into a building he thought that radiation from the walls was turning his brain into sand would usually be considered to have made a pathological premise that led to an understandable but pathological decision.

Since by some estimates there are 2 to 3 million homeless people in the United States, one-third of them families with children (Kozol, 1988), it is important to distinguish among those people living on the street who are clearly ill and either are dangerous or have such impaired thinking that they cannot be said to be freely choosing their lifestyles, those who are making a rational but unpopular choice, and those who, though normal, find themselves in abnormal circumstance. Our feelings about the homeless, which may range from pity to admiration, from impatience to fear, from disgust to guilt, do not help us to make a diagnosis, and they may get in the way. The first case of this casebook, which concerns a homeless family that was described in a picture essay in *Life* magazine (Fadiman, 1987), may help to define normality in the context of homelessness.

THE DAMM FAMILY

The Damm family as described in *Life* had their share of problems. To introduce the family, there is mother Linda (age twenty-seven), father Dean (age thirty-three), daughter Crissy (age six), and son Jesse (age four). And then there is the family dog Runtley, as well as their 1971 Buick Skylark, which provides them not only with transportation but with shelter. The Damm family lives in their car.

Originally from Colorado Springs, the family moved to the Los Angeles area after Linda and Dean were unsuccessful in finding jobs for two years. Linda had worked as a nursing-home aide, and Dean as a truck driver. They heard that work was more plentiful in California than Colorado. Further, California welfare allotments are the highest in the nation.

Once in California, they did not find work. And since the family arrived with an empty gas tank and less than 10 cents, their life became a constant struggle to find money to buy necessities. They sold parts of their car. They pawned their wedding rings. Dean regularly sold blood. Not only was he given $10 for each visit, but a meal as well. He remarked that the blood center is one of the few clean places he ever visited.

The Damms were homeless, broke, and unemployed. Even more problems followed. They found a federally subsidized shelter in which to stay, but they were evicted because they had children; the federal grant for homeless families had expired. If they had been childless, they could have continued to stay. Then they applied for welfare and faced a number of bureaucratic hassles. A check was mysteriously delayed. Another check was made out for too much money, and the family had to return it instantly or risk further problems. In one incident, Dean lost his temper at the guard in the welfare office. "I'm sick of your goddamn system . . . you're jerking my family around! You're treating us like garbage! *We are not garbage!"*

Homelessness took a toll on the children. The little girl, Crissy, became agitated whenever she saw her parents pack up their belongings to move, which of course was frequently. She was enrolled in a school, and Linda and Dean worried about how she would be treated by classmates and teachers. Crissy's clothes, from charitable organizations, didn't fit. She had no food to bring for lunch. In one poignant scene, the Damm family dropped her off at school in the morning, along with other parents doing the same. The car behind them was a Porsche.

Jesse reacted to the stress of homelessness by becoming timid and overly obedient. He was too young for school, and the family was unable to find subsidized child-care for him. So he accompanied Linda and Dean on their rounds: to the welfare office, to look for inexpensive apartments, to the trade schools that his parents attended.

They constantly searched for a place to live. Although it is illegal to discriminate against individuals on welfare, this was apparently a common practice among landlords. Even if someone was willing to rent to such individuals, the typical demand for a damage deposit, plus first month's rent, and last month's rent, was simply too much for the family to provide up front. Another problem resulted from having no telephone: no landlord could ever call them back about an apartment. The little money they did have went into pay telephones, 25 cents at a time.

Are you surprised that Dean and Linda sometimes fought? Are you surprised that they had feuds with their relatives in the Los Angeles area? But were they abnormal?

ABNORMALITY AND NORMALITY

Remember the elements of abnormality that Rosenhan and Seligman present. How many of these apply to the Damm family? First there is *suffering.* Certainly, on this score, the family qualifies as abnormal. Their situation is difficult, physically and mentally. They must go without food. They must suffer the scorn of others, perhaps even their own scorn at times.

Second there is *maladaptiveness.* Aspects of the Damms' existence may strike us as maladaptive. They are unable to find work. They have trouble providing a roof over their heads. They cannot raise their children optimally.

Conversely, Linda and Dean do things that show intelligence and industry. Each is enrolled in technical classes, Linda to learn emergency medical care and Dean to learn telephone installation. Each is the best student in his or her respective class. If they complete a twenty-six-week program, they quite possibly will find skilled work. While doing all this, they are able to care for Jesse and to keep Crissy in school. Here Linda and Dean are acting in an extremely adaptive fashion, and don't seem at all abnormal.

Irrationality and incomprehensibility are more difficult criteria to apply. On the face of it, the existence of the Damm family is irrational. Why would anyone live in a car? But when we learn something about their history, it is not difficult to understand how they ended up on the street.

What about *unpredictability and loss of control?* By the account we've been presented, the Damm family does not exemplify this criterion of abnormality. Dean loses his temper, but only occasionally. The rest of the family is extremely disciplined in their behavior. Despite not being able to control their circumstances, they do not become passive or bitter; they just keep trying.

Are these people *vivid and unconventional?* Yes, certainly, at least to those of us with middle-class sensibilities. The pictures in Life magazine that accompany the story of the Damms are haunting. Their car is missing the hood and windows on the driver's side. The upholstery is torn. They have ninth-hand clothing. It is difficult for them to keep themselves clean. Linda owns no underwear.

The Damms elicit *observer discomfort* in those who are in contact with them. Who wouldn't be uncomfortable seeing their circumstances? In some places, discomfort with the homeless has become an excuse to attack the homeless physically; it makes one wonder who it is that is sick.

This leads us to the next criterion: *violation of moral and ideal standards.* The homeless are at odds with what we think is right. They ought to have a home, a career, and a clean family. If they had chosen to keep their family on the street, if they preferred not to work, Dean and Linda would be violating societal standards. Is the same true if the problem is not volitional?

So, the Damm family would meet some but not all the criteria for abnormality outlined in Chapter 1 if their behavior is considered in a vacuum. If their behavior is examined in its social context, the positive findings might have to be reconsidered. For instance, it would be abnormal *not* to suffer if one's family were on the street. Instead of exhibiting maladaptive behavior, the Dam family may have made the best possible adaptation to an abnormal situation. If anything, the family's situation may prove that society is irrational, not them; look at how difficult it was to negotiate the system and find shelter and a job. Instead of looking for an unconventional life-style, the family seemed to have been doing what they could to retain some sense of conventionality. any discomfort they experienced was likely to have been a natural reaction to their situation rather than their behavior. We have already discussed the question of violation of moral standards.

Just as we cannot assess abnormality merely by looking at the Damm family's circumstances, we cannot attribute any problems that they might exhibit only to the environment. People's inner strengths are not a direct reflection of their circumstances; they interact with them. To the extent that a family has psychological vulnerabilities to begin with, it may handle economic hardship very badly. To the extent that it exhibits flexibility and cohesiveness, we would predict that it would endure and eventually find a way out of the abnormal situation. In the case of the Damm family, this is just what happened.

The Damms found an apartment they could afford, and they moved in. Linda walked by a barrel that day, with a sign saying "Help the Homeless." She dropped in a handful of pennies.

DISCUSSION QUESTIONS

1. Many people around the world find themselves in situations that are even more desperate than the one that was just described, situations that have no chance of improving in the foreseeable future. How should abnormality be defined in these settings? What would be abnormal in societies in which innocent civilians are randomly bombed, starved, or taken off the streets by armed vigilantes?

2. In a more stable society, how should individual psychology be assessed under unusual circumstance? For example, when would it be "normal" for a heterosexual person to engage in homosexual behavior while in a situation in which no one of the opposite sex was around? When would it be "abnormal"?

3. At what point would you decide that the Damm family had made a poor adjustment to a bad situation? If you were a psychologist (as opposed to a social worker or politician), how would you help them? How would you know if your intervention was successful?

4. A subpopulation of the homeless consists of chronically mentally ill patients who were "deinstitutionalized" with the national reduction in the number of state hospital beds and who had made a better adaptation to the structure of the hospital than to society at large. What are the clinical, economic, moral, and political issues raised by discharging them into the community?

REFERENCES

Fadiman, A. (1987). A week in the life of a homeless family. *Life,* December 10, pp. 30–38.

Kozol, J. (1988). *Rachel and her children: Homeless families in America.* New York: Crown Publishers.

Wolf Madness

Chapter 2 describes evolving notions of the classification as well as the definition of abnormality. One example of a psychological illness that was limited to a particular time in history (horror movies notwithstanding) is lycanthropy, or wolf madness. This form of abnormality, present in Europe from about 300 to 1700 A.D. involved the belief that the person had become a wolf. Someone who was so afflicted acted out this belief:

> He will goe out of the house in the night like a wolfe, hunting about the graves of the dead with great howling, and plucke the dead mens bones out of the sepulchers, carrying them about the streetes, to the great feare and astonishment of all them that meete him . . . Melancholike persons of this kinde, have pale faces, soaked and hollow eies, with a weake sight, never shedding one teare to the view of the worlde, a drie toong, extreme thirst, and they want spittle and moisture exceedingly . . . . (Tommaso Garzoni, 1600, quoted by Jackson, 1986, pp. 346–347).

EXPLANATIONS OF WOLF MADNESS

Since wolf madness occurred during the animistic era, you might think that people afflicted with this disorder were thought to be werewolves, that is, people who turn into wolves when there was a full moon. Although people in the Middle Ages believed in werewolves, those with wolf madness were carefully distinguished from those who were werewolves: a werewolf was someone who became a literal wolf, whereas a person with wolf madness became a wolf only in his or her own mind. The first instance was obvious enchantment, and the latter instance was obvious insanity.

Animistic explanations were nonetheless applied to wolf madness. Hippocrates (460–377 B.C.) had proposed that good health (or being in a "good humor") was a function of the balance among the four humors—blood, yellow bile, black bile, and phlegm. The predominance of one or another humor, which might be caused by the star or planet that influenced it, produced specific forms of illness. Too much black bile, for instance, wandered around the body trying to get out. Finding no outlet, it lodged in the soul and gave it a black character. Melancholic people therefore were (and still are) called "bilious" or "saturnine," because black bile was under the influence of Saturn.

Hippocrates' concept had a certain amount of timelessness. In the Middle Ages, wolf madness was thought to be a type of melancholy caused by excess black bile. It was the extra bile that was thought to produce the continual thirst of the sufferer from wolf madness. Black bile corresponds with the element of earth. As the earth absorbs water, so too does the person with wolf madness.

In many ways, melancholia of the Middle Ages and depression of the twentieth century are related, although the way in which symptoms are described has changed. Since the melancholia of Hippocrates' time was caused by excess black bile, gastric symptoms were frequent, and black vomit confirmed the diagnosis. Today, loss of appetite and constipation are common symptoms of depression. It may be that popular explanations of the distress determined which symptoms were noticed, or folk wisdom may have modified the expression of symptoms that are similar throughout the generations.

What puts the humours out of balance? Wolf madness was thought to be more likely to occur in February; this again implied the influence of the stars. Rabies was another possible cause, one very much consistent with an animistic view of the world. Rabies is transmitted through the bite of a mad animal. Once bitten, you were thought to take on the character of that animal. Direct intervention by divine powers could also be responsible.

Divine intervention was the only cure for a kind of wolf madness that was described in the Bible, in the Book of Daniel. Nebuchadnezzar, the king of Babylon, conquered Judah, but he was too proud to recognize that it was only God's will that allowed his victory (Daniel 1:2). Nebuchadnezzar had a dream that foretold that he would be humbled for his pride as a lesson that great accomplishments come from God, not humans. Sure enough, as Nebuchadnezzar bragged to his court, "Is not this great Babylon, that I have built for the house of the kingdom by the might of my power, and for the honor or my majesty?" (Daniel 4:30), a voice said "The kingdom is departed form you" (Daniel 4:31). Nebuchadnezzar promptly went mad and began acting as a wild animal. He ate "grass as oxen, and his body was wet with the dew of heaven, till his hairs were grown like eagles' feathers, and his nails like birds' claws" (Daniel 4:33). He was then driven from his kingdom to live with the beasts. Nebuchadnezzar remained mad until he was made to realize that it was God, not him, to whom praise was due and that the kingdom of God, not the kingdom of humans, is eternal. At the moment of this inspired insight, his reason and his kingdom were restored.

What happened to other individuals with wolf madness? According to available accounts, some got better by themselves, others wasted away, and still others died. When treatment was possible, it followed two strategies. First, the amount of black bile was decreased through moistening with broths, syrups, and baths. Second, the other humors were strengthened through purging and bloodletting. Also thought to be helpful in restoring one's humours to good balance were soothing music and poetry. With the passing of the years, wolf madness faded away as a disease, only to be replaced by more contemporary culture-bound maladies.

DISCUSSION QUESTIONS

1. A form of madness in native Canadians involves the belief that they have been transformed into flesh-eating monsters called whitigos (or wendigos). Is this a modern form of lycanthropy? Why is it only encountered in this particular culture?

2. Why has the fascination with werewolves continued? What about the fascination with vampires?

3. Why was a wolf so frequently chosen in the Middle Ages as the animal into which people were transformed? Other popular choices were dogs. Why not butterflies? Why do some people judged to be abnormal today believe themselves to be machines?

4. From your reading or traveling, do you know any examples of psychological problems in different cultures that have no counterpart in our own? How are these explained in their native cultures? How would we explain them?

5. Which contemporary mental disorders will disappear? Which will remain? Will the symptoms of modern disorders change in full generations? Why?

REFERENCE

Jackson, S. W. (1986). *Melancholia and depression from Hippocratic times to modern times.* New Haven, CT: Yale University Press.

What Goes Around Comes Around: Witchcraft in America

With the rise of empiricism and modifications of church dogma about possession and witchcraft, supernatural explanations for mental illness faded into the woodwork in most cultures. During the 1990s, however, there has been a resurgence of belief in the devil as a cause of mental illness. In this case, we will see an interesting transformation of ancient beliefs into a modern setting.

You will recall that one thing that made witches so frightening during the Middle Ages was that it was impossible to identify them on sight. The way to be sure was to find a secret mark or conduct some sort of test, usually one that was fatal. Because they looked just like you and me, witches were free to perform extraordinary feats of evil mischief without anyone's knowing what they had done. In recent years, claims have again been made of the widespread influence of satanic cults that conduct bizarre rituals, animal sacrifices, kidnapping, and murder, right under the nose of the authorities. Indeed, those making the claims believe that one reason why the cults are able to remain secret is that the authorities are cult members too.

Concerns about satanic cults had their roots in the movement to bring child abuse out of the closet. Although abuse of children is as old as the aphorism "Spare the rod and spoil the child," the first attempt to document it as something bad was not until 1969, when a description of "the battered child syndrome" by pediatrician C. Henry Kempe and his colleagues at the University of Colorado School of Medicine appeared in the *Journal of the American Medical Association*. Until that time, physicians had never questioned the unlikely explanations of childrens' accidents, injuries, and illnesses and left the children to suffer continued abuse and even death at the hands of their parents. The Kempe article was the first in a long series of agonizing steps toward overcoming ignorance, denial, and rationalization to make child abuse a legitimate topic of study and treatment. To protect children whose parents deny their behavior, laws now exist in all states requiring clinicians to report to the appropriate social agency any reasonable suspicion of child abuse, even if the suspicion turns out on investigation to have been wrong.

One outgrowth of the changing attitude of society toward child abuse is that a number of prominent figures have revealed that they were secretly abused in families that seemed to have been pillars of society. These people had always been aware of the abuse, but they had never said anything because they were threatened with retaliation if they did, even as adults. At the same time, another group has emerged that "recovered" in adulthood memories of abuse in childhood that are not only horrific, but transcend human experience. Under the guidance of therapists they consulted for treatment of anxiety, depression, eating disorders, or difficulty functioning, these individuals gradually remembered being subjected to bizarre rituals involving devil worship, torture, and human sacrifice (Putnam, 1991).

"Ritual Satanic Abuse" has become such a common experience that patients now enter psychiatric hospitals with a diagnosis of "RSA." When RSA "survivors" compare notes, they find that they have had very similar experiences—a phenomenon that has been taken as proof that RSA must really exist. Of course, people from around the country who have been kidnapped by flying saucers also tell remarkably similar stories (Lanning, 1991), but psychiatrist John Mack contends that this proves that flying saucer abductions also are real (Mack, 1994). These kinds of contentions might be tempered by the realization that the same thing also happened to everyone in the Middle Ages who thought they had experienced witchcraft and satanism. It has been claimed that no physical evidence has been found of the 20,000 murders a year that would have been committed if each RSA report was accurate because the police either are inept or are in on the conspiracy (Lanning, 1991). But the police seem to have been competent enough to uncover conspiracies by the Mafia, spies, the World Trade Center bombers, and other secret groups.

Some parents who say that they are innocent assert that those who claim that they are victims of RSA are suffering from a "false memory syndrome." They believe that the patients have been encouraged by therapists and are as suggestible as the children in the Middle Ages who believed that their parents were witches and the adults in those times who actually confessed to practicing witchcraft (Putnam, 1991). False accusations of widespread witchcraft and satanism have been compared with the "blood libel," the falsehood promulgated during the Middle Ages that Jews kidnapped Christian children to obtain blood for the Passover ceremony (Putnam, 1991). RSA sufferers reply that such ideas are just one more attempt to discount experiences that society is afraid to acknowledge. If you reject the legitimacy of RSA, you reject the legitimacy of those who experience it. In the following case, which side of the debate seems most accurate?

THE CASE

Tabatha is a thirty-two year-old woman who has been depressed for most of her life. When she is finally able to get to sleep, she has bad dreams she cannot remember. She habitually overeats, feeling that being heavier will protect her from some unknown attack.

In psychotherapy a few years ago, Tabatha struggled to overcome the impact of having been molested from age ten to fifteen by her father and one of his brothers. Her rage at her father was bad enough, but she felt even greater disappointment in her mother, who seemed oblivious to what was going on. She realized that her chronic feelings of emptiness were the result of being treated like nothing more than an object. It became obvious that she had always felt that if her mother did not care enough about her to protect her, she was not worthy of being helped by anyone else. Her therapist helped her to understand that it was not her fault that she had been treated badly and that she deserved more than loneliness and unhappiness. At this point, she had to stop therapy to move to another city to take a new job.

It took a year for Tabatha to get back into therapy, and when she did, she consulted a therapist who specialized in the treatment of people who had had traumatic experiences as children. The therapist invited her to join a group whose members had all been victims of RSA, and Tabatha discovered that they had experienced similar symptoms. As she heard about their experiences, she began to remember times in her life that until then had been a blank. Gradually, she realized that the sexual abuse was not the only atrocity she had suffered: she remembered that her father was a member of a large group that had conducted ceremonies that involved torture and mutilation. She recalled that several of his friends' daughters had been forced to become pregnant so that babies whose births were never registered could be sacrificed on Halloween. She remembered that on one occasion she had found a human head in the refrigerator. She remembered that far from being a passive accomplice, her mother had assisted at the rituals.

Unlike her previous insights, Tabatha's new realizations seemed to make her feel that she had less control over her mind. The more she knew that she had been the victim of a monstrous conspiracy, the less safe she felt. She felt that no one who had not had similar experiences could understand what she was going through; they could not help, and they might even be agents of her father, sent to silence her for exposing the cult. Far from being unimportant and despised, she was now a member of an elite if tortured group.

DISCUSSION QUESTIONS

1. Which is worse—the mundane evil that Tabatha initially remembered or the dramatic events she remembered later?

2. How would you evaluate the veracity of Tabatha's memories? What would you do if they could not be verified?

3. in recent years, a number of cults based on worship of some individual or entity have emerged that create or exploit mental illness in their members. Consider, for example, the murderous and suicidal behavior of the Jim Jones cult and the Branch Davidians. Why do such cults continue to surface? Do their members exhibit the kind of mass hysteria that was common during the Middle Ages?

4. Will the antiscientific attitude of some segments of society increase claims of supernatural causes of mental distress?

5. How would you treat someone who was convinced that chronic headaches for which no medical cause could be found were caused by a hex when the patient's culture supports this belief?

6. In what ways does childhood abuse lead to adult psychopathology? Why doesn't everyone who was abused develop a mental illness?

REFERENCES

Lanning, K. V. (1991). Ritual abuse: A law enforcement view or perspective. *Child Abuse and Neglect, 15,* 171–73.

Mack, J. E. (1944). *Abduction: Human encounters with aliens.* New York: Scribner's.

Putnam, F. W. (1991). The satanic ritual abuse controversy. *Child Abuse and Neglect, 15,* 175–79.

Anna O. from
Different Perspectives

In the field of abnormal psychology, different theoretical approaches attempt to explain particular instances of abnormality. The text calls these approaches models. Each model consists of a set of related assumptions about human nature, about the nature of abnormality, and the treatment of abnormality.

The Freudian *psychodynamic model* regards people as energy systems, striving for quiescence. Conflicts between the pressures of drives and the prohibitions against expressing these drives inevitably lead to distress. Problems are cast in energy terms as well. Symptoms represent a bad investment, so to speak, of someone's finite psychological energy. According to modifications of this "hydraulic" model, symptoms may also represent weakened defenses and observing and synthetic capacities (ego psychology); deficits in a sense of personal cohesiveness, intactness, or meaning (self psychology); or pathological ways of balancing needs and the constraints of reality and the personality (the adaptational approach). The energy devoted to symptoms is not available for more productive use elsewhere. Depending on the theoretical approach, treatment might aim to free energy tied up in symptoms for more adaptive use of the mind, strengthening defenses, or stabilizing the sense of self and enhancing self-esteem.

The *biomedical model* regards people as physical systems, with psychological symptoms as direct or indirect manifestations of dysregulated biology. When problems develop, they are seen as due to physiologic damage or malfunction. Solutions to problems are similarly physical. The biomedically oriented therapist tries to undo or correct the presumed pathobiology, relying on drugs and related interventions.

The *learning (behavioral and cognitive) models* propose that people naturally try to maximize rewards and minimize punishments, and our cognitive abilities are brought into service to achieve this aim. When we have problems, the learning model looks either to the situation or at least to the way that we perceive it. Perhaps we have been rewarded for pathological behaviors or punished for healthy ones. Perhaps we lack the skills, behavioral and/or cognitive, to thrive in a particular environment.

The solution? Learn different ways of thinking and behaving and, if possible, change a pathological environment.

Each model has its own domain, a set of problems and treatments that it does a particularly good job of explaining. At the same time, no one model can ever fully capture everything important about abnormality. A model represents a deliberate narrowing of perspective in order to learn as much as possible about one aspect of a problem without trying to assimilate the entire problem at once. Each theory becomes a piece of a jigsaw puzzle that, when fully understood, will mesh with the other pieces to produce a coherent whole. The text warns that this goal is not always met. Sometimes models put blinders on psychologists.

In this case, you will see how different models can profitably be applied to the same instance of abnormality; each achieves its own insights. The inspiration for this case is a book that examines one of history's most famous patients—Anna O.—from fourteen contemporary perspectives (Rosenbaum & Muroff, 1984). We will only consider three of these to illustrate some of the models illustrated in your textbook. However, if these three models are so disparate, imagine how complicated it is to try to synthesize every reasonable viewpoint about psychopathology.

THE CASE OF ANNA O.

Anna O. is the name given to the *first* psychoanalytic case, a woman seen in therapy not by Sigmund Freud but by his early collaborator Josef Breuer. Anna O. was an intelligent young woman who showed a variety of puzzling symptoms (Breuer & Freud, 1895). At various times, she lost the ability to move her right arm, her legs, and her head. She was unable to feed herself. She had a chronic cough. She had trouble seeing, and thus could not read or write. Sometimes she spoke in broken sentences and complained that snakes were in the room with her. She often did not hear what people said to her. She was weak, yet she refused food that was offered to her. At times she was suicidal.

At the time she saw Breuer, Anna O. was given the diagnosis of hysteria, which means that she experienced loss of bodily functions that was presumed to have psychological rather than neurological causes. Because mental conflict was "converted" into a physical symptom, the condition was called "conversion hysteria." Breuer followed a common procedure for treating hysteria by hypnotizing Anna O. and suggesting that she give up her symptoms. It soon became clear, however, that it was not necessary to hypnotize her in order to relieve her various symptoms. Instead, she merely needed to talk about the symptoms and about when they had first appeared. This would bring her dramatic relief.

Some writers speculate that the patient rather than the doctor should be credited with inventing this new technique, which she called the "talking cure." Psychology has come to know it by the more formal name of *catharsis*. The technique of saying whatever comes to mind, without censoring, is now called *free association*. Freud developed free association into the principal technique of psychoanalytic therapy; he regarded it as a way of unearthing unconscious material and freeing the psychological energy that kept this material hidden.

There is more to the case. Although Breuer successfully treated her symptoms, Anna O. did not necessarily recover. Indeed, after Breuer ended therapy with her, Anna O. experienced a bizarre state in which she mistakenly yet vividly believed that she was giving birth to a child and the child was Breuer's! This phantom pregnancy shook Breuer greatly, but Freud saw it as compelling proof that the doctor-patient relationship could be a source of information about the patient's unconscious wishes. Freud made the examination of transference, or the transfer of feelings about other people onto the therapist, the central focus of psychoanalysis. To this day, the analysis of transference remains the most important way the psychoanalyst has of learning about the secret workings of the patient's mind. Today, Anna O.'s symptoms would raise suspicions of sexual contact or other transgression of the therapist-patient boundary.

Despite her continued symptoms Anna O., whose real name was Bertha Pappenheim, accomplished a great deal in life. In her later life, she was an active feminist and a pioneer in developing the field of social work in Germany. She was a leader in the Jewish community. She was a champion of women and children and the mentally retarded. When she died in 1936 at the age of seventy-seven, Bertha Pappenheim was an honored and respected citizen of the world.

THE PSYCHODYNAMIC MODEL

According to the psychodynamic model, Anna O.'s symptoms would be likely to represent an attempt to disguise an unacceptable drive. Breuer and Freud felt that Anna O. had an unacknowledged sexual attraction for her father. Some contemporary experts think that she might have been sexually abused by her father. Because this attraction (or the possible memory of having been molested) was threatening to her conscious mind, it was actively repressed. Because the energy of the repressed drive had no healthy outlet, it was converted into unhealthy symptoms. The particular symptoms she experienced bore a symbolic relationship to her underlying motives. By this view, the snakes she hallucinated were phallic symbols, representing her hidden desires for her father, and a dream she had about a "jewel box" represented her own genitals. She became attracted to Breuer because he stood for her father. Her false pregnancy seemed a rather blatant representation of her unconscious wishes. Her commitment to championing the rights of women and children could also be understood as an attempt to relive a childhood wish to have been protected from the desires or influences of men.

Therapy proceeded by freeing up psychological energy. Anna O. talked about the circumstances in which specific symptoms had first developed.

[handwritten margin note: She was sexually abused by her father, she was attracted to Breuer was like her father.*]*

In the course of her associations, she would come up with the heretofore unconscious motive that the symptom represented. Once brought into conscious awareness, the motive no longer had to be expressed in disguised form and the energy associated with keeping it repressed could be used for other purposes.

THE BIOMEDICAL MODEL

CASE OF DEPRESSION Does the psychodynamic model provide the only way to interpret the case *CONVERSION HYSTERIA* of Anna O.? Not at all. The biologically oriented therapist would try to find a medication that would relieve Anna O's distress and disability. But first it would be necessary to make a diagnosis, or at least to define the "target symptoms" for psychotropic medicines. Unfortunately, Freud and his colleagues did not collaborate with the descriptive psychiatrists of his time, who were the progenitors of the modern biological psychiatrists. Emil Kraepelin, Eugen Bleuler, and other descriptive psychiatrists devoted themselves to carefully cataloging signs and symptoms, defining diagnoses, and describing what happened to people with different diagnoses—an approach that was radically different from the inferred psychopathology of psychoanalysis. Bleuler felt that the two approaches complemented each other, but Freud did not want to collaborate with him because Bleuler did not want to work toward a worldwide analytic movement. Freud's school continued to emphasize process over content; it is therefore not nearly as easy to decide on possible diagnoses of Anna O. as it is to come up with her psychodynamics.

The Rosenbaum and Muroff book points out that Anna O. had some symptoms suggestive of depression, for example, loss of appetite and weight, withdrawal, decreased energy, and suicidal thinking. The physical symptoms could have been symptoms of conversion hysteria, or they could have been physical symptoms of depression or anxiety, or somatic hallucinations; visual hallucinations also seemed to have been intermittently present. If a diagnosis of depression were made, an antidepressant might be utilized. If depression were felt to be associated with hallucinations, an antipsychotic drug might be added, since the combination of the two kinds of medications works better than either one alone for depression with psychotic symptoms. Depression with hallucinations in younger individuals often indicates a bipolar (manic-depressive) mood disorder, and if this diagnosis were confirmed, lithium might be used, with or without an antipsychotic drug.

The best DSM-IV diagnosis in Anna O.'s case would probably be brief psychosis, which is characterized by delusions, hallucinations, disorganized speech, or disorganized behavior, lasting form one day to one month and occurring with or without a stress. Brief psychosis, which used to be called "hysterical psychosis," usually goes away with limit setting, especially on fantasies about the therapist. A low dose of an antipsychotic drug is helpful for some brief psychoses, but it may make others worse.

THE LEARNING MODEL

One more perspective on the case of Anna O. comes from the learning model. Proponents of this view of abnormality would start by locating the woman in her environment:

> [She was] a young woman of the last part of the nineteenth century. Although Anna O.'s formal education had ended at age sixteen, she was a quick and avid learner and continued to educate herself. No matter how closeted she was by the religious orthodoxy of her family, she could not have helped by absorb the intellectual ferment of her time. Like a true Viennese, she must have visited the coffee houses, enjoyed the theater and music, read the journals and books of her day. . . . Certainly her achieving self was fostered by the excitement of what was occurring in the world around her . . . (Steinmann, 1984, p. 119).

Now let us sketch the more immediate environment of this intelligent young woman living in a fascinating city in a fascinating era. Anna O. spent her days nursing her dying father. Despite the possibilities that beckoned her, Anna O.'s day-to-day life was narrow and boring.

According to the learning model, no matter how much she might have wanted to have a fuller life, Anna O. was a woman in Victorian Austria, and the male-dominated culture was not interested in her aspirations. Conversely, in an era in which doctors were more interested in the function of the body than the problems of the mind, her unusual physical symptoms made her the center of attention of a group of important male doctors.

Continued reinforcement for getting rid of some symptoms, so that Breuer thought that he was helping her, but coming up with new symptoms that kept his interest engaged could have prolonged therapy indefinitely, and at least gotten her away from her depressing surroundings while she saw the doctor. Her physical disability also could have excused her failure to fulfill role expectations. However, as soon as Anna O. expressed transference feelings, Breuer dropped her; this confirmed any unconscious impression she may have had of the power that her illness gave her over social reinforcers.

A therapist working from the vantage of the learning model would pay great attention to the details of Anna O.'s situation in life. The therapist might encourage Anna O. to continue her education, to find friends and activities outside her immediate family, and to articulate her desires and find ways to satisfy them. Attempts might be made to get people to stop rewarding the expression of symptoms and disability ("illness behavior") and start reinforcing more adaptive behaviors. If women's groups existed, she might have been referred to one instead of having to invent them for herself.

DISCUSSION QUESTIONS

1. Which of the three explanations of the case of Anna O. do you find most compelling? Which is the least compelling? Explain your reasons.

2. The three models of abnormality need not contradict each other. How might the psychodynamic, biomedical, and learning approaches be combined to explain the problems of Anna O. and how to treat them?

3. According to the approach to abnormality known as family systems, all problems are best conceived and treated as problems of the family. By this view, Anna O. would simply be the "identified patient." How would a family systems therapist treat the Pappenheim family?

4. The case of Little Hans is another important psychoanalytic study (Freud, 1909). It is described in Chapter 8 of the text. How might this case be interpreted from the perspective of the biomedical model? From the perspective of the learning model?

5. What would a unified model of abnormality look like? What about a unified model of treatment?

REFERENCES

Breuer, J., & Freud, S. (1895). Studies on hysteria. In J. Strachey (Ed. and Trans.), *The complete psychological works* (Vol. 2). New York: Norton, 1976.

Freud, S. (1909). Analysis of a phobia in a five-year-old boy. In J. Strachey (Ed. and Trans.), *The complete psychological works* (Vol. 10). New York: Norton, 1976.

Rosenbaum, M., & Muroff, M. (Eds.) (1984). *Anna O.: Fourteen contemporary reinterpretations.* New York: Free Press.

Steinmann, A. (1984). Anna O.: Female, 1880–1882; Bertha Pappenheim: Female, 1980–1982. In M. Rosenbaum & M. Muroff (Eds.), *Anna O.: Fourteen contemporary reinterpretations.* New York: Free Press.

Watson, J. B., & Rayner, R. (1920). Conditioned emotional reactions. *Journal of Experimental Psychology, 3, 1–14.*

The Office as Laboratory: Clinical Applications of the Experimental Method

Chapter 6 describes a number of methods used in psychological research. Because each method examines a question from a different angle, many different studies using different methods are usually necessary to get a comprehensive view of any important issue. Although most clinical psychologists agree that this kind of painstaking research ultimately leads to better diagnoses and treatments, they do not see the relevance of a given report to their everyday work, and a few think that it is a waste of time even to conduct research. Dr. Harol Eist, a psychoanalyst, said in an interview that "the doctor-patient relationship is as much ruled by art as by science. . . . [I]ndividuals and their experiences differ so much . . . that looking at outcome studies can never direct you to what the appropriate treatment for any individual would be." (*Sunday Oregonian,* April 17, 1994, p. G15).

The sentiment that whatever feels right is right notwithstanding, the majority of responsible clinicians want to know whether their therapies are scientifically sound and whether new techniques have been developed that might help their patients, but their eyes glaze over as soon as they pick up a complicated research protocol. They would like to skip the description of the method and get right to the bottom line. What did the researchers find? Did the new treatment work or not? The only problem is that it is impossible to know whether the conclusions that are drawn at the end of all research reports are valid without knowing something about the validity of the methods.

Of the research methods you learned about in Chapter 6, the "gold standard" for the establishment of treatment efficacy is the randomized, prospective, placebo-controlled study in which patients with the same disorder are assigned by a process like flipping a coin to different active treatments and a placebo and then followed over time to see who does best. Whoever interprets the results should be unaware of (blind to) the treatment being administered to avoid biased conclusions. A study that compares a psychotherapy with no treatment does not have the same power as a comparison with a placebo psychotherapy containing non-specific support and a therapeutic relationship but not the technique that is supposed to be the active ingredient. A study that includes a reference treatment that is known to be effective can provide even more information: a new psychotherapy might be better than a placebo, but it might not be as good as another therapy that is known to be useful in clinical practice.

To interpret whether research really demonstrates what the authors allege, a number of other questions must be asked. For example, is the population that was studied representative of most people with the problem under investigation? Does a change on a rating scale mean that patients were really better? Are comparisons with no treatment or with alternative therapies valid? If the results are statistically significant, does it mean that they were clinically significant? How sure can one be that the results are not being presented in a way that favors the researchers' biases? The next case shows how some of these issues might apply in making everyday recommendations for therapy.

THE CASE

Vanna Woolfe became depressed as she entered her senior year in college. She had been depressed once before, when she finished high school, but she never sought treatment and the depression went away after about six months. This time, the depression was still there as she approached graduation. She has heard that psychotherapies have been specifically developed for depression, and she wants to know which, if any of them, might be right for her. Is one of these therapies more likely to help her than another? She does not want to waste her time and money on something that is not as likely to be useful as another treatment.

Ms. Woolfe's therapist could find several studies comparing different kinds of psychotherapy for depression with no therapy, and even with the antidepressant imipramine used as a reference treatment with an established response rate (see Chapter 11). These studies suggested that several psychotherapies reduced symptoms of depression in mildly to moderately depressed outpatients. However, there did not seem to be much scientific data on which to base a recommendation of one treatment over another or to tell the patient exactly what to expect from each therapy.

There was, however, one large study (Elkin et al., 1989), supported by the National Institute of Mental Health, in which 250 patients at three universities were randomly assigned to two psychotherapies designed specifically for depression, interpersonal therapy, and cognitive-behavioral therapy and to two control treatments. One control was imipramine combined with "clinical management," a combination of dosage adjustment and nonspecific supportive psychotherapy. To be certain that a comparison with imipramine would be reasonable, a placebo medication combined with a clinical management group was also included; if the active medication did not turn out to be better than the placebo, it might be concluded that clinical management was the active agent or that all treatments were basically placebos. Patients were treated for sixteen weeks, and their progress was assessed by two primary measures completed by interviewers, the Hamilton Rating Scale for Depression (HRSD), consisting of numerical ratings on seventeen depressive symptoms, and the Global Assessment Scale (GAS), a single number indicating an overall judgment of impairment. Patients also filled out two questionnaires, the Beck Depression Inventory (BDI), a self-rating of depressive symptoms, and the Hopkins Symptom Checklist (HSCL-90), a self-rating scale of ninety different kinds of symptoms.

Of the 250 patients who entered the study, 239 began treatment. About one-third of the latter group (77 patients) dropped out before receiving twelve sessions, or fifteen weeks of treatment. When the rating scale scores were analyzed at the end of sixteen weeks, there was a statistically significant decrease in symptom ratings in all four groups. Overall, there was no difference in the average reduction of rating scale scores between the psychotherapies or between either psychotherapy and the medication. However, the three active treatments also did not produce better results than the placebo combined with clinical management. Brief nonspecific therapy and a placebo therefore seemed to be as effective as psychotherapies designed for depression or as a medication in this group of mildly to moderately depressed patients.

A reduction in depression scores is not the same thing as not being depressed anymore. To examine which treatments produced meaningful improvement, the investigators defined recovery as having few or no depressive symptoms on the HRSD at the end of the study—an assumption that might or might not be valid. Using this criterion, 43 percent of patients receiving interpersonal therapy and 42 percent receiving imipramine recovered, compared with 21 percent of patients receiving placebos. The recovery rate (32 percent) for cognitive-behavioral therapy was not significantly worse than the other treatments, but it was also not significantly better than the placebo. Dividing patients who completed the study into those with more severe and those with less severe depression (assessed by degree of impairment on the GAS) at the beginning of the study showed that compared with the placebo–clinical management group, those who were more depressed initially had a greater reduction on all measures with imipramine and a greater reduction on only HRSD scores with interpersonal therapy. In the more severely depressed group, cognitive-behavioral therapy did not perform better than a placebo.

The investigators concluded form these results that for mildly depressed patients, a placebo and a therapeutic relationship are as good as any specific treatment, whether it be medication or psychotherapy. If the goal is recovery rather than just a reduction in symptoms, interpersonal therapy and imipramine but not cognitive-behavioral therapy are superior to a placebo. For more severely depressed patients, imipramine plus clinical management is the best treatment and cognitive-behavioral therapy is not effective, whereas interpersonal therapy helps on some measures but not others.

If structured psychotherapy for mild depression is unnecessary and if cognitive-behavioral therapy does not cure depression, why do so many clinicians use such therapies and why has cognitive-behavioral therapy been found to work in other studies of the same kinds of depression? Should psychologists not bother to learn new psychotherapies for mild depression and refer the more severely depressed patients for an antidepressant? A reanalysis of the data from this study addresses some of these questions.

One issue is that the NIMH study used a statistical method called "end-point analysis," in which the last measure obtained is used as the final value, even if the subject dropped out of the study after a few weeks. Assuming that dropouts would look the same after twelve or fifteen weeks more of treatment is not a trivial assumption considering the large number of dropouts in the study. What if some subjects dropped out of the psychotherapy groups just before they started to improve, so that their final scores would have been much better if they had stayed in, while people dropped out of the medication group after three or four weeks because they had received maximum benefit and therefore would not have looked better after sixteen weeks? If everyone had been followed through the entire study, the psychotherapy groups might have been found to have done much better than the antidepressant groups.

Another potential statistical problem is that patients whose rating scale scores were not as good at sixteen weeks, when the final measures were taken, might have been doing much better at fifteen or seventeen weeks if the final reading was the result of a random fluctuation. In addition, in most longitudinal studies not all measures are obtained for all subjects. Patients may forget an appointment, they may get sick, or they may feel better (or worse) and not want to bother filling out the rating scales. How do we know that the measures that got recorded reflect the true status of each subject?

Using a "random regression model" that creates a more realistic projection of final results when there are missing data points, the NIMH group reanalyzed its data a few years later (Gibbons et al., 1993); it constructed an individual curve for each subject that predicted what every data point would have been for HRSD scores. Whereas the original study suggested that interpersonal therapy was better than cognitive-behavioral therapy, the reanalysis found the psychotherapies to be equally effective. The antidepressant was now found to produce recovery a little faster, but by the end of sixteen weeks the psychotherapies had caught up. Interestingly, the investigators continued to reveal their bias: they showed a graph illustrating that by raw numeric scores, both psychotherapies were intermediate between placebo and imipramine in reducing HRSD scores. However, as the results were not statistically significant, the careful reader would have to conclude that there was no real difference in the efficacy of these treatments, at least as far as the HRSD was concerned.

In addition to the method of data analysis, we must consider the actual data in studies like this. One of the most important considerations in this and most other psychotherapy studies is that "improvement" is defined as a 50 percent decrease in rating scale scores, and sure enough in the NIMH study, average HRSD scores dropped from about 19 to around 8. Although the decrease may be statistically significant, would you settle for being half as symptomatic after sixteen weeks of treatment? The results are not too much more impressive when you remember that at most 43 percent of treated patients had few or no symptoms at the end of the study, especially since the patients were not that depressed in the first place (a minimum HRSD score of 21 is required to get into many antidepressant studies). The NIMH group thought that clinical management was so good that other treatments could not perform better, but another interpretation is that none of the treatments, including clinical management, was really that good for mild depression.

DISCUSSION QUESTIONS

1. No one would expect every clinical psychologist to be an expert statistician. How much is it necessary to know about statistics in order not to be misled by published research?

2. Statistical analysis is inherently boring to most people. Is there any way to make learning about it more enjoyable and more relevant?

3. What sorts of studies would have to be performed before you could tell a patient that a type of psychotherapy has been proven to be effective for a given condition?

4. Most psychotherapy studies have involved patients with mild forms of unipolar depression (see Chapter 11). What can we say about more severe depressions? If there is no scientific evidence supporting the use of psychotherapy in these conditions, does that mean that it doesn't work?

5. "Biological" disorders like schizophrenia are clearly helped by medications. Does this make psychotherapy irrelevant? How would you study the use of psychotherapy in conditions also treated with medications?

6. How would you develop hypotheses and gather data while treating a single patient? What would you do if your outcome data (e.g., the patient is not functioning better despite working well in therapy) did not support your hypothesis (e.g., this approach to psychotherapy should help the patient)?

7. What are the consequences of using as the major outcome variable the therapist's global impression that the patient seems to be getting something out of therapy? Should patient and therapist do anything else to reassure themselves that therapy is achieving its goals?

REFERENCES

Elkin, I., Shea, T., Watkins, J. T., Imber, S. D., Sotsky, S. M., Collins, J. F., Glass, D. R., Pilkonis, P. A., Leber, W. R., Docherty, J. P., Fiester, S. J., & Parloff, M. B. (1989). National Institute of Mental Health Treatment of Depression Collaborative Research Program: General effectiveness of treatments. *Archives of General Psychiatry, 46*:971–82.

Gibbons, R. D., Hedeker, D., Elkin, I., Waternaux, C., Kraemer, H. C., Greenhouse, J. B., Shea, T., Imber, S. D., Sotsky, S. M., & Watkins, J T. (1993). Some conceptual and statistical issues in analysis of longitudinal psychiatric data. Application to the NIMH Treatment of Depression Collaborative Research Program dataset. *Archives of General Psychiatry, 50,* 739–750.

Projective Test Protocols

To diagnose psychopathology, a psychologist requires a variety of sources of information. He or she will ascertain the individual's psychological history and talk to friends and family members. He or she will conduct a mental status exam, the psychological equivalent of the physical exam that a physician carries out. He or she will observe how the individual behaves and utilize the results of psychological tests.

In arriving at a final diagnosis, and along with it a treatment recommendation and a likely prognosis, a psychologist integrates all the available information. As you know, the judgment of abnormality is inherently fuzzy, and diagnoses are far from foolproof. Projective tests like the Rorschach Inkblot Test (Rorschach, 1942) and the Thematic Apperception Test (Morgan & Murray, 1935) are not as objective as they may seem.

As you read these protocols, try to make inferences about the individuals who produced the responses. However, actual diagnosticians do not work from such protocols alone. They have available a wealth of other information about the person. The purpose of this case is not to illustrate the whole process of diagnosis but simply to let you see some of the raw ingredients involved.

RORSCHACH PROTOCOL

As the text describes in Chapter 7, the Rorschach test consists of a series of ten symmetric inkblots printed individually on heavy card stock. These are shown to an individual one at a time. First the person is asked to say what the blot looks like. The subject gives as many answers as possible, and then is asked specific questions about each perception. Where does it occur in the blot? What makes it look like whatever it looks like?

A number of features in addition to the content of a subject's response are important. For instance, does the individual locate a perception in part or all of the blot? Although the blot is ambiguous, some perceptions nevertheless "fit" better with the actual stimulus than do others in that most people have similar responses. What proportion of responses show a good versus a poor fit? Does the individual respond quickly or slowly when cards are first presented? And so on.

Here are responses given to the ten Rorschach cards by a subject who was unusually productive; the subject gave many more than the typical number of responses to each card. The inkblots are not shown, since psychologists try not to make these images widely available. Nevertheless, do your best to make sense of the responses. What commonalities do you find?

Card #1

1. a bug or beetle about to fly
2. two monks
3. a shark
4. the ocean crashing on rocks
5. African mask used in initiation rite
6. a person's face in profile
7. two dogs
8. a map: the coast of Maine
9. a bell
10. the face of a rhinoceros

Card #2

1. two roosters doing a dance
2. a film negative of a face
3. the inside of a shell
4. two elephants reaching for God knows what
5. two rabbits
6. a tern
7. a bust of Beethoven
8. a flower
9. dancers in the Nutcracker ballet
10. a top

Card #3

1. two guys sitting around a fire
2. two waiters pulling on something
3. seagulls
4. a seedpod
5. a bowl with an elaborate top
6. a panda bear climbing a tree
7. a woman with big boobs laughing
8. a pancreas
9. a Chinese urn
10. an monkey making a gesture
11. an ice shaker

Card #4

1.   a Chinese dragon
2.   seaweed
3.   an iris
4.   a dead duck—really, I mean it!
5.   nodes on the inside of a violin

Card #5

1.   a bat
2.   a butterfly
3.   a guy's face

Card #6

1.   a dragonfly
2.   a boar on its back

Card #7

1.   garden statues . . . in poor taste
2.   an hourglass
3.   the top of a castle
4.   a bedpost

Card #8

1.   a flower, kind of an orchid but not exactly
2.   a uterus
3.   a an animal crawling around on rocks
4.   a biology textbook page

Card # 9

1.   the wizard in the Wizard of Oz
2.   a baby's head
3.   a guy playing a saxophone

Card #10

1.   fantastic-looking flowers
2.   all sorts of flowers
3.   a snapdragons surrounded by dragonflies
4.   a caricatures of two boys bickering
5.   a poodle
6.   a waterfall

THEMATIC APPERCEPTION TEST PROTOCOL

The Thematic Apperception Test, or TAT, also presents subjects with ambiguous stimuli printed on heavy card stock, although in this case the images carry more meaning in themselves than do inkblots. Many TAT pictures contain people. What are they doing? That's for the respondent to say.

There are thirty different TAT cards, but not all are shown to the same individual. Some are intended for children; others for adults. Some are for females; others for males. So each person gets a subset of the cards and is asked to tell a story about what is going on in the pictures. No constraints are placed on the story, except that it must have a beginning, middle, and end. A TAT protocol therefore consists of a description of the scene, what led up to it, and what will follow from it.

Protocols from adults are usually 300 words in length. What follow here are edited stories. These stories are shorter than the actual ones told. As you did for the Rorschach protocol, try to get some sense of the person telling these stories. What themes recur? What defenses seem important? What can you say about the subject's self-esteem?

Card #1

The young boy here is attempting to envision what the future will hold for him. He has been playing his violin with great passion, and he has stopped to wonder if he might be able to have a career as a musician. He envisions a ballet for which he has composed the music. He plays first violin for the orchestra at the opening. The scene is very exciting and grand, but it is difficult for him to hold it in focus.

Card #2

The woman in the left of the picture is a college student, back home for a brief time with her family. The family is a farm family, and their life is hard, simple, and satisfying. The young woman is wondering if she is making the right decision in going to college and following such a different direction. Her mother is again pregnant, and the thought confuses the young woman. She cannot reconcile her belief that women should pursue professions with her mother's obvious happiness about being pregnant.

Card #4

These characters look like they're out of a 1940s movie billboard. He is an adventurer, a reckless do-gooder who takes far greater chances than common sense would dictate. But he always succeeds. After all, this is Hollywood. He has curly black hair and intense blue eyes. The woman is a nurse, in a hospital where our hero has been recovering from a bullet wound to his shoulder. She has fallen in love with him, and is trying to discourage him from leaving the hospital to search for the men who shot him. They are greasy and immoral bandits, and our hero intends to rid the country of them.

Card #5

She has opened the door because she has heard a loud crash. It seems as if a large potted plant, hanging from the ceiling, has fallen to the floor and scattered dirt all over the carpet. She is relieved that the noise signified nothing more serious, but she is also annoyed because she must now clean up the mess.

DISCUSSION QUESTIONS

1. What are your inferences about the person who produced the Rorschach protocol? Is this a male or female? What age? What kind of personality does this person have? What issues are important to this person? What problems does he or she have?

2. Make the same inferences about the person who produced the TAT protocol. And have you considered whether this person is the same as the one who responded to the Rorschach?

3. Compare your impressions with those of your classmates. Do you agree or disagree? What do you conclude about the reliability and validity of projective tests?

4. Take a step back from the controversy that surrounds the usefulness of projective tests in diagnosis. Why would a clinical psychologist favor these tests? Why would another clinical psychologist find them of no value? Does the model of psychopathology that a psychologist has have anything to do with his or her reaction to projective tests?

5. What additional information would you like to have about each subject? How would you gather it?

6. A patient gave just one response to the first three Rorschach cards. In card #1, he saw "impending doom." His response to card #2 was "more impending doom." When presented with card #3, he said, "another kind of impending doom." As he did not seem to be joking, the psychologist stopped the test at this point. What do you think was done next?

REFERENCES

Morgan, C. D., & Murray, H. A. (1935). A method for investigating fantasies. *Archives of Neurology and Psychiatry, 34,* 289–306.

Rorschach, H. (1942). *Psychodiagnostics: A diagnostic test based on perception.* Berne: Huber.

Dread of Church Steeples:
Specific Phobia

A phobia is a fear of some object or situation that is greatly out of proportion to the danger actually posed. The textbook describes two models of phobias. The psychodynamic model holds that the phobic object or situation is the focus of anxiety that is displaced from an unconscious conflict, in which case the object of the phobia symbolizes some aspect of the conflict. According to the behavioral model, a phobia is the result of conditioning fear to a neutral stimulus because both were present at the same time. The only meaning of the stimulus is that fear happened to occur in its presence. A related model holds that readiness to experience fear toward certain things that could be dangerous in the wild such as snakes or heights has evolved in human biology. Psychodynamic and behavioral explanations are not mutually exclusive: conditioned fears can have symbolic meaning, and people can learn to associate increasing anxiety with situations they began avoiding for psychological reasons.

While conditioning and innate vulnerabilities to anxiety probably account for the majority of specific phobias, some cases, perhaps those that do not involve such universal phobic objects as bugs, snakes, and closed in spaces, seem to be more directly related to unconscious conflict. One classic example was described by Morton Prince (1914). Prince's patient had a phobia of steeples and towers that seemed clearly symbolic, although figuring out exactly what they symbolized required some ingenuity.

THE CASE

Here is how Prince presents the symptoms of his patient:

> The patient . . . dreaded and tried in consequence to avoid the sight of [church steeples and towers of any kind]. . . . When she passed by such a tower she was very strongly affected emotionally, experiencing always a feeling of terror or anguish accompanied by the usual marked physical symptoms.

> Sometimes even speaking of a tower would at once awaken this emotional complex which expressed itself outwardly in her face. . . . Considering the frequency with which church and schoolhouse towers are met with in everyday life, one can easily imagine the discomfort arising from such a phobia. . . . She was unable to give any explanation of the origin or meaning of this phobia and could not connect it with any episode in her life, or even state how far back in her life it had existed. Vaguely she thought it existed when she was about fifteen years of age and that it might have existed before that. Now it should be noted that an idea of a tower with bells had in her mind no meaning whatsoever that explained the fear. (Prince, 1914, pp. 389–390).

These symptoms along with others that Prince described seem to meet the six DSM-IV criteria for a diagnosis of specific phobia (simple phobia in DSM-III-R). First, there was "marked and persistent fear that is excessive or unreasonable, cued by the presence or anticipation of a specific object or situation" (American Psychiatric Association, 1994). Second, every time she encountered the phobic stimulus, she immediately became anxious. Consistent with the third DSM-IV criterion, the patient recognized that her fear was excessive but continued to either avoid the phobic situation or endure it only with intense anxiety. In DSM-IV, avoidance, anxious anticipation, or distress must interfere with functioning, relationships, or normal routines, or the patient should be upset about having the phobia, and the symptoms should not be attributable to another mental disorder.

What else should we note about this fear? Although the particular stimulus is somewhat unusual, in other ways this fear is typical of a specific phobia. The patient is a female. The phobia seems to date from her adolescence. And it shows remarkable endurance.

HISTORY

Prince thought that fear of church steeples suggested a psychoanalytic explanation, so he used Freud's method of free association with the patient to uncover the thoughts and feelings she linked to steeples. This failed to reveal any associations. Then he used hypnosis, and again failed to find any deeper meaning to the phobia. Finally, he again hypnotized the woman and put a pencil in her hand. While talking about another subject altogether, the woman "automatically" began to write:

> G _____ M_____ church and my father took my mother to Bi _____ where she died and we went to Br _____ and they cut my mother. I prayed and cried all the time that she would live and the church bells were always ringing and I hated them. (Prince, 1914, pp. 391).

Here then was a clue about the etiology of the phobia. Prince proceeded to question the patient concerning the events that surrounded the death of her mother.

When the patient was about fifteen years of age, her mother was taken to a famous surgeon in another town for an operation needed to save her life. While her mother was in the hospital, the patient went twice a day to a nearby church to pray for her recovery. The church bells chimed while she prayed. Further, she could hear the church bells chime fifteen minutes from the hotel where she and her father were staying. The bells therefore came to be strongly associated with the fear that the patient experienced about her mother's possible death.

Her mother finally died. It had so happened that on one occasion, the patient had neglected her prayers. At that time, the thought occurred to her that her lapse might have caused of her mother's death. So the bells also came to be strongly associated with the guilt that the patient subsequently experienced.

It turned out that the patient's guilt went deeper than forgetting to pray once. When she was thirteen years old, i.e., two years before her mother's death, the family was abroad, and the girl fell ill. The family subsequently delayed its return home. The patient believed that had the family returned home sooner, her mother's illness would have been diagnosed sooner, with a happier outcome. Had she not fallen ill, then her mother would not have died.

The patient's considerable guilt had been linked with the church bells. To avoid this association, she avoided the bells, as well as the steeples that contained them. She was thus able to repress her painful feelings; she experienced anxiety only when she was around the objects that unconsciously reminded her of those feelings. Displacement of anxiety was complicated by classical conditioning in that when thoughts about her mother's illness (the US) were paired with the church bells (CS), distress about the thoughts (UR) came to be evoked by the bells; i.e., anxiety became a CR. Distress extended to the steeple as a result of stimulus generalization.

TREATMENT

Today, Prince's treatment of his patient would be considered a combination of psychoanalytic psychotherapy and cognitive therapy (see Chapter 19). First, he focused on her self-reproach. Was it really the case that the family delayed its return home because the young girl was ill? Upon examination, this belief seemed to have no basis whatsoever. Relying on the patient's own memories, Prince convinced her that she was not particularly ill. After all, she was not taken to doctors or hospitals. She was not housebound. And the family traveled extensively. Her mother and father were not worried about her health. They were just looking for an excuse to prolong their vacation!

Had the unfortunate death of her mother not followed on the heels of this vacation, the patient would have probably forgotten about her own illness or perhaps remembered it for the minor incident that it was. But because of the way that events unfolded, her illness took on great meaning and provided the foundation of her phobia. As these ideas were made clear, the patient remarked to Prince:

> Why, of course, I see it now! My mother did not stay in Europe on account of my health but because she enjoyed it, and might have returned if she wanted to. I never thought of that before! It was not my fault at all! (Prince, 1914, p. 410)

With this realization, the phobia was gone.

DISCUSSION QUESTIONS

1. The modern therapist might have used behavioral techniques such as systematic desensitization or flooding. If one of these methods had worked, would it invalidate the psychodynamic explanation of the cause of the phobia?

2. How could the success of insight in this case be explained in behavioral terms?

3. How might psychodynamic and behavioral approaches be combined in the treatment of a specific phobia?

4. What is the relationship between specific phobias and more complex disorders such as agoraphobia?

5. How might test-taking phobia be treated?

6. Why are women more likely to have specific phobias than men?

REFERENCES

American Psychiatric Association (1994). *Diagnostic and Statistical Manual of Mental Disorders* (4th ed.). Washington, DC: American Psychiatric Press.

Prince, M. (1914). *The unconscious: The fundamentals of human personality normal and abnormal.* New York: Macmillan.

The Hidden Crisis:
Masked Post-Traumatic
Stress Disorder

You learned in Chapter 8 that during the development of DSM-IV there was considerable debate about how severe trauma should be before post-traumatic stress disorder (PTSD) is diagnosed. Some argued that when depression, anxiety, multiple personality, eating disorder, personality disorder, and other syndromes are felt to be caused by early childhood trauma, they should all be include in a category of "disorders of extreme stress not otherwise specified" (DESNOS) on the grounds that they are all forms of PTSD. The DSM-IV committee eventually decided that there was not enough credible research or even agreement about what would constitute "extreme stress" to subsume so many conditions under a DESNOS category. Instead, they stipulated that PTSD should be diagnosed after the patient experiences or witnesses events that involved actual or threatened death or serious injury to him- or herself or others (American Psychiatric Association, 1994). The experience should have evoked intense fear, helplessness, or horror in adults and disorganization or agitation in children.

The resulting PTSD symptoms that are described in Chapter 8 fall into the categories of reexperiencing the trauma, avoiding stimuli or situations associated with the trauma plus numbing of general responsiveness, and symptoms of arousal. In DSM-IV, these symptoms must last more than a month and must impair functioning or cause significant distress if a diagnosis of PTSD is to be made. DSM-IV permits diagnoses of acute or chronic PTSD and of PTSD with delayed onset if symptoms begin at least six months after exposure to the stress.

PTSD can be easy to recognize in victims of rape, war, earthquake, and other disasters. It may be overdiagnosed in situations in which there are powerful incentives to use any sort of stressful experience to legitimize being compensated or getting out of the consequences of committing a crime. On the other hand, PTSD may be underrecognized following mundane events, especially if no one was hurt or killed, when compensation is not an issue. The next case shows how PTSD can assume subtle but nevertheless incapacitating forms.

THE CASE

Anna Francis, a thirty-year-old executive, was driving to work when the driver of a car going in the other direction lost control and struck her vehicle. Her car rolled over, and she was trapped inside for an hour. While rescue attempts proceeded, she wondered whether her car was going to catch fire before she got out.

When Anna was finally freed, she was rushed to the hospital and kept overnight for observation. She was found to have a mild concussion that seemed to be causing a bad headache that gradually got better over the next few weeks. She did not feel particularly upset about her experience and was mainly grateful not to have ended up in worse shape.

About six months later, Anna was driving to work when someone cut in front of her. Momentarily startled, she was able to avoid an accident and continued on her way. Although nothing happened, she could not sleep that night. Her sleep continued to be disturbed, and lack of sleep brought on a severe headache. When rest and aspirin did not help, she consulted a neurologist, who, not finding anything wrong, suggested that the headache would probably go away in a few more days.

Not only did the headache not improve, it became complicated by pain in her neck and arms and by severe dizziness that prevented her from driving. She felt too tired to go to work, and she was too uncomfortable to get anything done anyway. After several weeks, her activities were so restricted that she got worried and went back to the neurologist. There were still no findings, and the neurologist thought that it might help to consult a psychologist.

Discovering that Anna's mother had died at about the same time of year, the consultant encouraged her to express unresolved grief, and this seemed to help somewhat. However, the dizziness persisted and even got worse. As Anna became more unhappy, irritable, and withdrawn, the diagnosis was changed to depression, but treatment for this problem did not help the dizziness and headache, and her neck and back pain became nearly unbearable.

Admitting that treatment based on the presumptive diagnoses was not working, the therapist decided to discard any preconceptions and start over by finding out more about the symptoms instead of taking them at face value. When the patient was asked to describe what the dizziness felt like, she mentioned that it was something like being upside down. The psychologist was struck by this unusual description and asked whether she had ever actually been upside down. "Just when I was trapped in the car," was her reply. "Were you frightened?" asked the therapist. "I didn't have time to be scared. And it wouldn't have done any good to worry about it after it was over."

The psychologist began to wonder whether ignoring her reaction to the life-threatening situation had created an underlying state of arousal that was activated with such intensity by the brief scare she had six months later that she could no longer shut it off. Perhaps the "upside-down" feeling was a way of remembering being trapped in the car in "body language" so that she would not have to think about it in words. The headache could have been a physical memory of the shock following getting out of the car. Her inability to drive might represent avoidance of situations that might recall the accident, and her withdrawal could be an expression of emotional blunting rather than depression.

When this possibility was discussed with Anna, she suddenly remembered that the reason why she was having trouble sleeping was that she was repeatedly awakened by some kind of nightmare about driving that she could not exactly remember. It also turned out that while her memory of some aspects of her experience was excellent, she could not remember anything about the actual crash, even though she was never knocked out. When she began to try to reconstruct the event, she suddenly felt tense, and this made her back and neck pain much worse. The pain, it turned out, was caused by muscle tension associated with chronic hypervigilance.

The therapist explained that although it might be desirable not to feel frightened by life-threatening events once they were over, human physiology is programmed to respond to danger so that it can mobilize mind and body to respond. It might be possible to block out conscious awareness of the danger, but the only way to shut off the underlying arousal was to let it out and perhaps recondition it. Acknowledging and remembering the incident in detail helped Anna to put the event into perspective, and progressive relaxation helped the muscle tension and headaches. The dizziness went away once she remembered the fear of being trapped upside down in a car that might burst into flame, as well as the spinning feeling of the actual collision. Feeling a greater sense of control over body and mind, she was no longer as tense.

Why had Anna had to repress her memory of the initial trauma? Her mother had died in an automobile accident.

DISCUSSION QUESTIONS

1. How might previous traumatic experiences predispose to the development of PTSD after a later, milder trauma?

2. How could preexisting anxiety or depression make a person more susceptible to PTSD?

3. Is there anything about individual psychology and physiology that might make one person develop incapacitating PTSD whereas someone else exposed to the same trauma handles it well?

4. The textbook points out that Israeli soldiers fighting in Lebanon were found to be more likely to get PTSD if their parents were Holocaust survivors. What might be the cause of this vulnerability?

5. The Israeli Army has also found that putting soldiers with early PTSD right back on the battlefield produces a remission. During the Vietnam War, the U.S. Army evacuated soldiers with PTSD. Who do you think had a better outcome? Why?

6. If you were on one of the debriefing teams for survivors of disasters like the recent earthquakes or floods in California, how would you reduce the risk of PTSD in the people you interviewed?

7. Under what circumstances might medications be useful for PTSD? When might they be harmful?

REFERENCE

American Psychiatric Association (1994). *Diagnostic and Statistical Manual of Mental Disorders* (4th ed.). Washington, DC: American Psychiatric Press.

The Insistent Ideas
of Miss M.: Obsessive-
Compulsive Disorder

You learned in Chapter 9 that obsessive-compulsive disorder (OCD) continues to be classified with anxiety disorders because trying to resist obsession or compulsion evokes anxiety. However, this does not prove that anxiety *causes* obsession or compulsion. You might feel anxious if you were kept from going to class or studying in your usual way for an examination, but not because your only reason for learning or studying were nonspecific anxiety. If your favorite route home were under construction, you might feel distress, but not because your anxiety drove you in that direction. If anxiety is an innate response to disruption of any routine, it may be the routine that is abnormal in OCD, not the anxiety.

The hypothesis that OCD is a disorder of routines rather than conflicts, perhaps involving loss of regulation of areas of the brain involved in smooth and coordinated movement (the basal ganglia and frontal cortex) (Rapoport and Wise, 1988), receives some support from observations of associations between obsessions and compulsions with movement disorders. Almost 40 percent of OCD patients meet criteria for tic disorder (Putnam et al., 1987), and up to 75 percent of patients with Tourette's disorder have obsessions and compulsions (Frankel et al., 1986). It has even been suggested that OCD is the only human mental disorder for which a naturally occurring animal model exists. This takes the form of compulsive grooming that can lead to chronic self-injury in horses who bite themselves compulsively (Murphy, 1991). Stable owners have found that the same medications that improve OCD in people reduce this kind of behavior in their animals.

Your textbook points out that although the form of obsessions and compulsions has remained stable over the years, their content has changed. Some of the more enduring types of obsessions, such as concerns about contamination or harm to a loved one, are also described. When such obsessions occur in the context of a mood disorder or schizophrenia, as when a woman with a postpartum depression develops obsessive fears of harming her newborn, they may represent the breakthrough of destructive impulses, and it may be necessary to take steps to protect the subject of the obsessions. In such settings, clinicians also have to distinguish obsessions from delusional beliefs, for example, that the infant is doomed and would be better off dead, and even from responses to hallucinated voices telling the patient to commit some harmful act. Obviously, all these situations require urgent intervention.

Conversely, people with OCD (as opposed to obsessions or compulsions that are brought out by some other disorder) rarely if ever act on obsessive thoughts that they will hurt someone. Psychoanalysts have traditionally interpreted these kinds of obsessions as representing forbidden wishes, with the rage that really belongs with these thoughts being removed (isolation of affect) and the patient experiencing only dismay at an abhorrent thought. However, attempts to make OCD patients aware of the unconscious wish are notoriously unsuccessful in curing obsessions; if anything, they provide more to obsess about. As you learned in Chapter 9, behavioral treatments and serotonin reuptake inhibitor antidepressants such as clomipramine (Anafranil), fluoxetine (Prozac), and fluvoxamine (Luvox) are much more effective, although they reduce by 40 to 50 percent rather than cure symptoms, especially in severe cases.

The failure of attempts to unravel the meanings of obsessions to resolve them could mean that the presumed meanings are wrong. Perhaps some obsessional fears represent minor irritations and jealousies that become amplified by the inability to regulate repetitive thoughts that conflict with a person's self-image. It is also possible that obsessions represent an amplified experience of a person's idea of the worst thing that could happen. Certainly, killing someone you love would fall into this category. This was an issue in a case of OCD that was described more than a century ago by Edward Cowles (1888).

THE CASE

When Cowles first met the patient, she was twenty-eight years old.

> She was of a good family . . . both the parents were then living, and over seventy years of age. She was the youngest of ten children. . . . The patient had a good physique, was a little above the average in stature, and in good bodily health in all particulars. She [was] . . . a person of more than ordinary intelligence and good sense . . . usually amiable, pleasing, and dignified in manner; though reticent, she was not unsocial. She was disposed, however, to dress very plainly and to be negligent in this regard. . . . She was well-informed, read good books, chose the most intelligent persons as companions, . . . was keen of insight and quick at repartee. . . . In brief, she was in many respects an interesting person (Cowles, 1888, pp. 230–231).

So what was the problem that brought Miss M. to the mental hospital where Dr. Cowles worked? The main problem was that she believed that ordinary acts she might commit would bring harm to a close female friend, Miss C. Although Miss M. recognized that her beliefs were absurd, that there could be no actual connection between her acts and anything that would befall her friend, she nonetheless could not rid her mind of them. These beliefs caused her great distress, and she despaired of ever ridding herself of them.

Her obsession dated to adolescence and revolved around Miss C., by all accounts a lovely, charming young woman. Although Miss M. cared deeply for Miss C., she felt jealous of the attention that was paid to her friend's beauty. She had fleeting thoughts of wanting to hurt Miss C. that felt so reprehensible that she immediately reprimanded herself. But instead of going away, her thoughts just intensified. The obsessions got much worse when Miss M. spent a few months living with Miss C., so much so that Miss M. made a threatening gesture toward her friend. This made her feel extremely guilty, and she became frightened about how she would feel if anything bad did happen to Miss C.

Miss M. discovered a way of allaying some of her anxiety. When she started to think of something bad happening to Miss C., she substituted another person in her mind and let that person take the brunt of the injury.

> This worked well for a while, but soon began to be refined upon. It became necessary to choose for the substituted person someone with many opposite characteristics to C.; for example, there had to be a difference in age, sometimes of sex, initials of name, color of eyes and hair, stature, distance as to residence from C., and at last peculiar requirements as to time, place, etc., etc., to an endless extent. Next it became necessary to have ready in mind a number of chosen persons, two, or three, or four of whom, as the case might be, must be thought of in a certain order, etc. After a while, thinking of these persons ceased to give mental relief and another set had to be chosen, to wear out in turn (Cowles, 1888, p. 241).

Miss M.'s growing obsession was accompanied by compulsions.

> It affected the taking of certain articles of food, or going to certain places; interdicted certain things, or permitted them on certain days and not on others. Colors, pictures, and ornaments were banished from her room. She was fond of dress, but certain materials and many colors could not be worn, although she most liked them. Certain days were tabooed for shopping . . . and certain shops could not be entered (Cowles, 1888, pp. 244–245).

Although Miss M. was treated many years ago, she would meet DSM-IV criteria for OCD. She had obsessions and compulsions that caused considerable distress, took a great deal of time, and interfered with her ordinary life. Indeed, her rituals became her life. Although she had been an outstanding student, she left school, unable to study. She had trouble reading, because what she read frequently triggered her obsessions, which in turn triggered her compulsions. She gave up many of her friends.

To compound her difficulties even more, Miss M. did not discuss her problems with anyone. She kept her mental and behavioral routines a secret. Immediately prior to her hospitalization, Miss M. attempted suicide. Her motive was not to die but to have herself taken to a hospital, which was what happened. It was then that she confided in the attending physician.

HISTORY

According to Cowles, the first hint of Miss M.'s disorder appeared as early as age ten or twelve, when she was occasionally depressed and had worries about death. During early adolescence, she experienced several severe illnesses, during which her fears increased. At this time, she found herself repeating acts several times because her initial performance didn't quite seem "right" and might thereby bring harm to her. As her illnesses resolved, so too did these tendencies. With puberty, however, Miss M. again began to repeat everyday actions, particularly those associated with dressing or undressing. She felt insecure about her own attractiveness, and she became quite jealous of other young women, notably the lovely Miss C.

As the years passed and the number of "substitute" victims increased, some of them died. Having "wished" that they would die, her fears of the power of her own thoughts were intensified.

Miss M. did not improve much during her hospitalization, so she devised her own solution to her problems. Perhaps if she suffered physically, she would no longer suffer mentally. On a walk away from the hospital, she obtained a pistol and shot herself in the shoulder and hip, hoping to damage her joints and cripple herself. The wounds she inflicted were only superficial, though, and quickly healed. Miss M. was left with her obsessive-compulsive disorder. Cowles closes by saying that he was unaware of her subsequent history. Granted what we know about the prognosis of these disorders, though, we can assume that Miss M. probably continued to suffer.

DISCUSSION QUESTIONS

1. Is it normal to be jealous of an attractive friend? If so, what would a psychoanalyst say about why Miss M. developed OCD whereas someone else in the same situation might not? What would the cognitive-behavioral therapist postulate? What about the biologically oriented therapist?

2. Miss M. seemed to have been open with Cowles in discussing the meaning of her symptoms. Yet, we can assume that she still got worse since she engaged in increasingly pathological behavior to try to control her obsessions. Why might she have had this paradoxical treatment response?

3. Miss M. seems to have become depressed during the course of the OCD, as occurs in about half the patients with this disorder. Why do some people with OCD become depressed and others not become depressed despite equally severe obsessions? How might OCD and depression interact?

4. What is the difference between an obsession and a delusion? Between a compulsion and an impulsive act? Between a fear and a wish?

5. If Miss M. came to you for treatment, what would you do? How would you discuss the prognosis without making her feel more demoralized?

REFERENCES

Cowles, E. (1888). Insistent and fixed ideas. *American Journal of Psychology, 1,* 222–270.

Frankel, M., Cummings, J. L., Robertson, M. M., Trimble, M. R., Hill, M. A., and Benson, D. F. (1986). Obsessions and compulsions in Gilles de la Tourette's syndrome. *Neurology, 36,* 378–82.

Murphy, D. L. (1991). The serotonin connection in OCD. *Neuropsychopharmacology, 5,* 11–12.

Pittman, R. K., Green, R. C., Jenike, M. A., & Mesulami, M. M. (1987). Clinical comparison of Tourette's disorder and obsessive-compulsive disorder. *American Journal of Psychiatry, 144,* 1166–71.

Rapoport, J. L., & Wise, S. P. (1988). Obsessive-compulsive disorder: Evidence for basal ganglia dysfunction. *Psychopharmacology Bulletin, 24,* 380–84.

George's Magic Bullet: Obsessive-Compulsive Disorder

When salversan (arsphenamine) was introduced as a treatment for syphilis (Chapter 3), it was called "Doctor Ehrlich's magic bullet" because it was a specific and near magical treatment for a disabling and fatal mental disease. Miss M., in Case 9, tried a more concrete kind of bullet therapy: by crippling herself, she hoped to give herself a tangible focus of worry that would distract her from her obsessions. This was not a terribly unusual strategy: psychotic patients sometimes feel better emotionally when they develop physical illnesses that occupy all their attention and activity. In Miss M.'s case, however, "bullet therapy" was not effective. One hundred years later, the *San Francisco Chronicle* reported an instance in which this approach did work. George, a man with a severe obsessive-compulsive disorder, shot himself in the head with a .22-caliber bullet. His motive was not as complex as that of Miss M. He merely wanted to die, so distressed was he by his symptoms. When George recovered form his suicide attempt, the obsessions and compulsions were gone. Presumably, the bullet interrupted the pathological input from the frontal lobes that either sustained or failed to suppress repetitive mental and physical behavior. Remarkably, this happened without any loss of intellectual function. He returned to school, finished high school, and started college.

George was nineteen years old when he tried to kill himself. His disorder had revolved around fear of germs. He had obsessed about contamination. He had washed his hands hundreds of times a day and taken frequent showers. He could not attend school or hold a job. When the stories about George appeared, it had been five years since his suicide attempt. His disorder had not returned, although it is reported that George washes his dishes much more thoroughly than most people. George lives alone. Apparently, he is a somewhat isolated individual.

DISCUSSION QUESTIONS

1. Although they have received terrible press over the years, most of it justified, neurosurgical interruption of various brain tracts, especially from the frontal cortex (Rapoport and Wise, 1988), still is used occasionally as a treatment of last resort for intractable OCD. How might this treatment work?

2. Under what circumstances might surgery for OCD be justified? Would an obsessional patient have trouble understanding and accepting the potential risks and benefits?

3. What common mechanisms might exist for surgery, medications that increase brain serotonin levels, and behavior therapy?

4. How would you test the hypothesis that George had a spontaneous remission of OCD or that there were psychological reasons why the suicide attempt cured him? What psychological factors might produce remission of OCD after a suicide attempt? After a lobotomy?

REFERENCES

Bullet in the brain cures man's mental problem. *San Francisco Chronicle*, February 23, 1988, pp. 1+.

Rapoport, J. S., & Wise, S. P. (1988). Obsessive-compulsive disorder: Evidence for basal ganglia dysfunction. *Psychopharmacology Bulletin, 24,* 380–84.

Mr. P.'s Travels:
Dissociative Fugue

Pierre Janet, the French psychiatrist who figures prominently in the history of abnormality as described in Chapter 2 of your text, visited Harvard University in the early part of this century to give a series of lectures. One of the cases he described was that of Mr. P., a man with dissociative fugue. Fugue remains a rare type of dissociative disorder (dissociative fugue in DSM-IV) in which a person suddenly leaves home, loses memory of the past, and partially or fully assumes a new identity.

If we did not have the capacity to process a large amount of information unconsciously, we would be so overwhelmed by the sheer number of perceptions and thoughts it is possible to have that it would be impossible to pay attention to the simplest task. When we are studying or working on a project, we pay no attention to what we did yesterday or last year. When we are concentrating intensely on something, for example, driving on an icy road, we may not be aware of anything else—perhaps not even what just happened on the road. However, when we redirect our attention, we can recover memories of events that were not in our conscious awareness. We may not remember everything that we were not actively thinking about, but there is usually nothing systematic about memories that are lost.

A fugue state is an exaggeration of the tendency to split off or dissociate aspects of experience, not because it is inconvenient or distracting to pay attention to them, but because they feel threatening, overwhelming, or confusing. As a result, personal memories cannot be recalled. Conscious experience is not fragmented, but is organized to exclude important memories.

The person in a fugue state is unaware that large segments of personal history are separated from the rest of active mental life. Janet describes the fugue state as

> . . . a system of images which has separated from the totality of consciousness and has an independent development. It brings about two things: a blank in the general consciousness, which is represented by an amnesia, and an exaggerated and independent development of the emancipated idea. . . . The

feeling that arises from the fear of an ignominious charge, the feeling of curiosity for distant countries, the feeling of love and jealousy toward a lover . . . these are systems of thoughts . . . not always easy to express in words . . . but they nonetheless possess a mental unity. (Janet, 1920, pp. 64–65).

THE CASE

Janet provides the background of Mr. P.'s fugue:

> The subject is a man, P., thirty years old, employed in a railway station in a town in the east of France. Although an active and clever fellow, he was a little eccentric, and had already led a somewhat adventurous life. In his youth he had had frequent fits of somnambulism, sometimes in the day, but mostly at night. Moreover, the tendency to somnambulism is to be found in his family. . . . This man, P., was also very affected, predisposed to fixed ideas. One day, in the notary's office where he worked, he was slightly suspected, though not accused of stealing a trifle. He fell ill, and was very distressed. Night and day he discussed that suspicion, and, although everybody tried to prove to him how trifling it was, he could not remain in that office. Moreover, he had a tendency to exaggerated fears. He had left Lorraine after its annexation to Germany, and during many years he was haunted by the fear of the German police, whom he always believed to be running after him . . .
>
> At the age of twenty, he got a situation in a railway company, and was soon in easy circumstances. He married, and had a child he dearly loved. His wife was again pregnant when the following incident took place. Although he led a quiet and rather happy life, he was uneasy in his mind, and gave himself up to intellectual labours too hard for a man who had no great acquirements. To his work in the railway office he added bookkeeping . . . He was made uneasy in his mind by family quarrels: his brother, who was jealous of him, had just quarrelled with him and had charged him with shameful and dishonest acts. The charge was groundless, and nobody around him troubled about it, but we know how easily upset, how susceptible he was in that quarter . . .
>
> It is in these conditions that we come to the third of February, 1895. He was alone . . . he went to a coffee-house where he was well known. During the afternoon, a part of which he spent with some friends at this coffee-house in playing billiards, he drank a cup of coffee, two glasses of beer, and a small glass of vermouth . . . He told us himself all these circumstances, which he remembers quite well. . . . He left that coffee-house about five . . . but a few yards off, while crossing the Stanislas bridge over the railway line, just as he got to the middle (that also he perfectly remembers), he felt a violent

pain in his head, as if he had been struck . . . immediately after that something must have changed in the mental state of
our patient, as he entirely lost the memory of all that happened afterwards on that Sunday, the third of February, 1895.
(Janet, 1920, pp. 45–48).

When Mr. P.'s normal state of consciousness returned nine days later,
he found himself not in France but in Belgium, near Brussels. He was
lying in a snow-covered field. He had no recollection of what had ensued
during this period.

Mr. P. sought assistance. He was taken to Paris and then to the
Salpetriere, where he came under the care of Dr. Janet. Although Janet
skips over just how he helped Mr. P. recapture his lost memories, here is
what was discovered:

- On the Stanislas Bridge, Mr. P. became overwhelmed with fear over
  the accusations by his brother.
- He went home, continuing to worry about the charges, and became
  even more anxious.
- He wandered the streets, wondering how to escape the consequences
  of the accusations.
- He returned home for money and then checked into a hotel to spend
  the night.
- The next morning, he went to a railway station (not the one where
  he worked) and traveled to another city.
- He got off the train and walked to a nearby town, all the time hiding
  from the police he supposed were pursuing him.
- He took another train to yet another city, then another city, then still
  another city.
- The idea occurred to him that he should eventually seek refuge in a
  distant country.
- He came to Brussels and set out to find a job, in order to save money
  for his long journey.
- He was unsuccessful in finding work.
- His finances dwindled, and he sought help in a shelter; a man there
  took pity on him and wrote a letter of introduction to a local charity.
- Mr. P. attempted to enlist for service in the Dutch Indies but was
  turned down.
- Exhausted, broke, and thwarted, he stretched out in a field of snow
  to die.

As Mr. P. prepared himself for death, he thought of his family. (He had
not thought of his family for the previous nine days.) He was jarred, since
his memories struck him as so vague. He read the letter of introduction
that was still in his pocket, which recounted part of his story, and his
memory returned, except for what had transpired during the last nine
days.

DISCUSSION QUESTIONS

1. How do you think Janet helped the patient regain his memories? Would you do anything differently nowadays?

2. Why is fugue such a rare disorder? Why is it most prevalent during wartime or in the wake of a natural disaster?

3. Janet says that Mister P.'s fugue began in the context of intense emotional arousal and feelings of helplessness. The same state can lead to psychosis, suicide, or sudden death. Why would some people develop dissociation, and others different forms of mental or even physical breakdown in the same setting?

4. What is the relationship between somnambulism (sleepwalking) and fugue?

5. Does Mister P.'s family history of somnambulism suggest an inherited component of fugue or other dissociative disorders? What sort of inherited malfunction might lead to dissociation? How would you distinguish between a dissociation factor that is inherited in families from one that is learned in families?

REFERENCE

Janet, P. (1920). *The major symptoms of hysteria.* New York: Macmillan.

The Two Faces of Eve: Genuine and Pseudo Multiple Personality Disorder

You learned in Chapter 9 that multiple personality disorder, or MPD (dissociative identity disorder in DSM-IV), is being recognized with increasing frequency. In part, this reflects an increasing awareness of a disorder that was until recently thought to be rare or nonexistent (Prince, 1905). The textbook also points out that MPD may be overdiagnosed in some cases. Criminals like the Hillside Strangler may claim innocence on the grounds that an alternate personality or "alter" committed the crime without the perpetrator's conscious knowledge—another version of the "it was the devil, not me" defense.

Pretending to have MPD (i.e., malingering) is rare. However, the unconscious simulation of MPD may be more common. Since people who develop MPD learn to hypnotize themselves readily as children, it is possible that people with a tendency toward dissociation may be encouraged by therapists, other patients, or even the patients themselves to magnify that tendency until lapses in consciousness seen to be organized into different personalities. In this case, treatment of dissociation may increase the very symptom it is supposed to help, not only by suggestion but by producing emotional arousal that calls forth more dissociation and by paying more attention to evidence of emerging MPD than evidence of adaptation.

Isn't the diagnosis of something as dramatic as MPD obvious? Isn't MPD an inevitable outgrowth of dissociation, just a little further down the road from fugue? It is true that dissociation is the core mechanism of MPD, but it is also prominent in any number of other syndromes, including not only other dissociative disorders but also mood disorders, psychoses, post-traumatic stress disorder, and borderline personality disorder. In any of these conditions, dissociation may be called into play to an extent that it fragments the personality temporarily, but this is not necessarily the defining problem. If the depression or psychosis is treated, reactions to the trauma are overcome, or the personality disorder is addressed, less dissociation is needed to handle overwhelming emotion or conflict. Conversely, suggesting subtly that perhaps the patient was another person during times that cannot be remembered may provide a cohesive explanation for everything that has ever troubled the patient, an exciting partnership with the therapist, and as was mentioned in the discussion of Case 3, membership in an elite if tortured group that can provide at least a modicum of identity and self-esteem for someone who has been abandoned, abused, despised, or confused.

There have also been political and economic inducements to the proliferation of MPD. Since MPD occurs almost exclusively in people with a history of childhood abuse, legitimizing it has become linked to movements to acknowledge child abuse and help its victims. Not believing that a patient has MPD can seem to some patients (and their therapists) like not believing that they have suffered or that they are entitled to feel bad or to be treated. There has been a certain symbiosis between the victims' rights movement and certain psychiatric hospitals that have been able to keep up their income by opening inpatient units specializing in the treatment of MPD.

Many patients who get admitted to these units have complicated problems that lead to prolonged hospitalization at a time when hospitalization for virtually every other psychiatric disorder has been limited by cost containment strategies. These kinds of pressures add to clinical uncertainty in deciding whether the apparent experience of different personalities actually represents MPD, which requires a different treatment than disorders that can masquerade as it. The next two cases illustrate some of the differences between MPD that develops spontaneously and an MPD-like syndrome that emerges later in life, often during the course of treatment.

THE CASE OF EVE WHITE

Eve White had been having problems for most of her life. Trouble concentrating in school made her a mediocre student, and she never was able to live up to her potential. She thought that her drinking was the cause of frequent lapses of memory, but these were not typical of alcoholic blackouts. She might find herself in the middle of a conversation with no idea what she had been talking about, or she might end up in an unfamiliar place with no memory of how she got there. She never said anything about these interruptions of awareness but covered them up by pretending to be aware of what was going on.

Ms. White married a man who was away on business for at least six months of every year. Far from being an inconvenience, this amount of distance proved desirable for both of them. When he was promoted to a position that no longer required so much travel, the couple could not tolerate spending more time together and they began arguing. Mr. white had an affair, and the couple separated.

Eve did not seem to feel any different after the separation, but her memory got worse. She began to find clothing in her closet that she did not remember buying. While going through the mail, she found an unstamped letter addressed to her in a handwriting she did not recognize that told her about something she had done that she did not remember.

When Eve consulted a psychologist for help in understanding what was happening to her, the therapist was struck with what seemed to be random fluctuations in the patient's manner. Sometimes, she was withdrawn, passive, and unhappy, while the next moment she was irritable and sarcastic. Her mind seemed well organized at any particular moment, but she was not always aware of statements she had just made. At first, she seemed to have an odd tic, but on closer inspection it appeared that she was "spacing out," completely unaware of what was going on.

Eve initially resisted the idea that she might have multiple personality disorder. Using videotapes, however, the psychologist was able to demonstrate the dissociative episodes to her. They were gradually able to trace her drastically different behaviors back to three personalities that had varying awareness of each other. One personality was a pessimistic, withdrawn, dependent person; one was an angry, vengeful woman who wanted to punish her husband for leaving her; and one was a willful, promiscuous adolescent. The personalities had first appeared when her father began molesting her, as a way of dealing with contradictory feelings about someone she loved who also betrayed her. Eve was gradually able to see these personalities as different aspects of the problems handling anger, intimacy, and sexuality that emerged from these experiences.

THE CASE OF EVE BLACK

Like Eve White, Eve Black forgot things that happened in one state of mind when she was in another state of mind. However, this did not progress to organized activities in dissociated states such as buying things, writing letters, or behaving like a completely different person. On the other hand, she had a long-standing history of severe mood swings in which periods of irritable or exhilarated hyperactivity and decreased need for sleep alternated with sluggish withdrawal and a constant sleep. It was these states of contradictory mood that drove contradictory thoughts and behaviors, rather than the other way around.

Ms. Black was also married to a man who left her, and in response she, too, became more disorganized. She began forgetting large segments of the day, and her manner changed continually. She could not remember what she had done five minutes earlier, and when reminded of conversations she had had, she could recall nothing about them.

Eve Black began psychotherapy with a therapist who specialized in treating MPD. Just as a surgeon is more likely to tell you that you need an operation for a given problem whereas an internist will tell you that a medication will work, this therapist's bias was that *dissociation* equaled a dissociative *disorder,* and the therapist began asking the patient about different personalities. With encouragement from the therapist to report anything that might provide evidence of multiple personalities, the patient became aware that two alters—one called "Fast Eddie" and the other called "Slowpoke"—were competing with her dominant personality for control of her mind. Fast Eddie was jovial, impulsive, hyperactive, and a spendthrift, with a great interest in sex. Slowpoke was withdrawn, lethargic, demoralized and depressed, and disinterested in everything.

Eve Black's therapist also tried to make her more aware of the personalities she exhibited so that she could reintegrate the different sides of herself that had been dissociated from each other. It was presumed that dissociation had been the result of early abuse that the patient could not remember because it had been dissociated too. Unlike Eve White, Eve Black readily talked about her alters, and as she continued to focus on them, they not only became more definite, they split off more and more from each other. To deal with the increased dissociation, the frequency of therapy sessions was increased so that the therapist could work on emerging evidence of even more personalities. After a year of therapy, patient and therapist had counted 741 different personalities, and the tally was still increasing.

In contrast to Eve White, Ms. Black's functioning deteriorated the more therapy she received. In considering the reasons for this failure of treatment, it was recognized that the loss of Eve Black's husband had precipitated a bipolar mood disorder (see Chapter 11), with increasingly severe mood swings from mania to depression. Dissociation in this case was an attempt to organized chaotic and randomly fluctuating moods that pushed her mind in one direction or another in response to minor provocations by placing experience in different moods in different mental categories. When the unstable mood was treated with lithium and the patient was encouraged to grieve the loss of her husband, the other personalities went away. It turned out that she had not been abused but that her family was loaded with people with the same kinds of mood swings.

DISCUSSION QUESTIONS

1. Would you expect Eve White and Eve Black to have different symptoms that might be clues that they had different problems?

2. What is the difference between dissociation and a dissociative disorder?

3. What problems would you anticipate in the treatment of Eve White?

4. Why did Eve Black develop so many personalities?

5. Why does one person who has been abused in childhood utilize dissociation as a defense when someone else who has not been abused employs other defenses? What might make a person who has not

had traumatic experiences dissociate? Would a family history of fugue and other dissociative states change your answer?

6. Why is MPD more common in women than men?

7. Is the proliferation of hospital units specializing in the treatment of MPD the result or the cause of the increasing frequency with which MPD is being diagnosed?

REFERENCE

Prince, M. (1905). *The dissociation of a personality.* New York: Longmans, Green.

Psychosomatic Medicine: The Mirsky Ulcer Study

Chapter 10 reviews the evolving concept of psychosomatic illness. As Rosenhan and Seligman imply, it is very unlikely that a single psychological factor directly causes any specific medical illness. Nonspecific psychological and psychophysiologic processes such as reactions to loss, helplessness, anger, arousal, and withdrawal seem to interact with inborn and acquired response styles and physical predispostions to set the stage for the emergence of a range of bodily conditions. As the body changes, it can feed back to the mind to solidify attitudes that may contribute to more physical pathology. As researchers have understood the two-way interactions between mind and body, theories of psychosomatic illness have become much more complex.

One of the classic studies supporting all three psychosomatic models discussed in Chapter 10 was the "Mirsky study" of peptic (duodenal) ulcer, published in 1958. I. Arthur Mirsky, a gastroenterologist trained in psychoanalysis, had noted that most peptic ulcer patients had elevated levels of pepsinogen, a hormone that stimulates gastric secretion. However, it was well known that not everyone with high pepsinogen levels got ulcers. At the same time psychiatrists with an interest in internal medicine such as Franz Alexander and Thomas French had noted that ulcer patients who happen to undergo psychoanalysis had excessive dependency needs that they were afraid to express because to do so might threaten relationships for which the patients had a strong need.

The investigators postulated a possible interaction between inborn hypersecretion of pepsinogen and dependency that might lead to peptic ulcer in some patients with both problems. Since pepsinogen is a hormone of digestion, chronically high levels might produce ongoing hunger and abdominal discomfort that would only be relieved by food. Since feeding during infancy and early childhood usually occurs in the context of being held, soothed, and generally cared for, an excessive need to be fed to relieve physical distress could easily generalize to an excessive need for caregiving. This would not be a problem if parents could meet the increased neediness of the high-pepsinogen child. But if they withdrew or got angry, the child might learn to be afraid of expressing dependency and might go through life pretending not to need anyone. This would make it harder to get needs met later in life, and so would build up even more dependency.

Since dependency and pepsinogen were both found to be present whether or not an ulcer was active, Mirsky hypothesized that an ulcer would develop only in a situation that stimulated an increased need for dependency in a person who could not respond to it, and thus aroused the physiology of approach-avoidance conflict described in Chapter 10 and overwhelmed bodily defenses worn down by the chronic attack of hypersecretion on the duodenum.

Mirsky and his associates tested their hypothesis by examining 2,073 men aged eighteen and nineteen who had just been inducted into the army. The investigators assumed that for most of these men, being away from home for the first time would be a threat to dependency, but it would only be stressful for those with unresolved conflict about these needs, which would make it harder to handle the stress. It was predicted that only patients with ulcerogenic traits and high pepsinogen would develop ulcers under these circumstances. Prior to beginning basic training, conflicts over dependency were measured in all subjects with psychological tests for dependency, immaturity, need to please others, and difficulty dealing with hostility. Pepsinogen levels were measured with a blood test. Upon arrival for basic training, and then again eight to sixteen weeks later, all subjects also got a set of gastrointestinal barium X rays (GI series) to see if ulcers developed.

At the beginning of the study, 3 inductees had healed peptic ulcers and 1 had an active duodenal ulcer. By the end of basic training, 5 more men had developed ulcers. The ulcers were all asymptomatic, but they could be clearly visualized. The 9 men with ulcers were among 63 with high pepsinogen levels; none of 57 men with low pepsinogen levels developed an ulcer.

What was the difference between the 9 men who developed ulcers either just before or during basic training and the 2,064 who did not? It was not just high pepsinogen levels, since 54 of the 63 men with this finding remained well. It turned out that the results of the psychological tests were crucial. Only 10 soldiers had the kind of intense dependency conflicts that were thought to be associated with ulcers; of these, 7—all of whom also had high pepsinogen levels—developed ulcers. Only 2 of the 9 ulcer patients did not have the characteristic psychological profiles, although they did have elevated pepsinogen.

The finding that only 10 of 2,073 young men undergoing the same stress had a combination of high pepsinogen and strong dependency conflicts, and 7 of these had ulcers in the context of their first separation from home, was highly significant statistically. The intimate relationship between the psychology and the physiology of dependency was further illustrated by a second result: without any knowledge of the blood tests, the investigators could identify 85 percent of high pepsinogen secretors just from the presence of dependency and related traits on the psychological tests.

Although the results of the Mirsky study were dramatic, they were never replicated by anyone else. For one thing, these kinds of investigations are expensive and time consuming. Another problem is that diseases like peptic ulcer are so rare that it is difficult to find a population with enough members who are likely to get sick to produce statistically meaningful results. Since there are few reliable markers of disease risk that would make it possible to select people at increased risk of getting a particular illness, more recent studies take people who are already ill and try to determine whether a psychological factor seems to predict the outcome.

DISCUSSION QUESTIONS

1. Given the small number of subjects who had evidence of ulcer disease, how would the results of the Mirsky study be interpreted if one or two low-risk subjects developed ulcers?

2. What do you think of Mirsky's definition of "ulcer," since none of the subjects was clinically ill and there was no way of knowing exactly when the process of developing the ulcer began?

3. What other psychological factors, associated with dependency, could have been the "true" risk factors for ulcer? What physical factors, associated with high pepsinogen, could have been more directly causative of ulcer?

4. How would a study be designed to test the hypothesis that hopelessness increases the risk of death in people with cancer?

5. Would psychotherapy of "dependency conflicts" reverse ulcer disease? What is the chance that focusing on unresolved conflict would intensify emotional arousal and make the ulcer worse?

6. What are the implications of studies like the Mirsky study for clinical practice?

REFERENCE

Mirsky, I. A. (1958). Physiologic, psychologic and social determinants in the etiology of duodenal ulcer. *American Journal of Digestive Disease, 3,* 285–311.

Hopelessness: The Interface between Research and Practice

The case described in Chapter 10 of the woman who died on schedule is one of many reports in which hopelessness about a life event or illness presaged a fatal outcome, even in people who did not appear sick. Indeed, ever since Biblical times, it has been known that "A heart that is joyful does good as a curer, but a spirit that is stricken makes the bones dry" (Proverbs 17:22).

The toxic effect on the body of negative emotions may be indirect, as when depressed people do not take care of themselves or are accident prone, or feeling states may have a direct effect on bodily function. Hopelessness seems to mobilize he stress response in two different directions at the same time and produce rapid alternations between activating and withdrawal systems. One result may be abrupt slowing of the heart followed by sudden increases in heart rate leading to arrhythmias, heart failure, and sudden cardiac death, especially in people who already have heart disease (Frasure-Smith et al., 1993). Changes in input to the heart from the autonomic nervous system as well as metabolic consequences of a chaotic stress response may contribute to the development o coronary heart disease. Hormonal consequences of a dysregulated stress response can directly affect the immune response and possibly mechanisms by which cancer cells are kept from going out of control (Reichlin, 1993).

Attempts to treat peptic ulcer and other "classic" psychosomatic illnesses with psychotherapy were not very successful, perhaps because the treatment aroused the very conflicts that were aggravating physical pathology in the first place. However, as more has been learned about the nature of mind-body connections that may contribute to physical disease, attempts to add psychological interventions to the medical armamentarium have been more successful. As long as twenty years ago, for example, it was demonstrated that the mortality rate of a coronary care unit could be reduced by one-third just by having a psychiatrist meet with the nursing staff, even if the patients themselves were never seen; changing the hospital milieu seemed to have a positive effect on people with acute heart disease (Dubovsky et al., 1975).

The study by psychiatrist David Spiegel that was described in your textbook is one of a number of impressive formal demonstrations that the fatal physical consequences of mental states like hopelessness can be reduced psychologically (Spiegel et al., 1989). Similar results have been reported with other kinds of illnesses. For example, ten of thirty-four patients receiving six weeks of group therapy during treatment for malignant melanoma but only three of thirty-four patients receiving no group therapy died five to six years later—a significant and enduring reduction in mortality with just a brief intervention (Fawzy et al., 1993).

Most of the psychological interventions that have been thought to have an impact on the course of cancer provide education, social support, a sense of mastery, enhanced coping skills, and encouragement of hope; as Fawzy et al. (193) put it, "Don't minimize, mobilize!" In making sure that patients were informed about their disease, for example, Spiegel was able to give them at least a sense of intellectual mastery in a setting in which everyone was struggling against a common foe. Self-hypnosis was a way to gain control of pain, one of the most frightening aspects of cancer; its mastery solidifies the feeling that at least the pain aspect of the disease could be conquered. The group approach may be particularly useful not only because it provides an opportunity for sharing coping strategies, but also because the human contact directly combats the physiology of despair.

When results as dramatic as those in the Spiegel study are reported, it would seem imperative to begin to apply them to clinical practice. However, the leap from psychosomatic research to clinical practice is not always obvious. For one thing, positive results in a few people do not necessarily generalize to everyone. In addition, not everyone is suited to the kinds of interventions that are studied. Some people are uncomfortable in groups or become disorganized when they try to learn hypnosis. Some people become overwhelmingly upset if they are taught too much about their diseases. If the psychological interventions are effective, they must have adverse effects too; the only treatment that never does anything bad is a placebo, and even that can make people sick.

Another reason why it is important not to accept this kind of research uncritically is that people may be tempted to substitute psychological treatments for medical therapy. No study has shown that psychotherapy cures physical disease, just that it may be a useful adjunct. Patients may understandably want psychotherapy to replace other cancer treatments, but if they act on this hope, they may delay getting medical therapies that are crucial for recovery and end up feeling disappointed when one approach does not substitute for the other.

As Chapter 10 indicates, however, there has been enough research into the power of the mind over the body to encourage clinicians to consider psychological interventions as part of any comprehensive treatment plan for hypertension, many forms of heart disease, and some cancers. However, the ways in which these approaches should be integrated with other aspects of patient care are not always obvious. The treatment of Ms. McBette illustrates some of the complexities of holistic clinical decision making.

THE CASE

Ms. McBette had felt trapped in an unhappy marriage for fifteen years. Her husband was unresponsive to all attempts to get him to work on their problems, but whenever she thought about leaving, she became frightened of being on her own. In her helpless state she concluded that she did not deserve to be happy and began to see that the only way out of her misery would be to die.

When she developed heart failure, Ms. McBette saw it as a possible escape from her unhappy life. The news that the replacement of a heart valve could restore normal functioning therefore did not necessarily fill her with hope. She felt obligated to agree to surgery, but with the underlying hope that it would kill her rather than cure her.

Ms. McBette's surgeon was aware of research cited in Chapter 10 indicating that mental attitude can adversely affect the heart. She knew that helplessness and hopelessness increase the risk of death from heart disease, and she wondered whether the chronic state of arousal from experiencing insoluble conflict could have contributed to Ms. McBette's heart disease in the first place. Worried that the patient's wish to die might come true during surgery, she asked a psychologist consultant whether she should postpone the operation until the patient could be helped to feel more hopeful.

"How should I know"? Was the consultant's answer. "I'm not in a position to decide how urgently the patient needs surgery. But if you make your best judgment as a surgeon, I'll work with the psychological side of the patient's illness."

On the basis of an examination and laboratory studies, the surgeon decided to operate in two days. As she waited for surgery, Ms. McBette was visited twice a day by the psychologist, who encouraged her to form a positive relationship. The next task was to generate a beginning feeling of hope. The psychologist approached this by demonstrating repeatedly that the patient's belief that her situation could not be changed was not necessarily true. She began to feel a little curious about techniques the psychologist might teach her to decide what to do about her marriage. "If I die, none of this will matter," she said. "If you die," the psychologist answered, "you won't get to find out whether I really can help you." The patient had to admit that the therapist had a point.

When the surgeon got to the valve that needed replacement, she found an enormous clot that was ready to fragment. Had this occurred, it would have traveled through the bloodstream (embolized) to the patient's brain. The clot was removed, the valve was replaced, and the patient recovered uneventfully. As she continued to see the psychologist every day, she became more curious about what options might exist in her life. Somehow, she was able to get her husband to agree to try couples therapy, and she left the hospital.

DISCUSSION QUESTIONS

1. How would you devise a study to decide whether this kind of intervention actually benefited the patient? What might have been the physiologic mechanisms of having no complications of surgery?
2. Can any kind of stress affect the heart, or just certain kinds of stress?
3. What would have happened if the psychologist had not been able to come up with a way to help the patient to feel a greater sense of control? Was this risk worth taking?
4. The surgeon's ability to make routine decisions was paralyzed by her attempts to take psychological factors into account, and possibly by identification with the patient's inability to resolve conflict. Was it a good idea for the psychologist to make the surgeon's approach less "holistic"?
5. Medical care has become so subspecialized that it is impossible for any one specialist to keep track of all aspects of a patient's care. In addition, physicians who must deal with terrible illnesses and invasive procedures often must keep a certain amount of emotional distance in order to avoid feeling overwhelmed by their work. How can the inevitable dichotomization of mental and physical aspects of disease encouraged by these processes be prevented? How should clinicians of different disciplines integrate mental and physical approaches in clinical decision making?

REFERENCES

Fawzy, F. I., Fawzi, N. W., Hyan, C. S., Elashoff, R., Guthrie, D., Fahey, J. L., & Morton, D. L. (1993). Malignant melanoma. Effects of an early structured psychiatric intervention, coping, and affective state on recurrence and survival 6 years later. *Archives of General Psychiatry, 50,* 681–689.

Frasure-Smith, N., Lesperance, F., & Talajc, M. (1993). Depression following myocardial infarction. Impact on 6-month survival. *Journal of the American Medical Association, 270,* 1819–1825.

Reichlin, S. (1993). Neuroendocrine-immune interactions. *New England Journal of Medicine, 329,* 1246–1253.

Spiegel, D., Bloom, J. R., Kraemer, H. C., & Gottheil, F. (1989). Effect of psychosocial treatment on survival of patients with metastatic breast cancer. *Lancet, 2,* 888–891.

Comprehensive Treatment of Unipolar Depression

Chapter 11 discusses some of the psychological, social, and biological hypotheses of depression. One reason why there are so many ideas about the cause of depression is that there are many different kinds of depression. Subdividing mood disorders into unipolar, bipolar, and seasonal subtypes is just the beginning. Some cases of depression are accompanied by melancholia (vegetative symptoms like changes in sleep and appetite), whereas others are not. Depression accompanied by psychotic symptoms (hallucinations and delusions) is a drastically different syndrome from other forms of depression (Dubovsky, 1994). Depression that recurs frequently is probably a different disorder from depression that only strikes once or twice. Various causes probably figure more or less prominently in each of the many depressive subtypes.

Even within a given depressive subtype, the many causes of depression that have been postulated are not mutually exclusive. Loss or helplessness may act on bodily systems that have been sensitized by previous experience, conflict, and/or heredity to induce neurotransmitter changes, and neurotransmitter changes make it impossible to overcome loss and conflict. As the textbook points out, learned helplessness alters neurotransmitter function and can be prevented by antidepressants. Negative thinking makes it much more difficult to overcome grief, and repeated loss can induce the pessimistic mind set of depression. By the same token, interpersonal therapy improves physical symptoms of depression (i.e., melancholia), and antidepressants improve the psychological symptoms of depression.

Since different kinds of psychopathology can contribute to depression, a combination of psychotherapeutic approaches is often necessary. In addition, although psychotherapy and pharmacotherapy have been found to be approximately equally effective in the treatment of mild to moderate depression (American Psychiatric Association, 1993), psychotherapy may have to be combined with medications in more severe or treatment-resistant cases. In the case of Mr. Lear, who became acutely depressed when his company restructured and his job was terminated, a combination of psychotherapeutic approaches proved effective. Most people would become upset under these circumstances, but Mr. Lear's reaction was not normal because it produced enduring symptoms and interfered with his ability to function.

THE CASE

Mr. Lear had been an effective middle manager, but after his position was abolished during restructuring, a relative of one of the members of the Board of Directors got the only job left for which someone with Mr. Lear's skills was qualified. Faced with the choice of taking another post at the company at two-thirds the pay or accepting severance pay and trying to find another job, he felt psychologically paralyzed. Not only could he not decide what to do about his career, but he could not decide anything—not what to do when he got up in the morning, not what to eat, not what to read or think.

Lacking any energy during the day, ruminations about what he should do kept him up at night. His family could sympathize with his growing unhappiness and indecision, but not with his irritability. Everything stopped feeling pleasurable to him, including eating, and he lost ten pounds. He felt that he was a burden to everyone and thought about ending it all, but he decided that he would not act on this thought for the sake of the family.

Although he felt that there was nothing unusual about the way he was feeling under the circumstances, Mr. Lear had a sufficient number of the symptoms described in Chapter 11 to warrant a DSM-IV diagnosis of a major depressive episode. These included a depressed mood most of the day, markedly diminished interest and sense of pleasure, loss of more than 5 percent of his body weigh tin a month, insomnia nearly every day, loss of energy nearly every day, indecisiveness nearly every day, and recurrent thoughts of suicide. DSM-IV requires five of a list of symptoms including these symptoms, agitation or slowing, and feeling of worthlessness or guilt. The symptoms must be present for at least two weeks and must cause significant distress or impairment of functioning and not be due to an illness, medication, or drug. DSM-IV attempts to differentiate depression from grief by stipulating that depression should not be diagnosed within two months of the loss of a loved one unless there is marked functional impairment, significant feelings of worthlessness, suicidal thinking, psychological and behavioral slowing, or psychosis. This scheme may make it difficult to recognize less severe cases of depression precipitated by a loss, which is of course one of the most common causes of depression.

In Mr. Lear's case, earlier experiences had sensitized him to developing depression and helplessness in response to the loss of his job. His father died when he was five, and he was given no opportunity to grieve by a family that did not tolerate sadness because several of them had been depressed. After his father's death, the family lost its social status and

was forced to move. For the next few years Mr. Lear felt helpless to resolve his sadness about the loss of his father or to change his circumstances.

Finally, when Mr. Lear's rumination and hostility became intolerable,
his wife insisted that he see a psychologist. The therapist made a diagnosis of major depression and suggested a course of psychotherapy. She also
let him know that an antidepressant might be added later if the depression did not respond as expected.

The first crisis in psychotherapy occurred when Mr. Lear reluctantly
agreed to psychotherapy, but said that he was sure that it would not work.
The therapist replied that this statement seemed like an excellent example of Mr. Lear's negative thinking and suggested that they start cataloging other negative cognitions. Still insisting that it would not help, the
patient agreed at least to write down negative cognitions as they occurred
and to rate the severity of depression as he did so. This kind of
"homework" is an essential component of psychotherapies that have been
proven effective for depression. Homework provides a structure for carrying the work of therapy outside the office and for practicing more adaptive approaches to thinking and behaving.

To teach Mr. Lear not to accept his incorrect beliefs as facts, he was
shown how to frame them as testable hypotheses. "Let's begin by examining the evidence for and against the belief that you're helpless," the
therapist suggested. At first, the patient said that the proof was that he
wasn't accomplishing anything, but the therapist pointed out that this
was a self-fulfilling prophecy: he was not accomplishing important goals
because he wasn't working on them. Mr. Lear was then asked to make a
list of things he had and had not accomplished. It turned out that he had
built a playhouse for the children and had kept up with his investments
despite being depressed. When he realized this, he rated his mood as
slightly improved. At first, the improvement seemed meaningless, but
only because anything short of an immediate total cure didn't count.

The latter statement is an example of a global, all-or-nothing assumption (schema) that leads to negative cognitions when the positive side of
the assumption inevitably cannot be fulfilled. For example, the negative
cognitions "I can't do anything right now that I lost that job" and "I'm
helpless to change anything now" were the consequences of the schemata
"If I don't succeed at everything, I'm a complete failure" and "If I can't
control everything, I can't control anything." Stating these assumptions
openly made it easier to examine their logic and discard it.

Further steps in reversing all-or-nothing thinking involved developing
goals that could be achieved in increments. For example, instead of setting the goal of immediately getting a better job, Mr. Lear was given the
assignment of making a graded list of goals leading up to finding a new
job. The first item on the list was noting companies that might use his
services. Next in order of difficulty was updating his resume. Next was
calling just one person he knew who might be able to help him evaluate
the job market.

The cognitive approach was supplemented by techniques drawn from interpersonal therapy. Once he reconsidered his belief that there was no point in grieving for something that was lost if it cannot be brought back, Mr. Lear was encouraged to express grief over the loss of status and friendships that had gone along with his job. He was also able to get around to resolving the grief left over from the unmourned death of his father.

After twelve sessions of psychotherapy, Mr. Lear no longer felt depressed or irritable. With more awareness of his strengths and accomplishments, he no longer believed that "Anyone who can't keep his company form downsizing can't get a new job." He opted for severance pay and found himself a better job. In view of evidence that "maintenance" psychotherapy may decrease the risk of relapse of depression (Frank et al., 1990), he saw the psychologist periodically for reviews of tendencies toward negative thinking and negative global assumptions.

DISCUSSION QUESTIONS

1. Would psychotherapy have been as effective if the patient had not been encouraged to practice therapeutic techniques at home?

2. How did unexpressed grief contribute to depression years later? How much work is it necessary to do on reactions to past losses in order to resolve depression in the future?

3. How do the learned helplessness and the interpersonal models complement each other?

4. At what point would a medication be added to psychotherapy for depression? How might an antidepressant facilitate psychotherapy? How might it get in the way?

5. Can anyone get depressed under the right circumstances? If so, why doesn't this happen?

6. What are the relative contributions of heredity and experience to the risk of becoming depressed?

REFERENCES

American Psychiatric Association (1993). Practice guidelines for major depressive disorder in adults. *American Journal of Psychiatry, 150* (4, Suppl.), 1–23.

Dubovsky, S. L. (1994). Challenges and concepts in psychotic mood disorders. *Bulletin of the Menninger Clinic, 58,* 197–214.

Frank, E., Kupfer, D. J., Perel, J. M., Cornes, C., Jarrett, D. B., Mallinger, A. G., & Thase, M. E. (1990). Three-year outcomes for maintenance therapies in recurrent depression. *Archives of General Psychiatry, 47,* 1093–99.

Moods and Great Men: Bipolar Disorder

In bipolar disorder, also known as manic-depression, manic or hypo-manic symptoms alternate or are mixed with depression. Artists and successful business executives have been found to have an above average incidence of bipolar disorder in themselves or their families. By definition, mania creates substantial psychological, legal, financial, and interpersonal problems. The high energy, rapid thought, pressure of activity, and grandiosity of hypomania can contribute to high productivity, but it can also create irritability and impulsivity, and so lead to alienation of friends and loved ones and rash professional decisions. In addition, it rarely if ever happens that hypomania, even if it is sustained, does not end with a "crash" into depression.

Chapter 11 points out that three well-known historic figures—Abraham Lincoln, Theodore Roosevelt, and Winston Churchill—have also been thought to have suffered form bipolar disorder. A book by psychiatrist Ronald Fieve (1976) examines these men's lives in a little more detail. Historical figures cannot really be given diagnoses at a distance in the same way that a flesh-and-blood patient can be given a diagnosis when observed and questioned up close. Such interpretations can be informative but must be regarded as highly speculative, because there is no way to check them out. Any "literary" diagnosis must therefore be taken with a large grain of salt.

Lincoln, Roosevelt, and Churchill were not great men because they had manic episodes. Rather, their intelligence, vision, and leadership abilities were independent of any affective abnormality they may have experienced. Do you think that their tremendous accomplishments were related to hypomania?

ABRAHAM LINCOLN (1809–1865)

We all know something about Honest Abe. Does what you recall from grade school include any of the following details that Fieve recounts?

Possible depressive episodes. Lincoln's contemporaries and biographers commented on his bouts with melancholy. At age 29, for instance, following the death of Ann Rutledge, whom he greatly loved, he was profoundly depressed. His friends feared that he would kill himself, and they hid knives and razors from him. This episode lasted for many months and was marked by not only sadness but fatigue, indecision, and self-doubt.

Another well-documented episode of depression occurred when Lincoln and Mary Todd were engaged to be married. He didn't show up at the wedding! Friends later found him wandering about—restless, desperate, and unhappy. Again, those around Lincoln believed that suicide was a distinct possibility, and they kept a close watch over him until the threat passed. As in many cases of bipolar disorder an external cause was not obvious.

There is also frequent documentation of Lincoln's slowness, lack of energy, and indecision. As you know, these are typical manifestations of depression. Perhaps the worst episode in his later life occurred when his son Willie died. Although Lincoln was at that time President and the Civil War was going on, he spent long periods of time sitting alone, doing nothing except mourning his son.

Possible manic episodes. Fieve acknowledges that one must read between the lines of the historic record to find any evidence that Lincoln was sometimes manic. Reportedly, as a young man, Lincoln went through a wild phase that might have been a manic episode. He was overtalkative and got involved in a series of fistfights. He was bombastic and insulting.

Once his political career began, Lincoln showed bursts of prodigious energy, which Fieve interprets as manic episodes. Fieve emphasizes that Lincoln often gave numerous speeches in a short period of time, and this was in the days when a speaker wrote his own lines (by hand!). Lincoln was described by his contemporaries as agitated and nervous during these bursts of activity. He pushed himself hard. He was impulsive and slept little.

Family history. As you know from Chapter 11, recent research shows that bipolar disorder has a genetic predisposition. Accordingly, a positive family history may strengthen the diagnostician's confidence that a particular individual's symptoms exemplify this disorder, especially if mood disorders run in consecutive generations. What about Abraham Lincoln's family? The evidence here is extremely weak. Fieve describes Lincoln's father as restless, moody, and impulsive, but he refrains from calling him bipolar.

THEODORE ROOSEVELT (1858–1919)

As the twenty-sixth President of the United States, Theodore Roosevelt at times seemed bigger than life. (Among other things, he inspired the teddy bear!) He was a bundle of energy, and his life story is a series of accomplishments, each greater than the preceding one. Here is a brief chronology:

- Although a sickly child, Roosevelt built up his body to become an excellent athlete and boxer.
- Attending college at Harvard, Roosevelt was regarded as too ambitious, too talkative, and in too much of a hurry; he had a good but not distinguished academic career.
- As a young politician in Albany, New York, he became a member of the State Assembly; again, he is remembered as doing too much and talking too much.
- He was appointed to the U.S. Civil Service Commission and set about to weed out corruption; he became famous for his quarrels with those who dared to contest him.
- In 1895, Roosevelt became the head of the police board in New York City. He worked during the days in the office, and then patrolled the streets at night, on the lookout for police officers straying from their duties; he slept but one or two hours out of each twenty-four.
- When the Spanish-American War broke out, Roosevelt became a colonel and led the cavalry regiment that came to be known as the Rough Riders. He was an inspirational but reckless leader; losses in his regiment were incredibly high.
- In 1899, Roosevelt became governor of New York State.
- In 1900, he was elected Vice President, and following McKinley's assassination, Roosevelt became President.
- He worked eighteen hours a day, slept little, and pursued uncountable activities; for instance, it is estimated that he wrote some 150,000 letters while Governor and President.
- After stepping down from the presidency in 1908, he kept busy, touring Africa and Europe; he sent reports of his adventures back to newspapers in the United States.
- In 1912, he ran again for president but did not succeed; he made strategic and perhaps impulsive mistakes in his campaign and was at times inappropriate.

Are you exhausted just reading about this man's life?

Possible depressive episodes. Was Roosevelt ever depressed? According to Fieve, he had periods of depression at college and while in the New York Assembly. For the rest of his life, though, he showed no evidence of depression. Let us note that this does not rule out a diagnosis of bipolar disorder. Although some individuals with this disorder show a regular and rapid cycle of depressive and manic episodes, and others have mixtures of the two syndromes (e.g., depression with increased energy), there are many other individuals whose mood swings show no pattern.

Possible manic episodes. Indeed, the historical record seems to suggest that Roosevelt's manic episodes lasted for decades at a time. There is lit tle ambiguity in describing his activity, particularly when he came into national prominence, as manic. He had an expansive mood. He needed little sleep. He was reckless. He was argumentative. He was talkative. He was incredibly active. He charmed many of his contemporaries and alarmed others. Was Roosevelt indeed manic? This fascinating and frenetic man can at least be described as what Hagop Akiskal (1992) calls "hyperthymic" (chronically elevated mood and energy integrated into the personality).

WINSTON CHURCHILL (1874–1965)

Churchill is the third great man suggested by Fieve to have had bipolar disorder. Churchill was the prime minister of England during World War II, and his leadership is widely credited with helping the Allies prevail.

Churchill's early life shows some parallels to that of Roosevelt. He did not distinguish himself as a student. He enlisted in the army and fought in India. Then he served with the Nile expeditionary force. Once he got a taste of adventure, he took off on a career that made him the most important person in England throughout most of his life, a period when England was the most important nation in the world.

Churchill first made his mark as a brilliant writer, as he recounted his war experiences. Then he took on a series of political appointments and marked himself as energetic, confident, and tireless. His opponents found him aggressive and quarrelsome. Eventually, Churchill became prime minister and led his country in its fight with Hitler. Needing almost no sleep and capable of working around the clock, he contributed more ideas than the rest of the cabinet combined.

Possible depressive episodes. Despite his accomplishments, Churchill experienced frequent bouts with depression, which he termed "Black Dog" and made few efforts to disguise. He thought of suicide, became apathetic, and sat for hours in what Fieve characterizes as a stupor. During the episodes, Churchill was beset with self-doubt and complained that he had accomplished nothing important in his life. Sometimes his depressions were triggered by his political frustrations and defeats, but at other times they occurred spontaneously.

Possible manic episodes. As in the case of Roosevelt, Churchill could be described as chronically hypomanic. All viewed him as brilliant, but his critics added impetuous and hotheaded to their characterizations. His decisions were sometimes questioned as reckless. Certainly, he was domineering and irritable. He talked nonstop and pursued numerous projects simultaneously.

Family history. Fieve firmly concludes that bipolar depression ran through the Churchill family, and hence Winston's disorder had an inherited factor.

DISCUSSION QUESTIONS

1. Some writers "diagnose" contemporary celebrities just as Fieve diagnoses figures from history. Under what circumstances, if any, can this be done without being a sideshow? What are the ethical issues here? How skeptical should we be of their "authoritative" pronouncements?

2. Do you think that political charisma can be a symptom of hypomania? Are there any risks of electing a manic person to high office? Would it be discriminatory not to do so?

3. Psychoanalytic accounts of bipolar disorder propose that mania is a defense against depression. Is this persuasive to you? How might you test this hypothesis? Specify the sequencing of manic and depressive episodes that should be observed. How would this hypothesis explain people who are manic and depressed at the same time?

4. Many patients with bipolar disorder do not comply with their lithium prescription. This is partly because lithium may have uncomfortable physical side effects. But there are psychological effects as well that patients dislike, especially the loss of symptoms like boundless energy and enthusiasm. In addition, lithium may cause emotional blunting and memory problems. What can be done to encourage compliance with a medication that may make life less fun?

5. Suppose Lincoln, Roosevelt, and Churchill were given lithium. Would world history have been different?

6. In light of recent findings that support the biomedical conception of bipolar disorder, some are tempted to dismiss the role of psychology in this disorder. Drawing on these three cases, why should we pay attention to psychological factors if we wish to understand this problem?

7. Should unipolar and bipolar disorders be classed together? How are they different or similar?

REFERENCES

Akiskal, H. S. (1992). Depression in cyclothymic and related temperaments: Clinical and pharmacologic considerations. *Journal of Clinical Psychiatry Monograph, 10,* 37–43.

Fieve, R. R. (1976). *Moodswing: The third revolution in psychiatry.* New York: Bantam.

Causative Factors and Outcome in Schizophrenia

Emil Kraepelin originally divided the psychoses into dementia praecox and manic-depressive insanity on the basis of his assessment of their outcomes. He believed that manic-depressive illness always got better, whereas schizophrenia always deteriorated. Yet you learned in Chapter 12 that not all cases of schizophrenia are chronic, and bipolar disorder is chronic at least 30 percent of the time.

Chapter 12 indicates that research into the causes and outcome of schizophrenia may be so contradictory because different conditions are lumped together that share content (e.g., hallucinations or delusions) or form (e.g., disturbed associations or logic) disorders but differ in other ways. As Rosenhan and Seligman point out, such symptoms, somewhat akin to fever or seizures, are fairly nonspecific no matter how dramatic they may be. Even "typical" schizophrenic hallucinations, delusions, and disorders of logic are seen in mood disorders, especially bipolar ones (Pope and Lipinski, 1978). And there are many other kinds of psychoses—schizoaffective disorder, delusional disorder (paranoia), brief psychotic disorder, shared psychotic disorder (*folie-à-deux*), and psychoses caused by general medical conditions, to name a few. Psychoses diagnosed in Europe such as paraphrenia (a type of late-onset schizophrenia) and cycloid psychoses (highly recurrent psychotic disorders accompanied by confusion, ecstasy, or changes in activity) are not even well enough studied in the United States to have been included in DSM-IV.

Your textbook shows how twin studies can be used to identify a genetic component to schizophrenia; these studies can also be used to clarify environmental factors. One interesting approach to this issue is to study monozygotic (identical) twins who are *discordant* for schizophrenia (i.e., one twin has schizophrenia and the other does not) and attempt to find out what distinguishes the schizophrenic from the nonschizophrenic twin. In one such study, National Institute of Mental Health psychiatrists Richard Suddath, E. Fuller Torrey, Daniel Weinberger, and their associates found that the schizophrenic twins had enlarged cerebral ventricles (the fluid-filled space within the brain), while the normal twins did not. They hypothesized that schizophrenia was the result of an interaction between an insult acquired after birth with the inherited vulnerability. The insult could have been a virus, an injury of some kind, or something else (Suddath et al., 1990).

What are the clinical implications of the data that have accumulated about the biology of schizophrenia? Regardless of subtype, negative symptoms such as withdrawal, lack of interest, and asociality convey more chronicity and do not respond nearly as well to treatment as positive symptoms. Enlarged ventricles seem primarily linked to negative symptoms and may indicate a component of neurological dysfunction for which no clearly effective treatment has yet been found. However, about one-third of chronic schizophrenic patients with prominent negative symptoms improve dramatically when they receive clozapine or risperidone, two "atypical" antipsychotic medications that have a more significant action on serotonin receptors than on dopamine receptors. Schizophrenic patients whose symptoms are primarily positive (hallucinations, delusions, and agitation) have a better treatment response to standard therapies (although atypical antipsychotics work too) and are less likely to have evidence of neurological dysfunction.

As you learned in Chapter 12, the modern treatment of schizophrenia involves social therapies as well as medications. These include minimizing unrealistic expectations and emotional overstimulation in the family, teaching social and occupational skills, and enhancing reality testing. The prognosis with these treatments is often much better than was once thought, even for patients with negative symptoms.

THE CASE

Ronnie was well behaved and outgoing until he entered adolescence. His teenage years were no more stressful than average, but he seemed overwhelmed by teenage social demands. He became more withdrawn and adopted a number of weird mannerisms that made people stay away from him even more. He mumbled to himself, often in response to a conversation no one else could hear. He stopped changing his clothes and washing regularly and seemed increasingly suspicious.

By age twenty, Ronnie had decided that there was a conspiracy afoot that he could not exactly describe but was nevertheless vast. Part of the conspiracy involved monitoring his thoughts and actions. This delusion obviously had the effect of keeping him away from other people, but it had a more complicated hidden meaning. If everyone was monitoring him, they must find him important enough to want to keep in touch with him, and he was not really alone. The secret ambivalent wish to have some sort of relationship hidden behind his withdrawal could also be discerned in his response to questions about how he was feeling. Instead of saying "None of your business," he would reply, "Well, you know . . . it's nothing . . . You know," as if the questioner actually did know what was going on in his mind.

Ronnie was finally brought to treatment by his parents, who were told that the prognosis was mixed. A bad prognosis was suggested by the insidious onset and prominent negative symptoms such as withdrawal and apathy. On the other side of the coin, some of his withdrawal might have been a reaction to paranoia rather than a primary symptom. In addition, he had several specific indicators of a more positive prognosis, including a good adjustment prior to the onset of his symptoms, the presence of confusion and depression, and the absence of a family history of schizophrenia. A CT scan of his head indicated that he did not have enlarged ventricles, which are associated with a worse outlook, but he might not yet have had time for them to enlarge.

When Ronnie was treated with the antipsychotic drug thiothixene (Navane), his suspiciousness decreased enough for him to describe his symptoms in more detail. He revealed for the first time that he frequently heard voices telling him to "watch out" as well as other strange voices. Sometimes, he saw men in trench coats. All the hallucinations went away with further treatment with the antipsychotic drug, but he could not stand the stiffness and tremor caused by the medicine. Clozapine (Clozaril) did not produce these side effects, but it made him too sleepy. Risperidone (Risperdal), a new antipsychotic medicine with actions similar to those of clozapine, was better tolerated, and it was more effective than the other medications in controlling the delusions and hallucinations. It also seemed to reduce the drive toward withdrawal.

The medication was far from a cure, but it did decrease his anguish and make him more accessible to other people. This made it possible to begin the process of rehabilitation. One issue that had to be addressed was that, having missed adolescence, Ronnie did not even know how to have an adult conversation. As he felt more comfortable around other people, he was able to engage in group treatments that taught him social interactions. He had to learn to suppress his tendency to make cryptic comments that put people off.

The family also had to be involved in treatment. While they were not abusive or psychotic, they could not relinquish their belief that Ronnie was just going through a "phase" or their expectation that he would still be able to join the family business. The more they pushed Ronnie to do more—to go back to school, to work part time for Ronnie's father—the more withdrawn and disorganized Ronnie had become. Thinking that this was a motivational problem, they got upset; this only made Ronnie more psychotic. When they finally were helped to stop expecting so much and the level of "expressed emotion" in the family decreased, Ronnie felt less pressured and began to accomplish more. In this respect, he was not different from many young adults who do not respond well to being told what to do by their parents, but he responded with psychosis rather than other kinds of opposition.

Ronnie did not get married, as his parents had hoped, but he did establish several friendships and was able to live in an apartment complex. He did not become a business executive, but he did develop a career. Ronnie channeled his paranoia, which became much less blatant but did not go away entirely, into the realm of fantasy, and he became a mystery writer. You may even have read one of his books.

DISCUSSION QUESTIONS

1. Is schizophrenia more "biological" or "psychological"? Why?

2. How is prognosis assessed in schizophrenic patients? How accurate are these assessments?

3. Are there any ways to decrease the risk of severe illness in someone with several schizophrenic relatives?

4. How might you convince a paranoid person to take a medication that you knew would decrease the paranoia?

5. Schizophrenia was defined during the Kraepelin-Bleuler era as a deteriorating disorder, and this definition persists in DSM-IV. How should patients be classified who have all the symptoms of schizophrenia but do not deteriorate? What about those who do badly for a number of years and then seem to get better?

REFERENCES

Pope, H. G. & Lipinski, J. (1978). Diagnosis in schizophrenia and manic-depressive illness: A reassessment of the specificity of "schizophrenic" symptoms in the light of current research. *Archives of General Psychiatry, 35,* 811–28.

Suddath, R. L., Christison, G. W., Torrey, E. F., Casanova, M. F., & Weinberger, D. R. (1990). Anatomical abnormalities in the brains of monozygotic twins discordant for schizophrenia. *New England Journal of Medicine, 322,* 789–94.

The Genain Quadruplets: Schizophrenia

As Chapter 12 of the text makes clear, psychologists have debated the causes of schizophrenia since the disorder was first delineated. Most of these debates have revolved around the issue of biological versus environmental causation, the familiar nature-versus-nurture issue played out so often in the biological and social sciences. Family studies can help to address this question.

One of the most interesting cases in the whole of abnormal psychology is that of the Genain children: identical quadruplets concordant for schizophrenia (Rosenthal, 1963). The likelihood of such a coincidence is about 1 in 15 billion, and fewer than 8 billion people have ever lived on the planet!

THE CASE

The name "Genain" was made up by the researchers in order to protect the identity of the family. It is an acronym from Greek words meaning "dire birth." In all published reports, the four sisters are referred to as Nora, Iris, Myra, and Hester. These are made-up names as well, with the first letters coming from the initials NIMH. They were raised in a Midwestern town called Envira (for environment).

The Genain quadruplets were born in the 1930s, to great fanfare. Their parents, Henry and Gertrude, were overwhelmed. Nothing in their background prepared them for the task of simultaneously raising four children.

Henry was the son of immigrants from Europe. His mother had a history of mental breakdowns and hospitalizations. She was manipulative and controlling. Henry was not a wanted child. When his mother became pregnant with him, she tried to induce an abortion by working herself to exhaustion and lifting heavy items. His father was meek and gentle, and he left the rearing of the children to his wife. Henry grew up a shy and fearful child. He stuttered, had a history of blacking out, and drank too much. He did not finish high school, and he worked at a series of un-skilled jobs. At the time that the quadruplets were born, Henry was un-employed.

Gertrude was the daughter of farmers, the eldest child in a family of eight children. Her parents are described as kind and congenial, but nei-ther spent much time with their older children. Gertrude did more than her share of household chores, and she helped care for her younger broth-ers and sisters. Her father greatly preferred his sons, and Gertrude re-sented the fact that he felt she needed little education. She was kept at home until she was seven and a half years old, and only then started school. At about this time, both her parents became ill, so Gertrude went to live with her grandmother. When Gertrude expressed her preference to stay on with her grandmother, her father disowned her in an ugly scene. Supporting herself, Gertrude finished high school and started working as a practical nurse.

When Gertrude met Henry, she was not impressed. He annoyed her, but they eventually started to see each other. She was ambivalent about the courtship, but he threatened suicide if she would not marry him. Be-fore they were married, they had a frank conversation. She asked him to stop drinking, which he did. He asked her to treat him as his mother had. Gertrude replied that she did not want to act in this way, but he appar-ently did not take her seriously.

Their married life did not start off on the right foot. Henry worked only occasionally. He was awkward around other people. He had little to say to Gertrude. Evenings were spent sitting alone at home, staring at each other but not talking. Neither of them particularly wanted to have chil-dren, but after three years of marriage, Gertrude became pregnant. Ac-cording to her, Henry left for days at a time and neglected her. According to him, he helped with the cooking and housework.

In the fifth month of her pregnancy, her doctor predicted that she would have twins. He was wrong. She had quadruplets: four girls, weighing a total of 15 pounds, 1 ounce. The babies were small and sickly and were difficult to feed. However, after six weeks in the hospital, all were in good condition and were sent home.

Gertrude and Henry could not afford to raise four babies, and so the lo-cal newspaper got involved with the family. There was a contest to name the children, and some modest contributions were raised. A new house was donated to them, and they moved in, along with Henry's mother. Gertrude shouldered the major burden in caring for the infants, and it was difficult work. This was before disposable diapers, paper towels, ready-made formula, automatic washers and driers, and Sesame Street.

A steady stream of visitors came to see the babies, and the Genains started to charge each 25 cents per peek. Eventually visitors were turned away as Henry became worried about the safety and privacy of his family. He locked the doors and windows. Both Henry and Gertrude feared kid-nappers, and an atmosphere of suspicion colored the household.

Although the four children were identical, they were treated by their family as two sets of twins. The two larger babies, Nora and Myra, were grouped together, as were the two smaller ones, Iris and Hester. Nora and Myra were favored by their parents. All four were weaned at five months apparently because Gertrude thought it would be funny to make this event coincide with a national holiday. (Was this a schizophrenic thing to do?) She attempted to toilet train them at six months, but her efforts failed. Gertrude tried again when the quadruplets were nine months old, and finally succeeded after a year of trying. All four girls, however, continued to wet the bed at night until their middle teens.

Both parents accepted the belief that the four girls really represented one person split by unusual circumstance into four people. This is also at least a bizarre idea; we do not know if it might have been a delusion. Accordingly, the girls were not expected to be particularly hardy. They were kept separate from other children. They never had playmates other than each other. Gertrude took a dislike to Hester, and described her as just like Henry, always trying to undermine her. At age three, Hester developed the habit of masturbating; this caused her mother to see her as oversexed.

What was Henry up to during these first few years? He was in the basement of the new house, making illegal moonshine. He also started drinking again. When Gertrude tried to make him get a job, he campaigned for public office in the town. With the fame that the quadruplets brought him, he was easily elected to a position he held for more than twenty years. He continued to drink heavily. This did not interfere with his job, but it created havoc at home. He frightened his children greatly when he was drunk.

Other problems plagued the household. Gertrude suffered a lengthy depression. She and Henry stopped having sex. Henry's mother had seizures and became senile. She criticized Gertrude and accused her of having affairs with other men. But it was Henry who had a series of rather open affairs. He contracted a venereal disease. Once, while drunk, he shot a revolver at his wife, thinking she was an intruder.

The girls started kindergarten at age five, and their first day of school was widely covered in the newspapers. Teachers considered them normal students, with the exception of Hester, who had some trouble with reading. The girls tried hard at school, but did average to somewhat less than average work. Henry and Gertrude, in contrast, believed that Nora and Myra—their favorites—were excellent students, whereas Iris and Hester were far behind. At the insistence of their teachers, all four girls repeated the fifth grade and part of the sixth. Everyone outside the family thought the girls were overprotected and highly restricted by their parents. In retrospect, we might wonder whether Gertrude and Henry were not just overprotective, but suspicious or even paranoid.

At school, the other children were never able to distinguish among the quadruplets. They made fun of the girls and called them dumb. At least some of this teasing came from resentment at the attention and privileges given to the girls. Also important is the fact that the girls did not know how to play any of the common childhood games. Hester continued to bear the brunt of criticism from Gertrude, who blamed her for the social problems of all four girls. In Gertrude's mind, Hester was too intent on masturbating to have any interest in developing friendships.

When the girls were about six, they started to take private dancing and singing lessons. They performed around town, appeared on radio shows, and were featured in several Hollywood newsreels. They made a small amount of money, but most of it was used to buy costumes for them. The girls apparently enjoyed singing and dancing. They had some natural talent, and they were appealing to audiences when they performed in unison. They continued to perform until they were about twelve, when their schoolwork began to require more of their time.

Life at home became ever more stressful as the girls entered adolescence. Gertrude and Henry continued to fight. Each developed health problems. Henry's mother died, and Gertrude refused to go to the funeral. And the girls were faced for the first time with household chores.

The pairing of the girls into two sets continued, although often it was three against one, with Hester being the odd one out. The other three girls were always urged to "protect" her, which they did, but with more than a little resentment. Gertrude continued to worry about Hester's masturbation, and alerted her teachers to be on the outlook for it. She constantly punished the girl; once she even swabbed her clitoris with carbolic acid.

Gertrude brought Hester to a clinic, where she was assured that masturbation was normal and harmless. Nonetheless, Gertrude was not placated and she continued to punish Hester. Henry got into the act as well; he told the girls that masturbation led to insanity. The whole family became extremely upset about masturbation. When Hester and Iris, still sleeping together at age twelve, were discovered by their mother engaged in mutual masturbation, one would have wondered whether this behavior was a cause or a result of the family's preoccupation with it.

The parents found a doctor who would "circumcise" the two girls, i.e., remove part of the clitoris in the hope of deadening pleasurable sensations. But the girls continued to masturbate, breaking the stitches from the operation. For thirty days thereafter, their hands were tied to their beds when they were put to sleep. They continued to masturbate anyway.

In junior high school, the girls did better work than in elementary school. Teachers regarded them as meek, quiet, and shy. But they were too well behaved, in the eyes of some who were interviewed years later. Nora was the spokesperson for the quadruplets; Hester continued to be the most backward. The girls made few friends, and for the most part were ignored by the other students.

Gertrude and Henry were particularly adamant that the girls should have nothing to do with boys. Sex was a taboo topic except when its dangers were emphasized. The parents suspected that numerous boys and men were molesting their girls, especially Hester. It should be noted, though, that Henry insisted on watching his daughters dressing and undressing. He even watched when they changed their sanitary pads.

These patterns continued into high school, although the girls began to participate in some extracurricular activities and started to make some friends and take a few steps toward independent activity. Classmates warmed a bit toward them. Hester, however, began to have problems. She fell behind in her schoolwork. She became irritable and depressed. Her behavior became at times destructive and bizarre. Hester "confessed" to her mother about a series of sexual activities dating back to elementary school.

We can easily appreciate that Hester was probably developing her first psychotic episode, but her parents thought that she had become mentally retarded from masturbation. Hester was removed from school and kept at home. She complained of feeling lost and insecure. She was treated with sedatives. Nora and Iris started to experience physical symptoms: allergies, stomach spasms, menstrual irregularities, and fainting spells. They finished high school, though, and all the girls except Hester received their degrees.

Nora was the first to take a job, and she worked for two years as a stenographic clerk. Because she worked with a woman recently discharged from a tuberculosis sanitarium, Henry insisted that she wash the office telephone with alcohol twice a day. He dropped in at her office several times a day, and stood around watching her. Myra found a job as a legal secretary, at which she worked for four and a half years. Iris worked at a series of temporary jobs, in which she was overly slow and meticulous.

These three young women each had minor involvements in social groups. Henry fretted and fumed about this and warned his daughters of the dangers that other people represented. He forbade them to date. At the same time, he started to fondle both Nora and Myra, touch their breasts and buttocks, and he continued to watch all his daughters dress and undress.

In the next few years, first Nora, then Iris, then Myra, and finally Hester had psychotic episodes requiring them to be hospitalized. They were all diagnosed with schizophrenia, and showed the gamut of symptoms described in your text: hallucinations, delusions, neglect of self-care, and so on. The family was unable to pay the medical bills, and so the National Institute of Mental Health offered to provide free treatment in return for the opportunity to study them. Numerous studies were carried out, and resulted in the book from which this story was obtained (Rosenthal, 1963).

POSTSCRIPT

What happened to the Genain quadruplets? Twenty years after the initial NIMH investigations, a follow-up study was conducted (Buchsbaum, 1984). Although all four continued to have problems, they showed different outcomes. Hester and Iris spent most of the ensuing years in hospitals. Nora had successfully held several jobs, as had Myra. Myra was the only one of the four to marry and have children.

DISCUSSION QUESTIONS

1. Each of the four sisters was given a diagnosis of schizophrenia, but with a different subtype, from paranoid to disorganized to catatonic. Since the girls were genetically identical, what does this say about the nature of the genetic risk for schizophrenia?

2. Do you think that the parents were delusional? Could they have been schizophrenic too?

3. What were the relative roles of heredity and environment in the case of the Genain quadruplets? What are the implications for a general theory of the etiology of schizophrenia?

4. What could have been done to prevent or minimize the severity of psychosis in the quadruplets?

5. Every state now has laws requiring that clinicians report to the appropriate authorities any reasonable suspicion of child abuse so that the child can be protected and the parent treated. Would a clinician working with the Genain family have been required to report Henry? What about Gertrude?

6. Why did Nora and Myra do so much better than the other quadruplets? Given the combination of genetic risk and psychotic and probably abusive parents, why did any of the girls have a favorable outcome?

REFERENCES

Buchsbaum, M. S. (1984). The Genain quadruplets. *Psychology Today, 18*(8), 46–51.

Rosenthal, D. (Ed.) (1963). *The Genain quadruplets.* New York: Basic Books.

Does a Diagnosis of Schizophrenia Tell the Whole Story?

DSM-III-R and DSM-IV represent a fundamental shift of psychological diagnosis from a more informal approach to a *categorical* method based on constellations of signs and symptoms. With the exception of some considerations on the course of the illnesses (e.g., the disorder must be continuously present for at least six months to qualify for a diagnosis of schizophrenia), most modern diagnoses are cross-sectional; that is, the diagnosis is based on a certain number of symptoms at a particular point in time. In the case of schizophrenia, there are five criteria, four of them cross-sectional, that must be fulfilled. These include:

Category A: Characteristic symptoms present for a month, or less if successfully treated, including delusions, hallucinations, disorganized or incoherent speech, grossly disorganized or catatonic behavior, and negative symptoms such as emotional blunting and lack of motivation. Only one symptom from this category is necessary if delusions are bizarre or hallucinations involve a voice commenting on the patient's actions or thoughts, or voices talking to each other; otherwise, two symptoms are necessary.

Category B: Deterioration of social or occupational functioning, or failure to achieve interpersonal, academic, or occupational milestones in childhood and adolescence.

Category C: Duration of the disorder of at least six months. At least one month of the total duration must consist of Category A symptoms; the rest may consist of prodromal and/or residual phases that may include only negative symptoms or attenuated versions of Category A symptoms such as odd beliefs or unusual perceptions.

Category D: Psychotic mood disorders (unipolar) and schizoaffective disorder (a mixture of schizophrenic symptoms with depression or mania, with at least two weeks of psychosis in the absence of a major mood change) have been ruled out.

Category E: Not due to substance abuse or a medical illness.

Category F: Not just an extension of a pervasive developmental disorder like autism. (American Psychiatric Association, 1994).

Although categorical diagnoses increase the likelihood that two clinicians who make the same diagnosis are talking about approximately the same condition, they ignore clinically important differences between patients with the same diagnosis. For example, some patients hear certain kinds of voices all the time, and some just hear them intermittently. Some patients like being psychotic, and others are terrified of the experience. Some patients have multiple psychotic symptoms, and some with the same diagnosis have only a few. Some have mainly negative symptoms, some have only positive symptoms, and some have both. Some schizophrenic individuals have only hallucinations to keep them company, whereas others have more adaptive friendships.

According to Scottish psychiatrist R. D. Laing (1965), schizophrenia consists not of signs and symptoms, but of the patient's experience of the illness. Extending a tradition that goes back to Adoph Meyer, who felt that each psychological disorder was unique to the individual who had it, Laing feels that the categorical diagnosis of schizophrenia aggravates the feeling of inhumanity that is central to the experience of being schizophrenic. He proposes that many of the concepts used to explain schizophrenia inadvertently serve as roadblocks to understanding because they make the schizophrenic individual seem to be a thing rather than a person. "Things" don't have experiences, and "things" don't assign meanings to events. If a schizophrenic is rendered a thing by a theory, and a broken thing at that, we are tempted not to listen to what that person has to say.

Laing, believes that it is important to be aware of this because one of the central problems of schizophrenia is that the patients regard themselves as things. When they act on this conception, the rest of society views them as abnormal, but their actions are perfectly understandable given their basic assumptions. In *The Divided Self*, Laing (1965) describes how schizophrenics come to view themselves in these terms. Let us present one of the cases that Laing describes to make his point.

THE CASE

Peter is a large and robust man in his middle twenties. When he first came to see Laing, he looked the picture of health. But Peter had an unusual complaint. An unpleasant smell constantly surrounded him. He was not sure that other people could detect the smell, but it was clear to him. (Many people think that olfactory and tactile hallucinations always indicate epilepsy, structural disease of the brain or drug intoxication, but these hallucinations also occur in "functional" psychoses like schizophrenia and psychotic depression.)

In Peter's case, the smell seemed to emanate from the lower part of his body, particularly his genitals. Sometimes it smelled like something was burning. Other times it smelled like something old and decayed. Although he bathed several times a day, Peter could not rid himself of the smell.

He later described frequent attacks of anxiety, centering around the conviction that he was a hypocrite. He knew himself to be a sham, someone whose "real" feelings consisted largely of sadistic sexual fantasies. It was just a matter of time before others found him out. In one incident that greatly frightened him, Peter masturbated in the bathroom at work, all the time thinking of assaulting one of his female coworkers. When he left the bathroom, he immediately encountered the woman, who looked directly at him. He had a panic attack, fearing that she could read his mind and learn of his evil thoughts. He began to worry that people could smell his semen and thereby know that he had masturbated.

These beliefs and fears affected the way that Peter went about his daily life. He drifted, attempting to be as anonymous as possible. He was most comfortable in the role of the stranger. He would go to a place where he was unknown, always using a different name in his travels. Only as a stranger could he act spontaneously around other people. As long as he went incognito, Peter felt safe from his fear that others could see through him and detect his "real" nature.

A PHENOMENOLOGICAL DESCRIPTION

Schizophrenia certainly seems to be an appropriate diagnosis in Peter's case. He experiences bizarre hallucinations and delusions, has a phase of active illness lasting more than a month, and has had a deterioration of functioning. He does not seem to have a mood disorder, and medical illnesses and substance abuse are not present. But is this the end of the diagnostic evaluation?

Laing tells the mental health profession to slow down. Regardless of the cause of Peter's hallucinations and delusions, he is still a human being. What is it like to be Peter? And how did Peter develop his present way of being?

One starts to get a glimpse of Peter from the inside by knowing about his childhood. Here is Laing's account:

> His parents were not happy people but they stuck close to each other. They had been married ten years before he was born. They were inseparable. The baby, the only child, made no difference to their life. He slept in the same room as his parents from birth until he left school. His parents were never openly unkind to him and he seemed to be with them and yet

they simply *treated him as though he wasn't there*. . . . He was bottle-fed and put on weight well, but he was never cuddled or played with. . . . His mother . . . hardly noticed him at all. She was a pretty woman, and was always fond of dressing up and admiring herself . . . though the father was very fond of the boy in his way, something seemed to stop him from being able to show his affection to him. He tended to be gruff, to pick on faults, occasionally to thrash him for no good reason, and to belittle him with such remarks as, "Useless Eustace," "You're just a big lump of dough" (Laing, 1965, pp. 120–121; emphasis in original).

Laing believes that Peter failed to learn what was real and what was not. His parents gave him no clues. Inner and outer reality were never particularly distinct for Peter. How could they be? When you are treated as if you are not there, you regard yourself as not really present. Some of his "symptoms" start to make sense. Most of us define reality as what is interpersonally validated. Smells that other people confirm are real ones; smells that only you detect are not. But if you were raised by parents who never confirmed any of your sensations as real, or disconfirmed others, then hallucinations are apt to occur.

Further, the hallucinated smell has a meaning to Peter. The smell symbolized Peter's shame. He later came to interpret the smell less literally: "'It was more or less the regard I had for myself. It was really a form of self-dislike.' That is to say, he stank so badly in his own nostrils that he could hardly endure it" (Laing, 1965, p. 130). Had a central problem been felt to be low self-esteem, the diagnosis might have been different. If the hallucinations and delusions had not been so obvious, Peter might have been diagnosed depressed, obsessional, or perhaps just insecure. On the other hand, the unique meaning to Peter of the hallucination does not mean that he was not schizophrenic. Schizophrenia, like any distortion of experience of the internal and external world, interacts with the totality of the personality of the person who suffers from it.

A poignant episode from early in Peter's life further illustrates the usefulness of paying attention to a schizophrenic's experience. Peter had but one friend when he was a child. So, we might say that he was socially estranged and leave it at that. But pause and discover that his friend was a little girl about his own age who had been blinded in an air raid (during World War II). For several years, Peter spent a great deal of time with the girl; he showered her with patience and kindness and helped her adjust to life without sight. She later said that she owed her life to Peter's kindness, because no one else took any time to be with her.

Do you see the meaning of this relationship? If you were raised as Peter was raised, by parents who treated you as though you were invisible, what would you look for in a friend? Like his mother, the little girl did not see him. But unlike his mother, she needed him.

On one level, Laing's account of Peter is consistent with some of the theories reviewed in Chapter 12 of your text, those that stress the causal role of disordered family communication in the origin of schizophrenia.

But on another level, there is an important difference. Family theorists argue that particular styles of interaction can produce schizophrenia in a child. Laing's point is that schizophrenia can be an inevitable and even "healthy" adaptation to pathological circumstances. However, Laing makes the logical error of assuming that because certain childhood experiences occurred in patients with delusions of worthlessness, one caused the other. If innate factors do not play a role in adaptation to a pathological environment, why do some people whose families do not validate their existence develop schizophrenia, others personality disorders, others depression, and others no symptoms at all?

DISCUSSION QUESTIONS

1. Does Peter's family have anything in common with the Genain family (Case 18)? Does Laing argue for the existence of "schizophrenogenic" parents, a notion that was discarded when biological theories of schizophrenia became popular and researchers concluded that schizophrenic children made their parents schizophrenogenic, not the other way around?

2. How are Laing's theories affected by observations that the incidence of schizophrenia is the same in developing as well as in industrialized countries?

3. Discuss Laing's description of Peter in light of the distinction in the text between positive and negative symptoms of schizophrenia. Is phenomenology incompatible with biology?

4. Laing can be described as an existentialist. Discuss the case of Peter in terms of the important existential concepts presented in Chapter 4 of the text.

5. The prophet Ezekial had a vision of a man clothed in flaming brightness who instructed him to lie on his left side without moving for 390 days, and then to do the same on his right side for 40 days. Later, Ezekial cut off his hair and beard and divided it into three piles; he burnt one pile, struck the second pile with a sword, and scattered the remaining third of the hair to the wind (Ezekial 1:25– 5:2). Although it might have seemed bizarre, his behavior, like Peter's and like the behavior of the man described in Chapter 12 who shook his finger when asked a question, Ezekial's behavior had a very specific meaning. The two phases of lying immobile for a specified number of days stood for the number of years of rebellion of the house of Israel and the house of Judah. The fate of the three piles of hair symbolized the fate of the nation of Israel.
    Unlike the schizophrenic patients you have read about, Ezekial was following instructions from God, who had foretold that "they will not want to listen to you, for they are not wanting to listen to

me" (Ezekial 3:7). How would you decide whether Ezekial was inspired or psychotic?

6. How would you design a therapy to correct the kinds of pathological communication observed in Peter's family? What impact would you expect the therapy to have on the course of the schizophrenia? Could anything else have been done to reduce Peter's chance of growing up to be so disabled?

REFERENCE

American Psychiatric Association (1994). *Diagnostic and Statistical Manual of Mental Disorders* (4th ed.). Washington, DC: American Psychiatric Press.

Laing, R. D. (1965). *The divided self: An existential study in sanity and madness.* New York: Penguin.

Please Tread on Me: Paraphilia

A paraphilia is a misdirection of sexual arousal that interferes with re-ciprocated, affectionate sexual activity. In other words, a paraphilia is a disorder to the degree that it interferes with healthy sexual relationships.

A classic description of paraphilia was given by Wilhelm Stekel (1930). Stekel's patient was a man who was aroused when a woman walked on him while he was lying on his back. As she trod on his throat and chest, he became increasingly excited. When she eventually stepped on his erect penis, he had an orgasm. The individual in the case, Mr. P., was not at all distressed by his paraphilia. He was not psychotic. And he was not estranged from other people. He was, however, prevented by the paraphilia from establishing a fulfilling relationship with a woman.

THE CASE

Mr. P., a thirty-two-year-old man, described his paraphilia like this:

> If I meet a woman who appears attractive to me . . . it is not my wish to have sexual contact with her in the usual sense of the word, but rather to lie down prone on the floor and have her walk over me and tread me underfoot. The curious wish occurs seldom and only when the woman in question is a real lady and well built. She must be elegantly dressed, preferably in evening clothes with low shoes that have very high heels . . . Even though I may appreciate the spiritual or beautiful qualities of a woman, there is, after all, nothing about her that could arouse me like that part of her from the knee down, es-pecially the foot. . . . Comparatively few women have a leg or ankle or foot beautiful enough to command my undivided or permanent attention. If such nevertheless turns out to be the case, I lose no time or energy in trying to get under her feet

and then await being trod with most anxious anticipation.

The treading must last several minutes and must include the chest, abdomen . . . and finally the penis which is by then far too stiffly erect to suffer any damage thereby. I might say that I am also thrilled when a female foot compresses my throat. . . .

I imagine that the woman who treads upon me is my mistress and I her slave, and that she does it as a punishment for some transgression I have committed or perhaps out of pure pleasure for her self (Stekel, pp. 277–278).

Mr. P. occasionally has intercourse with women, and thereby experiences pleasure. But he derives greater satisfaction from being walked on. He estimates that he has had about one hundred different partners in this activity. Few comply with his request more than once. Mr. P. believes that a small number of the women involved derive some pleasure from walking upon him, but that most initially comply without fully appreciating the sexual nature of what he has requested. He regards the process as a "conquest" of the woman in question and derives particular satisfaction when she is from the upper class. Most of his partners, however, have been prostitutes.

How did this practice begin? Mr. P. traces it to a sexual encounter when he was fourteen years old. Friends of his family had a pretty daughter, some years older than he. The two of them spent a great deal of time together. He found her ankles and feet extremely attractive, and she was aware of his attention. They would take walks together, and she seemed to go out of her way to step on things and crush them beneath her feet: flowers, fallen fruit, acorns, hay, and the like.

One evening Mr. P. was stretched out on a thick carpet in front of a fire. The young woman walked across the room. Instead of walking around him, she playfully stepped on him and made a joke, saying that she was stepping on him just as she stepped on things during their walks. He laughed with her, and she remained standing on his body. He became aroused, grabbed her foot, and kissed it. The he pressed it against his erect penis, and he instantly had an orgasm.

They played out this scene many times in the next few years. She would buy lovely stockings and shoes and demonstrate each new purchase to him by treading on his body and stimulating him to orgasm. She seemed to enjoy the activity as much as he did, although they never talked about it. In her absence, Mr. P. would masturbate using one of her shoes. She eventually married someone else, and she and Mr. P. never again engaged in this sexual activity. Nor did they ever allude to it when they met. He wished to resume, but this was not to be. And so he turned his attention to other women.

DISCUSSION QUESTIONS

1. The text describes several theoretical accounts of how a paraphilia comes to be established. How does each apply to the present case? Do you find these compelling as explanations or just descriptions of Mr. P.'s history? Remember that in the initial sexual episode with the young woman, Mr. P. was already aroused when it began. Was this a critical event in the development of his paraphilia, or not?

2. Stekel hypothesizes that Mr. P.'s paraphilia and indeed all fetishes represent hostility toward women. He thinks that this is an unconscious process, and is alerted to it by Mr. P.'s preference for women of high social status. How would you test this hypothesis more definitively in the present case?

3. Mr. P.'s paraphilia seems to have elements of fetishism, masochism, and possibly exhibitionism. What does this imply about attempts to classify the paraphilias?

4. Some theorists reserve the term "fetish" for a nonliving object. Other theorists say that a part of a body can be termed a fetish if a person is interested in the body part to the exclusion of the body to which it belongs. Does this make sense to you? What does this mean for someone with a preference that his partners, let us say, have green eyes or rippling muscles?

5. Would Mr. P. Have a psychological disorder if it did not bother him?

6. Suppose Mr. P. was distressed by his paraphilia and went to a behavior therapist for treatment. How would his therapy proceed? How would it proceed with a psychoanalyst?

7. Could paraphilia be considered compulsive behavior? If so, would any of the treatments described in Chapter 9 be useful? The serotonin reuptake inhibitors, which are used to treat obsessive-compulsive disorder, sometimes reduce the frequency of exhibitionism. Do you think that this is a primary therapeutic effect, or could it be due to decreased sex drive (a side effect of this class of medications)?

REFERENCE

Stekel, W. (1930). *Sexual aberrations: The phenomena of fetishism in relation to sex.* New York: Liveright.

What's the Real Illness?

The status of homosexuality as a psychiatric disorder has had a complicated history, some of which is summarized in Ronald Bayer's 1987 book, *Homosexuality and American Psychiatry.* In DSM-I and DSM-II, homosexuality was considered a disorder. The major reason for this was probably that the clinicians who participated in the development of these manuals had never seen a homosexual patient who did not have emotional problems. In retrospect, the reason for this seems obvious: who else would consult a therapist? Later research with homosexual populations that did not request treatment indicated that there was no special psychopathology attached to homosexuality beyond that associated with experiencing the disapproval of families and society at large.

The classification of homosexuality as a mental disorder probably had additional roots in the stigmatization of homosexuality, an attitude from which the mental health professions were not immune. Everyone is familiar with the anxiety generated by homosexuality in many quarters, especially political and religious conservatives. While mental health professionals tend to be more liberal as a group, the notion first proposed by Freud that homosexuality was the result of distorted psychosexual development could be considered a form of bias that homosexuality is inferior to heterosexuality, the most desirable outcome of the growth of sexual preference. Bias may have interacted with muddled scientific thinking when the hypothesis was proposed that homosexuality was caused by having a passive or absent father because some male homosexuals presenting for treatment had this history. As you have already learned, many patients who are not homosexual—indeed many people who are not even patients—feel that they had absent or passive fathers.

More recent attitudes toward homosexuality have been changed somewhat by political and economic action, public education, movies, and other media. Destigmatization in the mental health community has also been facilitated by research discussed in Chapter 13 suggesting a possible inherited anatomical and/or hormonal substrate of homosexuality that makes it seem less volitional. These kinds of findings will undoubtedly fuel better scientific studies of the psychology of normal versus abnormal homosexuality.

Changing attitudes toward homosexuality and accumulating knowledge led to a change in the diagnostic status of sexual orientation. This process began with a vote of the membership of the American Psychiatric Association about whether homosexuality should be classified as a mental disorder in DSM-III. The majority doesn't rule on a diagnosis of schizophrenia, and certainly not on a diagnosis of heart failure, so why vote on a question that should have been based on scientific data? The problem was that such data did not exist. Ideally, homosexuality would not have been included in the first place without sufficient scientific support, but since earlier drafts of the *Diagnostic and Statistical Manual* did include it as a disorder, it was left to the political process to restore a more appropriately skeptical approach.

As you already know, the majority ruled that homosexuality alone was not a disorder, but as a compromise they held onto the disorder diagnosis in the form of "ego dystonic homosexuality." The difference between the latter disorder and adjustment disorder was only that the stress was supposedly internal rather than external. In DSM-III-R homosexuality moved a little further away from being equated automatically with pathology with the diagnosis of "ego dystonic homosexuality," indicating that there is no evidence that dissatisfaction with sexual orientation or functioning or with their impact on self-esteem and social and occupational status is inherently different in homosexuals than in anyone else. In fact, people are equally likely to be dissatisfied with anything else about themselves that places them at odds with the majority culture in which they live.

The notion of homosexuality per se having a primary impact on diagnosis or illness was finally condemned to the dustbin of history by DSM-IV, which left it out entirely. However, therapists remain confused about how to differentiate between homosexuality as a primary problem and homosexuality as a focus of attention in someone with another problem that may or many not be related to it continues to be a source of confusion for patients and therapists. This process is illustrated in the next case.

THE CASE

Robert, a twenty-four-year-old engineer, consulted a psychologist for help changing his sexual orientation. He had dated as a teenager, but after an impulsive homosexual experience during his teen years, he had only been aroused sexually by other men. For the past year, he had had a male "roommate," Charles, with whom he was physically intimate. His family liked Charles but knew nothing about the nature of their relationship. An uncle who became homosexual had been a big disappointment to the entire family.

After a thorough review of Robert's history, the therapist could find no evidence that he had ever been sexually aroused by a woman. All Robert's sexual dreams and fantasies involved men. He had not had any traumatic experiences and was not delusional. There were no current stresses other than his concern about his sexuality.

When pressed about his desire to change his sexual orientation, Robert replied that he was tired of being gay. What exactly did this mean, the therapist wondered, when there was nothing to indicate that he had any heterosexual interests? In continued discussion, it turned out that what Robert was really tired of was that Charles had a drinking problem. When Robert had told Charles that he thought that Charles had had too much to drink at a party, Charles became defensive and angry and said that the subject was closed as far as he was concerned. Robert had become frightened of alienating his friend and backed off. This was not the first time that Robert had been unwilling to push an issue because he was afraid of being abandoned.

Now the connection between Robert's problem and his homosexuality was clear. If he were not gay, he would not be involved with Charles in the first place and would not be confronted with the anxiety engendered by thinking about standing up for himself. He would also be able to ask his family for help without fear that they would find out about his homosexuality.

Although attempts to change sexual orientation are rarely if ever successful, there are established techniques for dealing with interpersonal crises, conflicts about assertiveness, and alcoholism. Yet these issues were much more daunting to Robert. Challenging the global assumptions that he either had to be subservient to Charles or get him to change everything Robert did not like and that the problem with Charles had to be solved immediately or it could not be solved at all helped Robert to plan a series of increasingly strong confrontations that were limited to the drinking problem. The most strenuous of these were never needed, since Charles revealed that he was defensive because he was afraid that he would never be able to stop drinking. He was invited to join Robert and the therapist in figuring out what to do.

DISCUSSION QUESTIONS

1. When he presented for treatment, what psychological defenses was Robert using to deal with the problem with Charles?

2. What treatment plan would you suggest to Robert and Charles? What problems might you encounter implementing the plan? How would you deal with them?

3. Which disorders in homosexual patients might be presented with requests to change sexual orientation?

4. When would it be reasonable to try to change a patient's sexual orientation? How would this be accomplished?

5. Is a homosexual therapist the only clinician who could understand a homosexual patient sufficiently to provide effective treatment? If so, are female therapists the only ones who can treat female patients? Should schizophrenics only be treated by schizophrenic therapists?

6. Should psychologists participate as professionals (as opposed to individuals) in the debate about whether homosexuality is morally or spiritually wrong? What is the overlap between psychology and religion? In which ways do they not interact?

REFERENCE

Bayer, R. (1987). *Homosexuality and American psychiatry: The politics of diagnosis.* Princeton, NJ: Princeton University Press.

Famous Substance Abusers

We hear about substance dependence and abuse in rock stars, sports fig-ures, and show business personalities so frequently that it almost seems to be an inevitable component of being famous. But substance abuse is more likely to end up being fatal than glamorous. Elvis Presley, Jimmy Hen-drix, Jim Morrison, Janis Joplin, Kurt Cobain, and many other celebrities died of substance abuse, and many others have been impaired. There is no evidence that substance abuse enhances creativity, performance, or anything else; it is only a question of how long it takes for its adverse ef-fects to become manifest.

Being famous offers no protection against the risks of substance abuse; indeed it can insulate against potentially lifesaving interventions People who are rich and prominent have more resources that permit them to evade or nullify attempts to control their use of drugs or alcohol. The case of John Belushi, the comic actor who died of an accidental overdose of cocaine and heroin ("speedball"), is a well-documented example of how self-defeating a celebrity's resources can be. Belushi's life and death, which are detailed in the controversial book *Wired* by Bob Woodward (1985), teaches us not to idealize substance abuse in the public figures we idealize.

Although the term "substance abuse" is used generically in this hand-book to refer to pathological use of psychoactive substances such as alco-hol, stimulants, hallucinogens, inhalants, narcotics, nicotine, sedatives, and stimulants, DSM-IV draws a distinction between substance depend-ence and substance abuse. Both of these terms are defined as maladaptive patterns of substance use producing clinically significant impairment or distress. A diagnosis of substance dependence is made when three or more of the following symptoms have been present in the same year:

1. Tolerance, manifested by a need for increased does to produce the same effect or by decreased effect with the same dose
2. Withdrawal, manifested by a substance-specific physical and/or psy-chological syndrome when the substance is withdrawn or by the use of the same or a related substance to relieve or avoid withdrawal
3. Using more of the substance than the person intended
4. Unsuccessful attempts or wishes to reduce substance use

5. Spending inordinant amounts of time trying to obtain the substance, use it, or recover from its effects
6. Giving up or reducing important social, occupational or recreational activities because of substance use
7. Continued use of the substance despite knowing that it is harmful (e.g., using cocaine even though it makes the person depressed)

DSM-IV specifies two subcategories of substance dependence: with and without physiologic dependence (i.e., with or without item 1 or 2).

Substance abuse is diagnosed when at least one of the following is present.

1. Failure to fulfill major role obligations (e.g., missing days at work, failing to complete school assignments, being unable to care for children) as a result of substance use
2. Recurrent use of the substance in situations in which it is dangerous (e.g., drinking and driving)
3. Recurrent substance-related legal problems (e.g., arrests for driving under the influence or disturbing the peace)
4. Continued use of the substance despite social or interpersonal problems that are caused or made worse by the substance (e.g., getting into barroom brawls, arguing with a spouse)

DSM-IV considers substance dependence and substance abuse to be distinct diagnoses. Substance abuse is not diagnosed in someone who meets the criteria for substance dependence since the latter includes many characteristics of the former. However, it is clear that either of these disorders spells trouble for anyone who has it.

THE CASE

John Belushi grew up in Wheaton, a small suburb of Chicago. He graduated from high school in 1967. As an adolescent, Belushi was a gifted athlete and actor. He was offered a football scholarship to college, but the opportunity of a summer job acting in a small company set him on his way to a show business career. His talent for comedy was soon apparent, and when he was just 22 years old, he became the youngest member of Chicago's famous Second City comedy troupe.

Early in his career, Belushi began to use marijuana and hallucinogens. Compared to his peers, this drug use was not unusual, except that he used drugs while working, and he used a prodigious amount before showing any effects. Because of the permissive attitude toward drug use of his culture, the fact that Belushi was in trouble from the beginning was overlooked.

His next notable career step was a major part in a satirical musical called *Lemmings*, which spoofed the Woodstock generation. The job took him to New York, and the musical was a great hit. Its highlight was John Belushi doing a Joe Cocker imitation. Here was where John was introduced to cocaine, and it quickly became his preferred substance. He used the drug not only after the show—which was common practice—but before as well. Sometimes it spoiled his performance. Friends suggested he not perform when he was high, but he resisted. "I can handle it," he assured them.

In 1975, NBC television executives decided that a live comedy show pitched at the counterculture might work. There was the danger that a live camera might let nasty words slip uncensored over the airwaves, but this possibility made the show exciting as well. And so "Saturday Night Live" was born. A cast was assembled, including Jane Curtin, Dan Aykroyd, Chevy Chase, Gilda Radner, and John Belushi. None of these actors was well known at that time, and "Saturday Night Live" was their vehicle to fame. Chevy Chase became the first real star on the show, and Belushi was reportedly jealous.

When Chevy Chase left the show to pursue movies, Belushi became the acknowledged star, and his various routines became the rage of the country: the Joe Cocker imitation, the buzzing bees, the samurai, the greasy diner that served only cheeseburgers and Pepsis, and the Blues Brothers. He helped make "Saturday Night Live" the hippest show on television. Some of the biggest names in comedy and show business appeared as guest hosts for the show: George Carlin, Richard Pryor, Candace Bergen, and so on. Even consumer advocate Ralph Nader hosted a show.

Belushi's drug use continued to increase. In 1976, he visited a doctor who specialized in drug addiction. The following summary appeared in the doctor's notes:

> Smokes 3 packs a day.
> Alcohol drinks socially.
> Medications: Valium occasionally.
> Marijuana 4 to 5 times a week.
> Cocaine—snorts daily, main habit.
> Mescaline—regularly.
> Acid—10 to 20 trips.
> No heroin.
> Amphetamines—four kinds.
> Quaaludes. (Woodward, 1985, p. 111)

The doctor told him he had to stop because he was killing himself. Belushi refused. He was convinced that drugs were his only relief in an otherwise hectic life.

In keeping with the tenor of the times, drug use pervaded the humor of "Saturday Night Live." The prevailing belief in the 1970s was that only drugs injected with a needle were harmful. Few thought cocaine addictive, and most laughed at the idea that marijuana could be harmful. As your text explains, it is now known that marijuana causes more lung damage than cigarettes and lowers the threshold for the use of other drugs.

It is doubtful that Belushi would have stopped using drugs even if at the time they had been widely recognized as harmful. But these prevailing notions perhaps explain why so many of his friends and associates stood to the side and watched him slowly poison himself. Perhaps they were awed by his growing success. As you probably know, Belushi moved from the television show to star in movies, including the highly successful *Animal House* and *The Blues Brothers*. He made a record album that sold well. He also did a sell-out concert tour. John Belushi was not only famous, he was wealthy.

As his drug use escalated, his reputation began to suffer. Some of his show business projects failed because his performances were hampered by intoxication. Belushi's drug use was clearly out of control; this caused those closest to him to despair. It got so bad that his wife left him.

At this point, an around-the-clock bodyguard was hired by his manager to protect Belushi . . . not from other people but from himself. The guard labored mightily to keep Belushi away from drugs. Eventually he left the job. Baby-sitting is not easy work under any circumstances, much less when the baby has the resources to thwart your attempts to help him.

Then John discovered heroin. As a beginner, he had another person inject the drug for him. Like every other drug he had ever tried, he liked heroin very much. He once enthused that using heroin was "like kissing God" (Woodward, 1985, p. 321)—A statement that illustrates that drugs are primarily rewarding; people take them because it feels good, even if the consequences are bad. On or about March 5, 1982, John Belushi died of an overdose. The coroner's report attributed his death to acute toxicity from heroin and cocaine. He was thirty-three years old.

DISCUSSION QUESTIONS

1. What would the DSM-IV diagnosis be in Belushi's case?

2. With potent and highly rewarding drugs like crack cocaine, many users report feeling addicted after the first dose. How can adolescents, who think that nothing can harm them, be warned of this risk in a credible manner?

3. Would legalizing drugs like cocaine and heroin increase or decrease their use? What is the difference between the clinical and the legal (e.g., stealing to get drugs) aspects of pathological substance use?

4. Is there a difference between using speed to stay awake in order to study for an examination or drive across the country and pathological substance use? Does using cocaine or heroin "recreationally" differ from dependence or abuse?

5. How would you approach a fellow student who was exhibiting evidence of drug or alcohol abuse?

6. Cigarettes kill more people than all illicit drugs combined. Nicotine produces tolerance and withdrawal, and people continue to smoke despite awareness that it is harmful. Attempts to cut back on smoking are often unsuccessful. Is smoking a form of substance dependence? If so, how should it be treated?

REFERENCES

American Psychiatric Association (1994). *Diagnostic and Statistical Manual of Mental Disorders* (4th ed.). Washington, DC: American Psychiatric Press.

Woodward, B. (1985). *Wired: The short life and fast times of John Belushi*. New York: Pocket Books.

Does Treating Stress Cure Alcoholism?

The interaction between substance dependence and abuse and other Axis I disorders is complex. Many alcoholics become depressed, more often than not as a result of the effect of alcohol on their brains or of their recognition of the mess that alcohol has made of their lives. Anxiety in alcoholics may represent intermittent alcohol withdrawal as well as realistic worry about life circumstance. Irritability, memory problems, sleep disorders, and sexual dysfunction are other common toxic effects of alcohol on mental function.

Conversely, alcohol is the most common self-treatment for depression, anxiety, and insomnia. Initially, the sedative effect creates a feeling of well-being and tension relief that seems to dissolve a depressed or anxious mood. However, the longer-term action of alcohol is to aggravate depression, and intermittent withdrawal due to the short duration of the effect of the alcohol increases anxiety. People who have a few drinks to get to sleep may fall asleep right away, but they are awakened in the middle of the night by the mini-withdrawal syndrome that results when alcohol leaves the brain. Repeated episodes of alcohol withdrawal during sleep teach the brain to get into a state of arousal before it is time to wake up, and to create a sleep disturbance that may persist for a year or more after alcohol use is discontinued.

Not realizing that the cure is contributing to the disease, many drinkers have another drink when they cannot stay asleep or when anxiety or depression returns, but tolerance to the sedative effect of alcohol just comes on that much faster. In addition, with greater peaks of blood-alcohol concentration, the level of concentration falls more precipitously between doses and withdrawal intensifies. The higher the dose of alcohol and the more frequent and intense the withdrawal, the more abnormal function becomes programmed into the brain; this ensures that symptoms will persist long after the alcohol intake is stopped.

Another interaction between alcoholism and other conditions is comorbidity, or the cooccurrence of two mental disorders at a greater than expected frequency. There is a good deal of comorbidity between alcoholism and a number of mental disorders, especially depression, bipolar disorder, panic disorder, social phobia, simple phobia, and antisocial personality disorder (Kessler, McGonagle, and Zhao, 1994). In some of these cases, alcohol is not a cause or a self-treatment of the other problem, but a separate condition. The risk for alcoholism is acquired or inherited along with the other problem, or alcoholism is more easily expressed when the other problem is present.

The next case illustrates some of the interactions between alcoholism and depression. We will see that even if emotional conflict precipitates substance abuse, treatment of the substance abuse cannot be made subservient to treatment of the other problem.

THE CASE

Barry Behan's friends introduced him to alcohol when he was sixteen. By age eighteen, he was drunk every weekend and was emptying liquor bottles in the house and filling them with water. Over the years, he experimented with marijuana and cocaine, but alcohol was his drug of choice. During his college years, no one thought it odd that he drank most days and was intoxicated several times a week, since most of his fraternity brothers did the same thing. In fact, they thought that it was hilarious when he drove after consuming two or three six-packs of beer, and they laughed when he could not remember things that he had done when he had been drinking (i.e., when he experienced blackouts).

Following graduation from college, Barry entered law school. He found that it was getting too difficult to make up work he missed when he did not go to class because he was hung over. His grades suffered even more when he found that his concentration was not as good as it once was, and he found himself tending to lose his temper under the kind of aggressive questioning that is common in law school classes. He began to wonder whether he should stop drinking or at least cut back, but his friends were still heavy drinkers and he did not feel comfortable being around them if he was not at least a little high, too.

Luckily, Barry began dating a woman named Marianne who quickly realized that he was never in any social setting without a drink. She asked him to reduce his drinking and he tried, but despite the problems he was having, he could not do so. A promise not to drink was always followed by a week or two of abstinence, but just when she thought that things were finally under control, Barry would show up drunk. And each time, he told the same story: he meant not to drink, but everyone else was doing it, so it did not seem like a big deal. Anyway, he was under control. What about the time he drove home from a study session right after having a few drinks to relax? There was nothing wrong with his driving, he insisted. She pointed out that one of his drinking buddies was killed a few months ago while driving drunk, but he felt that this was an entirely different situation: he never drank that much, and he was always careful when he drove.

As she began to realize that Barry could not keep from drinking for any length of time, Marianne began to push a little harder. In response, Barry got angrier and told her to grow up and stop nagging him. They had a number of confrontations during which Barry was sarcastic and demeaning but not assaultive. He was always remorseful the next day, and Marianne kept forgiving him. However, she finally remembered that her father had been an alcoholic who was not a bad person normally but, when he had been drinking, became mean and devaluing. Marianne's mother felt helpless to do anything about it, and as she got older, Marianne had tried on several occasions to tell him that she was worried about his drinking. He humiliated her so badly that she gave up and finally left home. She now realized that she was unconsciously drifting toward a relationship that was similar to her parents', and she told Barry that she was going to leave him if he did not stop drinking.

Seeing that she really meant it, Barry decided that giving up Marianne would be worse than giving up drinking. He tried an Alcoholics Anonymous meeting and did not like it, but she encouraged him to try again and he finally found a meeting of lawyers—one of its regular members a professor of his—that suited him. He relapsed while doing a summer clerkship that required him to interact with people he did not feel comfortable with, and Marianne did not catch on at first because he only drank before events that she did not attend. But when she realized that he was laughing inappropriately and acting as though he was concealing something, she confronted him. At first, he had the usual counterattack, but he finally stopped drinking. He did not go back to A.A. because he did not think that he had the same kind of problem the other members had.

After law school, Barry and Marianne got married and he joined a prestigious law firm. Marianne was included in the firm's social gatherings, and Barry found it easier not to drink because his new associates were not heavy drinkers. However, even though he was learning how to handle social stress without drinking, he did not know how to handle other kinds of distress, and whenever he felt uncomfortable emotionally, he would find himself having a few secret drinks. He would then go on drinking for a few months before he finally stopped.

The approach broke down when Marianne found a half-empty vodka bottle hidden under the bathroom sink. During the ensuing confrontation, Barry admitted that he had begun drinking after the death of a senior partner whom Barry had regarded as a father figure. Barry had not bee aware of feeling sad, but he did feel tense and irritable, and he found that alcohol helped to relax him and to get him to sleep. His old friend alcohol had come through again, although it had prevented him from turning to Marianne for help with his feelings.

Even Barry could see the need for treatment at this point. Before going back to A.A., he thought that he might consult a psychologist. The therapist's diagnoses were alcoholism and complicated grief, possibly with an underlying depression. There was a significant familial risk for the first problem in that Barry's brother, grandfather, and an uncle were alcoholic. His father, whom he idealized, had died of cirrhosis when Barry was eighteen. Barry seemed to have had so much trouble after the death of his colleague because, like his father, he saw himself as a stoical person who would be humiliated by getting upset about normal events in life. The colleague had been sick for a long time, and there was no point feeling bad about something that he could not do anything about. The same trait had prevented Barry from mourning for his father, and some of that unresolved grief undoubtedly was trying to come out now.

As the therapist explained this formulation, Barry saw that his problem was simple: all he had to do was to learn how to grieve and he would not have to drink anymore. In the meantime, there was no hurry to cut back yet. There was no point in getting any more treatment for alcoholism, since this was not a relapse but self-treatment for sadness. "I can't agree with you for three reasons," replied the therapist. "First, having problems feeling sad and the pressure of unresolved grief may have lowered the threshold for your drinking, but what it did was to precipitate a relapse of drinking, so that now you have two problems; even if you do resolve this crisis, there is no guarantee that the drinking will stop. Second, the chances of resolving whatever depression may be underneath are much less if you keep drinking because the alcohol will keep you from resolving it by affecting your mood and concentration. Third, any emotional learning you do when you are drinking may not carry over to the nonintoxicated state. So I'm afraid you'll have to stop drinking if you want me to be of any help."

Barry brought Marianne to the next session, and she agreed with the therapist. She had also come to feel that she could not tolerate any more drinking episodes and that Barry needed a comprehensive approach if she were to stay with him. He went back to A.A., and he agreed to take disulfiram (Antabuse) to get over the immediate difficult period of strong temptation to drink. When he stopped drinking, his mind cleared more than he thought it would, and he was better able to examine the all-or-nothing belief that he either had to ignore his feelings or be completely overwhelmed by them. He was able to begin to express sadness about no longer having someone at work he admired and enjoyed talking to. Expressing grief in the present facilitated a discussion of his feelings about his father. He even wondered whether he had been able to hold onto some part of his father by drinking heavily.

These approaches helped Barry's emotional state, but what decreased the risk of another relapse of drinking was teaching him to tell Marianne whenever he had the urge to drink. The couple set aside time each day to talk about important issues, and Barry practiced telling her when he was upset instead of keeping it to himself. As Barry finally admitted that he could not control his feelings without help from anyone else, he came to see that he could not control his drinking by himself either. Making a long-term commitment to A.A. not only helped him to break down his isolation from the people he needed the most and his denial of his own weaknesses, but it provided insurance against the realistic risk of future relapse.

DISCUSSION QUESTIONS

1. In contingency contracting, the patient writes a letter surrendering something important such as a medical license or notifying an employer, superior, or spouse about relapse. The letter is mailed by the therapist in the event of noncompliance with substance-abuse treatment or of finding drugs or alcohol in a random urine sample. Contingency contracting may also involve a spouse's decision to leave a substance-abusing partner in the event of refusal to get treatment or relapse. Do you think that this approach is too coercive?

2. What do you think would have happened if the therapist had addressed Barry's grief but not his drinking?

3. What would be the implications of Marianne not following through with her threat?

4. In what ways might alcoholism interact with schizophrenia? What about personality disorders?

5. What are the biological dimensions of Barry's family history of alcoholism? What are its psychological dimensions?

6. What are the chances that Barry would have stopped drinking if he had realized that this behavior solidified his identification with his father?

REFERENCE

Kessler, R. C., McGonagle, K. A., & Zhao, S. (1994). Lifetime and 12-month prevalence of DSM-III-R psychiatric disorders in the United States. *Archives of General Psychiatry, 51,* 8–19.

The Mask of Sanity:
Antisocial Personality Disorder

As Chapter 15 indicates, agreement among investigators is good when they make a diagnosis of antisocial personality disorder. For all other personality disorders, independent evaluators may concur on what they see, but not on what it means. For example, there may not be much question about the presence of aggressive behavior, inflated self-esteem, and mood swings, but different experts might say that they are symptoms of borderline, narcissistic, histrionic, paranoid, or even no personality disorder. For this reason, agreement even among trained raters who are in accord about the presence of specific behaviors and traits is no greater than chance about the personality disorder diagnosis implied by those findings (Perry, 1992).

This kind of disagreement is inevitable, since no behaviors or symptoms are specific to any personality disorder. Pathological dependency is a trait shared by people with borderline, narcissistic, histrionic, and dependent personality disorders; people who are depressed or anxious; and people who do not have any other dysfunctions and therefore do not qualify for any diagnosis. Manipulative behavior is a feature of antisocial, histrionic, and borderline personality disorders, as well as factitious disorders, hypochondriasis, and just manipulativeness.

Individuals with antisocial personality disorder have an inflated view of their own importance and believe that everyone else is valuable only insofar as they can be manipulated. They do not feel guilty because they feel entitled to anything they get. Feeling above the law, they do not feel obligated to abide by it. A diagnosis of narcissistic personality disorder can be made on the basis of the presence of "a grandiose sense of self-importance," feeling "'special' and unique," having a "sense of entitlement," being "interpersonally exploitive," and lacking empathy (American Psychiatric Association, 1994). Does this mean that people with antisocial personality disorder also have narcissistic personality disorder? Or is pathological narcissism a feature of antisocial personality disorder? Irresponsibility, lying, irritability, thrill-seeking impulsivity, failure to conform to social norms, and lack of remorse are all DSM-IV criteria for antisocial personality disorder, but they are also characteristics of some bipolar individuals. Do the two groups share some common inability to regulate mood, arousal, or behavior? What is the impact on the outcome of one type of disturbance when features of the other are also present?

When personality is organized around blatant criminality, lack of remorse, and disregard for other people and their rules, the diagnosis of antisocial personality disorder is obvious. In other instances, the depth of destructiveness is hidden under a facade of superficial charm. In his classic book, *The Mask of Sanity,* psychiatrist Harold Cleckley (1964) demonstrated some of the many ways in which antisocial personality disorder can masquerade as something completely different, how a person who does not seem that disturbed can have what some have referred to as "cancer of the personality." The subtleties of antisocial personality disorder and the capacity of the person with it to draw other people into its deceptions are illustrated by the case of Alex Nord. This case will also illustrate that although it may not be possible to change an antisocial personality, it may still be possible to work constructively within the limits of personality to improve the outcome that would otherwise be expected.

THE CASE

Mr. Nord was twenty-four when he consulted a therapist for help controlling the impulse to break into houses and steal things. He had already cased a number of homes and knew exactly which ones would be easy pickings. He even knew just what he would like to take from each place. He had gone so far as to get into two of the houses and rummage through some dresser drawers. He left a few of the drawers slightly open so that the owners would suspect but not be entirely certain that someone had been there.

Alex did not seek help with this impulse because he thought that it was wrong. He was just afraid that the breaking and entering and stealing would escalate until he began making impulsive mistakes and got caught. His concern was justified by past experience: as a child he had stolen a neighbor's 10-speed bicycle. He then moved up to a mountain bike and then an expensive racing bicycle. He was caught shoplifting but released; he was finally charged after his fourth offense and was relieved to be sentenced to psychotherapy instead of jail.

While in therapy Alex discovered that the impulse to steal was a result of having gone from one foster home to another as a child. Never feeling that he would have anything of his own to take from placement to placement, he began taking other peoples' things. It never really occurred to him that they might miss an item; wanting it was reason enough. It seemed that there would no longer be a pressure to steal now that he realized why he did it, and the requirement to attend therapy was dropped. Alex immediately stopped attending therapy sessions, stating that he had received enough help to be on the road to recovery.

Alex was on the road, but it was not to stopping his antisocial behavior. He graduated to stealing car stereos, and then to stealing the cars themselves. He was finally apprehended while stealing a car in front of a police officer's house. This time, he received probation and more therapy. The therapist helped him to realize that the relapse of stealing was caused by fear of growing up and having to be more responsible. Stealing was a way of reassuring himself that he would still be able to get the things he wanted.

Mr. Nord had had a difficult childhood. His father, who was later killed in a brawl, left the family before he was born. His mother, who expressed little interest in him, had a succession of boyfriends who either paid no attention to him or beat him. He was removed from the home and lived in a series of foster homes. He was up for adoption several times, but before each one could be finalized, he would steal something important, and the prospective parents would change their minds. He was taken to treatment several times, but he never told the therapist anything meaningful, because he felt that it was none of the therapist's business.

Alex had been too bored to pay attention in school, and he preferred to cut classes and hang out with his friends. He dropped out at age sixteen, but almost immediately got a G.E.D. Despite his lack of a formal education, he fancied himself a great writer, and indeed he had a unique flair for the written word that paralleled his glib ability to explain almost anything and his quick insight into other peoples' motivations. Unfortunately, his insight was the cornerstone of manipulation rather than empathy, and he lost interest in any writing project soon after starting it. His failure to complete anything did not deter him from believing that his writing would one day be recognized, as had the work of other writers who lived on the fringe of the law like Jean Genet and Ezra Pound. Stealing was just another kind of poetic experience that would enhance his art.

Stealing was not only an artistic experience; it was a way of feeling alive. Alex felt bored and inconsequential if he was not doing something risky, something that excited him and made him feel alive. When he got away with an illegal act, he felt smarter than anyone else, at least until he had to prove it to himself again. Each time, it took a little more excitement and a little more outsmarting to make himself feel excited and clever, and he was a little less able to control his behavior. In Freudian terms, his fear of getting caught represented a modicum of conscience combined with a perception by the ego of id impulses that an insufficiently developed superego could not control.

THE TREATMENT

In psychotherapy for the first time without being sentenced to it, Alexander was eager to discuss the meaning of stealing as a way of dealing with conflict, especially loss, and exciting himself. But even as he talked about these motivations, he could not seem to keep himself from showing the therapist how much he knew, certainly more than she did. The therapist acknowledged that he was in fact very intelligent and that he seemed to have figured out a great deal about himself. However, even though there was much to be said for his insights, he seemed to be using them as rationalizations for not controlling his behavior: as long as he understood what he was doing, he did not feel obligated to do anything about it. This attitude had been reinforced by the authorities, who did not want to punish him for something that was a psychological problem

After thinking this over, Alex suggested that the thing that had been most helpful to him was to have had supportive relationships with his previous therapists. However, the therapist pointed out that these relationships had mainly been important so long as he was able to use the relationship with the therapist to get out of trouble or just manipulate therapists in order to feel superior to them. This bluntness impressed Alex, who suggested that more intensive therapy might really work this time. But the therapist felt that an open-ended treatment approach might be an invitation to her patient to try to find ways to outsmart her. Perhaps it would be more prudent for them to work concretely on strengthening adaptive defenses like reality testing and impulse control, especially since his primary goal was to avoid ending up in jail, which his lawyer had assured him would certainly happen the next time he got caught.

Alex said that he was impressed with the therapist's willingness to stay focused on an achievable goal and not seek insight as a substitute for action. The therapist did not know or care whether this statement was sincere, but she agreed to try to stick to the point. First, she got him to stop going near the neighborhood he had been frequenting to decrease the likelihood that he would act on his impulses. To try to find a way to enhance the patient's self-esteem that did not involve outsmarting the law, she reviewed his latest "masterpiece," which did in fact have much to recommend it although she doubted that he would have the persistence to complete it. Most important, she supported the ego assessment and whatever superego the patient had by a type of contingency contracting: Alex signed a "contract" permitting the therapist to notify the police about his behavior if she heard about any burglaries in the area he had been investigating.

Alex soon lost interest in his impulses, and then in the therapy. The psychologist did not hear from him again for several years, when he dropped in to say hello. Immediately suspicious, she asked him why he had chosen to see her at that particular time. He replied that nothing was new, he was just curious about whether she still had the same office. He was vague when she asked him about his antisocial impulses, but he seemed reassured when she told him that she would be there for some time to come and that their agreement still stood as far as she was concerned. He seemed reassured and said that he might check back some time in the future. Nothing had changed in his personality, but he had seemed to incorporate her presence into whatever capacity he had to suppress dangerous behaviors.

DISCUSSION QUESTIONS

1. Contingency contracting was discussed in Chapter 14 as a treatment for substance abuse. What do you think of this approach to antisocial behavior?

2. In not focusing on the unconscious motivations for Alex's behavior, did the therapist imply that such motivations did not exist?

3. Many people with antisocial personality behavior have been abused and/or neglected in childhood. So have half of all psychiatric patients. How might early abuse specifically cause antisocial personality?

4. How would you determine whether discussing past experiences is a means of understanding current problems or a way of not dealing with them?

5. In most states, a diagnosis of antisocial personality disorder does not qualify for a plea of not guilty by reason of insanity even though it is classified as a mental disorder. Cleckley (1964) argues that underneath a facade of charm and pseudo-insight, the sociopathic individual experiences the kind of emptiness, mental chaos, and disturbed sense of self that are experienced by psychotic patients. Are these views incompatible?

6. Is it possible to have an antisocial personality disorder and not to be in trouble with the law? Do any successful public figures with questionable ethics, superficial relationships, no enduring loyalties beyond their own self-interest, and inability to learn from repeated negative experiences qualify for this diagnosis?

REFERENCES

American Psychiatric Association (1994). *Diagnostic and Statistical Manual of Mental Disorders* (4th ed.). Washington, DC: American Psychiatric Press.

Cleckley, H. M. (1964). *The mask of sanity, an attempt to clarify some issues about the so-called psychopathic personality.* St. Louis: Mosby.

Perry, J. C. (1992). Problems and considerations in the valid assessment of personality disorder. *American Journal of Psychiatry, 149,* 1465–53.

The Agony and the Ecstasy: Borderline Personality Disorder

The concept of a disorder on the border between neurosis and psychosis was broached when Rorshach, the inventor of the famous projective psychological test, noticed that patients who seemed well organized on the surface gave psychotic interpretations of the inkblots. At first, it seemed that schizophrenia was latent in these patients, and so they were said to have latent or pseudoneurotic schizophrenia (Hoch and Palatin, 1949). However, when follow-up studies found that these patients remained stable over time and did not become schizophrenic, it was decided that the syndrome was a kind of personality disorder (Grinker et al., 1968).

Subsequent reviews of these and later studies on the topic (Gunderson and Zanarini, 1987) concluded that the bulk of research showed that borderline personality disorder (BPD) was indeed a type of personality disorder characterized by superficial adaptability, but a capacity to become psychotic (mainly paranoid) in response to certain stresses, especially close relationships. DSM-IV (American Psychiatric Association, 1994) codifies BPD as a personality disorder with enduring disturbances of relationships, self-image, emotional regulation, and impulse control, requiring five of the following symptoms for the diagnosis:

1. Attempts to avoid real or imagined abandonment
2. Unstable and intense relationships that the patient alternately idealizes and devalues
3. Disturbed or unstable self-image
4. Impulsive self-defeating behavior distinct from suicidal behavior or self-mutilation (e.g., promiscuity, substance abuse, binge eating)
5. Recurrent suicide attempts or threats or nonsuicidal self-mutilation (e.g., cutting or burning oneself)
6. Intense moodiness, irritability, or anxiety lasting hours to days at a time
7. Chronic feelings of emptiness
8. Inappropriate intense anger or difficulty controlling one's temper
9. Transient paranoia or severe dissociation in response to stress

Describing psychological functioning in BPD rather than symptoms, psychoanalyst Otto Kernberg (1975) has conceived of it as a personality organized around the use of pathological defense mechanisms that impair an organized experience of the self and others, especially denial, projective identification, and splitting. Denial involves ignoring the existence of emotionally crucial information such as rage at someone who is desperately needed. Projective identification supports denial in that it gets rid of unacceptable emotions and attitudes by inducing them in someone else and then responding to them as if they originated in that person. For example, someone who is burdened by unconscious anger might act in provocative ways to make another person, say a therapist, angry. One kind of provocation might be to refuse to get better while insisting that "it's not your fault; you're trying as hard as you can." Another might be to disagree, but cordially, with everything that the other person says. After hundreds of such interactions, the target of this behavior eventually becomes annoyed. Surprised, the patient becomes angry in response to what seems to be completely inappropriate behavior on the other person's part. While the anger has been "projected," therefore, the patient still feels it, although ostensibly only because the other person had the feeling first.

Splitting is a process of separating contradictory emotions and experiences. Kernberg speculates that early experiences taught BPD patients to fear that normal feelings of rebelliousness and anger would make primary caregivers abandon them or retaliate in some other way. To avoid even the inclination to risk this disaster, they split off or relegate all negative feelings to one part of their minds and remain aware only of positive feelings. This approach temporarily solves the conflict between good and bad feelings about the same person, but it makes it impossible for good feelings and bad feelings to interact with each other so that positive ideas can become less unrealistic and negative ideas less intense. Concepts of oneself and others become split into all good and all bad, until almost all of psychology is polarized. This makes it harder and harder to develop realistic views of anything as the intrusion of any negative feeling threatens to ruin completely anything positive. Kernberg would understand the identity disturbance of BPD as a reflection of this chaotic oscillation of attitudes, the self-destructive behavior as the consequence of emergence of hidden negativism, and the chronic emptiness as the result of the subtle destruction of feelings of optimism by underlying split off destructiveness.

Although there are many ways in which the psychodynamics that Kernberg describes could lead to specific symptoms and behaviors, he is really describing a personality *organization* rather than a personality *disorder* (Kernberg, 1975). This is an important distinction, because people with many disorders in addition to borderline personality disorder may have the same psychological constellations. For example, depression, mania, schizophrenia, and a variety of personality disorders may be associated with denial, splitting, and projective identification as attempts to handle intolerable anger at loved ones, and it is hard to see how dissociation, the defining mechanism of dissociative disorders like multiple personality, differs from splitting. Many people with multiple personality behave just as BPD patients in many other ways as well.

Whether we are talking about borderline personality disorder or borderline personality organization, the personalities of BPD patients are built on such shifting sands that they seem to be drastically different people at different times and in different situations. Alternating between contradictory all-or-nothing mental states, they often get other people to identify with one side or the other of their psychology; this results in half of the people they know loving them and the other half hating them, or half of their friends thinking that they are always right and the other half that they are always wrong. Similarly, there is often an ongoing split between functioning and inner experience and between mental states from one moment to the next.

For many years, it was felt that even though they threatened suicide, BPD patients rarely succeeded, but this impression may have represented a denial of the severity of BPD: suicide can be a very real risk in BPD, as we shall see in the next case.

THE CASE

The poet Sylvia Plath (1932–1963) was born in 1932 in Massachusetts. Her parents had both immigrated to the United States from Europe. Not much more is known about her early life until age eight, when her father died. Her mother then had to raise the family alone.

Sylvia began winning prizes for her poetry in high school, and in 1950 she entered Smith College on two writing scholarships. Despite continued awards and honors, she felt that "I've gone around for most of my life as in the rarefied atmosphere under a bell jar." Indeed, every success seemed to be negated by feelings of self-doubt and emptiness. The sense of the destruction of anything good by abandonment is already developed in her poem "Mad Girl's Love Song," which emerged at a time of triumph: it was published in an issue of *Mademoiselle* magazine for which she served as guest managing editor, while only a junior in college:

> I shut my eyes and all the world drops dead;
> I lift my lids and all is born again.
> (I think I made you up inside my head).
> . . . I should have loved a thunderbird instead;
> At least when spring comes they roar back again.
> I shut my eyes and the world drops dead.
> (I think I made you up inside my head).

That summer, Sylvia again followed the abrupt transition from happiness to despair:

> All in all, I felt unborn on a wave of creative,
> social, and financial success— The six month, crash,
> however, was to come— (Plath, 1971, p. 208).

In her only published novel, *the Bell Jar*, Sylvia gives an account of the progressive disintegration of her personality of the kind that has been reported since the time of Rorshach. The breakdown seems to have been precipitated by being left by a man she loved, and possibly also by her inability to tolerate her success. Plath tells us that her superficial ability to get along with people belied an underlying sense of fragmentation:

> . . . the cracks in her nature which had been held
> together as it were by the surrounding pressures of New
> York widen and gape alarmingly. More and more her warped
> view of the world around—her own vacuous
> domestic life and that of her neighbors—seems the one
> right way of looking at things." (Plath, 1971, p. 208).

In this and other statements, Sylvia indicates that she can feel good about herself and others until she loses one of the props that is keeping her personality together, in this case, her boyfriend. As soon as she is unable to maintain her "one right way" of looking at things, the persona she tries to maintain starts to disintegrate. Instead of wanting to destroy the person who leaves her, the positive, sustaining force within her is destroyed, and ultimately she wants to destroy herself completely. Dark feelings she ignores when things are going well seem released at these times with destructive and even hateful results.

Perhaps Sylvia learned to hide her negative side from her mother, who "secretly . . . hated [her father] for dying and leaving no money because he didn't trust life insurance salesmen" (Plath, 1971, p. 32). Whatever its origin, she seems to have alternated between the successful and the unfulfilled, the competent and the empty, the idealized and the devalued. Inevitably, bad feelings would emerge and ruin anything good that seemed to be going on. We can see the thinly disguised potential for harm at the very moment when something happens that could be helpful in Sylvia's thoughts about her first psychiatrist, whom she consulted at the beginning of the breakdown she experienced in college:

> Doctor Gordon's features were so perfect he was almost
> pretty. I hated him from the minute I walked in through the
> door. (Plath, 1971, p. 105).

Having lost whatever it was in the superficially positive relationship that had been keeping her destructive impulses in check, Sylvia was unable to withstand the assault of the destructive side of her personality on her functioning, and on her life. She made several serious suicide attempts, one by trying to hang herself and another by trying to drown herself. As she felt that she had lived against her will, she was hospitalized.

> . . . I saw that my body had all sorts of little tricks, such as
> making my hands go limp at the crucial second, which would
> save it, time and again, whereas if I had the whole say, I
> would be dead in a flash. (Plath, 1971, p. 130).

In other words, there was such a dramatic split between the life-affirming and the life-destroying sides of her personality that Sylvia could only experience one side at a time. She was not ambivalent in the sense that she felt "I want to die, but I also want to live." Instead, she experienced the wish to live as a force that was located in her body, not her mind. Sylvia may have learned splitting from her mother, who said, when Sylvia was finally released after a prolonged and nightmarish hospitalization, "We'll act as if all this were a bad dream." Instead of getting angry, or even annoyed, at this blatant dismissal of intense suffering that was still present, instead of withdrawing from her mother, Sylvia had a more global negative response and withdrew from the human race:

> To the person in the bell jar, blank and stopped as a dead
> baby, the world itself is the bad dream. (Plath, 1971, p. 193).

It is not clear whether the treatment Sylvia received, which consisted of psychotherapy and several courses of electroconvulsive therapy, had anything to do with it, but she began to reestablish a connection with her positive dimension. Perhaps she had experienced such an intense period of negativism that she could afford psychologically to pay attention to the other side again. Or perhaps the real therapeutic event was meeting British poet Ted Hughes. The two hit it off and got married, which seemed to reestablish the psychological glue that kept her negativism under control.

Sylvia started writing again, and more honors followed. However, her all-or-nothing thinking made it impossible to treat the inevitable rejections as minor setbacks that could be overcome. Instead, she felt that "nothing stinks like a pile of unpublished writing" (Plath, 1971, p. 211). She got a grant to write *The Bell Jar,* but she faced other responsibilities that she could not begin to integrate with each other, let alone with her professional responsibilities. As a result, she felt "like a very efficient tool or weapon, used and in demand from moment to moment" (Plath, 1971, p. 215).

Sylvia's difficulty integrating emotionally diverse states was further complicated by her husband's comings and goings, which made him a less-than-perfect stabilizing force and subjected her to fits of despair when he was unavailable. It was probably these repeated abandonments that added so much to the secret storehouse of rage that it overwhelmed her tenuous controls and became predominant again. She became increasingly suicidal, but this did not make her husband more available and she apparently had no other way of communicating her distress. In the same year that she finished *The Bell Jar,* she committed suicide by gassing herself with the oven. Her husband was expected home, but he did not return in time to save her.

DISCUSSION QUESTIONS

1. Was suicide inevitable in this case? What might have been done to prevent a fatal outcome?

2. If you had been Sylvia's therapist, how do you think she might have reacted to you? What would the most important problems in therapy have been?

3. Sylvia's extreme sensitivity to abandonment, suicidal behavior, periods of intense emotional discomfort, chronic feelings of emptiness, impulsivity, and intense relationships alternating between idealization and devaluation would be sufficient for a diagnosis of borderline personality disorder. These traits, as well as her all-or-nothing thinking and intolerance of loneliness are also characteristics of depression. How would you differentiate these two conditions from each other? In the significant number of cases of comorbidity between borderline personality and depression, how would you determine how much each was contributing to the overall clinical picture?

4. Borderline personality organization could interact with a variety of disorders to produce a range of clinical syndromes. What might some of them look like?

5. One reason why poetry like that of Sylvia Plath is popular is that it strikes a responsive chord in everyone. Does this mean that her perceptions are normal? Does anyone who identifies with Plath's poetry have a personality disorder?

REFERENCES

American Psychiatric Association (1944). *Diagnostic and Statistical Manual of Mental Disorders,* (4th ed.). Washington, DC: American Psychiatric Press.

Grinker, R. R., Werble, B., Drye, R. (1968). *The borderline syndrome.* New York: Basic Books.

Gunderson, J. G., Zanarini, M. C. (1987). Current overview of the borderline diagnosis. *Journal of Clinical Psychiatry, 48* (Suppl.) 5–14.

Hoch, P. H., Polatin, P. (1949). Pseudoneurotic forms of schizophrenia. *Psychiatric Quarterly, 23,* 248–76.

Kernberg, O. F. (1975). *Borderline conditions and pathological narcissism.* New York: Jason Aronson.

Plath, S. (1971). *The Bell Jar.* New York: Bantam Books.

Predicting the Unpredictable: Childhood Emotional Disorders

The fact that a single chapter can summarize childhood mental disorders is one indication that not as much is known about these conditions as about adult disorders. One of the many unanswered questions about childhood mental disorders is whether they are precursors of adult conditions, prodromal (early) forms of adult disorders, early onset versions of adult conditions that should be more severe because it takes less to bring them on, or whether they have nothing to do with adult syndromes of the same name. Adults with depression often report having been depressed as children, and adults with a diagnosis of attention-deficit–hyperactivity disorder (ADHD) must have a childhood history of ADHD to qualify for the diagnosis (Wender et al., 1985). However, even if adults with a given diagnosis had a similar problem in childhood, it does not mean that the childhood version will necessarily turn into the adult form.

New York University psychiatrists Alexander Thomas and Stella Chess (1984) have shown that difficult childhood temperaments can be precursors of later psychological disturbances, but no one had followed childhood emotional disorders to see whether they get better, get worse, change their form, or go away. In the absence of good scientific data about what to expect, all there is to go on is clinical experience, which teaches that some childhood emotional disorders become more severe with time, while some become much less troublesome. Some recur more frequently, and some do not. Even worse, there are few if any credible studies of psychotherapy for childhood emotional disorders.

Diagnosis and treatment planning for childhood emotional disorders is made more complicated by the symptomatic overlap of conditions with very different treatments. One problem that always arises is whether depression in a child could be the first manifestation of a bipolar disorder. After an adult has had four episodes of depression without any evidence of mania or hypomania, the chance of becoming manic later in life is small but a child or adolescent experiencing a first depressive episode is well within the risk period for having a manic episode later. Since the treatment of bipolar depression is much different from the treatment of unipolar depression, it is important to distinguish between them before treatment is administered that could induce mania. Induced mania can make the long-term course of the mood disorder worse.

Another area of diagnostic confusion is between ADHD and childhood bipolar disorder. DSM-IV (American Psychiatric Association, 1994) requires that at least six symptoms of inattention *or* hyperactivity-impulsivity be present for six months or more to diagnose ADHD. Symptoms of inattention include:

1. Failing to pay attention to details or making careless mistakes
2. Difficulty sustaining attention in tasks or play
3. Seeming not to listen when spoken to directly
4. Failure to complete schoolwork, chores, or other assignments (not due to oppositionalism or failure to understand)
5. Difficulty organizing tasks and activities
6. Avoidance or dislike of tasks that require sustained mental effort
7. Inability to keep track of things that are necessary for tasks or activities
8. Distractibility
9. Forgetfulness

Symptoms of hyperactivity-impulsivity include:

1. Fidgeting or squirming
2. Inability to sit still
3. Running around or excessive climbing
4. Inability to play quietly
5. Hyperactivity
6. Excessive talking
7. Blurting out answers before questions have been completed
8. Inability to wait one's turn
9. Interrupting or intruding on others

Many bipolar children would meet criteria for ADHD by virtue of symptoms that are also diagnostic for mania such as hyperactivity, rapid speech, and impulsive behavior, as well as symptoms that frequently accompany bipolar disorder such as intrusiveness, inability to sit still, and inability to pay attention. When a child also exhibits clearcut bipolar symptoms such as elation, decreased need for sleep, hypersexuality, buying sprees, grandiosity, or psychotic symptoms, DSM-IV would not permit a diagnosis of ADHD if the ADHD symptoms were only present at the same time as the manic ones. However, manic children are much more likely to be irritable and display behavioral problems than to appear typically manic (Carson and Weintraub, 1993), and clinicians are much more accustomed to diagnosing ADHD in children anyway.

Examples of these kinds of diagnostic issues are illustrated by the next two cases of two kinds of childhood depression with different outcomes. These cases also underline the point made in the textbook that genetic factors, problems parenting by people who are psychologically ill, and assortative mating (marriage of people with similar traits) make childhood emotional disorders a family affair.

JACKIE: CHILDHOOD DEPRESSION

Jackie came from a family of overachievers. To nobody's surprise she was an excellent student, but at age fourteen she lost interest in school. She no longer liked being around her friends and spent most of her time in her room sleeping or listening to heavy metal music. Her parents had shown great interest in her intellectual development and had done as much as they could do to foster her performance at school. She, in turn, had always readily discussed her schoolwork with her parents. But now she had nothing more than a surly grunt when asked about her classes.

As she had reached adolescence, Jackie had begun to experience the normal teenage drive for autonomy. Unfortunately, while she had been taught everything she needed to know about trigonometry, no one had taught her how to negotiate conflict. Her parents, a surgeon and a physicist, were excellent role models or professional success, but they were too busy to pay much attention to feelings of annoyance, unhappiness, or disagreement. So long as she had the same basic orientation as the family, everyone felt good. But once she started feeling disagreeable, they did not know how to respond. Jackie felt helpless to forge a new identity for herself—a feeling that generalized to a negative view of anything she tried. The reason that she spent so much time in bed was that once she felt distracted, she no longer got perfect scores on her examinations. Feeling that if she did not perform perfectly, she was a failure, she began to avoid school; this of course made it even more difficult to perform perfectly.

This episode of depression was treated aggressively with confrontation of negative cognitions and all-or-nothing thinking. It was slow going, since Jackie was skeptical about getting help with anything and had a hard time participating in the treatment. Her parents were involved in the therapy, but they felt ill at ease talking about feelings. Eventually, they realized that, never having gone through rebellious stages themselves, they did not know how to help Jackie with her wish to be independent. Indeed, intellect was so important to them that they had not bothered learning how to recognize let alone deal with emotions. However, with a good deal of encouragement and modeling by the therapist, they were able to start talking to Jackie about topics other than school; this made her feel that they valued her as a person and not just as an extension of their own academic interests.

Jackie's mood gradually improved, and she resumed her previous activities. Her school performance improved again, although she still tended to miss classes whenever she felt that her performance was not perfect. She went back to spending time with her friends, but although she felt more valued as a person, her transition to independence consisted mainly of moving from spending all her time at home to being gone most of the time.

Jackie continued to do well for about four years, but when she got into college the new step toward independence proved to be too much for her and her family. Pointing out that they had left home when they were eighteen, her parents encouraged her to go away to attend school. Unfortunately, even though they were trying to follow by rote the advice they had received in psychotherapy to help Jackie become more independent, they were out of phase with her attempts to find a middle ground between remaining enmeshed with them and being completely on her own. She interpreted their stance as representing a desire to get rid of her. Even though she did not experience them as fully supportive, they were still important, and the threat of being pushed out precipitated another episode of depression. Once again, her energy was low, she slept all the time, she became irritable and sensitive to rejection, and everything seemed negative.

Cognitive therapy was reinstituted right away, and Jackie was much quicker to generate alternative hypotheses to such global assumptions as "If I'm not completely independent, I'll never be able to survive on my own" and "If I don't understand everything in a course immediately, I might as well give up." It only took a few family sessions to help Jackie's parents to see that they were pursuing a similar all-or-nothing approach in feeling that if Jackie did not move out right away, she would never become independent. Everyone was then able to develop a realistic plan for more but not complete independence. Whether because of a change in the nature of the disorder, the previous treatment, or more maturity in Jackie and her parents, the depression, even though recurrent, had become easier to treat.

TOMMY: CHILDHOOD BIPOLAR DISORDER

Tommy's mother felt that he was on the go from the day he was born. Much of the time, he seemed to need much less sleep than a normal toddler, but by the time he started school, he was unable to get out of bed in the morning and complained of feeling tired all the time. He was extremely clever and could be very endearing, but whenever he was frustrated, he threw tantrums that would last for hours during which he spoke rapidly, used profanity, and broke things. Even when nothing was different in his life, he went from being moody and irritable to being excessively happy-go-lucky and claiming that he could do anything.

Tommy's grades were good, but he was in constant trouble in school. Easily bored, he became the class clown to keep himself amused. He could grasp almost any concept rapidly, but he was readily distracted. On its own, his mind jumped from one thing to another so quickly that he had trouble paying attention to anything for any length of time, but he also had the capacity to become completely absorbed by a video game or book.

As Tommy got older, he began picking fights with anyone he thought had insulted him. He felt bad later, but during a fight he became so angry that it did not matter who he hurt or how much he hurt them. In addition, when he got angry, he was as likely to hurt himself as anyone else. His parents enrolled him in a special education course, but he was expelled. Finally realizing that he would not grow out of his problem, they took him for a psychological evaluation.

Based on the presence of hyperactivity, poor attention span, aggressive behavior, and impulsivity, a diagnosis of ADHD was made and Tommy was treated with the behavioral techniques discussed in Chapter 16. His fighting decreased at first, but it picked up again soon thereafter. His pediatrician gave him stimulants, which seemed to calm him down, but a year later he was moodier than ever. Because he frequently seemed depressed, he was given psychotherapy, but he seemed to become angrier when the therapist began focusing on self-esteem and feelings of control. Extensive discussions with the family mainly resulted in its being made clear that they were feeling increasingly helpless not only because no one had been able to help their son, but also because every clinician they consulted seemed to misunderstand how ill he really was. The pediatrician changed to an antidepressant, in response to which Tommy virtually stopped sleeping.

By age sixteen, Tommy was experiencing bouts of serious depression, but they only lasted a week or so at a time and they alternated with increasingly frequent periods of hyperactive irritability. Very rarely, he would say that he felt "on top of the world," but even when he was irritable he was grandiose, repeatedly overestimating his prowess; this lead him to take dangerous chances. More and more, his depressive states became mixed with manic symptoms such as racing thoughts, irritability, and not needing to sleep, while his irritable states were increasingly contaminated with suicidal and other depressive thoughts.

Tommy was experiencing a problem that is disturbingly common in bipolar adolescents. Treatment with stimulants and antidepressants had brought out more manic symptoms, which were making his behavior worse. Open-ended psychotherapy had stimulated more emotions in a patient whose every mood was already magnified beyond his capacity to control. Without effective treatment, the bipolar mood disorder was following its tendency to accelerate and become more complex. Later in its course, it was therefore much harder to treat.

Getting Tommy's mood and behavior under control involved a more intensive approach than had been necessary for Jackie. First, firm limits were set on impulsive and aggressive behavior. Instead of trying to explain why Tommy should not speak out of turn, take dangerous chances, or talk back, it was simply stated that he would not be permitted to do so. Since confrontations stimulated his emotions, interactions were broken off as soon as he started to become too excited and he was encouraged to go off by himself. The therapist was then able to point out that underneath his bravado was a view of himself as someone who was out of control of his emotions. He was better able to discuss this perception when lithium helped to keep the shame and helplessness he felt about it from escalating out of control.

DISCUSSION QUESTIONS

1. Why was Jackie's depression not a normal reaction to the challenges of adolescence?

2. Could all Tommy's problems be explained by ADHD? By bipolar disorder? Could he have had both disorders?

3. What similarities do you see between the unipolar and bipolar depression in these two patients and the same disorders in adults? What differences?

4. What psychological, social, and biological mechanisms might be involved in making Tommy worse as he got older? Why did Jackie get easier to treat?

5. What developmental processes might be involved in making depression look different in a child than in an adult?

6. How capable is a child of understanding diagnostic impressions and treatment recommendations? At what age does informed consent become possible?

7. If you were Tommy's psychologist, how would you react if he saw you once and then refused to come back? What would you tell his parents if they did not think that he needed treatment despite severe behavioral problems, truancy, and depression?

8. Tommy's mood disorder was aggravated by a stimulant and an antidepressant and helped by lithium. What level of formal study of such medications should be necessary before they are given to children and adolescents? What are the potential dangers? How might they help?

REFERENCES

American Psychiatric Association (1994). *Diagnostic and Statistical Manual of Mental Disorders* (4th ed.). Washington, DC: American Psychiatric Press.

Carson, G. A., Weintraub, S. (1993). Childhood behavior problems and bipolar disorder—relationship or coincidence? *Journal of Affective Disorders, 28,* 143–53.

Thomas, A., & Chess, S. (1984). Genesis and evolution of behavioral disorders: From infancy to early adult life. *American Journal of Psychiatry, 141,* 1–9.

Wender, P. H., Reimherr, F. W., Wood, D., & Ward, M. (1985). A controlled study of methylphenidate in the treatment of attention deficit disorder, residual type, in adults. *American Journal of Psychiatry, 142,* 547–52.

CASE 27 [CHAPTER 16]

The Hollow Idol:
Anorexia Nervosa

You learned in Chapter 16 that anorexia nervosa is a potentially life-threatening disorder characterized by refusal to maintain body weight at a "minimally normal weight for age and height" (which DSM-IV defines as a body weight of 85 percent of expected weight), intense fear of gaining weight or getting fat even though the patient is underweight, inaccurate perception of body weight or shape or denial of the seriousness of low body weight, and cessation of menstrual cycles in females (American Psychiatric Association, 1994). DSM-IV subdivides anorexia nervosa into the restricting type, which is not associated with bingeing or purging, and the binge-eating–purging type, in which weight restriction is accompanied by binge eating and/or attempts at weight loss through self-induced vomiting or use of laxatives, diuretics, or enemas.

Anorexia nervosa may seem to be a modern illness the incidence of which is increasing as a result of Western society's preoccupation with thinness. But as far back as the seventeenth century physician Richard Morton described what seems to have been anorexia nervosa in a chapter on "nervous consumption" in his textbook on tuberculosis. Morton thought that there was a group of apparently consumptive (tubercular) patients who, even though they wasted away, did not have tuberculosis. Instead, they had an abnormal nervous system that was thrown out of alignment by violent emotions or unwholesome air. One such patient was a young woman Morton called Mr. Duke's daughter.

THE CASE

Mr. Duke's daughter in St. Mary Axe, in the year 1684 and the eighteenth Year of her Age, in the month of July fell into a total suppression of her monthly courses from a multitude of Cares and Passions of her Mind, but without any Symptom of the Green-Sickness following it. From which time her appetite began to abate, and her Digestion to be bad; her flesh also began to be flaccid and loose, and her looks pale, with other symptoms usual in an Universal Consumption of the Habit of the Body, and by the extream and memorable cold Weather which happened the Winter following, this consumption did seem to be not a little improved; for that she was wont by her studying at Night, and continual poring over books, to expose herself both Day and Night to the injuries of the Air, which was at that time extreamly cold, not without some manifest Prejudice to the System of her Nerves. The Spring followed by the Prescription of some Emperick, she took a Vomit, and after that I know not what Steel Medicines, but without any Advantage. So from the time loathing all sorts of Medicaments, she wholly neglected the care of her self for two full Years, till at last being brought to the last degree of a Marasmus, or Consumption, and thereupon subject to Frequent Fainting Fits, she apply'd her self to me for Advice.

I do not remember that I did ever in all my Practice see one, that was conversant with the living so much wasted with the greatest degree of a Consumption (like a Skeleton only clad with skin) yet there was no Fever, but on the contrary a coldness of the whole Body; no cough or difficulty of Breathing nor an appearance of any distemper of the Lungs, or of any other Entrail . . . Only her Appetite was diminished, and her Digestion uneasie, with Fainting Fits, which did frequently return upon her. Which Symptoms I did endeavor to relieve by the outward application of Aromatick Bags made to the Region of the Stomach . . . [and] by the internal use of Bitter Medicines, Chalybeates, and Juleps made of Cephalik and Antihysterick Waters, sufficiently impregnated with Spirit of Salt Aromoniack, and Tincture of Castor. . . . Upon the Use of which she seemed to be much better, but being quickly tired with Medicines, she beg'd that the whole Affair might be committed again to nature, whereupon . . . she was after three months taken with a Fainting Fit and died (Morton, 1694).

In other words, Mr. Duke's daughter was 18 years old when she stopped eating and having periods. On the surface, she seemed to have tuberculosis, but she did not have most of the typical symptoms. She seemed to kike going out in the cold (to exercise?), stayed up all night reading, and lost tremendous amounts of weight. She is said to have lost her appetite, but perhaps Morton did not specifically ask about refusal to eat as the real cause of weight loss. At the very least, she did not seem upset enought about looking "like a Skeleton only clad with skin" to have seen this as a reason to consult a physician (her chief complaint was fainting spells) or to remain in treatment. Indeed, discontinuing treatment even though she was getting worse could well be another indication of denial.

Elsewhere in his book, Morton wrote that this "disease" flatters and deceives patients; in other words, they like it. For this reason, he went on to say, physicians are rarely called until things have gone too far for them to help. Morton's observations proved timeless, since the combination of denial and a drive toward excessive activity while continuing to lose body mass that made this a fatal illness for Mr. Duke's daughter can still be fatal today.

It might be coincidental, but it is still interesting to speculate that this young woman fits the demographic and psychological profile of the modern anorexic. She was a female. She was from the upper class (which we know because she could read). The onset of her anorexia was during adolescence (remember that puberty occurred later in one's life in the seventeenth century). Morton speculated that "this Disease does almost always proceed from Sadness and anxious Cares," thereby implicating psychological risk factors.

At the same time, Mr. Duke's daughter and her problem are very much a part of her era—the seventeenth century. Note the frequent references to the air and how it can hurt someone's health. The germ theory of illness had not yet been proposed, and so other explanations of disease were in vogue. The air was particularly suspect. In fact, have you noticed how some older colleges are built on top of hills? The goal in many cases was not to be picturesque but rather to keep the students and faculty safe from bad air! Morton probably viewed her disorder in terms of disturbed humors (remember Case 2). He probably prescribed medicine not to kill germs but to put her humors back in balance. Ironically, "treatments"— vomiting and laxatives—are misused by many anorectics as part of their illness.

HOLY ANOREXIA

Fasting and weight loss have long been entwined with some religious practices. Medieval Christians battled not only the pleasures of sexuality but also those that came from eating. In a fascinating book, Rudolph Bell (1985) surveyed the lives of 261 Italian women who lived between the twelfth and twentieth centuries. All were honored by the Catholic Church for their exemplary lives. Some were made saints. In every case, they had demonstrated their venerability by starving themselves to death. Bell termed this phenomenon "holy anorexia."

He presented the lives of some of these women in great detail. Obviously, they did not consume very much food. But when they did eat, they used this as a further opportunity to triumph over the desires of the body. They chose extremely unappetizing food: seeds, bitter herbs, uncooked vegetables, even vomit and pus!

On the face of it, holy anorexia differs from its counterpart in DSM-IV in that thinness per se is not the individual's goal but rather holiness. Both, however, utilize self-starvation to achieve a kind of transcendence over physical reality. In the twentieth century, being thin has achieved the status of an ideal, just as holiness was an ideal in centuries past. Perhaps all anorexics, holy and secular, are pursing an ideal state. We need to learn more about the psychology of subordination of the body to the pathology of the mind.

DISCUSSION QUESTIONS

1. If you were in Morton's shoes, how would you have responded to Mr. Duke's daughter's lack of interest in receiving more of a therapy that seemed to be helping?

2. Morton seems to have treated his patient at one point with emetics, a common treatment of the day. What effect could this treatment have had on a patient with anorexia?

3. Proponents of behavior therapy and psychodynamic psychotherapy have been at odds over the years about treatment approaches for anorexia nervosa. Behavior therapists recommend setting goals of small but definite increases in weight that the patient must achieve in order to obtain rewards such as being allowed to exercise. The psychotherapists contend that this approach intensifies the power struggles that are expressed in the first place as refusal to eat. If the patient cannot maintain a sense of control over her life and over others through control of her weight, the only way left to assert herself may be through suicide. Which of these approaches is correct? Is there a middle ground?

4. If you decided not to try to use behavior techniques to make the patient gain weight, what would you do if her weight declined to a life-threatening level?

5. Many anorexic patients exercise compulsively as a means of not gaining weight, producing predictable bodily sensations, and achieving a sense of mastery over their bodies. Some compulsive exercisers share many traits with these patients, including preoccupation with maintaining a low body weight, dietary obsessions, and absence of menstruation in women. Are some forms of compulsive exercise types of anorexia nervosa?

6. In the case of Mr. Duke's daughter a psychological illness masqueraded as a physical one. Can any physical illnesses masquerade as anorexia nervosa?

REFERENCES

American Psychiatric Association (1994). *Diagnostic and Statistical Manual of Mental Disorders* (4th ed.). Washington, DC: American Psychiatric Press.

Bell, R. M. (1985). *Holy anorexia.* Chicago: University of Chicago Press.

Morton, R. (1694). *Phthisiologica—or a treatise of consumptions.* London.

Nate G.: Down's Syndrome

Mental retardation has two principle causes: neurological deficits that are inherited or acquired early in life, and severe social and intellectual deprivation. One example of a congenital (present at birth) cause of retardation is Down's syndrome, which is caused by an extra copy of chromosome 21. Down's syndrome has become a subject of great interest for several reasons. First, a genetic form of Alzheimer's disease has also been linked to chromosome 21, and many people with Down's syndrome develop Alzheimer's if they live long enough. Second, changing attitudes toward mental retardation have led to rehabilitative programs that help many Down's individuals to lead productive and happy lives. On a disturbing note, with increasing pressure in society not to pay for any medical care that cannot guarantee a good outcome, questions may arise about how many resources to commit to the treatment of the cardiac defects Down's patients often develop when they are likely to develop dementia on top of the retardation at some point in their lives. The ability to make a prenatal diagnosis of Down's syndrome with great accuracy raises another important ethical issue.

Down's syndrome was first described in 1866 by the English physician Langdon Down. The condition was originally called "mongolism" because Down thought the children resembled Asians due to their slanting eyes. In retrospect, this is regarded as a misguided and possibly racist analogy. Asian children with Down's syndrome are as easy to recognize as their counterparts among Caucasian children. The physical characteristics associated with Down's syndrome are described in your text.

Children with Down's syndrome have lower IQs than other children and show less ability to fend for themselves when they become adults. But the things these children can do are not as limited as was once thought. At one time, their parents were routinely advised to institutionalize them, and many did. Research then began to show, however, that institutionalized children fared much worse than those kept at home (Edgerton, 1979). Presumably, a stimulating home environment boosts the intellectual and interpersonal attainments of children with Down's syndrome, just as it can for other children.

Another boost for Down's patients came from the 1975 federal law mandating public education for handicapped people. Children with

Down's syndrome began to receive instruction heretofore withheld from them, with new plateaus' being reached all the time. As Down's children began to receive more rigorous evaluation I the educational system, it was discovered that some of their problems were not a direct result of the retardation. For example, individuals with Down's syndrome may show language deficits that were thought to be obvious manifestations of the intellectual deficit. However, it has been found that in some cases there are peculiarities of the muscles of articulation (e.g., the tongue) that produce this problem. Once the cause was found to be mechanical, educators were able to provide speech therapy that helped Down's students to acquire needed language skills.

As with any concept, such discussions are more meaningful in the context of a real person with the problem. In this case, the person is Nate G., a teenager with Down's syndrome who was featured in a newspaper story several years ago (Ogintz, 1988).

THE CASE

Nate G. is a fifteen-year-old male with Down's syndrome, an eighth-grade student at a suburban school in the Chicago area. In many ways, his activities are the same as those of his classmates. He uses a computer to do his schoolwork, and he uses its graphics capacity to create his own comic strips. He likes girls, basketball, and acting.

Nate's condition was obvious at birth, but his parents never considered treating him as anything but normal. He was the first child with Down's syndrome to attend his elementary school, but he has since been joined by four other Down's children. He learned to read and write, and he takes some regular classes as well as some special education classes. His parents report that he has a good image of himself. He is aware that he is different from other children. He doesn't like having Down's syndrome and accepts that some things will be hard for him to master. He simply persists at them.

For the most part, Nate's classmates accept him. He has been teased occasionally, and one must realistically expect that at least some of the gaps between Nate and his peers will widen in the years to come. It is difficult enough to be an adolescent, much less one with Down's syndrome. Whether Nate will someday find work and how he will then live are matters that understandably concern his parents.

THE FUTURE FOR THOSE WITH DOWN'S SYNDROME

An expert quoted in the story about Nate G. predicted that "the majority will be able to go to school and read and write and do a job" (Ogintz, 1988, p. 1). Life expectancy has greatly increased as well. Not too long ago, most of those with Down's syndrome died in their early twenties, which explains why previous discussions of this disorder almost always focused on Down's children: There were no adults to talk about.

But now most of these individuals are expected to live into their fifties. In large part, the increased life expectancy reflects earlier and more aggressive medical intervention for common intercurrent illnesses such as heart disease and infections. We can read between the lines, perhaps, and deduce that earlier generations saw no good reason to try to increase the life expectancy of those with the syndrome. Moreover, today, people with Down's syndrome are no longer locked away in institutions; this means that the rest of us are more familiar with them. A young actor with Down's syndrome who played a leading role in the television series *Life Goes On* did a great deal to humanize the syndrome. With familiarity comes greater acceptance on our part. Perhaps this contributes as well to their greater mental and physical well-being.

DISCUSSION QUESTIONS

1. Further insight into Down's syndrome can be found in two published diaries kept by young men with this condition (Seagoe, 1964; Hunt, 1967). If you can, read one of these diaries and discuss the implications for how we ought to think about Down's syndrome and those with it.

2. DSM-IV defines mental retardation by the presence of an IQ on an individually administered IQ test of below about 70 and impairment in at least two of the areas of communication, self-care, ability to live at home, social-interpersonal skills,, use of community services, self-motivation, meaningful academic abilities, work, leisure, health, and safety. Are both the intelligence and adaptation criteria necessary? Why?

3. Should DSM-IV distinguish among different kinds of mental retardation?

4. How would you distinguish between mental retardation and autism?

5. A common cause of mental retardation during the early part of this century was goiter (hypothyroidism), an entirely treatable condition usually caused at that time by lack of dietary iodine. Are there any reversible psychological causes of mental retardation?

6. What can be done to make the world in general more hospitable for people like Nate, whose physical and intellectual characteristics set them apart from most others?

7. Discuss the ethical issues raised by the availability of prenatal testing for Down's syndrome.

8. Men with Down's syndrome are apparently all infertile, but some women with Down's syndrome can bear children. About half of

these children have the syndrome. What are the moral issues raised by Down's women's having children?

REFERENCES

Edgerton, R. B. (1979). *Mental retardation.* Cambridge, MA: Harvard University Press.

Hunt, N. (1967). *The world of Nigel Hunt: The diary of a mongoloid youth.* New York: Garrett.

Ogintz, E. (1988). In the mainstream. *Chicago Tribune*, May 3, Section 5, pp. 1–2.

Seagoe, M. V. (1964). *Yesterday was Tuesday, all night and all day.* Boston: Little, Brown.

Mind and Brain:
Alzheimer's Disease

Chapter 17 presents the classical distinction between "organic" and "functional" disorders. Alzheimer's disease, a neuropathological condition characterized by changes in structure (e.g., senile plaques, neurofibrillary tangles) and function (e.g., decreased activity of acetylcholine, a neurotransmitter of memory) of the brain, would appear to be a good example of a purely organic condition. Some cases of Alzheimer's disease are sporadic, and others are familial. The familial form acts as an autosomal (non-sex-liked) dominant trait (that is, you only need one copy of the abnormal gene to get the disease that at least some of the time is located on chromosome 21, the same chromosome that is reduplicated in Down's syndrome (Mohs and Green, 1994). The Alzheimer's gene may in some instances demonstrate age-dependent penetrance, in other words, the likelihood that someone carrying the gene will become ill increases with age. This could explain why Alzheimer's disease becomes more frequent in older individuals. By some accounts, the incidence of Alzheimer's disease would be even higher if people with the gene did not die of other causes before the Alzheimer's had a chance to manifest itself.

Even in the face of these findings, the organic-functional differentiation is not absolute. The initial symptoms of Alzheimer's disease are mental, depression, irritability, insomnia, and socially inappropriate behavior, for example. As the textbook points out, Alzheimer's disease affects functions that are at the very core of the personality. Another complication is that depression, which in itself can cause cognitive deficits (pseudodementia) indistinguishable from those of a primary dementia, can aggravate the deficits of Alzheimer's disease. Since Alzheimer's and other dementias can impair the capacity to express emotion normally and many older people have vegetative symptoms like changes in sleep, it may not be at all obvious that depression is complicating Alzheimer's, making the patient's functioning worse than would otherwise be the case (Dubovsky, 1986). The complicated interaction between depression and dementia is illustrated by the case of Robert Jones.

THE CASE

Bob Jones, a sixty-two-year-old married man, just retired as chief executive officer of a small company. He was always an effective administrator and a dedicated family man, but he became uncharacteristically short tempered about two years ago. Everyone attributed his inappropriate comments to stress, and when he did not run errands he had promised to take care of, his wife assumed that he just did not want to do them.

Mr. Jones became increasingly forgetful and finally went to see his family physician, who reassured him that he was just getting a little older. When he became so irritable that nothing seemed right, his wife took him back to the physician, who found no focal evidence of brain damage—no paralysis or sensory loss, no aphasia or apraxia. An MRI scan of the head was normal. The physician did, however, think that the insomnia, difficulty concentrating, and loss of interest Mr. Jones was experiencing were evidence of depression. She prescribed an antidepressant and referred Mr. Jones to a psychologist for psychotherapy.

The psychologist agreed that Mr. Jones did seem to feel demoralized and helpless and began psychotherapy. He also performed a careful mental status examination, which revealed deficits of attention, short-term memory, and ability to learn new information. He thought that Mr. Jones could be depressed because he was having trouble thinking, the cognitive symptoms could be symptoms of depression, or most likely, he had both problems, each one aggravating the other.

The combination of psychotherapy and the antidepressant helped. His mood and sleep improved, and so did his attention and intellectual performance. The mental status findings reverted almost to normal, at least sufficiently for him to go back to work. He did well for a year, but he then became more obviously forgetful. He had continued to take the antidepressant, but he thought that more psychotherapy for depression might make the returning symptoms go away again.

Realizing that the patient was worried but no longer depressed, the psychologist saw the problem as one of denial: no one becomes permanently demented from depression, and the patient and his family wanted their problem to be reversible. The therapeutic task therefore was to help the to acknowledge that the memory problem was more marked than the other symptoms. What had probably happened was that depression had lowered the threshold for expression of an underlying dementia, possibly through a facilitatory action on memory centers linked to the limbic system. When the depression was successfully treated, the dementia was not obvious anymore. As it continued to progress, however, it manifested itself even without the depression. Sure enough, an MRI scan at this point showed enlarged ventricles, and Mr. Jones had developed mild apraxia. A diagnosis of Alzheimer's could now be made.

Over the next year, Mr. Jones' memory continued to deteriorate and he could not work at all. The psychologist taught him how to compensate for his memory problems, for example, by writing everything down. He also learned to get enough rest, eat well, and avoid any unnecessary medication. Giving up his regular nightcap seemed to help, too.

Nevertheless, his memory continued to deteriorate gradually but progressively. To try to slow the progression of the Alzheimer's disease, Mr. Jones was offered tacrine (THA, Cognex), a medication approved by the Food and Drug Administration in 1993. Tacrine inhibits acetylcholinesterase, an enzyme that breaks down acetylcholine. Increasing the availability of this neurotransmitter should improve memory, and tacrine had been shown to produce improvement in patients with Alzheimer's disease (Farlow et al., 1992). However, the benefit is modest at best, and the disease continues to progress, as would be expected with the eventual loss of so many neurons using acetylcholine that decreasing breakdown of the neurotransmitter would not do much to its overall activity. Another problem with tacrine is that nausea, vomiting, and reversible liver damage are such common side effects that only about one-third of Alzheimer's patients who take this medication both tolerate it and benefit from it (Dubovsky, 1994). One recent study showed that higher doses of tacrine produce more reliable improvement, but they also produced more side effects (Knapp et al., 1994).

Tacrine was not of great help to Mr. Jones, who tried a number of other medications without much success. Two years later, he had so much confusion between left and right that he could not get his clothes on without assistance. Problems orienting parts of his body in space made it increasingly difficult for him to eat without assistance. On several occasions, he made himself a cup of coffee while his wife was out and forgot to turn the stove off. If he went out of the house, he promptly became lost. As time went on, he started getting lost in the house.

Feeling that this further deterioration must be a sign of further depression, his wife brought him back to the psychologist, complaining that his depression was interfering with his daily functioning. It did not take much insight to realize that she was the one who was depressed, since by this time he was too confused and forgetful to sustain any mood for long and, if anything, seemed mercifully indifferent to his fate. Mrs. Jones, on the other hand, had come to feel increasingly desperate. She thought that she should continue to care for her husband at home, but was becoming too frustrated to do so. Worse yet her children, who did not have to live with him every day, did not think that Mr. Jones was that impaired. With no acknowledgment of her plight, Mrs. Jones felt increasingly isolated and helpless.

Having the psychologist, who was able to evaluate Mr. Jones regularly, acknowledge that her husband had become too disabled to care for made Mrs. Jones feel less helpless, but more guilty. How could she complain, after all he meant to her? Even worse, she had felt for the last year that it was not her husband she was caring for, but a stranger. He looked the same, but he was not the same person. As the years had gone by and he had lost virtually all the traits that made him a unique individual, she had gradually grieved for the loss of the person to whom she was once married. Since grief is the psychological process of removing an attachment to someone who has been lost, for Mrs. Jones it was as if her husband were dead emotionally, even though he was alive physically. She had not wanted to admit that she could not take care of him anymore because she felt too guilty at the thought that she did not want to take care of him anymore. Recognizing this source of guilt made it possible to begin making more realistic plans for arranging caretaking, first in the home and later in assisted living. The children's denial of the seriousness of the problem also had to be confronted for them to be able to be more supportive of their mother.

DISCUSSION QUESTIONS

1. Was it abnormal for Mr. Jones to deny that his problem was Alzheimer's disease and not depression or for his children to deny that his disease was severe? Can denial be healthy? When should it be confronted?

2. Do you think that Mr. Jones should have gone to a nursing home? would you do if the Jones family insisted on nursing-home placement when the patient's illness clearly did not justify such a step?

3. In preliminary studies, a number of alternatives to tacrine have appeared to slow further deterioration of severe dementia. What are the ethical considerations in developing such medications for patients who are already severely disabled?

4. Why did treatment for depression stop working for the memory problem?

5. If a disease like Alzheimer's is "organic," does this mean that psychological treatments are not useful? What is the role of the psychologist in the treatment of "organic" dementia?

6. How might realistic hope be maintained for someone with an incurable disease without encouraging pathological denial?

REFERENCES

Dubovsky, S. L. (1986). Using electroconvulsive therapy for patients with neurological disease. *Hospital and Community Psychiatry, 37,* 819–25.

Dubovsky, S. L. (1994). Geriatric neuropsychopharmacology. In Coffey, C. E., & Cummings, J., *Textbook of geriatric neuropsychiatry.* Washington, DC: American Psychiatric Press.

Mohs, R. C. & Green, C. R. (1994). Alzheimer's disease and related dementias. *Current Opinion in Psychiatry, 7,* 95–98.

Farlow, M., Gracon, S. I., Hershey, L. A., Lewis, K. W., Sadowsky, C. H., & Dolan-Ureno, J. (1982). A controlled trial of tacrine in Alzheimer's disease. *Journal of the American Medical Association, 268,* 2523–9.

Knapp, M. J., Knopman, D. S., & Solomon, P. R. (1994). A 30-week randomized controlled trial of high-dose tacrine in patients with Alzheimer's disease. *Journal of the American Medical Association, 271,* 985–91.

Witty Ray: Tourette's Syndrome

The overlap of neurology and psychology is particularly obvious in Tourette's disorder. In DSM-IV, Tourette's disorder is diagnosed in patients with multiple motor tics and at least one vocal tic (sudden involuntary, nonrhythmic, recurrent, stereotyped movements or vocalizations). To qualify for the diagnosis, tics must have begun before age 18, and they must occur many times per day over the course of a year, with no more than a three-month period free of tics. People with tics often achieve a sense of control by turning involuntary movements into voluntary ones, making the entire action seem purposeful.

Interestingly, a DSM-IV criterion for Tourette's disorder is that "the disturbance causes marked distress or significant impairment in social, occupational, or other important areas of functioning." Neurologists, in contrast, base their diagnoses of the same disorder on signs and symptoms, not on the patient's reactions to them. Perhaps this is a sign of the dimension of humanism of the mental health professions. Perhaps it is a throwback to the days in which each patient had her or his own diagnosis.

Tics may be symptoms of a number of other illnesses that cause neurological and mental symptoms. One example is Huntington's disease, the incurable inherited illness that killed Woody Guthrie. Wilson's disease, a degenerative disease of the eye, liver, and brain, may also produce abnormal movements, including tics, in addition to a variety of psychological symptoms. Wilson's disease is important because it frequently produces mental symptoms severe enough to warrant psychiatric hospitalization long before the neurological component becomes obvious. The disease is fully treatable at this stage, but if it is allowed to progress, it leads to irreversible dementia. No one treating mental disorders can afford to be unaware of neurological diseases that affect the mind.

THE SYNDROME

Tourette's syndrome was first described in 1885 by the French neurologist Gilles de la Tourette, one of Charcot's students (see Chapter 2). Motor tics involve the head and upper body. A person so afflicted snaps and jerks about. Vocal tics are sounds like yelps, barks, sniffs, or coughs. Words may also occur, blurted out with great force, and in about one-third of the cases, these are obscenities. The tics may be grotesque to the observer, particularly when they include a stream of profanity.

The cause of Tourette's disorder seems to lie in a malfunction of the basal ganglia and possibly other parts of the brain. However, as with Alzheimer's disease, this does not mean that it does not have important mental dimensions. In addition to producing behavioral symptoms, Tourette's disorder can have a profound influence on personality development. The interaction between neurological dysfunction and personality is illustrated by the case of Witty Ray, who was described by neurologist Oliver Sacks (1985). Sacks is of course famous for his participation in the development of drug therapy for Parkinson's disease.

THE CASE

At twenty-four years of age, Ray was an intelligent young man with a profound problem. Since the age of four, he had experienced multiple tics every few seconds of his waking life. In view of the typical symptoms, the diagnosis of Tourette's syndrome was unambiguous.

In the face of a disorder that might have proven completely debilitating, Ray had achieved some remarkable accomplishments. He had finished high school and college. He had several close friends and a wife who greatly valued him, tics and all. But the Tourette's syndrome created incredible difficulties for him. Because of his unusual grimaces and uncontrollable profanity, people thought that he was an oddball and avoided him. He had lost a series of jobs, always because of the tics. His marriage had problems. When Ray would become sexually excited, his involuntary profanities would increase. Needless to say, cries of "Fuck!" and "Shit!" get in the way of making love.

Witty Ray was an impatient and pugnacious individual, but he had a sudden wit and clowning manner. These personality traits are not part of Tourette's syndrome, but in Ray's case at least, they seem related. Some of his impetuous actions may have been elaborated tics. Some of his negative behavior may have been a way of feeling more control over his environment by getting as much attention for purposeful negative behavior as for uncontrollable negative behavior. In many ways, Ray and the Tourette's had accommodated to each other. One example of this was Ray's weekend activity as a jazz drummer. He was quite accomplished and had a reputation for his wild improvisations, which would start as an uncontrollable tic but then be turned into an appropriate and exciting aspect of the music. Covering up involuntary movements with superimposed voluntary movements is a way of achieving a sense of control over them.

TREATMENT

Sacks treated Ray with haloperidol (Haldol), a neuroleptic medication. The neuroleptics (from the Greek "to clasp the neuron") are a class of medications that ameliorate psychosis and produce neurological effects. The basis of these effects is complex, but it depends in part on blockade of a type of dopamine receptor (the D_2 receptor) that is found in movement centers of the brain as well as in centers for emotion, information processing, reward, and vomiting. Blockade of the D_2 receptor in the basal ganglia produces a paucity of movement in normal people, whereas it decreases the excessive movements of Tourette's. Pimozide (Orap) is another neuroleptic frequently used to treat Tourette's disorder.

The haloperidol decreased Ray's symptoms significantly. However, the result was not entirely to Ray's liking. Although the tics were diminished, so were some of the behaviors that arose in response to them that Ray had prized, and so were some aspects of his experience that he considered central to his identity. As a trifling example, Ray found himself unable to navigate revolving doors. Before he had been able to dart in and out of them, and he enjoyed doing so. Now he had a black eye and a broken nose! As a serious example, Ray lost his ability to improvise as a drummer. Most generally, he lost the spark and playfulness that defined who he was. Ray expressed the fear that his personality was based on the tics. If these were taken away, nothing would be left but a shell.

In response to Ray's concerns, Sacks took Ray off the medication, and the two of them embarked on several months of talking therapy. They explored Ray's "true" personality and his dependency on the symptoms with which he had lived for 20 years. Only when Ray knew that he would be able to replace his Tourette's syndrome symptoms with something positive was he able to go back on haloperidol.

POSTSCRIPT

At the time that Sacks (1985) described Witty Ray, Ray had been on taking haloperidol for nine years. Ray held a steady job. His marriage had stabilized, and he was now a father. But in order not to miss the excitement that accompanied Tourette's syndrome, Ray did not take haloperidol on the weekends, when he became frenetic and frivolous. During the week, he resumed his medication, and led a calm and sober life.

DISCUSSION QUESTIONS

1. Sacks thought that it was strange for Ray to stop a medication that was helping. What do you think?

2. Under what other circumstances might a medication that is effective in relieving symptoms be discontinued?

3. If you were a psychologist consulting to Sacks, how would you help Ray to integrate his two contradictory experiences of himself, that is, with and without the tics? Do you think that he would need help grieving the loss of his old personality?

4. The point was made in Chapter 17 that neurologists are better at diagnosing disease than treating it. Do you think that they would have better luck if they addressed the person as well as the illness? In what ways might psychosocial treatments benefit patients with stroke, amnesia, and frontal-lobe syndromes? What aspects of these disorders would not be helped by the addition of psychological approaches?

5. At least half of all medically ill patients do not take medications as prescribed, and a significant number do not take them at all. (When was the last time you followed the directions in an antibiotic prescription to "take all these pills" after you no longer felt sick?) Why is noncompliance so common? What can be done about it? What about noncompliance with psychotherapy?

REFERENCE

Sacks, O. (1985). Witty Ticcy Ray. In *The man who mistook his wife for a hat and other clinical tales.* New York: Summit.

Give Me Liberty and
Give Me Death:
Involuntary Treatment

The tension between the right to be safe and the right to be free is addressed in Chapter 18: On one side of the argument is the desire not to abridge individual liberty any more than is absolutely necessary to provide basic protection for society. On the other side is the need to acknowledge that there are people who make decisions that are free but dangerous, either to themselves or someone else. The danger may be physical, or it may be emotional, psychological, or financial. At what point does the need to protect the individual's free will supersede the need to protect people from themselves and others? And how should free will be defined?

In the mental health field, these questions are not merely academic. Clinicians know that mental illness can reversibly but totally impair the capacity to make a truly informed choice, including the choice to be treated or not to be treated, or even to live or to die. Free choice may be disrupted by faulty premises (e.g., delusions), by illogical thought, or by inability to remember or catalog information. On the other hand, even being psychotic does not necessarily interfere with decision making. For example, a person might be paranoid but still might be aware that it is wrong to steal or that an illness is present that requires treatment. And it is possible to hear voices and know that one is schizophrenic.

The question of liberty versus safety moves from the mental health to the legal system when clinicians want to require that a patient be hospitalized and/or treated involuntarily. At these times, there is often a clash of standards of proof. The judge would like to know that a psychologist is at least 75 percent sure that a patient is a danger to self or others. The clinician knows that certain features, for example, hopelessness, severe depression, psychosis, high levels of anxiety, and a plan that can be carried out, predict a high risk of suicide in a depressed individual but has no scientific basis for predicting a numerical risk of suicide in a given depressed patient who has some of these features. Even if such figures were available, what good would they do? Would a patient with a 50 percent risk of suicide be hospitalized but not one with a 35 percent risk? What would a clinician say to the family of a patient who had "only" a 15 percent risk but committed suicide?

Clinical experience shows that just because a patient whose risk of suicide was judged to be high does not actually die, it does not mean that it was wrong to take steps to protect a patient who did not think that protection was necessary. The fact that a truck labeled "Danger! Explosives!" does not blow up does not mean that there was no danger. Pundits like Thomas Szasz (1961) who hold that suicide is always a matter of free will and should never be prevented cannot have worked with patients with severe forms of disorders that produce suicidal thinking, especially depression, schizophrenia, alcoholism, and personality disorder. Anyone who has treated these patients knows that suicidal plans that sound carefully considered and even "rational" simply go away when the acute disorder or the exacerbation of a chronic disorder is adequately treated. For its part, the court wants to be assured that the intention to override a patient's wish not to be treated or hospitalized is based on a sound clinical appraisal.

Even after the clinician has determined that it is justified to override a patient's wish not to be hospitalized and protect the patient until acute suicidality can be treated, it is up to the court to decide whether the clinical arguments outweigh the basic assumption of the patient's right to make choices, even if they are self-destructive. Because discussions in a court always consist of two sides arguing contrary positions, clinicians are sometimes in the position of trying to make their case by leaving out mitigating factors that make the situation sound more complicated, while attorneys assigned to protect the patient's rights try to "get the patient off," as if it were a jail term and not treatment that was being proposed.

Interactions between psychologists and the law have been complicated further by another recent twist. Attorneys have become interested not only in protecting mental patients from receiving unnecessary treatment, but also in protecting them from *not* receiving necessary treatment. There has been a dramatic increase in lawsuits on behalf of patients who have been injured or killed as a result of suicide attempts that were not prevented by involuntary treatment—a common problem since 15 percent of suicides occur in patients who have been offered hospitalization but refused it.

Whether they argue in favor of treatment or against it, lawyers, and many other people, would like to think that the assessment of dangerousness is not only an established science, but a static decision: a person either is suicidal or is not. A patient is either competent to make a rational decision about whether to accept treatment or is not. In real life, however, dangerousness and competence shift with a patient's mental state; this greatly complicates decision making. This problem is illustrated by the case of Nat Hale.

THE CASE

Nat performed brilliantly in high school. He was something of a loner, and he seemed a little eccentric, but isn't this true of many creative people? His father was the only one who ever understood him, but his father committed suicide when Nat was in high school.

In college, Nat majored in philosophy. He did well, although his professors thought that what to him seemed to be brilliant insights seemed to them to be weird ideas. After graduation from college, Nat entered graduate school in another state, and it was here that his problems became more obvious. Deprived of the structure of his family and places that were familiar to him, he became increasingly anxious. He was very uncomfortable around people, and he rarely spoke to anyone outside class. Even in the classroom, he was at times too preoccupied to respond to direct questions.

Nat finally broke through his shell when he joined a local church. However, his ideas were at odds with everyone else's. For example, the doctrine of the church emphasized forgiveness of sin, but Nat was preoccupied with the idea that guilt was an essential truth that would prevent redemption for all mankind. The church elders knew of other groups whose beliefs were perhaps a little closer to Nat's, but he saw it as his mission to reform the church he was already in as a first step toward notifying the entire earth of its impending doom. Finding that his mind was now so clear that he could understand every word of the Bible instantly, he stopped going to class in order to devote himself to his mission. He often stayed up all night writing tracts on the end of the world, and he went on a prolonged fast to purify himself.

When Nat told the church elders that he was in contact with Abraham and the apostle Paul, they became alarmed and called his mother. Mrs. Hale took Nat to a psychologist, who asked him whether he had been depressed. Nat replied that far from feeling down, he was ecstatic. He had been assured, by means of communications he refused to describe, that he alone of all humankind would be saved. Guilt had doomed all people to death, but he alone would never die. When the psychologist asked whether Nat was planning to test his theory, Nat replied that it was time to shed his physical body. This statement was made even more ominous by a history of suicide not only of Nat's father, but also of his grandfather and an uncle.

Taking this statement seriously, the psychologist suggested that Nat enter the hospital so that he could be watched closely and so a diagnosis could be made. However, after a night in the hospital Nat claimed that he had never said anything about dying. He had decided that the only reason for keeping him in the hospital was to persecute all the members of his religion, and he insisted on being discharged. He would not say anything more about how he was feeling and what he was planning, since to do so would be to transact with the devil, something he had never mentioned before.

Fearful for Nat's safety, the therapist insisted that he would have to remain an inpatient until it could be determined that his life was not in immediate danger; he continued to refuse to divulge whether he still planned to "shed his physical body." As Nat continued to demand discharge, in accordance with local laws he was provided with an attorney, and after three days of hospitalization he had a court hearing. Nat's behavior in the courtroom seemed normal, and the judge was at a loss to see what all the concern was about until Nat was asked if he had anything to add. Nat said that he was relieved to hear that the judge was planning to release him because if he was not let out immediately Abraham would destroy the court, and then the entire city, with a particle beam.

Since Nat thought that he was not ill, but was merely under attack for his religious ideas, he refused treatment of any kind. Upon further discussion with Nat, the judge realized that he was unable to understand his illness, the nature of the treatments being offered, the alternative therapies that might be effective, or the consequences of assenting to or refusing treatment. A guardian, Nat's mother, was appointed by the court to interpret treatment recommendations and make decisions she believed Nat would make if he could decide rationally.

Within three weeks of receiving individual and group therapy as well as lithium and an antipsychotic drug, Nat's point of view changed drastically. While he retained an intense interest in learning more about the Bible, he conceded that his ideas represented not religious insight but an attempt to come to terms with the fact of death, which had preoccupied him since his father died, and probably before. He now admitted that he had in fact had a suicide plan, to have been enacted on the day he came into the hospital, in which he would drive his car off a cliff he had picked out over several weeks of scouting around. He had thought that he would either survive, and thus prove that he could escape whatever curse had affected his father, or he would die and join his father. He remembered that the ecstasy he had reported had been mixed with despair, but he did not remember any of the ideas about Abraham or Paul.

Nat also now thought that he had been ill for quite some time. He felt that treatment had helped, and he no longer wanted to see if he could transcend death by trying to kill himself. However, he thought that he could handle things on his own from now on. The therapist agreed that Nat was ready for discharge but warned him that without continued treatment the symptoms could well return. Nat understood the risk, but it was a risk he wanted to take. Since he understood the illness, the reasons why treatment was being recommended, and the possible consequences of refusing treatment, he was competent at this point to refuse treatment. As he was no longer an immediate danger to himself, there was no justification for requiring treatment he did not want. Nat thanked the therapist and the staff for their help and left. He declined the offer of continued medication.

Nat went back to school. He continued to attend church regularly, but he no longer thought that he had a special mission. Within six months, however, he became more reclusive and began making incomprehensible allusions to special instructions from the apostles. He stopped going to class and once again stopped eating and sleeping. The church elders and Nat's mother urged him to go back to the psychologist, but Nat had determined that psychology was the work of the antichrist and he refused. While Mrs. Hale was trying to figure out how to force him back into treatment, Nat shot himself in the head.

DISCUSSION QUESTIONS

1. If Nat had been hospitalized at the onset of the relapse of what was probably a manic or schizoaffective psychosis, he could have been prevented from killing himself and the treatment that had worked before could have been reinstituted. Someone else with a similar disorder might have gotten better spontaneously without involuntary treatment. How many people (if any) who will not die if they are not hospitalized should be admitted involuntarily to protect those who will die if hospitalization is not instituted? How many people who will commit suicide if they sign out of the hospital should be allowed to leave in order to prevent inappropriate use of the psychiatric hospital?

2. Szaz (1961) asserts that people with free will should have the option to commit suicide if they choose to do so. Was Nat's suicide chosen freely, or was it constrained in ways he could not control?

3. Even though Nat's beliefs had religious connotations, they were delusional because they were fixed, false ideas (Abraham did not destroy the courtroom) that, by the testimony of church officials, were clearly out of keeping with the beliefs of his subculture and that could not be corrected by appeals to reason or church doctrine. How would a psychologist approach a patient with apocalyptic beliefs calling for suicide that were entirely consistent with the patient's religion and subculture?

4. There were two differences between Nat and the patients described in the textbook who were unjustly hospitalized. First, they were able to make an informed judgment about themselves and any treatment they might be offered, whereas Nat's views of the hospital and of his condition were delusional. Second, they did not present an immediate danger to themselves that was driven by a mental illness. What should be the criteria for determining when a patient is psychologically capable of considering all the issues to make an informed decision about whether help is needed?

5. When, if ever, is a decision to commit suicide "rational" or informed?

6. While it deprives a person of liberty, involuntary hospitalization is less of a personal invasion than involuntary treatment. When should a patient who is involuntarily hospitalized because of an imminent risk of suicide be permitted to refuse treatment for the illness that produced that risk?

7. The text, and most of the case discussion so far, addressed the problem of patients who refuse treatment. What about a patient who *agrees* to treatment for delusional reasons, for example, out of a belief that the treatment will turn him or her into a supernatural being or that the doctor will impose treatment in some supernatural way if the patient refuses? Does the capacity to consent to therapy require the same evaluation as the capacity to refuse?

8. What would be the clinical and ethical considerations in dealing with a mental patient who no longer needs hospitalization but refuses to leave? Or a patient who demands a treatment that a therapist does not feel is necessary but would not hurt either?

REFERENCES

Szasz, T. S. (1961). *The myth of mental illness.* New York: Dell.

Sale of the Century:
Adversarial Psychology

Thanks to lawsuits, writs of habeus corpus, and a new generation of practitioners who came of age during the civil-rights-conscious sixties and seventies, many of the abuses of psychology and psychiatry described in Chapter 18 have become much less common. State hospitals are no longer permitted to warehouse patients without treating them. Even if these hospitals wanted to keep patients indefinitely, their budgets would not permit it. Progressive cutbacks in state hospital funding without any cutbacks in the populations that must be served have made it necessary to discharge patients almost immediately in order to make room for the long lines of patients waiting to get in. Indeed, it is now much harder to get into these hospitals than to get out of them—sometimes harder than getting into Harvard.

The courts have played an important role in defining the limits of power of the mental health professionals over individual freedom. One example discussed in Chapter 18 is the case of Jackson versus Indiana. You will recall that Jackson was a mentally retarded deaf mute accused of a minor crime who was deemed incapable of understanding the charges against him or participating in his own defense. He was committed to a state hospital until his reasoning capacity could be restored sufficiently for him to understand why he was in trouble; this in the experts' estimates would be never.

Jackson appealed his commitment, which amounted to lifetime hospitalization without any hope that he could be "cured" sufficiently to proceed with his case, and the case eventually reached the Supreme Court. In June 1972, the Court ruled that this type of commitment violated Jackson's constitutional rights to due process and a speedy trial and reversed the commitment (*Supreme Court Reporter,* 1972). To comply with this ruling, the states now have laws requiring that people accused of a crime who have mental defects rendering them incompetent to stand trial and who are not expected to be restored to competence must either be released or civilly committed. If they do not meet criteria for commitment (mental retardation would not be such a criterion unless the person also represented an immediate danger), they must be released. Such laws hold that the balance between individual liberty and the authority of the mental health expert is weighted too heavily in the latter direction in instances of commitment to futile treatment. They also help to differentiate between restricting someone's liberty to protect her or him or someone else and locking the person up to provide treatment that she or he does not want or need or that will not help.

One of the most egregious abuses of the mental health system to be reported in the media in recent years concerned chains of private psychiatric hospitals that were paying various personnel, including doctors, school counselors, and freelance "bounty hunters," for referral of patients for inpatient treatment. Many of these hospitals also advertised aggressively; they suggested, for example, that bad grades or normal teenage rebelliousness could be cured in the hospital. Some patients were allegedly kept in the hospital involuntarily without any justification whatsoever, but were discharged as soon as their insurances ran out.

Reports of this kind of behavior led not only to lawsuits and investigations, but to the passage of "safe-harbor" laws, prohibiting clinicians from owning an interest in facilities to which they refer and requiring practitioners to disclose any financial interest they may have in referral to a given institution (for example, that the practitioner's value to the institution may be enhanced by the referral) as well as all other institutions that might provide comparable care. However, changes in health care financing have gone even further in eliminating unnecessary treatment motivated by greed.

"Managed care" of mental health, which consists of external review of hospitalization and inpatient treatment, has imposed severe limitations on whether a patient is hospitalized and how long the hospitalization will last. It is now rare for a clinician simply to be able to admit a patient to the hospital, keep the patient there as long as is desired, and do whatever treatment seems best, at least not if the clinician and the hospital want to get paid. Parenthetically, it has also become more difficult to provide any kind of treatment. Practitioners who must spend hours attempting to justify each day of necessary and even lifesaving care to reviewers who get paid for saving the insurance company money and begin with the assumption that the clinician is trying to cheat them have little motivation to keep patients in the hospital, no matter how great the need.

Another change in mental health practice has been a growing willingness of practitioners to oversee each other's work. Most professional boards require that licensed professionals who know that another professional is impaired or is practicing unethically must report that person or risk sanctions themselves. Reports to professional boards, and meaningful disciplinary actions by those boards, have become much more common. These kinds of developments have not stopped mental health abuses completely, but these abuses have become less frequent, and it has become harder to get away with them.

Shifting financial and legal pressures have removed the incentives for some activities by mental health professionals, but they have created incentives for new ones. One example of a role that has been created by the increasing interaction between the legal and mental health systems, a role that seems even more appealing because it has not been subjected to cost containment, is that of the *expert witness.* As you learned in the textbook, the courts must determine whether people charged with criminal acts are capable of understanding the charges against them and, if so, whether they were able to formulate the intention to commit the crime. It is also up to the courts to decide whether involuntary hospitalization and/or treatment can be instituted and to judge whether an individual who feels mistreated received therapy that was not within the standard of care for the profession, that is, whether most competent professionals in that field would have done things the same way. Although courts are able to interpret opinions about a patient's mental state, they are not capable of generating such opinions and must rely on experts in the field.

As was mentioned in the discussion of the previous case, courts would like the information they must evaluate to be clearcut, and lawyers take contradictory positions in a case, each trying to prove that there is only one interpretation of the available information. Unfortunately, the diagnostic process, which involves conflicting data, all of which have elements of truth, does not lend itself well to a struggle between two adversaries, only one of whom can win. When clinicians become agents of this adversarial process, they often end up being polarized along with everyone else. This problem is illustrated by the work of Dr. Blacke and Dr. Whitte as expert witnesses in the case of Dr. Gray.

THE CASE

Dr. Gray was a psychologist treating a twenty-four-year-old graduate student for recurrent depression when his patient took a handful of aspirin in front of her boyfriend, who immediately called the paramedics. There were no medical consequences of the overdose, and when the patient returned for her next session, she said that she had just been angry at her boyfriend and had not had any intention of dying. The patient continued to work on dealing with situations that made her feel angry and helpless. She did not express any suicidal thoughts.

After several months of therapy during which the patient appeared to be doing well, her mother requested a meeting with Dr. Gray. Dr. Gray discussed the call with the patient, who said that she did not want him to talk to her mother because it would interfere with her attempts to become more independent. Dr. Gray thought that this was reasonable and informed the mother that he did not have permission to meet with her. A week later, the patient took a fatal overdoes of two bottles of aspirin and a fifth of vodka.

The patient's mother sued Dr. Gray for malpractice, claiming that he had a duty to protect the patient, who had indicated that she was at risk by making the first suicide attempt. In addition, she had become more reclusive, distractible, and irritable over the two weeks prior to her death and had muttered something about "doing it right next time." The mother had been trying to tell Dr. Gray about this drastic deterioration in the patient's mental state when she called to set up the appointment.

Dr. Gray's attorney hired an expert witness, Dr. Whitte, and the lawyer for the patient's mother hired Dr. Blacke. Dr. Whitte testified that Dr. Gray's work was well within the standard of care for psychologists. Dr. Whitte pointed out that the patient fell into a low-risk group, and in any event it is impossible to predict suicide in an individual patient. The patient had denied having any suicidal thoughts, and the therapist had no way of knowing that she had deteriorated since she had apparently concealed the change in her mental state while appearing to continue to progress in psychotherapy. To have obtained the mother's observations, the therapist would have had to violate the patient's confidentiality.

Dr. Blacke testified that the previous suicide attempt, even though it was not serious, increased the risk of a second, more serious, attempt. She argued that Dr. Gray could have asked what the patient's mother had to say without telling her anything about the patient, and thereby protected the patient's confidentiality. It was clear to Dr. Blacke that a competent psychologist would have been more aggressive in pursuing the risk of suicide, for example, by repeatedly asking the patient about it directly. Dr. Gray also should have pushed the patient harder to find out why she did not want him to talk to her mother.

Who was right? The clinical truth is that both experts had points. The therapist might have been alerted by the suicide gesture, which was uncharacteristic of the patient, and he could have found out what the patient's mother had to say without violating confidentiality and used the patient's concerns about the intrusion on her autonomy as grist for the psychotherapeutic mill. On the other hand, no therapist can be expected to be a mind reader and intuit changes in a patient's mental state that the patient does not report. Should every therapist be required to ask repeatedly about suicide even if it does not seem clinically indicated? Wouldn't the patient experience such questions as unempathic? In addition, developing an independent identity was a central focus of psychotherapy, so talking with the mother would have been an important event.

In the clinical setting, Dr. Whitte and Dr. Blacke might compare notes with Dr. Gray to come up with better strategies for dealing with patients who conceal or minimize serious symptoms and for gathering information from significant others when the patient does not wish to authorize it and the circumstances do not appear to justify violating the patient's wishes. As there are no studies of any of these issues, the best that can be hoped for is some consensus based on the accumulated experience of the field. In the courtroom, in contrast, the goal is to assert a point of view that will be most favorable to one side of the case. With rare exceptions, there can only be one "correct" answer, not a consensus that takes into account the truth of each side's assertions.

Even the most-balanced clinician finds it difficult not to identify with the adversarial nature of legal proceedings when questions are framed in a way that will polarize the answers as much as possible, especially if conceding that the other side's expert's opinion is also valid could lose the case. Since earning a living as an expert witness does not require endless discussions with managed care reviewers about the necessity of the work or reduction of fees, the prospect of not being hired again may provide a little extra motivation to see things the same way as the attorney who has hired the expert. In the absence of safe-harbor laws and third-party reviews of expert opinions, we may see more all-or-nothing evaluations of cases the truth of which is really in the middle.

DISCUSSION QUESTIONS

1. Is it possible to devise an expert-witness system that would place a higher premium on truth than on winning?

2. Some experts make a living evaluating patients for insurance companies, worker's compensation, and similar groups, which feel that the treatment or benefits a patient is receiving are not justified by the illness. Such evaluations are said to be "independent," but is this true if the expert is paid by the third party and is more likely to be hired again if the findings are against continued benefits? What if the expert is hired by the patient?

3. What besides money might motivate abuses of psychology? How could these issues be dealt with?

4. What are the ethical responsibilities of an expert witness who feels that another expert not only is wrong, but is purposely misrepresenting the field?

5. What are the obligations of psychologists to protect the public from incompetent or unethical practitioners in their field?

6. What considerations hold in restoring an insane convicted murderer to competence so that the prisoner could be executed?

REFERENCE

Supreme Court Reporter (1972). Theon Jackson, Petitioner v State of Indiana. Argued Nov. 18, 1971. Decided June 7, 1972. 406 U.S. 715 (1845)–741 (1859).

So Many Psychotherapies, So Little Time

Chapter 19 contains descriptions of some of the more established of the hundreds of psychotherapies now being offered to sufferers of psychological distresses. As you learned in that chapter, the average person who gets psychotherapy is better off than 80 percent of those who need but do not receive it, but there is no evidence that any particular psychotherapy is better than any other or that longer psychotherapy is better than shorter psychotherapy (Smith et al., 1980; Karasu, 1984). It seems obvious that the experience of the therapist must be a relevant factor, especially for more severe or complex problems, but the best overall predictor of psychotherapy outcome is the match between patient and therapist. This finding must be taken with a grain of salt, however, since most studies comparing experienced and inexperienced therapists do not include patients with major mental disorders of great severity.

Common sense dictates that certain psychotherapies are best suited to some types of problems. However, although specific therapies (e.g., cognitive therapy) have been developed for specific disorders (e.g., depression) and have been found effective in those disorders, they do not seem better than other psychotherapies for the same problems (e.g., interpersonal therapy), and they also work in other disorders (e.g., panic disorder) (Beck et al., 1992). The consumer therefore must be in a position to evaluate competing claims of practitioners of different psychotherapies to make an informed decision about whether the therapy, and its practitioner, seem suited to the problem, and to the sufferer. Therapists who insist that there is only one way to treat a particular problem are not accurately representing the state of knowledge summarized in the textbook.

The purpose of this case is to illustrate ways in which someone with a common problem, anxiety in public and social situations, would be treated by practitioners of a few of the therapies described in Chapter 19 that would be expected to be helpful for this problem.

THE CASE

Eli Jahn is a nineteen-year-old college sophomore majoring in journalism. He is a good student, but he freezes whenever he has to make comments in class. The problem began when Eli participated in a debate as part of his public-speaking course. He thought that he had made a number of good points, but his opponent replied with a blistering attack that made Eli feel that he had made a complete fool of himself. In fact, he had not done badly, it was just that the other student was more aggressive. But he could not sleep that night as he went over and over what he had done wrong.

When he gave an oral report in an English Literature class a few weeks later, Eli was convinced that he would do badly again. He did a good job, but his heart was racing so much and his mouth was so dry that he was convinced that it was obvious to everyone how shaky he was. Once again, he was aware mainly of what he had done wrong and he came away from the experience feeling humiliated instead of satisfied. He was beginning to learn an association between public speaking and anxiety. He did not sleep for three nights before the next time he had to speak in public because he was so preoccupied with the fear of humiliating himself again. Even though he never performed poorly, he was becoming anxious at just the thought of speaking in public.

The association between anxiety and performance generalized, so that it became difficult to give answers in class. He interpreted the decline in his grades that resulted from his failure to participate more as evidence that he was doing a bad job on the occasions when he did speak up. This made him even more inhibited.

Eli continued to feel comfortable with people he knew, but his performance anxiety began to intrude whenever he met someone new. The prospect of being unable to think of anything to say or, even worse, of saying something stupid made the prospect of going to a party too intimidating to contemplate. Just being introduced to someone he did not know made him wonder what he was about to do wrong next. He wanted to make new friends, but he felt like a failure so much of the time that it was harder to reach out the next time. The irony was that he never really said or did anything embarrassing; it was his fear that he would embarrass himself that made him so inhibited. His isolation finally became so painful that he decided he must seek treatment to avert social and professional disaster.

BEHAVIOR THERAPY

Eli's inhibition in social situations can be conceptualized as a learned response. The surprise attack he experienced during the debate was an unconditioned stimulus (US) that evoked the unconditioned response (UR) of anxiety. Being in a situation in which others scrutinized him was a conditioned stimulus (CS), which by virtue of its association with the UR, came to produce the same response (i.e., anxiety was the conditioned response to being in a public setting). It is well known that classical conditioning can occur after a single trial if the UR is intense, and each subsequent experience of anxiety reinforced the association between the CS and the UR. Treatment of the problem would involve unlearning the association between anxiety and performing in public situations by learning the contradictory association between relaxation and performance.

One way to accomplish reconditioning would be with systematic desensitization. First, Eli would be taught to relax using progressive muscle relaxation, meditation, biofeedback, self-hypnosis, or a related technique. Next, he would make a list of situations that made him anxious ranked from least to most anxiety provoking (i.e., an anxiety hierarchy). Under the therapist's direction, Eli would visualize each situation, starting with the least bothersome, and induce a relaxed state until he could picture the situation and feel relaxed instead of anxious. He would then move up the anxiety hierarchy, pairing visualization of each situation with relaxation until the conditioned anxiety response was extinguished.

This "in vitro" desensitization in the office would be followed by "in vivo" desensitization, in which Eli would actually go into each situation, again starting with the least anxiety provoking, using his relaxation technique in order to solidify the association between being in the situation and feeling relaxed. A mock classroom situation or even an actual classroom experience might be utilized. The therapist or some other reassuring figure who could help with the relaxation technique might be present during the in vivo phase. It would be important to move up the anxiety hierarchy gradually so that the only experience in public settings would be of comfort. Extinction of a CR can be interrupted by even one pairing of the CS and the UR.

COGNITIVE THERAPY

The emphasis in cognitive therapy would be on negative expectations that lead to self-fulfilling prophecies that reproduce Eli's symptoms. For example, Eli might make the global assumption, "If everyone doesn't approve of everything I say, everything about me is unacceptable," leading to the negative cognition "I'm a failure" every time he did not perform perfectly. Expecting to fail, he would be too nervous to perform well in the next interaction. He would then pay attention only to the negative aspects of each experience; convincing himself that he had in fact failed each time, he would reinforce the negative belief.

Therapy would involve systematically tracing back such negative cognitions to the underlying assumptions (schemata) and then examining them rationally. Eli might be encouraged to list reasons for and against the belief that he is a failure and might be assigned the task of gathering data that he performed well (e.g., "Despite feeling anxious, I was able to give a report anyway," or "People did say that I did a good job") to debunk the belief that his performance was all bad. Cognitive therapy would include the behavioral techniques of exposure to anxiety—provoking situations with tools for feeling comfortable such as a plan to reassess the meaning of being in a social setting. By the same token, behavior therapy provides the means for cognitive restructuring.

PSYCHODYNAMIC PSYCHOTHERAPY

The psychodynamic therapist would help Eli to figure out why he was so vulnerable to feeling humiliated the first time and what unconscious factors might be contributing to his continued hypersensitivity to others' scrutinies. A briefer, time-limited version of dynamic psychotherapy would focus on the here and now and would examine Eli's feelings in depth every time he felt anxious in a public setting. In the time-limited version, there would not be much discussion of the therapist-patient relationship unless feelings about the therapist threatened to interfere with the treatment. More-extended forms of dynamic psychotherapy would encourage Eli to report concerns about how the therapist viewed him and fears of speaking to the therapist as a model of anxieties about relationships and fears of humiliation that were learned earlier in life.

Psychodynamic psychotherapy may focus on unconscious conflict, but it includes many behavioral techniques. For example, in encouraging the patient to expose himself to public situations and figure out what is really going on, the therapist will provide desensitization by pairing a feeling of intellectual mastery with these situations. The therapist will also model adaptive behavior and help the patient to feel more relaxed by promoting the feeling that the problem can be understood and overcome. There will also be a certain amount of confrontation of negative expectations and generation of alternative hypotheses, albeit informally.

GROUP THERAPY

Since Eli's symptoms are only experienced when he is around other people, treatment might be most effective in the context of social interactions. In group therapy, he would be able to get feedback from other people about whether he was really as ineffective as he believed. If he was making socially inappropriate mistakes, he could be given advice about how to correct them. Positive feedback and encouragement from the group would encourage him to take chances in other settings.

As with the other psychotherapies, group therapy would not be a pure technique in Eli's case. Positive experiences in the group would provide desensitization, while being with other people who are able to function in a group would furnish modeling. Negative cognitions would be confronted by other group members, who might also have insights into Eli's basic sensitivity to becoming so preoccupied by fears of humiliating himself in the first place.

PHARMACOTHERAPY

Eli's problem could be conceptualized from a psychobiological standpoint as an arousal response gone awry. The first time he was surprised by the attack on his point of view, he was startled, and this naturally caused anxiety, alertness to the possibility of danger, and physiological arousal. Ordinarily, the feeling of being startled would go away once he was out of the situation. However, whether by virtue of previous experiences of being surprised or anxious or an innate sensitivity of arousal mechanisms, the response could not be turned down normally and had become autonomous. Physical symptoms of arousal such as hyperventilation, rapid heart beat, dizziness, dry mouth, and tremulousness could then serve as cues to the mental state of expecting something terrible to happen. Even subclinical arousal with each reexposure to the same kind of social situation might be sufficient to reevoke the pathological expectations.

The psychopharmacologist (who would have to be a psychiatrist, whereas the other treatments could be provided by any mental health practitioner) would want to determine whether Eli's anxiety was an isolated symptom or part of an Axis I disorder such as social phobia, generalized anxiety disorder, panic disorder, or depression. If a specific diagnosis could be made, a medication known to be effective for that disorder would be prescribed. Social phobia (social anxiety disorder in DSM-IV), for example, is characterized by fear of acting in a way or displaying symptoms that will be humiliating in social or performance situations in which unfamiliar people or scrutiny by others is present. Social anxiety disorder, which causes either avoidance of the feared situation or intense anxiety on remaining in the situation, has been shown to respond to two classes of medication (Liebowitz, 1987). The monoamine oxidase (MAO) inhibitors seem to reduce interpersonal sensitivity, possibly by decreasing arousal in situations to which a person feels sensitive. Medications such as propranolol (Inderal) and atenolol (Tenormin), which block a type of receptor for norepinephrine called the beta receptor, may decrease bodily symptoms of arousal such as rapid heart rate, tremulousness, and sweating, as well as the stimulation of arousal centers in the brain. Feeling less uncomfortable physically decrease anxiety and feelings of loss of control and makes it easier to remain in the phobic situation. The beta blockers are also used intermittently to treat performance anxiety in people who do not have more global anxiety symptoms such as public speakers, musicians, and sometimes students taking examinations.

To the extent that Eli's brain had "learned" to become aroused excessively in response to the minor threat of social scrutiny, medications by themselves might not cure so much as suppress the symptoms. However, by making it possible for Eli to remain in social situations without becoming anxious, they would facilitate desensitization, perhaps without any need for formal systematic desensitization. Medications that dampened global responsiveness might also make it easier to address underlying conflicts or negative cognitions without becoming overwhelmed by the anxiety that talking about these topics might arouse, and thereby facilitate psychotherapy.

DISCUSSION QUESTIONS

1. What factors might govern the selection of one treatment over another? When should treatments be combined?

2. You will recall that to give truly informed consent for a particular therapy, a person must know about available alternative treatments. Should psychotherapists inform all patients that many types of therapy are available for their problems, including therapies that the clinician offering a particular approach may not know how to do?

3. What factors are shared by all effective psychotherapies? How can these be maximized in any psychotherapy?

4. To what standards of proof of efficacy should psychotherapies be held before they can be used? Since any effective treatment, including psychotherapy, has the potential to do harm as well as good, should psychotherapy be regulated in the same way as medications?

5. Psychotherapy studies use a variety of outcome measures, usually involving scores on symptom assessment scales, to determine whether a type of psychotherapy is having a positive effect. How should the clinician decide whether psychotherapy is working for an individual patient? How is a consumer of psychotherapy to know if it is really helping?

6. The textbook makes the point that some psychotherapies may be said to be working if the patient likes them. When is this not a satisfactory standard? How should psychotherapy be evaluated if the patient seems to work hard in the office and feels helped but still has all the symptoms for which the treatment is being applied?

REFERENCES

Beck, A. T., Sokol, L., Clark, D. A., Berchick, R., & Wright, F. (1992). A crossover study of focused cognitive therapy for panic disorder. *American Journal of Psychiatry, 149*, 778–83.

Karasu, T. B. (1984). Recent developments in individual psychotherapy. *Hospital and Community Psychiatry, 35*, 29–39.

Liebowitz, M. R. (1987). Social phobia. *Modern Problems in Pharmacopsychiatry, 22*, 141–73.

Smith, M. (1980). *The benefits of psychotherapy.* Baltimore: Johns Hopkins Press.

Study Guide

CHAPTER 1

The Meanings of Abnormality

CHAPTER OVERVIEW

The textbook begins with a discussion of abnormality. How is it best to define it? Abnormality, like many concepts in ordinary language, has fuzzy boundaries. Although it is easy to recognize extreme examples of abnormality, it is not as easy to classify less extreme instances—the gray areas. The notion of "family resemblance" is introduced to help explain the fuzzy nature of abnormality. When instances of a concept like abnormality are said to have a family resemblance, they have elements in common. However, no given element is necessary or sufficient to define that concept.

For abnormality, these elements include (a) suffering; (b) maladaptiveness; (c) irrationality and incomprehensibility; (d) unpredictability and loss of control; (e) vividness and unconventionality; (f) observer discomfort; and (g) violation of moral and ideal standards. The more of these elements present, the more confident we are that abnormality is present.

Abnormality is a social judgment, and, like all such judgments, it is fallible. Disagreement sometimes occurs about who or what is abnormal. However, this does not mean that abnormality does not exist or that it is not a useful concept.

Normality is defined here simply as the absence of abnormality—i.e., possessing few of the elements that count toward a judgment of abnormality. There is more to life than the mere absence of abnormality, though, and the positive side of life is termed *optimal living*. Optimal living includes (a) positive attitudes toward oneself; (b) ability to grow and develop; (c) autonomy; (d) accurate perception of reality; (e) competence at life's tasks; and (f) satisfying relationships with other people.

ESSENTIAL TERMS

family resemblance	notion that instances of a concept possess elements in common, but no given element is necessary or sufficient (p. 6)
flexible control	ability to retain control or to give it up as self and situation require (p. 9)
intern's disease	illness created by suggestion, as by reading of symptoms and "discovering" their presence(p. 19)
necessary condition	property that all instances of a given concept possess (p. 5)
normality	absence of abnormality (p. 19)

optimal living

pleasures, maturities, insights, achievements, and wisdoms of life (p. 17)

residual rules

unwritten rules of behavior (p. 10)

sufficient condition

property that only instances of a given concept possess (p. 5)

CENTRAL CONCEPTUAL ISSUES

Recognizing abnormality.   Although abnormality may seem to be widely and readily recognized, there are no specific elements common to all instances of abnormality (necessary conditions), nor are there elements that consistently distinguish abnormal cases from normal ones (sufficient conditions). This lack of precise definition does not imply that abnormality does not exist or cannot be recognized, only that there is some flexibility in the term's meaning and usage.

Defining abnormality: Family resemblance.   In contrast to the logical rigor of necessary and sufficient conditions, the "family resemblance" approach is used to define the concept of abnormality. In this approach, the various characteristics or properties that are generally held to indicate abnormality are compared with the behavior of the individual in question to determine the extent, if any, of a "resemblance." If there is a match to a significant degree between the case and any or some subset of the elements, then it is likely to be regarded as abnormal.

Abnormality as a social judgment.   Elements may be judged to indicate abnormality by the individual him or herself (e.g., suffering, maladaptiveness), by an observer (e.g., irrationality/incomprehensibility, unpredictability/loss of control, vividness/unconventionality, observer discomfort), or by the culture of subculture (e.g., violation of moral or ideal standards). In the first case the judgment is subjective. In the latter two cases, the determination of abnormality is a social one. In no case is the judgment truly objective or independent of context. Because some of the elements in the set reflect evolving social norms, "family resemblance" allows for diagnosis of abnormality yet denies certainty in categorization.

Normality versus abnormality.   Normality means simply *not abnormal:* either there are few if any elements of abnormality present and/or the elements that are present are mild in intensity or impact. In other words, there is minimal or no family resemblance. Because no strict definition of abnormality exists (i.e., stipulating necessary and sufficient conditions), the implications of diagnosing or labeling an individual as abnormal raises important and ongoing moral, legal, philosophical, and medical questions.

Optimal living.   Just as abnormality may be distinguished from normality by the presence of certain elements, so may optimal living be contrasted with normal living by specific recognizable characteristics. In each case, the elements exist to a matter of degree and, just as in the case of abnormality, may be highly situation- and time-specific.

SAMPLE EXAM

1. Which of these statements was made about abnormality?
   a. It is easy to define abnormality.
   b. Abnormality exists in all cultures.
   c. There is no such thing as abnormality.
   d. Although it is difficult to define abnormality, it is easy to recognize it.
   e. Abnormality is the absence of normality.

2. Which of these is a necessary condition for "dog"?
   a. four legs
   b. bark
   c. fur
   d. Domesticated
   e. have a master

3. Which of these is a sufficient condition for "triangle"?
   a. equal angles
   b. three sides
   c. each angle less than 90 degrees
   d. equal sides
   e. not a square

4. Which of these is a necessary condition for "abnormality"?
   a. suffering
   b. irrationality
   c. unpredictability
   d. observer discomfort
   e. none of the above

5. Which of these is a sufficient condition for "abnormality"?
   a. suffering
   b. irrationality
   c. unpredictability
   d. observer discomfort
   e. none of the above

6. The idea of a family resemblance is that
   a. first cousins look more alike than second cousins.
   b. there are necessary and sufficient conditions for belonging to a family.
   c. members of a family tend to share characteristics in common.
   d. identical twins look alike.
   e. mad people all look alike.

7. The more elements of abnormality present,
   a. the more abnormal a person is.
   b. the more complex abnormality is.
   c. the more certain it is that abnormality is present.
   d. the more difficult it is to cure abnormality.
   e. the more expensive the treatment.

8. Which of these statements is true?
   a. Abnormality always implies suffering.
   b. Suffering always implies abnormality.
   c. Abnormality never implies suffering.
   d. Suffering never implies abnormality.
   e. Abnormality sometimes implies suffering.
   f. Suffering sometimes implies abnormality.

9. In biology, adaptiveness involves all except
   a. survival of species.
   b. population growth.
   c. well-being of individual.
   d. well-being of society.
   e. successful offspring.

10. Which of these is most incomprehensible?
    a. grief
    b. thought disorder
    c. arson
    d. ingratiation
    e. residual rules

11. Flexible control is the ability to
    a. bend but not break.
    b. change one's mind about the causes of behavior.
    c. retain or relinquish control as required.
    d. control actions in several ways.
    e. delegate authority.

12. Unconventionality characterizes all but
    a. genius.
    b. abnormality.
    c. trend-setters.
    d. high moral standards.
    e. optimal living.

13. When broken, residual rules of behavior result in
    a. judgments of abnormality.
    b. misdemeanors.
    c. observer discomfort.
    d. irrational behavior.
    e. felonies.

14. Violation of moral standards
    a. may be conventional.
    b. always results in observer discomfort.
    c. always is abnormal.
    d. always is normal.
    e. none of the above

15. The *Diagnostic and Statistical Manual* (Fourth Edition) is a
    a. list of fees charged by psychiatrists.
    b. set of criteria for different mental disorders.
    c. discussion of global abnormality.
    d. specification of necessary and sufficient conditions for different mental disorders.
    e. a medical textbook.

16. Which one of the following statements is *not* a hazard of the family-resemblance approach?
    a. Society may be wrong about abnormality.
    b. There may be no family resemblance for abnormality.
    c. Observers may disagree about abnormality.
    d. Actors and observers may disagree about abnormality.
    e. all of the above are hazards.

17. Normality is
    a. absence of abnormality.
    b. adaptation.
    c. conventionality.
    d. lack of suffering.
    e. indistinguishable from abnormality.

18. Optimal living is
    a. self-actualization.
    b. normality.
    c. the positive side of life.
    d. different in kind from normality.
    e. lack of abnormality.

19. Optimal living involves all of the following but
    a. positive attitudes toward self.
    b. autonomy.
    c. conventionality.
    d. environmental competence.
    e. accurate perception of reality.

20. Interns' syndrome is caused by
    a. stress.
    b. germs.
    c. congenital defect.
    d. suggestion.
    e. exams.

Answer Key for Sample Exam

1.	b	(p. 4)	11.	c	(p. 9)
2.	a	(p. 5)	12.	a, d	(p. 10)
3.	b	(p. 5)	13.	c	(p. 10)
4.	e	(p. 6)	14.	a	(p. 10)
5.	e	(p. 5)	15.	b	(p. 13)
6.	c	(p. 6)	16.	b	(p. 13)
7.	c	(p. 6)	17.	a	(p. 16)
8.	e, f	(p. 7)	18.	c	(p. 17)
9.	b	(p. 7)	19.	c	(p. 17)
10.	b	(p. 8)	20.	d	(p. 20)

SELF-TEST

1. Abnormality is recognized in _____ cultures.

2. If all cases of abnormality shared some single property, the property would be a _____ for abnormality.

3. If only cases of abnormality shared some single property, the property would be a _____ for abnormality.

4. Just because abnormality is difficult to define does not mean _____ or _____.

5. The idea that cases of abnormality share elements in common, although none of these elements is necessary or sufficient, is called _____.

6. The more elements of abnormality present, the more _____.

7. The elements of abnormality include _____, _____, _____, , _____, _____, and _____.

8. An instance of loss of control that is not abnormal is _____.

9. Unwritten rules of behavior are called _____.

10. Unlike many judgments in science, the judgment of abnormality is a _____.

11. The catalog currently in use of ways in which people are abnormal is _____.

12. The three hazards of the family resemblance approach to abnormality are _____, _____, and _____.

13. Normality is _____.

14. The positive side of life is _____ _____.

15. The elements of optimal living are _____ _____, _____, _____, _____, and _____.

16. Illness brought about by suggestion is _____ _____.

Answer Key for Self-Test

1. all
2. necessary condition
3. sufficient condition
4. it does not exist; it cannot be recognized
5. family resémblance
6. certain we are that abnormality is present
7. suffering; maladaptiveness; irrationality and incomprehensibility; unpredictability and loss of control; vividness; observer discomfort; violation of moral and ideal standards
8. flexible control
9. residual rules of behavior
10. social judgment
11. *Diagnostic and Statistical Manual of Mental Disorders* (Fourth Edition) (or DSM-IV)
12. society may be wrong; observers may disagree; observers and actors may disagree
13. absence of abnormality
14. optimal living
15. positive attitudes toward self; growth and development; autonomy; accurate perception of reality; environmental competence; positive interpersonal relations
16. interns' syndrome

MATCHING ITEMS

_____   1. necessary condition

_____   2. moral or ideal standards

_____   3. unpredictability

_____   4. adaptiveness

_____   5. observer discomfort

_____   6. incomprehensibility

_____   7. sufficient condition

_____   8. accurate reality perception

_____   9. family resemblance

_____   10. optimal living

A. irrationality

B. distinguishing element

C. oughts

D. positive mental health

E. well-being

F. tolerating ambiguity

G. diagnosis

H. inconsistency

I. common element

J. residual rules

Answer Key for Matching Items

1. I	6. A
2. C	7. B
3. H	8. F
4. E	9. G
5. J	10. D

SHORT-ANSWER QUESTIONS

1. What is meant by the terms "necessary" and "sufficient" conditions? How do they apply when defining abnormality?

2. Why does the text describe abnormality as a social judgment? Which of the elements of abnormality are good illustrations of this and why?

3. What are the possible hazards of using a family resemblance approach to define abnormality?

4. According to the text, optimal living has six elements. Think about these with respect to your own life. In each area, what are you doing, planning on doing, or could you be doing to enhance optimality?

TYING IT TOGETHER

This chapter introduces two important ideas that will aid in understanding the material presented in the rest of the textbook. First, abnormality is described as a category with fuzzy boundaries. There are neither necessary nor sufficient conditions for abnormality. Instead, instances of abnormality bear a family resemblance to each other; they tend to share elements in common, although no given element is critical in defining abnormality. The idea of family resemblances should be kept in mind throughout your reading of the textbook. It helps explain why clinical research (Chapter 6) and clinical diagnosis (Chapter 7) are less than exact. It helps explain why treatment (Chapter 9) is less than 100 percent successful.

The disorders described in Chapters 8 through 17 are also characterized by family resemblances. Any given disorder has a number of elements that count toward its diagnosis, but in most cases these elements are neither necessary nor sufficient. Further, elements may count toward more than one diagnosis. Anxiety, for instance, is pertinent not just to the anxiety disorders (Chapters 8 and 9), but also to such difficulties as psychosomatic disorders (Chapter 10), sexual dysfunctions (Chapter 13), and the schizophrenias (Chapter

12). Similarly, depressed mood is central to many disorders of mood (Chapter 11) and also may play a role in eating disorders (Chapter 15) and somatoform disorders (Chapter 9).

Chapters 3 through 5 describe popular approaches to understanding and treating abnormality. Most of these approaches propose that some factor is a necessary and sufficient cause of abnormality. The family resemblances idea suggests that none of these approaches will always be reasonable. Indeed, it is frequently concluded throughout the textbook that a combination of models is needed to explain a given disorder.

The examples given of each disorder tend to be good examples—i.e., they possess many of the elements that count toward a diagnosis.

However it should be realized that such good examples are rarely encountered. In reality, most instances of a disorder lack some of the important elements.

The second important idea introduced in this first chapter is that identification of abnormality is a social judgment. Theory (Chapters 3 through 5), research (Chapter 6), and assessment (Chapter 7) aid this judgment, but inherently it involves one person making a decision about another person, even in the case of neurological disorders (Chapter 17). Mistakes may occur (Chapter 18). The social context of abnormality and its identification (Chapter 2) should not be forgotten even though attention is usually drawn to the so-called abnormal individual.

FURTHER READINGS

Campbell, A. (1976). Subjective measures of well-being. *American Psychologist, 31,* 117–124.

Cantor, N., Smith, E., French, R. de S., & Mezzich, J. (1980). Psychiatric diagnosis as prototype categorization. *Journal of Abnormal Psychology, 89,* 181–93.

Foulks, E. F., Wintrob, R. M., Westermeyer, J., & Favazza, A. R. (1977). *Current perspectives in cultural psychiatry.* New York: Spectrum.

Goffman, E. (1963). *Stigma.* Englewood Cliffs, NJ: Prentice-Hall.

Greenblatt, M. (1978). *Psychopolitics.* New York: Grune & Stratton.

Scott, W. A. (1958). Research definition of mental health and mental illness. *Psychological Bulletin, 55,* 29–45.

Scott, W. A. (1968). Conceptions of normality. In E. G. Borgotta & W. W. Lambert (Eds.), *Handbook of personality theory and research* (pp. 974–1006). Chicago: Rand McNally.

TERM-PAPER TOPICS

1. Critics of the mental health professions, like Thomas Szasz, argue that diagnoses of abnormality constitute moral judgments in the guise of scientific statements. Evaluate this claim. Discuss the idea of family resemblances and its pertinence to your thesis.

2. It can be argued that the family resemblances idea is too easy a way out for psychologists who have been unable to discover the essence of abnormality. The natural sciences—physics, chemistry, and biology—have proceeded without resorting to family resemblances. What about the field of abnormal psychology? Take a strong stand, and defend it.

3. The textbook does not discuss positive mental health (optimal living) in much detail. However, other writers have devoted considerable thought to the topic. Review some of these formulations. Can positive mental health be actively brought about, or can it at best merely not be inhibited?

EXERCISES

Exercise One—The Elements of Abnormality

The purpose of this exercise is to illustrate the idea that the elements of abnormality are neither necessary nor sufficient.

Consider the following descriptions. Most people would consider at least some of the actions described to be abnormal. In each case, which elements of abnormality are present? Which are absent? Compare your judgments with those of your classmates.

a. Your neighbors encourage their children to watch twelve hours of television per day.

b. Your uncle consumes a quart of whiskey per day; he has trouble remembering the names of those around him.

c. Your ten-year-old neighbor calls the police to tell them that her parents keep marijuana in the house.

d. Your neighbor divorces her husband in order to devote more time to her career.

e. All visitors to your parents' home must wash their hands immediately upon arriving, or else they are not allowed to stay.

f. Your neighbors allow their children to watch while they make love.

g. Your cousin is pregnant, and she smokes three packs of cigarettes per day.

h. Your roommate is a highly successful college football player who uses steroids to increase his strength, despite their negative effects on his long-term health.

Exercise Two—Abnormality: How Does It Look?

How common are the different elements of abnormality described in the text in people's actual judgments of abnormal behavior? Poll a number of your friends with the question "I'm taking a class in abnormal psychology, and I'm trying to understand what makes some people think others are abnormal. Think of someone you think is psychologically abnormal in some way and tell me what it is about them that makes you think that." Categorize the answers according to which of the elements they entail. Which are most common? Which are least? Why might each be the case? If you have a large enough sample you might be able to examine whether any particular kind of explanation was more common by the sex or ethnicity of the observer or by the sex or ethnicity of the observed.

Exercise Three—Actor-Observer Differences in Explanation

The purpose of this exercise is to show that people often explain their own behaviors differently than do people who observe these behaviors. Specifically, "actors" often point to situational demands or requirements, while "observers" often point to dispositions of the actor.

Ask several different individuals you know to explain (a) why they received a poor grade on an exam; (b) why they went to a party; (c) why they have a part-time job; (d) what attracted them to their current or past boy/ girlfriend. Then ask other people who know these individuals to explain the same events. Do actor-observer differences occur?

Jones, E. E., & Nisbett, R. E. (1971). *The actor and observer: Divergent perceptions of the causes of behavior*. Morristown, NJ: General Learning Press.

Exercise Four—Examples of Concepts: Family Resemblances

The textbook introduced the idea of family resemblances to explain why instances of abnormality do not always have elements in common. The purpose of this exercise is to show that the idea of family resemblances has wide application.

Think of a large number of examples of common concepts like these:

a. fruit (e.g., apple, orange)

b. dog (e.g., collie, shepherd)

c. game (e.g., baseball, billiards)

d. joke (e.g., cartoon, pun)

For each concept, what appear to be critical elements? Does every example possess these elements?

Wittgenstein, L. (1953). *Philosophical investigations*. New York: Macmillan.

Rosch, E., & Mervis, C. B. (1975). Family resemblances: Studies in the internal structure of categories. *Cognitive Psychology, 7,* 573–605.

Exercise Five—Ethics and Abnormality

Consider your ethics and behavior in light of a foreign culture or local subculture. How might *your* behavior be construed as abnormal? How should you adjust to a foreign culture ("When in Rome do as the Romans do" or "stick to your principles")? How should an individual behave in society that he or she believes is destructive, evil, or unjust? How should society treat that individual?

Exercise Six—Am I Normal?

Consider some aspect of your behavior that you fear is abnormal. What criteria or knowledge would help you to resolve this question or prompt you to address it?

CHAPTER 2

Abnormality across Time and Place

CHAPTER OVERVIEW

This chapter provides a brief history of abnormality. How has it been explained across time and place? How has it been treated? Changing conceptions of madness underscore the point of the first chapter: abnormality is not some invariant thing. Rather, it is explained and treated within a cultural and historical context.

Over the years, the causes of abnormality have variously been viewed as (a) animistic; (b) physical; and (c) psychological. Animistic explanations included the belief that madness resulted from possession by evil spirits as well as the notion that madness could be caused by witches. Such explanations largely gave way to physical-illness explanations and psychological explanations, which remain the prevalent conceptions today.

Each explanation of madness has an asso

ciated strategy for treatment. When thought to be animistic in origin, madness was treated by religious means such as exorcism. When thought to be an illness, it is treated medically—with drugs, operations, and diet. And when thought to be psychological, it is treated psychologically—with, for example, hypnosis or psychotherapy.

Important in the history of abnormality is the rise of the psychiatric hospital. Hospitals originated as asylums for the underprivileged, which included the mad. These individuals were given worse treatment than other inmates, especially severer physical abuse, since it was believed that they were like animals and experienced little pain. Eventually, this belief was replaced by the idea that humane treatment was more ethical and more effective.

ESSENTIAL TERMS

animalism	belief that animals and mad people are similar (p. 29)
animism	belief in spirits (p. 25)
animal magnetism	according to Mesmer, "universal magnetic fluid" which causes physical disease when distributed unequally in the body (p. 30)
baquet	large wooden tub filled with water and magnetized iron filings, used by Mesmer to restore the health of patients in whom animal magnetism was unequally distributed (p. 32)

166

catharsis	release of psychic energy resulting from uncovering and reliving early traumatic conflicts (p. 35)
exorcism	ceremonial ritual during which demons are thought to be dispelled from the victim's body (p. 33)
hospital	charitable institution for the needy, infirm of all ages (p. 36)
hypnotism	techniques originally associated with Mesmer's theory of animal magnetism (p. 32)
hysteria	disorder with symptoms such as fits, pains, paralysis, blindness, lameness, listlessness, and melancholia; at one time thought to be caused by a wandering uterus (p. 27)
lycanthropy	form of psychopathology in the Middle Ages in which groups of people believed themselves to be wolves and acted accordingly (p. 25)
mesmerism	another term for animal magnetism (p. 32)
moral treatment	approach to treating mental disorders emphasizing kindness and the virtues of work (p. 42)
ostracism	casting out of a person believed to be possessed by demons (p. 33)
tarantism	form of dancing mania in the Middle Ages thought to be caused by the tarantula (p. 25)
trephines	holes found in the skulls of some Paleolithic cave dwellers; believed to have been created to release evil spirits trapped inside (p. 25)
Witches' Hammer *(Malleus Maleficarum)*	1486 manual describing how to identify and dispose of witches (p. 26)

CENTRAL CONCEPTUAL ISSUES

History as context.   Because social standards and norms of behavior have changed through history, what has been classified as abnormal behavior has changed as well. In addition, changes in cultural and intellectual climate have produced different theories of the cause of abnormal behavior, and these theories and accompanying attitudes have determined the kinds of treatment employed. Interestingly, not only have the criteria for deciding what is abnormal changed, but the particular forms through which psychological disorders are expressed have also varied (e.g., hysteria).

Explanations of abnormality.   Specific explanations for abnormality develop from more general cultural views of the meaning and mechanisms of reality. There have been three dominant general theories of abnormality, each reflecting the prevailing beliefs and values of its period: animism (i.e., abnormal behavior is due to psychological possession by spirits, animals, the devil, etc.); physical (i.e., psychological symptoms result from malfunctioning organs, disease states); and psychogenic (i.e., psychological conditions produce an abnormal psychological states).

Treatments for abnormality.   The varied theories of abnormality spawned their own convictions about appropriate treatment. In the case of animistic theories, supernatural means of treatment were employed (e.g., exorcism to expel the invading spirit, ostracism to cast out sufferer and spirit as one). When physical origins were assumed, the treatment was aimed at remedying the dysfunction (e.g., purging, bleeding, vomiting, aromatherapy; and more recently, surgery, pharmacology). When psychogenic explanations prevailed, treatments were developed to intervene at the psychological level (e.g., hypnosis, catharsis, free association, psychotherapy).

Serendipity in treatment findings.   Although some theories were later discredited or abandoned, they occasionally led to effective treatments which endured (e.g., mesmerism and hypnosis).

Inhumane treatment.   What is now considered to be the inhumane treatment of the mentally ill in the seventeenth and eighteenth centuries, actually grew out of theories of insanity of that time. It was believed that the insane had lost their reason and were, as a consequence, more animal than human, and that reason could be restored only through punishment and fear. In this view, confinement, severe conditions, and extreme treatment were considered appropriate to their subject. Thus, in addition to the social and political needs the early hospitals served, their therapeutic ethos was consistent with the prevailing scientific dogma.

Humane treatment.   In response to the growing recognition of the abject suffering and lack of improvement of the incarcerated mentally ill, theoretical and treatment alternatives were sought. Treatment consistent with theories which emphasized the ethics of kindness, work, self-esteem, and internalized controls (vs. external physical restraints) led to more humane conditions and practices in hospitals and "retreats" beginning in the late eighteenth century.

SAMPLE EXAM

1. All of these have changed across time except
   a. elements of abnormality.
   b. theories of abnormality.
   c. concern with abnormality.
   d. treatment of abnormality.
   e. manifestations of abnormality.

2. Which of these disorders is uncommon today?
   a. depression
   b. schizophrenia
   c. hysteria
   d. phobia
   e. alcoholism

3. Over time, explanations of abnormality fall into which categories?
   a. animistic, physical, and psychological
   b. historical, political, and economic
   c. religious, racial, and ethnic
   d. pessimistic, optimistic, and neutral
   e. ancient and modern

4. The idea that all behavior has causes is first encountered in which approach to abnormality?
   a. animistic
   b. medical
   c. psychodynamic
   d. behavioral
   e. animalistic

5. How were evil spirits thought to cause abnormality?
   a. by upsetting brain chemistry
   b. by leading to faulty learning
   c. by inhabiting the brain and controlling actions
   d. by stealing one's possessions
   e. by controlling others

6. Which of these disorders was not common in the Middle Ages?
   a. tarantism
   b. anorexia
   c. animal possession

d. lycanthropy
e. all of the above were common

7. All of these historical events provided the context of the witch hunts in the Middle Ages except
   a. decay of cities.
   b. rise of capitalism.
   c. schism in the Roman Catholic church.
   d. breakdown of the family.
   e. weakening of traditional authority.

8. *The Witches' Hammer* was a
   a. machine used in exorcism rituals.
   b. tool used by a witch's familiar.
   c. manual for hunting witches.
   d. cookbook for magical brews.
   e. none of the above

9. At the heart of *The Witches' Hammer* is
   a. fear of women's sexuality.
   b. distrust of ethnic minorities.
   c. intolerance of socialism.
   d. disgust with conventional morality.
   e. sadistic impulses.

10. All of these were considered *weak* tests of witchcraft except
    a. body marks
    b. confessions
    c. improbable coincidences of bad events
    d. improbable coincidences of good events
    e. failure to bleed after wounding

11. The Salem witch trials seemed to begin in
    a. disagreement over tobacco tariffs.
    b. children's games.
    c. suggestions in a sermon.
    d. letters from England.
    e. magical phenomena.

12. Historically, hysteria was most common among
    a. children.
    b. elderly men.
    c. women who were virgins or widows.
    d. adolescent boys.
    e. physicians.

13. According to the Greeks, hysteria was caused by
    a. an inadequate diet.
    b. a ruptured spleen.
    c. fallen arches.
    d. a wandering uterus.
    e. anxiety.

14. Galen believed that hysteria was caused by
    a. lack of exercise.
    b. sexual abstinence.
    c. red meat.
    d. interpersonal conflict.
    e. anxiety.

15. Proponents of animalism pointed to all of these characteristics of the mad except that
    a. the mad could live without protest in miserable surroundings.
    b. the mad could not control themselves.
    c. the mad could be unusually loyal.
    d. the mad could be suddenly violent.
    e. the mad lost their reason.

16. When abnormality began to be regarded as a physical illness, it was treated with all of the following except
    a. purges.
    b. rebirthing.
    c. bleeding.
    d. forced vomiting.
    e. aroma therapy.

17. The view that abnormality has psychological causes is
    a. a twentieth-century idea.
    b. a nineteenth-century idea.
    c. present in Roman writings.
    d. present in Stone Age cave paintings.
    e. undisputed.

18. Which of these terms does not belong?
    a. anthropomorphism
    b. animal magnetism
    c. hypnotism
    d. mesmerism
    e. all of the above belong

19. How did Mesmer define animal magnetism?
    a. musk-based perfume
    b. universal magnetic fluid
    c. communication among animals
    d. sexual pheromones
    e. mutual attraction

20. What was the purpose of a baquet?
    a. to concentrate magnetic fluid
    b. to distract hysterics from their symptoms
    c. to provide nourishment to anemics
    d. to exorcise evil spirits
    e. none of the above

21. Mesmer was criticized for his
    a. therapy success.
    b. theory of animal magnetism.
    c. taste in clothes.
    d. fees.
    e. lack of credentials.

22. Charcot was all of the following except a
    a. physician
    b. neurological researcher.
    c. clinical psychologist.
    d. professor.
    e. teacher of Freud.

23. Charcot used the technique of hypnosis to
    a. redistribute universal magnetic fluid.
    b. distinguish hysteria from epilepsy.
    c. bring unconscious conflicts to the
       surface.
    d. see whether or not an accused crimi-
       nal was guilty.
    e. do public shows.

24. Charcot's research into hypnotism was
    sabotaged by
    a. overzealous students.
    b. cuts in government funding.
    c. overprotective ethics committees.
    d. jealous fellow scientists.
    e. lack of equipment.

25. Over time, treatment of abnormality has
    often
    a. not been considered possible.
    b. reflected theories of underlying
       causes.
    c. followed the suggestions of the
       patient.
    d. treated body and mind
       simultaneously.
    e. declined.

26. Which of the following does not belong?
    a. exorcism
    b. ostracism
    c. anomie
    d. prayer
    e. all of the above belong

27. All of the following were treatments for
    hysteria except
    a. garlic and burning dung.
    b. lithium.
    c. massage.
    d. perfume.
    e. hypnosis

28. Mesmer's theory of hysteria is an example
    of
    a. a supernatural explanation.
    b. an illness explanation.
    c. a cognitive explanation.
    d. a psychological explanation.
    e. charlatanism.

29. Who first introduced catharsis?
    a. Galen
    b. Cotton Mather
    c. Josef Breuer
    d. Sigmund Freud
    e. Pinel

30. Catharsis belongs with
    a. "A stitch in time saves nine."
    b. "Thanks, I needed that."
    c. "Walk softly but carry a big stick."
    d. "I am not a crook."
    e. "Grin and bear it."

31. Freud showed that catharsis results from
    a. hypnosis.
    b. early sexual experience.
    c. neurological disorder.
    d. talking about problems.
    e. all of the above.

32. Historically, hospital meant
    a. an asylum for the underprivileged.
    b. a workplace for physicians.
    c. an inn for travelers.
    d. a spa for workers.
    e. a restaurant.

33. The Hôpital Général of Paris was founded
    in
    a. 1532.
    b. 1606.
    c. 1656.
    d. 1789.
    e. 1801.

34. Inmates of early hospitals had what in
    common?
    a. illness
    b. insurance
    c. unemployment
    d. abnormality
    e. criminal histories

35. The first hospital in the United States was
    founded in
    a. New York.
    b. Virginia.
    c. Pennsylvania.

d. Maryland.
e. San Francisco.

36. Treatment of the mad in the early hospitals embodied what belief about abnormality?
    a. lycanthropy
    b. animalism
    c. medical model
    d. psychogenic explanation
    e. animism

37. Gheel is best known
    a. for its humane treatment of abnormality.
    b. for using exorcism as a cure of abnormality.
    c. for first using psychosurgery.
    d. as the source of Freud's patients.
    e. for Bedlam hospital.

38. If you were a psychiatric patient in Paris in the late eighteenth century, which of the following physicians would be most likely to free you from your shackles?
    a. Tuke
    b. Cullen
    c. Galen
    d. Lavoisier
    e. Pinel

39. Philippe Pinel advocated
    a. liberty and equality.
    b. a supernatural explanation of abnormality.
    c. catharsis.
    d. the psychological control of abnormality.
    e. all of the above.

40. The Retreat at York was founded by
    a. secular authorities.
    b. physicians.
    c. Quakers.
    d. mesmerists.
    e. Mormons.

41. Moral treatment embodied
    a. a supernatural view of abnormality.
    b. an illness view of abnormality.
    c. a psychological view of abnormality.
    d. Mesmer's view of abnormality.
    e. an animalistic view of abnormality.

Answer Key for Sample Exam

1. c (p. 23)	22. c (p. 33)	
2. c (p. 23)	23. b (p. 32)	
3. a (p. 24)	24. a (p. 33)	
4. a (p. 25)	25. b (p. 33)	
5. c (p. 25)	26. c (p. 33)	
6. b (p. 25)	27. b (p. 34)	
7. a (p. 27)	28. b (p. 35)	
8. c (p. 26)	29. c (p. 35)	
9. a (p. 26)	30. b (p. 35)	
10. e (p. 26)	31. d (p. 35)	
11. b (p. 28)	32. a (p. 36)	
12. c (p. 27)	33. c (p. 36)	
13. d (p. 27)	34. c (p. 36)	
14. b (p. 29)	35. c (p. 38)	
15. c (p. 29)	36. b (p. 38)	
16. b, e (p. 29)	37. a (p. 39)	
17. c (p. 29)	38. e (p. 39)	
18. a (p. 32)	39. d (p. 39)	
19. b (p. 30)	40. c (p. 41)	
20. a (p. 31)	41. c (p. 41)	
21. b (p. 31)		

SELF-TEST

1. Over the years, concepts of abnormality have _____.

2. Treatment of abnormality reflects _____.

3. Over the years, the three major explanations of abnormality have been _____, _____, and _____.

4. Holes drilled in skulls of Paleolithic cave dwellers are called _____ and are thought to have been drilled in order to _____.

5. Abnormality thought to be caused by supernatural forces was treated by

   _____.

6. Witch hunts in Europe resulted _____ _____ occurring

   _____.

7. The 1486 manual for recognizing witches was _____.

8. Most "witches" persecuted in Europe were _____.

9. *The Witches' Hammer* seems to reflect a strong fear of _____.

10. Evidence regarding a suspected witch was obtained _____ and

    _____.

11. One of the first psychological disorders thought to have a physical cause was
    _____; the cause was believed to be _____.

12. The belief stressing the similarity between animals and mad people was
    _____; it was in part responsible for the seemingly cruel _____.

13. Abnormality thought to be caused by physical factors was treated by _____.

14. The theory of animal magnetism was proposed by _____.

15. Mesmer used a device called a _____ to treat hysteria; the device was thought to cure hysteria by _____.

16. Mesmer came under criticism not for _____ but for _____.

17. Mesmerism came to be known as _____.

18. Charcot used hypnosis to distinguish between _____ and _____.

19. Abnormality thought to be caused by psychological factors was treated by _____.

20. The first psychological therapy was used to treat _____.

21. Emotional relief that accompanies the reliving of painful experiences is _____.

22. Freud discovered that catharsis could occur without the use of _____.

23. Hospitals date as far back as _____.

24. Inmates of the first hospitals shared one common characteristic: _____.

25. Compared to the treatment of other inmates, the treatment of the insane in the first hospitals was _____.

26. The idea that the insane should not be treated like animals was called _____.

27. The Belgium town that pioneered humane treatment was _____.

28. The director of the Paris Hospital who removed the chains from the insane was

    _____.

29. The approach emphasizing the therapeutic value of work and the need for self-esteem was

    called _____.

30. Moral treatment in the United States resulted in _____ percent of patients being dis-

    charged within one year as recovered or improved.

Answer Key for Self-Test

1. changed
2. the perceived cause of abnormality
3. animistic explanations; physical explanations; psychological explanations
4. trephines; let demons escape from the
   skull
5. supernatural means
6. social upheaval; at the end of the fifteenth
   century
7. *The Witches' Hammer (Malleus Malefi-
   carum)*
8. women
9. women's sexuality
10. body marks; confessions
11. hysteria; wandering uterus
12. animalism; ways mad people were treated
13. physical means

14. Franz Anton Mesmer
15. baquet; redistributing magnetic fluid
16. his cures; his theories
17. hypnosis
18. hysteria; epilepsy
19. psychological means
20. hysteria
21. catharsis
22. hypnosis
23. the seventeenth century
24. unemployment
25. brutal
26. humane treatment
27. Gheel
28. Philippe Pinel
29. moral treatment
30. 70

MATCHING ITEMS

_____ 1. catharsis

_____ 2. refuge

_____ 3. hypnosis

_____ 4. witch hunts

_____ 5. animalism

_____ 6. psychoanalysis

_____ 7. hysteria

_____ 8. shaman

A. priest

B. Charcot

C. Breuer

D. Freud

E. mesmerism

F. Gheel

G. fear of women's sexuality

H. rejected by Pinel

_____   9.   moral treatment

_____   10. animalism

I.   soul

J.   Tuke

Answer Key for Matching Items

1. C		6. D	
2. F		7. B	
3. E		8. A	
4. G		9. J	
5. H		10. I	

SHORT-ANSWER QUESTIONS

1. Discuss how each of the three explanations of abnormality described in the text dictates its own specific form to treatment.

2. Briefly, what are the benefits and hazards, as you see them, of animistic versus physical versus psychological explanations of abnormality?

3. What lessons were learned about the causes and treatment of abnormality through the use of hypnosis by each of Mesmer, Charcot, Breuer, and Freud?

4. Trace the changing functions of the psychiatric hospital from the sixteenth to nineteenth centuries, and the conditions that prompted this evolution.

TYING IT TOGETHER

This chapter illustrates the idea introduced in Chapter 1 that judgments of abnormality are social. The history of how abnormality has been explained and treated underscores the idea that abnormality is not an invariant property of an individual. Rather, explanation and treatment reflect the particulars of a given social and historical context. As the disorders in Chapters 8 through 17 are described, you should entertain the possibility that some are mainly problems of contemporary Americans. For instance, drug abuse (Chapter 14), anorexia nervosa (Chapter 16), and infantile autism (Chapter 16) are relatively "new" disorders that may reflect reactions to aspects of contemporary society. Schizophrenia (Chapter 12) may be similarly interpreted. And perhaps depression (Chapter 11) is the psychological manifestation of twentieth-century alienation.

Treatment of abnormality usually reflects theories about underlying causes. This strategy seems to have been followed by primitive people who drilled holes in the skulls of their fellows to let demons escape. Similarly, today's treatments (Chapter 19) for the various disorders (Chapter 8 through 17) usually attempt to undo their presumed causes. Thus, if schizophrenia is viewed as a biologically determined disorder, it is treated with drugs (see Chapter 12). Although this strategy is often reasonable, it is not guaranteed to be. There are biological disorders that can be treated psychologically (see Chapter 17) and psychological disorders that can be treated biologically. As emphasized in Chapter 3, one of the dangers in adhering to a given model of abnormality is blindness to better ways of conceiving and treating disorders.

Chapter 2 describes the rise of humane treatment in psychiatric hospitals. Compare humane treatment with the factors that characterize successful psychotherapy (Chapter 19). They are strikingly similar. One of the important elements that characterize abnormality is observer discomfort (Chapter 1). To the degree that individuals with psychological difficulties can be approached without discomfort, the better off they may be.

FURTHER READINGS

Foucault, M. (1965). *Madness and civilization.* New York: Random House.

Hare, E. H. (1974). The changing content of psychiatric illness. *Journal of Psychosomatic Research, 18,* 283–289.

Jackson, S. W. (1986). *Melancholia and depression from Hippocratic times to modern times.* New Haven, CT: Yale University Press.

Kraepelin, E. (1917/1962). *One hundred years of psychiatry.* Baskin, W. (Ed.). New York: The Citadel Press.

Kuhn, T. S. (1970). *The structure of scientific revolutions* (2nd ed.). Chicago: University of Chicago.

Maher, W. B., & Maher, B. (1982). The Ship of Fools: Stultifera Navis or Ignis Fatuus. *American Psychologist, 37,* 756–761.

Porter, R. (1987). *A social history of madness.* New York: Weidenfeld & Nicholson.

Roosens, E. (1979). *Mental patients in town life: Gheel, Europe's first therapeutic community.* Beverly Hills, CA: Sage.

Spanos, N. P., & Gottlieb, J. (1979). Demonic possession, mesmerism, and hysteria: A social psychological perspective on their historical interrelations. *Journal of Abnormal Psychology, 88,* 527–546.

Torrey, E. F. (1986). *Witchdoctors and psychiatrists.* New York: Harper & Row.

Zilboorg, G. (1941). *A history of medical psychology.* New York: Norton.

TERM-PAPER TOPICS

1. What were the causes of the witch hunts in the Middle Ages? In Salem? Were psychological factors of overriding importance?

2. Why did Mesmer run afoul of French authorities? Was his theory that much at odds with dominant thought, or did political factors enter into his difficulties?

3. The deinstitutionalization movement of the 1960s represents a further revolution in the cultural perception and treatment of the mentally ill. According to Torrey, what are the antecedents and consequences of this sociopolitical movement? In what ways is the existence of the current epidemic of homeless mentally ill similar to, and different from, the plight which faced the mentally ill in centuries past?

   Torrey, E. F. (1988). *Nowhere to go—The tragic odyssey of the homeless mentally ill.* New York, Harper & Row.

4. Transposing present trends to the future, speculate about psychiatric hospitals in the year 2050.

EXERCISES

Exercise One—Animistic Accounts of Abnormality

This exercise has the purpose of illustrating how abnormality can be explained and treated from an animistic point of view.

Go to a popular horror movie. What are the abnormal things that the characters in the movie are driven to do? How are animistic forces depicted as responsible for these instances of abnormality? How are these forces combated?

Exercise Two—A Witch on Trial

In a famous scene from the Monty Python film, *The Holy Grail,* a woman is accused of being a witch and put on trial. What tests (strong and weak) did her prosecutors use to determine her guilt or innocence? What were the results? In what ways do you believe that this film depiction captures and/or fails to capture the essence (ironic and otherwise) of the witch-hunting of this period?

Exercise Three—Mental Health Treatment

The purpose of this exercise is to illustrate the close relationship between theories of abnormality and treatments of abnormality. As Chapter 2 of the textbook stresses, through history these have usually been congruent. They still are today.

Contact local mental health facilities and arrange tours for the class. Inquire about the philosophy of each facility. Do treatment philosophies reflect assumptions about the causes of abnormality?

Exercise Four—Beliefs about Mental Illness

The purpose of this exercise is to show how diverse beliefs about mental illness—its causes and its treatments—can be.

Ask acquaintances questions like "What is mental illness?" "Who is at risk for mental illness?" "How is mental illness treated?" "What are people like after treatment for mental illness?" Try to talk to a variety of people. What range of opinions is represented? As you read the rest of the textbook, keep in mind these opinions. Which are consistent with current knowledge in psychology? Which are inconsistent?

Nunnally, J. C. (1961). *Popular conceptions of mental health.* New York: Holt, Rinehart & Winston.

Exercise Five—Failure: Then and Now

According to the text, in seventeenth-century France "the poor, the mad, the aged, the infirm, and even the petty criminal" (p. 37) were lumped together by the common property of being unemployed and were institutionalized. "Unemployment was viewed, not as a result of economic depression, technological change, or bad luck, but as a personal, indeed a moral, failure" (p. 37). Compare and contrast these attitudes with their prevailing counterparts in the present day.

CHAPTER 3

The Biomedical Model

CHAPTER OVERVIEW

This chapter is the first of three that deal respectively with the most prevalent contemporary approaches to abnormality: (a) the biomedical model; (b) the psychodynamic and existential approaches; and (c) the learning model, including behavioral and cognitive approaches. A model helps in approaching abnormality. It suggests how to describe, explain, and treat. However, the risk in using models is that important aspects of abnormality may be overlooked.

The chapter describes the biomedical model, which views abnormality as something wrong with the body—an illness, an injury, a defect. Described in detail is the account of how general paresis—a psychological disorder—was discovered to result from untreated syphilis—a physical disorder. Also described is the contemporary search for the cause of obsessive-compulsive disorder in biological factors. Research findings of genetic contributions to everything from schizophrenia to criminal behavior to normal personality are also examples of the biomedical approach.

ESSENTIAL TERMS

concordant twins	both members of a set of twins have the same disorder (p. 54)
discordant twins	one member of a set of twins has a disorder, and the other does not (p. 54)
dopamine hypothesis	explanation of schizophrenia proposing that the disorder results from too much dopamine (a neural transmitter) in the brain (p. 58)
etiology	causal explanation of a disorder (p. 49)
general paresis	disorder characterized by delusions of grandeur, mental deterioration, and eventual paralysis and death; caused by untreated syphilis (p. 50)
learning model of abnormality	model of abnormality that stresses situational determinants; outgrowth and combination of behavioral and cognitive models; also known as the environmentalist model (p. 48)
lithium	drug used to treat bipolar depression and mania (p. 63)

model	approach to defining and explaining some phenomenon by emphasizing presumably critical aspects of the phenomenon while de-emphasizing other, presumably non-critical aspects (p. 48)
behavioral model of abnormality	model of abnormality conceiving it as learned behavior (p. 48)
biomedical model of abnormality	model of abnormality holding that it is an illness or malfunction of the body (p. 48)
cognitive model of abnormality	model of abnormality holding that it is the product of certain thoughts and beliefs (p. 48)
psychodynamic model of abnormality	model of abnormality regarding it as the result of unconscious conflicts within the person (p. 48)
PET (positron emission tomography) scan	assessment of brain metabolism (p. 59)
reductionism	philosophy that holds that all psychological phenomena can be explained by and reduced to biological phenomena (p. 68)
syndrome	a group of diverse symptoms that tend to co-occur (p. 49)
tardive dyskinesia	nonreversible neurological side effect of antipsychotic drug treatment; symptoms include sucking, lip smacking, and peculiar tongue movements (p. 62)

CENTRAL CONCEPTUAL ISSUES

The biomedical model.   The model one uses to understand abnormal behavior guides the type of research conducted, the choices made concerning treatment, the metaphors employed to describe the phenomenon, and the theories developed to explain it. This can lead to new insights into human behavior and successful new treatments for disordered conditions, but it can also limit the resources brought to bear on a particular problem. Of the three dominant approaches—biomedical, psychodynamic, environmental—the biomedical approach is the one which describes abnormal behavior as "mental illness" and explains it as a product of malfunctioning biological mechanisms in the brain. Because physiological mechanisms are involved, treatments derived form this model are most likely to include physical interventions (e.g., surgery, ECT, pharmacology).

The biomedical approach.   The biomedical approach to mental illness involves three stages. First, co-occurring symptoms are identified and grouped together as a syndrome. Next, four areas—biological organisms (germs), genetics, neurochemistry, and neuroanatomy—are examined for the possible cause (etiology) of the symptoms. A mechanism is sought which can most fully explain all of the symptoms believed to constitute the syndrome. Finally, once such a mechanism is identified, treatment is aimed at correcting or controlling the physical condition. Sometimes, however, the process works in reverse and a medical treatment is discovered that treats particular symptoms. This in turn leads the biomedical scientist to investigate which mechanisms of the body are being affected by the treatment (usually a drug). If this process yields insight into a particularly basic mechanism, it may then prompt a re-definition of the syndrome.

Genes and mental illness.   Twin studies are often used to investigate possible genetic contribu-tions to mental illness. Because identical twins have the same genetic makeup, a strictly ge-netic explanation for a disorder would require a concordance of nearly 100 per cent. The ex-ample of schizophrenia, in which concordance is approximately 50 percent—a strong but far from complete correlation—suggests an interaction of genetic vulnerability and environment stressors: a diathesis-stress model. Currently, this model is widely applied in our under-standing of the role of genes in various mental disorders.

Genes and personality.   Recent genetic studies have indicated that there are heritable compo-nents of normal as well as abnormal personality. These elements interact in complicated ways with each other and with the environment such that the probability of "gross" or com-plex behaviors can be affected. Strong genetic loadings of some of these characteristics may be socially desirable (e.g., IQ, cheerfulness, self-control), or they may be unwanted (e.g., de-pressiveness, pessimism, antisocial behavior). Because personality and social behavior in-volve such complex interactions, it is unlikely that specific genes for these traits exist.

Biomedical treatments.   The biomedical approach to mental illness has yielded numerous help-ful treatments; treatments that alleviate much suffering and inconvenience. However, the treatments, especially drugs, are by and large cosmetic, and may have serious side effects. They do not prepare the sufferer for functioning independently of the drug. With few excep-tions, conditions are rarely correctable in 100 percent of sufferers through biomedical inter-ventions alone. Nevertheless, many otherwise intractable conditions are made manageable with biomedical interventions, and may become amenable to additional treatment ap-proaches once brought under some degree of pharmacological control. Interestingly, psycho-logical interventions also sometimes work on the very conditions for which drugs are used, and not infrequently psychological approaches work where drugs are unsuccessful. These facts have kept the reductionist/anti-reductionist debate very much alive.

Reductionism.   In general, the biomedical model assumes a reductionist position: that psycho-logical phenomena can be reduced to and explained by biological phenomena. Opponents argue that there are at least some psychological phenomena for which biology is not a suffi-cient explanation. Clearly the interaction of biology and psychology is not yet fully under-stood.

The biomedical view of normality and abnormality.   In contrast to the psychodynamic or learn-ing models, according to the biomedical model, the symptoms of psychological abnormality indicate an underlying *physiological* disorder or dysfunction which may originate in genes, neurochemistry, neuroanatomy, or a disease state. Psychological normality then, reflects nor-mal physiological functioning.

SAMPLE EXAM

1. A model of abnormality is
    a. psychopathology in children caused by parents.
    b. a pictorial representation of uncon-scious conflicts.
    c. a means of defining and approaching abnormality.
    d. unnecessary if the causes of abnor-mality are of primary interest.
    e. unnecessary in determining treatment.

2. The risk in using models of abnormality is that
   a. society may be wrong about abnormality.
   b. actors and observers may disagree about abnormality.
   c. investigators may be blinded to other possibilities.
   d. biological determinants may be de-emphasized.
   e. investigators may be wrong about abnormality.

3. The idea that abnormality results from unconscious conflicts within the self is the
   a. biomedical model.
   b. psychodynamic model.
   c. behavioral model.
   d. cognitive model.
   e. existential model.

4. The idea that abnormality results from illness or injury to the body is the
   a. biomedical model.
   b. psychodynamic model.
   c. behavioral model.
   d. cognitive model.
   e. existential model.

5. The idea that abnormality results from the failure to confront successfully fundamental questions about living is the
   a. biomedical model.
   b. psychodynamic model.
   c. behavioral model.
   d. cognitive model.
   e. existential model.

6. The idea that abnormality results from certain thoughts and beliefs is the
   a. biomedical model.
   b. psychodynamic model.
   c. behavioral model.
   d. cognitive model.
   e. existential model.

7. The idea that abnormality results from the acquisition of certain ways of acting is the
   a. biomedical model.
   b. psychodynamic model.
   c. behavioral model.
   d. cognitive model.
   e. existential model.

8. If an individual acting abnormally were found to have a brain tumor, this would support the
   a. biomedical model.
   b. psychodynamic model.
   c. behavioral model.
   d. cognitive model.
   e. existential model.

9. If an individual acting abnormally were found to have deep doubts about the meaning of life, this would support the
   a. biomedical model.
   b. psychodynamic model.
   c. behavioral model.
   d. cognitive model.
   e. existential model.

10. If an individual acting abnormally were found to have idiosyncratic beliefs about the ways things should be if happiness is to be achieved, this would support the
    a. biomedical model.
    b. psychodynamic model.
    c. behavioral model.
    d. cognitive model.
    e. existential model.

11. A syndrome is
    a. a set of symptoms that cohere.
    b. an illness with an unknown cause.
    c. a pathological way of behaving.
    d. an instance of thought disorder.
    e. the origin of symptoms.

12. An advocate of the biomedical model looks for the cause of abnormality among all these except
    a. germs.
    b. genetics.
    c. biochemistry.
    d. church attendance.
    e. neuroanatomy.

13. Abnormality with a physical etiology might be treated in any of these ways except
    a. catharsis.
    b. drugs.
    c. fumigations.
    d. massage.
    e. surgery.

14. Which discovery provided important support for the biomedical model of abnormality?
    a. Patients exposed to the moral treatment often improved dramatically.
    b. Hysteria was not caused by a wandering uterus.

c. General paresis resulted from untreated syphilis.
d. Penicillin was isolated.
e. Hypnosis can treat hysteria.

15. General paresis is characterized by all these symptoms except
a. delusions of grandeur.
b. paralysis.
c. stupor.
d. weakness.
e. low self-esteem.

16. One reason why the link between general paresis and syphilis was not discovered earlier is that
a. many individuals with general paresis denied ever having syphilis.
b. abnormality was thought to be caused by psychological factors.
c. most cases of syphilis had been successfully cured.
d. general paresis had a social stigma.
e. all of the above

17. The experiment showing that untreated syphilis caused general paresis was based on the
a. careful use of a control group.
b. fact that general paresis was more common among cigar smokers than nonsmokers.
c. fact that one could contract syphilis only once.
d. fact that general paresis was more common among men than women.
e. none of the above

18. The experiment showing that untreated syphilis caused general paresis was conducted by
a. Sigmund Freud.
b. Richard von Krafft-Ebing.
c. Josef Breuer.
d. August von Wassermann.
e. Sir Randolph Churchill.

19. Nowadays, the prevalence of general paresis is
a. as common as always.
b. more common than it used to be.
c. less common than it used to be.
d. difficult to estimate.
e. no longer of interest.

20. Fraternal twins have
a. the same genes.

b. more genes in common than non-twin siblings, but fewer in common than identical twins.
c. two-thirds of their genes in common.
d. as many genes in common as non-twin siblings.
e. none of the above

21. Twins have been studied extensively by researchers interested in the role of
a. communication in schizophrenia.
b. genetics in schizophrenia.
c. birth order in schizophrenia.
d. facial appearance in schizophrenia.
e. personality traits in schizophrenia.

22. Which pattern of results provides support for the biomedical model?
a. Fraternal twins and identical twins are equally concordant for schizophrenia.
b. Identical twins are concordant for schizophrenia.
c. Identical twins are more concordant for schizophrenia than are fraternal twins.
d. Fraternal twins are discordant for schizophrenia.
e. Fraternal twins are more concordant for schizophrenia than are identical twins.

23. Which pattern of results would disprove the biomedical model?
a. if fraternal twins and identical twins were equally concordant for schizophrenia
b. if identical twins were concordant for schizophrenia
c. if fraternal twins were discordant for schizophrenia while identical twins were concordant for schizophrenia
d. if fraternal twins were discordant for schizophrenia
e. none of the above

24. Schizophrenia research using twins makes a number of simplifying assumptions, including all of the following except that
a. identical and fraternal twins have the same environment.
b. identical twins have the same genes.
c. diagnosis of schizophrenia is reliable.

d. all instances of schizophrenia have the same causes.
e. schizophrenia research assumes all of the above.

25. The current view about genetics and schizophrenia is that
a. schizophrenia is caused by genes.
b. schizophrenia is caused by the environment.
c. schizophrenia is caused by both genes and the environment.
d. schizophrenia is caused by neither genes nor environment.
e. there is not enough known to draw any conclusions.

26. Recent research suggests that there may be a genetic basis for each of the following complex characteristics except
a. criminality.
b. beauty.
c. religiosity.
d. neuroticism.
e. all of the above

27. The dopamine hypothesis proposes that schizophrenia
a. involves diminished intellectual ability.
b. results from untreated general paresis.
c. is caused by too few neurons in the brain.
d. results from too much neural transmitter.

28. Support for the dopamine hypothesis comes largely from
a. drug research.
b. twin studies.
c. epidemiological research.
d. psychosurgery investigations.

29. The dopamine hypothesis is an example of the
a. biomedical model.
b. psychodynamic model.
c. behavioral model.
d. cognitive model.
e. existential model.

30. Recent research that compares brain activity in the brains of patients with OCD before and after drug or behavior therapy finds that

a. only behavior therapy works on OCD.
b. when therapy works, activity in the caudate nucleus increases.
c. when therapy works, activity in the caudate nucleus decreases.
d. only drug therapy works on OCD.
e. none of the above.

31. The possible side effects of treating schizophrenia with major tranquilizers include
a. addiction.
b. tardive dyskinesia.
c. confusion.
d. insomnia.
e. all of the above.

32. The treatment of choice for bipolar depression is
a. anti-anxiety medication.
b. antidepressive medication.
c. antipsychotic medication.
d. lithium.
e. major tranquilizers.

33. Criminality can be best understood as a product of
a. genes.
b. environment.
c. gene-environment covariances.
d. a and b.
e. all of the above.

34. Strengths of the medical model include all but one of the following
a. concepts are objective.
b. methods are well defined.
c. its history is one of successes.
d. the side effects of drugs are minimal.
e. concepts are measurable.

35. A reductionist believes that
a. psychopathology represents a problem in living.
b. psychological events cause biological events.
c. all psychological phenomena can be explained by biological phenomena.
d. some psychological phenomena cannot be explained by biological phenomena.
e. all biological events can be reduced to psychological events.

Answer Key for Sample Exam

1.	c	(p. 48)	10.	d	(p. 48)	19.	c	(p. 52)
2.	c	(p. 49)	11.	a	(p. 49)	20.	d	(p. 53)
3.	b	(p. 48)	12.	d	(p. 49)	21.	b	(p. 53)
4.	a	(p. 48)	13.	a	(p. 49)	22.	c	(p. 54)
5.	e	(p. 48)	14.	c	(p. 52)	23.	a	(p. 54)
6.	d	(p. 48)	15.	e	(p. 50)	24.	b	(p. 54)
7.	c	(p. 48)	16.	a	(p. 50)	25.	c	(p. 54)
8.	a	(p. 48)	17.	c	(p. 51)	26.	e	(p. 55)
9.	e	(p. 48)	18.	b	(p. 51)	27.	d	(p. 58)

28.	a	(p. 55)
29.	a	(p. 58)
30.	c	(p. 59)
31.	b	(p. 62)
32.	d	(p. 63)
33.	e	(p. 66)
34.	d	(p. 67)
35.	c	(p. 68)

SELF-TEST

1. An approach to identifying, explaining, and treating abnormality is a _____.

2. The danger of adhering to a given model is that one may _____.

3. The model that views abnormality as an illness or injury of the body is the _____.

4. The model that views abnormality as the product of unconscious conflicts is the

   _____.

5. The model that views abnormality as the result of learning is the _____.

6. The model that views abnormality as caused by thoughts and beliefs is the

   _____.

7. The model that views abnormality in terms of the failure to confront fundamental questions about life is the _____.

8. Diverse symptoms that tend to occur together are a _____.

9. Proponents of the biomedical model look for the cause of abnormality to involve

   _____, _____, and/or _____.

10. The sixteenth-century disorder characterized by delusions of grandeur and caused by untreated syphilis was _____.

11. The cause of a disorder is referred to as its _____.

12. Syphilis is like measles in that once someone has contracted it, he or she _____.

13. The crucial experiment linking syphilis to general paresis was conducted by _____. In this experiment, individuals with _____ were exposed to _____. The result was that they _____.

14. The current treatment of general paresis is to treat syphilis with _____.

15. Schizophrenia afflicts about _____ percent of the world's population.

16. Twins who have all the same genes are _____ twins, while twins who do not have all the same genes are _____ twins.

17. If schizophrenia is genetically transmitted, the _____ for schizophrenia would be greater among _____ twins than among _____ twins.

18. The concordance rate of schizophrenia among identical twins is approximately _____ percent.

19. The concordance rate of schizophrenia among fraternal twins is approximately _____ percent.

20. In the case of complex characteristics such as beauty, it is now thought that traits rather than _____ configurations of DNA are the level at which natural selection operates.

21. The best method for separating the learning from the genetic contribution to personality is to study twins who have been _____ and _____.

22. Research in Denmark found that having a criminal for an adopted father does not increase your risk of becoming a criminal unless _____.

23. The neurotransmitter thought to be involved in schizophrenia is _____. Schizophrenia may involve too _____ of this neurotransmitter in the brain.

24. Drugs used to treat schizophrenia seem to work by _____ dopamine receptors in the brain.

25. PET brain scans of untreated patients with OCD have found _____ activity in the area of the _____ when compared to scans of successfully treated patients.

26. About _____ percent of depressed patients improve noticeably on antidepressants.

27. Manic-depression can often be treated with _____.

28. Although anti-anxiety drugs may have less _____ than anti-psychotics or anti-depressants, they may be more _____.

29. Causal agents in the environment that produce a trait but are also correlated with genes and so do not appear causal are called _____.

30. Problems with the biomedical model include _____ and _____.

Answer Key for Self-Test

1. model of abnormality
2. overlook other possibilities
3. biomedical model
4. psychodynamic model
5. behavioral model
6. cognitive model
7. existential model
8. syndrome
9. germs; genetics; biochemistry
10. general paresis
11. etiology
12. cannot contract it again
13. Richard von Krafft-Ebing; general paresis; syphilis; did not contract syphilis
14. penicillin
15. 1
16. identical; fraternal
17. concordance; identical; fraternal
18. 50
19. 10
20. Molar; molecular
21. adopted away; reared apart from birth
22. your natural father was also a criminal
23. dopamine; much
24. blocking
25. higher; caudate nucleus
26. 65
27. lithium
28. side effects; addictive
29. gene-environment covariances
30. neglect of psychological factors; side effects of medication

MATCHING ITEMS

_____ 1. etiology
_____ 2. von Krafft-Ebing
_____ 3. discordant
_____ 4. degree of heritability
_____ 5. schizophrenia
_____ 6. syndrome
_____ 7. Prozac
_____ 8. "second revolution" in psychiatry
_____ 9. "revolving door"
_____ 10. Valium
_____ 11. PET scan
_____ 12. Paul Ehrlich

A. introduction of antipsychotics
B. dopamine hypothesis
C. cause
D. 606
E. psychoanalysis
F. dissimilar with respect to a trait or disease
G. antidepressant
H. glucose metabolism
I. compare trait correlations in fraternal and identical twins
J. general paresis
K. anti-anxiety
L. a group of symptoms that co-occur

Answer Key for Matching Items

1.	C	7.	G
2.	J	8.	E
3.	F	9.	A
4.	I	10.	K
5.	B	11.	H
6.	L	12.	D

SHORT-ANSWER QUESTIONS

1. Describe five main areas of support for the biomedical model of mental illness and give an example of experimental evidence for each.

2. If identical twins had a .7 positive correlation for a particular trait, and fraternal twins had a .4 correlation for that same trait, what conclusions could you draw and why?

3. What were the consequences, both positive and negative, of the widespread introduction of anti-psychotic medications?

4. Discuss the relative strengths and weaknesses of the biomedical model.

TYING IT TOGETHER

The biomedical model was the first cohesive approach to abnormality. The successful identification of untreated syphilis as the cause of general paresis provides an example still followed by researchers who hope to find biological bases—illness, injury, genetics, biochemistry—for other disorders. In some cases, their search has uncovered biological factors: psychosomatic disorders (Chapter 10), depression (Chapter 11), personality disorders (Chapter 15), schizophrenia (Chapter 12), childhood disorders (Chapter 16), and neurological disorders (Chapter 17). In other cases, an understanding of biology is essential to an understanding of what otherwise are psychological problems: neuroses (Chapter 8 and 9), sexual dysfunctions (Chapter 13), and drug abuse (Chapter 14). However, in almost no case are biological factors alone responsible for a disorder. The contemporary view of many disorders is a diathesis-stress model, which attributes the disorder to a constitutional weakness (diathesis) coupled with an environmental trauma (stress) (Chapter 10).

The biomedical model is at the base of several well-known treatments—in particular, drugs and electroconvulsive shock therapy (Chapter 19). Again, though, these treatments are rarely 100 percent effective in themselves. The case of drug treatment and rehabilitation (Chapter 14) illustrates this well. Biological treatments of drug abuse are often of limited effectiveness, since they ignore the reasons that an individual has for using drugs. Drug abuse is like an illness, but it is not quite the same thing. No one has pneumonia for a reason, but everyone who drinks too much alcohol does have a reason. Successful treatment must address not just the biological aspect of drug abuse but also the psychological aspect (Chapter 14). The same seems to be true for schizophrenia; the neuroleptics alleviate certain schizophrenic symptoms, but they do not solve the psychological problems faced by the schizophrenic patient (Chapter 12).

As you read about disorders that have been conceptualized in terms of the biomedical model, keep in mind its limitations. Because the biomedical model is the oldest of the contemporary approaches to abnormality, its problems are the easiest to recognize.

FURTHER READINGS

Andreasen, N. C. (1984). *The broken brain: The biological revolution in psychiatry.* New York: Harper & Row.

Bouchard, T. J., Jr., Lykken, D. T., McGue, M., Segal, N. L., & Tellegen, A. (1990). Sources of human psychological differences: The Minnesota study of twins reared apart. *Science, 250,* 223–228.

Dubos, R. J. (1950). *Louis Pasteur: Free lance of science.* Boston: Little, Brown.

Engel, G. L. (1980). The clinical application of the biopsychosocial model. *American Journal of Psychiatry, 137,* 535–544.

Heston, L. L. (1992). *Mending minds: A guide to the new psychiatry of depression, anxiety, and other serious mental disorder.* New York: W. H. Freeman.

Lykken, D. T., McGue, M., Tellegen, A., & Bouchard, T. J. (1992). Emergenesis: Genetic traits that may not run in families. *American Psychologist, 47:12,* 1565–1577.

Mazur, A., & Robertson, L. S. (1972). *Biology and social behavior.* New York: Free Press.

Painter, T. I. (1981). Tuskegee experiment.

Encore, 10(11), 32–33.

Sochurek, H. (1987). Medicine's new vision. *National Geographic, 171*(1), 2–41.

Wrightsman, L. S. (1974). *Assumptions about human nature: A social-psychological approach.* Monterey, CA: Brooks/Cole.

TERM-PAPER TOPICS

1. Is the biomedical model outmoded in medicine? Compare and contrast the biomedical model as described in your textbook with current ideas about holistic medicine.

2. Was the Krafft-Ebing experiment in which he exposed individuals suffering from general paresis to syphilis really necessary? Why did he not include a comparison group?

3. Consider this statement: All models of abnormality embrace the medical model in the sense that they look for a metaphorical "germ" or "deficiency" within the person. Do you agree or disagree with this statement? Defend your answer with examples.

4. As particular diseases are linked to genetic predispositions, the possibility of testing people for these genes must be considered. Discuss the ethical issues involved here.

5. Twin studies are used to isolate genetic versus environmental causes of disorders like schizophrenia. What are the simplifying assumptions necessary for such studies to serve their stated purpose? Are these overlimiting assumptions?

6. Consider the evidence that both genes and childhood environment contribute to the risk of adult criminality. What public policy implications might there be, for example, in the case of guidelines for adoption? In general, what are the ethical and practical considerations raised by the fact of our growing knowledge of the contribution of inheritance to adult personality?

7. Though one can hardly argue with using medications to relieve suffering, what if the drug makes normal people fell "better than well?" What if it does not simply remedy an illness but actually changes personality in a positive way? Is this the job of a drug prescription? Discuss the implications and dilemmas posed by the thesis of Peter Kramer's controversial book.

   Kramer, P. D. (1993). *Listening to Prozac.* New York: Viking.

EXERCISES

Exercise One—Working with a Model

The purpose of this exercise is to illustrate one of the consequences of working within a given model of abnormality—in this case the biomedical model. If one believes abnormality to be an illness or injury of the body, then one tends to treat it with medical means.

Look at recent issues of a psychiatry journal that accepts advertising, like *Archives of General Psychiatry.* Notice the treatments of abnormality that are advertised (drugs) and the benefits that are touted (rapid relief). How might ads be different if the journal did not adhere to the biomedical model of abnormality?

Exercise Two—Twins and the Environment

Twin studies are frequently used to disentangle the effects of nature (heredity) and nurture (environment). In order for these studies to serve their stated purpose, several assumptions must be made. The purpose of this exercise is to examine critically one of these assumptions:

that the "environment" of identical twins is the same as the "environment" of fraternal twins.

One person of every eighty-six people is a twin. Find some of these individuals, and talk to them about being a twin. Ask these individuals if they are identical or not. Ask about their social environment—which includes their twin—as they were growing up. Do identical twins describe a different environment than fraternal twins?

Scheinfeld, A. (1967). *Twins and supertwins.* Philadelphia: Lippincott.

Exercise Three—Adoption and Resemblance

Just like twins, adopted children are also often studied to separate the contributions of genes and upbringing. Locate some adoptees and ask them how they view the nature-nurture question. Which factor do they believe contributed the most to who they are now? Are there char-acteristics of their personality that they attribute almost exclusively to the influence of their adopted family? Are there aspects of themselves that they feel to be independent of their environment—features that they believe would have developed just as they did regardless how they had been raised? Why do they believe this?

Exercise Four—Selection of Complex Traits

Consider the heritable traits listed in the text (p. 54):

1) How might extremes on a subset of these traits (very high or very low trait charac-teristics) interact with each other and with your society to produce highly de-sirable or undesirable behavior?

2) How might these traits be very produc-tive or counterproductive in different subcultures within your society or at different times in your country's history?

CHAPTER 4

Psychodynamic and Existential Approaches

CHAPTER OVERVIEW

This chapter describes one of the important psychological approaches to abnormality, the psychodynamic model, which originated in the work of the Viennese physician Sigmund Freud. The psychodynamic model views abnormality as resulting from unconscious conflicts within the individual. These conflicts typically occur between instinctive sexual impulses and societal prohibitions internalized by the individual. Conflicts produce anxiety, which is thought to be at the root of abnormality.

Psychodynamic explanation is complex because of Freud's assumption that behavior is overdetermined, the product of numerous factors. Important to all of these factors is psychic energy, which seeks an outlet in pleasurable activities. The developing individual is thought to use this energy differently as maturation occurs. Development involves the passage through psychosexual stages defined by that part of the body with which pleasure is obtained: the mouth, the anus, the genitals.

Present at birth is the *id*, the seat of the instincts. As a result of socialization, there emerges the *superego*, or the conscience, and the *ego*, the arbitrator between id and superego. Because id impulses are threatening to the superego, the ego has at its disposal a variety of techniques called defense mechanisms that disguise one's true motives from one's conscious self.

Abnormality occurs when the individual's ego is weak relative to the id or the superego. Psychic energy is tied up in symptoms and is not available for more constructive purposes. Psychodynamic therapy attempts to bring underlying conflicts into consciousness.

Freud inspired a number of other theorists to propose energy-based conflict theories of abnormality, notably Carl Jung and Alfred Adler. These theorists did not emphasize sexuality to the degree that Freud did. Other theorists—the Neo-Freudians Karen Horney, Harry Stack Sullivan, and Erik Erikson—were also inspired by Freud and proposed theories that viewed people as inherently social.

Psychoanalytic theory suffers from two problems. First, it is difficult to verify. Second, it was based on observations of a small number of individuals: clients in psychoanalytic therapy. Modern approaches have tried to correct these flaws and in particular concern themselves with the self, which gives personality its unity.

This concern overlaps with the existential approach, which sees abnormality resulting from one's failure to deal successfully with fundamental questions about life and existence. People are viewed as responsible for their actions and their destinies; and they are seen as intrinsically motivated to fulfill their inner potentials.

ESSENTIAL TERMS

anal character	personality traits of orderliness, stinginess, and stubbornness thought to result from fixation at the anal stage of psychosexual development (p. 64)
anxiety	in psychoanalytic theory, psychic pain (p. 79)
realistic anxiety	expectation that real-world events may be harmful (p. 79)
neurotic anxiety	expectation that one will be overwhelmed by one's own unconscious impulses (p. 79)
moral anxiety	expectation that one's behavior will violate one's moral standards; conscience (p. 80)
archetype	in Jung's psychodynamic theory, a universal idea obtained in the collective unconscious (p. 81)
authenticity	in existential theories, acting to achieve attainable goals (p. 98)
castration anxiety	fear among young boys that their father will castrate them because of their incestuous desire (p. 75)
catharsis	in psychoanalytic theory, the release of psychic energy resulting from uncovering and reliving early traumatic conflicts (*see* also Chapter 2, "Essential Terms") (p. 104)
client-centered therapy	therapy founded by Carl Rogers that attempts to change the self-regard of an individual through unconditional positive regard and empathy on the part of the therapist (p. 106)
collective unconscious	in Jung's psychodynamic theory, memory traces of experience of past generations (p. 81)
core self	sense of physical separateness and unity (p. 84)
counterphobia	a reaction formation in which individuals pursue deeply feared activities (p. 90)
death anxiety	in existential theories, the central human fear: fear of dying (p. 97)
defense mechanism	in psychoanalytic theory, the technique used by the mind to cope with painful psychological events (p. 87)
denial	in psychoanalytical theory, active ignoring of distressing external events (p. 92)
displacement	in psychoanalytic theory, replacement of a true objective with a less threatening objective (p. 90)
ego	in psychoanalytic theory, mental representation of reality requirements (p. 76)
erogenous zones	pleasure centers (p. 73)
exhortative will	in existential theories, the ability to force oneself to do things at odds with immediate desires (p. 100)

fixation	in psychoanalytic theory, not progressing from one stage of psychosexual development to the next (p. 73)
fusion	in existential theories, a way to deal with death anxiety by attaching oneself to others and making oneself indistinguishable from them (p. 97)
goal-directed will	in existential theories, the ability to work toward future goals, to make specific wishes come true (p. 100)
hypochondriasis	conviction in the absence of medical evidence that one is ill or about to become ill (p. 93)
id	in psychoanalytic theory, mental representation of biological processes (p. 76)
identification	process by which characteristics of others are internalized (p. 90)
intellectualization	in psychoanalytic theory, repression of emotional components of experience and their restating in abstract and analytic terms (p. 92)
intersubjectivity	the sense of understanding another's intentions and feelings, sharing of experiences (p. 84)
introcosm	subjective psychological space that is the storehouse of personal experience within each person (p. 83)
isolation	in psychoanalytic theory, repression of affective components of a threatening experience and retention of informational components (p. 92)
libido	psychic energy associated with a variety of pleasurable activities (p. 72)
Neo-Freudians	theorists like Horney, Sullivan, and Erikson who followed Freud, emphasizing unconscious motives but downplaying sexuality and stressing the social nature of people (p. 81)
Oedipus complex	desire among young children to do away with the same-sex parent and to take the opposite-sex parent for themselves (p. 74)
oral character	personality traits of dependence and distrust thought to result from fixation at the oral stage of psychosexual development (p. 73)
overdetermined behavior	in psychoanalytic theory, the notion that every behavior has numerous determinants (p. 108)
penis envy	desire among young girls to have a penis (p. 75)
perceptual consciousness	refers to the small number of mental events to which the individual is presently attending (p. 78)
pleasure principle	immediate impulse gratification that characterizes the id (p. 76)

preconscious	consists of the information and impulses that are not at the center of attention but can be relatively easily retrieved (p. 78)
projection	in psychoanalytic theory attribution of private under-standings and meanings to others (p. 88)
assimilative projection	projection of a quality of which one is aware (p. 89)
disowning projection	projection of a quality that one denies having (p. 89)
psychic energy	in psychoanalytic theory, energy that fuels psychological life (p. 72)
psychoanalysis	Freud's psychodynamic theory; also, his methods of studying and changing personality (p. 72)
psychodynamic theory	theory of behavior concerned with unconscious psycho-logical forces (p. 71)
psychosexual development	in psychoanalytic theory, description of development em-phasizing passage through stages defined by the means by which pleasure is achieved: oral, anal, phallic, latency, and genital (p. 72)
psychosocial development	in psychodynamic theory, description of development em-phasizing passage through stages defined by dominant means of interaction with others (p. 81)
rationalization	in psychoanalytic theory, assignment to behavior of so-cially desirable motives (p. 92)
reaction formation	in psychoanalytic theory, repression of one impulse and substitution of its opposite (p. 90)
reality principle	delayed and realistic impulse gratification that charac-terizes the ego (p. 76)
repression	in psychoanalytic theory, active deflection of material from consciousness (p. 87)
responsibility	in existential theories, awareness that one has created one's own self, life, and destiny (p. 99)
self-coherence	sense that one is physically unified (p. 84)
self-history	perception of one's continuity through time (p. 84)
self-objects	people and things providing support to personality cohe-siveness (p. 85)
self theory	contemporary psychodynamic theory that emphasizes the self: how it develops, is experienced, and is defended (p. 83)
specialness	in existential theories, a way to deal with death anxiety by regarding oneself as special and not subject to the laws of nature (p. 97)
sublimation	in psychoanalytic theory, transfer of libido to socially val-ued activities (p. 93)

subjective self	sense of understanding each others' intentions and feelings, as well as the sharing of experiences about things and events (p. 84)
superego	in psychoanalytic theory, conscience and ideals (p. 76)
transference	in psychoanalytic theory, transfer by clients of emotions, conflicts, and expectations from diverse sources on to their therapist (p. 105)
unconditional positive regard	in client-centered therapy, the therapist's acceptance of and respect for the client regardless of what is said or done (p. 106)
unconscious	material not available to awareness (p. 79)
verbal self	self as a storehouse of knowledge and experience (p. 84)

CENTRAL CONCEPTUAL ISSUES

Freud in his time.   In the context of the burgeoning industrial revolution, with scientists exploring the possibilities of hydraulics and electricity and having great success in converting energy into mechanical work, Sigmund Freud developed the concepts of psychic energy (e.g., libido) and its conversion to human industry (action/behavior) through the controlling influences of the id, the ego, and the superego.

Psychodynamic assumptions.   The term psychodynamic is used to describe Freud's model of human behavior and those models which have evolved from one or more of Freud's theoretical contributions. The term captures the insight that psychic energy and the interaction of forces within the individual drive human behavior. Freud's proposition that these forces may work at an *unconscious* level is of equal importance in defining the class of theories labeled psychodynamic. Together, these two postulates clearly distinguish psychodynamic theories from the cognitive, behavioral, or biomedical schools of psychology.

Energy, conflict and resolution.   Using the indepth analysis of individuals afforded by case studies, Freud constructed theories to explain the development of individuals from infancy to adulthood as an interplay between three processes—*id, ego, and superego*—which guide the expression of psychic energy. Freud posited that the manner in which these conflicts are resolved determines whether the individual moves successfully through each psychosexual stage or becomes fixated at a particular level in development. Unsuccessful or maladaptive resolution of conflict at any stage results in forms of abnormal behavior specific to the level of development at which the failure occurred.

Id, ego, and superego.   The two irrational processes of *id* and *superego*—which direct psychic energy along the lines of the pleasure principle and unfettered conscience, respectively—are medicated by the reality testing "executive" of the personality, the *ego*. In Freudian theory, the "normal" personality is one in which psychic energy is appropriately distributed among these three processes. Proper allotment of energy to the ego gives it the wherewithal to direct or restrain the influences of the id and superego through the use of defense mechanisms. An unbalanced distribution of energy to the id or superego results in the expression of biological energy without regard for consequences or appropriateness, hence abnormal behavior. If the id is insufficiently inhibited or directed by the ego, the individual will lack impulse control, indulging every urge as it arises. If the superego is not kept in check, it will follow the edict of "Thou shalt not . . ." and will unduly restrict the expression of biological energy making the individual uncomfortable with pleasure and hounded by conscience. The task of the ego is to mediate between the goals of the id and superego and the constraints of reality, in the management of this energy system.

Anxiety.   In Freud's view, anxiety indicates a conflict between the various personality processes that may be threatening to break through to consciousness or influence behavior. In response, the mind deploys defense mechanisms to cope with the conflict and reduce the anxiety. Nevertheless, because this is a dynamic model, the energy inhibited by the superego or ego, or kept from consciousness by defense mechanisms, sometimes finds a way to the surface even in normal individuals through, for example, dreams, slips of the tongue, or other symbolic behaviors. Poorly developed defense mechanisms or anxiety that overwhelms attempts at coping can result in serious psychopathology.

Psychodynamic treatment.   To remediate psychopathology (e.g., neuroses, psychoses), Freud developed a system of therapy whereby a patient can become conscious of the conflict underlying his or her state, and through understanding and insight into the origins and meaning of the conflict is able to defuse the energy associated with it, energy that may be tied up in the defense mechanisms developed to manage it and/or expressed in the psychopathological symptoms prompted by it. This therapeutic approach, which includes such methods as free association, dream analysis, catharsis, and analysis of transference and resistance, is called *psychoanalysis.*

For existential theorists, fear of dying, failure to take responsibility for one's life, and disorders of will can all subvert an individual's natural tendency toward psychological growth and result in inauthentic modes of behavior. Confrontation and resolution of these issues is essential to the process of personal growth. Through both empathy, respect, and unconditional positive regard, *client-centered therapists* make their clients fell both heard and accepted thereby creating an environment conducive to learning and change.

The psychodynamic view of normality and abnormality.   Of particular importance to the modern conceptions of abnormality is Freud's suggestion that the fundamental processes that underlie both normal and abnormal behaviors are the same. It is the *outcome* of the conflict and the *nature* of the defense mechanisms that determine whether behavior will be normal or abnormal. Two important implications of this are that normal and abnormal persons are fundamentally the same, and that behavior, even "crazy" behavior, is potentially tractable.

SAMPLE EXAM

1. Psychodynamic theories are so named because of their concern with
    a. strong personalities.
    b. biological processes.
    c. psychological forces.
    d. personality disorders.
    e. physical urges.

2. Freud's theory of studying and changing personality is called
    a. dynanalysis.
    b. ego therapy.
    c. self psychology.
    d. psychoanalysis.
    e. depth psychology.

3. One of the most important concerns of Freud was
   a. physical forces.
   b. psychic energy.
   c. will power.
   d. mental telepathy.
   e. animal magnetism.

4. Which of the following does not belong?
   a. psychic energy
   b. libido
   c. lust
   d. IQ
   e. id energy

5. A child gains pleasure from sucking. In what stage of psychosexual development is this child?
   a. oral
   b. anal
   c. phallic
   d. genital
   e. latency

6. A child gains pleasure from eliminating. In what stage of psychosexual development is this child?
   a. oral
   b. anal
   c. phallic
   d. genital
   e. latency

7. A child gains pleasure from masturbating. In what stage of psychosexual development is this child?
   a. oral
   b. anal
   c. phallic
   d. genital
   e. latency

8. In *The Odd Couple*, Felix is fixated at what stage of psychosexual development?
   a. oral
   b. anal
   c. phallic
   d. genital
   e. latency

9. In *The Odd Couple*, Oscar is fixated at what stage of psychosexual development?
   a. oral
   b. anal
   c. phallic
   d. genital
   e. latency

10. All of the following are part of the Oedipal complex for boys except
    a. desire to do away with same-sex parent.
    b. desire to possess opposite-sex parent.
    c. desire to become the opposite sex.
    d. fear of retaliation.
    e. thinking females have been castrated.

11. Who was Oedipus?
    a. a character of Greek legends
    b. one of Freud's first patients
    c. the mayor of Vienna
    d. one of Freud's teachers
    e. a hungry dog

12. Castration anxiety is to little boys as what is to little girls?
    a. hysteria
    b. penis envy
    c. genital fixation
    d. womb worry
    e. frigidity

13. According to Freud, the result of the successful resolution of the Oedipal complex is
    a. schizophrenia.
    b. hysteria.
    c. identification.
    d. deviance.
    e. fixation.

14. The Oedipal complex occurs during which stage of psychosexual development?
    a. oral
    b. anal
    c. phallic
    d. latency
    e. genital

15. In which stage of psychosexual development is sexuality repressed?
    a. oral
    b. anal
    c. phallic
    d. latency
    e. genital

16. Which of these processes is present first?
    a. id
    b. ego
    c. superego
    d. sublimation
    e. none of the above

17. Id is to pleasure principle as what is to reality principle?
    a. libido
    b. ego
    c. superego
    d. sublimation
    e. none of the above

18. Freud characterized the relationship among id, ego, and superego as
    a. harmonious.
    b. hierarchical.
    c. independent.
    d. conflicting.
    e. mutually supportive.

19. Most of the time, one's telephone number is
    a. conscious.
    b. pre-conscious.
    c. unconscious.
    d. subconscious.
    e. metaconscious.

20. According to Freud, material is unconscious because it
    a. has been poorly learned.
    b. has been forgotten.
    c. is not interesting.
    d. it is too interesting.
    e. has been repressed.

21. The fear of real-world events is termed
    a. realistic anxiety.
    b. high anxiety.
    c. neurotic anxiety.
    d. moral anxiety.
    e. social anxiety.

22. The fear of one's impulses is termed
    a. realistic anxiety.
    b. high anxiety.
    c. neurotic anxiety.
    d. moral anxiety.
    e. social anxiety.

23. The fear that one's behavior will violate one's standards is termed
    a. realistic anxiety.
    b. high anxiety.
    c. neurotic anxiety.
    d. moral anxiety.
    e. social anxiety.

24. The text criticizes early psychoanalytic theory on grounds of
    a. a principle.

    b. generalizability.
    c. verifiability.
    d. both b and c
    e. neither b nor c

25. The collective unconscious is associated with
    a. Sigmund Freud.
    b. Carl Rogers.
    c. Carl Jung.
    d. Alfred Adler.
    e. Erich Fromm.

26. According to Jung, an archetype is
    a. a universal idea.
    b. a dream.
    c. a myth unique to a culture.
    d. a signature.
    e. a product of learning.

27. Who among the following does not belong?
    a. Alfred Adler
    b. Karen Horney
    c. Carl Rogers
    d. Harry Stack Sullivan
    e. Erich Fromm

28. The Neo-Freudians differed from Freud by
    a. de-emphasizing sexuality.
    b. de-emphasizing social aspects of people.
    c. ignoring defense mechanisms.
    d. downplaying consciousness.
    e. re-emphasizing the unconscious.

29. Modern psychodynamic theories focus mainly on
    a. development.
    b. instincts.
    c. needs.
    d. the self.
    e. sexual identity.

30. The first "self" to emerge is the
    a. core self.
    b. intersubjective self.
    c. surface self.
    d. subjective self.
    e. verbal self.

31. Physical unity is the province of the
    a. core self.
    b. intersubjective self.
    c. subjective self.
    d. verbal self.
    e. surface self.

32. The "self" that allows us to understand others is the
    a. core self.
    b. surface self.
    c. subjective self.
    d. verbal self.
    e. intersubjective self.

33. Self theory terms the important others in one's life
    a. meaningful relationships.
    b. other objects.
    c. self objects.
    d. ego objects.
    e. them.

34. A defense mechanism is a
    a. response to external threat.
    b. coping strategy of the ego.
    c. biochemical process that combats infection.
    d. means of winning arguments with others.
    e. good offense.

35. An individual forgets the details of a painful experience. This is an example of what defense mechanism?
    a. repression
    b. sublimation
    c. regression
    d. projection
    e. reaction formation
    f. displacement
    g. denial
    h. isolation
    i. rationalization
    j. intellectualization

36. An individual keeps the bedroom of a dead relative intact. This is an example of what defense mechanism?
    a. repression
    b. sublimation
    c. regression
    d. projection
    e. reaction formation
    f. displacement
    g. denial
    h. isolation
    i. rationalization
    j. intellectualization

37. An individual pursues medicine as a career. This is an example of what defense mechanism?
    a. repression

    b. sublimation
    c. regression
    d. projection
    e. reaction formation
    f. displacement
    g. denial
    h. isolation
    i. rationalization
    j. intellectualization

38. An individual says that she hates someone who is dear. This is an example of what defense mechanism?
    a. repression
    b. sublimation
    c. regression
    d. projection
    e. reaction formation
    f. displacement
    g. denial
    h. isolation
    i. rationalization
    j. intellectualization

39. Counterphobia is an example of what defense mechanism?
    a. repression
    b. sublimation
    c. regression
    d. projection
    e. reaction formation
    f. displacement
    g. denial
    h. isolation
    i. rationalization
    j. intellectualization

40. An individual who cannot play professional sports becomes a Little League coach. This is an example of what defense mechanism?
    a. repression
    b. sublimation
    c. regression
    d. projection
    e. reaction formation
    f. displacement
    g. denial
    h. isolation
    i. rationalization
    j. intellectualization

41. Identification is the opposite of what defense mechanism?
    a. repression

b. sublimation
c. regression
d. projection
e. reaction formation
f. displacement
g. denial
h. isolation
i. rationalization
j. intellectualization

42. Identification with the aggressor is thought to
a. be a way to ridicule powerful others.
b. occur frequently among happy individuals.
c. help overcome fear and inadequacy.
d. result from jealousy.
e. require empathy.

43. An individual matter-of-factly discusses the recent death of her child. This is an example of what defense mechanism?
a. repression
b. sublimation
c. regression
d. projection
e. reaction formation
f. displacement
g. denial
h. isolation
i. rationalization
j. intellectualization

44. An individual argues against clear evidence that his child is seriously ill. This is an example of what defense mechanism?
a. repression
b. sublimation
c. regression
d. projection
e. reaction formation
f. displacement
g. denial
h. isolation
i. rationalization
j. intellectualization

45. A student studies hard but fails a test. He then claims that the material was not worth knowing. This is an example of what defense mechanism?
a. repression
b. sublimation
c. regression
d. projection

e. reaction formation
f. displacement
g. denial
h. isolation
i. rationalization
j. intellectualization

46. A recently divorced individual provides an elaborate explanation of why her marriage failed. This is an example of what defense mechanism?
a. repression
b. sublimation
c. regression
d. projection
e. reaction formation
f. displacement
g. denial
h. isolation
i. rationalization
j. intellectualization

47. Which of these defense mechanisms is the most mature?
a. denial
b. sublimation
c. projection
d. displacement
e. repression

48. Which of these defense mechanisms is the least mature?
a. denial
b. sublimation
c. projection
d. displacement
e. humor

49. The study of Harvard graduates between 1939 and 1942 revealed that mature defense mechanisms were associated with
a. psychological adjustment in later life.
b. social adjustment in later life.
c. medical adjustment in later life.
d. career adjustment in later life.
e. all of the above.

50. According to existential psychologists, the central human fear is
a. castration fear.
b. fear of death.
c. fear of self-actualization.
d. fear of childhood.
f. fear of failure.

51. How are specialness and fusion similar?
a. Both are means of self-actualization.

b. Both are ways to cope with fear of death.
c. Both are innate defense mechanisms.
d. Both are instances of Pavlovian conditioning.
e. Both are disorders.

52. The workaholic may be exemplifying
a. specialness.
b. catharsis.
c. authenticity.
d. fusion.
e. transference.

53. The individual who identifies himself as a Jaycee may be exemplifying
a. specialness.
b. catharsis.
c. authenticity.
d. fusion.
e. transference.

54. Existential psychology is particularly opposed to psychoanalysis and behaviorism with regard to
a. the role of responsibility.
b. the role of the environment.
c. the role of thought processes.
d. the role of conflict.
e. the role of anxiety.

55. All of the following ways of talking avoid responsibility except
a. the use of the passive voice.
b. the avoidance of first-person pronouns.
c. reference to freedom.
d. mention of the past.
e. losing control.

56. Goal-directed will is concerned with
a. the past.
b. the present.
c. the future.
d. death.
e. none of the above.

57. According to existential psychologists, all of the following are true about wishes except that
a. wishes are general.
b. wishes make willing possible.
c. wishes may be confused.
d. wishes create vulnerability.
e. wishes may be unclear.

58. Psychoanalytic therapy attempts to free psychic energy because
a. psychic energy can be used in other, more constructive ways.
b. neurotic individuals have no libido.
c. there is an energy crisis.
d. conscious conflicts are harmful.
e. psychic energy is destructive.

59. A client confesses that he loves his therapist. This is an example of
a. sublimation.
b. transference.
c. repression.
d. moral anxiety.
e. catharsis.

60. Client-centered therapy is characterized by all of the following except concern with
a. feeling accepted.
b. responsibility.
c. experience.
d. freedom.
e. early experiences.

61. Which one of the following is *not* important for client-centered therapy?
a. diagnosis
b. unconditional positive regard
c. empathy
d. reflection
e. all of the above are important.

62. Among the shortcomings of psychoanalytic theory are all these except
a. reliance on individual cases.
b. demystification of abnormality.
c. neglect of situation.
d. relative inefficacy of psychoanalytic therapy.
e. difficult to prove or disprove.

63. Overdetermined behavior means that
a. lower mental abilities are caused by higher mental abilities.
b. each behavior has numerous determinants.
c. all behavior is determined by an overriding sexual drive.
d. important behaviors have causes, but unimportant behaviors do not.
e. behavior is controlled by the superego.

Answer Key for Sample Exam

1.	c	(p. 71)	17.	b	(p. 76)	33.	c	(p. 85)	49.	e	(p. 94)
2.	d	(p. 72)	18.	d	(p. 78)	34.	b	(p. 87)	50.	b	(p. 97)
3.	b	(p. 72)	19.	b	(p. 78)	35.	a	(p. 87)	51.	b	(p. 97)
4.	d	(p. 72)	20.	e	(p. 79)	36.	g	(p. 92)	52.	a	(p. 97)
5.	a	(p. 73)	21.	a	(p. 79)	37.	b	(p. 93)	53.	d	(p. 98)
6.	b	(p. 73)	22.	c	(p. 79)	38.	e	(p. 90)	54.	a	(p. 99)
7.	c	(p. 74)	23.	d	(p. 80)	39.	e	(p. 90)	55.	c	(p. 99)
8.	b	(p. 73)	24.	d	(p. 80)	40.	f	(p. 90)	56.	c	(p. 100)
9.	b	(p. 73)	25.	c	(p. 81)	41.	d	(p. 90)	57.	a	(p. 101)
10.	c	(p. 74)	26.	a	(p. 81)	42.	c	(p. 90)	58.	a	(p. 102)
11.	a	(p. 74)	27.	c	(p. 81)	43.	h	(p. 92)	59.	b	(p. 105)
12.	b	(p. 74)	28.	a	(p. 81)	44.	g	(p. 92)	60.	e	(p. 106)
13.	c	(p. 75)	29.	d	(p. 82)	45.	i	(p. 92)	61.	a	(p. 106)
14.	c	(p. 74)	30.	a	(p. 83)	46.	j	(p. 92)	62.	b	(p. 107)
15.	d	(p. 75)	31.	a	(p. 84)	47.	b	(p. 95)	63.	b	(p. 108)
16.	a	(p. 76)	32.	c	(p. 84)	48.	a	(p. 95)			

SELF-TEST

1. Psychodynamic theories are concerned with inner _____ that are _____ to the individual.

2. Freud's psychodynamic theory is called _____.

3. The most important psychoanalytic concept is that of _____.

4. The five psychosexual stages are _____, _____, _____, _____, and _____; they are defined by the way in which _____ is obtained.

5. If an individual does not pass through a stage of psychosexual development, he is _____ at that stage.

6. People fixated at the oral stage show _____ as adults.

7. People fixated at the anal stage show _____, _____, and _____ as adults.

8. The important conflict during the phallic stage of psychosexual development is the _____, in which the child wishes to _____ the same-sex parent and _____ the opposite-sex parent.

9. Accompanying the Oedipus complex is _____ among boys and _____ among girls.

10. The outcome of the Oedipus complex is thought to be _____ with the _____ parent.

11. The transfer of libidinal energy to socially valued activities is called _____ and occurs during the _____ stage of psychosexual development.

12. Freud described three interacting processes that comprise personality. The _____ is the source of instincts; the _____ is the internalization of societal demands; and the _____ arbitrates between the two.

13. The id operates according to the _____ principle, while the ego operates according to the _____ principle.

14. The three levels of consciousness described by Freud are _____, _____, and _____.

15. Material is unconscious because it has been _____.

16. According to Freud, conflicts are accompanied by the signal of _____.

17. Fear of real-world events is _____ anxiety.

18. Fear of one's impulses is _____ anxiety.

19. Fear that one will violate one's personal standards is _____ anxiety.

20. Theorists who build upon the ideas of Freud are called _____.

21. Jung proposed that we not only have a personal unconscious but also a _____ made up of memories from our ancestors; among these memories are universal ideas called _____.

22. In contrast to Freud's psychosexual stages, the Neo-Freudians describe development in terms of _____ stages.

23. Modern psychodynamic theories emphasize the _____.

24. According to self theory, the three aspects of the self are the _____, _____, and _____ selves.

25. The coping strategies deployed against anxiety are _____.

26. The defense mechanism that forces undesired thoughts into the unconscious is _____.

27. The defense mechanism in which undesired characteristics and impulses are attributed to others is _____.

28. The defense mechanism in which an impulse is substituted for its opposite is _____.

29. The defense mechanism in which the target of an impulse is replaced with a less threatening target is _____.

30. The defense mechanism that is the opposite of projection is _____.

31. The striking phenomenon observed in concentration camps in which some Jewish inmates imitated the Nazi guards is _____.

32. The defense mechanism in which objective facts are ignored is _____.

33. The defense mechanism in which only the affective components of experience are deleted from consciousness is _____.

34. The defense mechanism in which a painful experience is given an elaborate interpretation is _____.

35. The defense mechanism in which implausible excuses are offered is _____.

36. Research suggests that _____ defense mechanisms such as _____ result in social, psychological, and medical well-being.

37. The issues of primary concern to the existential psychologists are _____, _____, and _____.

38. According to existential psychologists, people cope with fear of death through _____ and _____.

39. A false mode of acting, one that attempts to achieve unattainable goals, is _____.

40. Existential psychologists are strongly opposed to traditional psychoanalysts and behaviorists on the issue of whether people have _____ for their lives.

41. One of the ways in which people seem to avoid taking responsibility is through their _____.

42. The two forms of will are _____ will and _____ will.

43. Goal-directed willing arises from the capacity to _____.

44. Psychoanalytic therapy attempts to make conflicts _____.

45. When clients transfer their own emotions, conflicts, and expectations to their therapists, this is called _____.

46. In _____ therapy, the therapist attempts to provide unconditional positive regard.

47. Shortcomings of the psychodynamic model of abnormality include _____, _____, _____, _____, and _____.

48. According to psychoanalytic theory, behavior is _____.

Answer Key for Self-Test

1. conflicts; unconscious
2. psychoanalysis
3. psychic energy
4. oral; anal; phallic; latency; genital; pleasure
5. fixated
6. dependency
7. orderliness; stinginess; stubbornness
8. Oedipus complex; do away with; possess
9. castration anxiety; penis envy
10. identification; same-sex
11. sublimation; genital
12. id; superego; ego
13. pleasure; reality
14. perceptual consciousness; preconscious; unconscious
15. repressed
16. anxiety
17. realistic
18. neurotic
19. moral
20. Neo-Freudians
21. collective unconscious; archetypes
22. psychosocial
23. self
24. core; subjective; verbal
25. defense mechanisms
26. repression
27. projection
28. reaction formation
29. displacement
30. identification
31. identification with the aggressor
32. denial
33. isolation
34. intellectualization
35. rationalization
36. mature; sublimation
37. fear of dying; responsibility; will
38. specialness; fusion.
39. inauthenticity
40. responsibility
41. language
42. exhortative; goal-directed
43. wish
44. conscious
45. transference
46. client-centered
47. reliance on individual cases; difficulty of proof; lack of scientific support; neglect of situation; ineffectiveness of therapy
48. overdetermined

MATCHING ITEMS

_____	1.	catharsis	A.	psychic energy
_____	2.	libido	B.	unconditional positive regard
_____	3.	Horney	C.	memory
_____	4.	transference	D.	collective unconscious
_____	5.	intersubjectivity	E.	social anxiety
_____	6.	identification	F.	neurotic anxiety
_____	7.	ego	G.	internalize
_____	8.	superego	H.	connectedness
_____	9.	id	I.	control
_____	10.	repression	J.	coping strategies
_____	11.	Freud	K.	psychosocial development
_____	12.	defense mechanisms	L.	castration anxiety
_____	13.	Erikson	M.	abstract analysis

_____ 14. Rogers

_____ 15. archetypes

_____ 16. intellectualization

_____ 17. sublimation

_____ 18. penis envy

_____ 19. anal

_____ 20. oral

N. reliving traumatic conflicts

O. conscience

P. projecting own expectations, attributions

Q. psychosexual development

R. dependent

S. constructive rechanneling

T. reality principle

Answer Key for Matching Items

1.	N	11.	Q
2.	A	12.	J
3.	E	13.	K
4.	P	14.	B
5.	H	15.	D
6.	G	16.	M
7.	T	17.	S
8.	O	18.	L
9.	F	19.	I
10.	C	20.	R

SHORT-ANSWER QUESTIONS

1. Describe each of the first three psycho-sexual stages of development proposed by Freud. What are the specific consequences for developing child's personality if he or she fails to adequately navigate through the challenges faced at any of these stages?

2. According to Freud, anxiety is central to a great deal of psychopathology. Where does it originate and why? Explain the role of defense mechanisms in this view.

3. What are the "mature" defense mechanisms and why does the text say we should strive for them?

4. In what ways are classical psychoanalysis and brief psychotherapy similar?

5. How would a Freudian explain a case of multiple personality? How might he or she treat it?

6. Compare and contrast the assumptions and psychotherapeutic methods of psychoanalytic and existential approaches to psychopathology.

7. What are the relative strengths and weaknesses of psychodynamic theories?

TYING IT TOGETHER

Although Freud discovered that disorders could have psychological causes instead of physical causes, the psychodynamic approach shares some characteristics with the biomedical approach (Chapter 3). Both look beyond the behavior of a troubled individual to presumed underlying causes. Psychic energy is analogous to physical energy, and Freud wrote about mental processes as if they were literal "things" within a person, like viruses or bacteria. Clinical case histories (Chapter 6) were patterned after medical histories. Freud's training as a neurologist is shown in the psychodynamic approach, which embodies many neurological principles (Chapter 17).

Psychological assessment and testing have been greatly influenced by the psychodynamic model (Chapter 7). In particular, projective tests like the Rorschach and past diagnostic schemes like DSM-II look beyond what the individual is doing on the surface to find an underlying basis to his or her "symptoms." To a large degree, the diagnostic scheme currently in use, DSM-IV, embodies less of a biomedical/psychodynamic flavor. However, it still retains terminology originating with Freud, particularly in his theorizing about anxiety disorders (Chapters 8 and 9).

The psychodynamic model proposes explanations of most of the disorders covered in Chapters 8 and 17. Some of these explanations seem more reasonable than others. In particular, psychodynamic explanations fare well when applied to disorders with some "depth" to them: hysteria (Chapter 9), amnesia (Chapter 9), and depression (Chapter 11). Like biomedical explanations, psychoanalytic explanations can be faulted for neglecting the role of environmental factors and conscious thought (Chapter 5). To the degree that disorders reflect the influence of these, psychoanalytic explanations fall short.

The existential approach is more interested in psychological health than in psychological disorder, in experience than in research. Accordingly, it is not surprising that this approach has little to say about how to explain disorders (Chapters 8 through 17) or how to remediate them (Chapter 19). Indeed, since the existential approach usually disavows any strict determinism, it has not given rise to much traditional research, which is concerned with the isolation of causes (Chapter 6).

Nevertheless, the existential approach offers an important criticism of what is neglected by the other models. Other approaches sometimes fail because they neglect the questions of choice and meaning deemed important by the existential approach. Thus, drug abuse is not fully understood until an individual's reasons for choosing to use drugs are addressed (Chapter 14). Schizophrenia may be as much a statement about the meaning of life in an insane world as it is an insufficiency of neurotransmitter (Chapter 12). Successful psychotherapies are those in which the client and the therapist treat each other as human beings (Chapter 19).

Of all the models surveyed in the textbook, the existential approach is most compatible with common-sense notions. Not surprisingly, it is the only model that seems to fit with legal aspects of abnormality (Chapter 18) since the legal system is importantly based on the idea of free will and individual responsibility. As you read about how the other models explain and treat disorders, you should consider whether these disorders involve deficiencies in will and responsibility, perhaps occasioned by an oppressive environment. The existential approach shares with the psychodynamic approach a view of the environment as coercive. Both models assume a human nature that is easily thwarted by others.

FURTHER READINGS

Allport, G. W. (1955). *Becoming: Basic considerations for a psychology of personality.* New Haven, CN: Yale University.

Brown, J. A. C. (1966). *Freud and the Post-Freudians.* Baltimore: Penguin.

Erikson, E. H. (1963). *Childhood and society* (2nd ed.). New York: Norton.

Erikson, E. H. (1968). *Identity: Youth and crisis.* New York: Norton.

Eysenck, H. J. (1985). *Decline and fall of the Freudian empire.* New York: Penguin.

Fancher, R. (1973). *Psychoanalytic psychology: The development of Freud's thought.* New York: Norton.

Freud, A. (1946). *The ego and the mechanisms of defense.* New York: International Universities Press.

Freud, S. (1952). *On dreams.* New York: Norton.

Freud, S. (1963). *Jokes and their relation to the unconscious.* New York: Norton.

Freud, S. (1963). *Three case histories.* New York: Collier.

Freud, S. (1966). *Introductory lectures on psychoanalysis.* New York: Norton.

Freud, S. (1976). *The interpretation of dreams.* New York: Norton.

Fromm, E. (1941). *Escape from freedom.* New York: Rinehart.

Fromm, E. (1974). *The art of loving.* New York: Perennial Library.

Greenberg, J. R., & Mitchell, S. A. (1983). *Object relations in psychoanalytic theory.* Cambridge, MA: Harvard University Press.

Hall, C. S. (1954). *A primer of Freudian psychology.* New York: New American Library.

Horney, K. (1945). *Our inner conflicts: A constructive theory of neurosis.* New York: Norton.

Jones, E. (1953–57). *The life and work of Sigmund Freud* (3 vols.). New York: Basic Books.

Jung, C. (1964). *Man and his symbols.* New York: Dell.

Kohut, H. (1977). *The restoration of the self.* New York: International Universities Press.

Malcolm, J. (1982). *Psychoanalysis—The impossible profession.* New York: Random House.

Masson, J. M. (1985). *The assault on truth: Freud's suppression of the seduction theory.* New York: Penguin.

May, R. (1969). *Existential psychology* (2nd ed.). New York: Random House.

Rogers, C. (1961). *On becoming a person.* Boston: Houghton Mifflin.

Sullivan, H. S. (1953). *The interpersonal theory of psychiatry.* New York: Norton.

Vaillant, G. E. (1977). *Adaptation to life.* Boston: Little, Brown.

Wertheimer, M. (1978). Humanistic psychology and the humane but tough-minded psychologist. *American Psychologist, 33,* 739–745.

Yalom, I. D. (1980). *Existential psychotherapy.* New York: Basic Books.

TERM-PAPER TOPICS

1. Compare and contrast Freud and the Neo-Freudians. Does the work of the Neo-Freudians represent an extension of Freud's work or a drastic break from Freud's work?

2. Recent critics have charged that Freud's theory development was influenced by conflicts in his own life and corresponding defense mechanisms. Specifically, Jeffrey Masson has argued that Freud suppressed his personal knowledge of the widespread childhood sexual abuse of his time in favor of promoting his own formulation which cast childhood sexuality in terms of fantasy rather than stark reality. Evaluate the evidence which Masson offers in support of this view.

   Masson, J. M. (1985). *The assault on truth: Freud's suppression of the seduction theory.* New York: Penguin.

3. Existential psychology is antagonistic to research. Evaluate this claim. Take a strong stand, and defend it with examples.

4. Why is the effectiveness of psychoanalytic therapy so difficult to ascertain?

5. Compare and contrast DSM-II and DSM-IV. The former clearly embodies psychodynamic theory. What about the latter?

EXERCISES

Exercise One—Dream Analysis

This exercise allows you to evaluate an important Freudian hypothesis: dreams represent unconscious wishes.

Keep a notebook and pencil next to your bed. For a week, write down the dreams that you remember. Do this immediately upon awakening, and provide as much detail as you can. After the week, analyze what you have written. Are there recurrent themes? Do these themes pertain to important aspects of your life—parents, romance, achievement? Do they seem to represent wishes that you may have? Do any of your dreams illustrate Freudian defense mechanisms such as displacement or reaction formation?

Freud, S. (1952). *On dreams*. New York: Norton.

Exercise Two—Freudian Slips

In this exercise you will evaluate another important Freudian hypothesis: "errors" such as slips of the tongue or slips of the pen reveal one's true motives.

Talk to individuals about "errors" they have made while speaking or writing. Are these slips sexual or aggressive in nature? Do they correspond with motives that these individuals would prefer not to acknowledge?

A favorite example of mine comes from a colleague who had a student who wrote an essay on the absurdity of Freudian symbolism. In that paper the sentence "A pen is not a phallic symbol" was typed without a space between "pen" and "is"—perhaps the result of the very process against which the student was arguing!

Freud, S. (1965). *The psychopathology of everyday life*. New York: Norton.

Exercise Three—Prejudice and Projection

The defense mechanism of projection involves the attribution to others of characteristics one does not like in oneself. In this exercise, you will look for examples of projection.

Talk to some individuals you know well about people or groups that they dislike. Ask them what it is that they dislike. Do these characteristics have anything to do with their own make-up?

Freud, S. (1936). *The problem of anxiety*. New York: Norton.

Exercise Four—Language and Responsibility

In this exercise, you will investigate an important existential hypothesis—that individuals may avoid taking responsibility for events in their life by the use of certain expressions.

Talk to graduate students about their thesis or dissertation research, and unobtrusively note if they refer to their research as *the* thesis or *the* dissertation—e.g., "When *the* dissertation is done, I can get a good job." Also ask them about their progress. Do students who objectify their research, who speak of it as if they have little to do with its start or finish, also have difficulties doing the research, as the existentialists predict?

Sometimes one sees a similar phenomenon well illustrated on rehabilitation wards in hospitals where many patients have suffered some loss of bodily function, through a stroke, an accident, and so on. Patients with paralyzed limbs sometimes refer to their arm or leg as *the* arm or *the* leg, as if it were no longer part of them. In one way this is a psychologically healthy way of speaking, because it helped the patients make a short-term adjustment to a serious loss. But in another way this is not a helpful way of speaking, because it encourages the patients not to take responsibility for solving their problems.

Exercise Five—Choice and Responsibility

The purpose of this exercise is to illustrate the existential idea that some individuals fail to make choices because they are afraid of being wrong.

Talk to friends who are graduating seniors about what they will be doing in the next few years. Pay attention to students who speak of "keeping options open." Are these the same individuals who do not have a good idea about what they will be doing? Are these the same individuals who are traumatized at the thought of leaving college?

Fromm, E. (1941). *Escape from freedom*. New York: Rinehart.

Exercise Six—Being a Good Listener

In this exercise, students will practice an empathic technique suggested by Carl Rogers.

When you talk to a friend, "reflect" back to him things that he says. That is, if he mentions that he is worried about a pending event, ask him to elaborate on his feelings about the event. If he says that he is happy, ask him to tell you about his happiness. And so on.

According to Rogers, by accepting what your friend says, you will help your friend accept himself. Above and beyond this possibility, I suspect that your friend will find you a good "conversationalist" since good conversationalists are usually those who help other people talk.

Rogers, C. R. (1951). *Client-centered therapy: Its current practice, implications, and theory*. Boston: Houghton Mifflin.

CHAPTER 5

The Learning Models: Behavioral and Cognitive Approaches

CHAPTER OVERVIEW

This chapter is concerned with behavioral and cognitive approaches to abnormality. According to the behavioral view, abnormal behavior is determined by the environment: it is the result of learning. The behavioral model thus regards therapy as a process of relearning, and it is optimistic that all disorders can thereby be treated.

The roots of the behavioral model lie in animal learning research, which distinguishes between two types of learning. The first is Pavlovian conditioning, in which individuals come to learn what goes with what as a result of pairings among stimuli in the environment. For instance, in Pavlov's original experiments, dogs learned to salivate at the sight of the experimenter since his presence had previously been paired with food, which reflexively elicits salivation. The second type of learning is operant conditioning, in which individuals come to learn what to do in order to obtain rewards and avoid punishments as a result of environmental response to behaviors. Thus, a child may learn to help with housework because he is given a special dessert after doing so.

Each type of learning gives rise to several therapy techniques. Pavlovian techniques such as flooding and desensitization are usually deployed against undesired emotional reactions. Operant techniques such as selective positive reinforcement and behavioral contracting are used to increase desired behaviors and decrease undesired ones.

The cognitive model regards abnormality as due to maladaptive thoughts. Cognitive therapy attempts to change the thoughts that give rise to abnormality. Among the targets of cognitive therapy are unrealistic and irrational expectations, appraisals, attributions, and beliefs. Depressed individuals may believe, for instance, that they are responsible for all the bad events in the world. Cognitive therapy would attempt to dissuade these people from their depressing beliefs.

ESSENTIAL TERMS

acquisition — process by which learning occurs; in Pavlovian conditioning, pairing of conditioned stimulus with unconditioned stimulus; in operant conditioning, pairing of an operant with reinforcement or punishment (p. 118)

appraisals	our evaluations about what happens to us and what we do; cognitive therapists believe that these automatic thoughts often precede and cause emotion and so may target them in therapy (p. 131)
associationism	movement that believes ideas congeal in the mind because they have been experienced together (p. 114)
attribution	individual's conception of why an event occurred; the consequences of an attribution depend on its qualities on three dimensions: external or internal, stable or unstable, and global or specific (p. 132)
avoidance learning	form of learning that involves both Pavlovian conditioning (learning what stimulus predicts an aversive event) and operant conditioning (learning to escape the stimulus, thereby avoiding the aversive event) (p. 127)
BASIC ID	notion of Arnold Lazarus that disorder occurs at seven different levels (B = behavior; A = affect; S = sensation; I = imagery; C = cognition; I = interpersonal relations; D = drugs) and that there are therapies appropriate to each of these modalities (p. 135)
behaviorism	movement within psychology that stresses overt actions and their shaping by the environment (p. 114)
beliefs	long-term cognitive processes that can, when irrational or illogical, yield distorted expectations, appraisals, and attributions; cognitive therapy often attacks or disputes faulty belief systems (p. 133)
cognitive-behavioral therapy	approach to therapy employing techniques based on the learning model and the cognitive model (p. 135)
cognitive therapy	therapy techniques based on the cognitive model of abnormality, which views mental events as causing disorder (p. 129)
conditional reflex (conditioned response; CR)	behavior acquired by Pavlovian conditioning (p. 117)
continuous reinforcement	reinforcement that occurs after every operant (p. 123)
discriminative stimulus	stimulus that signals that reinforcement is available if an operant is made (p. 122)
efficacy expectancy	person's estimate that he or she can successfully execute behavior necessary to produce a desired outcome (p. 130)
empiricism	movement that regards all ideas as resulting from experience (p. 113)
environmentalism	movement that regards all organisms, including humans, as being shaped by the environment (p. 114)
epiphenomenon	process that is not causal but that reflects an underlying process that is causal (p. 128)
extinction	process by which learning is "lost"; in Pavlovian conditioning, cessation of pairing of a conditioned stimulus with

	an unconditioned stimulus; in operant conditioning, cessation of pairing of an operant with reinforcement or punishment (p. 118)
flooding	therapy technique based on Pavlovian conditioning in which stimuli that elicit fear are repeatedly encountered (p. 120)
law of effect	Thorndike's principle of learning: when a response is followed by positive consequences, it tends to be repeated; when it is followed by negative consequences, it tends not to be repeated (p. 122)
multi-modal therapy	therapy that combines behavior, cognitive, and other techniques to address psychopathology at its different levels using techniques appropriate to each modality (see BASIC ID above) (p. 135)
nature-nurture issue	debate whether behavior is determined by heredity (nature) or environment (nurture) (p. 113)
negative reinforcer	stimulus that by its removal increases probability that a response preceding it will occur again (p. 122)
operant	response whose probability can be either increased by positive reinforcement or decreased by negative reinforcement (p. 122)
operant conditioning (instrumental conditioning)	form of learning described by Edward Thorndike and B. F. Skinner in which behaviors come to be associated with environmental consequences (rewards and punishments); trial-and-error learning (p. 121)
outcome expectancy	person's estimate that a given behavior will lead to a desired outcome (p. 130)
partial reinforcement	reinforcement that occurs after only some operants (p. 123)
Pavlovian conditioning (classical conditioning)	form of learning described by Ivan Pavlov in which environmental events (stimuli) come to elicit behaviors (responses) because they have been paired with other environmental events that do so reflexively (p. 116)
positive reinforcer	stimulus that by its presentation increases probability that a response preceding it will occur again (p. 122)
punisher	a stimulus whose onset decreases the probability that a response preceding it will occur again (p. 122)
rational-emotive therapy	therapy founded by Albert Ellis that attempts to change the irrational beliefs of an individual (p. 133)
rationalism	movement that regards certain basic ideas as inborn or innate (p. 113)
selective positive reinforcement	therapy technique based on operant conditioning in which probability of a desired target behavior is increased by delivering positive reinforcement contingent on this behavior (p. 125)

selective punishment | therapy technique based on operant conditioning in which the probability of an undesired target behavior is decreased by delivering punishment contingent on this behavior (p. 126)

stimulus generalization | tendency of a response conditioned to one stimulus to occur to similar stimuli (p. 118)

systematic desensitization | therapy technique based on Pavlovian conditioning in which stimuli that elicit fear are paired with relaxation or other pleasant experiences (p. 121)

CENTRAL CONCEPTUAL ISSUES

Behaviorism and empiricism.   As with most scientific schools of thought, the behavioral approach to psychology grew out of pre-existing philosophical doctrine, in this case empiricism. Building on the idea that all knowledge derives from experience—implying that a newborn infant's mind is *tabula rasa*—the behaviorists adopted the tenet that all behavior is therefore a product of the environment. Because the causes of behavior are external they can be best examined with controlled experimentation, and only that which can be measured empirically is considered suitable for study.

Avoidance learning.   Many relationships in life are learned initially through association (Pavlovian conditioning: this goes with that) and then maintained through the reinforcement (operant conditioning: doing this will get me that). Indeed, some maladaptive behaviors—particularly those related to anxiety—involve a combination of these lessons. In the avoidance learning model of psychopathology, the person has learned both what predicts the feared event (e.g., the presence of a phobic object or situation), and what to do to reduce the accompanying fear (i.e., to get away from it or to diminish the anxiety felt). Even if the original association was random or of low probability, because the individual immediately acts to reduce the anxiety through some secondary operant behavior, the power of the original lesson is never extinguished or countered with new learning.

Behavioral therapy.   Just as behaviorists view abnormal behavior to be a result of a maladaptive learning history, they seek its remedy in new learning. The tools employed by behavioral therapists to adjust inappropriate or ill-serving behaviors are derived directly from principles of Pavlovian (classical) conditioning and operant (instrumental) conditioning. Pavlovian therapies capitalize on the process of extinguishing learned associations through (1) *flooding,* in which fears diminish in the face of prolonged exposure to the feared stimulus without the traumatic outcome, and with (2) *systematic desensitization,* in which imagining the frightening scene or object is paired with physical relaxation—a response incompatible with sustaining the feeling of fear.

Operant therapies change the environmental contingencies maintaining a maladaptive response or construct new contingencies to elicit a target behavior by using selective reinforcement, punishment, or extinction (removal of reinforcement). The patient learns quickly to emit a more adaptive behavior to continue to get what is desired.

Cognitive therapy.   Because cognitive therapists view cognitive processes as the medium of much psychopathology, their therapeutic techniques tend to focus on trying to change the client's negative expectations, appraisals, and attributions, and the fundamental beliefs in which they are grounded. To do this, the therapist actively helps the client recognize, confront, and dispute his or her own faulty or irrational thoughts.

The behavioral view of normality and abnormality.   According to behaviorism, all behavior, normal and abnormal, is learned from and in response to environmental associations and contingencies. Consequently, psychological dysfunction may be therapeutically approached as an issue of changing the environment or changing one's response to it. Unlike psychodynamic theory, which stresses unconscious conflict and anxiety, and cognitive theory, which stresses disordered thinking, behavioral psychology considers mental events to be causally irrelevant and merely reflective of behavior (i.e., they are epiphenomena). In behaviorism, the symptom (the maladaptive behavior) *is* the disorder.

The cognitive view of normality and abnormality.   The cognitive approach to psychopathology holds that abnormal behavior follows from distorted thinking or irrational beliefs. In this model, maladaptive behavior and debilitating psychological states (e.g., depression, anxiety, etc.) are a direct result of specific conscious or preconscious thought processes. Cognitive therapy directly attacks the logic of the client's thinking and the implicit beliefs hypothesized to underlie it. As such, cognitive theory assumes the importance of mental events, but only conscious or inferable ones. Unlike psychodynamic theory, truly unconscious forces are not considered significant; and unlike strict behaviorism, actions are seen to be prompted by thought.

SAMPLE EXAM

1. What is the stance of the behavioral model with respect to the nature-nurture issue?
   a. agrees with the nature position
   b. agrees with the nurture position
   c. agrees with both positions
   d. disagrees with both positions
   e. does not take a position

2. Descartes is to Locke as
   a. mind is to body.
   b. dopamine is to schizophrenia.
   c. rationalism is to empiricism.
   d. Freud is to Erikson.
   e. learned is to innate.

3. Which of the following terms does not belong?
   a. empiricism
   b. associationism
   c. materialism
   d. behaviorism
   e. all of the above belong

4. Which of the following terms does not belong?
   a. environmentalism
   b. rationalism
   c. experimentalism
   d. optimism
   e. all of the above belong

5. The behavioral model of abnormality regards abnormal behavior and normal behavior as
   a. different in kind.
   b. learned in the same way.
   c. similar only on the surface.
   d. related by association learning.
   e. biologically determined.

6. Ivan Pavlov's initial interest was in
   a. mental phenomena.
   b. learning.
   c. digestion.
   d. obedience.
   e. memory.

7. When Pavlov's dog learned to salivate to the sight of Pavlov, what was the conditional reflex?
   a. the sight of Pavlov
   b. food
   c. the taste of food
   d. salivation to the sight of Pavlov
   e. salivation to the sight of food

8. Suppose you ate too many cookies and became ill. If you became nauseated the next day when you saw the cookie jar, what was the conditional reflex?
   a. sight of the cookie jar
   b. cookies
   c. the taste of cookies
   d. nausea at the sight of the jar.
   e. nausea after over-eating.

9. For the situation in question 8, how could you extinguish this learning?
   a. ignore the cookie jar
   b. wait until time passed
   c. continue to see the cookie jar
   d. eat more cookies
   e. don't over-eat

10. Pavlovian conditioning best explains
    a. thought.
    b. memory.
    c. emotion.
    d. libido.
    e. hunger.

11. According to the Pavlovian conditioning model of phobias, an individual afraid of cats
    a. does not know why he or she has the fear.
    b. has had past experiences with cats.
    c. has no past experience with cats.
    d. really likes cats.
    e. has always avoided cats.

12. According to the behavioral model, abnormality resides in
    a. the symptoms of the disorder.
    b. underlying drives.
    c. one's conflict with the environment.
    d. personality traits.
    e. faulty beliefs.

13. Which of the following types of therapy does not belong?
    a. flooding
    b. behavioral contracting
    c. systematic desensitization

d. Pavlovian extinction
e. exposure

14. Systematic desensitization is effective with
    a. schizophrenia.
    b. general paresis.
    c. phobias.
    d. anorexia.
    e. depression.

15. In systematic desensitization, what is the conditional reflex?
    a. fear in the presence of the feared object
    b. the feared object
    c. relaxation in the presence of the feared object
    d. early learning
    e. imagining

16. If you wished to treat someone who was afraid of mice with the technique of flooding, you would
    a. expose the individual to mice.
    b. have the individual read about Disneyland.
    c. ask the individual to speak freely about mice.
    d. discover if the person has had experience with mice.
    e. have the individual imagine mice.

17. Which of the following corresponds to the "law of effect"?
    a. "A stitch in time saves nine."
    b. "Pretty is as pretty does."
    c. "You can catch more flies with honey than with vinegar."
    d. "It don't rain in Indianapolis."
    e. "penny wise, pound foolish"

18. Your cat learns to ring the doorbell to be let in when she sees your car in the driveway. In this example, what is the operant?
    a. ringing the doorbell
    b. your car in the driveway
    c. being let in
    d. seeing your car
    e. your cat

19. In question 18, what is the reinforcer?
    a. ringing the doorbell
    b. your car in the driveway
    c. being let in
    d. seeing your car
    e. your cat

20. In question 18, what is the discriminative stimulus?
    a. ringing the doorbell
    b. your car in the driveway
    c. being let in
    d. seeing your car
    e. your cat

21. In question 18, you could decrease the frequency with which your cat rang the doorbell by all of these except
    a. selling your car.
    b. stopping answering the door.
    c. kicking the cat when she comes in.
    d. feeding the cat when she comes in.
    e. not coming home.

22. Intermittent reinforcement results in all of the following except
    a. behavior that is learned slowly.
    b. behavior that is extinguished quickly.
    c. behavior that is persistent.
    d. behavior that is maintained with little payoff.
    e. behavior that resists extinction.

23. Selective positive reinforcement as a treatment of anorexia involves
    a. ignoring bizarre behaviors.
    b. convincing the client to eat.
    c. finding a desired reinforcer.
    d. prescribing minor tranquilizers.
    e. convincing the client she is too thin.

24. Avoidance learning involves
    a. only Pavlovian conditioning.
    b. only operant conditioning.
    c. both Pavlovian and operant conditioning.
    d. neither Pavlovian nor operant conditioning.
    e. not learning.

25. In avoidance learning, what is the reinforcer?
    a. avoidance
    b. fear
    c. decrease of fear
    d. signal
    e. feared object

26. The cognitive model of abnormality views abnormality as residing in
    a. faulty learning.
    b. demonic possession.
    c. irrational thoughts.

    d. bodily injury.
    e. childhood trauma.

27. Behaviorists may concede that mental life exists, but they further argue that it is
    a. epiphenomenal.
    b. literal.
    c. norepinephral.
    d. dual.
    e. ethereal.

28. A cognitive therapist is mainly interested in the
    a. early childhood experiences of clients.
    b. physical well-being of clients.
    c. thought and beliefs of clients.
    d. unconscious impulses of clients.
    e. maladaptive behavior of clients.

29. All of the following are cognitive processes except
    a. expectation.
    b. reuptake.
    c. attribution.
    d. appraisal.
    e. belief.

30. What is the difference between an outcome expectancy and an efficacy expectation?
    a. An outcome expectancy is a belief about what will happen, and an efficacy expectation is a belief about how hard one will try.
    b. An outcome expectancy is an optimistic belief, and an efficacy expectation is a pessimistic belief.
    c. An outcome expectancy is a belief about whether a given response leads to an outcome, and an efficacy expectation is a belief about whether one can perform a given response.
    d. An outcome expectancy is a belief about end states, and an efficacy expectation is a belief about processes.
    e. external attribution and an internal attribution

31. You are taking an examination, and another student turns in her test after a few minutes and leaves. You think: "I must be stupid. I'm going to flunk." This is an example of
    a. appraisal.
    b. attribution.
    c. epiphenomenon.

d.   castration fear.
e.   outcome expectancy.

32. You go out on a date, and you have a bad time. You explain your bad time by saying: "I was too tired this evening to enjoy a movie." This causal attribution is
a.   internal, stable, and global.
b.   external, unstable, and global.
c.   internal, unstable, and specific.
d.   external, stable, and specific.
e.   internal, stable, and specific.

33. You cannot finish all the work given to you. You explain this failure by saying: "The boss is overly thorough when it comes to this kind of project." This causal attribution is
a.   internal, stable, and global.
b.   external, unstable, and global.
c.   internal, unstable, and specific.
d.   external, stable, and specific.
e.   internal, stable, and specific.

34. You give a speech, and the audience reacts negatively. You explain this reaction by saying: "I am an inept person." This causal attribution is
a.   internal, stable, and global.
b.   external, unstable, and global.
c.   internal, unstable, and specific.
d.   external, stable, and specific.
e.   internal, stable, and specific.

35. Cognitive therapy for depression attempts to change the way people explain bad events. This involves changing
a.   external attributions to internal attributions.
b.   internal attributions to external attributions.
c.   specific attributions to global attributions.
d.   unstable attributions to stable attributions.
e.   none of the above.

36. Which of the following is *not* an irrational belief identified by Albert Ellis?
a.   One should take the bad with the good.
b.   One should be thoroughly competent in all respects.
c.   One must be loved by all people.
d.   There is a right way to do everything.
e.   Our past determines our present.

37. Cognitive therapy and behavior therapy
a.   are similar.
b.   are not incompatible.
c.   are both concerned with underlying causes.
d.   are unsuccessful.
e.   both developed out of Pavlov's findings.

38. Arnold Lazarus suggests the mnemonic BASIC ID to describe the seven different levels of disorder. The A refers to
a.   autonomy.
b.   assertion.
c.   affect.
d.   adrenaline.
e.   appraisal.

39. Arnold Lazarus suggests the mnemonic BASIC ID to describe the seven different levels of disorder. The I stands for
a.   id.
b.   independence.
c.   indolamine.
d.   interpersonal relations.
e.   intelligence.

40. Arnold Lazarus suggests the mnemonic BASIC ID to describe the seven different levels of disorder. The D stands for
a.   drugs.
b.   dependence.
c.   displacement.
d.   discomfort.
e.   dysphoria.

41. Which one of the following is *not* a strength of the cognitive approach?
a.   Cognitive therapy is usually brief.
b.   Cognitive therapy is often successful.
c.   Cognitive therapy addresses the whole person.
d.   Cognitive therapy is based on research.
e.   Cognitive therapy is usually unexpensive relative to psychodynamic therapy.

Answer Key for Sample Exam

1. b	(p. 113)	5. b	(p. 115)
2. c	(p. 113)	6. c	(p. 116)
3. c	(p. 114)	7. d	(p. 116)
4. b	(p. 114)	8. d	(p. 117)

9. c	(p. 118)	18. a	(p. 122)	26. c	(p. 128)	34. a	(p. 132)
10. c	(p. 118)	19. c	(p. 122)	27. a	(p. 128)	35. b	(p. 133)
11. b	(p. 119)	20. b	(p. 122)	28. c	(p. 129)	36. a	(p. 134)
12. a	(p. 119)	21. d	(p. 122)	29. b	(p. 130)	37. b	(p. 135)
13. b	(p. 120)	22. b	(p. 123)	30. c	(p. 130)	38. c	(p. 135)
14. c	(p. 121)	23. c	(p. 125)	31. a	(p. 131)	39. d	(p. 135)
15. c	(p. 121)	24. c	(p. 127)	32. c	(p. 132)	40. a	(p. 135)
16. a	(p. 120)	25. c	(p. 127)	33. d	(p. 132)	41. c	(p. 137)
17. c	(p. 122)						

SELF-TEST

1. The sixteenth-century French philosopher _____ proposed that basic ideas were innate. This position is termed _____.

2. The position that all ideas are acquired through experience is _____ and is associated with the philosophers _____ _____.

3. According to the empiricists, the "mental glue" that holds together ideas is called an

   _____.

4. Behaviorism is a world view based on assumptions of _____, _____, and

   _____.

5. The two major forms of learning _____ conditioning and _____ conditioning.

6. The major difference between Pavlovian conditioning and operant conditioning is that in Pavlovian conditioning one _____, while in operant conditioning one learns

   _____.

7. Pavlov was originally interested in _____ reflex.

8. When Pavlov's dogs began to salivate at the sight of him, it was because he had become a

   _____.

9. _____ is the process by which one learns that a CS is associated with a US.

10. _____ is the process by which one learns that a CS is not associated with a US.

11. According to the behavioral model, emotional states and emotional disorders are acquired through _____.

12. The behaviorists feel that symptoms of a disorder _____.

13. Behavior therapies attempt to rid the client of _____.

14. Joseph Wolpe developed the therapy technique known as _____.

15. In systematic desensitization, the phobic object is paired with _____.

16. Flooding is based on Pavlovian _____.

17. Thorndike discovered that learning among cats was not sudden but rather _____.

18. According to the "law of effect," behaviors with positive consequences are _____, while behaviors with negative consequences are _____.

19. An event that increases the probability that a response preceding it will occur again is a

_____.

20. An event that decreases the probability that a response preceding it will occur again is a

_____.

21. A signal that reinforcement is available if the operant is made is a _____.

22. Reinforcement delivered after every operant is _____ reinforcement, while reinforcement delivered only after some operants is _____ reinforcement.

23. Partial reinforcement makes responses more difficult to learn, but it also makes them more resistant to _____.

24. Selective positive reinforcement is a therapy technique in which a target behavior is chosen to be _____.

25. A type of learning that involves both Pavlovian conditioning and operant conditioning is

_____.

26. Behaviorists may concede the existence of mental events, but they dismiss them as

_____.

27. According to the cognitive model of abnormality, thoughts and beliefs _____ disorders.

28. The approach to therapy that attempts to change what a client believes _____.

29. Short-term cognitive processes include _____ (anticipations about future events), _____ (evaluations), and _____ (causal explanations).

30. _____ expectancy is a person's estimate that a given behavior will lead to the desired outcome, while _____ expectancy is the belief that he or she can successfully execute the behavior that produces the desired outcome.

31. An attribution for an event that points to an individual's lack of intelligence is _____, _____, and _____.

32. _____ developed rational-emotive therapy, which is based on the argument that psychological disorder stems largely from beliefs that are _____.

33. When therapy combines techniques from the behavioral approach and the cognitive approach, it is called _____ therapy.

34. Arnold Lazarus has argued that disorder exists on seven levels; _____, _____ _____, _____, _____, _____, _____, and _____.

35. Cognitive therapy has been criticized for being too _____.

Answer Key for Self-Test

1. René Descartes; rationalism
2. empiricism; John Locke; David Hume
3. association
4. environmentalism; experimentalism; optimism
5. Pavlovian (classical); operant (instrumental)
6. what goes with what; what to do to get what one wants
7. salivary
8. conditional stimulus
9. acquisition
10. extinction
11. Pavlovian conditioning
12. are the disorder
13. symptoms
14. systematic desensitization
15. relaxation
16. extinction
17. gradual
18. repeated; not repeated
19. reinforcer
20. punishment
21. discriminative stimulus
22. continuous; partial (intermittent)
23. extinction
24. increased in frequency
25. avoidance learning
26. epiphenomena
27. cause
28. cognitive therapy
29. expectations; appraisals; attributions
30. Outcome; efficacy
31. internal; stable; global
32. Albert Ellis; irrational
33. cognitive-behavioral
34. behavior; affect; sensation; imagery; cognition; interpersonal relations; drugs
35. narrow

MATCHING ITEMS

_____ 1. Locke

_____ 2. flooding

_____ 3. Lazarus

_____ 4. negative reinforcement

_____ 5. outcome expectancy

_____ 6. efficacy expectancy

A. "tyranny of should's"

B. belief about one's ability to execute necessary behavior

C. exposure

D. doctrine of innate ideas

E. adaptive behavior

F. empiricism

_____ 7. Ellis

_____ 8. Descartes

_____ 9. punishment

_____ 10. response prevention

_____ 11. target behavior

_____ 12. appraisals

G. decreases probability of a future response

H. cognitive-behavioral

I. operant-Pavlovian

J. increases the probability of a future response

K. automatic thoughts

L. estimate that behavior will lead to desired outcome

Answer Key for Matching Items

1.	F	7.	A
2.	C	8.	D
3.	H	9.	G
4.	J	10.	I
5.	L	11.	E
6.	B	12.	K

SHORT-ANSWER QUESTIONS

1. There is a cat named Oedipuss who loves to eat. If you were a behaviorist how would you explain his following behaviors? (Use behaviorist terminology.) (a) Whenever he sees cat food he gets hungry; (b) He rubs against your legs whenever you walk into the kitchen; (c) When he hears the electric can opener he gets hungry; (d) When he hears the coffee grinder he gets hungry.

2. In what ways are Pavlovian and operant conditioning similar, and in what ways different?

3. Describe two kinds of Pavlovian therapies, how they work, and under what conditions they are employed.

4. Why is punishment not necessarily the best way to decrease maladaptive behaviors? What else might be used as an alternative strategy and how?

5. How is the cognitive school an outgrowth from, and reaction to, the behavioral school?

6. Attributions can be external or internal, stable or unstable, and global or specific. What kinds of attributions, and under what conditions, would cognitive therapists be interested in changing and why?

7. Describe how expectations, appraisals, attributions, and beliefs might each affect your performance on an exam. (Give at least one specific example for each.)

TYING IT TOGETHER

The behavioral model was the first approach to abnormality to be identified mainly with psychologists and not with physicians or biologists. It is based largely on experimental research (Chapter 6). Historically, advocates of the behavioral model have been less interested in diagnosis than in careful description of the behaviors involved in abnormality (Chapter 7). Thus, the behavioral model does not regard behaviors as symptoms of an underlying biological or psychodynamic cause; instead, behaviors are regarded as the problem itself. The behavioral model is associated with careful studies of therapy outcome in which the frequencies of target behaviors are assessed following treatments.

The behavioral approach seems to do its best job in explaining and changing problems that involve circumscribed behaviors with emotional components: fears and phobias (Chapter 8), obsessive-compulsive disorders (Chapter 9), paraphilias (Chapter 13), sexual dysfunctions (Chapter 13), and drug abuse (Chapter 14). It is less successful when difficulties are "deeper" or more diffuse.

In part a reaction against psychoanalysis, the behavioral model also has served as a foil for the cognitive approach and the existential approach. According to cognitive psychologists, behaviorists inappropriately ignore mental life. According to existential psychologists (Chapter 4), behaviorists are guilty of a narrow determinism that overlooks essential aspects of human experience. The emergence of a cognitive-behavioral approach suggests that these criticisms have been valid, and that they can be answered within the behavioral framework.

One of the achievements of the behavioral approach has been the development, implementation, and evaluation of a number of simple and successful therapy techniques to treat problems that have defied previous therapeutic attempts (Chapter 19).

The cognitive approach to abnormality developed both from the behavioral model and in reaction to it. Like the behavioral model, it is largely associated with psychologists. It has generated its own assessment devices, like the Rep Test (Chapter 7), and it is closely tied to empirical research (Chapter 6).

The cognitive model is at its best when explaining disorders in which conscious thought plays a causal role. Thus, fear and anxiety disorders (Chapter 9) and depression (Chapter 11) are clarified by the cognitive approach since these disorders are partly brought about by characteristic ways of thinking. Cognitively based therapies have been successfully used to treat such disorders (Chapter 19), and in some cases they may be as effective as drug therapy without the side effects of medication.

The psychodynamic model is concerned with mental processes, but it differs from the cognitive model in emphasizing the unconscious (Chapter 4). In contrast, the cognitive approach is concerned largely with conscious thought. Accordingly, it co-exists more easily with existential approaches (Chapter 4) than do the other models of abnormality. However, there is a tendency for cognitive explanations to focus on "small" aspects of thought, such as expectations and appraisals, rather than on "larger" belief systems. Perhaps this is the reason why the cognitive model is largely silent about schizophrenia, a so-called thought disorder (Chapter 12).

The cognitive model is the most recently articulated psychological approach to abnormality. Its applicability to the range of disorders has not been fully explored. As you read Chapter 8 through 17, you may speculate about which disorders could be profitably approached in terms of an individual's thoughts and beliefs. Sexual behavior is inherently symbolic behavior, not just an activity of the physical body; accordingly, the sexual dysfunctions (Chapter 13) may merit reexamination from a cognitive perspective. Similarly, drug use and abuse (Chapter 14) are embedded in a life style that includes a belief system. Couldn't this belief system help maintain drug-related behavior? Perhaps cognitive therapy could be effective in dissuading individuals from a destructive life-style.

FURTHER READINGS

American Psychological Association (1992). Reflections on B. F. Skinner and Psychology. *American Psychologist, 47,* 1.

Bandura, A. (1969). *Principles of behavior modification.* New York: Holt, Rinehart & Winston.

Beck. A. T. (1976). *Cognitive therapy and the emotional disorders.* New York: International Universities Press.

Begelman, D. A. (1975). Ethical and legal issues of behavior modification. In M. Hersen, R. Eisler, & P. Miller (Eds.), *Progress in behavior modification* (vol. 1, pp. 159–189). New York; Academic Press.

Burns, D. D. (1980). *Feeling good: The new mood therapy*. New York: Morrow.

Carrera, F., & Adams, P. L. (1970). An ethical perspective on operant conditioning. *Journal of the American Academy of Child Psychiatrists, 9*, 607–634.

Ellis, A. (1962). *Reason and emotion in psychotherapy*. New York: Stuart.

Ellis, A. & Harper, R. A. (1975). *A new guide to rational living*. North Hollywood, CA: Wilshire Book Co.

Huxley, A. (1946). *Brave new world*. New York: Harper & Row.

Kelly, G. A. (1963). *A theory of personality: The psychology of personal constructs*. New York: Norton.

Lazarus, A. A. (1989). *The practice of multimodal therapy*. Baltimore, MD: The John Hopkins University Press.

Mahoney, M. J. (1974). *Cognition and behavior modification*. Cambridge, MA: Ballinger.

Masters, J. C., Burish, T. G., Hollon, S. D., & Rimm, D. C. (1987). *Behavior therapy—techniques and empirical findings*, 3rd edition. Fort Worth, TX: Harcourt Brace Jovanovich.

Meichenbaum, D. (1977). *Cognitive-behavior modification*. New York: Plenum.

Mowrer, O. H. (1948). Learning theory and the neurotic paradox. *American Journal of Orthopsychiatry, 18*, 571–610.

Skinner, B. F. (1971). *Beyond freedom and dignity*. New York: Knopf.

Skinner, B. F. (1976). *Walden two*. New York: Macmillan.

Wachtel, P. (1977). *Psychoanalysis and behavior therapy: Toward an integration*. New York: Basic Books.

Watson, J. B. (1970). *Behaviorism*. New York: Norton.

TERM-PAPER TOPICS

1. How does social learning theory build upon the behavioral model? How does it break with this model? Does social learning theory have more to do with the cognitive model than with the behavioral model?

2. Consider this statement: Behavior therapy techniques are effective only for mild problems. Do you agree or disagree? Support your answer with examples from research.

3. What are the ethical issues raised by behavior modification? Are they any different than the ethical issues raised by other approaches to therapy?

4. Read the first chapter in Gilbert Ryle's *Concept of Mind* (1949). In light of his arguments, evaluate the cognitive model's claims that thoughts and beliefs are at the basis of psychological disorders.

5. It has been claimed that cognitive therapy for depression is as effective as antidepressant medication. Read some of the original studies that made this comparison. What qualifications need to be made? What factors may be considered in pursuing cognitive therapy versus drug therapy?

6. *Irrational* is a complex term with several meanings. In what sense does Albert Ellis use the term? In what sense does Aaron Beck use the term? Does cognitive therapy as practiced by Ellis and Beck make clients more rational, or is there a better way to describe its effects?

EXERCISES

Exercise One—Taste Aversion and Pavlovian Conditioning

In this exercise you will evaluate the Pavlovian-conditioning explanation of taste aversions.

According to Pavlovian conditioning, if a taste is paired with an unpleasant experience, that taste will become unpleasant. Talk to people about tastes of foods or drinks that make them nauseous. Were these tastes originally associated with illness or some other aversive experience?

Logue, A. W., Logue, K. R., & Strauss, K. E. (1983). The acquisition of taste aversions in humans with eating and drinking disorders. *Behaviour Research and Therapy, 21,* 275–289.

Seligman, M. E. P., & Hager, J. L. (1972). Biological boundaries of learning: The sauce-Bearnaise phenomenon. *Psychology Today, 6*(3), 59–61; 84–87.

Exercise Two—Increasing the Frequency of Your Studying

In this exercise you will use principles of operant conditioning to increase the frequency of an important operant—your studying.

A reinforcer is any stimulus that increases the probability of an operant that precedes it. This is a circular definition, and a number of attempts have been made to characterize a reinforcer in noncircular terms. One of these attempts is the Premack principle, which proposes that the opportunity to engage in a high-frequency behavior will reinforce any low-frequency behavior. If this is the case, then you can increase your studying in a simple way. Identify some behavior that you perform a great deal (e.g., watching television, playing sports). Impose on yourself the rule that you will only perform this behavior if you have first studied, say, one hour more per day than you have been studying in the past. According to the Premack principle, your studying should increase.

Premack, D. (1959). Toward empirical behavior laws: I. Positive reinforcement. *Psychological Review, 66,* 219–233.

Exercise Three—Thoughts and Mood

In this exercise, you will test the premise of the cognitive model that thoughts cause emotions.

Have some of your friends read the following statement out loud:

> I have just failed an examination. It is entirely my fault that I failed this test. The teacher made her help available, but I did not take it. The course material was interesting, and my classmates said that it was simple, but I could not understand the ideas no matter how hard I tried. My failure on this examination is just one of many disappointments that I have had throughout my life. I have no close friends, and even my family takes no interest in what I do. There is nothing that I'm good at, and there is nothing that I'll ever be good at. Failure seems to result from everything I do.

Have other friends read this statement out loud:

> I have just failed an examination. It was a hard test, and the teacher didn't help in making the ideas easier to understand. I guess I could have studied a bit harder, but I had some other things to do that were more important. They turned out fine, so I can't look at the failed exam as a big deal. What's really important to me are my friends and my family, and doing things with them that are rewarding. So I can't complain. Anyway, I usually do well on exams and in my courses in general, so I'm pretty sure that I'll pull my grade up before the course is over. Things usually turn out pretty successfully for me.

Ask your friends about how they feel after they have read the statements. Do the two statements have different effects on mood?

Velten, E. (1968). A laboratory task for the induction of mood states. *Behaviour Research and Therapy, 6,* 473–482.

Exercise Four—Test Anxiety and Automatic Thoughts

According to the cognitive model, emotions like guilt and sadness are brought about by negative statements that people make to themselves, almost without being aware of what they are doing. The purpose of this exercise is to demonstrate this idea.

Arrange this exercise with the instructor of a large class. During an examination, have a student hand in her test in the front of the classroom shortly after receiving it. She should do so confidently, as if she breezed through all the questions. Thirty seconds later, the instructor should ask the other students in the class to write down what they thought when the test was handed in so early.

How many students wrote down self-deprecating statements? Are these the same individuals who experience a great deal of anxiety while taking tests?

Sarason, I. G. (1980). *Test anxiety: Theory, research, and applications.* Hillsdale, NJ: Erlbaum.

1. My mood has been sad.
   a. not at all
   b. sometimes
   c. all the time
2. My appetite has been poor.
   a. not at all
   b. sometimes
   c. all the time
3. My sleep has been irregular.
   a. not at all
   b. sometimes
   c. all the time
4. My interest in activities has decreased.
   a. not at all
   b. sometimes
   c. all the time
5. My concentration has been poor.
   a. not at all
   b. sometimes
   c. all the time
6. My self-esteem has been low.
   a. not at all
   b. sometimes
   c. all the time

Score each question a = 1, b = 2, and c = 3. The higher the score, the more depressed the person is.

Peterson, C., & Seligman, M. E. P. (1984). Causal explanations at a risk factor for depression: Theory and evidence. *Psychological Review, 91,* 347–374.

Exercise Five—Depression and Attributions

The purpose of this exercise is to test the prediction of learned helplessness theory that depression is associated with a characteristic style of explaining bad events.

Talk to individuals who are sad and individuals who are not. (You may gauge their mood by administering the questionnaire below.) Ask them to explain the causes of several recent bad events they have experienced. Are the sad individuals more apt to offer internal, stable, and global attributions as explanation for bad events?

Ask people to respond to these questions in terms of how they have been feeling for the last two weeks:

Exercise Six—Applying the Theories

Consider the four approaches to psychology that you have studied thus far (biomedical, psychodynamic, behavioral, cognitive). Of these, which is most antithetical to your personal views? Which appears to most violate your sense of yourself? Now consider a behavior of yours or of someone else's which stands out as particularly maladaptive. How might the selected approach be used to explain this behavior? Repeat with a particularly laudable behavior. How well does it do? Does it account for aspects of the behavior that your personally-favored model does not? Does the attraction or utility of the theory seem to make more sense now that you've used it?

CHAPTER 6

Investigating Abnormality

CHAPTER OVERVIEW

There are a number of ways in which abnormality and its causes may be investigated, and these are described in Chapter 6. The hope of all abnormality researchers is that effective means for preventing and/or curing disorders will result from discovery of their causes.

The two principal methods of investigation, which possess complementary strengths and weaknesses, are clinical case histories and experimental studies. A clinical case history is a record of part of the life of an individual seen during therapy. Case histories are useful as a source of hypotheses and as a nonartificial means of studying rare phenomena. However, case histories cannot definitively isolate causes. In contrast, an experimental study is able to evaluate possible causes of a disorder by manipulating them and assessing the consequences. Among the drawbacks of experiments are artificiality as well as practical and ethical limitations in applying them to certain disorders.

To overcome some of these limitations, researchers use three other techniques of investigation. All attempt to isolate causes, but they cannot do so definitively. Correlational studies observe the relationships among variables without manipulating them. Experiments of nature capitalize on striking accidents to provide a "manipulation" of some factor of interest, the consequences of which are assessed. Finally, laboratory models of psychopathology attempt to create in the laboratory under controlled circumstances phenomena analogous to disorders that can be studied with fewer limitations than the disorders themselves.

What is the best method of investigation? There is none. Different questions and different circumstances require different research approaches. Method is a means to an end. In the case of methods for studying abnormality, the desired end is an understanding of disorders that allows assistance to those suffering from them. If research using different methods converges in the understanding provided, then a good research strategy has been followed.

ESSENTIAL TERMS

clinical case history

record of part of the life of an individual seen during therapy (p. 144)

confound

factor other than the independent variable that could produce an experimental effect (p. 148)

control group	a group of subjects similar to those in an experimental group, who experience everything the experimental group does, except the independent variable (p. 148)
correlation	linear covariation of two variables (p. 159)
negative correlation	correlation in which increases in one variable are associated with decreases in the other variable
positive correlation	correlation in which increases in one variable are associated with increases in the other variable
uncorrelated correlation	correlation in which changes in one variable are not associated with changes in the other variable
correlational study	alternative to experimental studies in which the co-occurrence of two factors is assessed without manipulation (p. 160)
correlation coefficient	strength of correlation between two variables, ranging from +1.00 (perfect positive correlation) through 0.00 (no correlation) to −1.00 (perfect negative correlation) (p. 161)
demand characteristics	clues in an experimental setting which may induce subjects to invent hypotheses about how they should behave (p. 152)
dependent variable	in an experimental study, the effect, appearance of which depends on whether the cause precedes it (p. 147)
double-blind experiment	experiment in which both subject and experimenter are "blind" as to which drug or treatment has been provided (p. 152)
experimental effect	change in a dependent variable determined by manipulation of an independent variable (p. 147)
experimental group	a group of subjects who are given experience with an independent variable (p. 148)
experimental study	method of isolating causes by manipulating possible causes and assessing the consequences (p. 147)
experimenter bias	subtle influence of the experimenter on subjects, producing an expected result (p. 152)
experimenter-blind experiment	experiment in which the experimenter is "blind" as to which drug or treatment has been provided (p. 152)
experiment of nature	alternative to experimental studies in which the occurrence of a striking event is regarded as a "manipulated" factor and its consequences are assessed (p. 165)
false alarms	conclusions that effects are true when they are actually false (p. 155)
independent variable	in an experimental study, the hypothesized cause, which is manipulated by the experimenter (p. 147)
laboratory model of psychopathology	production under controlled conditions of phenomena analogous to naturally occurring mental disorders (p. 167)

lifetime prevalence	the proportion of people in a sample who have experienced a particular disorder (p. 163)
longitudinal study	investigation that follows the same subjects over time (p. 166)
meta-analysis	statistical technique for combining the results of different investigations (p. 150)
misses	conclusions that effects are false when they are actually true (p. 155)
operational definition	set of observable and measurable conditions under which a phenomenon is said to occur (p. 147)
placebo	useless drug or treatment that produces an effect because of subject bias (p. 152)
population	the entire set of potential observations (p. 153)
prospective study	longitudinal investigation in which subjects are chosen at one point in time and followed into the future (p. 166)
random assignment	in an experimental study, an equal chance of each subject to be assigned to each condition (p. 150)
repeatability	the chance that, if an experimental manipulation is repeated, it will produce similar results (p. 155)
retrospective	investigation in which systematic observation begins after the precipitating event (p. 166)
sample	a selection of items or people from the entire population of similar items or people (p. 153)
single-blind experiment	experiment in which the subject is "blind" as to which drug or treatment has been provided (p. 152)
single-subject experiment	experimental study with only one subject (p. 155)
statistical inferences	procedures used to decide whether a sample or set of observations is truly representative of the population (p. 153)
statistical significance	probability that a given result occurred by chance; when sufficiently low, it is concluded that the effect is real (p. 155)
subject bias	in an experimental study, the subtle tendency of a subject to produce an expected result (p. 152)

CENTRAL CONCEPTUAL ISSUES

Trade-offs in research design.   The three general approaches to the investigation of abnormal psychology—clinical case histories, experimental manipulation, and correlational studies—present trade-offs in several major areas: amount of information, practicality, replicability, and narrowness of interpretation. Scientific discovery requires insight and the recognition of relationships previously unseen or unexplained. Clinical case histories offer the kind of depth and complexity which can be a fertile breeding ground for the development of new theories. However, the very richness and uniqueness of information acquired with clinical case histories is a practical barrier to large scale or controlled investigations and to replicability of findings. Experimentation, which systematically minimizes the amount of information presented, is more often controllable and replicable, but by its very nature is artificial and less conducive to broad insight. Moreover, the very controlled conditions which can give an experiment its rigor makes the results, even robust ones, only narrowly applicable. Correlational studies occupy a middle ground by looking at large amounts of information by way of a circumscribed number of variables. In the vast majority of cases, scientific experiments, clinical case histories, and correlations are suggestive rather than conclusive. One's world view or theoretical bias inevitably informs and constricts which questions we ask and what information we consider to be important. Sometimes a study will present us with results or implications which run counter to our expectations. Such counter-intuitive findings offer a valuable opportunity to see beyond our theoretical blind spots and to question our presuppositions. Such experimental "failures" can be the most exciting and fruitful events of the process of scientific investigation.

Statistical significance.   The statistical analysis of experimental results yields a conclusion expressed in probability or in confidence level. Thus the results of a study are said to be *statistically significant* when they have a likelihood of less than 5 percent of having occurred by chance. Put another way, such a result still has a one in twenty chance of being a random finding (i.e., wrong). The possibility of random findings underscores the importance of replicating a result. It also illuminates the value that psychologists place on convergent studies—that reach the same conclusion from different methods and approaches.

Controlling for confounds.   All approaches to scientific investigation must wrestle with the problem of confounds. To isolate the effect of the variable of interest from the contributions of other unintended variables *control groups* are employed. Subjects in the control group are exposed to exactly the same experimental conditions as subjects in the experimental group with the exception of the independent variable. This procedure obviates the almost impossible task of trying to anticipate and eliminate in advance all possible confounds from affecting the experimental group. Instead, the effect of the independent variable, if there is one, can seen over and above the effects, if any, of being in the experiment. In the case of non-experimental studies, subjects are matched with control subjects on any variables that may be related to the variable of interest. For example, in a study of whether depressed patients experience their lives as more stressful, one could compare them to other subjects matched on factors such as age, sex, and socioeconomic level in order to rule out these factors as possible confounds. If the groups are equivalent in these factors then we can assume that a positive finding is not merely a product of the possible independent effects of age, sex, or SES on stress.

Besides controlling for confounds, the results of experimental manipulation and correlation studies must always be considered in reference to a base rate for the population being studied. Without some point of reference (e.g., a control group) results cannot be interpreted. For example, if a study found that 30 percent of patients improved while taking a new drug, it would be incorrect to conclude that the drug was quite effective, because we do not know how many patients would have improved during the same time without the drug (or with a placebo treatment which controls for the potentially confounding effects of believing one is taking a drug). If the base rate of recovery without treatment (or with placebo) is approximately 30 percent, then, in fact, the drug is without additional effect.

Correlation does not equal causality.   One of the easiest mistakes to make when interpreting patterns in data is to conclude that because two events are consistently associated with each other their relationship is therefore causal. In the example above, a finding that depression is associated with more reported stress does not necessarily imply any particular causal relationship. Experiencing more stressors may cause depression, being depressed may make life feel more stressful, or both may be causally related to some other factor (e.g., some biological condition). Drawing a causal interpretation is particularly tempting when the association fits our expectations. An amusing example is captured by the finding that in the Old West the number of saloons in a town was positively correlated with the number of churches. Were the ministers driving parishioners to drink? Were drunks turning to God for their solace? How are we to interpret this? In fact, as is often the case in correlations, a third variable was responsible for both: growth in town population increased the demand for drink and deliverance.

SAMPLE EXAM

1. The benefit of an experimental study as opposed to a clinical case history is that
    a. experiments are richer in detail.
    b. experiments are more scientific.
    c. experiments isolate causes.
    d. experiments have greater applicability.
    e. experiments are a source of more hypotheses.

2. All of the following are alternatives to experimental studies except
    a. correlational studies.
    b. introspective studies.
    c. experiments of nature.
    d. laboratory models of psychopathology.
    e. all of the above are alternatives.

3. The best method of investigating abnormality is
    a. clinical case histories.
    b. correlational studies.
    c. experiments of nature.
    d. laboratory models of psychopathology.
    e. none of the above.

4. Sigmund Freud used which method of investigation?
    a. clinical case histories
    b. correlational studies
    c. experiments of nature
    d. laboratory models of psychopathology
    e. none of the above

5. Which one of the following is a disadvantage of the clinical case history?
    a. It is not artificial.
    b. It lacks generalizability.
    c. It is a rich source of hypotheses.
    d. It can provide evidence that disconfirms a generally accepted theory.
    e. none of the above

6. Which one of the following is *not* a disadvantage of the clinical case history?
    a. It uses retrospective evidence.
    b. It lacks repeatability.
    c. It lacks generality.
    d. It overemphasizes causality.
    e. possible therapist bias

7. In an experimental study, the scientist manipulates
    a. the hypothesized cause.
    b. the hypothesized effect.
    c. the number of subjects.
    d. the dependent variable.
    e. the statistical significance.

8. Which of these is an operational definition of temperature?
    a. the movement of atoms
    b. the lack of cold
    c. the reading of a thermometer
    d. the amount of heat
    e. all of the above

9. Which of these is an operational definition of happiness?
    a. the number of smiles per hour

b. the amount of joy
c. the degree of pleasure
d. the operation of brain processes

10. Which of these does not belong?
    a. independent variable
    b. dependent variable
    c. effect
    d. experimental effect
    e. results

11. How would you conduct an experiment to
    see if ice cream causes happiness?
    a. Feed individuals ice cream and see if
        they are happy.
    b. Do not feed individuals ice cream and
        see if they are unhappy.
    c. Feed some individuals ice cream, and
        do not feed it to other individuals; see
        which group of individuals is more
        happy.
    d. Conduct a survey in which individu-
        als are asked if ice cream causes them
        to be happy.
    e. any of the above

12. A factor that occurs along with the inde-
    pendent variable is
    a. a cause.
    b. a confound.
    c. an overdetermined behavior.
    d. an operational definition.
    e. an experimental effect

13. Why do experimenters employ control
    groups?
    a. to achieve symmetry
    b. to check for random error
    c. to rule out confounds
    d. to replicate findings
    e. to keep things in order

14. The ideal control group in an experiment
    a. is exactly the same as the experi-
        mental group.
    b. is one that introduces the suspected
        confound.
    c. is studied before the experimental
        group is studied.
    d. is studied after the experimental
        group is studied.
    e. is exactly the same as the experi-
        mental group except that the hypoth-
        esized cause is not present.

15. Meta-analysis is a(n) _____ technique.
    a. assessment

b. deductive
c. epidemiological
d. statistical
e. therapy

16. According to meta-analysis, the average
    client in psychotherapy does better than
    _____ of untreated clients.
    a. 1%
    b. 25%
    c. 50%
    d. 75%
    e. 99%

17. All of the following are potential con-
    founds except
    a. nonrandom assignment.
    b. experimenter bias.
    c. yoking.
    d. demand characteristic.
    e. subject bias.

18. In the "executive" monkey study, what
    was the confound?
    a. nonrandom assignment
    b. experimenter bias
    c. yoking
    d. demand characteristic
    e. non-human subjects

19. Placebo treatments work because of
    a. experimenter bias.
    b. nonrandom assignment.
    c. subject bias.
    d. sublimation.
    e. the lack of control groups.

20. What confound does a double-blind ex-
    periment attempt to avoid?
    a. experimenter bias
    b. subject bias
    c. nonrandom assignment
    d. a and b
    e. a and c
    f. b and c

21. What confound does an experimenter-
    blind experiment attempt to avoid?
    a. experimenter bias
    b. subject bias
    c. nonrandom assignment
    d. a and b
    e. a and c
    f. b and c

22. What confound does a single-blind ex-
    periment attempt to avoid?

a. experimenter bias
b. subject bias
c. nonrandom assignment
d. *a* and *b*
e. *a* and *c*
f. *b* and *c*

23. Demand characteristics assume that an experimental subject usually tries to be
    a. objective.
    b. helpful.
    c. belligerent.
    d. humorous.
    e. honest.

24. Sensory-deprivation experiments have sometimes been subject to what confound?
    a. experimenter bias
    b. nonrandom assignment
    c. demand characteristics
    d. yoking
    e. hallucinations

25. Statistics are used to make inferences about
    a. whether a population represents a sample.
    b. whether a sample represents a population.
    c. individual cases.
    d. both *a* and *b*.
    e. none of the above.

26. At statistically significant effect is one that
    a. occurs more than 95 percent of the time.
    b. has a less than 95 percent chance of occurring by chance.
    c. has greater than a 5 percent chance of occurring by chance.
    d. has a less than 5 percent chance of occurring by chance.
    e. gets published.

27. If a scientist concludes that a therapy technique is successful when it is not successful, she has made what kind of mistake?
    a. a statistically significant error
    b. a false alarm
    c. a miss
    d. an experimenter bias
    e. a confound

28. If a scientist concludes that a therapy technique is unsuccessful when it really is successful, she has made what kind of mistake?
    a. a statistically significant error
    b. a false alarm
    c. a miss
    d. an experimenter bias
    e. a confound

29. What is the biggest drawback of a single-subject experiment?
    a. It does not isolate causes.
    b. It lacks repeatability.
    c. It lacks generality.
    d. It is liable to subject bias.
    e. It cannot be double-blind.

30. A scientist may not conduct an experiment for all these reasons except
    a. ethical considerations.
    b. financial considerations.
    c. time considerations.
    d. practical considerations.
    e. scientific considerations.

31. Correlational studies involve
    a. manipulation without observation.
    b. observation without manipulation.
    c. both manipulation and observation.
    d. neither manipulation nor observation.
    e. inferences about causality.

32. The correlation between height and weight is
    a. positive.
    b. negative.
    c. zero.
    d. one.
    e. none of the above.

33. Individuals who study a lot also receive good grades. This means that
    a. studying results in good grades.
    b. good grades result in studying.
    c. conscientiousness results in studying and good grades.
    d. all of the above.
    e. none of the above.

34. Which correlation coefficient is most likely to describe the correlation between height and weight?
    a. $r = +1.00$
    b. $r = +0.50$
    c. $r = 0.00$
    d. $r = -0.50$
    e. $r = -1.00$

35. Which one of the following is *not* an ad-
    vantage to the correlational method?
    a. It is quantitative and rigorous.
    b. It is not artificial.
    c. It can avoid ethical problems.
    d. It can isolate causes.
    e. It is repeatable.

36. Are confounds more likely in experiments
    or in experiments of nature?
    a. experiments
    b. experiments of nature
    c. equally likely in both
    d. unlikely in either
    e. none of the above

37. In an experiment of nature, what corre-
    sponds to the independent variable?
    a. the effect
    b. the operational definition
    c. the accident
    d. the confound
    e. the dependent variable

38. A longitudinal study explicitly incorpo-
    rates
    a. childhood factors.
    b. manipulations.
    c. projective tests.
    d. survey questions.
    e. the element of time.

39. Which one of the following is *not* a
    strength of experiments of nature?
    a. They are not artificial.
    b. They are repeatable.
    c. They avoid ethical problems.
    d. They isolate gross causes.
    e. They document something real.

40. Laboratory models are based on
    a. simplicity.
    b. analogy.
    c. animals.
    d. physiology.
    e. computer models.

41. Which one of the following is *not* a
    strength of laboratory models?
    a. They isolate causes.
    b. They are repeatable.

c. They avoid ethical problems.
d. They are not artificial.
e. They can be used when direct experimentation is impossible.

42. If one were most interested in conveying
    the reality of a disorder, one would use
    which method of investigation?
    a. clinical case history
    b. experimental study
    c. correlational study
    d. laboratory model
    e. single subject design

43. Research using different methods is most
    useful when it
    a. supports experimental findings.
    b. converges.
    c. diverges.
    d. supports insights from clinical case
       histories.
    e. supports laboratory analog findings.

Answer Key for Sample Exam

1.	c	(p. 143)	23.	b	(p. 152)
2.	b	(p. 143)	24.	c	(p. 153)
3.	d	(p. 144)	25.	b	(p. 153)
4.	a	(p. 144)	26.	d	(p. 155)
5.	b	(p. 146)	27.	b	(p. 155)
6.	d	(p. 146)	28.	c	(p. 155)
7.	a	(p. 147)	29.	c	(p. 155)
8.	c	(p. 147)	30.	e	(p. 158)
9.	a	(p. 147)	31.	b	(p. 159)
10.	a	(p. 147)	32.	a	(p. 159)
11.	c	(p. 148)	33.	e	(p. 162)
12.	b	(p. 148)	34.	b	(p. 162)
13.	c	(p. 148)	35.	d	(p. 165)
14.	e	(p. 148)	36.	b	(p. 167)
15.	d	(p. 150)	37.	c	(p. 165)
16.	d	(p. 150)	38.	e	(p. 166)
17.	c	(p. 150)	39.	b	(p. 167)
18.	a	(p. 150)	40.	b	(p. 167)
19.	c	(p. 152)	41.	d	(p. 168)
20.	d	(p. 152)	42.	a	(p. 170)
21.	a	(p. 152)	43.	b	(p. 170)
22.	b	(p. 152)			

SELF-TEST

1. The two principle methods of investigating abnormality are _____ and _____.

2. Case histories cannot isolate _____.

3. Alternatives to experimental studies include _____, _____, and _____.

4. Sound method is a _____, not an _____.

5. Clinical case histories have several strengths. First, they are not _____; second, they can be used to study _____ phenomena; and third, they are a rich source of _____.

6. Clinical case histories have several disadvantages. First, their evidence may be _____; second, they lack _____; third, they lack _____; and fourth, they cannot identify _____.

7. In an experiment, the hypothesized cause is the _____ and the effect of interest is the _____.

8. An _____ is the set of observable conditions under which a phenomenon occurs.

9. Factors other than the independent variable that may produce an experimental effect are _____.

10. To eliminate confounds in an experiment, one uses _____ groups.

11. Meta-analysis has been used to investigate _____.

12. Among the common experimental confounds are _____, _____, _____, and _____.

13. Statistical inference is used to decide whether the _____ truly represents the _____.

14. Conclusions that say x is false when it is true are _____, while conclusions that say x is true when it is false are _____.

15. Single-subject experiments can demonstrate _____ but not _____.

16. The experimental method has several strengths. First, it is the foremost method for _____; second, it is _____; and third, it is _____.

17. Among the weaknesses of the experimental method are that it is _____; inferences are _____; and it is sometimes _____ or _____.

18. Studies in which variables are observed without being manipulated are _____.

19. If variable *A* increases while variable *B* decreases, and vice versa, then the correlation between variables *A* and *B* is _____.

20. If variable *C* increases while variable *D* also increases, and vice versa, then the correlation between variables *C* and *D* is _____.

21. The strength of the relationship between two variables can be expressed by a _____.

22. On the positive side, correlational studies are not _____; they are _____; they are _____; and they avoid _____ problems; on the negative side, they are not able to _____.

23. Studies that capitalize on the occurrence of a striking event are _____.

24. Experiments of nature have several strong points. First, they are not _____; second, they avoid _____ problems; and third, they isolate gross _____.

25. There are several weaknesses in experiments of nature. First, they cannot specify _____ in the gross cause; second, they are not _____; and third, they may be subject to _____ bias.

26. The production under controlled conditions of a phenomenon analogous to an actual psychopathology is a _____.

27. The strengths of laboratory models are: first, they specify _____; second, they are _____; and third, they minimize problems with _____.

28. On the negative side, laboratory models are _____, and _____ is limited.

29. The best method is _____.

Answer Key for Self-Test

1. clinical case histories; experimental studies
2. causes
3. correlational studies; experiments of nature; laboratory models of psychopathology
4. means; end
5. artificial; rare; hypotheses
6. selective; repeatability; generality; causes
7. independent variable; dependent variable
8. operational definition
9. confounds
10. control (comparison)
11. psychotherapy effectiveness
12. nonrandom assignment; experimenter bias; subject bias; demand characteristics
13. sample; population
14. misses; false alarms
15. repeatability; generality
16. isolating causes; repeatable; general
17. artificial; probabilistic; impractical; unethical
18. correlational studies
19. negative
20. positive
21. correlation coefficient
22. artificial; quantitative; repeatable; ethical; isolate causes

23. experiments of nature
24. artificial; ethical; causes
25. active elements; repeatable; retrospective
26. laboratory model

27. causes; repeatable; ethics
28. artificial; generality
29. none

MATCHING ITEMS

_____ 1. confound

_____ 2. false alarm

_____ 3. miss

_____ 4. experiments

_____ 5. correlations

_____ 6. operational definitions

_____ 7. meta-analysis

_____ 8. frequency distribution

_____ 9. population

_____ 10. placebo

A. used in control group

B. causality

C. saying x is false when it is true

D. entire set of potential observations

E. saying x is true when it is false

F. used to define the variables

G. used to integrate conflicting findings

H. nonrandom assignment

I. relationships

J. number of occurrences in each given class observed

Answer Key for Matching Items

1.	H	6.	F
2.	E	7.	G
3.	C	8.	J
4.	B	9.	D
5.	I	10.	A

SHORT-ANSWER QUESTIONS

1. If you were to launch a major line of investigation into a completely new, uncharted research area, and you had to use each of the five methods described in the chapter, but only one at a time, what would be your research plan and why? Describe the order and logic of your choices of methodology (i.e., explain and justify them).

2. Issues of ethics can arise whenever we try to investigate abnormality. Describe the ethical issues which face experimenters in each of the following methods: clinical case studies, experimental studies, correlational studies, experiments of nature, and laboratory models of psychopathology. Why are some methods more or less likely to raise questions of ethics? In each case, what may be traded off?

3. Single-subject research designs can be very useful in demonstrating many psychological phenomena. Imagine you want to investigate a hunch (i.e., you have a hypothesis) about a possible confound in your own research. You think that the way some of your research assistants are administering the test materials may be subtly affecting the results. Specifically, you have noticed that some RAs uncon-

sciously nod or say "uh-huh" after a subject gives a right answer but maintain a neutral expression when subjects give incorrect answers. You speculate that subjects working with these RAs learn this distinction and continue elaborating their answers (thereby contaminating the results) until they see a sign of "success." Explain how you would apply a single subject design to test this hypothesis? What conclusions could you draw?

TYING IT TOGETHER

This chapter surveys the ways in which abnormality is investigated. The first major strategy of investigation is the clinical case history, which is associated with the psychodynamic approach as well as with the existential approach (Chapter 4). You will encounter clinical case histories throughout the text as they are used to illustrate the various disorders (Chapter 8 through 17). For rare disorders such as multiple personality (Chapter 9), transsexuality (Chapter 13), and certain forms of aphasia (Chapter 17), they provide the only information available.

The second major strategy of investigation is the experiment, which is associated mainly with the behavioral model (Chapter 5) but also with the biomedical (Chapter 3) and cognitive (Chapter 5) approaches. The more circumscribed a disorder, the more amenable it is to investigation with experimentation.

Correlational investigations are frequently cited throughout the text. You have already seen how such a strategy led researchers to suspect that general paresis may be linked to syphilis and to conduct the critical experiment described in Chapter 3. Correlations are at the basis of epidemiological research, which has shed light on the origins of psychosomatic disorders (Chapter 10), depression (Chapter 11), sexual difficulties (Chapter 13), drug abuse (Chapter 14), and schizophrenia (Chapter 12). The elegant twin studies and adoption studies, undertaken to unravel nature and nurture, are essentially correlational investigations.

Experiments of nature also occur throughout the textbook. They have provided important information about post-traumatic stress disorders (Chapter 8), dissociative disorders (Chapter 9), depression (Chapter 11), childhood disorders (Chapter 16), and neurological disorders (Chapter 17). Biological accidents such as hermaphroditism (Chapter 13) and the XYY chromosome disorder (Chapter 15) should be recognized as experiments of nature.

Finally, laboratory models of psychopathology have been used to investigate phobias (Chapter 8), peptic ulcers (Chapter 10), hypertension (Chapter 10), sudden death (Chapter 10), schizophrenia (Chapter 12), and so on. In many cases, these models have suggested therapy techniques that have proven successful in the clinic (Chapter 19).

This chapter makes the point that the best research metaphorically resembles a woven fabric; it occurs when results from different strategies converge in the understanding provided. As you read about the disorders and their treatments, decide which disorders seem most understandable. Are these the ones that have converging research?

FURTHER READINGS

American Psychological Association (1992). Ethical principles of psychologists and the code of conduct. *American Psychologist, 47,* 1597–1611.

Barber, T. X. (1976). *Pitfalls in human research: Ten pivotal points.* New York: Pergamon.

Becker, H. (1986). *Writing for social scientists.* Chicago: University of Chicago Press.

Huff, D. (1954). *How to lie with statistics.* New York: Norton.

Jung, J. (1971). *The experimenter's dilemma.* New York: Harper & Row.

Kazdin, A. E. (1980). *Research design in clinical psychology.* New York: Harper & Row.

Kazdin, A. E. (1981). Drawing valid inferences from case studies. *Journal of Consulting and Clinical Psychology, 49,* 183–192.

Maser, J. D., & Seligman, M. E. P. (1977). *Psychopathology: Experimental models.* San Francisco: Freeman.

Runyan, W. M. (1984). *Life histories and psychobiography: Explorations in theory and method.* New York: Oxford.

Schmidt, F. L. (1992). What do data really mean? Research findings, meta-analysis, and cumulative knowledge in psychology. *American Psychologist, 47*:10, 1173–1181.

Smith, M. L., & Glass, G. V. (1977). Meta-analysis of psychotherapy outcome studies. *American Psychologist, 32,* 752–760.

TERM-PAPER TOPICS

1. Describe the pros and cons of experimentation as a means to understanding complex human behavior. What are the implications of these arguments for the use of experiments in understanding abnormality?

2. Describe the pros and cons of laboratory models of psychopathology. When are models most useful? When are they least useful?

3. Is the relationship between laboratory research and therapy techniques based on this research really as straightforward as the textbook suggests? Evaluate the evidence with respect to a particular therapy technique. Take a stand, and defend it.

EXERCISES

Exercise One—Find the Confound

In this exercise, you will criticize the research designs of hypothetical investigations.

In a few sentences describe what is wrong with the conclusion of the researcher in each of the following:

1. A psychology teacher hypothesized that students who know little in the first place will learn more effectively than students who known a great deal to begin with. Thus, he administered to his students the identical multiple-choice test at the beginning and end of a course. He subtracted the number correct at the beginning from the number correct at the end to obtain a measure of improvement. This measure was negatively correlated with the number of correct answers on the first test.

The instructor concluded that his hypothesis was therefore correct.

2. A hospital director approached her hospital board with a request to continue a program of deep muscle massage for depressed patients. She provided statistics showing that among patients who had been massaged within the preceding five years, 20 percent were able to leave the hospital within one month after the massage and another 50 percent were able to leave within two months.

3. A group of elementary school children first learned a list of ten five-letter words and then a list of ten two-digit numbers. Two days later, they were asked to recall as many words and numbers as they could. The mean number of words recalled was 5.3, while the mean number of numbers was 1.2. It was concluded

that numbers are more difficult to recall than words.

4. A study used a large number of clinical tests and interviews to show that 37 of 112 patients given a new drug for hypertension exhibited inappropriate aggressiveness. It was, therefore, concluded that the drug should be discontinued because of its dangerous effect on behavior.

5. In a follow-up of patients treated with a new form of psychotherapy, it was found that 68 percent of the individuals treated with the new approach reported that they were satisfied with its effects. In contrast, 43 percent of the patients in a comparison group given traditional psychotherapy by the same therapists reported satisfaction. The researchers concluded that the new psychotherapy approach was an improvement over the traditional approach.

Exercise Two—Designing Psychological Research

Many questions of interest to psychologists can be approached with a variety of research strategies. In this exercise, you will demonstrate this idea to yourself.

For each of the following questions, design a brief experiment, correlational study, experiment of nature, and laboratory model to answer it.

1. Is depression the result of insufficient positive reinforcement?

2. Can phobias result from classical conditioning?

3. What are the characteristics of a good psychotherapist?

4. Does drug use cause psychopathology, or does psychopathology cause drug use?

5. Does loneliness lead to overeating?

Exercise Three—The Human Side of Research

The purpose of this exercise is to take you behind the scenes of psychological research by asking you to read some autobiographies by famous psychologists.

These volumes contain autobiographies by important researchers:

Boring, E. G., & Lindzey, G. (Eds.). (1967). *A history of psychology in autobiography* (Vol. 5). New York: Appleton-Century-Crofts.

Boring, E. G., Werner, H., Yerkes, R. M., & Langfeld, H. S. (Eds.). (1952). *A history of psychology in autobiography* (Vol. 4). Worcester, MA: Clark University Press.

Lindzey, G. (Ed.). (1974). *A history of psychology in autobiography* (Vol. 6). Englewood Cliffs, NJ: Prentice-Hall.

Murchinson, C. (Ed.). (1930–1936). *A history of psychology in autobiography* (3 vols.). Worcester, MA: Clark University Press.

As you read a given autobiography, contrast the life depicted with the common stereotype of the detached and eccentric scientist.

Exercise Four—Research by Psychologists and Others

In this exercise, you will compare and contrast the goals and methods of research by psychologists with the goals and methods of research by other scientists.

Arrange for your class a panel discussion by a research psychologist, biologist, chemist, physicist, and anthropologist. Have these scientists discuss research in their respective fields. What is common? What is different?

CHAPTER 7

Psychological Assessment and Classification

CHAPTER OVERVIEW

This chapter explains how psychologists diagnose abnormality. Diagnosis—or classification—is unavoidable in treating disorders, and when done well, it serves several purposes: (a) communication shorthand; (b) treatment recommendation; (c) etiology suggestion; (d) scientific investigation; and (e) payment for treatment. Psychologists use a variety of assessment devices in diagnosis, and these devices should be reliable (giving the same information on different occasions) and valid (serving the purpose intended).

A number of assessment techniques are described in this chapter, among them clinical interviews, psychological tests (inventories, projective tests, and intelligence tests), behavioral assessments, and psychophysiological assessments.

The diagnostic system in widest current use is the *Diagnostic and Statistical Manual of Mental Disorders,* Fourth Edition, of the American Psychiatric Association, DSM-IV. This system is described along with its strengths and weaknesses. The chapter ends with a discussion of factors that may bias diagnosis.

ESSENTIAL TERMS

behavioral assessment	record of the behaviors and thoughts targeted for change in therapy (p. 183)
Bender Visual-Motor Gestalt Test	widely used neuropsychological test (p. 186)
clinical interview	assessment technique in which a clinical psychologist or psychiatrist obtains information by face-to-face talking with a patient (p. 174)
structured interview	clinical interview in which questions are predetermined (p. 175)
unstructured interview	flexible clinical interview in which questions are not predetermined (p. 174)

239

Computerized Axial
   Tomography (CAT scan)
an X-ray technique used in neurological diagnosis for constructing a two-dimensional cross-sectional view of brain areas (p. 187)

diagnosis
classification into categories of disorder based on information about a pattern of symptoms for purposes of efficient communication, selection of treatment, suggestion of etiology, and/or facilitation of scientific investigation (p. 188)

clinical diagnosis
diagnosis given to patient in therapy (p. 188)

research diagnosis
diagnosis given to subject in scientific research (p. 203)

Diagnostic and Statistical Manual of Mental Disorders (DSM)
diagnostic system adopted by the American Psychiatric Association in 1952 (p. 190)

Diagnostic and Statistical Manual of Mental Disorders, Second Edition (DSM-II)
revision of DSM adopted by the American Psychiatric Association in 1968 (p. 190)

Diagnostic and Statistical Manual of Mental Disorders, Third Edition (DSM-III)
revision of DSM-II adopted by the American Psychiatric Association in 1980 (p. 191)

Diagnostic and Statistical Manual of Mental Disorders, Third Edition, Revised (DSM-III-R)
revision of DSM-III adopted by the American Psychiatric Association in 1987, currently in use (p. 191)

Diagnostic and Statistical Manual of Mental Disorders, Fourth Edition, Revised (DSM-IV)
revision of DSM-III-R adopted by the American Psychiatric Association in 1994 (p. 191)

electromyograph (EMG)
psychophysiological assessment instrument for measuring muscle contractions (p. 185)

functional analysis
behavioral assessment that includes a record of stimuli presumed to increase or decrease behaviors of interest (p. 183)

Halstead-Reitan
   Neuropsychological Battery
time-intensive battery of neuropsychological tests which can be used to provide information about cognitive and motor functioning, and to isolate the location of an impairment (p. 186)

illusory correlation
in psychological tests, the false belief that certain responses indicate certain disorders (p. 181)

intelligence quotient (IQ)
score from Wechsler intelligence tests (p. 182)

performance IQ
score reflecting nonverbal skills, such as design comprehension, ability to associate symbols with numbers (p. 182)

verbal IQ
score reflecting verbal skills, such as vocabulary, verbal comprehension, general information (p. 182)

intelligence test
psychological test that samples behaviors that predict success in school; used by clinicians to assess mental retardation and brain damage (p. 181)

interview schedule
protocol for a structured clinical interview (p. 175)

Kappa	statistic for estimating agreement between two interviews that corrects for chance (p. 195)
Luria-Nebraska Neuropsychological Battery	battery of neuropsychological tests which taps a broad spectrum of functioning (p. 187)
mental disorder	behavioral or psychological pattern that causes an individual distress or disables the individual in one or more significant areas of functioning, distinct from social deviance (p. 191)
Minnesota Multiphasic Personality Inventory (MMPI)	widely used personality inventory (p. 176)
Minnesota Multiphasic Personality Inventory-2 (MMPI-2)	most recent edition of MMPI with updated language and larger standardization sample (p. 178)
Nuclear Magnetic Response Imaging (MRI)	a noninvasive brain-imaging technique in which the neural organization of hydrogen atoms in a magnetic field produce readable signals that are translated into a cross-sectional computer image of a brain section (p. 188)
personality inventory	psychological test in written form that inquires about conscious experiences and feelings; e.g., MMPI (p. 176)
Positron Emission Tomography (PET scan)	a brain-imaging technique in which a radioisotopic substance is injected into the bloodstream and brain activity is recorded; useful for locating brain processes (p. 188)
projective test	psychological test that presents individuals with ambiguous stimuli to which they respond; so named because respondents are thought to project their unconscious conflicts onto the ambiguous stimuli; e.g., Rorschach (p. 179)
psychological test	standardized assessment technique, usually highly reliable (p. 175)
psychophysiological assessment	psychological testing that measures physiological characteristics (p. 185)
reliability	characteristic of an assessment device: capacity to generate the same findings on repeated use (p. 174)
test-retest/test reliability	ability of the instrument to yield the same results with repeated trials (p. 193)
inter-judge reliability	ability of the instrument to yield the same results with different observers (p. 193)
Rorschach test	projective test consisting of ten bilaterally symmetric inkblots; patients are asked to describe everything each inkblot resembles (p. 179)
Schedule for Affective Disorders and Schizophrenia (SADS)	structured interview used for diagnosing affective and schizophrenic disorders (p. 175)
Structured Clinical Interview for the DSM (SCID)	structured clinical interview used for making DSM diagnoses (p. 175)
Thematic Apperception Test (TAT)	projective test consisting of a series of ambiguous pictures; patients are asked to look at each picture and make up a story about it (p. 181)

validity   characteristic of an assessment device: utility for intended purposes (p. 174)

   descriptive validity   ability of an assessment device to differentiate patients in one category from those in another (p. 198)

   predictive validity   ability of an assessment device to predict the course and outcome of treatment (p. 198)

Wechsler Adult Intelligence
Scale—Revised (WAIS-R)   intelligence test for adults (p. 181)

Wechsler Intelligence Scale for
Children—Revised (WISC-R)   intelligence test for children (p. 181)

Wechsler Preschool and Primary
Scale of Intelligence (WPPSI)   intelligence test for young children (p. 181)

CENTRAL CONCEPTUAL ISSUES

Theoretical overview.   Psychological assessment and classification go right to the heart of what makes psychology such a complex and difficult science. The tools of assessment are very often theory-bound and domain-specific and run into the problem of quantifying and qualifying human behavior and psychology. The more subtle and complex they seek to be, the greater the difficulty of achieving satisfactory reliability and validity. The same can be said of classification. Yet without each of these, experimental analysis is impossible. Without some way to operationalize the object of study there is no way to systematically evaluate therapeutic approaches. These difficulties, together with a scientist's natural desire to obtain firm and reliable results, provide a powerful incentive to value those areas which can be most quantified, and partially explains the popularity of psychological theories. For this reason, psychological theories can be driven simply by reliance on that which we can measure, while down-playing that which we can observe or intuit. It is therefore not surprising that practicing therapists and research psychologists can have dramatically different perspectives. However, many of the greatest advances in psychology have been the product of the attempt to understand and classify psychology in new ways in order to resolve this a tension.

Reliability.   To say that an assessment tool is reliable is to say *only* that use of the tool yields consistent results. That is, repeated use of the tool to quantify or categorize the same phenomenon must achieve equivalent outcomes. A tool may be 100 percent reliable and still be a completely invalid measure of a given phenomenon. In general, reliability may be affected by many of the sources of bias which may hamper any scientific endeavor, including chance variation or consistency, improper administration, illusory correlation, experimenter bias, subject bias or resistance, environmental influence, and uncontrolled variables.

Validity.   The fact that a tool reliably measures *something* tells you nothing about the implications or applicability of the result. The validity of an assessment measure is the degree to which the results reflect the phenomenon which the tool is believed to be measuring. Consequently, it gauges the instrument's true usefulness. The sources of validity error include the entire domain of potential error in any observation, experiment, or interpretation. The nature of the claims made about the results of a reliable measure strongly influences its validity. Thus a conclusion that a measure indicates a strong correlational relationship between two factors may be valid, while a conclusion that the same measure indicates a causal relationship may be invalid. Very often consistent cultural or theoretical biases of the investigators may lead to highly reliable results which are entirely invalid as support for the investigator's conclusions. (Such a test might be a highly valid measure of the scientist's biases!)

Diagnosis.   Compared to medical diagnosis, psychological diagnosis is often one step removed from the phenomena of true interest. Rather than relying on physical data, it depends on the patient's reported symptoms or observable behavioral signs. It is the constellation of these pieces of evidence that is compared to a diagnostic check list. To make a diagnosis, both qualitative (such as the presence of specific symptoms) and quantitative (such as severity or duration) issues usually need be considered. Because diagnosis depends so heavily on observation of the manifest characteristics of a condition (whether it be from the clinician's external view or from the patient's vantage point of internal experience), it can be influenced by a number of social psychological factors, including the context in which the behavior is observed, expectations about normality or abnormality, and the credibility of other information considered to be relevant to the diagnostic judgment being made.

Systems of classification: The DSM-IV.   The DSM-IV and its predecessors have been accurately criticized both in terms of reliability and validity. Nevertheless it remains a valuable tool. By laying out a broad system of classification it allows scientists and therapists to begin organizing their approaches and research. In providing a structure, it allows psychologists and psychiatrists both to investigate what may be, as well as to argue what is not. In other words, to form and to test hypotheses. One danger of the prevalence and use of the DSM, is that it can blind psychologists to other ways of classifying, studying, diagnosing, or treating abnormal behavior. As significant as this may be, it is an inevitable pitfall of all paradigms or systems for organizing thought and observation.

SAMPLE EXAM

1. An assessment device generates the same findings with repeated use. It is, therefore,
   a. reliable.
   b. valid.
   c. standardized.
   d. both reliable and valid.
   e. neither reliable nor valid.

2. An assessment device proves useful for the purpose intended. It is, therefore,
   a. reliable.
   b. valid.
   c. standardized.
   d. both reliable and valid.
   e. none of the above.

3. In general, the reliability of an assessment device used in clinical diagnosis
   a. should be as high as the reliability of an assessment device used in research.

   b. should be higher than the reliability of an assessment device used in research.
   c. should be lower than the reliability of an assessment device used in research.
   d. is not as important as its validity.
   e. is the same as its validity.

4. In a clinical interview, information is obtained from
   a. what people say.
   b. how people say what they say.
   c. body posture.
   d. what people don't say.
   e. all of the above.

5. An interview schedule is
   a. a list of daily appointments for a clinical psychologist.
   b. a list of possible diagnoses to be ascertained during an interview.

c. a list of questions to be asked during an interview.

d. a list of techniques for increasing the flexibility of an interview.

e. the order of a test battery.

6. All of the following are strengths of an unstructured interview except
a. reliability.
b. spontaneity.
c. flexibility.
d. sensitivity.
e. all of the above are strengths

7. Kappa is used to estimate
a. inter-judge reliability.
b. inter-judge validity.
c. intra-judge reliability.
d. intra-judge validity.
e. none of the above.

8. Which does not belong?
a. DSM
b. MMPI
c. SCID
d. SADS
e. all of the above belong

9. Which of these does the patient fill out?
a. DSM
b. MMPI
c. SCID
d. SADS
e. none of the above

10. In general, compared to interviews, psychological tests are
a. more valid.
b. less valid.
c. more reliable.
d. less reliable.
e. more valid but less reliable.

11. Which is an example of a personality inventory?
a. MMPI
b. SNAFU
c. SADS
d. WAIS-R
e. SCID

12. The MMPI was developed by
a. writing questions that operationalized DSM-III-R categories.
b. seeing how people with known characteristics responded to questions.

c. choosing statements reported verbatim in Freud's case histories.
d. borrowing questions from WAIS-R.
e. none of the above.

13. The validity scales of the MMPI
a. ascertain the reliability of the test.
b. distract the respondent from the true purpose.
c. contain items that are not scored.
d. check for distortions.
e. measure the amount of guessing.

14. Projective tests are used by psychologists who favor the
a. biomedical model.
b. psychodynamic model.
c. behavioral model.
d. cognitive model.
e. existential model.

15. If a psychologist asked you to look at inkblots, you would be taking a
a. TAT.
b. BDI.
c. Rorschach.
d. Rep Test.
e. SCID.

16. Why are projective tests called projective tests?
a. They are administered on 35-mm slides.
b. The psychologist uses her imagination to score them.
c. The respondent is thought to reveal his unconscious conflicts.
d. They ask about future events.
e. none of the above

17. The Rorschach inkblots are all
a. black.
b. multicolored.
c. round.
d. symmetric.
e. of animals.

18. Which one of the following is *not* scored from the Rorschach?
a. what is seen
b. where it is seen
c. how common the response is
d. the order of the cards
e. whether color is used

19. Interpretation of the Rorschach is plagued by difficulties with

a. reliability.
b. validity.
c. distortion.
d. literacy.
e. the subject lying.

20. Rorschach interpretations may be distorted by
a. negative correlations.
b. zero correlations.
c. nonsignificant correlations.
d. illusory correlations.
e. any of the above.

21. If a psychologist asked you to tell a story about a fuzzy picture, you would be taking a
a. TAT.
b. WPPSI.
c. SADS.
d. GRE.
e. SCID.

22. The TAT has been frequently used to measure
a. intelligence.
b. motives.
c. attributions.
d. hallucinations.
e. personal constructs.

23. The TAT is used by psychologists who favor the
a. biomedical model.
b. existential model.
c. behavioral model.
d. cognitive model.
e. psychodynamic model.

24. Intelligence tests tend to be
a. reliable.
b. valid.
c. reliable and valid.
d. reliable but not valid.
e. either reliable or valid.

25. Intelligence tests are most useful for predicting success at
a. a profession.
b. school.
c. interpersonal relations.
d. telling jokes.
e. sports.

26. Clinical psychologists sometimes use intelligence tests to assess
a. sexual conflicts.

b. brain damage.
c. norepinephrine depletion.
d. creativity.
e. defense mechanisms.

27. If you wished to give an intelligence test to a twenty-five-year-old man, you would administer a
a. WAIS-R.
b. WISC-R.
c. WPPSI.
d. WHAT.
e. none of the above

28. If you wished to give an intelligence test to a ten-year-old boy, you would administer a
a. WAIS-R.
b. WISC-R.
c. WPPSI.
d. WHAT.
e. none of the above

29. If you wished to give an intelligence test to a three-year-old girl, you would administer a
a. WAIS-R.
b. WISC-R.
c. WPPSI.
d. WHAT.
e. none of the above

30. Behavioral assessment tends to be used by psychologists who favor the
a. biomedical model.
b. existential model.
c. behavioral model.
d. cognitive model.
e. psychodynamic model.

31. Functional analysis is to behavioral assessment as what is to operant?
a. instincts
b. personal constructs
c. rewards and punishments
d. discriminative stimuli
e. association

32. If a psychologist wished to measure contractions of your muscles, she might employ an
a. EKG.
b. EMG.
c. EEG.
d. EFG
e. ESP.

33. An assessment device that is different for men and women is
    a. Rorschach.
    b. TAT.
    c. EMG.
    d. WAIS-R.
    e. none of the above.

34. Which one of the following is *not* a reason to make a diagnosis?
    a. Diagnosis aids communication.
    b. Diagnosis guides treatments.
    c. Diagnosis suggests etiology.
    d. Diagnosis aids research.
    e. Diagnosis increases vigilance.

35. All of the following are diagnostic schemes except
    a. *The Witches' Hammer.*
    b. DSM.
    c. DSM-II.
    d. SADS.
    e. Aesop's fables.

36. Who does not belong?
    a. Bleuler
    b. Butler
    c. Kraepelin
    d. Kretchmer
    e. Pinel

37. DSM-IV improves on previous diagnostic schemes because it
    a. is contemporary.
    b. provides precise criteria.
    c. specifies necessary and sufficient conditions for mental disorders.
    d. recommends preferred treatments.
    e. specifies etiologies.

38. Mental disorder is not the same as
    a. mental illness.
    b. emotional disturbance.
    c. social deviance.
    d. behavioral disability.
    e. psychological syndrome.

39. DSM-IV describes mental disorders along how many dimensions?
    a. two
    b. three
    c. five
    d. seven
    e. ten

40. Which one of the following is *not* a strength of DSM-IV?

    a. More diagnoses are possible.
    b. Reliability has been ascertained.
    c. Reliability is acceptably high.
    d. It aids in planning treatment.
    e. It is consistent with international classification.

41. Reliability studies of DSM-III are criticized for all these reasons except
    a. Axis II disorders are more reliable than Axis I diagnoses.
    b. judges are not always independent.
    c. reliabilities are reported for clusters of diagnoses only.
    d. multiple diagnoses increase likelihood of agreement.
    e. all of these are criticisms.

42. DSM-IV has very good
    a. descriptive validity.
    b. outcome validity.
    c. predictive validity.
    d. both *a* and *b*.
    e. none of the above.

43. All of these conditions bias diagnosis except
    a. context.
    b. reliability.
    c. expectation.
    d. source credibility.
    e. all of the above can bias diagnosis

44. Patients in mental hospitals tend to
    a. engage in writing behavior.
    b. hear voices.
    c. be regarded as abnormal.
    d. be seen as malingering.
    e. be under-medicated.

45. Psychological diagnosis is plagued by all of these except
    a. suspect reliability.
    b. suspect validity.
    c. bias.
    d. lack of treatments.
    e. expectation.

46. On the whole, psychological diagnosis is
    a. useless.
    b. unavoidable.
    c. accurate.
    d. simple.
    e. wholly inaccurate.

Answer Key for Sample Exam

1.	a	(p. 174)	13.	d	(p. 176)	25.	b	(p. 182)	36.	b	(p. 190)
2.	b	(p. 174)	14.	b	(p. 179)	26.	b	(p. 182)	37.	b	(p. 192)
3.	b	(p. 203)	15.	c	(p. 179)	27.	a	(p. 181)	38.	c	(p. 191)
4.	e	(p. 174)	16.	c	(p. 179)	28.	b	(p. 181)	39.	c	(p. 192)
5.	c	(p. 175)	17.	d	(p. 179)	29.	c	(p. 181)	40.	c	(p. 195)
6.	a	(p. 175)	18.	d	(p. 179)	30.	c	(p. 183)	41.	a	(p. 196)
7.	a	(p. 195)	19.	a, b	(p. 181)	31.	c	(p. 183)	42.	e	(p. 199)
8.	b	(p. 176)	20.	d	(p. 181)	32.	b	(p. 185)	43.	b	(p. 200)
9.	b	(p. 176)	21.	a	(p. 181)	33.	e	(p. 185)	44.	c	(p. 200)
10.	c	(p. 176)	22.	b	(p. 181)	34.	e	(p. 189)	45.	d	(p. 203)
11.	a	(p. 176)	23.	e	(p. 181)	35.	e	(p. 190)	46.	b	(p. 203)
12.	b	(p. 176)	24.	c	(p. 181)						

SELF-TEST

1. Without _____, science is impossible.

2. Classification of psychological disorders is also called _____.

3. If an assessment device gives the same results on repeated occasions, it is _____.

4. If an assessment device serves its stated purpose, it is _____.

5. How reliable an assessment device should be depends partly on the consequences of

   _____.

6. The favorite assessment technique of clinicians is the _____.

7. The Schedule for Affective Disorders and Schizophrenia (SADS) is a

   _____ interview.

8.   Advantages of personality inventories include _____ and the _____ with which they can be administered.

9. The most commonly used personality inventory is the _____; its results are presented in terms of a _____.

10. Psychodynamic clinicians tend to favor _____ tests to measure _____ conflicts; two of the most common of these tests are the _____ and the _____.

11. Interpretations of the Rorschach may be distorted by _____ correlations.

12. When a client takes the TAT, she is asked to _____.

13. The most reliable and valid psychological tests _____.

14. The Wechsler test for adults is the _____; for children it is the _____; and for preschoolers it is the _____.

15. Wechsler tests provide two scores, _____ IQ and _____ IQ.

16. Intelligence tests were originally developed to distinguish _____ from _____; psychologists may also use these tests to diagnose _____ and _____.

17. Psychologists who favor the behavioral model tend to use _____ assessment, which usually is done in conjunction with _____.

18. The electromyograph is used in _____ assessment.

19. The _____ and the _____ are neuropsychological batteries used to assess the nature and location of brain impairment.

20. The CAT scan and MRI allow visualization of the specific _____ in the brain, while the PET scan allows visualization of specific _____ therein.

21. Reasons for diagnosis include _____, _____, _____, _____, and _____.

22. Diagnosis of psychological disorders is modeled on the example of _____ classification.

23. The first comprehensive system of classifying psychological disorders was created by _____; he based diagnosis on _____.

24. The current system of diagnosis endorsed by the American Psychiatric Association is _____.

25. DSM-IV attempts to improve DSM-II by making the criteria for diagnosis more _____.

26. DSM-IV diagnoses employ _____ axes.

27. According to DSM-IV, mental disorders should be distinguished from _____.

28. The reliabilities of DSM-IV diagnoses are _____ than the reliabilities of DSM-II.

29. The reliability and validity of DSM-IV diagnoses are an _____.

30. Conditions that may bias diagnosis include _____, _____, and _____.

31. The reliability of research diagnoses may be _____ than the reliability of clinical diagnoses. The validity of research diagnoses may be _____ than the validity of clinical diagnoses.

Answer Key for Self-Test

1. classification
2. diagnosis
3. reliable
4. valid
5. errors
6. clinical interview
7. structured
8. reliability; efficiency
9. MMPI; profile
10. projective; unconscious; Rorschach; TAT
11. illusory
12. tell a story
13. intelligence test
14. WAISR; WISCR; WPPSI
15. verbal; performance
16. bright students; dull students; mental retardation; brain damage
17. behavioral; treatment
18. psychophysiological
19. Halstead-Reitan; Luria-Nebraska
20. locations; processes
21. communication shorthand; treatment recommendation; etiology suggestion; scientific investigation, third-party payments
22. biological
23. Emil Kraepelin; symptoms
24. DSM-IV
25. precise
26. five
27. social deviance
28. higher
29. open question
30. context; expectation; source credibility
31. less; less

MATCHING ITEMS

_____	1.	PET scan
_____	2.	Bender Gestalt
_____	3.	electromyagraphs
_____	4.	validity
_____	5.	reliability
_____	6.	Rorschach
_____	7.	SCID
_____	8.	MMPI-2
_____	9.	MRI
_____	10.	Kappa statistic
_____	11.	clinicians' beliefs
_____	12.	TAT

A. draw from memory
B. useful
C. brain structure
D. projective test
E. brain activity
F. personality profile
G. inter-judge reliability
H. structured clinical interview
I. muscle tension
J. stable
K. motives
L. illusory correlation

Answer Key for Matching Items

1.	E	7.	H
2.	A	8.	F
3.	I	9.	C
4.	B	10.	G
5.	J	11.	L
6.	D	12.	K

SHORT-ANSWER QUESTIONS

1. In conducting a clinical interview, information may be elicited using structured or unstructured formats. What are the benefits and limitations of each?

2. What are projective tests? What do they examine? What are their assumptions? (Give examples.)

3. What are the major issues to consider when developing a diagnostic system? How does the DSM classification system address these? What are its shortcomings?

4. What are the five axes used for classification in the DSM system and what does each assess?

5. What are the two major kinds of validity? How do issues of reliability impact them?

6. Even with a reliable and valid diagnostic classification system in hand, diagnosis can be biased by a number of factors. Discuss these.

TYING IT TOGETHER

Diagnostic approaches reflect models of abnormality. Each approach surveyed in Chapters 3 through 5 is associated with characteristic assessment techniques. Thus, the biomedical approach (Chapter 3) gives rise to psychophysiological and neuropsychological assessment (see also Chapter 17), the psychodynamic approach to projective tests (Chapter 4), the behavioral approach (Chapter 5) to functional analysis, and the cognitive approach (Chapter 5) to the Rep Test. Even the supernatural approach (Chapter 2) had an associated diagnostic strategy presented in *The Witches' Hammer*.

Regardless of the type of assessment, the fuzzy nature of abnormality must be remembered. The family resemblance idea puts upper limits on the reliability and validity of an assessment device that measures a single sign of abnormality (Chapter 1). To the degree that this idea is neglected, problems in research (Chapter 6) and legal decisions (Chapter 18) may seem more puzzling than they may otherwise.

As you read the remaining chapters, keep in mind how the various assessment devices described in Chapter 7 can be used to make a diagnosis (Chapter 8 through 17), to justify involuntary commitment (Chapter 18), and to assess the effectiveness of psychotherapy (Chapter 19). Remember the less-than-perfect reliability and validity of any assessment device.

DSM-IV attempts to make assessment easier. It proposes behavioral criteria (see Chapter 5) for most disorders, and it rarely proposes necessary and sufficient conditions (see Chapter 1) for diagnosis. Again, as you read the remaining chapters, keep in mind the clarity of DSM-IV criteria for a given diagnosis. In some cases, such as phobias (Chapter 8), diagnosis is simple. In other cases, such as personality disorders (Chapter 15), diagnosis is more complicated and may ultimately prove nonviable. As illustrated in Chapter 2, conceptions of abnormality have changed over the years. Perhaps the future will see further change in diagnostic categories in response to difficulties in reliable and valid diagnoses.

FURTHER READINGS

Chapman, L. J., & Chapman, J. P. (1969). Illusory correlation as an obstacle to the use of valid psychodiagnostic signs. *Journal of Abnormal Psychology, 74,* 271–287.

Kendell, R. E. (1991). Relationships between the DSM-IV and the ICD-10. *Journal of Abnormal Psychology, 100*:3, 297–301.

McLemore, C. W., & Benjamin, L. S. (1979). Whatever happened to interpersonal diagnosis? A psychosocial alternative to DSM-III. *American Psychologist, 34,* 17–34.

Persons, J. B. (1986). The advantages of studying psychological phenomena rather than psychiatric diagnoses. *American Psychologist, 41,* 1252–1260.

Schact, T., & Nathan, P. E. (1977). But is it good for psychologists? Appraisal and status of DSM-III. *American Psychologist, 32,* 1017–1025.

Singerman, B. (1981). DSM-III: Historical antecedents and present significance. *Journal of Clinical Psychiatry, 42,* 409–410.

Wakefield, J. C. (1992). The concept of mental disorder: On the boundary between biological facts and social values. *American Psychologist, 47,* 373–388.

Wakefield, J. C. (1993). Limits of operationalization: A critique of Spitzer and Endicott's (1978) proposed operational criteria for mental disorder. *Journal of Abnormal Psychology, 102*:1, 160–172.

Zigler, E., & Phillips, L. (1961). Psychiatric diagnosis: A critique. *Journal of Abnormal and Social Psychology, 63,* 607–618.

Zimmerman, M. (1990). Is DSM-IV needed at all? *Archives of General Psychiatry, 47,* 974–976.

TERM-PAPER TOPICS

1. The use of intelligence tests in the school system is controversial, yet this is where they seem to be most valid. How are intelligence tests used in diagnosis of abnormality? What is controversial about this use?

2. Describe the evidence for the reliability and validity of a particular projective test.

3. How has illusory correlation been investigated? Do these investigations convince you that psychological testing should be viewed with skepticism?

4. Review the popular approaches to interviewing. Identify which model of abnormality is most compatible with which interviewing approach.

5. The MMPI has recently been revised to bring it up to date. As the text points out this has had several consequences; one of which being that the old and new versions of the tests yield different results. Discuss why this might be. How might changing social norms effect test writing or results? How might a theoretical or cultural bias change? What would this imply about validity and diagnosis? Would these questions be taken into account?

6. Discuss the implications of the correlational nature of the MMPI. Is it possible that a person's profile might precisely resemble that of a well documented "pattern" and yet be incorrectly classified or yield poor predictions?

7. How might a test be useful for research but not for application? How might a test be useful in application but not for research?

EXERCISES

Exercise One—Invalidity of Trait Description

In this exercise, you will see how "personality" sketches that describe people in terms of their traits may not capture their unique selves as well as you may think.

Ask a group of five or six people who know each other well to describe each other in terms of his or her striking traits. Remove the names from these descriptions, and show them to all the group members. Ask them to identify who has been described. You may find that correct identification is no better than chance.

Forer, B. R. (1949). The fallacy of personal validation: A classroom demonstration of gullibility. *Journal of Abnormal and Social Psychology, 44,* 118–123.

Mischel, W. (1968). *Personality and assessment.* New York: Wiley.

Rodin, M. J. (1972). The informativeness of trait descriptions. *Journal of Personality and Social Psychology, 21,* 341–344.

Exercise Two—Validity of Behavior Description

The purpose of this exercise is to assess the validity of behavioral assessment compared to "personality" assessment.

Repeat Exercise One, but this time ask the individuals to describe each other in terms of characteristic actions and behaviors. It may be that correct identification is greatly increased by the use of descriptions based on discrete and observable characteristics.

What do you conclude about behavioral assessment versus more traditional "personality assessment?

Exercise Three—Psychological Assessment

The purpose of this exercise is to gain some first-hand knowledge about the use of psychological tests.

Arrange a class presentation by a clinical psychologist about his or her use of psychological assessment. What tests are used by this psychologist? What tests are not used? Does the psychologist adhere to a given model of abnormality?

Exercise Four—Expectations and Assessment

The textbook describes how expectations can bias assessment. In this exercise, you will demonstrate this.

Introduce someone to several of your friends. To some of your friends, mention that this individual has just returned from a year abroad in which he traveled widely. To your other friends, mention that the individual has just returned from a year abroad in which he stayed in a mental hospital. Pay attention to how the individual is treated during the ensuing conversation. What is said about him after he leaves?

A colleague tells a story about arriving at a new teaching job after working on an inpatient psychiatric ward. Upon meeting new people he would say matter-of-factly, "Oh, I just spent two years on a psychiatric ward, and now it's interesting to be in such a different place." Strange reactions always ensued, and it finally occurred to him that his new acquaintances had not heard him say what he intended to say.

Farina, A., Holland, C. H., & Ring, K. (1966). The role of stigma and set in interpersonal attraction. *Journal of Abnormal Psychology, 71,* 421–428.

Langer, E. J., & Abelson, R. P. (1974). A patient by any other name . . . : Clinician group difference in labelling bias. *Journal of Consulting and Clinical Psychology, 42,* 4–9.

CHAPTER 8

Phobia, Panic, and the Anxiety Disorders

CHAPTER OVERVIEW

This is the first of ten chapters that describe the major types of abnormality. The subject of this chapter is disorders in which fear or anxiety is consciously experienced. Subsequent chapters describe disorders in which anxiety is not consciously experienced but is inferred.

Disorders in which anxiety is consciously experienced are of two major types: fear disorders (phobias and post-traumatic stress disorders) and anxiety disorders (panic disorders, agoraphobia, and generalized anxiety disorders). A phobia involves fear of an object out of all proportion to the actual danger posed. Post-traumatic stress disorders are reactions to a catastrophic experience in which the individual suffers anxiety, depression, numbness, and reliving of the catastrophe. In a panic disorder, an individual is suddenly overwhelmed by apprehension and terror that are unattached to any specific object in the environment. Generalized anxiety disorders are the chronic experience of anxiety.

The chapter describes the four components of fear: (a) cognitive, (b) somatic, (c) emotional, and (d) behavioral. The components of anxiety are the same except for cognitive component. In fear expectation of harm is associated with a specific danger, but in anxiety expectation of harm is general.

Phobias are the best understood of these disorders and are described in some detail in this chapter. The psychodynamic account and the behavioral account of phobias are explained. When the idea of prepared classical conditioning is introduced, the behavioral model better handles the evidence regarding phobias than does the psychodynamic model. Successful therapies for phobias are based on the behavioral model: systematic desensitization, flooding, and modeling.

The other fear and anxiety disorders are briefly described.

ESSENTIAL TERMS

adrenal glands	glands that secrete hormones involved in emergency reaction (p. 213)
adrenergic system	physiological system using adrenaline and noradrenaline as chemical messengers to produce an emergency reaction; e.g., SNS (p. 213)

agoraphobia	anxiety disorder characterized by fear of places of assembly and open spaces (p. 255)
anxiety	emotion involving expectation of diffuse danger, physiological emergency reaction, and fight-or-flight behavior (cf. fear) (p. 215)
state anxiety	transient anxiety (p. 260)
trait anxiety	anxiety displayed across time and situation (p. 260)
anxiety disorder	disorder in which no specific object is feared (cf. fear disorder) (p. 250)
applied tension therapy	therapy technique for blood phobia in which deliberate tensing of muscles raises blood pressure and heart rate and prevents fainting (p. 232)
autonomic nervous system (ANS)	part of the nervous system that controls internal organs composed of sympathetic and parasympathetic nervous systems (p. 213)
avoidance responding	flight response in which a harmful event is fled from before it is encountered (p. 215)
blood phobia	phobia characterized by anxiety in situations involving the sight of blood, injections, and injuries; physiological pattern of anxiety is unique, involving a marked drop in blood pressure and heart rate which may result in fainting (p. 221)
central nervous system (CNS)	brain and spinal cord (p. 212)
cholinergic system	physiological system using acetycholine as a chemical messenger to produce the relaxation reaction; e.g., PNS (p. 213)
counterconditioning	therapy technique for fear disorders in which responses that are incompatible with fear are caused to occur at the same time as the fear object; e.g., systematic desensitization (p. 229)
emergency reaction	physiological response to danger; increased heart beat, breathing, sweating; contraction of spleen; blood-content change (p. 213)
escape responding	flight response in which a harmful event actually occurs and then is fled from (p. 214)
exposure therapy	(*see* flooding)
fear	emotion involving expectation of specific harm, physiological emergency reaction, and fight-or-flight behavior (cf. anxiety) (p. 210)
fear disorder	disorder characterized by dread of specific objects (cf. anxiety disorder) (p. 249)
flooding	therapy technique for fear disorders in which stimuli that elicit fear are repeatedly encountered; also known as exposure (*see* Chapter 5, "Essential Terms") (pp. 230, 257)

generalized anxiety disorder (GAD)	disorder characterized by chronic anxiety (p. 258)
hypothalamus	brain structure influencing eating, drinking, and sexual behavior, and regulating fundamental bodily processes (p. 213)
illness and injury phobia	(*see* nosophobia)
inanimate object phobias	a class of specific phobias in which particular situations or objects such as dirt, heights, closed places, darkness, and travel, are anxiety-provoking (p. 220)
incidence	rate of new cases of a disorder in a given time period (cf. prevalence) (p. 218)
mantra	a syllable repeated to oneself in a meditation exercise (p. 261)
meditation	a relaxation technique that blocks the thoughts that produce anxiety; involves sitting eyes-closed in a quiet setting repeating a mantra (p. 261)
modeling	therapy technique for fear disorders in which client watches someone who is not fearful perform a behavior of which the client is not capable (p. 231)
nosophobia	phobia of a specific illness or injury; not the same as hypochondria (*see* Chapter 4, "Essential Terms"), which is anxiety about a variety of illnesses (p. 220)
panic disorder	disorder characterized by recurrent attacks of sudden and intense anxiety (p. 250)
parasympathetic nervous system (PNS)	part of the autonomic nervous system responsible for producing the relaxation response, which counteracts the emergency reaction (p. 213)
phobia	disorder characterized by fear of an object out of all proportion to the reality of danger (p. 217)
post-traumatic stress disorder	following a catastrophic event, a disorder characterized by numbness, reliving of event, and symptoms of anxiety (p. 238)
prepared classical conditioning	rapidly acquired Pavlovian conditioning thought to be predisposed by natural selection (p. 235)
prevalence	percentage of population having a disorder at any given time (cf. incidence) (p. 218)
progressive relaxation	a relaxation technique that blocks the motor components of anxiety; involves tightening and releasing the major muscle groups (p. 261)
rape trauma syndrome	post-traumatic stress disorder following rape, including acute (disorganization) and long-term (reorganization) reactions (p. 224)
social phobia	phobia characterized by fear of social situations (p. 221)

specific phobias

a category of phobias that includes animal phobias, phobias of inanimate objects, illness and injury phobias (nosophobias), and blood phobias (p. 219)

survival guilt

aspect of post-traumatic stress disorder in which the individual feels guilty for having survived a traumatic event while others did not (p. 241)

sympathetic nervous system (SNS)

part of the autonomic nervous system responsible for producing emergency reaction (p. 213)

systematic desensitization

therapy technique for fear disorder in which stimuli that elicit fear are paired with relaxation or other pleasant experiences (*see* Chapter 5, "Essential Terms) (p. 229)

CENTRAL CONCEPTUAL ISSUES

Identifying anxiety disorders.   Abnormal phobia and anxiety differ from normal fear and anxiety in terms of degree of appropriateness, but they are not fundamentally different in kind. As is commonplace in psychology, fear, phobia, and anxiety are categorized and distinguished from other psychological events and disorders on a family resemblance basis. The four components which comprise the family of signs and symptoms common to fear, phobia, and anxiety are cognitions, somatic events, emotional/subjective experience, and behaviors.

Distinguishing anxiety disorders.   Phobia and anxiety share the same signs and symptoms within the somatic, emotional/subjective, and behavioral categories, but they differ in cognitions. Fears and phobias are of specific objects, situations, or events. Anxiety disorders involved non-specific fears in which the threatening event or situation cannot be specifically identified. Thus abnormal fears of elevators or public speaking have specific referents and are categorized as phobias. Panic disorder, in contrast, involves a desperate fear that something dreadful will happen, but without an apparent source of threat. Because phobias are generally quite circumscribed, phobics can often function well in other areas of their life: the phobia itself is the only problem. In contrast, an anxiety disorder, which does not present a specific source of threat, is much more difficult to manage. Without the sense that a particular threat can be avoided, the individual may grow to fear all matter of exposure, severely limiting his or her ability to go out and function in the world. Moreover, with spontaneous panic attacks, the individual may become conditioned to fear a variety of stimuli.

The behavioral understanding of phobias.   Significant progress in understanding and treating phobias has come through behavioral analysis. In this model, phobias are classically conditioned through particularly traumatic experiences. Avoidance behavior around the fear-conditioned object prevents reality-testing and the phobia persists. Very effective treatments employing extinction have been developed using this model. The four major treatments (systematic desensitization, flooding, modeling, applied tension), each using different methodologies, strive to present the individual with the phobic situation, thereby gradually extinguishing the phobic response. In the case of systematic desensitization, the individual is also counterconditioned by pairing deep relaxation with the phobic stimulus.

Prepared to fear.   While classical conditioning is an adequate explanation of the genesis of fears in general, it has several shortcomings in fully explaining phobias: (1) phobias tend to be limited to a small subset of possible—and on the surface, likely—conditioned stimuli; (2) the irrationality of phobias which persist in the face of overwhelming counter-argument evidence and adverse effects of phobic behaviors; and (3) the existence of phobias that arise seemingly spontaneously or from less-than-traumatic events. All of these issues are addressed by the idea of *prepared classical conditioning*. Prepared classical conditioning assumes that organisms have adaptively evolved to be prepared to fear common situations which may have been threatening to early humans (e.g., snakes, heights, etc.). This seems to explain the prevalence of particular phobias. By virtue of the biological substrate to these phobias—and because they may be localized in a more primitive area of the brain than that responsible for the higher intellectual functions—prepared phobias would be resistant to rational argument. Being genetically prepared to be frightened would explain why typical objects of phobias become conditioned stimuli much more readily than other classically conditioned fears.

Panic.   The dispute about the origins of panic disorders provides an unusually clear example of the ways in which theoretical orientations treat particular evidence, the differing implications for treatments, and the method by which scientists attempt to resolve conflict. The biological approach seizes upon the physiological data as evidence of a biological etiology, and attempts treatment through pharmaceutical intervention. The cognitive approach sees the essential link between physiological events and panic as being one of interpretation, and prescribes a cognitive treatment. Evidence in favor of one or the other orientation is sought in a clinical trial based on implications of the two theories. Converging support is sought by comparing the efficacy of the implied treatments.

Phobic and anxiety disorders.   Cognitive, behavioral, and biological analyses have all been important in understanding and treating phobic and anxiety disorders. Each orientation has contributed to some very effective treatments. However, they leave unresolved the questions of who will become afflicted and why certain situations are particularly anxiety-inducing. Psychoanalytic theorists point to an individual's developmental history and to the symbolic meaning of his or her symptoms or the objects of fear to explain these issues. However, the insight-oriented treatment prescribed by this model has a poor overall track record of success.

SAMPLE EXAM

1. All of these are neuroses in which anxiety is experienced except
   a. phobia.
   b. hysteria.
   c. post-traumatic stress disorder.
   d. panic disorder.
   e. agoraphobia.

2. The text distinguishes fear disorders from anxiety disorders by
   a. their relative seriousness.
   b. whether the object or situation is truly dangerous.
   c. whether they can be treated.
   d. whether or not the reaction is normal.
   e. the role or presence of a specific object.

3. According to the text, the fear disorders include
   a. phobias and post-traumatic stress disorder.
   b. hysteria and obsessive-compulsive disorder.
   c. panic disorder, agoraphobia, and generalized anxiety disorder.
   d. obsessive-compulsive disorder, phobia, and agoraphobia.
   e. panic disorder, phobias.

4. All of these are disorders in which anxiety is *not* experienced except
   a. amnesia.
   b. fugue.
   c. phobia.
   d. multiple personality.
   e. conversion disorder.

5. The most important element of fear is
   a. cognitive.
   b. somatic.
   c. emotional.
   d. behavioral.
   e. none of the above.

6. What is the cognitive component of fear?
   a. appraisal
   b. expectation
   c. attribution
   d. belief
   e. reaction

7. All of the following are reactions to fear except
   a. flushed skin.
   b. goosebumps.
   c. sweat.
   d. tense muscles.
   e. clammy palms.

8. What is the emergency reaction?
   a. flight or fight response
   b. body's reaction after danger has passed
   c. response to sudden infection
   d. resolution of the approach-avoidance conflict
   e. a reaction specific to anxiety and fear disorders

9. The emergency reaction follows which order?
   a. danger to SNS to hypothalamus to cortex
   b. danger to cortex to hypothalamus to SNS
   c. danger to cortex to SNS to hypothalamus
   d. danger to hypothalamus to cortex to SNS
   e. none of the above

10. The parasympathetic nervous system is to the sympathetic nervous system as what is to the emergency reaction?
    a. vigilance
    b. excitation
    c. exhaustion
    d. relaxation
    e. inhibition

11. The SNS is to the PNS as
    a. cholinergic is to adrenergic.
    b. behavioral is to cognitive.
    c. adrenergic is to cholinergic.
    d. cognitive is to behavioral.
    e. fight is to flight.

12. What is the difference between escape responding and avoidance responding?
    a. Escape responding occurs frequently, while avoidance responding does not.
    b. Escape responding is easily learned, while avoidance responding is not.
    c. Escape responding is easily extinguished, while avoidance responding is not.
    d. Escape responding is successful while avoidance responding is not.
    e. Escape responding occurs when an event is encountered, while avoidance responding occurs before an event is encountered.

13. Which element of abnormality do phobias have?
    a. suffering
    b. maladaptiveness
    c. observer discomfort
    d. irrationality
    e. all of the above

14. All of the following are common phobias except
    a. agoraphobia.
    b. anthophobia.
    c. social phobia.
    d. animal phobia.
    e. nosophobia.

15. At any given time, 10 percent of the population has a certain disorder. Every year, 1 percent of the population acquires this disorder. What is its prevalence?
    a. 10 percent
    b. 1 percent per year
    c. 9 percent
    d. 11 percent
    e. none of the above

16. In the above question, what is the incidence of the disorder?
    a. 10 percent
    b. 1 percent per year

c.   9 percent
d.   11 percent
e.   none of the above

17. Social phobics are afraid of all of the following except
    a.   crowds.
    b.) people.
    c.   being seen.
    d.   speaking in public.
    e.   doing things in public.

18. Animal phobias begin during
    a.) early childhood.
    b.   puberty.
    c.   early adulthood.
    d.   middle age.
    e.   old age.

19. Which is *not* true about animal phobics?
    a.   Most are women.
    b.   Most outgrow their phobia.
    c.) Most have other problems.
    d.   Most can point to a precipitating trauma.
    e.   all of the above are true

20. Which one of the following is *not* true about nosophobics?
    a.   Most are healthy.
    b.   Most are not hypochondriacs.
    c.) Most are women.
    d.) Most have other problems.
    e.   all of the above are true

21. A friend of yours confides that he is extremely concerned that he might have contracted AIDS. When you ask him whether he has put himself at any risk of exposure or has any symptoms, he answers "no" to both questions but mentions that ever since an acquaintance at work announced that he was HIV positive, he has been very concerned about how common it seems to be. You begin to consider that your friend might be suffering from
    a.   hypochondriasis.
    b.   agoraphobia.
    c.   homophobia.
    d.   blood phobia.
    e.) nosophobia.

22. According to Freud, the development of a phobia involves all but
    a.   castration fear.
    b.   displacement
    c.) sublimation.

d.   anxiety.
e.   reaction formation.

23. According to Freud, the phobic object is a
    a.   real danger.
    b.   symbol.
    c.   non sequitur.
    d.   fantasy.
    e.   dream component.

24. According to Freud, phobias are cured through
    a.   desensitization.
    b.   flooding.
    c.   insight.
    d.   tricyclics.
    e.   none of the above.

25. Little Hans was afraid of
    a.   cats.
    b.   homosexuals.
    c.   horses.
    d.   white rats.
    e.   wolves.

26. Which one of the following is *not* true about the psychoanalytic account of phobias?
    a.   Psychoanalytic therapy does not cure phobias.
    b.   There exist better explanations.
    c.   It explains only phobias among men.
    d.   It is based on loose reasoning.
    e.   all of the above are true

27. According to the behavioral account, phobias arise by
    a.   classical conditioning.
    b.   operant conditioning.
    c.   modeling.
    d.   desensitization.
    e.   flooding.

28. Little Albert was afraid of
    a.   cats.
    b.   horses.
    c.   homosexuals
    d.   white rats.
    e.   wolves.

29. The Little Albert investigation was an early example of
    a.   clinical case history.
    b.   experimental study.
    c.   correlational study.
    d.   experiment of nature.
    e.   laboratory model of psychopathology.

30. How does the behavioral model account for the persistence of phobias?
    a. escape learning
    b. avoidance learning
    c. modeling
    d. flooding
    e. it cannot

31. All of these are effective therapies for most phobias except
    a. flooding.
    b. insight.
    c. desensitization.
    d. modeling.
    e. all of the above are effective

32. In desensitization, the phobic object is paired with
    a. drugs.
    b. terror.
    c. relaxation.
    d. social support.
    e. shock.

33. The cure rate of specific phobias by systematic desensitization is approximately
    a. 10 percent.
    b. 33 percent.
    c. 50 percent.
    d. 85 percent.
    e. 100 percent.

34. Symptom substitution following treatment of phobias by systematic desensitization is predicted by the
    a. biomedical model.
    b. psychodynamic model.
    c. behavioral model.
    d. cognitive model.
    e. existential model.

35. Flooding involves
    a. modeling.
    b. escape responding.
    c. avoidance responding.
    d. extinction.
    e. insight.

36. Modeling involves
    a. behavioral change.
    b. cognitive change.
    c. either behavioral or cognitive change.
    d. both behavioral and cognitive change.
    e. neither behavioral nor cognitive change.

37. Antidepressant drugs may be used to treat phobics who
    a. have specific fears.
    b. have spontaneous panic attacks.
    c. have illness phobias.
    d. have little insight.

38. The most effective treatment for blood phobics is
    a. flooding.
    b. modeling.
    c. systematic desensitization.
    d. relaxation.
    e. applied tension.

39. Which one of the following is *not* a problem with the behavioral account of phobias?
    a. It fails to explain which therapies prove effective.
    b. It fails to explain the selectivity of phobias.
    c. It fails to explain the irrationality of phobias.
    d. It fails to explain the lack of a traumatic event for some phobias.
    e. All of the above are problems with the behavioral account.

40. Prepared classical conditioning is thought to be "prepared" by
    a. learning.
    b. evolution.
    c. briefing.
    d. drugs.
    e. expectation.

41. Which one of the following is *not* true about prepared classical conditioning?
    a. It is involved in taste aversions.
    b. It has been demonstrated with people.
    c. It is rational.
    d. It may be a model of phobias.
    e. It is inherited.

42. The prepared-classical-conditioning account does not explain
    a. why phobias persist.
    b. why phobias occur in some people but not in others.
    c. why phobias are irrational.
    d. why phobias entail suffering.
    e. why some phobias are more common than others.

43. A child wearing a sunhat while playing outdoors in the backyard is bitten by a spider. If she were to develop a phobia following this experience, which of these would it most likely be?
   a. agoraphobia.
   b. claustrophobia.
   c. an inanimate object phobia.
   d. nosophobia.
   e. an animal phobia.

44. Post-traumatic stress disorders are characterized by all of the following except
   a. numbness.
   b. reliving the trauma.
   c. loss of contact with reality.
   d. anxiety.
   e. avoidance of trauma-related stimuli.

45. Survival guilt occurs among those with
   a. agoraphobia.
   b. nosophobia.
   c. post-traumatic stress disorder.
   d. panic disorder.
   e. blood phobia.

46. The rape trauma syndrome is an example of
   a. agoraphobia.
   b. nosophobia.
   c. post-traumatic stress disorder.
   d. panic disorder.
   e. blood phobia.

47. Following a catastrophic hurricane a young boy is rescued having apparently survived in the wilderness for four days with a broken ankle. The child is very anxious and you consider his most likely diagnosis to be
   a. agoraphobia.
   b. nosophobia.
   c. post-traumatic stress disorder.
   d. panic disorder.
   e. generalized anxiety disorder.

48. Fear and anxiety are the same with respect to all of the following components except
   a. cognitive.
   b. somatic.
   c. emotional.
   d. behavioral.
   e. all of the above.

49. A panic disorder consists of anxiety that is
   a. chronic.
   b. infrequent.
   c. spontaneous.
   d. rational.
   e. unconscious.

50. Recent explanations of panic disorders emphasize _____ factors.
   a. biological
   b. cognitive
   c. emotional
   d. behavioral
   e. both a and b.

51. Cognitive explanations of panic disorders point to _____ bodily sensations.
   a. absence of
   b. exaggerated
   c. fluctuating
   d. misinterpreted
   e. under-estimation of

52. Agoraphobics are afraid of all of the following except
   a. open spaces.
   b. traveling.
   c. the dark.
   d. streets.
   e. smooth bodies of water.

53. Most agoraphobics are
   a. children.
   b. adolescents.
   c. men.
   d. women.
   e. the elderly.

54. A generalized anxiety disorder consists of anxiety that is
   a. chronic.
   b. infrequent.
   c. spontaneous.
   d. rational.
   e. unconscious.

55. Panic disorder is to generalized anxiety disorder as
   a. Freud is to Beck.
   b. mind is to body.
   c. state is to trait.
   d. Freud is to Jung.
   e. before is to after.

Answer Key for Sample Exam

1.	b	(p. 210)	15.	a	(p. 218)	29.	e	(p. 227)	43.	e	(p. 237)
2.	e	(p. 210)	16.	b	(p. 218)	30.	b	(p. 228)	44.	c	(p. 238)
3.	a	(p. 210)	17.	b	(p. 222)	31.	b	(p. 229)	45.	c	(p. 241)
4.	c	(p. 209)	18.	a	(p. 219)	32.	c	(p. 229)	46.	c	(p. 244)
5.	e	(p. 211)	19.	c	(p. 219)	33.	d	(p. 230)	47.	c	(p. 238)
6.	b	(p. 211)	20.	c	(p. 221)	34.	b	(p. 230)	48.	e	(p. 249)
7.	a	(p. 213)	21.	e	(p. 221)	35.	d	(p. 230)	49.	c	(p. 250)
8.	a	(p. 213)	22.	c	(p. 223)	36.	d	(p. 231)	50.	e	(p. 230)
9.	b	(p. 213)	23.	b	(p. 223)	37.	b	(p. 232)	51.	d	(p. 252)
10.	d	(p. 213)	24.	c	(p. 223)	38.	e	(p. 232)	52.	c	(p. 255)
11.	c	(p. 213)	25.	c	(p. 223)	39.	a	(p. 233)	53.	d	(p. 256)
12.	e	(p. 215)	26.	c	(p. 224)	40.	b	(p. 235)	54.	a	(p. 258)
13.	e	(p. 218)	27.	a	(p. 226)	41.	c	(p. 234)	55.	c	(p. 260)
14.	b	(p. 219)	28.	d	(p. 227)	42.	b	(p. 237)			

SELF-TEST

1. There are two types of "neuroses"— those in which anxiety is _____ and those in which anxiety is _____.

2. Fear disorders include _____ and _____.

3. Anxiety disorders include _____ and _____.

4. A phobia involves fear of an object; this fear is _____ of the danger represented by the object.

5. The four elements of fear are _____, _____, and _____.

6. The cognitive component of fear is an expectation of _____.

7. The internal state that accompanies fear is the _____; it prepares the body for _____ or _____.

8. The chain of command in fear proceeds from the cortex to the _____ to the _____ to the _____.

9. The autonomic nervous system is composed of the _____ nervous system and the _____ nervous system.

10. The SNS is an _____ system, and the PNS is a _____ system.

11. In _____ responding, a bad event is actually encountered, and in _____ responding, it is not.

12. The percentage of people with a disorder at a given time is _____, and the rate of new cases in a given time period is _____.

13. The most common phobias are _____ and _____...

14. The specific phobias include fear of _____ and fear of _____.

15. The most crippling phobia is _____, and it tends to occur among _____.

16. Most animal phobias occur among _____ and _____.

17. Fear of illness is called _____. Fear of blood is best treated with _____.

18. Comprehensive theories of phobias have been proposed by the _____ model and by the _____ model.

19. The famous psychoanalytic case in which Freud proposed his theory of phobias was the _____ case.

20. According to Freud, Little Hans was not really afraid of horses. Instead, he was afraid of his _____.

21. The psychoanalytic account of phobias is _____.

22. In Pavlovian conditioning terms, the phobic object is a _____.

23. In their study of _____, Watson and Rayner showed that fear could be learned.

24. The behavioral account of phobias explains their persistence in terms of _____ responding.

25. The three behavioral treatments of phobias are _____, _____, and _____.

26. _____ drugs may be helpful in treating phobias that involve _____.

27. Problems with the Pavlovian conditioning account of phobias are several. First, phobias are usually _____; second, they are _____; and third, they are not always preceded by _____.

28. The problems with the Pavlovian conditioning account of phobias are solved by _____.

29. Prepared classical conditioning is thought to be "prepared" by _____.

30. The behavioral account of phobias does not explain _____.

31. In contrast to phobias, the event feared in post-traumatic stress disorders is not _____.

32. The symptoms of post-traumatic stress disorder are _____ to the world, _____ the trauma, and symptoms of _____.

33. When an individual feels guilty for surviving a trauma in which others died, he is experiencing _____.

34. Reactions to rape follow a sequence known as the _____.

35. Prognosis for post-traumatic stress disorders appears _____.

36. Unlike fear disorders, anxiety disorders do not involve fear of a _____ object.

37. Panic disorders are more common among _____.

38. Panic disorders have recently been explained by _____ theorists.

39. In generalized anxiety disorders, anxiety is _____.

40. Transient anxiety is called _____ anxiety, and chronic anxiety is called _____ anxiety.

Answer Key for Self-Test

1. experienced; inferred
2. phobias; post-traumatic stress disorders
3. panic disorders; generalized anxiety disorders
4. out of proportion to the reality of the danger
5. cognitive; somatic; emotional; behavioral
6. specific impending harm
7. emergency reaction; flight; fight
8. hypothalamus; sympathetic nervous system; adrenal medulla
9. sympathetic; parasympathetic
10. adrenergic; cholinergic
11. escape; avoidance
12. prevalence; incidence
13. social phobias and specific phobias
14. animals; illness
15. agoraphobia; women
16. children; women
17. nosophobia; applied tension
18. psychodynamic; behavioral
19. Little Hans
20. father

21. unsatisfactory
22. CS (conditioned stimulus)
23. Little Albert
24. avoidance
25. systematic desensitization; flooding; modeling
26. Antidepressant; spontaneous panic attacks
27. selective; irrational; trauma
28. prepared classical conditioning
29. evolution
30. who becomes a phobic
31. commonplace
32. numbness; reliving; anxiety
33. survival guilt
34. rape trauma syndrome
35. bleak
36. specific
37. women
38. biological and cognitive
39. chronic
40. state; trait

MATCHING ITEMS

_____	1.	generalized anxiety disorder	A.	applied tension
_____	2.	nosophobia	B.	public speaking
_____	3.	blood phobia	C.	misinterpretation of sensations
_____	4.	parasympathetic nervous system	D.	survivor guilt
_____	5.	sympathetic nervous system	E.	disorganization
_____	6.	panic disorder	F.	avoidance responding
_____	7.	rape trauma syndrome	G.	heart slows down
_____	8.	Joseph Wolpe	H.	heart speeds up
_____	9.	agoraphobia	I.	chronic anxiety
_____	10.	hypochondriasis	J.	fear of injury or illness
_____	11.	social phobia	K.	systematic desensitization
_____	12.	post-traumatic stress disorder	L.	somatoform disorder

Answer Key for Matching Items

1.	I	7.	E
2.	J	8.	K
3.	A	9.	F
4.	G	10.	L
5.	H	11.	B
6.	C	12.	D

SHORT-ANSWER QUESTIONS

1. Describe the precipitants, components, and development of the emergency reaction.

2. What are the six characteristics that contribute to a diagnosis of phobia?

3. Compare and contrast the psychodynamic and behavioral views of the role of anxiety in the origin and development of phobias.

4. What is meant by the term "prepared classical conditioning?" To what aspect of the phobic experience is this concept relevant? Explain.

5. In what ways are the therapeutic techniques of systematic desensitization, flooding, and modeling the same, and in what ways do they differ?

6. What are the central features of post-traumatic stress disorder? Under what conditions is it most likely to develop?

7. Recent evidence suggests that panic disorder may be a disease of the body. Summarize these findings.

8. How are panic disorder and agoraphobia related? What treatments are most successful for treating each and under what conditions?

9. How does generalized anxiety disorder differ from everyday anxiety? How is it similar to panic disorder?

TYING IT TOGETHER

Freud wrote extensively about neurosis (Chapter 4), and used the term to refer not just to symptoms of a disorder, but also to the pre-sumed underlying process; defense against anxiety. However, research (Chapter 6) and therapy (Chapter 19) suggest that the behavioral account (Chapter 5) of neurosis is more reasonable. Symptoms are regarded as the problem, and they are assumed to arise because they have been learned. Therapy consists of new learning. Laboratory models of psychopathology (Chapter 6), often employing animals, have been fruitful in the study of neurosis.

Fear and anxiety are present in a number of other disorders as well: obsessions (Chapter 9), psychosomatic disorders such as peptic ulcers and hypertension (Chapter 10), sexual dysfunction (Chapter 13), drug abuse (Chapter 14), and childhood disorders (Chapter 16). Not surprisingly, the behaviorally based therapy techniques often prove useful in treating these disorders as well as the fear disorders (Chapter 19). Antisocial personality disorder may involve too little fear and anxiety (Chapter 15).

Although neuroses have historically been contrasted with the psychoses, schizophrenia (Chapter 12) often is associated with fear and anxiety. The neuroleptic drugs used to treat schizophrenic symptoms are tranquilizers. Deficits caused by neurological damage (Chapter 17) are exacerbated by anxiety.

Fear and anxiety are often experienced by "normal" people. These emotions are part of the observer discomfort that counts toward a judgment of abnormality (Chapter 1). To the degree that an individual's behavior is unconventional and inexplicable, it will be reacted to with trepidation. Erroneous diagnoses may be made (Chapter 7), and involuntary commitment (Chapter 19) and other extreme measures may be undertaken (see Chapter 2). Some have observed that even research may be distorted if experimental subjects are overly fearful and anxious; subject bias is increased, and demand characteristics are potentiated (Chapter 6).

FURTHER READINGS

Burgess, A. W., & Holmstrom, L. L. (1974). *Rape: Victims of crisis.* Bowie, MD: Brady.

Figley, C. R. (1977). *The American Legion study of psychological adjustment among Vietnam veterans.* Lafayette, IN: Purdue University.

Figley, C. R., & Leventman, S. (1980). *Strangers at home: Vietnam veterans since the war.* New York: Praeger.

Holmstrom, L. L., & Burgess, A. W. (1978). *The victim of rape: Institution reactions.* New York: Wiley.

Hunt, C. & Singh, M. (1991). Generalized anxiety disorder. *International Review of Psychiatry, 3,* 215–229.

Jones, J. C., & Barlow, D. H. (1990). The etiology of post-traumatic stress disorder. *Clinical Psychology Review, 10,* 299–328.

Joyce, P., Bushness, J., Oakley-Browne, M., & Wells, J. (1989). The epidemiology of panic symptomatology and agoraphobic avoid-ance. *Comprehensive Psychiatry, 30,* 303–312.

Laughlin, H. P. (1967). The soterial reactions: Security from an external object choice. In *The neuroses* (pp. 607–638). Washington, DC: Butterworth.

Levin, A., Scheier, F., & Liebowitz, M. (1989). Social phobia: Biology and pharmacology. *Clinical Psychology Review, 9,* 129–140.

Marks, I. M. (1969). *Fears and phobias.* New York: Academic Press.

McNally, R. J. (1990). Psychological approaches to panic disorder: A review. *Psychological Bulletin, 108,* 403–419.

Öst, L-G., Sterner, U., & Fellenius, J. (1989). Applied tension, applied relaxation, and the combination in the treatment of blood phobia. *Behavior Research and Therapy, 27,* 109–121.

Rachman, S. & Maser, J. (Eds.) (1988). *Panic: Psychological perspectives.* Hillsdale, NJ: Erlbaum.

Regier, D., Narrow, W., & Rae, D. (1990). The epidemiology of anxiety disorders: The Epidemiological Catchment Area (ECA) experience. *Journal of Psychiatric Research, 24,* 3–14.

Rothman, B., Foa, E., Riggs, D. Murdock, T., & Walsh, W. (1992). A prospective examination of post-traumatic stress disorder in rape victims. *Journal of Traumatic Stress., 5:3, 455–475.*

Marks, I. M. (1970). Agoraphobic syndrome (phobic anxiety state). *Archives of General Psychiatry, 23,* 538–553.

Tuma, A. H., & Maser, J. D. (1985). *Anxiety and the anxiety disorders.* Hillsdale, NJ: Erlbaum.

TERM-PAPER TOPICS

1. What is the evidence against the behavioral account of phobias? (Include evidence against the preparedness idea.)

2. Agoraphobia is mainly a problem experienced by women, and it has been argued that the "disorder" reflects sexism in our society. Review these arguments, and then agree or disagree with them.

3. How was combat fatigue treated in World War II? With which model of abnormality was this treatment compatible?

4. Of recent interest is the plight of Vietnam veterans. In particular, these individuals may suffer from post-traumatic stress disorders to a greater degree than have veterans from other eras. Is this true? If so, what about the Vietnam War may be responsible for this? If not, why has the claim been made?

EXERCISES

Exercise One—Phobias and Classical Conditioning

In this exercise, you will evaluate the classical conditioning explanation of phobias.

Talk to individuals who have phobias. What were the circumstances under which their fears first appeared? Do these correspond to the Pavlovian account?

For years, a colleague of mine was afraid of dogs. According to his parents, when he was three years old, the family pet, a collie who looked like Lassie, developed the un-Lassie-like habit of knocking him down as he explored the backyard. This may have been the origin of his fear of dogs. Almost twenty years later, he was "cured" through flooding occasioned by his summer job: a letter carrier in the suburbs of Chicago. Almost every house to which he delivered mail was guarded by a large dog, and he quickly became used to them. The only time he was bitten was by a three-year-old girl. However, he did not develop a fear of children.

Seligman, M. E. P. (1971). Phobias and preparedness. *Behavior Therapy, 2,* 307–320.

Exercise Two—Sex Differences in Fears

The purpose of this exercise is to ascertain whether men and women fear different things.

Ask men and women of your acquaintance to list the objects and situations of which they are afraid. What are the sex differences? How do you explain them?

Cornelius, R. R., & Averill, J. R. (1983). Sex differences in fear of spiders. *Journal of Personality and Social Psychology, 45,* 377–383.

Marks, I. M. (1969). *Fears and phobias.* New York: Academic Press.

Wilson, G. D. (1967). Social desirability and sex differences in expressed fear. *Behaviour Research and Therapy, 5,* 136–137.

CHAPTER 9

Obsession, Hysteria, and Dissociation: Anxiety Inferred

CHAPTER OVERVIEW

Disorders in which underlying anxiety has often been inferred as the cause—i.e., obsessive-compulsive disorders, somatoform disorders, and dissociative disorders—are the subject matter of this chapter.

Obsessive-compulsive disorders involve uncontrollable, repulsive thoughts (obsessions) and senseless rituals (compulsions). Obsessions and compulsions are thought to be defenses against anxiety. The psychodynamic model attempts to explain vulnerability to obsessive-compulsive disorders, while the behavioral model attempts to explain their persistence. Recent studies find a biological predisposition to obsessive-compulsive disorders. Behavioral and drug therapies for these disorders are described.

Somatoform disorders (conversion disorder, somatization disorder, and pain disorder [psychalgia]) are characterized by the loss of physical functioning in the absence of any physical problem. Instead, somatoform disorders are thought to result from psychological factors. Cautions in diagnosing somatoform disorders are discussed since they often resemble other problems. Three theories of somatoform disorders—the psychodynamic model, which proposes that these disorders symbolize underlying conflicts, the communicative model, which suggests that they communicate global distress and the percept blocking model, which argues that perception of the physical condition is blocked from awareness—are described along with treatments.

Dissociative disorders entail problems with memory. In amnesia, an individual forgets significant personal information, which may include identity. In the fugue state, the individual suffers amnesia and assumes a new identity. In multiple personality, more than one self exists within the same individual, and "they" may not always be aware of each other. Like obsessive-compulsive disorders and somatoform disorders, dissociative disorders are thought to be ways of dealing with anxiety.

ESSENTIAL TERMS

alexithymic	being unable to express feelings in words (p. 290)
amitriptyline	antidepressant drug with pain-killing effects used for pain disorder patients (p. 293)
amnesia	sudden loss of memory (p. 294)

anterograde amnesia	amnesia in which it is difficult to learn new material (p. 295)
global amnesia (generalized amnesia)	amnesia in which all details of one's personal memory are lost (p. 295)
post-traumatic amnesia	amnesia in which there is an inability to recall events after a trauma (p. 295)
retrograde amnesia	amnesia in which events prior to a trauma are forgotten (p. 295)
selective amnesia (categorical amnesia)	amnesia in which only events related to a particular theme vanish (p. 295)
belle indifference, la	symptom of somatoform disorders, wherein there is a lack of concern with physical symptoms (p. 289)
Briquet's syndrome	(*see* somatization disorder)
chronic fatigue syndrome	syndrome sometimes comorbid with somatoform disorders (p. 288)
clavus	somatoform disorder common at the time of World War I characterized by the painful sensation of a nail being driven into the head and severe low back pain producing a forwardly bent back (p. 291)
clomipramine	antidepressant drug that works markedly better than placebos on OCD (p. 279)
communicative model	theory of somatoform disorder proposing that symptoms are used to deal with distressing emotions and to negotiate difficult interpersonal transactions (p. 290)
conversion disorder	disorder in which it is thought that psychological stress is converted into physical symptoms; known as hysterical conversion in the nineteenth century (p. 281)
depersonalization	a form of dissociation in which one feels detached from oneself (p. 294)
derealization	a form of dissociation in which the world, not oneself, seems unreal (p. 294)
dissociative disorder	mental disorder in which some area of the memory is split off or dissociated from conscious awareness; e.g., amnesia, fugue, multiple personality (p. 294)
dissociative identity disorder (DID)	(*see* multiple personality disorder, p. 294)
factitious disorder (Münchhausen syndrome)	disorder resembling a somatoform disorder; in this disorder symptoms are voluntarily produced (p. 286)
fugue	amnesic state, wherein the person travels away from home and assumes a new identity (p. 295)
glove anesthesia	somatoform disorder in which nothing can be felt in the hand and fingers although sensation is intact from the wrist up; the disorder is neurologically impossible (p. 286)
identity alteration	a form of dissociation in which one displays a surprising skill that one did not know one had (p. 294)

identity confusion — a form of dissociation in which one is confused or uncertain about who one is (p. 294)

malingering — faking; symptoms are under the person's voluntary control (p. 284)

multiple personality disorder (MPD) — more than one personality existing in the same individual; also known as dissociative identity disorder (DID) (p. 297)

obsessive-compulsive disorder (OCD) — mental disorder in which the individual is plagued by the uncontrollable, repulsive thoughts (obsessions) and engages in seemingly senseless rituals (compulsions) (p. 265)

obsessive-compulsive personality — personality style characterized by methodical, meticulous, and ordered behavior (p. 270)

pain disorder (psychalgia) — disorder in which pain is the central symptom; thought to be psychological in origin (p. 283)

psychogenic amnesia (dissociative amnesia) — forms of amnesia which are thought to be due to psychological trauma rather than organic factors (p. 294)

psychosomatic disorder — disorder resembling a somatoform disorder but with a physical basis that can explain the symptom, e.g., peptic ulcer (p. 286)

recovery movement — a popular psychological view that holds that many adult problems may be traced to childhood sexual abuse (p. 298)

response prevention — therapy technique for obsessive-compulsive disorders in which the compulsive act is not allowed to occur (p. 278)

secondary gain — benefits from the environment as a consequence of abnormal symptoms (p. 284)

somatization disorder — mental disorder involving a dramatic and complicated medical history for a variety of bodily complaints not physically caused (cf. somatoform disorder) (p. 282)

somatoform disorder — mental disorder characterized by loss of physical functioning in the absence of physical cause (cf. somatization disorder) (p. 281)

CENTRAL CONCEPTUAL ISSUES

Dissociative and somatoform disorders: The origin of psychodynamic theory.   It is perhaps not surprising that the area of abnormal psychology which most looks to psychodynamic theory for its explication includes the very problems from which psychoanalytic theory was born. Psychodynamic theory, which postulates unconscious conflict and associated anxiety as the explanation for psychopathology, provides the best explanation to date for a class of disorders in which the symptoms have no known cause and seem to provide relief from psychological trauma. A number of psychodynamic precepts, including concepts such as defense and displacement, the symbolic meaning of symptoms, and the use of insight in treatment, find as strong a foothold here as anywhere in psychology, and seem to provide more compelling analyses than do cognitive, behavioral, or biomedical theories.

Why is anxiety inferred?   The text distinguishes between disorders in which anxiety is apparent, and those in which symptoms are seen as attempts to manage underlying anxiety or distress. In the case of obsessive-compulsive disorder, we infer anxiety for several reasons: patients report their obsessions to be anxiety-inducing; anxiety often erupts when compulsive behaviors are prevented; and the assertion of underlying anxiety and its relationship to specific conflicts goes a considerable distance in explaining both who is vulnerable to obsessions and what symbolic content they will manifest. In both dissociative disorders and somatoform disorders, anxiety is usually unfelt and unobservable, yet the symptoms can be readily understood as functioning for defensive purposes.

Treating anxiety.   The theoretical distinction between the "felt anxiety" and "inferred anxiety" classes of disorders is supported by the different success rates of therapies across these classes. In general, cognitive-behavioral theory does not adequately explain the disorders in which we infer anxiety to be the cause. Moreover, its therapies are usually more successful in treating disorders in which anxiety is manifest than those in which anxiety is presumed. Obsessive-compulsive disorder proves an exception to this rule, being very amenable to forms of extinction therapy, specifically in exposure and response prevention. Insight-oriented therapeutic interventions, in contrast, may prove much more successful in remediating the symptoms in somatoform and dissociative disorders—conditions in which anxiety is inferred.

Differential diagnosis in somatoform disorders.   Whenever making a specific diagnosis, it is essential to rule out any other conditions it may resemble. This can be particularly difficult with somatoform disorders (disorders of physical symptoms with a psychological rather than physical cause) because they must be distinguished from a number of other possible conditions, including undiagnosed physical disorder, psychosomatic disorders, a factitious disorder, or an instance of malingering. Misdiagnosing a physical illness as a somatoform disorder not only gives the patient the stigmatizing and mistaken message "it's all in your head," but also represents a lost treatment opportunity as well—a consequence that may be dire indeed. Just as with undiagnosed physical disorders, psychosomatic disorders are also distinguished from somatoform disorders by the physical origin of their symptoms (although psychological factors may play a role in the onset or course of the disorder). In both malingering (faking) and factitious disorders, the physical symptoms are voluntarily and willfully produced by the patient (they differ only in whether the patient is or is not conscious of his or her motivations), whereas in somatoform disorders, symptoms are believed to be psychological in origin and completely beyond voluntary control.

Why do we forget? Psychogenic and organic causes.   Varying kinds of amnesia may be associated with serious psychological trauma, like physical brain trauma. However, the organic and psychogenic amnesias differ not only in origin but in the specific characteristics of their memory loss. While psychogenic amnesics may forget both recent and remote past and their personal identity, they tend *not* to forget general knowledge or events that happen after the trauma, and their condition may reverse abruptly with a complete recovery of memory for the traumatic event that precipitated the memory loss. Amnesic states of organic origin tend to resolve only gradually, if at all, with memory of the trauma and events following it usually permanently lost. They are also more likely to involve memory loss for recent rather than remote events, for both personal *and* general knowledge, and for events following the trauma. Although psychogenic amnesias may manifest in ways that defy a neural damage explanation, and tend to be associated with personal stress (e.g., troubling marital, financial, or career situations) or more global threats (e.g., war, natural disaster), we can only speculate that the loss of memory acts as a "psychological escape hatch" or defense against unbearable anxiety—the actual mechanism is unknown.

SAMPLE EXAM

1. All of the following are disorders in which anxiety is *not* experienced except
   a. panic disorder.
   b. obsessive-compulsive disorder.
   c. somatoform disorder.
   d. dissociative disorder.
   e. conversion disorder.

2. Obsession is to compulsion as
   a. Lennon is to McCartney.
   b. behaviorism is to psychoanalysis.
   c. thought is to deed.
   d. cholinergic is to adrenergic.
   e. high is to low.

3. Obsessions are different from recurring thoughts in all of the following ways except that they
   a. are unwelcome.
   b. are difficult to control.
   c. are cognitive.
   d. arise from within.
   e. are excessive.

4. Common contents of obsessions today include all of the following except
   a. religion.
   b. illness.
   c. violence.
   d. orderliness.
   e. contamination.

5. Howard Hughes suffered from
   a. schizophrenia.
   b. depression.
   c. amnesia.
   d. obsessive-compulsive disorder.
   e. multiple personality disorder.

6. How do obsessives deal with anxiety?
   a. by crossing the street
   b. by acting out their compulsions
   c. by panic attacks
   d. by flooding
   e. by relaxing

7. Obsessive-compulsive disorders are made worse by
   a. depression.
   b. illness.
   c. alcoholism.
   d. schizophrenia.
   e. multiple personality disorder.

8. Obsessive-compulsive disorders
   a. are more common among men than women.
   b. are more common among women than men.
   c. are more common in children.
   d. are equally common among men and women.
   e. none of the above.

9. If you were told that you would soon meet an individual with an obsessive-compulsive personality, you would expect to encounter someone who is
   a. meticulous.
   b. sloppy.
   c. tall.
   d. flexible.
   e. empathic.

10. Which statement is true?
    a. Obsessive-compulsive personality leads to obsessive-compulsive disorder.
    b. Obsessive-compulsive disorder leads to obsessive-compulsive personality.
    c. Obsessive-compulsive personality and obsessive-compulsive disorder are the same thing.
    d. Obsessive-compulsive disorder is a mild form of obsessive-compulsive personality.
    e. Obsessive-compulsive personality and obsessive-compulsive disorder are not related.

11. People with obsessive-compulsive disorder may have
    a. abnormal neurological signs.
    b. a comorbid neurological disorder.
    c. brain-scan abnormalities.
    d. a positive response to clomipramine.
    e. all of the above.

12. The cognitive-behavioral account of obsessive-compulsive disorders does a good job explaining
    a. the genesis of the disorders.
    b. the maintenance of the disorders.
    c. the remission of the disorders.
    d. all of the above.
    e. none of the above.

13. The psychoanalytic account of obsessive-compulsive disorders does a good job explaining
    a. the genesis of the disorders.
    b. the maintenance of the disorders.
    c. the remission of the disorders.
    d. all of the above.
    e. none of the above.

14. According to the cognitive-behavioral model of obsessive-compulsive disorders, which one of the following is *not* true about obsessions?
    a. They are made worse by depression.
    b. They involve a vicious circle.
    c. They are temporarily relieved by compulsive rituals.
    d. It is virtually impossible to distract oneself from them.
    e. They are eventually extinguished.

15. Psychoanalysts see obsessions as all of the following except as
    a. a defense against more threatening thoughts.
    b. an instance of sublimation.
    c. a symbol of an underlying conflict.
    d. a neurosis.
    e. anxiety-related.

16. The most effective treatment overall for obsessive-compulsive disorders seems to be
    a. electroconvulsive shock.
    b. drugs.
    c. insight therapy.
    d. behavioral therapy.
    e. b and d

17. Which one of the following is *not* evidence that obsessive-compulsive disorders involve anxiety?
    a. Anxiety-reducing drug therapies are effective.
    b. Anxiety is common among those with obsessive-compulsive personalities.
    c. Anxiety is experienced if compulsive acts are not performed.

    d. Anxiety is reduced if compulsive acts are performed.
    e. Therapies involving extinction are effective.

18. Somatoform disorders include
    a. conversion disorders.
    b. psychosomatic disorders.
    c. factitious disorders.
    d. malingering.
    e. multiple personality disorder.

19. Somatoform disorders are characterized by all of the following except
    a. loss of physical functioning.
    b. lack of neurological damage.
    c. fear.
    d. lack of voluntary control.
    e. la belle indifference.

20. The night before leaving for college on an art scholarship a friend suddenly goes blind. All testing indicates normal functioning. Because you know how much she was looking forward to leaving, you are surprised at how well she is taking it. You begin to consider that she could
    a. have a conversion disorder.
    b. have a factitious disorder.
    c. be hypochondriacal.
    d. be malingering.
    e. have somatization disorder.

21. Hysterical conversion is to somatization disorder as
    a. phobia is to schizophrenia.
    b. one is to many.
    c. behaviorism is to psychoanalysis.
    d. East is to West.
    e. psychology is to physiology.

22. The most frequent somatoform disorder seems to be
    a. somatization disorder.
    b. pain disorder (psychalgia).
    c. conversion disorder.
    d. thought disorder.
    e. Briquet's syndrome.

23. All of the following may be confused with somatoform disorders except
    a. phobias.
    b. malingering.
    c. factitious disorders.
    d. psychosomatic disorders.
    e. undiagnosed physical illnesses.

24. Conversion disorders are particularly uncommon among
   a. children.
   b. adolescents.
   c. middle-aged individuals.
   d. old people.
   e. a and d

25. According to the psychodynamic model,
conversion disorders involve all except
   a. defense against anxiety.
   b. transformation of psychic energy.
   c. symbolic symptoms.
   d. fear.
   e. la belle indifference.

26. What is "la belle indifference"?
   a. indifference of individuals to their
      conversion symptoms
   b. inability of diagnosticians to distin-
      guish somatoform disorders from
      psychosomatic disorders
   c. ideas that hysterics are likely to be
      young women
   d. confusion accompanying somatoform
      pain disorder
   e. a personality trait which often pre-
      cedes the onset of conversion symp-
      toms

27. Which model best explains "la belle indifference"?
   a. biomedical model
   b. psychodynamic model
   c. behavioral model
   d. cognitive model
   e. existential model

28. According to the communicative model of
hysterical conversion, hysterics
   a. can tell you what is wrong.
   b. can be cured through social support.
   c. use their symptoms to communicate.
   d. are nonstop talkers.
   e. were punished for talking as children.

29. The communicative model does a good
job of explaining
   a. "la belle indifference."
   b. sex differences in conversion disor-
      ders.
   c. changing hysterical symptoms over
      time.
   d. double-binds.
   e. dissociative disorders.

30. Someone who is alexythimic has difficulty expressing
   a. abstractions.
   b. emotions.
   c. motives.
   d. thoughts.
   e. creativity.

31. The mechanism of hysterical conversion
may involve
   a. blocking of a percept from awareness.
   b. excess dopamine in the brain.
   c. too little serotonin in the brain.
   d. sensory overload.
   e. malingering.

32. All of the following seem to be successful
treatments for hysterical conversion except
   a. suggestion.
   b. electroconvulsive shock.
   c. insight.
   d. antidepressant drugs.
   e. b and d

33. All of these are dissociative disorders except
   a. amnesia.
   b. fugue.
   c. multiple personality.
   d. derealization.
   e. conversion.

34. Dissociative disorders all involve
   a. forgetting.
   b. willing.
   c. learning.
   d. concentrating.
   e. communicating.

35. Psychogenic amnesia is thought to result
from
   a. genetic factors.
   b. learning.
   c. anxiety.
   d. errors in logic.
   e. physical trauma.

36. An individual cannot remember events
immediately before a bad automobile accident that he caused. He is experiencing
   a. global amnesia.
   b. retrograde amnesia.
   c. anterograde amnesia.
   d. categorical amnesia.
   e. post-traumatic amnesia.

37. An individual cannot remember events immediately after a bad automobile accident that he caused. He is experiencing
    a. global amnesia.
    b. retrograde amnesia.
    c. anterograde amnesia.
    d. categorical amnesia.
    e. post-traumatic amnesia.

38. An individual cannot remember events related to a prior unhappy romance. She is experiencing
    a. global amnesia.
    b. retrograde amnesia.
    c. anterograde amnesia.
    d. categorical amnesia.
    e. post-traumatic amnesia.

39. An individual can remember no details of her personal life. She is experiencing
    a. global amnesia.
    b. retrograde amnesia.
    c. anterograde amnesia.
    d. categorical amnesia
    e. post-traumatic amnesia.

40. Which one of the following is false?
    a. Organic amnesia is caused by physical trauma, while psychogenic amnesia is not.
    b. Organic amnesia is not associated with prior life stresses, while psychogenic amnesia is.
    c. Organic amnesia involves forgetting the distant past, while psychogenic amnesia does not.
    d. Organic amnesia involves loss of both personal and general knowledge, while psychogenic amnesia does not.
    e. In organic amnesia the memory returns gradually, while psychogenic amnesia often reverses abruptly.

41. Which of these statements is true?
    a. Amnesia involves multiple personality.

b. Multiple personality involves amnesia.
    c. Multiple personality protects one from developing amnesia.
    d. Amnesia and multiple personality are the same thing.
    e. Amnesia and multiple personality have no relation.

42. Which is an example of multiple personality?
    a. Lenin and Marx
    b. Howard Hughes
    c. Dr. Jekyll and Mr. Hyde
    d. Little Hans and Little Albert
    e. none of the above

43. Which one of the following is *not* true about multiple personality?
    a. One of the personalities is aware of the other(s).
    b. One of the personalities is unaware of the other(s).
    c. The different personalities are essentially the same along important dimensions.
    d. The dominant personality is not always the most psychologically healthy.
    e. It always involves more than one personality.

44. All of the following seem involved in the etiology of multiple personality except
    a. tendency toward schizophrenia.
    b. severe trauma.
    c. susceptibility to self-hypnosis.
    d. relief of emotional burden through the creation of a different personality.
    e. amnesia.

45. Therapy for multiple personality is
    a. usually successful.
    b. usually unsuccessful.
    c. successful about half the time.
    d. of unknown success.
    e. none of the above.

Answer Key for Sample Exam

1.	a	(p. 265)	13.	a	(p. 275)	25.	d	(p. 288)	36. b (p. 295)
2.	c	(p. 267)	14.	e	(p. 275)	26.	a	(p. 289)	37. e (p. 295)
3.	c	(p. 266)	15.	b	(p. 273)	27.	b	(p. 289)	38. d (p. 295)
4.	a	(p. 267)	16.	d	(p. 279)	28.	c	(p. 290)	39. a (p. 295)
5.	d	(p. 268)	17.	b	(p. 280)	29.	c	(p. 291)	40. c (p. 296)
6.	b	(p. 269)	18.	a	(p. 281)	30.	b	(p. 290)	41. b (p. 298)
7.	a	(p. 269)	19.	c	(p. 281)	31.	a	(p. 291)	42. c (p. 299)
8.	c	(p. 270)	20.	a	(p. 281)	32.	e	(p. 293)	43. c (p. 300)
9.	a	(p. 270)	21.	b	(p. 282)	33.	d	(p. 294)	44. a (p. 302)
10.	e	(p. 271)	22.	b	(p. 283)	34.	a	(p. 294)	45. a (p. 304)
11.	e	(p. 276)	23.	a	(p. 284)	35.	c	(p. 297)	
12.	b	(p. 275)	24.	e	(p. 287)				

SELF-TEST

1. Disorders in which anxiety is inferred include _____, _____, and _____.

2. Dissociative disorders include _____, _____, and _____.

3. _____ are uncontrollable, repulsive thoughts, and _____ are senseless rituals.

4. Obsessions are distinguished from harmless recurring thoughts in three ways. First, they are not _____; second, they arise from _____; and third, they are _____.

5. The _____ of obsessions has changed over time.

6. If an obsessive does not act out her compulsion, she experiences _____.

7. Obsessions are _____ among men and women.

8. A methodical and meticulous person is said to have an _____ personality; such as a person is _____ to develop an obsessive-compulsive disorder than other people.

9. Obsessive-compulsive disorders tend to co-occur with _____ disorders, perhaps because of _____.

10. According to recent biological studies, obsessive-compulsive disorder is associated with neurological _____ and abnormal _____.

11. According to the cognitive-behavioral view of obsessive-compulsive disorders, compulsions serve to _____.

12. The cognitive-behavioral explanation of obsessive-compulsive disorders does a good job accounting for their _____, but a poor job accounting for _____.

13. According to the psychodynamic model, obsessions are _____ against more threatening impulses.

14. Psychodynamic theory explains _____ to obsessive-compulsive disorders as well as their _____.

15. The prognosis for obsessive-compulsive disorders is _____.

16. Among the behavioral therapy techniques for obsessive-compulsive disorders are _____, _____, and _____.

17. There are four reasons why anxiety is thought to underlie obsessive-compulsive disorders. First, therapy techniques that _____ are effective. Second, when an individual with an obsessive-compulsive disorder is not allowed to _____, anxiety is experienced. Third, obsessives experience some _____ during the obsession. And fourth, the content of the obsession can often be seen as a _____ of an underlying conflict.

18. Somatoform disorders are marked by loss of _____ in the absence of _____.

19. Three types of somatoform disorder are _____, _____, and _____.

20. Somatoform disorders are difficult to diagnose. They must be distinguished from _____, _____, and _____, as well as from _____.

21. Conversion disorders are _____ likely to occur among men than women.

22. About _____ percent of conversion disorders disappear within two years.

23. According to the psychodynamic model, conversions are _____.

24. _____ is the puzzling lack of concern among hysterics for their symptoms.

25. The _____ model of conversion disorders proposes that symptoms are a means of negotiating difficult interpersonal transactions.

26. One theory of conversion disorders suggests that they involve the blocking of perceptions from _____.

27. Among the treatments for somatoform disorders are _____ and _____.

28. All the dissociative disorders involve loss of _____, presumably to reduce _____.

29. Amnesia in which all memories are lost is _____ amnesia; when events immediately prior to a trauma are forgotten, it is _____ amnesia; when events immediately after a trauma are forgotten, it is _____ amnesia; and when events pertaining to a certain theme are forgotten, it is _____ amnesia.

30. In cases of multiple personality, one personality is usually _____ of the other personalities.

31. Multiple personality is often confused with _____, but these are different disorders.

32. Individuals susceptible to multiple personality are highly _____; as children, they often had _____ and experienced _____.

Answer Key for Self-Test

1. obsessive-compulsive disorders; somatoform disorders; dissociative disorders
2. amnesia; fugue; multiple personality
3. obsessions; compulsions
4. welcome; within; difficult to control
5. content
6. anxiety
7. equally common
8. obsessive-compulsive; no more likely
9. depressive; helplessness
10. soft signs; brain scans
11. reduce anxiety
12. persistence; individual susceptibility
13. defenses
14. individual susceptibility; content
15. not particularly good
16. response prevention; flooding; modeling
17. reduce anxiety; perform the ritual; anxiety; symbol
18. physical functioning; neurological damage
19. conversion disorders; somatization disorder; somatoform pain disorder
20. malingering; psychosomatic disorders; factitious disorders; undiagnosed physical illnesses
21. less
22. 50
23. defenses against anxiety
24. "La belle indifference"
25. communicative
26. awareness
27. suggestion; insight
28. memory; anxiety
29. global; retrograde; anterograde; categorical
30. unaware
31. schizophrenia
32. hypnotizable; imaginary playmates; sexual abuse

MATCHING ITEMS

_____ 1. fugue state	A. Munchausen syndrome
_____ 2. obsessive-compulsive disorder	B. la belle indifference
_____ 3. multiple personality disorder	C. difficulty expressing feelings
_____ 4. derealization	D. an extremely hypnotizable subset of the population
_____ 5. somatization disorder	E. difficulty remembering events immediately before a trauma
_____ 6. conversion disorder	F. childhood sexual abuse
_____ 7. hysteria	G. primitive content
_____ 8. obsessions and compulsions	H. travel
_____ 9. malingering	I. Briquet's syndrome
_____ 10. dissociation	J. cleaning, checking, doubting

_____ 11.   retrograde amnesia

_____ 12.   identity alteration

_____ 13.   factitious disorder

_____ 14.   Grade 5

_____ 15.   alexithymia

_____ 16.   anterograde amnesia

K.   some area of memory is split off from conscious awareness

L.   wandering womb

M.   display of a surprising skill

N.   alterations in time and space

O.   difficulty learning new material following a trauma

P.   faking

Answer Key for Matching Items

1.	H	9.	P
2.	J	10.	K
3.	F	11.	E
4.	N	12.	M
5.	I	13.	A
6.	B	14.	D
7.	L	15.	C
8.	G	16.	O

SHORT-ANSWER QUESTIONS

1. Briefly compare and contrast the psychodynamic and cognitive-behavioral views of obsessive-compulsive disorder.

2. Describe the four areas of evidence that have been offered in support of a biomedical theory of obsessive-compulsive disorder.

3. When diagnosing a somatoform disorder, it is important to rule out other possible causes of the symptoms. Name the four disorders with which somatoform disorders could be confused. What piece(s) of evidence would help you to rule out each alternative diagnosis and why?

4. What are the three major theories that explain the origin of conversion disorders and how does each account for the symptoms?

5. What questions would you need to ask a patient with amnesia (or her family) in order to identify the specific type of amnesia? And why?

6. What are the common individual characteristics, life events, and symptoms in multiple personality disorder?

7. Describe the typical progression of therapy when treating an individual with multiple personality disorder.

TYING IT TOGETHER

This chapter covers disorders in which anxiety is inferred to be the cause. These disorders—hysteria in particular—are historically important, since early workers debated whether they were biologically or psychologically caused (Chapter 2; see Chapter 17). Pioneers in the field of abnormal psychology such as Mesmer, Charcot, Janet, Breuer, and Freud were all concerned with hysteria (Chapter 2 and 4). These disorders are still explained with the psychodynamic model, although the behavioral model (Chapter 5) has made important contributions to our understanding of them.

Hysteria seems to be less common now than it was at the turn of the century. This may be due to increased sophistication on the part of individuals who "know" that physical functions do not suddenly cease without cause. It may also result from an increasingly liberal society in which conflicts around sexuality and aggression are not as prevalent as they once were (Chapter 2). Yet another factor contributing to the decline in hysteria is the increase in use of tranquilizing drugs and alcohol (Chapter 14). To the degree that "self-medication" decreases fear and anxiety, it also decreases disorders in which these are underlying causes. Of course, drug abuse may create more problems than it solves.

Obsessions and compulsions are sometimes components of other disorders, where they may serve a role in decreasing anxiety. Depressives (Chapter 11) often suffer repetitive thoughts involving themes of self-recrimination. Schizophrenic delusions (Chapter 12) are repetitive and may give rise to ritualistic behavior. Neurological disorders are sometimes associated with perseveration (Chapter 17).

The behavioral treatments are among the most successful for disorders brought about by fear an anxiety (Chapter 19).

FURTHER READINGS

Baer, L. (1992). *Getting control—Overcoming your obsessions and compulsions.* New York: Plume.

Bliss, E. L. (1980). Multiple personalities: A report of 14 cases with implications for schizophrenia and hysteria. *Archives of General Psychiatry, 37,* 1388–1397.

Classen, C. et al. (1993). Trauma and dissociation. *Bulletin of the Menninger Clinic, 57*:2, 178–194.

Fraser, S. (1987). *My father's house—A memoir of incest and of healing.* New York: Harper & Row.

Freud, S. (1963). Notes upon a case of obsessional neurosis. In *Three case histories.* New York: Collier.

Hirst, W. (1982). The amnesic syndrome: Descriptions and explanations. *Psychological Bulletin, 91,* 435–460.

Janet, P. (1907). *The major symptoms of hysteria.* London: Macmillan & Co., Ltd.

Loftus, E. F. (1993). The reality of repressed memories. *American Psychologist, 48*:5, 518–537.

Rapoport, J. L. (1989). *The boy who couldn't stop washing—The experience and treatment of obsessive-compulsive disorder.* New York: New American Library.

Schreiber, F. R. (1973). *Sybil.* New York: Warner Books.

Spiegel, D., & Cardena, E. (1991). Disintegrated experience: The dissociative disorders revisited. *Journal of Abnormal Psychology, 100*:3, 366–378.

Stevenson, R. L. (1906). *The merry men, and other tales and fables; Strange case of Dr. Jekyll and Mr. Hyde.* New York: Scribner's.

Thigpen, C. H., & Cleckley, H. M. (1957). *The three faces of Eve.* New York: Popular Library.

TERM-PAPER TOPICS

1. One of Freud's patients, known as the Wolf Man, has been the subject of two contemporary books—Gardiner, M. (1971). *The Wolf-Man.* New York: Basic Books; Obholzer, K. (1982). *The Wolf-Man—Sixty years later: Conversations with Freud's controversial patient.* New York: Continuum. Read these books and Freud's original case study. Evaluate Freud's account of neuroses and their treatment with psychoanalysis.

2. Evaluate the psychoanalytic explanation of psychogenic amnesia on the basis of case histories.

3. Cases of multiple personality are rare and exciting. Therapists can make a great deal of money by writing about such cases. Could these therapists ever be guilty of encouraging a patient to evidence multiple personalities? In short, decide if multiple personality is real.

EXERCISES

Exercise One—Superstitious Rituals and Sports

The purpose of this exercise is to investigate the rituals followed by athletes to reduce their anxiety while performing.

Talk to men and women of your acquaintance about superstitions they have while playing sports. Do these involve behaviors? Cognitions? How did these superstitions develop? Do these athletes experience anxiety if their rituals are interrupted?

Skinner, B. F. (1948). "Superstition" in the pigeon. *Journal of Experimental Psychology, 38,* 168–172.

Exercise Two—Superstitious Rituals and Tests

The purpose of this exercise is to investigate the rituals followed by students taking examinations to reduce their anxiety.

Repeating the procedure of the above exercise, talk to your classmates about their test-taking superstitions.

Exercise Three—Imaginary Playmates

According to the textbook, multiple personalities may develop from imaginary playmates that a child invents in stressful situations. The purpose of this exercise is to ascertain the frequency of imaginary playmates and the circumstances under which they "come out to play."

Talk to your friends about imaginary playmates they had when they were young. If possible, talk to young school children who may still have them. What are the characteristics of these playmates? Are they similar or different from the people who create them? What kinds of things do people do with imaginary playmates? Are these done in stressful situations?

Pines, M. (1978). Invisible playmates. *Psychology Today, 12*(9), 38–42, 106.

Exercise Four—Reactions to Stress

The purpose of this exercise is to ascertain if one's own aches and pains reflect stress reactions.

Among the possible responses to stress are headaches, stomach aches, insomnia, lower back pains, diarrhea, sore throats, and so on. Keep a daily log of such minor physical disturbances for at least a month. At the same time, keep track of how stressful each day was. You may want to rate each day on a scale like the following

1 = an incredibly laid-back day
2 = a relaxing day
3 = a somewhat relaxing day
4 = a somewhat stressful day
5 = a moderately stressful day
6 = a pretty stressful day
7 = an incredibly stressful day

Is there a relationship between the stressfulness of the day and the number of minor aches and pains you experienced? Try representing the information in graph form. Consider the possibility that you respond to stress several days following it. (Beware of illusory correlations in interpreting the information you have recorded!)

Kanner, A. D., Coyne, J. C., Schaefer, C., & Lazarus, R. S. (1981). Comparison of two modes of stress measurement: Daily hassles and uplifts versus major life events. *Journal of Behavioral Medicine, 4,* 1–39.

CHAPTER 10

Health Psychology

CHAPTER OVERVIEW

In contrast to somatoform disorders, psychosomatic disorders involve actual physical problems influenced by psychological factors. Peptic ulcers and coronary heart disease are two important examples of psychosomatic disorders. Each is interpreted in terms of a diathesis-stress model, in which a physical weakness (diathesis) is coupled with an environmental event (stress) to bring about the disorder.

A peptic ulcer is an erosion of the mucous lining of the stomach or esophagus. There are constitutional risk factors for peptic ulcers—oversecretion of gastric juice and weak mucous membrane—as well as environmental risk factors—conflict, unpredictability, and uncontrollability.

One risk factor for coronary heart disease is the Type A personality pattern, characterized by hostility, time urgency, and competitiveness. Research suggests that hostility is the active ingredient leading to heart disease, perhaps because it leads to chronic engagement of the body's emergency reaction.

A new area within psychosomatics is currently taking form: psychoneuroimmunology, which studies how psychological factors influence the body's ability to recognize and fight off disease. Described in detail is a line of research linking stressful events, helplessness, depression, and pessimism to poor immune function and hence to increased illness and death.

ESSENTIAL TERMS

approach-avoidance conflict	situation with aspects encouraging both approach and avoidance; thought to produce peptic ulcers (p. 318)
asthma	condition in which the air passages of the bronchia narrow, swell, and secrete excess fluid in response to a variety of stimuli, resulting in difficulty breathing (p. 337)
blood pressure	pressure exerted by the blood on the walls of blood vessels (p. 329)
cimetidine	drug that reduces stomach acid; treatment of choice for peptic ulcers (p. 321)
continual emergency reaction	constant state of anxiety and readiness for danger (p. 327)

diathesis-stress model — idea that disorder results from a combination of constitutional weakness (diathesis) and traumatic event (stress) (p. 313)

executive monkey study — well-known but confounded study ostensibly showing that monkeys given control (executives) develop more ulcers than monkeys not given control; subsequent research suggests lack of control produces ulcers (p. 320)

general adaptation syndrome — theory of stress proposed by Hans Selye that describes a sequence of three stages in response to stress: alarm reaction (i.e., emergency reaction), resistance, and exhaustion) (p. 339)

hardiness — personality characteristic associated with robust physical health (p. 345)

health psychology — field that investigates the psychological causes and consequences of health and disease (p. 311)

hypertension — technical term for high blood pressure (p. 324)

immune system — bodily system that recognizes and removes foreign material (p. 332)

antibody — material that inactivates antigens

antigen — material foreign to one's body

lymphocytes — cells that recognize antigens

macrophages — cells that eat antigens

neutrophils — cells that eat antigen-antibody complexes

immunocompetence — the degree to which the immune response proceeds efficiently and effectively to protect the organism (p. 333)

immunologic memory — describes immune system response of doing a better job of destroying antigens the second time it is challenged with them, because T-cells and B-cells originally involved multiply more rapidly; responsible for immunization (p. 332)

life stressors — theory of psychosomatic disorders proposing that illness follows stressful life events (p. 341)

entrances — life events involving gains (p. 342)

exits — life events involving losses, thought to result in more problems than entrances (p. 342)

uncontrollable events — events for which no response an individual can make changes their chances of occurring (pp. 319, 344)

unpredictable events — unsignaled life events (p. 318)

peptic ulcer — circumscribed erosion of the mucous membrane of the stomach (gastric ulcer) or duodenum (duodenal ulcer) (p. 313)

psychoneuroimmunology (PNI) — field that investigates how psychological states influence the immune system (p. 332)

psychosomatic disorder	disorder of the body (soma) influenced by the mind (psyche); e.g., peptic ulcer (p. 311)
specific organ vulnerability	theory of psychosomatic disorders holding that an individual inherits a tendency to react to stress with a characteristic part of the body (p. 338)
stigmata	marks on skin, usually bleeding or bruising, often of religious or personal significance, brought on by an emotional state (p. 312)
sudden death	death in the face of threat, thought to result from hopelessness and giving up (p. 329)
Type A behavior pattern	personality style that predisposes an individual to cardiovascular difficulties; the pattern consists of exaggerated time urgency, competitiveness and ambition, aggression and hostility in response to frustration(p. 322)
Type B behavior pattern	personality style in contrast to Type A pattern; such a pattern consists of no time urgency, as well as relaxation and serenity (p. 323)

CENTRAL CONCEPTUAL ISSUES

The mind/body problem finessed.   Health psychology raises fundamental questions about the relationships between personality, the mind, and the body. The classic philosophical mind/body problem is avoided by recourse to statistical relationships within a temporal chain of events. For example, depression is statistically linked to lowered immunocompetence. That is, changes in the variables used to quantify depression can be said to statistically account for changes in the variables used to quantify immunological capacity. Immunocompetence is then statistically tied to later health outcomes (e.g., disease or death). Once this chain of events is articulated, it can be used to devise treatments which intervene at particular stages of the process. In turn, the success of such treatments is seen as supporting (or countering) the hypothesized chain of events.

Diathesis-stress model.   In the general diathesis-stress model, a weakness or vulnerability (diathesis) combined with a stressor can result in physical or psychological disorders. This model is widely used throughout abnormal psychology and in health psychology. Severe childhood psychological trauma, for example, is sometimes seen as creating a diathesis which increases the likelihood of psychological problems or disorders much later in life. In schizophrenia, a constitutional diathesis (e.g., a physical vulnerability, perhaps inherited) is generally regarded as a necessary but not necessarily sufficient precondition for the development of the disorder in adulthood.

In health psychology, in which the contributions of psychological processes to physical disorders are examined, a number of factors are considered relevant to this model: among them, physiological weaknesses and natural adaptive response mechanisms, the number and degree of environmental stressors and support systems, and the extent of mediating or exacerbating psychological mechanisms (e.g., conflict, attributional style, conditioning). In health psychology, diathesis-stress mechanisms are seen as contributors to physical disorders, poor health outcomes, increased frequency of illness and other physical problems, and even death.

Theoretical applications of the diathesis-stress model.   The dominant theoretical orientations have all developed theories revolving around one or more aspects of the diathesis-stress model. The biomedical approach focuses particularly on the diathesis aspect, and suggests mechanisms whereby immunological systems or other physiological weaknesses or propensities (e.g., thin stomach linings in ulcer patients) are exacerbated as a result of external stressors. Psychodynamic theories emphasize the psychological conflicts (often unconscious) that link particular stressors (corresponding to the conflict), and the vulnerable organs onto which the energy from the aggravated conflict is displaced. The cognitive and behavioral approaches pay particular attention to stressors and the habitual ways that the individual responds. Behavioral analyses focus on conditioned behavior, while cognitive analyses focus on attributional styles and their sequelae (e.g., pessimism). Together, and in combination with physiological data, they have elucidated the roles that learned helplessness, hostility, and aggression play in health outcomes.

SAMPLE EXAM

1. Psychosomatic disorders involve
    a.   the mind.
    b.   the body.
    c.   the environment.
    d.   both the mind and the body.
    e.   none of the above.

2. All of the following are psychosomatic disorders except
    a.   stigmata.
    b.   somatoform disorder.
    c.   peptic ulcer.
    d.   high blood pressure.
    e.   asthma.

3. Stigmata usually possess
    a.   religious significance.
    b.   political significance.
    c.   economic significance.
    d.   historical significance.
    e.   no real significance.

4. DSM-IV describes psychosomatic disorders as
    a.   physical factors affecting a psychological condition.
    b.   psychological factors affecting a physical condition.
    c.   conscious factors affecting an unconscious condition.
    d.   unconscious factors affecting a conscious condition.
    e.   none of the above.

5. Diathesis is to stress as
    a.   mild is to severe.
    b.   phobia is to schizophrenia.
    c.   nature is to nurture.
    d.   conscious is to unconscious.
    e.   acute is to chronic.

6. All of the following may destroy the stomach lining except
    a.   antacids.
    b.   aspirin and alcohol.
    c.   hydrochloric acid.
    d.   pepsin.
    e.   bile.

7. The most obvious symptom of peptic ulcers is
    a.   abdominal pain.
    b.   fever.
    c.   flushed skin.
    d.   painful bowel movements.
    e.   nausea.

8. In general,
    a.   peptic ulcers are more frequent among men than women.
    b.   peptic ulcers are more frequent among women than men.
    c.   peptic ulcers are equally frequent among men and women.
    d.   sex differences in peptic-ulcer frequency have changed over the years.

e. peptic ulcers are so rare that data on possible sex differences is not available.

9. Which of the following statements are true?
    a. Social class does not influence the incidence of peptic ulcers.
    b. Peptic ulcers are less frequent after age thirty-five.
    c. Peptic ulcers run in families.
    d. Boys have more peptic ulcers than girls.
    e. All of the above are true.

10. According to research, gastric secretions increase during all of the following emotions except
    a. anxiety.
    b. anger.
    c. resentment.
    d. sadness.
    e. all of the above

11. Animal research has shown that all of the following situations increase the likelihood of ulcers except
    a. conflict.
    b. extinction.
    c. unpredictability.
    d. uncontrollability.
    e. approach-avoidance.

12. What was the confound in the "executive monkey" study?
    a. nonrandom assignment
    b. experimenter bias
    c. subject bias
    d. demand characteristics
    e. too small a sample

13. The best treatment for a peptic ulcer is
    a. antacids.
    b. a bland diet.
    c. cimetidine.
    d. thorazine.
    e. steroids.

14. Psychological treatment for a peptic ulcer has
    a. been conclusively proven effective.
    b. been conclusively proven ineffective.
    c. been inconclusive.
    d. not been attempted.
    e. not been appropriately tested.

15. Blood pressure increases under conditions of

a. threat.
b. anxiety.
c. depression.
d. hostility.
e. all of the above.

16. Hypertension is most likely to occur when an individual is
    a. constantly threatened and can retaliate.
    b. constantly threatened and cannot retaliate.
    c. periodically threatened and can retaliate.
    d. periodically threatened and cannot retaliate.
    e. never threatened but wants to retaliate.

17. The Type A behavior pattern is a
    a. personality prone to cardiovascular troubles.
    b. way to resolve approach-avoidance conflicts.
    c. tracking strategy for elementary education.
    d. defense against sexual inadequacy.
    e. protection from CHD.

18. All of the following are characteristics of the Type A behavior pattern except
    a. time urgency.
    b. forgetfulness.
    c. competitiveness.
    d. hostility.
    e. ambitiousness.

19. Suppose you were told that you would meet someone for lunch who had a Type A personality. You would be surprised if this individual
    a. arrived late.
    b. ate quickly.
    c. sent food back to the kitchen.
    d. started an argument.
    e. had a heart attack while eating French fries.

20. _____ kills more people in the Western world than any other disease.
    a. AIDS
    b. cancer
    c. coronary heart disease
    d. pneumonia
    e. ulcers

21. Which of these is a risk factor for coronary heart disease?
    a. female
    b. smoking cigarettes
    c. physical activity
    d. Type B personality
    e. low serum cholesterol

22. Type A personality predicts heart disease among
    a. males only.
    b. females only.
    c. the general population.
    d. people selected to be at high risk for heart disease only.
    e. people selected to be at low risk for heart disease only.

23. The active ingredient making Type A personality a risk factor for coronary heart disease is
    a. anger.
    b. competitiveness.
    c. time urgency.
    d. all of the above.
    e. none of the above.

24. Recent research has revealed that poor nonwhite males have the highest rates of
    a. hostility.
    b. poor health.
    c. coronary heart disease.
    d. none of the above
    e. all of the above

25. Which of the following has been found to best predict subsequent death from heart attack in males who survive an initial heart attack?
    a. damage to the heart from the first attack.
    b. pessimism.
    c. Type A personality.
    d. traditional risk factors.
    e. none of the above

26. Compared to Type B individuals, Type A's seem to be more involved in a
    a. struggle for control.
    b. conflict with unconscious impulses.
    c. need to self-actualize.
    d. desire to help others.
    e. low-stress lifestyle.

27. Compared to Type B individuals, Type A's respond to helplessness by

a. desperately trying to gain control and then by giving up.
b. half-heartedly trying to gain control and then by giving up.
c. only trying if they are competing.
d. giving up for a while and then by trying to gain control.
e. giving up immediately and then by leaving the situation.

28. When a person shows a chronic emergency reaction, his or her heart becomes
    a. efficient.
    b. overloaded.
    c. sluggish.
    d. unresponsive.
    e. enlarged.

29. Which of the following has been found to best predict death in the ten years following a stroke?
    a. depression following the stroke
    b. sex
    c. age
    d. amount of brain damage from the stroke
    e. all of the above equally predict death

30. Foreign materials that invade the body are
    a. antibodies.
    b. antigens.
    c. lymphocytes.
    d. T-cells.
    e. none of the above

31. Recent research by psychiatrist David Spiegel and colleagues has revealed that survival rates of metastatic breast cancer patients can be enhanced by
    a. routine physical treatment.
    b. higher expectations of survival.
    c. hypnotic exercises to attack the cancer.
    d. psychotherapy.
    e. none of the above.

32. All of these psychological states except _____ have been linked to poor immune function among people.
    a. anxiety
    b. depression
    c. helplessness
    d. hopelessness
    e. all have been linked to poor immune function

33. Sudden death seems to result from
    a. hopelessness and helplessness.
    b. fear and loathing.
    c. approach and avoidance.
    d. illness and exhaustion.
    e. all of the above.

34. When one's spouse dies, one's risk of death is
    a. increased.
    b. increased but only for six months.
    c. decreased.
    d. decreased but only for six months.
    e. unchanged.

35. Severity of colds has been found to be related to all but which of the following?
    a. degree of perceived stress
    b. number of recent negative events in one's life
    c. degree of negative affect
    d. long-term caregiving
    e. all of the above seem to influence the severity of colds

36. Research in nursing homes suggests that
    a. choice and control result in longer life.
    b. support and assistance result in longer life.
    c. rest and relaxation result in longer life.
    d. respect and deference result in longer life.
    e. predictability and lack of responsibility result in longer life.

37. Asthma always results from
    a. infection.
    b. allergy.
    c. psychological factors.
    d. none of the above.

38. All of the following have proposed accounts of psychosomatic disorders except the
    a. biomedical model.
    b. psychodynamic model.
    c. behavioral model.
    d. cognitive model.
    e. existential model.

39. Specific organ vulnerability is an instance of the
    a. biomedical model.
    b. psychodynamic model.
    c. behavioral model.

d. cognitive model.
e. existential model.

40. The idea of specific organ vulnerability is that
    a. after repeated psychosomatic disorders, individuals develop weakness in a specific part of the body.
    b. with repeated use, individuals develop weakness in a specific part of the body.
    c. without repeated use, individuals develop weakness in a specific part of the body.
    d. individuals inherit weakness in a specific part of the body.
    e. none of the above

41. According to Selye's general adaptation syndrome, stress results in which one of the following sequence of responses?
    a. alarm reaction to exhaustion to resistance
    b. alarm reaction to resistance to exhaustion
    c. resistance to alarm reaction to exhaustion
    d. resistance to exhaustion to alarm reaction
    e. exhaustion to resistance to alarm reaction

42. The psychodynamic account of psychosomatic disorders emphasizes all of the following except
    a. vulnerable organ.
    b. underlying conflict.
    c. precipitating event.
    d. adaptation.
    e. c and d

43. The account of psychosomatic disorders that argues that symptoms are acquired through learning the pairing of unconditioned and neutral stimuli is described in the text as the _____ view.
    a. conditioning
    b. association
    c. classical
    d. instrumental
    e. diathesis-stress

44. All of the following have been found to buffer the effects of life events on illness development except
    a. social support.

b. vigor.
c. uncontrollability.
d. a strong sense of self.
e. hardiness.

45. Life events that are most likely to result
    in illness are those that are
    a. controllable entrances.
    b. controllable exits.
    c. uncontrollable entrances.
    d. uncontrollable exits.
    e. major.

Answer Key for Sample Exam

1. d	(p. 311)	5. c	(p. 313)	
2. b	(p. 312)	6. a	(p. 315)	
3. a	(p. 312)	7. a	(p. 315)	
4. b	(p. 313)	8. d	(p. 316)	

9. c	(p. 316)	28. b	(p. 327)
10. d	(p. 318)	29. a	(p. 330)
11. b	(p. 318)	30. b	(p. 332)
12. a	(p. 320)	31. d	(p. 334)
13. c	(p. 321)	32. a	(p. 333)
14. e	(p. 321)	33. a	(p. 329)
15. a, d	(p. 324)	34. b	(p. 330)
16. b	(p. 324)	35. e	(p. 335)
17. a	(p. 323)	36. a	(p. 331)
18. b	(p. 323)	37. d	(p. 337)
19. a	(p. 323)	38. e	(p. 337)
20. c	(p. 322)	39. a, b	(p. 338)
21. b	(p. 322)	40. d	(p. 338)
22. c	(p. 324)	41. b	(p. 339)
23. a	(p. 324)	42. d	(p. 340)
24. e	(p. 325)	43. a	(p. 341)
25. b	(p. 331)	44. c	(p. 345)
26. a	(p. 327)	45. d	(p. 344)
27. a	(p. 327)		

SELF-TEST

1. Unlike somatoform disorders, psychosomatic disorders involve actual _____.

2. Among the psychosomatic disorders are _____ and _____.

3. Marks on the skin produced by an emotional state and having religious significance are

    _____.

4. The model used to explain psychosomatic disorders is the _____ model.

5. The process causing psychosomatic effects seems to be _____ for different organs.

6. A peptic ulcer is an erosion of the _____ of the _____ or the _____.

7. The most salient symptom of a peptic ulcer is _____.

8. Among the constitutional weaknesses that predispose peptic ulcers are an excess of

    _____, a weak _____, and a slow _____ stomach lining.

9. Twin studies suggest that peptic ulcers are _____.

10. Emotional states like _____ and _____ cause excess stomach acid. These

    states may be brought about by conditions of _____, _____, and _____.

11. The "executive monkey" study suggested that _____ causes peptic ulcers. However this study was confounded by _____, and its conclusion should really have been _____.

12. _____ is the treatment of choice for peptic ulcers.

13. The Type A behavior pattern characterizes individuals at risk for _____ difficulties. It involves exaggerated _____, _____ and _____, and _____ and _____.

14. Type A behavior pattern predicts coronary disease among _____.

15. _____ is probably the component of Type A personality that puts one at increased risk for heart disease, through _____.

16. Poor, nonwhite males have the highest rates of _____, _____, and _____.

17. The field that looks at how psychological states affect the body's immune system is _____.

18. The two tasks of the immune system are _____ and _____.

19. When the immune system does a better job of destroying antigens the second time it is exposed to them it is described as _____.

20. _____, _____, _____, and _____ affect immune functioning among people.

21. Sudden death seems to be caused by the psychological state of _____.

22. Following the loss of a spouse, one's chances of death are increased for about _____ months.

23. _____ has been found to increase the life span in women with metastatic breast cancer.

24. Hopelessness may be promoted in nursing homes that deprive individuals of _____.

25. Pessimistic _____ may be a risk factor for illness.

26. Emotional factors play a role in about _____ percent of asthma cases.

27. The notion of specific organ vulnerability proposes that people inherit _____ in a _____.

28. Research support for the notion of specific organ vulnerability is _____.

29. Hans Selye's general adaptation syndrome theory hypothesizes that psychosomatic disorders are _____.

30. Life events may influence illness if they are _____.

Answer Key for Self-Test

1. physical damage
2. peptic ulcers; coronary heart disease
3. stigmata
4. diathesis-stress
5. similar
6. mucous lining; stomach; duodenum
7. abdominal pain
8. hydrochloric acid; mucous membrane; regenerating
9. genetic
10. anger; anxiety; conflict; unpredictability; uncontrollability
11. control; nonrandom assignment; the opposite
12. Cimetidine
13. cardiovascular; time urgency; competitiveness; ambition; aggressiveness; hostility
14. the population at large
15. Hostility; chronic arousal of the emergency reaction
16. hostility; CHD; poor health
17. psychoneuroimmunology
18. recognizing foreign materials; removing them from the body
19. immunologic memory
20. Depression, helplessness, hopelessness, and stressful events
21. hopelessness
22. six
23. psychotherapy
24. control
25. explanatory style
26. 33
27. weakness; specific organ
28. mixed
29. general stress reactions
30. uncontrollable exits

MATCHING ITEMS

_____	1.	hostility
_____	2.	hypertension
_____	3.	stigmata
_____	4.	antigens
_____	5.	immunocompetence
_____	6.	Holmes and Rahe
_____	7.	health psychology
_____	8.	diathesis
_____	9.	stress
_____	10.	Selye

A. stressful life events

B. measure of protection efficiency of the organism

C. central component of Type A personality

D. psychological reaction to meaningful events

E. physical marks psychologically created

F. general adaptation syndrome

G. constitutional weakness

H. psychosomatic disorders

I. continual emergency reaction

J. foreign invaders

Answer Key for Matching Items

1.	C	6.	A
2.	I	7.	H
3.	E	8.	G
4.	J	9.	D
5.	B	10.	F

SHORT-ANSWER QUESTIONS

1. How are the psychosomatic symptoms of stigmata and the somatoform symptoms of conversion disorders alike and different?

2. Describe the diathesis-stress model of psychosomatic disorders. How might this model be applied to our thinking about cancer, for example?

3. What are the defining characteristics of the Type A personality? What factors appear to also be associated with it?

4. Describe the essential components of each of the biomedical, psychodynamic, behavioral and cognitive explanations of psychosomatic disorders.

TYING IT TOGETHER

The psychosomatic disorders are explained with a diathesis-stress model, which combines the biomedical approach (Chapter 3) with the behavioral approach (Chapter 5). This may become an increasingly popular way to explain other psychological disorders—e.g., depression (Chapter 11) and schizophrenia (Chapter 12)—and it may become a popular way to view physical disorders as well (Chapter 17). Chapter 10 describes how feelings of hopelessness may underlie illness. Similar feelings have been implicated in post-traumatic stress disorders (Chapter 8), depression, and suicide (Chapter 11).

The day may come when "psychological" disorders and "physical" disorders are seen as overlapping, as possessing fuzzy boundaries (Chapter 1). The idea behind holistic medicine is that all disorders—physical and psychological—are psychosomatic disorders. Treatments may become more eclectic, and therapists may become more broadly trained (Chapter 19). Contemporary models of abnormality (Chapter 3 through 5) may become outmoded and replaced with more integrative explanations.

The personality disorders described in Chapter 15 lead to social and occupational maladjustment. Perhaps these disorders should be expanded to include any pervasive life-style that results in problems. Thus, the Type A behavior pattern, shown by research to be associated with hypertension and other cardiovascular difficulties, is as much a disorder of personality as is sociopathy. Similarly, life-styles that entail drug abuse (Chapter 14) could be viewed as being akin to life-styles that result in psychosomatic difficulties.

Many of the psychosomatic disorders described in this chapter involve fear and anxiety (Chapter 8 and 9), and animal models of psychopathology have been used to understand them better (Chapter 6) and to develop effective treatments (Chapter 19).

FURTHER READINGS

Alexander, F. (1950). *Psychosomatic medicine: Its principles and applications.* New York: Norton.

Cannon, W. B. (1942). "Voodoo" death. *American Anthropologist, 44,* 169–181.

Cousins, N. (1979). *Anatomy of an illness.* New York: Norton.

Friedman, N., & Rosenman, R. H. (1974). *Type A behavior and your heart.* New York: Knopf.

Jaret, P. (1986). Our immune system: The wars within. *National Geographic, 169*(6), 702–735.

Locke, S., & Colligan, D. (1986). *The healer within.* New York: Dutton.

Moyers, B. (1993). *Healing and the mind.* New York: Doubleday.

Ornstein, R., & Sobel, R. (1987). *The healing brain.* New York: Simon & Schuster.

Richter, C. P. (1957). On the phenomenon of sudden death in animals and man. *Psychosomatic Medicine, 19,* 191–198.

Selye, H. (1956). *The stress of life.* New York: McGraw-Hill.

Spiegel, D. (1993). *Living beyond limits—New hope and help for facing life-threatening illness.* New York: Random House.

TERM-PAPER TOPICS

1. Does asthma fit a diathesis-stress model? Review the evidence, and come to a conclusion.

2. The textbook describes how feelings of hopelessness can be involved in cancer. What other psychological factors have been shown to foreshadow cancer? Is cancer a psychosomatic disorder?

3. How does the prevalence of ulcers vary across different occupational and economic groups? What theory of ulcer formation does the pattern support?

4. It has been suggested that so-called "crib death" may be an instance of sudden death. What is the evidence for and against this claim?

5. Suppose research continues to support the role of psychological factors in predisposing immunological disease. What role might psychologists play in the prevention and treatment of such illnesses?

EXERCISES

Exercise One—Type A Behavior Pattern and Achievement

The textbook described the Type A behavior pattern in terms of its negative effects on cardiovascular health. However, this way of living also has positive effects on achievement. The purpose of this exercise is to demonstrate the often superior academic performance of Type A individuals.

Categorize a number of your friends as Type A or Type B. Remember that Type A individuals are characterized by (a) an exaggerated sense of time urgency; (b) competitiveness and ambition; and (c) aggressiveness and hostility when things get in their way. Type B individuals are the opposite—relaxed and serene. Talk to these individuals about their approach to schoolwork. How much time do they spend studying? Do they study as much for courses they like as for courses they dislike? How well do they do? What are their future academic goals? You will probably find striking differences between Type A individuals and Type B individuals.

Glass, D. C. (1976). Pattern A and achievement striving. In *Behavior patterns, stress, and coronary disease* (pp. 36–50). Hillsdale, NJ: Erlbaum.

Exercise Two—Blood Pressure

In this exercise you will have your blood pressure checked. This will give you a better understanding of hypertension and how it is diagnosed. This may also start a habit that is life-long and life-protecting.

Contact your physician at home or at school and make an appointment to have your blood pressure checked. Is your blood pressure normal?

You may also be able to arrange a classroom demonstration by the American Red Cross in which the blood pressure of everyone in your class can be measured. What is the range of scores? What sorts of people have the highest blood pressure? What sorts of people have the lowest?

Exercise Three—Stomach aches and Ulcers

The purpose of this exercise is to learn about the causes and consequences of ulcers.

Talk to several individuals of your acquaintance who suffer or have suffered from stomach aches and ulcers. Does their experience correspond to what your textbook describes as the case about people with peptic ulcers. For instance, do their family members have similar problems? Does stress exacerbate their ulcer?

Kapp, F. T., Rosenbaum, M., & Romano, J. (1947). Psychological factors in men with peptic ulcers. *American Journal of Psychiatry, 103,* 700–704.

CHAPTER 11

Depression and Suicide

CHAPTER OVERVIEW

The depressive disorders, the most common form of abnormality, are covered in this chapter. These are disorders of mood and include unipolar depression (characterized by sadness), mania (characterized by euphoria), and bipolar depression (characterized by swings between sadness and euphoria). Depression is also associated with specific cognitive, motivational, somatic, and behavioral symptoms. Women are more apt to become depressed than men, and recent studies show that depression is much on the rise among both men and women.

The biological model of depression points to an insufficiency of the neurotransmitters norepinephrine and serotonin as the cause of depression. Antidepressant medication, which is successful in combating depression, increases the availability of these brain chemicals. The psychodynamic model proposes that depression results when excessively dependent and helpless individuals turn anger inward against the self. Psychodynamic therapy encourages depressed individuals to recognize and change their anger, dependency, and helplessness. Cognitive models emphasize negative thoughts, erroneous logic, and learned helplessness, and cognitive therapies try to undo these ways of thinking. Each model seems to capture something about depression.

Bipolar depression and mania are not as well understood as unipolar depression, but they involve a genetic component. Lithium is successful in controlling manic episodes, but in light of its serious side effects it is to be used with caution.

The chapter ends with a discussion of suicide, which is frequently preceded by depression. Descriptive information about suicide and suicide attempts is presented, and the presumed motives of suicidal individuals are discussed.

ESSENTIAL TERMS

affective disorder	mental disorder involving disturbance in mood; including unipolar depression, bipolar depression, and mania (p. 352)
anaclitic depression	psychological state among infants separated from their mother characterized by unresponsive apathy, listlessness, weight loss, increased susceptibility to illness; it is thought to be the earliest state related to depression (p. 366)
anger turned inward	in psychodynamic theories, the hypothesized cause of depressive disorders (p. 378)

Attributional Style Questionnaire (ASQ)	self-report questionnaire that assesses explanatory style (p. 340)
attributions in learned helplessness	in human helplessness, causal explanations of uncontrollable events thought to influence reactions to these events (pp. 387–389)
global-specific	explanation in terms of a pervasive (global) versus a circumscribed (specific) factor
internal-external	explanation in terms of oneself (internal) or other people/circumstances (external)
stable-unstable	explanation in terms of a recurring (stable) or transient (unstable) factor
automatic thoughts	according to Beck, discrete, negative statements told to oneself quickly and habitually that produce and maintain depression (p. 383)
Beck Depression Inventory (BDI)	self-report questionnaire developed by Aaron T. Beck that measures the prevalence and severity of twenty-one common depressive symptoms (p. 359)
biogenic amines	neurochemicals involved in neural transmission in the medial forebrain bundle and periventricular system (p. 371)
breakdown	process in which a neurochemical is chemically broken down and rendered inactive (p. 373)
catecholamine hypothesis	biological theory of depression proposing that depression results from decreased availability of norepinephrine, a biogenic amine (p. 372)
childhood depression	depressive disorder among children, once thought to be rare, currently thought to be much more common (p. 320)
chronic depression	*see* dysthmia
chronic hypomanic disorder	chronic low-level form of mania also known as hypomanic personality (p. 400)
cognitive therapy for depression	approach to therapy developed by Beck that attempts to change the thoughts and justifications of depressed patients (*see* Chapter 5, "Essential Terms") (p. 380)
cognitive triad	according to Beck, negative thoughts about the self, ongoing experience, and the future that produce depression (p. 380)
depressed mood	sad, blue, miserable feelings (p. 351)
depressive disorder	disorder characterized by a depressed mood, a negative view of oneself and the future, diminished motivation, loss of pleasure, and sleep and eating disturbances (p. 352)
bipolar depression	depression alternating with mania; manic-depression (p. 352)
unipolar depression	depression without mania (p. 352)

depressive personality	personality style characterized by excessive dependence on others for self-esteem and difficulty tolerating frustration; thought to predispose individuals to depressive disorders (p. 379)
double depression	suffering a depressive episode at the same time as an underlying dysthymic disorder (p. 360)
dysthymia	chronic low-level depression (p. 360)
electroconvulsive shock therapy (ECT)	therapy for depression in which an electric current is passed through the brain of the patient (p. 376)
endogenous depression	depressive disorder marked by psychomotor retardation, severe symptoms, lack of reaction to environmental events during depression, loss of interest in life, somatic symptoms; thought to arise from disordered biology; also known as depression with melancholia (cf. exogenous depression) (p. 360)
episodic depression	depressive disorder of less than two years' duration, marked by clear onset (p. 360)
errors in logic	according to Beck, erroneous reasoning that produces depression (p. 381)
arbitrary inference	drawing a conclusion in absence of evidence
magnification/minimization	evaluations that magnify bad events and minimize good events
overgeneralization	drawing conclusions on the basis of a single fact
personalization	taking responsibility for bad events in the world
selective abstraction	focusing on insignificant details and ignoring important features
exogenous depression	depressive disorder marked by less severe symptoms, reaction to environmental events during depression; thought to be precipitated by a life stressor (cf. endogenous depression) (p. 360)
explanatory style	the characteristic attributions made to explain successes and failures; a negative style that maximizes the expectation that responding will be ineffective may be a predisposition to helplessness and depression (p. 389)
flight of ideas	racing thoughts or ideas (p. 401)
fluoxetine (Prozac)	an effective, low side effect, antidepressant drug that inhibits the reuptake of serotonin (p. 374)
hopelessness theory	theory of depression that regards hopelessness about the future—stemming from stable and global attributions for negative events—as the proximal cause of depression (p. 389)
indoleamine hypothesis	biological theory of depression proposing that depression results from decreased availability of serotonin (p. 374)

learned helplessness	phenomenon in which organisms exposed to uncontrollable events display subsequent cognitive, motivational, and affective deficits; proposed as a model of depression (p. 385)
lithium	drug used to treat bipolar depression and mania (p. 404)
mania	excessive elation, expansiveness, irritability, talkativeness, inflated self-esteem, and flight of ideas (p. 352)
manic depression	now known as bipolar depression (p. 400)
manipulation	motive for a suicide attempt: desire to manipulate other people (p. 413)
MAO inhibitors	drugs that block breakdown of norepinephrine; used to treat depression (p. 373)
medial forebrain bundle (MFB)	brain structure involved in reward; thought to be involved in depression (p. 372)
melancholia	loss of pleasure in all activities and lack of reaction to pleasurable events (*see* endogenous depression) (p. 360)
negative explanatory style	attributing failure to internal, global, and stable factors, and success to external, unstable, and specific factors (also known as negative attributional style) (p. 389)
normal depression	sad mood occasionally experienced by most people in the course of everyday life (p. 352)
optimism	attributing negative events to unstable, specific, and external causes (cf. negative explanatory style) (p. 394)
periventricular system (PVS)	brain structure involved in punishment (p. 372)
premenstrual depression (premenstrual dysphoric disorder)	controversial diagnostic category, in which depressive symptoms among women occur just prior to menstruation (p. 365)
Prozac	(*see* fluoxetine, p. 374)
psychomotor retardation	symptom of severe depression, wherein physical movement—walking and talking—is markedly slowed (p. 358)
reattribution training	therapy technique for depression in which the patient is encouraged not to blame him- or herself irrationally for bad events (p. 384)
recurrence	a return of depressive symptoms following at least six months without significant symptoms (p. 370)
relapse	a return of temporarily relieved depressive symptoms within the same episode (p. 370)
reserpine	sedative given to patients with high blood pressure that can cause depression as a side effect presumably because it depletes norepinephrine (p. 374)
reuptake	process in which a neuron that has secreted a neurochemical reabsorbs it (p. 373)

seasonal affective disorder (SAD)	form of bipolar depression in which depressive episodes are triggered by short days (with little sunlight) (p. 406)
somatic therapy for depression	biological treatment of depression: ECT, MAO inhibitors, tricyclics, dream deprivation (p. 375)
suicide	killing of oneself (p. 407)
altruistic suicide	suicide required by society (p. 413)
anomic suicide	suicide precipitated by a shattering break in an individual's relationship to society (p. 413)
egoistic suicide	suicide by an individual with too few ties to fellow humans (p. 413)
surcease	motive for suicide: desire to see an end to problems (p. 413)
tricyclics	drugs used to treat depression that block the reuptake of norepinephrine (p. 373)

CENTRAL CONCEPTUAL ISSUES

The origins and mechanisms of depression.   Virtually every psychological orientation and form of therapy has been applied to the understanding and treatment of depression, each bringing with it a unique explanation of origin and mechanism. However, the fact that no one model can fully account for, nor any one therapy cure, all cases of depression, suggests that depressive symptoms may be just that: symptoms reflecting more than one possible origin and more than one possible underlying physiological or psychological process—not unlike the symptom of fever which is characteristic of a number of conditions requiring a variety of treatments. This aspect is highlighted in the traditional distinction between endogenous (coming from within) and exogenous (coming from outside) depression thought to reflect physiological versus psychological etiologies, respectively. (Some recent research suggests, however, that the distinction may be one of severity—with endogenous being more serious—rather than one of origin.) It may also be helpful to think of depression as a condition echoing many possible interacting levels of disorder: disordered physiology (e.g., norepinephrine and/or serotonin), disordered thought processes (e.g., illogical thinking, negative attributional style), disordered interpersonal relations and circumstances (e.g., issues of conflict, transition, and trauma), and disordered early experience (e.g., unresolved grief, negative self schemas, trauma). It is possible that depression can originate in any of these and then come to influence functioning in the rest. Moreover, if depression does reflect a complex interplay of somatic, cognitive, intrapsychic, and interpersonal factors, then intervention in any one of these domains may be predicted to have therapeutic effects in the others.

Treatment of mood disorders.   Although depression is the most common psychological disorder, and seems to be increasing, it can be positively affected in up to 90% of cases by using one form of treatment or another. Strategies for treating unipolar depression vary considerably among somatic, cognitive, psychodynamic, and interpersonal therapies, depending on the severity and profile of symptoms, and the orientation of the therapist. Somatic therapies alone (e.g., drug or ECT) do not have as successful long-term results after cessation of treatment as do psychotherapies alone or in combination with somatic therapies. This may be due to the failure of somatic therapies to effect any *permanent* change in underlying physiology. In contrast, cognitive and interpersonal therapies teach new ways of thinking and interacting that may be continued in practice long after formal therapy has ended, effectively inoculating the individual against depressive symptoms in the future. Bipolar disorder, which appears to have a strong genetic component, is unresponsive to psychotherapy alone, but can be well managed with drug therapies. However, relapse may follow discontinuation of drug use.

Electroconvulsive therapy (ECT).   Because the use of ECT is so controversial, it sharply highlights a number of issues—issues that arise, albeit less dramatically, with many other treatments in abnormal psychology. These include appropriate use and effectiveness of the treatment, public attitude about its use, and the state of knowledge within the psychological/psychiatric community about the mechanisms involved. ECT is used in cases of severe unipolar depression, typically when all other treatments have failed, are inappropriate (e.g., the patient has a condition that precludes the use of antidepressant drugs), or the sufferer is in need of relief *immediately* (e.g., they are suicidal, psychotic) and so cannot wait several weeks for the effects of antidepressants to remediate their symptoms. Once prescribed liberally for a wide variety of psychological ailments, its use has been considerably curtailed—in part because of public disapproval. For ECT to be effective, a seizure which lasts at least a minute must be induced in the brain through application of a brief electrical current to one or both hemispheres. The violent convulsions (if muscle relaxants are not administered), immediate side effects (including memory loss, disorientation, language impairment), frequency and breadth of its early usage, its failure to reduce relapse, and the mere idea of applying electric shock to the brain has led some critics to charge that its use is barbaric, callous, and even punitive. However, ECT is very successful at breaking up intractable depression in the short term, and better diagnostic techniques and classification, and the results of treatment outcome studies have allowed psychiatrists to narrow ECT use to those for whom it is most effective. As well, a greater understanding of the brain has allowed modifications in the treatment procedure (e.g., applying shock only to the nondominant (nonlanguage) hemisphere) which reduce apparent side effects. Public visceral discomfort notwithstanding, this treatment remains a valuable, if controversial, tool.

Suicide.   The most serious consequence of a depression is the possibility of suicide. Depressed individuals sometimes reach depths of despair unimaginable to the well, and in the face of which suicide seems to be the only option available to relieve the pain. The apparent rationality of suicide to the suicidal may be the hardest, most frustrating, and most frightening part of the illness for family members and friends who can readily see all the good reasons the depressed individual has to live. The nadir of a depressed episode may be when the suicidal intent is formed, but often it is only after the depressed individual begins to feel better and more energetic that the act is actually attempted: suicidal behavior requires energy along with intent. Moreover, the decision to commit suicide may itself bring some relief from depression, because it offers hope for surcease. Thus, it is particularly important to be vigilant during changes—for the worse, or for the better—in the state of the individual depressed.

SAMPLE EXAM

1. The most common psychological disorder is
   a. phobia.
   b. schizophrenia.
   c. psychosomatic disorder.
   d. depression.
   e. bipolar disorder.

2. Bipolar depression is the same as
   a. manic-depression.
   b. chronic depression.
   c. episodic depression.
   d. anaclitic depression.
   e. exogenous depression.

3. Normal depression differs from clinical depression in
   a. the number of symptoms.
   b. the severity of symptoms.
   c. the frequency of symptoms.
   d. the duration of symptoms.
   e. all of the above.

4. The most widespread symptom of depression is
   a. sadness.
   b. negative view of future.
   c. sleep disturbance.
   d. suicidal thoughts.
   e. helplessness.

5. The Beck Depression Inventory is used to
   a. diagnose depression.
   b. measure severity of depressive symptoms.
   c. recommend treatment.
   d. assess illogical thinking.
   e. all of the above.

6. A depressed person sees herself as
   a. negative.
   b. ambivalent.
   c. positive.
   d. variable.
   e. neutral.

7. Research suggests that depressives
   a. may see the world more accurately than individuals who are not depressed.
   b. may see the world as accurately as individuals who are not depressed.
   c. may see the world less accurately than individuals who are not depressed.
   d. refuse to see the world as accurately as individuals who are not depressed.
   e. none of the above.

8. How do depressed people respond to success?
   a. They increase their expectations of future success.
   b. They decrease their expectations of future success.
   c. They do not change their expectations of future success.
   d. They refuse to believe it.
   e. None of the above.

9. Psychomotor retardation refers to
   a. a form of mental retardation.
   b. an aspect of the emergency reaction.
   c. a slowing down of movement.
   d. a symptom of anxiety.
   e. an inability to use machinery.

10. Depressed individuals show all of the following except
    a. sleep disturbance.
    b. decreased appetite.
    c. loss of sexual desire.
    d. indifference to body.
    e. loss of concentration.

11. The endogenous-exogenous distinction is hoped to correspond to
    a. severe versus mild depressive disorders.
    b. unipolar versus bipolar depressive disorders.
    c. biological versus psychological depressive disorders.
    d. chronic versus episodic depressive disorders.
    e. helplessness versus hopelessness.

12. Endogenous is to exogenous as
    a. up is to down.
    b. former is to latter.
    c. right is to wrong.
    d. in is to out.
    e. mind is to body.

13. All of the following depressive symptoms are more common in endogenous depression than in exogenous depression except
    a. psychomotor retardation
    b. sadness
    c. sleep disturbance
    d. reaction to environmental events
    e. guilt

14. Studies over time suggest that during the twentieth century, the prevalence of depression has
    a. decreased over time.
    b. stayed much the same.
    c. increased over time.
    d. fluctuated.
    e. not been studied.

15. Which one of the following statements is true?
    a. Women are more likely to be depressed than men.
    b. Men are more likely to be depressed than women.
    c. Women and men are equally likely to be depressed.
    d. Sex differences in depression have changed over the years.
    e. Sex differences in depression depend on the time of year.

16. All of the following are symptoms in premenstrual depression except
    a. oversensitivity to rejection.
    b. sleep changes.
    c. fatigability.
    d. emotional lability.
    e. flight of ideas.

17. If a culture holds thinness as an ideal, we can predict that
    a. eating disorders will exist.
    b. women will have twice the rate of depression than men.
    c. there will be no sex difference in depression.
    d. more than half the dieters will be successful.
    e. both a and b

18. Depression is to anaclitic depression as
    a. up is to down.
    b. inside is to outside.
    c. abnormal is to normal.
    d. parent is to infant.
    e. mild is to severe.

19. For a child, loss associated with increased risk for depression may take the form of any of the following except
    a. divorce.
    b. parental turmoil.
    c. death of a parent.
    d. separation.
    e. moving.

20. All of the following increase the chances of depression except
    a. early childhood loss.
    b. absence of an intimate relationship.
    c. recent loss.
    d. serious religious commitment.
    e. stressors.

21. Among most inpatients depressions get better within
    a. one month.
    b. three months.
    c. six months.
    d. one year.
    e. two years.

22. After experiencing a depressive episode, one's chances of doing so again within the next ten years are
    a. 90 percent.
    b. 50 percent.
    c. 33 percent.
    d. 10 percent.
    e. less than 5 percent.

23. Chronic depression develops in what percent of people experiencing a depressive episode?
    a. 90
    b. 75
    c. 30
    d. 33
    e. 10

24. Biological accounts of depression focus on the
    a. brain.
    b. heart.
    c. immune system.
    d. spleen.
    e. endocrine system.

25. The MFB is to the PVS as
    a. dark is to light.
    b. reward is to punishment.
    c. inside is to outside.
    d. behaviorism is to cognitive theory.
    e. off is to on.

26. According to the biological model, depression is
    a. a thought disorder caused by too much dopamine.
    b. a motivational disorder caused by too little norepinephrine.
    c. a behavioral disorder caused by too much epinephrine.
    d. an emotional disorder caused by too much serotonin.
    e. none of the above

27. Of the biogenic amines, which is thought to be involved in depression?
    a. norepinephrine
    b. epinephrine
    c. dopamine
    d. serotonin
    e. histamine

28. Norepinephrine can be inactivated by
    a. sublimation.
    b. reuptake.
    c. breakdown.
    d. tolerance.
    e. habituation.

29. Depression is treated with all of the following drugs except
    a. thorazine.
    b. imipramine.
    c. tricyclics.
    d. MAO inhibitors.
    e. SSRIs.

30. Tricyclics are to MAO inhibitors as
    a. salt is to pepper.
    b. reuptake is to breakdown.
    c. thorazine is to valium.
    d. inside is to outside.
    e. breakdown is to block.

31. All of the following support the biomedical account of depression except
    a. effectiveness of drug therapies.
    b. depression is sometimes a side effect of medication.
    c. early loss predisposes an individual to depression.
    d. depression is sometimes a product of hormonal changes.
    e. effectiveness of ECT.

32. Electroconvulsive shock therapy for severe depression is
    a. highly effective.
    b. somewhat effective.
    c. ineffective.
    d. somewhat effective, but only for men.
    e. somewhat effective, but only for women.

33. Which of the following is true about ECT?
    a. Unilateral electrode placement is more effective than bilateral placement.
    b. The patient is awake during the procedure.
    c. Unilateral compared to bilateral electrode placement increases the likelihood of impaired speech following treatment.
    d. The effective ingredient in ECT is unknown.
    e. All of the above are true.

34. The psychodynamic account of depression emphasizes all of the following except
    a. fixation at the anal stage.
    b. anger turned inward.
    c. excessive dependence.
    d. helplessness.
    e. early loss.

35. Freud sought to understand depression by explaining the difference between
    a. id and superego.
    b. sexuality and aggression.
    c. mourning and melancholia.
    d. sadness and grief.
    e. libido and thanatos.

36. According to Freud, the depressed individual is actually angry at
    a. someone who is loved.
    b. someone who is hated.
    c. the self.
    d. someone who is not known.
    e. any of the above.

37. Suppose you were told that you would be introduced to someone with a depressive personality. You would expect this individual to be
    a. charming.
    b. oblivious.
    c. depressed.
    d. independent.
    e. boring.

38. Negative thoughts are to Beck as what is to Seligman?
    a. happiness

b. hopelessness
c. helplessness
d. helpfulness
e. optimism

39. According to Beck, the depressed individual has a negative view of all of the following except the
a. self.
b. past.
c. present.
d. future.
e. experience.

40. All of the following are errors of logic described by Beck except
a. arbitrary inference.
b. selective abstraction.
c. personalization.
d. depersonalization.
e. overgeneralization.

41. A depressed person says that she is a bad mother because her baby occasionally cries. What error in logic is she making?
a. arbitrary inference
b. selective abstraction
c. personalization
d. depersonalization
e. minimization

42. A depressed person says that he is responsible for the national debt. What error in logic is he making?
a. arbitrary inference
b. selective abstraction
c. personalization
d. depersonalization
e. minimization

43. A depressed person says that she is a bad person because her mother died. What error in logic is she making?
a. arbitrary inference
b. selective abstraction
c. personalization
d. depersonalization
e. minimization

44. All of the following are targets for cognitive therapy for depression except
a. anger turned inward.
b. automatic thoughts.
c. attributions.
d. assumptions.
e. beliefs.

45. Compared to drug therapy for depression, cognitive therapy
a. takes longer.
b. has less relapse.
c. is as effective.
d. a and b.
e. all of the above.

46. Learned helplessness was first discovered among
a. mice.
b. rats.
c. dogs.
d. monkeys.
e. people.

47. Learned helplessness deficits result from
a. unpredictable events.
b. uncontrollable events.
c. undesirable events.
d. unknown events.
e. unbelievable events.

48. Helplessness deficits include all of the following except
a. motivational deficits.
b. learning deficits.
c. emotional deficits.
d. unconscious deficits.
e. helplessness deficits include all of the above.

49. Learned helplessness in people involves
a. expectations.
b. appraisals.
c. attributions.
d. beliefs.
e. assumptions.

50. All of the following are dimensions along which helplessness theory describes attributions except
a. internal versus external.
b. controllable versus uncontrollable.
c. stable versus unstable.
d. global versus specific.
e. all of the above are attributional dimensions

51. Suppose you cannot work the crossword puzzle in the newspaper this morning. According to helplessness theory, the most depressing causal attribution for your failure is
a. "I didn't have my coffee."
b. "The light is bad."
c. "I'm stupid."

d. "Crossword puzzles are stupid."
e. "Crossword puzzle editors are stupid."

52. In the above example, the least depressing causal attribution is
a. "I'm stupid."
b. "I didn't have enough time this morning."
c. "Crossword puzzles are difficult."
d. "I'm not good at the puzzles in this paper."
e. "I must be getting old."

53. The parallel between learned helplessness and depression is evident in all of the following except
a. passivity.
b. cognitive deficits.
c. anger turned inward.
d. norepinephrine depletion.
e. explanatory style.

54. Learned helplessness can be prevented by
a. immunization.
b. stress.
c. relaxation.
d. avoidance.
e. none of the above.

55. The attributional reformulation as an explanation of depression has been investigated in studies of
a. children.
b. adults.
c. dogs.
d. children and adults.
e. none of the above.

56. Pessimistic explanatory style is a _____ of(for) depression.
a. necessary and sufficient cause
b. consequence
c. symptom
d. risk factor
e. side effect

57. Which of the following somatic treatments for depression in humans are also effective in remediating learned helplessness in animals?
a. ECT
b. serotonin enhancers
c. dream deprivation
d. MAO inhibitors
e. all of the above

58. Which one of the following is *not* a weakness of the cognitive approach to depression?
a. It is based on research.
b. It does not explain all forms of depression.
c. It does not explain why somatic therapies for depression are successful.
d. It is controversial.
e. It does not account for the somatic symptoms.

59. The best account of depression is that proposed by the
a. biomedical model.
b. psychodynamic model.
c. cognitive model.
d. behavioral model.
e. none of the above.

60. Mania that occurs without depression is
a. nonexistent.
b. rare.
c. frequent.
d. always the case.
e. called unipolar depression.

61. Symptoms of mania include all of the following except
a. a euphoric mood.
b. racing thoughts.
c. insomnia.
d. attribution of bad events to internal, stable, and global causes.
e. reckless behavior.

62. Bipolar depression
a. is more frequent among men than among women.
b. is more frequent among women than among men.
c. is equally frequent among men and women.
d. has seen a change in sex differences over the years.
e. is more frequent among female children than among male children.

63. In bipolar depression, the first episode of mania occurs in
a. childhood.
b. adolescence.
c. early adulthood.
d. middle age.
e. old age.

64. The current thinking about the role of genetics in mood disorders includes all of the following except
   a. identical twins have a higher concordance rate than fraternal twins.
   b. familial risk is probably more for manic-depression than for unipolar depression.
   c. relatives of manic-depressives have five times the normal risk.
   d. genetic inheritance may be involved in both unipolar and bipolar depressions.
   e. manic-depression does not run in successive generations.

65. The preferred treatment of bipolar depression is
   a. flooding.
   b. assertiveness training.
   c. lithium.
   d. MAO inhibitors.
   e. ECT.

66. Seasonal affective disorder is a form of
   a. unipolar depression.
   b. bipolar depression.
   c. mania.
   d. schizophrenia.
   e. any of the above.

67. Most suicides are preceded by
   a. anxiety disorders.
   b. affective disorders.
   c. schizophrenic disorders.
   d. somatoform disorders.
   e. psychosomatic disorders.

68. Who does not belong?
   a. Cleopatra
   b. Marilyn Monroe
   c. Sid Vicious
   d. Ronald Reagan
   e. Ernest Hemingway

69. Which one of the following is *not* a myth about suicide?
   a. Individuals who talk about killing themselves do not kill themselves.
   b. Individuals who are suicidal will always be suicidal.
   c. Individuals who attempt suicide may be rational.

   d. Women succeed at suicide less frequently than men.
   e. Suicide is more common in the rich.

70. Vulnerability to suicide is influenced by
   a. race.
   b. age.
   c. nationality.
   d. sex.
   e. all of the above.

71. Suicide is on the rise particularly among
   a. teenage males.
   b. teenage females.
   c. males in their twenties.
   d. females in their twenties.
   e. males and females in their thirties.

72. Suppose an individual attempted suicide because he wished to benefit his community. His motive is
   a. anomic.
   b. egoistic.
   c. altruistic.
   d. hedonistic.
   e. none of the above.

73. Suicide attempts motivated by surcease are
   a. a cry for help.
   b. less common than manipulative suicide attempts.
   c. precipitated by a break in an individual's relationship with society.
   d. apt to involve less lethal means.
   e. intended to end the individual's troubles.

74. Factors that predict suicide attempts include all of the following except
   a. intent.
   b. hopelessness.
   c. anger.
   d. depression.
   e. all of the above are factors

75. Suicide notes are usually
   a. grandiose.
   b. mundane.
   c. creative.
   d. angry.
   e. none of the above.

Answer Key for Sample Exam

1. d (p. 351)	20. d (p. 369)	39. b (p. 380)	58. a (p. 398)
2. a (p. 352)	21. c (p. 369)	40. d (p. 381)	59. d (p. 398)
3. e (p. 352)	22. b (p. 370)	41. b (p. 382)	60. b (p. 400)
4. a (p. 353)	23. e (p. 370)	42. c (p. 382)	61. d (p. 400)
5. b (p. 359)	24. a (p. 371)	43. a (p. 381)	62. c (p. 403)
6. a (p. 354)	25. b (p. 372)	44. a (p. 383)	63. c (p. 403)
7. a (p. 354)	26. b (p. 373)	45. g (p. 396)	64. e (p. 404)
8. c (p. 357)	27. a, d (p. 372)	46. c (p. 385)	65. c (p. 404)
9. c (p. 358)	28. b, c (p. 373)	47. b (p. 385)	66. b (p. 406)
10. d (p. 358)	29. a (p. 373)	48. d (p. 387)	67. b (p. 408)
11. c (p. 360)	30. b (p. 374)	49. a, c (p. 387)	68. d (p. 408)
12. d (p. 360)	31. c (p. 371)	50. b (p. 387)	69. c, d (p. 409)
13. b (p. 361)	32. a (p. 377)	51. c (p. 389)	70. e (p. 410)
14. c (p. 362)	33. d (p. 377)	52. b (p. 389)	71. c (p. 412)
15. a (p. 364)	34. a (p. 378)	53. c (p. 392)	72. c (p. 413)
16. e (p. 365)	35. c (p. 378)	54. a (p. 393)	73. e (p. 413)
17. e (p. 365)	36. a (p. 378)	55. d (p. 389)	74. c (p. 414)
18. d (p. 366)	37. a (p. 379)	56. d (p. 395)	75. b (p. 415)
19. e (p. 366)	38. c (p. 380)	57. e (p. 393)	

SELF-TEST

1. _____ is the most widespread psychological disorder and is _____.

2. The two types of depressive disorders are _____ depression and _____ depression.

3. Depression is widely regarded as a disorder of _____, but it also has characteristic _____, _____, and _____ symptoms.

4. Depressed people have a _____ view of the self, experience, and the future.

5. Research surprisingly suggests that depressed individuals may see reality more _____ than nondepressed individuals.

6. Depressed people tend not to _____ voluntary responses; extremely depressed people may show _____.

7. Common in depression is loss of _____.

8. _____ depression is thought to be precipitated by a life stressor, while _____ depression is thought not to be.

9. Women are _____ vulnerable to depression than men.

10. The earliest psychological state that may be related to depression is _____ depression.

11. Until recently, it was thought that childhood depression was _____.

12. Research shows that depressed individuals are more likely to have experienced early _____ than nondepressed individuals.

13. Brown and Harris identified four factors that help make an individual invulnerable to depression: first, whether the individual has an _____ relationship; second, whether the individual has a _____ away from home; third, whether the individual has fewer than _____ still at home; and fourth, whether the individual has a serious _____ commitment.

14. Among outpatients, the average depressive episode lasts about _____ months, and among inpatients, the average depressive episode lasts about _____ months.

15. There is evidence that bipolar depression is _____ inherited, while unipolar depression is only _____ inherited.

16. The biomedical model of depression proposes that the neurotransmitters _____ are involved.

17. Tricyclics affect the _____ of norepinephrine, while MAO inhibitors affect its _____.

18. About _____ percent of depressed patients improve with antidepressant medication.

19. Electroconvulsive shock therapy is _____ for severe depression. When it is administered to only one-half of the brain, it is _____.

20. The psychodynamic model of depression proposes that it results from _____ turned inward.

21. According to Freud, depressives _____ lost love objects.

22. The depressive personality is one in which a person is inordinately dependent on other people for _____.

23. Beck proposes two cognitive mechanisms for depression: the _____ and _____.

24. When a depressed individual draws a conclusion when there is little evidence, this is _____.

25. Focusing on one insignificant detail while ignoring more important features is _____.

26. A global conclusion based on a single fact is _____.

27. Gross errors of evaluation resulting from attention to an unimportant bad event are examples of _____.

28. Incorrectly taking responsibility for bad events is _____.

29. Cognitive therapy for depression is directed at the _____ of the depressive. It has four major techniques: first, detection of _____; second, _____ testing; third, _____ training; and fourth, changing _____.

30. Research suggests that cognitive therapy for depression may be _____ effective as drug therapy.

31. Learned helplessness theory proposes that depression results from the expectation that _____ and _____ will be independent.

32. Learned helplessness involves _____, _____, and _____ deficits.

33. Uncontrollable bad events are thought to produce depression when they are attributed to _____, _____, and _____ causes.

34. According to learned helplessness theory, self-esteem loss in depression results from _____ attributions for bad events.

35. Explanatory style can be changed by _____.

36. Problems of the cognitive model of depression are several. First, it is not clear is modeled. Second, it does not account for the _____ symptoms of depression.

37. The best model of depression seems to be _____.

38. Bipolar depressives alternate between _____ and _____.

39. The thoughts of a manic individual are _____.

40. Bipolar depression is _____ among women as it is among men.

41. The cause of bipolar depression is _____.

42. The treatment of choice for bipolar depression is _____; however, this treatment has serious _____.

43. The most disastrous consequence of depression is _____.

44. Approximately _____ percent of suicidal patients are depressed.

45. Women are _____ likely than men to attempt suicide, but _____ likely to succeed.

46. Suicide _____ with age.

47. Modern thinkers propose two fundamental motives for suicide: _____ and _____.

48. Most suicide notes are _____.

Answer Key for Self-Test

1. Depression; on the rise
2. unipolar; bipolar
3. mood; thought; motivational; physical
4. negative
5. accurately
6. initiate; psychomotor retardation
7. appetite
8. Exogenous; endogenous
9. more
10. anaclitic
11. rare
12. losses
13. intimate; job; three children; religious
14. three; six
15. strongly; weakly
16. norepinephrine and serotonin
17. reuptake; breakdown
18. 70
19. effective; unilateral
20. anger
21. incorporate
22. self-esteem
23. cognitive triad; errors in logic
24. arbitrary inference
25. selective abstraction

26. overgeneralization
27. magnification
28. personalization
29. thoughts; automatic thoughts; reality; reattribution; alternatives; depressogenic assumptions
30. as
31. responses; outcomes
32. cognitive; motivational; emotional
33. internal; stable; global
34. internal
35. cognitive therapy
36. what kind of depression; somatic
37. none
38. mania; depression
39. grandiose
40. as common
41. partly genetic
42. lithium; side effects
43. suicide
44. 80
45. more; less
46. increases
47. surcease; manipulation
48. mundane

MATCHING ITEMS

_____	1.	endogenous depression
_____	2.	catecholamine`
_____	3.	indoleamine
_____	4.	seasonal affective disorder (SAD)
_____	5.	Freud
_____	6.	arbitrary inference
_____	7.	recurrence
_____	8.	personalization
_____	9.	grandiosity
_____	10.	anaclitic depression
_____	11.	relapse
_____	12.	Beck
_____	13.	depressive explanatory style

A. return of symptoms during an episode
B. taking responsibility for bad events
C. anger turned inward
D. norepinephrine
E. serotonin
F. return of symptoms after six months symptom-free
G. melancholia
H. related to early separation
I. required by or to benefit society.
J. drawing a conclusion with little evidence
K. focusing on an insignificant detail
L. cognitive triad
M. learned helplessness

_____   14.   selective abstraction

_____   15.   dysthmia

_____   16.   flexible optimism

_____   17.   anomic suicide

_____   18.   altruistic suicide

_____   19.   manic-depression

_____   20.   exogenous depression

_____   21.   Seligman

_____   22.   psychomotor retardation

N.   making stable, global, internal attributions for bad events

O.   making unstable, specific, external attributions for bad events

P.   precipitated by a life stressor

Q.   bipolar disorder

R.   precipitated by a break with society

S.   may be treatable by light therapy

T.   chronic low level depression

U.   symptom of depression

V.   symptom of mania

Answer Key for Matching Items

1.	G	12.	L
2.	D	13.	N
3.	E	14.	K
4.	S	15.	T
5.	C	16.	O
6.	J	17.	R
7.	F	18.	I
8.	B	19.	Q
9.	V	20.	P
10.	H	21.	M
11.	A	22.	U

SHORT-ANSWER QUESTIONS

1. Give at least two examples of each of the emotional, cognitive, motivational, and somatic symptoms of depression.

2. Define dysthymia, double depression, endogenous/melancholic depression, and exogenous depression.

3. Describe the six hypotheses proposed to account for the higher incidence of depression among women.

4. The biological model of depression proposes somatic treatments for the condition. What are the three main types of antidepressants and how does each work? What is the fourth somatic treatment option and under what conditions is it indicated?

5. How did Freud explain the development of depression? What is this theory called?

6. Outline the three major steps in Beck's cognitive therapy for depression.

7. What is learned helplessness? In what ways is it similar to depression and in what ways does it differ?

8. Give at least two examples of each of the emotional, cognitive, motivational, and somatic symptoms of mania.

9. Define manic-depressive/bipolar depressive disorder, hypomania, and seasonal affective disorder.

10. What characteristics are particular risk factors for suicide?

TYING IT TOGETHER

Depression is one of the better-understood disorders largely because research employing a variety of strategies has converged in the understanding it has provided (Chapter 6). Depression is a disorder that exists on many levels: somatic (Chapter 3), emotional (Chapter 4), behavioral (Chapter 5), cognitive (Chapter 5), and experiential (Chapter 4). Individuals may become depressed because they have other disorders, such as schizophrenia (Chapter 12) and brain damage (Chapter 17). Traditionally, depression has been regarded as a disorder of mood (i.e., emotion), and this may have blinded investigators to the important role of other factors. However, depression is now being approached from a variety of directions, and successful therapies exist where none did before (Chapter 19).

One of the newest perspectives on depression is the cognitive model (Chapter 5). Research using laboratory models (Chapter 6) has shown depression to be as much a thought disorder as a mood disorder, and cognitive therapies for depression (Chapter 19) may be as effective as drug therapies.

Childhood depression illustrates the difficulties in conceiving and diagnosing disorders among children (Chapter 16). Developmental differences may alter the manifestation of depressive symptoms across the life-span, or at least the ease with which diagnosticians can recognize them. Indeed, psychodynamic theorists feel that children cannot be depressed because they lack a fully developed superego. Contemporary opinion is slowly embracing the notion that children can be depressed, but this is still a controversial idea. Behind this changing perspective is the increased use of behavioral assessment (Chapter 7). Some children act like depressed adults. Does it not make sense to view them as depressed, whether or not they verbalize sad and hopeless feelings?

Depression is one of the few fatal psychopathologies. Suicide attempts are frequently preceded by depressive symptoms, particularly hopelessness regarding the future (Chapter 5). The legal system must grapple with suicide and how to regard it (Chapter 18). Should intervention be undertaken if a suicidal individual is depressed (and, therefore, not thinking correctly)? Should intervention not be undertaken if a suicidal individual is not depressed? Are "suicidal" life styles like the Type A behavior pattern (Chapter 10) or alcohol abuse (Chapter 14) the province of the court?

FURTHER READINGS

Abramson, L. Y., Seligman, M. E. P., & Teasdale, J. D. (1978). Learned helplessness in humans: Critique and reformulation. *Journal of Abnormal Psychology, 87,* 49–74.

Beck, A. T., Rush, A. J., Shaw, B. F., & Emery, G. (1979). *Cognitive therapy of depression.* New York: Guilford Press.

Burns, D. D. (1980). *Feeling good: The new mood therapy.* New York: Morrow.

Durkheim, E. (1951). *Suicide.* New York: Macmillan.

Freud, S. (1976). Mourning and melancholia. In J. Strachey (Ed. and Trans.), *The standard edition of the complete psychological works of Sigmund Freud* (Vol. 14, pp. 243–258). New York: Norton. (Original work published 1917)

Gilman, C. P. (1989). "The yellow wallpaper," in *The yellow wallpaper and other writings.* New York: Bantam Books.

Kleinman, A., & Good, B. (1985). *Culture and depression: Studies in the anthropology and cross-cultural psychiatry of affect and disorder.* Berkeley, CA: University of California Press.

McKnew, D. H., Jr., Cytryn, L., & Yahraes, H. C., Jr. (1983). *Why isn't Johnny crying?* New York: Norton.

Nolen-Hoeksema, S. (1990). *Sex differences in depression.* Palo Alto, CA: Stanford University Press.

Peterson, C., & Seligman, M. E. P. (1984). Causal explanations as a risk factor for depression: Theory and evidence. *Psychological Review, 91,* 347–374.

Rado, S. (1929). The problem of melancholia. *International Journal of Psychoanalysis, 9,* 420–438.

Rosenthal, N. E., et al. (1986). Seasonal affective disorder in children and adolescence.

American Journal of Psychiatry, 143, 356–368.

Rutter, M., Izard, C. E., & Read, P. R. (1986). *Depression in young people: Developmental and clinical perspectives.* New York: Guilford.

Seligman, M. E. P. (1993). *Helplessness: On depression, development, and death.* San Francisco: Freeman.

Seligman, M. E. P. (1991). *Learned optimism.* New York: Alfred A. Knopf.

Shneidman, E. (1967). *Essays in self-destruction.* New York: Science House.

Styron, W. (1990). *Darkness visible.* New York: Random House.

TERM-PAPER TOPICS

1. Why are women more likely to be depressed than men? Review the possible explanations, and evaluate them in light of existing evidence.

2. What biological processes seem to be involved in bipolar depression? How does lithium affect these processes?

3. Post-partum depression is a depressive episode occurring to some women after childbirth. Is post-partum depression a special type of depression, or does it conform to what is known about other types of depression?

4. The learned helplessness theory of depression is controversial. What issues are involved? How may they be resolved?

5. Uncontrollable events may precede a number of disorders: phobias, peptic ulcer, sudden death, depression, and so on. It is obvious that uncontrollability is harmful, but what determines exactly how it is harmful? In other words, why does a given person become fearful rather than depressed following an uncontrollable event?

6. Discuss recent research into treatment of seasonal affective disorder. How solidly established is this supposed disorder?

EXERCISES

Exercise One—Depression and Uncontrollability

The purpose of this exercise is to demonstrate the basic premise of the learned helplessness model of depression: uncontrollable events result in feelings of helplessness and depression.

Talk to men and women who have just ended a serious romance. Ask them how much control they perceived over the end of the romance. Ask them how helpless and depressed they felt about the breakup. According to learned helplessness theory, the less control perceived by an individual over an important event like a breakup, the more depressed that person will be in response to it.

Hill, C. T., Rubin, Z., & Peplau, L. A. (1976). Breakups before marriage: The end of 103 affairs. *Journal of Social Issues, 32,* 147–168.

Seligman, M. E. P. (1975). *Helplessness: On depression, development, and death.* San Francisco: Freeman.

Weiss, R. S. (1976). The emotional impact of marital separation. *Journal of Social Issues, 32,* 135–145.

Exercise Two—Depression and Logical Errors

In this exercise, you will evaluate the hypothesis by Aaron Beck that depressed individuals make logical errors in their interpretation of events involving themselves.

Among your friends identify sad and happy individuals. (You may want to gauge their feelings by administering the questionnaire in Exercise Five of Chapter 5). Ask each individual to specify three bad events that occurred to him or her during the past year. Then ask the person to specify the major cause for each event and to provide evidence for believing the suggested cause to be the one.

According to Beck, the sad people should be likely to justify their suggested causes in illogical ways: by irrelevant evidence, by exaggerated evidence, by out-of-context evidence, and so on. Is this the case?

Beck, A. T. (1967). *Depression: Clinical, experimental, and theoretical aspects.* New York: Harper & Row.

Exercise Three—Learned Helplessness

In this exercise, you will perform a learned helplessness experiment.

The learned helplessness phenomenon is striking: following experience with uncontrollable events, individuals have trouble learning to control events that indeed are controllable. You can demonstrate this easily. Obtain twenty 3″ × 5″ index cards. On ten of them, write five letters (two vowels and three consonants) in a random order. Make sure that these letters do not spell a word regardless of how they are rearranged. On another ten, write five letters (two vowels and three consonants) in a random order that do spell a word when rearranged in the right order. Ask some individuals to try to solve these anagram problems. Give them thirty seconds per card. First, show them the ten cards with no answers. Do not let on that there really are no solutions. Then, show then the ten cards with answers. How many of the solvable anagrams do these individuals answer correctly? Compare this to the performance of other individuals who attempt to solve only the second set of problems—the solvable ones.

Hiroto, D. S., & Seligman, M. E. P. (1975). Generality of learned helplessness in man. *Journal of Personality and Social Psychology, 31,* 311–327.

The Schizophrenias

CHAPTER OVERVIEW

Chapter 12 is concerned with schizophrenia, a set of disorders entailing sweeping disturbances in thought, behavior, and mood. Its substantive criteria include a gross impairment in reality testing and the simultaneous disturbance of several psychological processes. The major types of schizophrenia are paranoid (characterized by delusions of persecution or grandeur), disorganized (characterized by silliness and incoherence), catatonic (characterized by enormously excited or strikingly frozen motor behavior), residual (absence of prominent symptoms but persistent peculiarities), and undifferentiated (not classifiable as one of the other types).

Theories of schizophrenia variously emphasize genetic, biochemical, familial, and societal determinants. Twin studies, adoption studies, family studies, and at-risk studies converge in their support for a genetic component to schizophrenia. Current biological theorizing suggests two independent clusters of schizophrenic symptoms, the first tied to excess dopamine and the second to abnormal brain structure. But biological factors do not make up the entire picture. Other investigations suggest that disordered communication within schizophrenic families may partly cause the disorder or precipitate relapse. It also has been suggested that schizophrenia is a sane reaction to an insane world—a withdrawal from a situation that is otherwise impossible.

Until the 1950s, treatment of schizophrenia was largely custodial. When neuroleptic drugs were introduced, they profoundly changed treatment. Thought to operate through the blocking of dopamine, these drugs decrease Type I schizophrenic symptoms and have made it possible for many individuals to leave mental hospitals. However, these drugs have severe side effects, and they are not the complete answer to the treatment of schizophrenia.

ESSENTIAL TERMS

adoption studies of schizophrenia
: technique for studying the etiology of schizophrenia, in which the prevalence of schizophrenia among children of schizophrenics who are adopted by nonschizophrenics is assessed (p. 444)

affect
: emotion (p. 436)

akathesis
: side effect of antipsychotic medication experienced as profound physical restlessness (p. 461)

antihistamine	synthetic drug that benefits individuals with asthma or allergies and that exerts a tranquilizing effect (p. 401)
at-risk studies of schizophrenia	technique for studying the etiology of schizophrenia, in which the prevalence of schizophrenia among children at risk for the disorder because of various factors is assessed (p. 445)
catatonic schizophrenia	schizophrenia characterized by motor behavior that is either enormously excited or strikingly frozen (p. 426)
clang association	association produced by rhyme of words (p. 429)
cognitive (or selective) filter	mechanism of attention that sorts out stimuli to determine which will be admitted to attention and which will not, thought to be disrupted in schizophrenia (p. 429)
communication deviance	inability of parent to establish and maintain a shared arena of attention with child (p. 453)
concealment of meaning	characteristic of communication in schizophrenic families in which individuals hide information when it is clear that it exists (p. 454)
concordant twins	both members of a set of twins have the same disorder (*see* chapter 3, "Essential Terms") (p. 441)
corpus striatum	brain area of high dopamine concentration (p. 449)
co-twin	in twin studies of schizophrenia, the twin examined for the presence or absence of schizophrenia after identification of the index case (p. 441)
delusion	false belief resisting all argument, sustained in the face of all contrary evidence (pp. 422, 432)
delusion of control	common schizophrenic delusion that one's thought or behavior is being controlled from without (p. 433)
delusion of grandeur	common schizophrenic delusion that one is especially important (p. 433)
delusion of persecution	common schizophrenic delusion that individuals, groups, or the government have malevolent intentions and are out to "get" the individual (p. 433)
delusion of reference	common schizophrenic delusion involving ideas of reference (p. 433)
somatic delusion	common schizophrenic delusion that something is terribly wrong with one's body (p. 434)
dementia praecox	term coined by Emil Kraepelin in 1896 to describe schizophrenia, literally meaning early or premature deterioration (p. 420)
denial of meaning	characteristic of communication in schizophrenogenic families in which individuals deny the reality of meanings and events, consciously or unconsciously (p. 454)

discordant twins	one member of a set of twins has a disorder and the other member does not (*see* Chapter 3, "Essential Terms") (p. 441)
disorganized (hebephrenic) schizophrenia	schizophrenia characterized by apparent silliness and incoherence (p. 426)
divided self	R. D. Laing's description of the schizophrenic self operating on two levels: the silent self, vulnerable and afraid to emerge, and the smokescreen self, disguised to conceal and protect the silent self (p. 438)
dizygotic twins (fraternal twins; DZ twins)	twins developed from two different eggs (p. 440)
dopamine hypothesis	explanation of schizophrenia that proposes that the disorder results from too much dopamine in the brain (*see* Chapter 3, "Essential Terms") (p. 448)
double-bind	characteristic of communication in schizophrenogenic families in which individuals are given mutually exclusive messages, which can neither be satisfied nor avoided (p. 445)
expressed emotion	style of expressing emotions within a family characterized by criticism, overinvolvement, and hostility directed at offspring (p. 453)
family studies of schizophrenia	technique for studying the etiology of schizophrenia, in which the prevalence of schizophrenia within families is assessed (p. 442)
frontal lobes	brain area important in attention, motivation, and in planning and organizing (p. 451)
hallucination	false sensory perception with a compelling sense of reality, occurring in the absence of stimuli that ordinarily provoke such a perception(p. 423)
idea of reference	belief that one is especially noticed by others (*see* Chapter 15, "Essential Terms") (p. 432)
index case (proband)	in twin studies of schizophrenia, the twin first seen at psychiatric clinic (p. 441)
injection of meaning	characteristic of communication in schizophrenogenic families in which the clear meaning of another's message is denied and another meaning substituted (p. 454)
milieu therapy	therapy technique in which the patient is provided with training in social communication, work, and recreation (cf. moral treatment—*see* Chapter 2, "Essential Terms") (p. 463)
monozygotic twins (identical twins; MZ twins)	twins developed from a single egg (p. 440)
mystification	characteristic of communication in schizophrenogenic families in which the individual is encouraged to doubt feelings, perceptions, and experiences (p. 453)

neologism	an invented word of idiosyncratic meaning (p. 429)
neuroleptic	drug used to treat schizophrenia; major tranquilizer; psychotropic agent; e.g., phenothiazine (pp. 439, 460)
neurotransmitter	chemical responsible for communication between neurons (*see* Chapter 11, "Essential Terms") (p. 448)
overinclusive thinking	characteristic of schizophrenic thinking: tendency to form concepts from both relevant and irrelevant information (p. 431)
paranoid schizophrenia	schizophrenia characterized by systematized delusions of persecution and/or grandeur (p. 425)
Parkinson's disease	neurological disease characterized by stiffness of the arms and legs, flat facial expression, and tremors, thought to result from too little dopamine in the brain (p. 449)
phenothiazine	neuroleptic that blocks brain receptors for dopamine (p. 449)
psychosis	marked impairment in contact with reality resulting in incorrect inferences about the world (p. 422)
reality testing	the ability to accurately assess one's thoughts and make correct inferences about them (p. 422)
schizophrenia	disorder of thinking from which flows troubled behavior and troubled mood (p. 419)
acute schizophrenia	schizophrenia marked by a rapid and sudden onset of very florid symptoms (p. 438)
chronic schizophrenia	schizophrenia marked by a prolonged history of withdrawal (p. 439)
residual schizophrenia	schizophrenia without prominent symptoms, marked by persistent peculiarities (p. 427)
Type I schizophrenia	schizophrenia characterized by positive symptoms (e.g., hallucinations and delusions) (p. 439)
Type II schizophrenia	schizophrenia characterized by negative symptoms (e.g., poverty of speech and flat affect) (p. 439)
schizophrenogenic family	family that fosters the emergence of schizophrenia in family members (p. 453)
substantia nigra	bundle of nerves connecting the brain stem to the corpus striatum (p. 450)
superphrenic	individual who is both related to schizophrenic(s) and recognizably outstanding in politics, science, or the arts (p. 447)
tardive dyskinesia	neurological disorder involving sucking, lip smacking, and tongue movements resulting from prolonged use of major tranquilizers (p. 461)
therapeutic community	therapy technique in which patients live and work under guidance (p. 464)

thought disorder	thinking which is disturbed either in process or content (p. 429)
twin studies of schizophrenia	technique for studying the etiology of schizophrenia, in which concordance and discordance of schizophrenia between monozygotic twins versus dizygotic twins are assessed (p. 441)
undifferentiated schizophrenia	schizophrenia not able to be classified as catatonic, disorganized, residual, or paranoid (p. 427)
ventricles	fluid-filled cavities in the brain (p. 452)

CENTRAL CONCEPTUAL ISSUES

Diagnosis and family resemblance in schizophrenia.   The schizophrenias may be categorized in a number of ways, many of which overlap. Current clinical diagnosis breaks schizophrenia into five categories based on groups of symptoms: paranoid, catatonic, disorganized (hebephrenic), undifferentiated, and residual. The virtue of this approach lies in the ability to convey broad information on the cluster of symptoms associated with each subtype diagnosis. In some ways, schizophrenia is the best example of how a "family resemblance" model must be applied for diagnosis. In clinical practice it is not uncommon to encounter two individuals diagnosed with schizophrenia who have no specific symptoms in common. For example, a paranoid schizophrenic may present with highly systematized delusions and hallucinations, while a disorganized schizophrenic may only display inappropriate affect, bizarre behavior, and incoherence. Diagnostic subtyping in schizophrenia is also useful in indicating appropriate treatment and prognosis. Indeed, the dimensions by which we categorize schizophrenia may reflect truly distinct disorders of different etiology and disease process, and that is why the text refers to them as "the schizophrenias."

Type I and II symptoms in schizophrenia.   A second approach to distinguishing between types of schizophrenia is to consider two broad categories of symptoms. By this system, Type I schizophrenia is associated with "positive symptoms"—symptoms that represent, in some ways, a pathological addition to normal functioning—such as the hallucinations, delusional thinking, and disordered thought and speech. Type II schizophrenia is defined by "negative symptoms"—symptoms that represent a diminution of normal functioning—such as blunted or flat affect, loss of volition, or poverty of speech. Many schizophrenics manifest, to a greater or lesser degree, both types of symptoms, though some present with almost pure Type I or Type II symptom profiles. The greatest strength of this system lies in its ability to predict treatment responsiveness and prognosis: Type I symptoms generally respond to neuroleptics and are associated with sudden onset and a better prognosis, while Type II symptoms are generally treatment refractory (i.e., resistant to treatment), and those afflicted with them tend to have a more chronic course with a poorer outcome. This dichotomy may also shed some light on understanding underlying pathology: Type II symptoms tend to be associated with structural brain changes (e.g., enlarged ventricles), while Type I symptoms are thought to reflect a disturbance in dopamine transmission (which is why they respond to neuroleptics).

Onset, course, and prognosis in schizophrenia.   A third way to categorize schizophrenia is by age of onset and course of the disorder. A gradual, insidious onset (i.e., difficult to isolate when it actually began) of symptoms beginning at an early age (e.g., adolescence), and seemingly unrelated to identifiable stressors, suggests a poorer prognosis associate with deterioration and ultimately a relatively chronic condition. This is traditionally called "process" schizophrenia. A sudden, acute onset, which may be precipitated by psychosocial factors (e.g., severe stressors), and which marks a sharp departure from premorbid functioning (level of functioning before onset), predicts a better prognosis. This is traditionally called "reactive" schizophrenia. The distinction here is sometimes conceptualized as endogenous versus exogenous.

Delusion formation in psychosis.   One of the most fascinating aspects of psychosis is the process of delusion formation. On the face of it, the presence of bizarre and irrational beliefs seems to be an essential feature or symptom of schizophrenia and other psychotic conditions. However, a closer examination suggests that some delusions may arise from, and be secondary to, other more fundamental pathological processes such as hallucinations or sensory impairments. For example, if the food you ate began to taste funny, and when you queried others about your experience they denied its reality, rather than abandon your perception, you might begin to suspect those around you of both tampering with your food and lying about it for some reason. In other words, you might develop a paranoid delusion to explain these apparent phenomena. In this view, the delusion is a theory or belief constructed to make sense out of experience, much as a scientist generates hypotheses to account for her data—the pathology lies with the data, not the hypothesis.

Dangerousness in schizophrenia.   Though it is widely believed, in part due to the extensive publicity given to "insanity pleas" and the bizarre behavior of some psychotic criminals, that schizophrenia is a dangerous condition, the reality is quite different. In general, schizophrenics tend to be too withdrawn, disorganized, frightened, and preoccupied to intentionally victimize others. In fact, although they can be difficult to manage when acutely psychotic—sometimes striking out in fear and anger at their real or perceived handling—they typically represent a much greater danger to themselves than to others. Suicide, motivated either by delusional beliefs or hallucinations when psychotic, or by despair upon some degree of recovery, is all too commonly attempted by schizophrenics, with fully 10 percent succeeding. It is a rare schizophrenic, and in most cases a paranoid one, whose delusions drive him or her to hurt others with criminal premeditation and intent.

SAMPLE EXAM

1. Schizophrenia involves
   a. thought.
   b. behavior.
   c. mood.
   d. perception.
   e. all of the above.

2. Which one of the following is *not* a myth about schizophrenia?
   a. Schizophrenics are dangerous.
   b. Schizophrenics have split personalities.
   c. Schizophrenia is a lifelong disorder.

   d. Schizophrenia only exists in technological cultures.
   e. all of the above are myths

3. Kraepelin described schizophrenia as
   a. general paresis.
   b. lycanthropy.
   c. dementia praecox.
   d. senility.
   e. manic-depression.

4. The term *schizophrenia* was coined by
   a. Galen.

b. Kraepelin.
c. Linnaeus.
d. Bleuler.
e. Breuer.

5. Both Kraepelin and Bleuler adhered to the
a. biomedical model.
b. psychodynamic model.
c. behavioral model.
d. cognitive model.
e. existential model.

6. Meyer adhered to the
a. biomedical model.
b. psychodynamic model.
c. behavioral model.
d. cognitive model.
e. existential model.

7. All of the following are people who are at increased risk for schizophrenia except
a. a person under forty-five years of age.
b. a male.
c. an urban resident.
d. a member of the lower class.
e. a person with a schizophrenic first-degree relative.

8. The substantive criteria for a DSM-IV diagnosis of schizophrenia include
a. impairment in reality testing.
b. excessive anxiety.
c. hallucinations.
d. delusions.
e. flat or blunted affect.

9. Delusion is to hallucination as
a. pea is to pod.
b. belief is to perception.
c. avoidance is to escape.
d. complex is to simple.
e. real is to false.

10. All of these are types of schizophrenia except
a. catatonic.
b. hebephrenic.
c. psychotic.
d. paranoid.
e. undifferentiated.

11. A schizophrenic patient acts silly. What type of schizophrenia is suggested?
a. paranoid
b. disorganized
c. catatonic

d. undifferentiated
e. residual

12. A schizophrenic patient acts suspicious. What type of schizophrenia is suggested?
a. paranoid
b. disorganized
c. catatonic
d. undifferentiated
e. residual

13. A schizophrenic patient does not move. What type of schizophrenia is suggested?
a. paranoid
b. disorganized
c. catatonic
d. undifferentiated
e. residual

14. A schizophrenic patient is difficult to assign to a category. What type of schizophrenia is suggested?
a. paranoid
b. disorganized
c. catatonic
d. undifferentiated
e. residual

15. A schizophrenic patient shows no prominent symptoms, just persistent and distressing behavior. What type of schizophrenia is suggested?
a. paranoid
b. disorganized
c. catatonic
d. undifferentiated
e. residual

16. What about schizophrenic thought is disordered?
a. content
b. process
c. perception
d. both a and b
e. all of the above

17. Attentional deficits in schizophrenia seem to be related to
a. no stimuli being let in.
b. too few stimuli being let in.
c. selective stimuli being let in.
d. too many stimuli being let in.
e. only hallucinations being let in.

18. Overinclusive thinking among schizophrenics is similar to which type of logi-

cal error described by Beck among depressives?

a. personalization
b. minimization
c. selective abstraction
d. arbitrary inference
e. all-or-nothing thinking

19. Which of these statements is true about schizophrenic patients' thinking?

a. Schizophrenics ignore common associations and attend to context.
b. Schizophrenic patients ignore context and attend to common associations.
c. The associations schizophrenic patients make are qualitatively different.
d. The associations schizophrenic patients make are quantitatively different.
e. none of the above

20. A schizophrenic patient believes that people on television are speaking to him. What kind of delusion is this?

a. delusion of grandeur
b. delusion of control
c. delusion of persecution
d. delusion of reference
e. delusion of somatic content

21. A schizophrenic patient believes that her doctor is manipulating her thoughts. What kind of delusion is this?

a. delusion of grandeur
b. delusion of control
c. delusion of persecution
d. delusion of reference
e. delusion of somatic content

22. A schizophrenic patient believes that he is directly in line for the British crown. What kind of delusion is this?

a. delusion of grandeur
b. delusion of control
c. delusion of persecution
d. delusion of reference
e. delusion of somatic content

23. A schizophrenic patient believes that the CIA is spying on him. What kind of delusion is this?

a. delusion of grandeur
b. delusion of control
c. delusion of persecution
d. delusion of reference
e. delusion of somatic content

24. A schizophrenic patient believes that she has no blood in her veins. What kind of delusion is this?

a. a delusion of grandeur
b. a delusion of control
c. a delusion of persecution
d. a delusion of reference
e. a delusion of somatic content

25. Delusions may result from the schizophrenic's attempt to make sense of his experience. This process is

a. different in kind from that maintaining the beliefs of normal individuals.
b. different in degree from that maintaining the beliefs of normal individuals.
c. different in form from that maintaining the beliefs of normals.
d. different in process from that maintaining the beliefs of normals.
e. the same as that maintaining the beliefs of normal individuals.

26. Schizophrenic affect is all of the following except

a. nonexistent.
b. inappropriate.
c. ambivalent.
d. seemingly flat.
e. blunted.

27. According to Laing's concept of the divided self,

a. schizophrenic communication is gibberish.
b. schizophrenic communication is literal.
c. schizophrenic communication is a disguise.
d. schizophrenic communication is coherent.
e. none of the above.

28. Acute schizophrenia is distinguished from chronic schizophrenia on the basis of all of the following except

a. suddenness of onset.
b. number of episodes.
c. precipitating incident.
d. presence of hallucinations.
e. length of hospitalization.

29. Type I schizophrenia is characterized by all these except

a. delusions.
b. flat affect.
c. hallucinations.
d. thought disorder.
e. sudden onset.

30. Type II schizophrenia is characterized by all these except
a. delusions.
b. flat affect.
c. poverty of speech.
d. social withdrawal.
e. poor prognosis.

31. Neuroleptics affect
a. positive symptoms.
b. negative symptoms.
c. neutral symptoms.
d. both a and b
e. none of the above

32. Twin studies indicate that
a. schizophrenia is caused by genes.
b. schizophrenia is caused by the environment.
c. schizophrenia is contagious.
d. both a and b.
e. none of the above

33. Family studies of schizophrenia indicate that one's chances of being schizophrenic are greatest if one has
a. a schizophrenic cousin.
b. a schizophrenic sibling.
c. a schizophrenic parent.
d. two schizophrenic parents.
e. a schizophrenic aunt.

34. Adoption studies of schizophrenia suggest that
a. schizophrenia is caused by genes.
b. schizophrenia is caused by the environment.
c. schizophrenia is contagious.
d. neither a nor b.
e. none of the above

35. Which of these statements is true?
a. Identical twins are more likely to be diagnosed schizophrenic than fraternal twins.
b. Fraternal twins are more likely to be diagnosed schizophrenic than non-twin siblings.
c. Fraternal twins are less likely to be diagnosed schizophrenic than non-twin siblings.

d. Identical twins are as likely to be diagnosed schizophrenic than fraternal twins.
e. Fraternal twins are as likely to be diagnosed schizophrenic than non-twin siblings.

36. What is a superphrenic?
a. a chronic schizophrenic
b. a creative relative of a schizophrenic
c. an alien schizophrenic
d. a long-lived schizophrenic
e. an acute schizophrenic.

37. The neurotransmitter thought to be involved in schizophrenia is
a. norepinephrine.
b. dopamine.
c. serotonin.
d. thorazine.
e. epinephrine.

38. Evidence for the dopamine hypothesis comes from investigations of
a. neuroleptics.
b. Parkinson's disease.
c. amphetamine-induced psychosis.
d. receptor distribution.
e. all of the above.

39. What happens when someone with schizophrenia is given amphetamine?
a. Schizophrenic symptoms increase.
b. Schizophrenic symptoms stay unchanged.
c. Schizophrenic symptoms decrease.
d. Parkinsonian symptoms, if he has them, may increase.
e. Parkinsonian symptoms, if he has them, may decrease.

40. What happens when someone with schizophrenia is given anti-Parkinson medicine?
a. Schizophrenic symptoms increase.
b. Schizophrenic symptoms stay unchanged.
c. Schizophrenic symptoms decrease.
d. Parkinsonian symptoms, if he has them, may increase.
e. Parkinsonian symptoms, if he has them, may decrease.

41. What happens when someone with schizophrenia is given neuroleptics for a long time?
a. Parkinson symptoms increase.

b. Parkinson symptoms stay unchanged.
c. Parkinson symptoms decrease.
d. Schizophrenic symptoms may increase.
e. Schizophrenic symptoms may decrease.

42. Amphetamine psychosis results from
a. too much dopamine.
b. making dopamine receptors too sensitive.
c. making dopamine receptors less sensitive.
d. too little dopamine.
e. killing dopamine receptors.

43. Neuroleptics
a. open dopamine receptors.
b. make dopamine receptors more sensitive.
c. make dopamine receptors less sensitive.
d. block dopamine receptors.
e. kill dopamine receptors.

44. Type II schizophrenia is associated with all of the following except
a. eye movement abnormalities.
b. enlarged brain ventricles.
c. smaller frontal lobes.
d. neuronal degeneration.
e. enhanced memory capacity.

45. Parents who are critical and overinvolved with their children are high in
a. communication deviance.
b. expressed emotion.
c. psychopathy.
d. Type I deviance.
e. Type II deviance.

46. Communication within schizophrenogenic families is characterized by all of the following except
a. mystification.
b. double-bind.
c. communication deviance
d. high expressed emotion.
e. all of the above

47. Suppose that one family member encourages another family member to doubt his perceptions of a situation. This is an example of
a. mystification.
b. double-bind.
c. denial of meaning.

d. injection of meaning.
e. high expressed emotion.

48. Suppose that one family member tells another family member to do something and then yells at him for not having a mind of his own. This is an example of
a. mystification.
b. double-bind.
c. denial of meaning.
d. injection of meaning.
e. high expressed emotion.

49. Suppose that one family member throws a brick through a window, and then tells another family member that the window is not broken. This is an example of
a. mystification.
b. double-bind.
c. denial of meaning.
d. injection of meaning.
e. high expressed emotion.

50. Suppose that one family member calls the police to complain about another family member and then tells that family member that he was just trying to be helpful. This is an example of
a. mystification.
b. double-bind.
c. denial of meaning.
d. injection of meaning.
e. high expressed emotion.

51. Recent research into the possible role of culture in schizophrenia outcome has found that
a. schizophrenics from developing nations fare better than those from developed nations.
b. schizophrenics from developed nations fare better than those from developing nations.
c. the incidence of schizophrenia changes across cultures.
d. schizophrenia has different clinical features across cultures.
e. culture plays no role in schizophrenia.

52. Schizophrenia seems to be overrepresented among the lower class. Research suggests that the reason for this is that
a. lower-class individuals are more apt to become schizophrenic than middle-class individuals.

b. schizophrenic individuals are more apt to move from the middle class to the lower class than nonschizophrenic individuals.
c. schizophrenic individuals are more likely to have lower class fathers.
d. both a and b.
e. all of the above

53. According to Laing, schizophrenia is
a. a learned behavior.
b. a social role.
c. withdrawal from an insane world.
d. a mental illness.
e. an illusion.

54. Which does not belong?
a. antihistamine
b. neuroleptic
c. amphetamine
d. major tranquilizer
e. phenothiazine

55. The neuroleptics alleviate
a. guilt.
b. depression.
c. thought disorder.
d. all of the above.
e. flat affect.

56. All of the following are side effects of the neuroleptics except
a. extra-pyramidal effects.
b. tardive dyskinesia.
c. diarrhea.
d. drowsiness.
e. akathesis.

57. Which statement is true?
a. Neuroleptics cure schizophrenia.
b. Neuroleptics alleviate some schizo-phrenic symptoms.

c. Neuroleptics cure psychological problems among schizophrenics.
d. Neuroleptics mask schizophrenic symptoms.
e. all of the above.

Answer Key for Sample Exam

1.	e	(p. 419)	30.	a	(p. 439)
2.	d	(p. 421)	31.	a	(p. 439)
3.	c	(p. 420)	32.	d	(p. 442)
4.	d	(p. 420)	33.	d	(p. 443)
5.	a	(p. 420)	34.	d	(p. 444)
6.	c	(p. 421)	35.	d, e	(p. 442)
7.	b	(p. 424)	36.	b	(p. 447)
8.	a	(p. 422)	37.	b	(p. 448)
9.	b	(p. 422)	38.	e	(p. 449)
10.	c	(p. 425)	39.	a, e	(p. 448)
11.	b	(p. 426)	40.	a, e	(p. 449)
12.	a	(p. 425)	41.	a, e	(p. 449)
13.	c	(p. 426)	42.	a	(p. 450)
14.	d	(p. 427)	43.	d	(p. 448)
15.	e	(p. 427)	44.	e	(p. 451)
16.	e	(p. 429)	45.	b	(p. 453)
17.	d	(p. 430)	46.	e	(p. 453)
18.	d	(p. 431)	47.	a	(p. 453)
19.	b, d	(p. 431)	48.	b	(p. 453)
20.	d	(p. 433)	49.	c	(p. 454)
21.	b	(p. 433)	50.	d	(p. 454)
22.	a	(p. 433)	51.	a	(p. 457)
23.	c	(p. 433)	52.	d	(p. 456)
24.	e	(p. 434)	53.	c	(p. 458)
25.	e	(p. 435)	54.	c	(p. 460)
26.	a	(p. 436)	55.	c	(p. 460)
27.	c	(p. 438)	56.	c	(p. 460)
28.	d	(p. 439)	57.	b	(p. 460)
29.	b	(p. 439)			

SELF-TEST

1. Schizophrenia is a disorder of _____, but it also involves disturbances in _____ and _____.

2. There are numerous myths about schizophrenia. In truth, schizophrenics are not _____; they do not have _____; and they are not necessarily schizophrenic for _____.

3. To describe what is now called schizophrenia, Kraepelin introduced the term _____, which means _____.

4. Kraepelin felt that schizophrenia was _____; in contrast, Meyer felt that schizophrenia was _____.

5. Schizophrenia occurs mainly among individuals who are under _____ years of age.

6. The two substantive criteria for schizophrenia are _____ and _____.

7. Delusions are false _____.

8. Hallucinations are false _____.

9. In _____ schizophrenia, the individual has systematic delusions about persecution.

10. In _____ schizophrenia, the individual is silly and incoherent.

11. In _____ schizophrenia, the motor behavior of the individual is enormously excited or strikingly frozen.

12. Schizophrenia that is not able to be classified as paranoid, disorganized, residual, or catatonic is _____ schizophrenia.

13. In _____ schizophrenia, there is an absence of prominent symptoms.

14. _____ difficulties may provide a fertile soil for hallucination.

15. The most common schizophrenic hallucinations are _____.

16. Schizophrenics' difficulties with attention seem to involve a _____ of the cognitive filter.

17. Schizophrenic thinking is _____ inclusive.

18. A belief that television newscasters are speaking to one is an _____.

19. Common schizophrenic delusions are delusions of _____, _____, _____, and _____.

20. Research suggests that delusions are a "normal" consequence of abnormal _____.

21. Schizophrenic affect often is either _____ or _____.

22. According to Laing, schizophrenics have a _____.

23. _____ schizophrenia involves positive symptoms like hallucinations and delusions, and _____ schizophrenia involves negative symptoms like flat affect and poverty of speech.

24. At least five factors may cause schizophrenia: _____, _____, _____, _____, and _____.

25. Twin studies suggest that schizophrenia has a _____ component; so, too, do _____ studies, _____ studies, and _____ studies.

26. Compared to the general population, the prevalence of schizophrenia among twins is _____.

27. Research suggests that the neurotransmitter _____ may be involved in schizophrenia. Specifically, it is thought that too _____ of this neurotransmitter may cause schizophrenia. There are several lines of evidence for this hypothesis. First, the neuroleptics _____ the availability of this neurotransmitter. Second, prolonged use of the neuroleptics may result in symptoms like those of _____, which seems to involve too _____ of this neurotransmitter. Third, amphetamine psychosis, which is indistinguishable from schizophrenia, involves too _____ of this neurotransmitter.

28. _____ families may encourage schizophrenia among their members through _____ communication.

29. Thought disorders may be influenced by _____ of meaning, _____ of meaning, and _____ of meaning.

30. The dopamine hypothesis applies particularly to _____.

31. Abnormal brain structure may be at the base of _____.

32. Schizophrenia is overrepresented among the _____ class.

33. Laing argues that schizophrenia is a _____ reaction to an insane world.

34. The drugs used to treat schizophrenia are called _____; three of the most common are _____, _____ and _____.

35. The neuroleptics reduce _____, but they do not reduce _____.

36. Two of the serious side effects of neuroleptics are _____ and _____.

37. The neuroleptics have greatly _____ the number of institutionalized schizophrenics. However, many of these patients are _____.

38. Two factors seem to dictate schizophrenic relapse: the _____ of the home and _____ the patient spends there.

39. The full treatment of schizophrenia may someday involve _____ or _____.

Answer Key for Self-Test

1. thought; mood; behavior
2. dangerous; split personalities; life
3. *dementia praecox*; early deterioration
4. biological; environmental
5. forty-five
6. gross impairment of reality testing; disturbance of several psychological processes
7. beliefs
8. perceptions
9. paranoid
10. disorganized
11. catatonic
12. undifferentiated
13. residual
14. Perceptual
15. auditory
16. breakdown
17. over
18. idea of reference
19. grandeur; control; persecution; reference
20. perceptions
21. flat; inappropriate
22. divided self
23. Type I; Type II
24. genetics; biochemistry; abnormal brain structure; family; society
25. genetic; adoption; family; at-risk
26. equal
27. dopamine; much; decrease; Parkinson's disease; little; much
28. Schizophrenogenic; disordered
29. injection; concealment; denial
30. Type I
31. Type II
32. lower
33. sane
34. neuroleptics; haloperidol; chlorpromaxine; clozapine
35. positive symptoms; negative symptoms
36. extra-pyramidal effects; tardive dyskinesia
37. reduced; readmitted
38. emotional quality; how much time
39. milieu therapies; therapeutic communities

MATCHING ITEMS

_____	1. Bleuler	A. negativism
_____	2. attentional deficit	B. positive symptoms
_____	3. delusion of grandeur	C. schizophrenia
_____	4. proband	D. dementia praecox
_____	5. disorganized schizophrenia	E. bang, rang, sang
_____	6. paranoid schizophrenia	F. "The devil made me do it."
_____	7. catatonic schizophrenia	G. hebephrenia
_____	8. Kraepelin	H. "I am the second coming."
_____	9. milieu therapy	I. negative symptoms
_____	10. Type I schizophrenia	J. approximately 50 percent
_____	11. Type II schizophrenia	K. approximately 10 to 15 percent
_____	12. double-bind	L. delusions of persecution
_____	13. overinclusiveness	M. breakdown of cognitive filter
_____	14. expressed emotion	N. index case
_____	15. somatic delusion	O. mutually exclusive messages which cannot be satisfied or avoided
_____	16. DZ schizophrenia concordance	P. criticism, over-involvement, hostility

_____ 17. delusion of control

_____ 18. MZ schizophrenia concordance

_____ 19. clang association

_____ 20. delusion of reference

_____ 21. psychosis

_____ 22. therapeutic community

Q. "*New York Times* editorials are sending me coded messages."

R. loss of ability to reality-test

S. "My brain is made of cottage cheese."

T. incapacity to resist distracting information

U. alternative to hospitalization

V. training in social communication, work, and recreation

Answer Key for Matching Items

1.	C	12.	O
2.	M	13.	T
3.	H	14.	P
4.	N	15.	S
5.	G	16.	K
6.	L	17.	F
7.	A	18.	J
8.	D	19.	E
9.	V	20.	Q
10.	B	21.	R
11.	I	22.	U

SHORT-ANSWER QUESTIONS

1. What did Kraepelin, Bleuler, and Meyer each contribute to the evolving views of schizophrenia?

2. In what ways is schizophrenia different from multiple personality disorder? (Review Chapter 9 for your answer.)

3. What are the temporal and substantive criteria for schizophrenia as outlined in the text?

4. Describe the incidence and prevalence statistics regarding schizophrenia. Who is most likely to get it? What proportion of people get it. What is the average age of onset?

5. What are the five major subtypes of schizophrenia and how do they differ from each other?

6. What are the major categories of symptoms in schizophrenia discussed in the text?

7. What is the difference between thought disorders of form and those of content? Use examples in your explanation.

8. Why does the text argue that delusion-formation is similar to normal thinking? If this is true, then why does it result in disordered thinking?

9. What characteristics are associated with Type I and Type II schizophrenia?

10. Summarize the evidence indicating that genetics play a role in schizophrenia.

11. What is the dopamine hypothesis of schizophrenia? What is the evidence supporting it?

12. In what ways might the family environment play a role in causing or exacerbating schizophrenia?

13. Describe the different treatments used for schizophrenia.

TYING IT TOGETHER

Schizophrenia is one of the "best" examples of abnormality since all of the elements that count toward a judgment of abnormality may be present in this disorder: suffering, maladaptiveness, irrationality, unpredictability, vividness, observer discomfort, and violation of standards (Chapter 1). Descriptions of schizo-phrenic-like disorders are found throughout history and across cultures (Chapter 2). When the legal system becomes involved with abnormal psychology (Chapter 18), it is often out of concern for schizophrenic individuals.

Schizophrenia is also one of the most complex disorders. Various explanations have been offered, representing most of the major approaches to abnormality (Chapters 3–5). Most explanations have been at least partly supported by a variety of research strategies (Chapter 6). Schizophrenia seems to have biological components—genetic inheritance, neurotransmitter imbalance, and abnormal brain structure (Chapter 3). The twin studies used to investigate the causes of schizophrenia are elegant, and the dopamine hypothesis has received converging support from a variety of sources, including laboratory models and experiments (Chapter 6). But schizophrenia also has psychological and social components. It may result from disordered patterns of communication within families. It is overrepresented among the lower class. Schizophrenia responds well to milieu therapy (Chapter 19), the modern equivalent of humane treatment (Chapter 2).

Granted the complexity of schizophrenia, perhaps it is not surprising that its diagnosis (Chapter 7) and treatment (Chapter 19) remain problematic. Some have expressed the opinion that schizophrenia is a myth, a label used to rationalize both inadvertent and willful persecution of powerless individuals who may be "marching to their own drummer." The relationship of schizophrenia to creativity is consistent with this interpretation, but the suffering and maladjustment of individuals with schizophrenic symptoms should not be forgotten.

FURTHER READINGS

Bateson, G., Jackson, D. D., Haley, J., & Weakland, J. (1956). Toward a theory of schizophrenia. *Behavioral Science, 1,* 251–264.

Bernheim, K. F., & Lewine, R. R. J. (1979). *Schizophrenia: Symptoms, causes, and treatments.* New York: Norton.

Fenton, W. S., & McGlashan, T. H. (1991). Natural history of schizophrenia subtypes. I. Longitudinal study of paranoid, hebephrenic, and undifferentiated schizophrenia. *Archives of General Psychiatry,* 48(11):969–977.

Gottesman, I. I. (1991) *Schizophrenia genesis: The origins of madness.* New York: Freedman.

Laing, R. D. (1965). *The divided self: An existential study in sanity and madness.* Baltimore: Pelican.

Laing, R. D., & Esterson, A. (1971). *Sanity, madness, and the family: Families of schizophrenics* (2nd ed.). New York: Basic Books.

Lidz, T., Fleck, S., & Cornelison, A. (1965). *Schizophrenia and the family.* New York: International Universities Press.

McGlashan, T. H., & Fenton, W. S. (1992). The positive-negative distinction in schizophrenia: Review of natural history validators. *Archives of General Psychiatry,* 49(1):63–72.

Murphy, H. B. M. (1978). Cultural influences on incidence, course, and treatment response. In L. C. Wynne, R. L. Cromwell, & S. Matthysse (Eds.), *The nature of schizophrenia: New approaches to research and treatment* (pp. 586–594). New York: Wiley.

Sass, L. A. (1992). *Madness and modernism: Insanity in the light of modern art, literature, and thought.* New York: Basic Books.

Suddath, R. L., Christianson, M. D., Torrey, E. F., Casanova, M., & Weinberger, D. R. (1990). Anatomic abnormalities in the brains of monozygotic twins discordant for schizophrenia. *New England Journal of Medicine,* 322:789–794.

Thornton, J. F. & Seeman, M. V. (1991). *Schizophrenia simplified—A field guide to schizophrenia for frontline workers, families, and professionals.* Toronto: Hogrefe & Huber.

Torrey, E. F. (1980). *Schizophrenia and civilization.* New York: Jason Aronson.

Torrey, E. F. (1995). *Surviving schizophrenia:* *A manual for families, consumers and providers.* New York: Harper Collins.

Sarbin, T. R., & Mancuso, J. C. (1980). *Schizophrenia: Medical diagnosis or moral verdict.* New York: Pergamon.

Vonnegut, M. (1975). *The Eden express.* New York: Praeger.

TERM-PAPER TOPICS

1. Evaluate R. D. Laing's claims about schizophrenia in *The Divided Self* with research investigating the long-term consequences of schizophrenia. Is Laing mostly right or mostly wrong? Take a stand and defend it.

2. The side effects of neuroleptics cause more distress than schizophrenia. Evaluate this claim, touching on both short-term and long-term side effects.

3. If schizophrenia has a genetic component, just what is it? In other words, what specifically is inherited that may bring about schizophrenia?

4. Describe the research investigating children at high risk for schizophrenia who did not develop the disorder. What are the implications of this research for theories about the cause of schizophrenia?

5. What are the implications of the distinction between Type I and Type II schizophrenia? Describe a future edition of DSM that takes this distinction into account.

6. Evaluate the controversy surrounding the plight of the homeless mentally ill, some large number of whom are schizophrenic, in light of what you know about the causes and treatments of schizophrenia.

7. Read David Rosenhan's (1973), "On being sane in insane places," *Science,* 179, 250–258. Would modern psychiatric/psychological practice (e.g., using the DSM-IV for diagnosis) change any of the findings of this study? If so, how? If not, why not?

EXERCISES

Exercise One—Beliefs about Schizophrenia

This exercise allows you to see the variability of beliefs about schizophrenia.

Talk to a number of individuals about schizophrenia. Ask them questions like

1. What is schizophrenia?
2. What are the symptoms of schizophrenia?
3. Do schizophrenics have split personalities?
4. Are schizophrenics dangerous?
5. What are the causes of schizophrenia?
6. Who is at risk for schizophrenia?
7. What are the treatments of schizophrenia?
8. Is schizophrenia incurable?
9. Do you know anyone who has had schizophrenia?

Also, repeat these questions for "nervous breakdown," which many people use in place of "schizophrenia."

What is the range of beliefs? Are there differences between beliefs about schizophrenia and beliefs about nervous breakdowns? Which beliefs are consistent with what is known about schizophrenia? Which are inconsistent?

Seeman, M. V. (1982). *Living and working with schizophrenia.* Toronto: University of Toronto Press.

Torrey, E. F. (1995). *Surviving schizophrenia: A manual for families, consumers and providers.* New York: Harper Collins.

Exercise Two—Chronic Patients

The purpose of this exercise is to gain first-hand knowledge of how chronic patients are treated in a mental hospital.

Arrange a tour for your class at a local psychiatric hospital. Ask to be told about the chronic wards. Who stays on them? What are their diagnoses? Prognoses? What kinds of therapy are they given? What are their lives like?

Exercise Three—Work on a Chronic Ward

The purpose of this exercise is to gain experience in the care of chronic psychiatric patients.

Volunteer to work as an aide in a chronic ward of a local psychiatric hospital. Use your work as an opportunity to examine your beliefs about how people with psychological problems should be treated.

CHAPTER 13

Sexual Dysfunction and Sexual Disorder

CHAPTER OVERVIEW

This chapter describes five layers of sexuality: sexual identify, sexual orientation, sexual interest, sex role, and sexual performance. Sexual problems and disorders can occur at any of these levels, and difficulty in treatment parallels the depth of level from which the problem or disorder arises.

The core layer described in the text is sexual identity. This primary identification is usually consistent with one's anatomy: those with a penis feel male, those with a vagina feel female. Transsexualism is a disorder of this primary association in which an individual feels that his or her identity is the opposite of the sex of his or her body.

Sexual orientation represents the next level and describes one's erotic and romantic attractions. Based on these preferences, one's sexual orientation is defined as heterosexual, homosexual, or bisexual. Although there is no longer a category of disorder associated with any of these orientations per se, some people do experience distress about their orientation and want to change it.

Sexual interest describes the specific objects of one's sexual fantasies and arousal, including types of persons, parts of the body, specific objects or situations. Disorders at this level arise when one's sexual interests conflict with the pursuit of affectionate, erotic, consensual relationships with others.

One's sex role is the public expression of one's sexual identity. Although there are no defined disorders at this layer, there may be some disparity between the sex role socially dictated for one's sex and the sex role one actually adopts.

The surface layer of these strata of erotic life is sexual performance. The stages of normal human sexual response include desire and arousal, physical excitement, and orgasm. A number of sexual dysfunctions are associated with each of these aspects of performance.

At each level the text describes the physical and psychological causes and treatments of the various sexual dysfunctions and disorders, including biomedical, psychoanalytic, behavioral, and cognitive views.

ESSENTIAL TERMS

androgen-insensitivity syndrome	hormonal problem in which fetus lacks receptors for the hormone androgen (p. 478)
androgyny	having both male and female psychological or physical characteristics (p. 497)

aversion therapy

treatment for paraphilias in which sexually arousing stimuli are paired with aversive stimuli (p. 495)

bisexuality

sexual activity with both men and women (p. 471)

cathexis

in psychoanalytic theory, the charging of a neutral object with psychical energy, either positive or negative (p. 493)

congenital adrenal hyperplasia (CAH)

condition in females that results from the fetus being exposed to excessive androgens in utero; associated with male-stereotyped behavior and toy preferences in childhood (p. 498)

covert sensitization

treatment for paraphilias in which imagined sexual stimuli are followed by aversive stimuli (p. 495)

direct sexual therapy

therapy for sexual dysfunction developed by Masters and Johnson in which patients are not treated individually but as couples who receive instruction while explicitly practicing sexual behavior under the systematic guidance of a therapist (p. 506)

erectile dysfunction

sexual dysfunction characterized by a recurrent inability to have or maintain an erection for intercourse (p. 501)

primary erectile dysfunction

erectile dysfunction in which an erection sufficient for intercourse has never been achieved

secondary erectile dysfunction

erectile dysfunction in which the ability to have an erection sufficient for intercourse has been lost

situation specific erectile dysfunction

erectile dysfunction in which the ability to have an erection is limited to specific situations or partners

erotic desire and arousal

response which may be elicited by a variety of stimuli; the first phase in human sexual response (p. 499)

exhibitionism

sexual disorder involving the exposure of genitals to unwitting and usually unwilling strangers (p. 489)

fetish

sexual object choice that is inanimate (p. 484)

homosexuality

sexual activity between individuals of the same sex (p. 477)

ego-dystonic homosexuality

sustained pattern of homosexuality that is a source of distress to the individual and is accompanied by a desire to acquire or increase heterosexual activity (p. 480)

ego-syntonic homosexuality

sustained pattern of homosexuality that is neither a source of distress nor something the individual desires to change (p. 480)

masochism

sexual disorder in which an individual becomes sexually aroused by having suffering or humiliation inflicted on him or her (p. 486)

masturbation

stimulation of one's own genitals (p. 469)

orgasm

emission (discharge of semen) and ejaculation triggered by rhythmic pressure on head and shaft of penis in males, reflexive contractions of vaginal muscles triggered by clito-

	ral stimulation in females; the third phase of human sexual response (p. 499)
orgasmic dysfunction	sexual dysfunction characterized by a recurrent inability to have an orgasm (p. 502)
primary orgasmic dysfunction	orgasmic dysfunction in which orgasm has never occurred
secondary orgasmic dysfunction	orgasmic dysfunction in which the ability to have an orgasm has been lost
situation specific orgasmic dysfunction	orgasmic dysfunction in which an orgasm can only be achieved under specific circumstances (pp. 501, 502)
paraphilia	sexual disorder characterized by sexual arousal to the unusual or bizarre; e.g., fetish (p. 483)
pedophilia	sexual disorder involving sexual relations with children below the age at which they can reasonably be expected to give mature consent (p. 491)
physical excitement	penile erection in the male, vaginal lubrication and swelling in the female; the second phase in human sexual response (p. 499)
premature ejaculation	recurrent inability to exert any control over ejaculation (p. 503)
preparedness	view that there is an evolutionarily determined limited set of objects that can become paraphilic (cf: phobias, see Chapter 8) (p. 494)
rape	the sexual violation of one person by another; not considered a paraphilia unless it is the individual's virtually exclusive mode of sexual release (p. 488)
retarded ejaculation	recurrent difficulty in ejaculating during sexual intercourse (p. 503)
sadism	sexual disorder in which an individual becomes sexually aroused by inflicting physical and psychological suffering or humiliation (p. 486)
sensate focus	direct sexual therapy technique that attempts to decrease anxiety during intercourse (p. 507)
sex role	public expression of one's sexual identity; what an individual does or says to indicate that he is a man or she is a woman; the fourth layer of erotic life (p. 497)
sexual disorder	problems with sexual identity, sexual orientation, or sexual interest (p. 470)
sexual dysfunction	problems involving sexual inabilities in desire, arousal, performance, or orgasm (pp 470, 500)
sexual identity	one's awareness of being male or female; the fundamental layer of erotic life (p. 470)
sexual interest	the objects and situations that are sexually arousing; the third level of erotic life (p. 483)
sexual object choice	sexual orientation (p. 477)

sexual orientation	to whom one is erotically and romantically attracted; the second layer of erotic life (pp. 471, 477)
sexual performance	capacities for desire, arousal, physical excitement, and orgasm; the surface layer of erotic life (p. 498)
sexual unresponsiveness	sexual dysfunction characterized by lack of sexual desire and impairment of physical excitement in appropriate situations (p. 500)
telephone scatologia	a sexual disorder in which there is a recurrent, intense sexual desire to make obscene phone calls to a nonconsenting individual; a paraphilia (p. 488)
transsexualism	sexual disorder of identity involving the belief that one is a woman trapped in the body of a man, or a man trapped in the body of a woman (p. 472)
transvestitism	sexual disorder in which a man persistently dresses in women's clothes in order to achieve sexual arousal (p. 485)
voyeurism	sexual disorder involving the observation of a naked body, disrobing, or the sexual activity of an unsuspecting victim (p. 490)

CENTRAL CONCEPTUAL ISSUES

Layers of sexuality.   The text presents sexuality as a composite of five layers organized metaphorically from deep to surface. A layer is considered deep insofar as it is biologically determined through genetics or developmental influences and therefore is more resistant to change (e.g., Layer I: Sexual Identity). At the most surface level (Level V: Sexual Performance) behaviors are viewed as subject to situational and flexible psychological influences and are therefore more easily affected both through dysfunction and by treatment.

Disorders and dysfunctions of sexuality can be viewed at any one of these levels of sexual functioning with a corresponding prognosis. At any level, behavior may be modifiable but at the deeper levels the underlying psychological state may be set. Thus a person who has, and has always had, exclusively homosexual desires may be able to act in stereotypical heterosexual fashion (e.g., get married, have children), yet such a person's deep sexual orientation may remain resistant to change.

What constitutes a disorder/dysfunction?   The distinctions between idiosyncratic thoughts and behavior; common thoughts and behaviors which everyone has but no one talks about; and truly abnormal, harmful, or dysfunctional thoughts and behaviors are at least as important, and as often misunderstood, in areas revolving around sexuality as in any area of human life. Much of the additional difficulty that arises around sexual issues stems from the cultural taboos that extend to sexual behavior and consequently limit open and honest discussion of sexual issues. This leaves many persons confused as to what is "normal" and what is "sick" or harmful. Moreover, the public norms for sexuality are among the most culturally determined—and variable—standards across human societies It is therefore important to understand what qualifies something as a sexual disorder or dysfunction.

The criteria which psychologists use to distinguish sexual problems from other sexual behaviors are much the same as those in any area of abnormal psychology. Rarely is a single thought or action sufficient to qualify an individual as having a problem. Many times the chief problem for the individual is not in the thoughts per se, but rather in the difficulties that arise as a result of the person's attitude and feelings about those thoughts. This highlights one of the principles and most broadly applied indication of a need for treatment: does the thought or behavior cause distress for the individual? It is easy to see how a cultural taboo against what would otherwise be seen as a normal biological urge could create anxiety, shame, guilt, or depression in an individual. A second major criterion is whether the thoughts or behaviors are experienced as intrusive or uncontrollable and therefore create difficulties with interpersonal relationships or the law. Whenever thoughts become obsessive or behavior becomes uncontrollable there is reason for concern. Thus, if a fetish for women's shoes (a desire which in itself is harmless) makes a mutually satisfying relationship impossible or if it drives an individual to harass strangers or steal shoes, then the individual has a problem which is in need of treatment. In contrast, the occasional erotic fantasy in which shoes play a significant role is not intrusive and does not create practical difficulties.

Sexual dysfunctions (low desire, low arousal, hindered physical excitement, problems with orgasm) also do not have absolute lines of demarcation, but are diagnosed along the general axes outlined above. For example, a particular level of sexual desire may not be problem if it is acceptable to one's mate and oneself. Both disorders and dysfunctions are considered to be abnormal when they grossly impair affectionate, erotic relations between human beings.

Transsexualism, homosexuality, and transvestitism.   Transsexualism, homosexuality, and transvestitism are often confused, but they are three distinct conditions operating at three distinct layers. Transsexualism is a disorder of sexual identity in which a person who is biologically one sex, profoundly and firmly feels him or herself to be psychologically of the other sex. This condition is believed to be the result of a disorder of timing or amount of hormones during a critical period of fetal development. In this view, sexual identity is determined in the womb by biological processes somewhat independently of one's sexual genotype or phenotype. A transsexual's sexual identity is therefore no more a matter of personal choice or subject to change in attitude than is that person's genital configuration. Indeed, sexual identity is so stable that it seems easier to change the body to match the psychology than vice versa. Transsexuality does not imply homosexuality.

Homosexuality is described in the next higher layer—sexual orientation. Here there is substantial data to indicate a strong genetic and developmental substrate. Although some influence may occur at the time of sexual maturation or through other experiences in life, it is not necessarily for it to be so. Because homosexuality typically has such a strong biological influence, it is also highly resistant to change. Homosexuality per se is no longer considered a disorder. Following the primary rule of diagnosing a disorder, homosexuality is only considered a problem if it is ego-dystonic. That is, if the individual is acutely distressed by and rejects his or her own homosexuality. In such cases, behavioral therapies have had some limited success in changing apparent sexual orientation, but even this has been questioned because it is difficult to determine whether a highly motivated individual has actually changed his or her orientation, or only his or her behavior. More often, treatment revolves around helping the individual to deal with the emotional consequences of violating what may be their own taboos or religious doctrines, and the attitudes of their culture. Often guilt, shame, and depression can result from diverging form the cultural norm, but these aspects can be well treated with the psychotherapies outlined in previous chapters. The treatments therefore focus on the conflict with an intolerant culture or with destructive self-judgment.

Transvestitism is a function of the third layer—sexual interest. At the level of disorder it is considered a paraphilia. Transvestitism is the desire to dress in clothes of the opposite sex (usually men dressed as women), in which the wearing of such clothes is sexually arousing and such arousal is an end in itself. Transvestites are typically not homosexual; they are not aroused by members of their own sex, but instead by wearing clothes of the opposite sex. Homosexual men who dress as women (e.g., drag queens) may do so to attract other men; a transsexual man who dresses as a woman does so because he believes himself to be a woman (who has a male body) and no because he is aroused by women's clothing.

Rape and other nonconsenting sexual acts.   Unlike voyeurism, exhibitionism, and pedophilia, rape is not usually a paraphilia because it does not meet the criterion of paraphilia in that it must be the individual's exclusive, or vastly preferred, mode of sexual release. Rapists typically can and do become sexually aroused and orgasmic in activities other than rape. A rapist may, however, have sadistic paraphilic urges to degrade, control, and inflict pain. Voyeurs and especially exhibitionists are not typically rapists. The object of the paraphilia, in this case illicit observation or surprise exposure, is the end in itself and not a prelude to an aggressive sexual assault.

SAMPLE EXAM

1. According to the text, all of the following are layers of erotic life except
    a. sex role.
    b. sexual orientation.
    c. sexual identity.
    d. sexual responsiveness.
    e. sexual interest.

2. Adventurous sexual attitudes in the past decade may have _____ due to _____.
    a. increased; the birth control pill
    b. increased; societal permissiveness
    c. decreased; the threat of AIDS
    d. decreased; political conservativeness
    e. stayed the same; stable sexual attitudes

3. The fundamental feeling of being male or female is described as
    a. sex role.
    b. sexual orientation.
    c. sexual identity.
    d. sexual performance.
    e. sexual interest.

4. An individual whose sexual identity differs from that indicated by his or her genitals is called
    a. a homosexual.
    b. androgen insensitive.
    c. a transvestite.
    d. a heterosexual.
    e. a transsexual.

5. All of the following are true about transsexualism except that
    a. the condition is chronic.
    b. males outnumber females about 2.5:1.
    c. they are always attracted to those of the opposite gender identity.
    d. they feel they are trapped in a body of the wrong sex.
    e. as children they engaged in behaviors consistent with their gender identity.

6. The origins of transsexuality seem to lie in
    a. a disruption of sexual identity phase of fetal development.

b. a disruption of the sexual organ development phase of fetal development.

c. a disruption of the resolution of the Oedipal complex.

d. a disruption of the socialization process in adolescence.

e. none of the above.

7. The treatment for transsexuality is
   a. changing the psychosocial identity.
   b. sexual reassignment.
   c. long-term psychoanalysis.
   d. sensate focus.
   e. aversion therapy.

8. Who one is erotically and romantically attracted to is described as
   a. sex role.
   b. sexual orientation.
   c. sexual identity.
   d. sexual performance.
   e. sexual interest.

9. Which of the following is not a sexual orientation?
   a. homosexuality
   b. bisexuality
   c. heterosexuality
   d. transsexuality
   e. all of the above are sexual orientations

10. There is evidence for all the following proposed sources of homosexuality except
    a. insufficient prenatal masculinizing hormone.
    b. structural brain differences.
    c. timing of sexual maturation.
    d. genetic factors.
    e. domineering mothers.

11. If a homosexual is distressed by his or her sexual orientation and wants it changed it is called
    a. a paraphilia.
    b. ego-syntonic.
    c. primary orgasmic dysfunction.
    d. ego-dystonic.
    e. primary erectile dysfunction.

12. The sources of ego-dystonic homosexuality include all of the following except

a. desire to have children.

b. rejection and disapproval of family and friends.

c. desire for a conventional family life.

d. societal pressures to conform to sexual norms.

e. conflict over gender identity.

13. The objects and situations that arouse a person indicate his or her
    a. sex role.
    b. sexual orientation.
    c. sexual identity.
    d. sexual performance.
    e. sexual interest.

14. The categories of paraphilias include all of the following except
    a. arousal and preference for nonconsenting partners.
    b. arousal and preference for situations involving humiliation and suffering.
    c. arousal and preference for consenting members of the same sex.
    d. arousal and preference or nonhuman objects.
    e. arousal and preference for consenting members of the opposite sex.

15. Which of the following does not belong in the category of fetishes?
    a. rubber
    b. animals
    c. underwear
    d. feet
    e. telephone scatologia

16. A male transvestite wears women's clothing
    a. to attract men.
    b. to achieve arousal.
    c. because he believes he is a woman trapped in a male body.
    d. to arouse his mate.
    e. to look pretty.

17. Sadism is to masochism as
    a. abnormal is to normal.
    b. reward is to punishment.
    c. giving is to receiving.
    d. suffering is to humiliation.
    e. voluntary is to involuntary.

18. Which of these statements is true?
    a. Sadism is more common in men than women; masochism is more common in women than men.
    b. Sadism is more common in women than men; masochism is more common in men than women.
    c. Sadism and masochism are both more common in men than women.
    d. Sadism and masochism are both more common in women than men.
    e. Sadism and masochism are equally common in men and women.

19. The category of paraphilias that involve nonconsenting partners includes all of the following except
    a. telephone scatologia.
    b. voyeurism.
    c. exhibitionism.
    d. pedophilia.
    e. all of the above involve nonconsenting partners

20. An exhibitionist seeks
    a. to be calmly confronted by his victim.
    b. a partner for sex.
    c. to shock and horrify his victim.
    d. to arouse his victim.
    e. admiration.

21. Voyeurs are often
    a. rapists.
    b. unhappily married.
    c. impotent.
    d. aroused by the illegal, secretive nature of the peeping.
    e. masochists.

22. The most common victims of child molesters are
    a. girls under age ten.
    b. girls over age ten.
    c. boys under age ten.
    d. boys over age ten.
    e. All children are equally at risk.

23. What proportion of adults report being approached sexually by an adult when they were children?
    a. 10 to 20 percent
    b. 25 to 33 percent
    c. 33 to 50 percent
    d. 50 to 66 percent
    e. 66 to 75 percent

24. All of the following generally characterize pedophiles except
    a. they have poor social skills.
    b. they are married.
    c. they are conflicted over religion and sexuality.
    d. they are older than other types of sex offenders.
    e. they are usually mentally retarded, senile, or schizophrenic.

25. The psychoanalytic account of paraphilia emphasizes
    a. cathexis.
    b. catharsis.
    c. sublimation.
    d. transference.
    e. none of the above.

26. The behavioral account of paraphilias emphasizes
    a. modeling.
    b. operant conditioning.
    c. Pavlovian conditioning.
    d. counterconditioning.
    e. none of the above.

27. The most successful treatment for paraphilias seems to be
    a. placebo.
    b. aversion therapy.
    c. psychoanalysis.
    d. drug therapy.
    e. all of the above are equally successful.

28. The most common sexual crime in America is
    a. exhibitionism.
    b. voyeurism.
    c. pedophilia.
    d. sadism.
    e. fetishism.

29. The way an individual expresses being male or female is called a
    a. sex role.
    b. sexual orientation.
    c. sexual identity.
    d. sexual preference.
    e. sexual interest.

30. Problems in a person's sexual response are described as dysfunctions in

a. sex role.
b. sexual orientation.
c. sexual identity.
d. sexual performance.
e. sexual interest.

31. The sexual response includes all of the following except
a. physical excitement.
b. arousal.
c. orgasm.
d. desire.
e. All of the above are aspects of sexual response.

32. Sexual dysfunction can occur in which stage of sexual response?
a. physical excitement
b. arousal
c. orgasm
d. desire
e. all of the above

33. The experiences of sexual response in men and women are
a. identical.
b. parallel.
c. complementary.
d. opposite.
e. incompatible.

34. Sexual unresponsiveness in women was formerly called
a. normal.
b. nymphomania.
c. frigidity.
d. orgasmic dysfunction.
e. none of the above.

35. The dysfunction in which men have lost the ability to maintain an erection sufficient for intercourse is called
a. situation specific erectile dysfunction.
b. hypoactive sexual desire.
c. primary erectile dysfunction.
d. retarded ejaculation.
e. secondary erectile dysfunction.

36. The dysfunction in which women can only have orgasms under specific cir-cumstance, such as during masturbation, is called
a. situation specific orgasmic dysfunction.
b. frigidity.
c. primary orgasmic dysfunction.
d. nymphomania.
e. secondary orgasmic dysfunction.

37. Direct sexual therapy includes all of the following except
a. explicit practice of sexual behavior with therapist guidance.
b. identifying which partner has the problem.
c. sexual problems are labeled as limited dysfunctions.
d. focus on the interaction of the couple.
e. All of the above are part of direct sexual therapy.

38. The premise of sensate focus therapy is that
a. depression leads to sexual dysfunction.
b. anxiety leads to sexual dysfunction.
c. boredom leads to sexual dysfunction.
d. overexcitement leads to sexual dysfunction.
e. none of the above.

39. The phases of sensate focus include all of the following except
a. masturbation.
b. nondemand intercourse.
c. pleasuring.
d. genital stimulation.
e. All of the above are phases in sensate focus.

40. Which of the following is/are most readily treated?
a. paraphilias.
b. problems with sexual orientation.
c. disorders of sexual identity.
d. sexual performance dysfunctions.
e. transsexualism.

Answer Key for Sample Exam

1.	d	(p. 469)	11.	d	(p. 480)	21.	d	(p. 490)	31. e (p. 499)
2.	c	(p. 469)	12.	e	(p. 481)	22.	a	(p. 491)	32. e (p. 499)
3.	c	(p. 472)	13.	e	(p. 483)	23.	b	(p. 491)	33. b (p. 500)
4.	e	(p. 472)	14.	c, e	(p. 483)	24.	e	(p. 492)	34. c (p. 500)
5.	e	(p. 473)	15.	e	(p. 484)	25.	a	(p. 493)	35. e (p. 501)
6.	a	(p. 474)	16.	b	(p. 485)	26.	c	(p. 494)	36. a (p. 502)
7.	b	(p. 476)	17.	c	(p. 486)	27.	b	(p. 495)	37. b (p. 506)
8.	b	(p. 477)	18.	c	(p. 488)	28.	a	(p. 489)	38. b (p. 507)
9.	d	(p. 477)	19.	e	(p. 488)	29.	a	(p. 497)	39. a (p. 507)
10.	e	(p. 480)	20.	c	(p. 489)	30.	d	(p. 498)	40. d (p. 508)

SELF-TEST

1. The layers of sexual life include _____, _____, _____, _____, and _____.

2. Problems related to sexual identity, sexual orientation, or sexual interest are called _____; problems with sexual response are called _____.

3. Transsexuality is a disorder of _____; while only _____ homosexuality is considered a disorder of _____.

4. The sexual response consists of three phases: _____, _____, and _____; dysfunctions can occur in _____ phases.

5. Difficulty in making changes at a particular layer are related to how _____ the layer is, which may be related to how _____ determined it is.

6. Lack of sexual desire is called _____.

7. A recurrent inability to have or maintain an erection is _____.

8. Orgasmic dysfunction in men includes _____ ejaculation and _____ ejaculation.

9. The majority of cases of sexual dysfunction are caused by _____ factors.

10. To treat sexual dysfunction, Masters and Johnson developed _____.

11. The major strategy of direct sexual therapy is _____, which attempts to reduce _____.

12. Direct sexual therapy usually involves the treatment of _____.

13. Masters and Johnson report that only _____ percent of patients fail to improve with direct sexual therapy.

14. Individuals who are neither exclusively heterosexual nor exclusively homosexual are called

    _____.

15. One type of paraphilia in which a person is sexually aroused by a nonliving object is called a

    _____; it is a disorder of sexual _____.

16. There are three major types of paraphilias: those that involve _____; those that in-

    volve _____ and _____; and those that involve _____.

17. _____ is when a man dresses in the clothes of a woman in order to achieve sexual
    arousal.

18. In _____, sexual arousal results from the infliction of suffering or humiliation on

    another; in _____, sexual arousal results from receiving suffering or humiliation
    from another.

19. Individuals who expose their genitals to unwitting strangers are _____; those who ob-

    serve the sexual activity of others are _____; and those who have sex with children

    are _____.

20. Paraphilias occur mainly among _____.

21. The psychodynamic model explains the paraphilias in terms of _____.

22. The behavioral model explains the paraphilias in terms of _____.

23. Behavioral therapy for the paraphilias includes _____ and _____.

24. One's dissatisfaction with his homosexuality may have several sources. First, he

    may wish to have _____. Second, _____ may disapprove. Third, his

    _____ may also disapprove.

25. Traditional psychotherapy is _____ in changing homosexual orientation.

26. A transsexual is a man who feels like a _____, or a woman who feels like a

    _____.

27. At present, the only treatment for transsexuality is a _____.

Answer Key for Self-Test

1. sexual identity; sexual orientation;
   sexual interest; sex role, sexual performance
2. disorders; dysfunctions
3. sexual identity; ego-dystonic; sexual orientation
4. desire and arousal; physical excitement;
   orgasm; all
5. deep; biologically
6. sexual unresponsiveness
7. erectile dysfunction
8. premature; retarded

9. psychological
10. direct sexual therapy
11. sensate focus; anxiety
12. couples
13. 24
14. bisexuals
15. fetish; interest
16. inanimate objects; suffering; humiliation; nonconsenting partners
17. Transvestitism
18. sadism; masochism
19. exhibitionists; voyeurs; pedophiles
20. men
21. cathexis
22. Pavlovian conditioning
23. aversion therapy; covert sensitization; reconditioning
24. children; society; family
25. ineffective
26. woman; man
27. sex-change operation

MATCHING ITEMS

_____   1.   sex role

_____   2.   cathexes

_____   3.   sexual interest

_____   4.   sexual response

_____   5.   sex reassignment

_____   6.   sexual performance

_____   7.   Androgen Insensitivity Syndrome

_____   8.   sensate focus

_____   9.   transsexual

_____   10. sexual orientation

_____   11. aversion therapy

_____   12. sexual identity

A. paraphilias

B. desire and arousal, physical excitement, orgasm

C. sexual identity therapy

D. homosexual, heterosexual, bisexual

E. pleasuring, genital stimulation, nondemand intercourse

F. public expression of sexual identity

G. male, female

H. what objects or situations are erotic

I. genotype male, phenotype female, sexual identity female

J. genotype male, phenotype male, sexual identity female

K. sexual dysfunctions

L. treatment for paraphilias

Answer Key for Matching Items

1.	F	7.	I
2.	A	8.	E
3.	H	9.	J
4.	B	10.	D
5.	C	11.	L
6.	K	12.	G

SHORT-ANSWER QUESTIONS

1. Briefly define the five levels of erotic life described in the text. What is an example of a disorder or dysfunction associated with each?

2. What are the differences between transsexuality, homosexuality, and transvestitism?

3. How are fetal hormones thought to be implicated in the development of transsexuality, homosexuality, and heterosexuality? Describe the three processes which are thought to be affected.

4. Under what conditions is homosexuality considered to be a disorder? What treatments have been applied, and with what results?

5. What is a paraphilia? Describe the characteristics of the major categories of paraphilias (i.e., fetishes, transvestitism, sadism, masochism, exhibitionism, voyeurism, pedophilia). Under what conditions would rape be considered a paraphilia?

6. How do the psychodynamic and behavioral schools explain paraphilias? What does each fail to explain?

7. Describe the behavioral, cognitive, and physical treatments for changing sexual interest. How successful is each?

8. What is the evidence for the contribution of social and biological factors to the development of sex roles? How does this change over time?

9. What are the major categories of impairment in sexual performance? What do each of the medical, psychodynamic, behavioral, and cognitive views have to say about the origins of sexual dysfunction?

10. What is "direct sexual therapy" and how is it practiced?

TYING IT TOGETHER

Although Freud was greatly concerned with sexuality, the psychodynamic model (Chapter 4) is not the model of choice with which to explain sexual problems. Sexual identity and orientation, and related disorders such as transsexuality, seem to be related to underlying biological factors such as genetic influences (Chapter 3), neuroanatomy (Chapter 17), or levels of fetal hormones, and are therefore difficult to change. However, many dysfunctions of sexual performance do not appear to have physical causes. Instead, the behavioral model (Chapter 5) has proven most useful in conceiving and treating these disorders, which often involve anxiety (cf. Chapters 8 and 9). Direct sexual therapy, as pioneered by Masters and Johnson, uses behavioral techniques to teach couples more satisfying ways of relating to each other sexually (Chapter 19). Like other behavioral techniques, these were developed through laboratory experimentation (Chapter 6) and careful behavioral and physiological assessment (Chapter 7).

Psychoanalytic theory is more helpful in explaining paraphilias, although again, the behavioral model seems viable. The behavioral approach leaves unanswered the questions of why men are more likely to have paraphilias than women. Perhaps cultural and historical factors (Chapter 2) explain this puzzling sex difference, but the possible role of biology should not be overlooked.

No theory gives a complete account of transsexuality. Although this disorder can be treated with a sex-change operation, the results are not always satisfactory. Changing societal conceptions of masculinity and femininity may mitigate the distress experienced by the transsexual.

That homosexuality is no longer considered a psychological disorder underscores the changing nature of abnormality (Chapter 2). As observer discomfort is reduced, so too is the tendency to judge a given life-style as abnormal (Chapter 1).

FURTHER READINGS

Bayer, R. (1987). *Homosexuality and American psychiatry.* Princeton, NJ: Princeton University Press.

Boswell, J. (1980). *Christianity, social tolerance, and homosexuality.* Chicago: University of Chicago Press.

Garfinkel, H. (1967). Passing and the managed achievement of sex status in an intersexed person. In *Studies in ethnomethodology.* Englewood Cliffs, NJ: Prentice-Hall.

Kinsey, A., Pomeroy, W., & Martin, C. (1948). *Sexual behavior in the human male.* Philadelphia: Saunders.

Heiman, J., LoPiccolo, L., & LoPiccolo, J. (1976). *Becoming orgasmic: A sexual growth program for women.* Englewood Cliffs, NJ: Prentice-Hall.

Kinsey, A., Pomeroy, W., Martin, C., & Gebhard, P. (1953). *Sexual behavior in the human female.* Philadelphia: Saunders.

Masters, W. H., & Johnson, V. E. (1966). *Human sexual response.* Boston: Little, Brown.

Money, J. (1988). *Gay, straight, and in between. The sexology of erotic orientation.* New York: Oxford University Press.

Money, J. (1986). *Sexual maps: Clinical concepts of sexual/erotic health and psychopathology, paraphilia, and gender transposition of childhood, adolescence, and maturity.* New York: Irvington.

Money, J., & Erhardt, A. A. (1972). *Man and woman/boy and girl.* Baltimore: Johns Hopkins.

Stoller, R. J. (1985). *Observing the erotic imagination.* New Haven, CT: Yale University Press.

Vance, E. B., & Wagner, N. N. (1976). Written descriptions of orgasm: A study of sex differences. *Archives of Sexual Behavior, 5,* 87–98.

Zilbergeld, B. (1978). *Male sexuality: A guide to sexual fulfillment.* Boston: Little, Brown.

TERM-PAPER TOPICS

1. Masters and Johnson have been credited with dispelling false beliefs about sexuality that originated in the theories of Freud. What were these beliefs? How did research suggest them to be incorrect?

2. Nancy Friday's books on women's erotic fantasies have catalogued and chronicled the variety and evolution of the subjects of women's arousal. Compare and contrast her findings in *My Secret Garden* and *Women on Top.*

3. Examine the cases of either serial sexual killer Ted Bundy or Jeffrey Dahmer in one of the popular biographies about them. How do their deviant sexual behaviors map onto the diagnostic categories presented in this chapter? Do they qualify for any other diagnoses as far as you can tell (e.g., a personality disorder, substance use or abuse disorder, psychotic disorder)?

4. How has the AIDS epidemic changed sexual behavior among homosexuals? Among heterosexuals?

EXERCISES

Exercise One—Attitudes toward Homosexuality

In this exercise, you will ascertain attitudes toward homosexuality.

Talk to a variety of people you know about homosexuality. Ask them these questions:

1. What is homosexuality?
2. How many people are homosexuals?
3. What causes homosexuality?
4. Are homosexuals crazy?
5. Are homosexuals ill?
6. Are homosexuals immoral?
7. Should one's homosexual orientation be changed?
8. Can one's homosexual orientation be changed?
9. Do you know any homosexuals?

You can expect a variety of opinions, and you can expect them to be strongly held. Anticipate the possibility that some people will not wish to speak to you at all about homosexuality, and respect their right not to do so.

Use this exercise as an opportunity to examine your own attitudes toward homosexuality. What are they? Why is homosexuality such an emotionally charged subject?

Bell, A., & Weinberg, M. (1978). *Homosexualities*. New York: Simon & Schuster.

Exercise Two—Perceptions of Sexual Practices

The purpose of this exercise is to demonstrate the discrepancies between the actual prevalence of certain sexual practices and people's perceptions of their prevalence.

Read through Kinsey's books and obtain his estimated figures for the prevalence of various sexual practices: homosexuality, masturbation, premarital intercourse, extramarital intercourse, and so on. Then ask people of your acquaintance to estimate these figures. Are they accurate or inaccurate? Do men and women make different estimates? Show them the actual estimates, and assess their reactions.

You will probably find considerable discrepancies between what people think and what they do. How do you explain these discrepancies?

Kinsey, A., Pomeroy, W., & Martin, C. (1948). *Sexual behavior in the human male.* Philadelphia: Saunders.

Kinsey, A., Pomeroy, W., Martin, C., & Gebhard, P. (1953). *Sexual behavior in the human female.* Philadelphia: Saunders.

Exercise Three—Erotic Fantasies

The purpose of this exercise is to gain an appreciation of the range of individuals, objects, situations, and occurrences that may be sexually arousing.

Talk to individuals you know well about the content of their erotic fantasies. How varied are these? Do they have much to do with these individuals' actual sexual practices? Do men and women report different fantasies?

What is your conclusion about "normal" and "abnormal" sexual fantasies?

Exercise Four—Knowledge Concerning AIDS

The purpose of this exercise is to understand what people do and do not understand about AIDS.

Talk to individuals you know well about their beliefs concerning AIDS. Do they understand common ways this disease is transmitted? Do they know what safe sex means? Do they believe that the population as a whole knows what they do about AIDS?

CHAPTER 14

Psychoactive Substance Use Disorders

CHAPTER OVERVIEW

Chapter 14 concerns itself with psychoactive drug abuse, which many consider the nation's major health problem. Although people abuse a variety of different drugs, all abused drugs share several properties: (a) their initial effect is pleasurable; (b) their continued effect is tolerance; and (c) their cessation is characterized by withdrawal. These temporal patterns can be explained by the opponent-process model of addiction.

Psychoactive drugs mimic the action of naturally produced compounds in one's brain that produce pleasure. For instance, endorphins are compounds that mitigate pain when released by the brain during times of pain and stress; narcotics like morphine and heroin are chemically similar to endorphins.

Early research attempts to find a personality

style predisposing drug abuse focused on the oral-dependent personality, but they met with little success. More recently, links between antisocial personality in adolescence and drug abuse in adulthood have been established.

The bulk of the chapter describes several types of drugs—alcohol, narcotics, stimulants like cocaine and amphetamine, hallucinogens like PCP and LSD, marijuana, tobacco, and sedative hypnotics—in terms of their effects on the person, their physiological mechanism, the medical and social complications they create, and current modes of treatment. In general, treatment for substance abuse disorders is difficult. Many strategies seem to have short-term success, but relapse of the treated individual remains common.

ESSENTIAL TERMS

addictive personality

psychological theory of addiction that assumes that a personality defect underlies the tendency to use and abuse drugs (p. 518)

affective contrast

the experience of processes A (initial positive emotions) and B (compensatory reaction or negative "after effect") in the opponent process model of addiction; the former diminishes with time and ultimately the latter dominates,

	cycle of negatively reinforced addictive behavior results (p. 520)
affective pleasure	pleasant emotional state induced initially by drug use (p. 519)
affective tolerance	loss of affective pleasure effects of drug use with repeated exposure (p. 520)
affective withdrawal	dysphoric emotional state following removal of drug reinforcer; opposite of affective pleasure (p. 520)
alcohol	a sedative-hypnotic psychoactive drug which may initially disinhibit behavior, but ultimately has depressant effects (p. 524)
Alcoholics Anonymous (AA)	self-help group for recovering alcoholics (p. 534)
blood-brain barrier	membrane which prevents certain compounds in the blood from entering the brain (p. 516)
conditioned withdrawal	physiological signs of withdrawal that may be elicited by classically conditioned environmental stimuli ("drug cues") (p. 523)
crack	potent and inexpensive free base form of cocaine (p. 537)
deactivation	process which removes neurotransmitter from the synapse by breaking it down with enzymes (p. 517)
delirium tremens (D.T.s)	severe alcohol withdrawal symptoms, including tremors, seizures, and delirium (p. 527)
disinhibition	drug-induced state in which individuals engage in behaviors which they would not normally because of fear of consequences (p. 525)
dissociative anesthetics	developed as anesthetics (e.g., phencyclidine (PCP), ketamine); user is awake but appears disconnected form the environment (p. 553)
drug	any chemical substance that can alter a biological system (p. 515)
ecstasy	street jargon for hallucinogen MDMA (p. 553)
endogenous opioids	naturally-occurring morphine-like substances in the brain which may modulate affect and reinforcement (p. 522)
fetal alcohol syndrome	syndrome of physical and mental abnormalities caused by maternal alcohol use during pregnancy (p. 536)
flashback	episode resembling drug intoxication months or even years after drug is discontinued (p. 552)
hallucinogens	psychoactive drugs that markedly alter sensory perception, awareness, and thinking (e.g., LSD, mescaline, psilocybin, phencyclidine (PCP), ecstasy (MDMA)) (p. 550)
lipid (fat) solubility	drug characteristic which determines whether a drug is absorbed and how fast it will reach the brain (p. 516)

mainlining	street jargon for intravenous injection of a drug (p. 516)
marijuana	a psychoactive drug made form the hemp plant (p. 554)
medical model of addiction	model in which addiction is viewed as a disease requiring medical or psychiatric treatment (p. 513)
methadone	long-lasting synthetic narcotic used in substitution therapy for addicts (p. 548)
neuroadaption	brain changes which result from repeated or chronic drug use (p. 517)
nicotine	a psychoactive drug found in tobacco; a stimulant (p. 557)
nucleus accumbens	brain region implicated in the reinforcing properties of many drugs; it receives input from the limbic system via the neurotransmitter dopamine (p. 521)
opiates (narcotics)	psychoactive drugs that reduce pain without producing a loss of consciousness (e.g., opium, morphine, codeine, heroin) (p. 543)
opponent-process model	biological theory of addiction that holds that systems react and adapt to drugs by compensating for their initial effects; increases motivation to continue drug use (p. 519)
physical dependence	normal functioning requires the drug and a withdrawal syndrome is experienced upon cessation of use (p. 517)
positive reinforcement model	model of addiction that holds that pleasurable, euphoriant effects explain drug use (p. 521)
psychoactive substance abuse	maladaptive, harmful pattern of drug use (p. 515)
psychoactive substance dependence	defined in DSM-IV as loss over control of use, impairment of functioning, continued use in spite of consequences, and a tolerance or withdrawal syndrome (p. 513)
sedative-hypnotics	class of psychoactive drugs that depress CNS activity (e.g., barbiturates, benzodiazepines) (p. 562)
stimulants	psychoactive drugs that increase alertness and decrease fatigue (e.g., cocaine, amphetamine) (p. 536)
reuptake	process which removes neurotransmitter from the synapse by taking it back up into the presynaptic terminal (p. 517)
tension reduction hypothesis	theory that people drink alcohol to relieve tension (p. 531)
THC	tetrahydrocannabinol; psychoactive ingredient in marijuana (p. 554)
tolerance	form of neuroadaptation in which response to drug is decreased; more drug is needed to obtain same effect (p. 517)
trait marker	an observable, biological indication of a genetic predisposition (p. 529)
withdrawal syndrome	changes in observable physical states associated with abrupt cessation of drug use; also known as abstinence syndrome (p. 518)

CENTRAL CONCEPTUAL ISSUES

The three "C's" of drug dependence.   Issues around drug use, abuse, and addiction are highly complex, transcending a simple physiological analysis of a drug's properties. Whether a drug is viewed as "good," benign, or "dangerous" involves much more than the effects of the drug on the human body. Cultural norms, individual experience, context, and differing reactions of individuals to a drug all inform the debate. Many people would not think twice about a two-martini lunch but would be aghast as the idea of someone they knew having a heroin fix once a month. This is true in spite of the fact that the regular martini drinker may be doing far more damage to his body than the occasional heroin user. Indeed, cultural norms can complicate a rational discussion, even when a drug can be demonstrated to have positive medicinal value (e.g., marijuana to reduce the nausea associated with chemotherapy for cancer patients, or relieve the symptoms of glaucoma) if that drug has been traditionally viewed as "bad" or is illegal.

Few drugs can be absolutely defined as inherently evil. It is when the use of a drug begins to affect a person's life in significantly negative ways—when it is maladaptive and harmful— that the drug use becomes problematic. This is the essence of the diagnostic criteria for substance dependence and abuse. In the DSM-IV a number of signs of dependence and abuse are enumerated and no single behavior is necessary or sufficient for the diagnosis. Rather , as with many psychological diagnoses, clusters of symptoms which indicate distress or disability are looked for. Three general aspects are indicative of a problem. Has the individual lost control over her use of the substance (e.g., consuming more of the drug, or for longer period, than intended or at inappropriate times)? Does use of the drug impair daily functioning and/or is there continued use despite clearly adverse consequences to the individual (e.g., drunkenness at the workplace; smoking during a bout of respiratory illness)? Has there been a physical or emotional adaptation to the drug such as tolerance or withdrawal (i.e., does the individual feel a compulsion to use the drug, perhaps in increasing quantities)? These are the three "C's": control, continued use, and compulsion.

The opponent-process theory of acquired motivation to continue drug use.   The opponent-process model does much to illuminate some central aspects of addiction. The driving mechanism of the opponent process is the body's tendency to maintain or restore homeostasis. The body responds to a psychoactive drug by compensating for (i.e., opposing) the effects of the drug. Process A, the primary action of the drug which results in *affective pleasure* (the euphoria or "high") is countered by the body (Process B) which produces affective states opposite to the high (dysphoria). With repeated exposures to the drug, Process B becomes stronger and Process A becomes weaker resulting in *affective tolerance* (i.e., the loss of affective pleasure) which may motivate an individual to increase the dose of the drug to maintain the same pleasurable effect. As the drug loses its positive effect, the opposing process (Process B) comes to dominate, and an unpleasant state is experienced which sharply contrasts with the memory of the positive state. The subjective experience of these disparate states is described as *affective contrast.* If the individual stops using the drug, Process A quickly dies out, and Process B which is now unopposed, is experienced. This is described as *affective withdrawal.* Withdrawal symptoms act as a negative reinforcer (recall that a negative reinforcer is one which, by its removal, *increases* the probability of a behavior)—so continued drug use comes to be reinforced by the removal of the negative effect (withdrawal symptoms). In simple terms, according to the opponent-process model an addictive cycle is created when motivation switches from taking drugs to achieve a pleasurable high to taking drugs to remove dysphoric withdrawal symptoms.

Conditioned tolerance and withdrawal.   Interestingly, when the dynamics of opponent-process and reinforcement are examined in the context of an individual's life and routine, an important corollary emerges. The rituals, the physical environment, the social milieu, etc., all may become conditioned stimuli signaling the body that drugs are to come. The body, ever vigilant to maintain homeostasis, may initiate Process B in anticipation of the drug, even if it is not actually taken. Thus cues from the environment alone may stimulate withdrawal symptoms and increase desire for the drug. This model predicts (and research has confirmed) that tolerance for a drug used in the habitual setting is higher than tolerance for the drug administered in a novel setting with novel rituals, even if the dosage is identical.

Positive reinforcement and addiction.   In addition to the opponent-process model of addiction, there is also a quite straight forward influence on drug taking—positive reinforcement. That is, many people think that drugs are pleasurable! Research has found that nearly all of the drugs abused by human beings affect the reinforcement center of the brain—the nucleus accumbens. This stimulation of the reinforcement center is in addition to whatever influence the drugs have on other parts of the brain. Hallucinogens such as LSD and psilocybin, which do not affect the nucleus accumbens, are notable in their lack of addiction potential.

SAMPLE EXAM

1. The focus of the concept of addiction has evolved historically from the role of _____ to the role of _____.
   a. habits; choices
   b. intrapsychic processes; learning
   c. morality; legality
   d. development; environment
   e. will; disease

2. Substance dependence is defined in the DSM-IV by which of the following criteria?
   a. compulsive use of the drug
   b. loss of control regarding drug use
   c. continued use despite consequences
   d. a and b
   e. all of the above

3. Substance abuse is defined in the DSM-IV by which of the following criteria?
   a. compulsive use of the drug
   b. loss of control regarding drug use
   c. continued use despite consequences
   d. a and b
   e. all of the above

4. When an individual has decreased response to a drug following repeated use, this is called
   a. tolerance.
   b. physical dependence.
   c. withdrawal.
   d. disinhibition.
   e. affective contrast.

5. When an individual requires the drug for normal functioning, this is called:
   a. tolerance.
   b. physical dependence.
   c. withdrawal.
   d. disinhibition.
   e. affective contrast.

6. Observable physical changes which appear upon stopping drug use, characterize
   a. tolerance.
   b. physical dependence.
   c. withdrawal.
   d. disinhibition.
   e. affective contrast.

7. The effectiveness and potency of a drug is influenced by all of the following except
   a. neuroadaptation.
   b. blood-brain barrier.
   c. lipid (fat) solubility.
   d. trait markers.
   e. All of the above have influence.

8. According to the opponent-process model of addiction, addictive drugs initially activate
   a. Process A.
   b. Process B.
   c. Process C.
   d. craving.
   e. tolerance.

9. The _____ grows with repeated drug use.
   a. Process A
   b. Process B
   c. Process C
   d. pleasure
   e. sensitivity

10. According to the opponent-process model of addiction, all of the following phenomena are associated with drug dependence except
    a. affective tolerance.
    b. affective withdrawal.
    c. affective contrast.
    d. affective pleasure.
    e. affective opposition.

11. Cues associated with drug use may elicit
    a. craving.
    b. conditioned withdrawal.
    c. tolerance.
    d. a and b.
    e. all of the above.

12. Which of these drugs affects neurotransmitters in the brains?
    a. alcohol
    b. cocaine
    c. narcotics
    d. tobacco
    e. all of the above

13. The morphine-like analogues to narcotic substances are called
    a. endogenous opioids.
    b. killer cells.
    c. methadone.
    d. neurotransmitters.
    e. exogenous opiates

14. Research shows the oral-dependent personality _____ associated with drug use, and the antisocial personality _____ associated.
    a. to be; to be
    b. to be; not to be
    c. not to be; to be

   d. not to be; not to be
   e. was in the past; to now be

15. Compared to the children of nonalcoholic parents, the children of alcoholic parents are _____ as likely to abuse alcohol.
    a. half
    b. just
    c. twice
    d. four times
    e. ten times

16. The theory of alcohol abuse that holds that people drink to reduce anxiety is called
    a. the endorphin compensation theory.
    b. the stress response theory.
    c. the tension reduction theory.
    d. the "addictive personality" theory.
    e. none of the above.

17. The type of alcoholism characterized by age of onset before twenty-five, passive-dependent personality traits, apprehension, and inhibition is called
    a. negative affect alchoholism.
    b. developmentally limited alcoholism.
    c. Type 1 alcoholism.
    d. Type 2 alcoholism.
    e. milieu-independent alcoholism.

18. Alcohol abuse costs the United States more than _____ dollars every year in terms of lost productivity, health care, and legal costs.
    a. ten million
    b. one hundred million
    c. one billion
    d. ten billion
    e. one hundred billion

19. Alcohol can be described as a
    a. depressant.
    b. hallucinogen.
    c. stimulant.
    d. narcotic.
    e. all of the above.

20. Alcohol withdrawal can be relieved by
    a. alcohol.
    b. strong coffee.
    c. exercise.
    d. cold showers.
    e. swearing never to drink again.

21. The major concern of alcohol rehabilitation programs is
    a. anxiety.
    b. depression.
    c. relapse.
    d. schizophrenia.
    e. withdrawal.

22. All of the following are used as treatments for alcoholism except
    a. disulfiram (antabuse).
    b. abstinence.
    c. skills training, cognitive restructuring, lifestyle intervention.
    d. naltrexone.
    e. systematic desensitization.

23. Alcohol use is involved in 40 to 50 percent of which of the following?
    a. homicides and suicides
    b. hospital admissions
    c. accidents
    d. a and c
    e. all of the above

24. Stimulants work by blocking the reuptake of
    a. dopamine.
    b. endorphins.
    c. norepinephrine.
    d. a and c.
    e. b and c.

25. Symptoms of withdrawal from cocaine are chiefly
    a. behavioral.
    b. emotional.
    c. physical.
    d. a and b.
    e. a and c.

26. In recent years, cocaine use has
    a. decreased.
    b. stayed the same.
    c. increased.
    d. peaked.
    e. not known.

27. Which of these drugs is made from opium?
    a. heroin
    b. morphine
    c. methadone
    d. codeine
    e. all of the above

28. Narcotics reduce one's
    a. consciousness.
    b. health.
    c. pain.
    d. tolerance.
    e. pleasure.

29. The consequences of heroin use include all of the following except
    a. serious medical complications.
    b. risk of disease transmission through needle sharing.
    c. risk for unborn fetuses.
    d. illegality.
    e. All of the above are consequences.

30. In substitution therapy for heroin, _____ is prescribed to the addict.
    a. methadone
    b. naloxone
    c. morphine
    d. opium
    e. antabuse

31. Compared to heroin, methadone has a _____ pharmacological effect.
    a. shorter
    b. longer
    c. similar
    d. painful
    e. more euphoric

32. Treatment for cocaine dependence may include all of the following except
    a. antidepressants.
    b. extinction of cravings.
    c. extinction of the physical responses to drug cues.
    d. rewarding abstinence to increase motivation.
    e. punishing relapse.

33. Which of the following is not a hallucinogen?
    a. mescaline
    b. psilocybin
    c. opium
    d. LSD
    e. MDMA

34. Hallucinogens are different in which of the following ways from other drugs of abuse?
    a. They seem to lack reinforcing properties.
    b. Users do not develop physical dependence or become addicted.

c. Use seems to reflect a desire for mind-altering rather than euphoriant effects.

d. a and b are true

e. all of the above

35. Which hallucinogen was initially thought to have potential for use in therapy?
   a. mescaline
   b. psilocybin
   c. opium
   d. LSD
   e. MDMA

36. THC is the active ingredient in
   a. cocaine.
   b. LSD.
   c. marijuana.
   d. PCP.
   e. MDMA.

37. The uses of marijuana across cultures have included all of the following except
   a. medicinal.
   b. recreational.
   c. religious.
   d. practical.
   e. All of the above have been uses.

38. Which of the following is most common in marijuana use?
   a. psychological dependence
   b. physical dependence
   c. abstinence syndrome
   d. cross-tolerance
   e. permanent brain damage

39. Surveys have found that smoking has decreased over the past twenty years _____ in the population.
   a. from 90 percent to 76 percent
   b. from 76 percent to 54 percent
   c. from 54 percent to 40 percent
   d. from 40 percent to 27 percent
   e. from 27 percent to 16 percent

40. The active ingredient in tobacco is
   a. endorphin.
   b. nicotine.
   c. PCP.
   d. tar.
   e. THC.

41. Tobacco use shows
   a. withdrawal.
   b. tolerance.
   c. dependence.

   d. both a and b.
   e. all of the above.

42. Which of these is not a major consequence of smoking?
   a. cancer
   b. coronary heart disease
   c. emphysema
   d. hypertension
   e. all of these are major consequences

43. Which theory of nicotine dependence stresses improving performance?
   a. coping model
   b. functional model
   c. positive reinforcement
   d. social factors
   e. none of the above

44. Which technique has shown some success in lowering relapse in nicotine addiction?
   a. hypnosis
   b. nicotine replacement
   c. group counseling
   d. behavior therapy
   e. physician advice

45. Sedative-hypnotic drugs are similar to which of the following in their central nervous system effects?
   a. alcohol
   b. narcotics
   c. stimulants
   d. hallucinogens
   e. marijuana

46. Benzodiazepines seem to affect the _____ neurotransmitter system most significantly.
   a. acetylcholine
   b. dopamine
   c. GABA
   d. norepinephrine
   e. serotonin

Answer Key for Sample Exam

1.	e	(p. 513)	8.	a	(p. 520)
2.	e	(p. 514)	9.	b	(p. 520)
3.	b	(p. 514)	10.	e	(p. 519)
4.	a	(p. 517)	11.	e	(p. 523)
5.	b	(p. 518)	12.	e	(p. 522)
6.	c	(p. 518)	13.	a	(p. 522)
7.	d	(p. 518)	14.	c	(p. 518)

15.	d	(p. 529)	23.	e	(p. 535)	31.	b	(p. 548)	39.	d	(p. 557)
16.	c	(p. 531)	24.	a	(p. 539)	32.	e	(p. 540)	40.	b	(p. 557)
17.	c	(p. 532)	25.	d	(p. 540)	33.	c	(p. 550)	41.	e	(p. 558)
18.	e	(p. 535)	26.	c	(p. 539)	34.	e	(p. 552)	42.	e	(p. 561)
19.	a	(p. 526)	27.	e	(p. 542)	35.	e	(p. 553)	43.	b	(p. 560)
20.	a	(p. 527)	28.	c	(p. 543)	36.	c	(p. 554)	44.	b	(p. 561)
21.	c	(p. 532)	29.	a	(p. 549)	37.	e	(p. 554)	45.	a	(p. 562)
22.	e	(p. 534)	30.	a	(p. 549)	38.	a	(p. 556)	46.	c	(p. 563)

SELF-TEST

1. _____ is the leading health problem in the United States today.

2. The modern view that the addict is a victim needing treatment is called the _____ model of drug addiction.

3. The DSM-IV diagnoses of dependence and abuse each require that there be a _____ pattern of use leading to clinically significant _____ or _____.

4. The DSM-IV criteria for substance dependence also include _____, _____, and _____.

5. The DSM-IV criteria for substance abuse do not include _____ or _____.

6. Factors that determine the effectiveness and potency of drugs include _____, _____, _____, _____, and _____.

7. Although evidence does not support the existence of an "addictive personality," there is a comorbidity of _____ with substance abuse.

8. Common to all drugs that produce dependence are _____, _____, and _____.

9. The brain area thought to mediate the rewarding properties of drugs is the _____.

10. According to the opponent-process model of addiction, _____ corresponds to the dose and duration of the drug, and is followed and opposed by _____, which grows in strength with _____.

11. Reminders of drugs may elicit _____.

12. Endogenous morphine, also called _____, is chemically similar to _____.

13. _____ may have a genetic predisposition.

14. The most commonly used psychoactive substance is _____.

15. According to the tension reduction hypothesis, people should drink _____ stressful situations.

16. Alcohol _____ central nervous system activity.

17. The severe form of alcohol withdrawal is called _____.

18. The best-known self-help group for alcoholism is _____.

19. The original source of narcotics was the _____.

20. The most frequently abused narcotic is _____.

21. There are _____ medical complications associated with narcotic use and withdrawal.

22. The two major treatments for opiate dependence are _____ and _____.

23. Two examples of stimulants are _____ and _____.

24. The exception to declining drug use in recent years is _____.

25. Stimulants work by blocking the reuptake of _____.

26. Withdrawal from stimulants resembles _____.

27. Treatments for cocaine addiction include _____ during the withdrawal phase, _____ therapy to increase motivation, and _____ of the craving and physical response elicited by the drug to prevent relapse.

28. Coffee, tea, soft drinks, cigarettes, and chocolate all have _____ properties.

29. _____ cause perceptual changes and hallucinations.

30. The hallucinogens include _____, _____, _____, _____, and _____.

31. The active ingredient in marijuana is _____.

32. Marijuana appears not to have a Process B because of the _____ of Process A.

33. Episodes that resemble intoxication that occur months after the discontinuation of drug use are _____.

34. Tobacco was first used by _____.

35. The addicting ingredient in tobacco is _____.

36. About _____ people die prematurely every year in the United States from smoking.

37. Smoking is medically harmful mainly because it leads to _____, _____, and _____.

38. Among those who quit smoking, as many as _____ resume within three months.

Answer Key for Self-Test

1. Substance abuse
2. medical
3. maladaptive; impairment; distress
4. loss of control over use; continued use despite consequences; compulsion to use the drug
5. physical dependence; compulsive use
6. route of administration; lipid solubility; blood-brain barrier; drug-receptor-neurotransmitter interactions; adaptation
7. antisocial personality disorder
8. affective pleasure; affective tolerance; affective withdrawal
9. nucleus accumbens
10. Process A; Process B; repeated drug use
11. conditioned withdrawal
12. endorphin; narcotics
13. Alcoholism
14. alcohol
15. before or during
16. depresses
17. delirium tremens
18. Alcoholics Anonymous

19. poppy
20. heroin
21. few
22. substitution; abstinence
23. cocaine; amphetamine
24. cocaine
25. dopamine
26. depression
27. antidepressants; behavioral; extinction
28. stimulant
29. Hallucinogens
30. LSD; mescaline; psilocybin, PCP, MDMA/Ecstasy
31. THC
32. long duration
33. flashbacks
34. Native Americans
35. nicotine
36. 350,000
37. coronary heart disease; cancer; emphysema
38. 70%

MATCHING ITEMS

_____ 1.   marijuana

_____ 2.   tolerance

_____ 3.   alcohol

_____ 4.   stimulant

_____ 5.   affective contrast

_____ 6.   opiate

_____ 7.   substance abuse

_____ 8.   hallucinogen

_____ 9.   sedative-hypnotic

_____ 10. nicotine

A.   decreased response to a drug following prior repeated exposure to it

B.   observable physical signs upon cessation of use of many drugs

C.   need for drug for normal functioning; withdrawal syndrome upon cessation of use

D.   intravenous injection

E.   normally inhibited behaviors released by some drug use

F.   delirium tremens

G.   narcotic

H.   cancer

I.   THC

J.   subjective experience of processes A and B in the opponent-process model

_____ 11. physical dependence

_____ 12. mainlining

_____ 13. disinhibition

_____ 14. withdrawal syndrome

K. mescaline

L. maladaptive, harmful pattern of drug use

M. a "downer"

N. cocaine

Answer Key for Matching Items

1.	I	8.	K
2.	A	9.	M
3.	F	10.	H
4.	N	11.	C
5.	J	12.	D
6.	G	13.	E
7.	L	14.	B

SHORT-ANSWER QUESTIONS

1. Discuss how cultural and historical factors affect perceptions (both the public's and government's) of drug use and abuse. Use specific examples from each of the general categories presented in the book (i.e., alcohol, stimulants, opiates, hallucinogens, marijuana, nicotine, and sedatives).

2. Define substance abuse and substance dependence. Give examples of behaviors that would reflect the criteria.

3. Describe each of the five factors discussed in the text that determine the effectiveness and potency of drugs.

4. What are the central features of the medical/biological, personality/physiological, conditioning/learning, opponent-process, and positive reinforcement theories of drug dependence?

5. Briefly describe the effects and characteristics of tolerance and/or dependence for each of the general drug categories presented in the book (i.e., alcohol, stimulants, opiates, hallucinogens, marijuana, nicotine, and sedatives).

6. Briefly describe the underlying mechanisms of action of each of the general drug categories presented in the book (i.e., alcohol, stimulants, opiates, hallucinogens, marijuana, nicotine, and sedatives).

7. Briefly describe the treatments used for each of the general drug categories presented in the book (i.e., alcohol, stimulants, opiates, hallucinogens, marijuana, nicotine, and sedatives).

8. What factors are thought to play a role in the etiology of alcoholism?

TYING IT TOGETHER

Chapter 2 makes the important point that abnormality must be placed within its cultural and historical context. This idea is important in understanding disorders of substance abuse. Not too long ago, all drug use was regarded as drug abuse, but in the 1960s and 1970s America became very much a drug-using society. Now the pendulum is swinging back, although tobacco and alcohol remain billion-dollar industries. Illicit drug use in some segments of our society is distressingly high. News stories about sports and politics are as apt to mention drug abuse as not. Drug treatment and rehabilitation are not as successful as desired (Chapter 19).

Drug abuse involves the body in important ways, and an understanding of drug effects must be based on an understanding of brain structure and function (Chapter 17). Nevertheless, the biomedical model (Chapter 3) is not the full answer to drug disorders. The recommendation by existential psychologists (Chapter

4) that our actions reflect willful choice must be incorporated into our explanations and treatments of drug abuse. And so must the fact that the behaviors associated with drug abuse reflect the prevailing rewards and punishments in one's environment, as well as people's beliefs about drugs (Chapter 5).

Other disorders may give rise to drug abuse, as individuals attempt to self-medicate. For instance, the lower rate of depression among men than women (Chapter 11) may reflect the greater rate of substance abuse found among men, who may be trading one problem (depression) for another (drug abuse). The fear and anxiety disorders (Chapter 8) may also lead to drug abuse as people attempt to allay their feelings of trepidation.

At the same time, drug abuse may lead to other disorders. Nicotine and alcohol may ex-

acerbate psychosomatic disorders like peptic ulcers and hypertension (Chapter 10) and such neurological disorders as amnesia (Chapter 17). Sexual dysfunctions (Chapter 13) may result from drug abuse, as may depression (Chapter 11) and a host of neurological problems (Chapter 17). Drug abuse weakens the body's immune system overall (Chapter 10), putting the abuser at risk for the spectrum of infectious diseases.

Prolonged use of stimulants like amphetamines and cocaine may result in hallucinations, delusions, and other schizophrenic-like symptoms (Chapter 12). Indeed, information about drug-induced psychoses has helped in the development of theories about the role of neurotransmitters in schizophrenia (Chapter 3).

FURTHER READINGS

Beecher, E. M. (1972). *Licit and illicit drugs.* Mount Vernon, NY: Consumers Union.

Bernstein, D. A., & Glasgow, R. E. (1979). Smoking. In O. F. Pomerleau & J. P. Brady (Eds.), *Behavioral medicine: Theory and practice.* Baltimore: Williams & Wilkins.

Desmond, E. W. (1987). Out in the open: Changing attributes and new research give fresh hope to alcoholics. *Time,* November 30, pp. 80–90.

Huxley, A. (1954). *The doors of perception* and *Heaven and hell.* New York: Harper &

Row.

Marlatt, G. A. (1983). The controlled-drinking controversy: A commentary. *American Psychologist, 38,* 1097–1110.

Vaillant, G. E. (1983). *The natural history of alcoholism.* Cambridge, MA: Harvard University Press.

Zimberg, S., Wallace, J., & Blume, S. B. (Eds.) (1985). *Practical approaches to alcoholism psychotherapy* (2nd ed.). New York: Plenum.

TERM-PAPER TOPICS

1. Survey recent evidence that alcoholism has a genetic predisposition. What possible mechanisms for this predisposition have been suggested? What are the treatment implications of this evidence? What, if anything, do they say about the role of individual responsibility in drug abuse?

2. Why are some drugs legal and other drugs illegal? Trace the history of drug legislation in this country. How does it reflect political considerations? (See Thomas Szasz's (1992), *Our right to drugs—The case for a free market,* for a discussion of these issues from a civil libertarian point of view.)

3. Compare and contrast the United States and England with regard to treatment of narcotics addicts. Which approach seems preferable?

4. What patterns in drug use and drug abuse seem likely to continue into the future? Be sure to take into account the AIDS epidemic. Describe patterns of drug use and drug abuse in the year 2050.

EXERCISES

Exercise One—Psychoactive Drugs and Opponent Processes

In this exercise, you will investigate some of the behavioral effects of two common psychoactive drugs: caffeine and chocolate. Can you detect the operation of Process A and Process B hypothesized by the opponent-process model of addiction?

If it does not offend you to do so, and if it is not medically inadvisable, use yourself as a subject in this drug study. While you may not think of caffeine and chocolate as psychoactive drugs, they satisfy all the criteria specified in the text. Drink three cups of strong coffee (not instant) within twenty minutes. Or eat three large chocolate bars in the same amount of time.

Pay attention to how your respond to these rather large does of drugs. What happens to your attention? Your energy level? Your mood? Your physical coordination? As time passes, what sorts of changes do you experience? Do you crave more coffee or chocolate?

If you are an "experienced" drug user, compare your experiences with someone who is not. Or vice versa. Does the opponent-process model describe the differences between the two of you?

Note: *Do not make yourself ill with this exercise!* Some people have an inordinate capacity for coffee or chocolate, probably because of habituation. But if you are a teetotaler, so to speak, do not get carried away.

Exercise Two—Addiction and Relapse

As satisfying as the opponent-process theory is in explaining the development and ongoing maintenance and reinforcement of addiction, it does not directly address the question of the longterm difficulties of abstention for the addict. Once the withdrawal symptoms have subsided and environmentally cued responses have been extinguished (in other words, no Process B is present), what causes the recovering addict to relapse? Why is it so difficult to maintain sobriety? What explanations might a cognitive, behavioral, or psychodynamic psychologist give?

Exercise Three—To Be or Not to Be an Addict

Other than a naturally occurring shortage or excess of neurotransmitters which might be self-medicated by the drug abuser, what mechanisms do you think might explain why some users become addicts and other do not? Does your theory borrow from cognitive, behavioral, and psychodynamic perspectives? What predictions could be made by your theory? How might they be tested? What would be the implications for treatment?

Exercise Four—Alcoholics Anonymous

The purpose of this exercise is to learn about Alcoholics Anonymous firsthand.

Contact a local AA group and arrange a classroom presentation by some of the members. Ask them to tell their stories, and to explain how AA helps them not to drink.

Bill W. (1976). *Alcoholics Anonymous: The story of how many thousands of men and women have recovered from alcoholism*

(3rd ed.). New York: Alcoholics Anonymous World Services.

Exercise Five—In Your Experience

If you are, or have been, a regular smoker, or if you have regularly used, abused, or been dependent on some other psychoactive drug (including alcohol, caffeine, or chocolate), what aspects of this chapter ring most true or false in your experience? If you have tried to quit using a substance (successfully or not) what worked for you and what did not? What undermined your efforts? How would these details fit into the described theories (e.g., opponent-process theory)? How do they contradict what you have read?

Exercise Six—On Any Given Sunday: Drugs and Sports

You will use the knowledge you have gained from the text to evaluate statements made in the sports pages about drug use and drug abuse.

Read your local sports pages, *Sports Illustrated,* or the *Sporting News.* Chances are that there will be a number of claims and counterclaims about drugs. Based on what you have learned, which claims make sense? Which claims make no sense? Why do some professional athletes use drugs? How may they be encouraged to stop using drugs? Is drug abuse by celebrities more prevalent than drug abuse by the general population? Numbers aside, how is it different?

CHAPTER 15

Personality Disorders

CHAPTER OVERVIEW

Personality disorders are pervasive and inflexible ways of behaving that result in social and/or occupational maladjustment. This chapter discusses the various personality disorders described in DSM-IV.

The best understood of these disorders is the antisocial personality disorder. Also termed *psychopathy* or *sociopathy*, this disorder is characterized by a rapacious attitude toward others manifested in lying, stealing, cheating, and worse. Antisocial personality is not the same thing as criminality, but it may involve considerable criminal activity. Research suggests that sociopaths are physiologically underaroused and deficient at avoidance learning. This may account for their failure to learn from mistakes. There may be a genetic basis to this underarousal.

The other personality disorders are not as well understood, and controversy exists over whether individuals indeed have the pervasive traits assumed by their descriptions: (a) para-noid personality disorder (characterized by inordinate suspicion and distrust); (b) histrionic personality disorder (marked by overdramatic emotional displays); (c) narcissistic personality disorder (characterized by outlandish sense of self-importance); (d) avoidant personality disorder (distinguished by social withdrawal combining hypersensitivity to rejection and desire for acceptance); (e) dependent personality disorder (characterized by excessive reliance on others to make important decisions for the self); (f) obsessive-compulsive personality disorder (marked by inappropriate preoccupation with details); (g) schizoid personality disorder (marked by deficiency in the ability to form social relationships); (h) schizotypal personality dis-order (characterized by odd behavior); and (i) borderline personality disorder (distinguished by unstable relationships, moods, and impulsive or self-destructive behaviors).

ESSENTIAL TERMS

antisocial personality disorder (sociopathy; psychopathy)
: personality disorder characterized by a rapacious attitude toward others: chronic insensitivity and indifference to the rights of others marked by lying, stealing, and/or cheating (p. 570)

avoidant personality disorder
: personality disorder characterized by turning away: social withdrawal combining hypersensitivity to rejection with a desire for acceptance and affection (p. 588)

borderline personality disorder — personality disorder characterized by instability in a variety of areas: interpersonal relationships, behavior, mood, and/or self-image (p. 591)

criminal — individual apprehended and convicted of a crime; not necessarily the same as an antisocial personality (p. 570)

dependent personality disorder — personality disorder in which an individual habitually allows others to make major decisions, to initiate important actions, and to assume responsibility for significant areas of his or her life (p. 588)

depersonalization — sense of estrangement from the self and the environment (p. 591)

electroencephalogram (EEG) — psychophysiological assessment device that measures electrical activity of the brain (p. 582)

galvanic skin response (GSR) — psychophysiological assessment device that measures moisture on the skin as a gauge of anxiety (p. 578)

histrionic personality disorder — personality disorder characterized by a long history of calling attention to oneself and of emotional displays in response to insignificant events (p. 586)

idea of reference — belief that one is especially noticed by others (p. 591)

machoism — term for histrionic personality disorder among males (p. 586)

moral insanity — nineteenth-century term for antisocial personality disorder, thought then to be a disorder of will (p. 571)

narcissistic personality disorder — personality disorder in which an individual has an outlandish sense of self-importance, shown by self-absorption, self-aggrandizing fantasies, and exhibitionistic needs for constant admiration (p. 587)

obsessive-compulsive personality disorder — personality disorder in which the individual consistently and pervasively strives for perfection (p. 589)

paranoid personality disorder — personality disorder in which an individual is always suspicious of others' motives (pp. 569, 585)

personality disorder — mental disorder in which an individual's traits are inflexible and a source of social and occupational maladjustment (p. 569)

schizoid personality disorder — personality disorder characterized by habitual inability to form social relationships, reflected in an absence of desire for social involvements, indifference to praise and criticism, insensitivity to feelings of others, and/or lack of social skill (p. 590)

schizotypal personality disorder — personality disorder involving long-standing oddities in thinking, perceiving, communicating, and behaving (p. 590)

trait — habitual and characteristic tendency to perceive and respond to the environment (pp. 570, 594)

XYY syndrome

chromosomal disorder in which a male has an extra male (Y) chromosome, thought to predispose criminal behavior, although the mechanism is not clear (p. 581)

CENTRAL CONCEPTUAL ISSUES

Personality disorders.   A personality disorder is characterized by a longstanding, inflexible approach to living. Where normal persons will adapt their behavior to suit life's demands and their various relationships, and to behave appropriately in social and work situations, an individual with a personality disorder will evince characteristic maladaptive behaviors across many situations which ultimately lead to difficulties at work and in forming and maintaining social relationships. The particular nature of the inflexible behaviors (i.e., traits) defines the particular personality disorder. Perhaps precisely because normal persons are flexible and adaptable in their approach to living, the very concept of traits—which are defined as characteristic behavior across situations—has been challenged. However, someone with a personality disorder demonstrates just this quality.

Those with personality disorders are usually socially defined. Indeed, they often come to treatment prompted by frustration about their interpersonal failures, or at the behest of those they are making unhappy. Personality disorders are believed to arise when stages of interpersonal development are unsuccessfully navigated, particularly those concerning attachment. It stands to reason, if one is raised in a dysfunctional family, that one learns destructive lessons about oneself and the social world. Because the traits characteristic of a particular disorder have developed early and over time, becoming a central aspect of the personality structure, they are notoriously difficult to treat.

Antisocial personality disorder: Antisocial personality disorder provides an important example of the ways in which physiological, behavioral, and social factors may combine to create and define abnormal behavior. It also raises numerous additional questions about human psychology. The current view holds that genetic and peri-natal biological influences may predispose an individual to sociopathy. These factors may include chronic underarousal; abnormalities in the limbic system of the brain which is the center of emotion and motivation (such bursts—"spikes"—in brain wave activity are associated with impulsive, aggressive behavior); and cortical immaturity (as indicated by slow brain wave patterns that are characteristic of children). It is believed that these physiological differences can lead to lack of control over bursts of emotion, sub-normal levels of fear, and stimulation-seeking behaviors. Born into a culture which has developed customs of childrearing, behavior, rewards, and sanctions geared to raising normal children, these kids will have a more difficult time controlling their behavior, and will be significantly less influenced by typical rewards and punishments. Thus, instrumental learning will be less successful at controlling behavior and structuring the developing personality. Indeed, such children might even seek out punishment and engage in forbidden behaviors as a way of attracting the stimulation they lack. Add to this the modeling of sociopathic, criminal, or emotionally and behaviorally maladjusted parents, and the influence of the home environment becomes significant. Moreover, a child manifesting these behaviors will have trouble in school and difficulty making and keeping friends resulting in fewer opportunities for reward for good behavior and more dismal future prospects. Sociopaths are not generally psychotic, and not necessarily unintelligent—their behavior simply clashes with social norms. When these behaviors are criminal, they harm others in society and society in turn takes notice. Thus the vast majority of those diagnosed as sociopaths are those with long criminal records—hence the "rap sheet" diagnosis.

This analysis raises as many questions as it answers. Is the sociopath just like any of us with the veneer of civilization provided by behavioral conditioning removed, or is there a difference in kind? What are we to make of the shallow depth of emotion characteristic of antisocial personality disorder? The strongest social influence mitigating against biological predisposition is a strong and nurturing mother. How does this influence the emotional development, conscience, and impulse control of the potential psychopath? What are the psychological mechanisms involved? And finally, why is antisocial personality disorder seen so much more frequently in men than in women? Is it cultural, biological, a combination, or an artifact of how we diagnose?

SAMPLE EXAM

1. Which of these does not belong?
   a. paranoid personality disorder
   b. antisocial personality disorder
   c. sociopathy
   d. psychopathy
   e. moral insanity

2. Antisocial personality disorders involve all of the following except
   a. unconventionality.
   b. observer discomfort.
   c. suffering.
   d. irrationality.
   e. violations of moral and ideal standards.

3. Which of these statements is true?
   a. Criminal behavior is a necessary condition for antisocial personality disorder.
   b. Criminal behavior is a sufficient condition for antisocial personality disorder.
   c. Antisocial personality disorder is a necessary condition for criminal behavior.
   d. Antisocial personality disorder is a sufficient condition for criminal behavior.
   e. None of the above.

4. Individuals with personality disorders
   a. are different in degree from individuals without personality disorders.
   b. are different in kind from individuals without personality disorders.
   c. have too much flexibility in their characteristic approach to work and relationships.
   d. have too little flexibility in their characteristic approach to work and relationships.
   e. are essentially the same as individuals without personality disorders.

5. A diagnosis of antisocial personality disorder is based on all of the following criteria except
   a. antisocial behavior.
   b. long-standing pattern.
   c. origin in early adulthood.
   d. manifestation in a variety of domains.
   e. all of the above are criteria

6. Sociopaths seem to lack
   a. motives for crimes.
   b. guilt over crimes.
   c. concern for others.
   d. deep emotions.
   e. all of the above.

7. Suppose you were told that you were to meet someone for lunch who had an antisocial personality disorder. You would expect this individual to be
   a. a male.
   b. married.

c. emotionally shallow.
d. dependable.
e. all of the above.

8. Current thought on the origins of sociopathy emphasizes all of the following except
    a. parental absence.
    b. learning deficits.
    c. genetics.
    d. underarousal.
    e. disharmonious home environment.

9. Which of these statements is true?
    a. Punishment for juvenile offenses leads to later offenses.
    b. Moderate punishment for juvenile offenses leads to later offenses.
    c. Severe punishment for juvenile offenses leads to later offenses.
    d. No punishment for juvenile offenses leads to fewer later offenses.
    e. None of the above.

10. Psychopaths seem to have difficulty with
    a. Pavlovian conditioning.
    b. operant conditioning.
    c. escape responding.
    d. avoidance responding.
    e. vicarious conditioning.

11. Underlying the learning deficits of psychopaths may be
    a. overarousal.
    b. underarousal.
    c. low intelligence.
    d. depression.
    e. anxiety.

12. Suppose you were told that a psychopath had just moved next door. You would be *least* wary of
    a. burglary.
    b. forgery.
    c. assault.
    d. con games.
    e. mail fraud.

13. Sociopaths seem to be sensitive to
    a. physical punishment.
    b. tangible punishment.
    c. social punishment.
    d. verbal punishment.
    e. none of the above.

14. Twin and adoption studies indicate that

a. criminality is determined by opportunity.
b. criminality may be partly genetic and partly environmental.
c. criminality is totally genetic.
d. criminality is totally environmental.
d. the relationship of genetics and environment to criminality is unclear.

15. Antisocial personality disorder is diagnosed up to four times more often in men than women. Current evidence suggests that this may be due to
    a. modeling by fathers.
    b. hormone differences between the sexes.
    c. a true base-rate difference in the prevalence of the disorder.
    d. genetic differences between the sexes.
    e. a sexual bias in diagnosticians.

16. The XYY chromosome has been linked to an increase in all of the following except
    a. violent crime.
    b. property crime.
    c. height.
    d. apprehension and conviction for crime.
    e. intelligence.

17. Findings of EEG abnormalities such as slow brain wave patterns and positive spiking in antisocial personality disorder suggest
    a. cortical immaturity.
    b. antisocial behavior should decline with age.
    c. possible limbic system dysfunction.
    d. poor avoidance learning may be due to faulty physiology.
    e. all of the above.

18. Abnormal EEG patterns among psychopaths are consistent with the
    a. biomedical model.
    b. psychodynamic model.
    c. behavioral model.
    d. cognitive model.
    e. existential model.

19. Suppose you met someone who was inordinately distrustful and suspicious. If this individual had a personality disorder, it would be
    a. paranoid personality disorder.
    b. schizoid personality disorder.

c. schizotypal personality disorder.
d. histrionic personality disorder.
e. narcissistic personality disorder.

20. Suppose you met someone who was inordinately emotional and dramatic. If this individual had a personality disorder, it would be
a. paranoid personality disorder.
b. schizoid personality disorder.
c. schizotypal personality disorder.
d. histrionic personality disorder.
e. narcissistic personality disorder.

21. Suppose you met someone who was inordinately preoccupied with the self. If this individual had a personality disorder, it would be
a. narcissistic personality disorder.
b. avoidant personality disorder.
c. dependent personality disorder.
d. obsessive-compulsive personality disorder.
e. antisocial personality disorder.

22. Suppose you met someone who was inordinately sensitive to rejection. If this individual had a personality disorder, it would be
a. narcissistic personality disorder.
b. avoidant personality disorder.
c. dependent personality disorder.
d. obsessive-compulsive personality disorder.
e. antisocial personality disorder.

23. Suppose you met someone who was inordinately unable to assume responsibility. If this individual had a personality disorder, it would be
a. narcissistic personality disorder.
b. avoidant personality disorder.
c. dependent personality disorder.
d. obsessive-compulsive personality disorder.
e. borderline personality disorder.

24. Suppose you met someone who was inordinately preoccupied with trivial details. If this individual had a personality disorder, it would be
a. narcissistic personality disorder.
b. avoidant personality disorder.
c. dependent personality disorder.

d. obsessive-compulsive personality disorder.
e. borderline personality disorder.

25. Suppose you met someone who was inordinately strange. If this individual had a personality disorder, it would be
a. paranoid personality disorder.
b. schizoid personality disorder.
c. schizotypal personality disorder.
d. histrionic personality disorder.

26. Suppose you met someone who was inordinately estranged from other people. If this individual had a personality disorder, it would be
a. paranoid personality disorder.
b. schizoid personality disorder.
c. schizotypal personality disorder.
d. histrionic personality disorder.

27. The most common personality disorder diagnosis is
a. avoidant.
b. borderline.
c. dependent.
d. narcissistic.
e. paranoid.

28. You expect that someone with a borderline personality disorder would be
a. labile.
b. weird.
c. emotionally flat.
d. withdrawn.
e. stable.

29. Self-theorists trace borderline personality disorder to difficulties experienced during
a. infancy.
b. childhood.
c. early adolescence.
d. late adolescence.
e. adulthood.

30. Problems in diagnosing personality disorders may arise from
a. the context of the behavior being overlooked.
b. misinterpretation of behaviors.
c. distortions in memory of longstanding behaviors.
d. lack of cross-situational consistency.
e. all of the above.

Answer Key for Sample Exam

1.	a	(p. 570)	9.	c	(p. 575)	17.	e	(p. 582)	24. d (p. 589)
2.	c	(p. 570)	10.	d	(p. 576)	18.	a	(p. 582)	25. c (p. 590)
3.	e	(p. 572)	11.	b	(p. 577)	19.	a	(p. 585)	26. b (p. 590)
4.	a, d	(p. 569)	12.	c	(p. 577)	20.	d	(p. 586)	27. b (p. 591)
5.	c	(p. 572)	13.	b	(p. 577)	21.	a	(p. 587)	28. a (p. 591)
6.	e	(p. 573)	14.	b	(p. 579)	22.	b	(p. 588)	29. b (p. 592)
7.	a, c	(p. 573)	15.	e	(p. 570)	23.	c	(p. 588)	30. e (p. 594)
8.	a	(p. 574)	16.	a, c	(p. 581)				

SELF-TEST

1. When an individual's _____ ways of perceiving and thinking are _____ and a source of _____, the person has a personality disorder.

2. The best known personality disorder is the _____ personality disorder, also known as _____ or _____.

3. Antisocial personality disorders are marked by _____ toward others.

4. _____ are not necessarily individuals with antisocial personality disorders.

5. DSM-IV criteria for antisocial personality disorder are threefold. First, the antisocial behavior must be _____; second, it must be evident before age _____; and third, it must be evident in at least _____ classes of behavior.

6. The criminal activities of psychopathic individuals do not _____.

7. Psychopathic individuals seem not to experience _____ as do other individuals.

8. Research shows that antisocial personality disorder is associated with a _____ childhood.

9. _____ punishment may dissuade a juvenile from future criminal activities.

10. Psychopaths are deficient at _____ learning, presumably because they are chronically _____.

11. Twin studies show that criminality may be _____, but the role of the should be underscored.

12. Adoption studies show that criminality may be _____.

13. Men with the _____ chromosome pattern have been thought to be prone to _____ crimes. Research suggests that this hypothesis is _____.

14. Sociopaths show abnormal _____ patterns, implying _____ immaturity.

15. Individuals who are chronically suspicious and distrustful may have a _____ personality disorder.

16. Individuals who habitually draw attention to themselves through inappropriate emotional displays may have a _____ personality disorder.

17. An outlandish sense of _____ is the hallmark of a narcissistic personality disorder.

18. Individuals with an avoidant personality disorder combine _____ to rejection with a desire for _____.

19. When a person habitually allows others to make the important decisions, this person may have a _____ personality disorder.

20. An inappropriate preoccupation with insignificant details characterizes the _____ personality disorder.

21. If an individual has a deficiency in the ability to form _____, he or she may have a schizoid personality disorder.

22. An individual who has a long history of odd behavior may have a _____ personality disorder, which is thought to predispose _____.

23. Markedly unstable individuals may be those with _____ personality disorders.

24. The entire idea of personality disorders may be criticized by doubting the assumption that people have pervasive _____.

25. Diagnostic reliability for the personality disorders is typically _____, except for _____ personality disorders.

Answer Key for Self-Test

1. characteristic; inflexible; maladjustment
2. antisocial; psychopathy; sociopathy
3. indifference
4. Criminals
5. long-standing; fifteen; three
6. make sense
7. emotions
8. difficult
9. Moderate
10. avoidance; underaroused
11. inherited; environment
12. inherited
13. XYY; violent; false
14. EEG; brain
15. paranoid
16. histrionic
17. self-importance
18. hypersensitivity; acceptance
19. dependent
20. obsessive-compulsive
21. relationships
22. schizotypal; schizophrenia
23. borderline
24. traits
25. poor; antisocial

MATCHING ITEMS

_____	1.	borderline personality disorder	A.	overprotective parenting
_____	2.	paranoid personality disorder	B.	superstitiousness
_____	3.	dependent personality disorder	C.	suspiciousness
_____	4.	schizoid personality disorder	D.	idealization and devaluation
_____	5.	avoidant personality disorder	E.	entitlement
_____	6.	schizotypal personality disorder	F.	seclusive and introverted
_____	7.	obsessive-compulsive personality disorder	G.	avoidance learning
_____	8.	histrionic personality disorder	H.	perfectionism
_____	9.	low arousal	I.	emotional poverty
_____	10.	narcissistic personality disorder	J.	flirtatious
_____	11.	antisocial personality disorder	K.	inflexible traits
_____	12.	personality disorders	L.	social phobia

Answer Key for Matching Items

1.	D	7.	H
2.	C	8.	J
3.	A	9.	G
4.	F	10.	E
5.	L	11.	I
6.	B	12.	K

SHORT-ANSWER QUESTIONS

1. Describe the similarities and differences between normal personality traits and full-blown personality disorders.

2. What three general characteristics were described by Cleckley as central to the sociopath's personality?

3. Summarize the four major theories of the origin of antisocial personality disorder, and the evidence supporting each.

4. Think about the ten personality disorders described in the text. If you were to clus-ter them into three groups, what would they be? What criteria would you use and why?

TYING IT TOGETHER

According to Chapter 1, the identification of abnormality involves a social judgment. This is nowhere better illustrated than in the case of personality disorders, which involves not simply disrupted "personality" but also disrupted relationships with other people. In one way or another, each personality disorder results in discomfort among observers (see Chapter 1). Treatments for personality disorders that do not take into account their inherently social nature are apt not to be successful (Chapter 19).

The best understood personality disorder—the antisocial personality—seems to be brought about by abnormally low levels of anxiety (see Chapters 8 and 9), resulting in deficiencies in avoidance learning (Chapter 5). Perhaps the capacity to experience fear and anxiety (Chapter 8) is necessary for the superego to develop (Chapter 4). Various research strategies have converged to provide our understanding of the antisocial personality (Chapter 6), and its explanation partakes of the several models of abnormality (Chapters 3–5).

Doubts have been raised about the existence of the other personality disorders. These disorders assume the existence of pervasive and stable traits, but research does not strongly support such an assumption. Contemporary personality psychology is increasingly attentive to the situational determinants of behavior. Thus, "personality" may be better described by the behavioral model (Chapter 4), and cross-situational regularities in behavior may be less common than has been presumed. Accordingly, diagnosis of personality disorders (Chapter 7) is not perfectly reliable or valid.

It has often been assumed that personality disorders predispose more serious psychopathologies when stress is encountered. Thus, individuals with obsessive-compulsive personality disorders are thought to be at risk for obsessive-compulsive disorders (Chapter 9), those with dependent personality disorders are thought to be at risk for depression (Chapter 11), those with schizotypal disorders are thought to be at risk for schizophrenia (Chapter 12), and so on. Research has not consistently supported this assumption, perhaps because of the aforementioned difficulties in diagnosing personality disorders.

The borderline personality disorder has an interesting history. Diagnostic schemes prior to DSM-III held that an individual was either neurotic (Chapter 8) or psychotic (Chapter 12). However, the line between the two is fuzzy, and individuals with both neurotic and psychotic manifestations had to be classified somewhere. Hence, the borderline-personality-disorder category was proposed for individuals who fall at the "border" of neurosis and psychosis. You will remember, however, that this disorder no longer has this meaning. At the present, it refers to individuals with markedly unstable lives.

FURTHER READINGS

Akhtar, S., & Thomson, J. A. (1982). Overview: Narcissistic personality disorder. *American Journal of Psychiatry, 139*:1, 12–20.

Beck, A. T., & Freeman, A. (1990). *Cognitive therapy of personality disorders.* New York: Guilford Press.

Cameron, N., & Rychlak, J. (1985). *Personality development and psychopathology: A dynamic approach.* Boston: Houghton Mifflin.

Clarkin, J. F., Widiger, T. A., Frances, A., Hurt, S. W., & Gilmore, M. (1983). Prototypic typology and the borderline personality disorder. *Journal of Abnormal Psychology, 93*, 263–275.

Cleckley, H. (1976). *The mask of sanity* (5th ed.). St. Louis: Mosby.

Gunderson, J. G. (1984). *Borderline personality disorders.* Washington, DC: American Psychiatric Press.

Jarvik, L. F., Klodin, V., & Matsuyama, S. S. (1973). Human aggression and extra Y chromosome: Fact or fantasy? *American Psychologist, 28*, 674–682.

Kendler, K. S, & Gruenberg, A. M. (1981). Genetic relationship between paranoid personality disorder and the "schizophrenic spectrum disorders." *American Journal of Psychiatry, 139*, 1185–1186.

Livesley, W. J. (1986). Trait and behavioral prototypes of personality disorder. *American Journal of Psychiatry, 143*:6, 728–732.

Loehlin, J. C., & Nichols, R. C. (1976). *Heredity, environment, and personality: A study of 850 sets of twins.* Austin: University of Texas.

Mailer, N. (1979). *The executioner's song.* Boston: Little Brown.

Millon, T., & Everly, G. (1985). *Personality and its disorders.* New York: Wiley.

Shapiro, D. (1965). *Neurotic styles.* New York: Basic Books.

Slavney, P. R. (1984). Histrionic personality and antisocial personality: Caricature of stereotypes? *Comprehensive Psychiatry, 25,* 129–141.

Walker, L. (1979). *The battered woman.* New York: Harper & Row.

TERM-PAPER TOPICS

1. In the past, psychologists have proposed that personality disorders set the stage for more serious disorders. What is the evidence for this idea?

2. Evaluate the research linking the XYY chromosome disorder to violence. What is your conclusion about genetics and criminality?

3. What alternative interpretation of the personality disorders is suggested by social learning theory?

4. Describe several additional personality disorders that fit the general definition and seem prevalent in our society. Speculate on their causes.

EXERCISES

Exercise One—Famous Personalities: Disordered or Not?

The purpose of this exercise is to demonstrate the difficulties involved in describing a person's life style in terms of a personality disorder.

Many celebrities seem eccentric. Some celebrities seem to have a personality disorder: a rigid and inflexible way of acting that results in problems for themselves and others. On the other hand, there are alternative ways of interpreting what these people are doing that does not mention personality disorders.

Read a biographical account of an eccentric celebrity. Does the person about whom you have read seem to have a personality disorder? Is there a better way to interpret his or her exaggerated and inflexible behavior? Possible biographies include:

Brodie, F. M. (1981). *Richard Nixon: The shaping of his character.* New York: Norton.

Devaney, J. (1982). *Blood and guts: The true story of General George S. Patton, USA.* New York: Messner.

Hanna, D. (1976). *"Come up and see me sometime": An uncensored biography of Mae West.* New York: Belmont.

Ludwig, E. (1940). *Three portraits: Hitler, Mussolini, Stalin.* New York: AMS Press.

Mailer, N. (1981). *Marilyn.* New York: Grosset & Dunlap.

Stock, N. (1982). *The life of Ezra Pound: An expanded edition.* Berkeley, CA: North Point Press.

Wells, R. (1977). *Vince Lombardi: His life and times.* Canoga Park, CA: Major Books.

Wicker, T. (1969). *JFK and LBJ.* Baltimore: Penguin.

Woodward, B. (1984). *Wired: The short life and fast times of John Belushi.* New York: Pocket Books.

Note: One cannot meaningfully diagnose an individual just from a biography; the best that one can do is to describe the public self presented there. What a celebrity is "really like" remains unknown.

Millon, T., & Everly, G. (1985). *Personality and its disorders*. New York: Wiley.

Exercise Two—Incorrigible Criminals

In this exercise, you will learn from a direct source about chronic criminals and their actions.

Arrange a classroom lecture by a local parole officer, judge, or attorney about incorrigible criminals. Does it make sense to describe some of these criminals as psychopaths? Is any form of punishment or rehabilitation effective?

Exercise Three—The Variability of Personality

The purpose of this exercise is to demonstrate that an individual's "personality" is not static.

Repeat the first part of Exercise One from Chapter 7. That is, ask a group of five or six people who know each other well to describe each member of the group in terms of striking personality traits.

Is there considerable variability in the way a given person is described? What are the implications for diagnosing personality disorders?

Mischel, W. (1968). *Personality and assessment*. New York: Wiley.

CHAPTER 16

Childhood Disorders and Mental Retardation

CHAPTER OVERVIEW

This chapter is concerned with problems suffered by children and adolescents. These problems are more difficult to understand than those of adults since they occur in the context of development and may be situationally specific and transient. Five major types are distinguished: disruptive behavior disorders, emotional disorders, habit and eating disorders, and developmental disorders. These are described in terms of its manifestation, presumed cause, and preferred treatment.

Behavioral disorders involve either aggression, rule breaking, and/or inappropriate attention. Boys are more likely to have these problems, which appear to have genetic and environmental causes. Treatment for the be-havioral disorders is not well developed. Emotional disorders are those in which fear, anxiety, and shyness predominate, and include childhood phobias. They seem similar to anxiety disorders among adults, and behavioral therapies may be promising in their treatment. Habit disorders involve habitual physical behaviors, such as enuresis, stuttering, anorexia nervosa, bulimia, and obesity. In most cases, therapy with behavioral techniques can be helpful. Intellectual disorders are instances of mental retardation, which result either from genetic and environmental influences or from injury and disease. Developmental disorders range from specific learning disabilities to mental retardation to autism.

ESSENTIAL TERMS

amniocentesis	*in utero* technique for detecting Down's syndrome (p. 628)
anorexia	habit disorder characterized by substantial loss of body weight and deliberate restriction of calorie intake (p. 620)
attention-deficit hyperactivity disorder	childhood disorder marked by inpulsivity, inattention, and hyperactivity (p. 602)
autism	pervasive developmental disorder characterized by a child's failure to develop the ability to respond to others (p. 633)

bulimia

habit disorder characterized by alternate gorging with food, and then purging of that food by vomiting, or using laxatives or diuretics (p. 621)

childhood depression

once thought to be unlikely due to developmental immaturity, now recognized but less prevalent than adult depression; family dysfunction is a significant risk factor (p. 615)

childhood sexual abuse

inappropriate sexual interactions with adults; puts children at increased risk for emotional and behavioral disorders both in childhood and as adults (p. 616)

conduct disorder

disorder characterized by aggression and rule breaking (p. 602)

delayed auditory feedback

therapy technique for treatment of stuttering in which the stutterer's speech is played back through earphones with a one-second delay (p. 619)

developmental disorder

childhood disorder involving enormous developmental tardiness (learning disorder, p. 632)) or gross developmental failure (pervasive developmental disorder, p. 633) (p. 624)

disruptive behavior disorder

general class of childhood disorders encompassing attention-deficit hyperactivity disorders, conduct disorders, and oppositional defiant disorders (p. 602)

Down's syndrome

mental retardation caused by chromosomal abnormality and accompanied by almond-shaped and slanted eyes and numerous physical anomalies (also called mongolism) (p. 628)

eating disorders

disorders, including anorexia and bulimia, usually developed in childhood or adolescence, characterized by unusual patterns of eating or weight control (p. 620)

echolalia

tendency to repeat or echo immediately or after a brief period precisely what one has just heard (p. 633)

emotional disorder

childhood disorder in which symptoms of fear, anxiety, inhibition, shyness, and overattachment predominate (p. 611)

enuresis

involuntary voiding of urine at least twice a month for children between five and six, and once a month for those who are older (p. 618)

habit disorder

childhood disorder with a habitual physical component; e.g., stuttering (p. 617)

hyperactivity

gross overactivity of motor behavior accompanied by developmentally inappropriate inattention and impulses (p. 609)

mainstreaming

educational strategy of educating mentally retarded children with other schoolchildren (p. 631)

mental retardation	subaverage intellectual functioning accompanied by deficient adaptive behavior and manifested before age eighteen (p. 624)
oppositional defiant disorder	childhood disorder in which a child is negative, hostile, and defiant (p. 602)
phenylketonuria (PKU)	mental retardation caused by a metabolic disorder in which phenylalanine cannot be digested, resulting in irreversible brain damage (p. 629)
pronominal reversal	tendency to use "I" where "you" is meant, and vice versa (p. 633)
Ritalin	brand name of methylphenidate, an amphetamine used to treat hyperactivity (p. 610)
school phobia	common childhood phobia characterized by refusal to attend school (p. 614)
separation anxiety disorder	childhood disorder centering around fear of separation from parents (p. 611)
shadowing	therapy technique for treatment of stuttering in which the therapist reads from a book while the stutterer repeats the words after they are heard (p. 619)
stuttering	habit disorder involving disturbed speech rhythm, often in pronouncing initial consonants in certain words (p. 619)
syllable-times speech	therapy technique for treatment of stuttering in which stutterers are required to speak in time to a metronome (p. 619)
Tay-Sachs disease	a metabolic disorder that results in fatal mental and physical deterioration before age 6 (p. 629)

CENTRAL CONCEPTUAL ISSUES

Diagnosing childhood disorders.   Diagnosing disorders in children is problematic in several respects. Because children are in process, their development ongoing, it may be difficult to distinguish between significant, potentially long-term problems and temporary lags or deviations. This may prove harder still if the problem behaviors are limited to specific domains, or are only marginally different from expected behaviors. Moreover, children have limited capacities to recognize and communicate their distress, and so it may go unvoiced or be channeled into other behaviors that are less readily recognized or interpreted as symptomatic by observers. Finally, labeling a child with a diagnosis, while helpful and necessary for purposes of intervention and treatment, brings with it the possibility of a number of troublesome secondary consequences, including the potential that a negative or damaged view of self will be incorporated into the developing identity, diagnosis-driven expectations in others, negative expectations about future prospects for self, loss of self-esteem, and the general social stigma of being diagnosed with a psychological condition. Needless to say, diagnosis of children should proceed with caution!

Continuity between childhood and adult disorders.   A number of childhood disorders appear to be juvenile versions of, or precursors to, adult conditions. For example, childhood emotional disorders such as depression and phobia, although sometimes different in specific symptom presentation and content, are close analogs to their adult counterparts. Similarly, children who display the disruptive behaviors that define conduct disorder and attention-deficit hyperactivity disorder are at increased risk for developing adulthood antisocial personality disorder. These worrisome long-term prospects, along with the pressing need to remediate the child's current distress, makes early intervention extremely imperative.

Trauma in childhood.   The disorders of children often reflect aberrations in their developmental environment. Current research suggests that traumatic childhood experiences can have profound, long-term sequelae. Most commonly, ongoing family stress of dysfunction can disrupt normal developmental processes and result in incompletely-resolved attachment, individuation, and separation issues. Many adult personality disorders, such as borderline, narcissistic, or dependent, seem to be related to such early disruptions. Similarly, some theorists believe that families who thwart a child's developing sense of autonomy or control, may put her at greater risk for developing eating disorders. Childhood sexual abuse represents a particularly egregious early trauma which research indicates may underlie some cases of conduct disorder, adult anxiety and depressive disorder, post-traumatic stress disorder, and substance abuse. Indeed, sexual abuse that is ongoing and severe has been isolated as the cause of some serious dissociative conditions such as multiple personality. Even a significant isolated trauma may have long-term effects: for example, childhood loss may result in the development of a psychological diathesis which predisposes the child to depression in adulthood following subsequent losses, and these issues must be kept in mind when treating children for psychological disturbances. Although the child may be viewed in treatment as the "identified patient," aspects of the family system or developmental environment may also require therapeutic intervention.

SAMPLE EXAM

1. It is perhaps more difficult to understand the disorders of children than those of adults for all the following reasons except that
   a. children's problems are often situationally specific.
   b. children's problems are not serious.
   c. children's problems arise in the course of development.
   d. children often cannot communicate a problem directly through language.
   e. all of the above make understanding more difficult.

2. If a child's problem involves habitual physical symptoms, she has
   a. a disruptive behavior disorder.
   b. an emotional disorder.
   c. a habit disorder.

   d. a pervasive developmental disorder.
   e. a learning disorder.

3. If a child's problem involves mental retardation, he has
   a. a disruptive behavior disorder.
   b. an emotional disorder.
   c. a habit disorder.
   d. a developmental disorder.
   e. an eating disorder.

4. If a child's problem involves shyness and fear, he has
   a. a disruptive behavior disorder.
   b. an emotional disorder.
   c. a habit disorder.
   d. a developmental disorder.
   e. an eating disorder.

5. If a child's problem involves hyperactivity, he has
    a. a disruptive behavior disorder.
    b. an emotional disorder.
    c. a habit disorder.
    d. a developmental disorder.
    e. an eating disorder.

6. If a child's problem involves the failure to learn language, she has
    a. a disruptive behavior disorder.
    b. an emotional disorder.
    c. a habit disorder.
    d. a developmental disorder.
    e. an eating disorder.

7. All of these are risk factors for delinquency except
    a. parental divorce or separation.
    b. school difficulties.
    c. being middle class.
    d. parental criminality.
    e. poverty.

8. The most effective treatments for conduct disorders are those suggested by the
    a. biomedical model.
    b. psychodynamic model.
    c. behavioral model.
    d. cognitive model.
    e. existential model.

9. Hyperactivity involves which of the following symptoms?
    a. short attention span
    b. impulsive actions
    c. inability to hold still
    d. boundless energy
    e. all of the above

10. Among the successful treatments for some hyperactive children are
    a. tranquilizers.
    b. antidepressants.
    c. stimulants.
    d. depressants.
    e. none of the above.

11. Behavioral techniques for treating hyperactivity are based on
    a. Pavlovian conditioning.
    b. operant conditioning.
    c. modeling.
    d. cognitive restructuring.
    e. all of the above.

12. Childhood emotional disorders correspond to which adult disorders?
    a. anxiety disorders
    b. affective disorders
    c. schizophrenic disorders
    d. psychosomatic disorders
    e. none of the above

13. The most common childhood emotional disorder is
    a. conduct disorder.
    b. hyperactivity.
    c. phobia.
    d. ADHD.
    e. separation anxiety.

14. Separation anxiety is often triggered by
    a. change.
    b. hormones.
    c. parental divorce.
    d. trauma.
    e. nightmares.

15. Childhood fears include all of the following except
    a. animal phobia.
    b. agoraphobia.
    c. school phobia.
    d. fear of the dark.
    e. imaginary creatures.

16. The risk factors for childhood depression include all of the following except
    a. low self-esteem.
    b. family dysfunction.
    c. pessimistic attitudes.
    d. family stress.
    e. immaturity.

17. Which does not belong?
    a. autism
    b. enuresis
    c. stuttering
    d. anorexia
    e. motor tics

18. The cause of enuresis is compatible with the
    a. biomedical model.
    b. psychodynamic model.
    c. behavioral model.
    d. cognitive model.
    e. existential model.

19. The most successful treatment for enuresis is that based on the
    a. biomedical model.

b. psychodynamic model.
c. behavioral model.
d. cognitive model.
e. existential model.

20. Someone who stutters would be expected to have particular difficulty saying
    a. "Please pass the potatoes."
    b. "I ironed out the idiotic ideas."
    c. "He had to have help."
    d. "Eat the edible eggplant."
    e. "She said it wasn't so."

21. All of the following are treatments for stuttering except
    a. shadowing.
    b. desensitization.
    c. delayed auditory feedback.
    d. syllable-timed speech.
    e. all of the above are treatments.

22. Anorexia nervosa most obviously involves
    a. weight loss.
    b. depression.
    c. anxiety.
    d. thought disorder.
    e. weight gain.

23. What percent of cases of anorexia are female?
    a. 10 percent
    b. 35 percent
    c. 50 percent
    d. 95 percent
    e. anorexics are always female

24. Theories explaining the development of anorexia include all of the following except
    a. the modern cultural norm of "ideal."
    b. a variant of mood disorders.
    c. autonomy needs.
    d. poor impulse control.
    e. low self-esteem resulting from abuse.

25. Bulimia usually involves
    a. binges.
    b. purges.
    c. depression.
    d. feelings of shame and distress.
    e. all of the above.

26. Purging in bulimia may take which of the following forms?
    a. fasting
    b. excessive exercise
    c. laxatives and diuretics

d. self-induced vomiting
e. all of the above

27. Treatment for eating disorders may include
    a. cognitive therapy.
    b. behavioral therapy.
    c. drug therapy.
    d. family therapy.
    e. all of the above.

28. An IQ score of less than _____ is traditionally regarded as the criterion of mental retardation.
    a. 25
    b. 50
    c. 70
    d. 100
    e. 125

29. Most individuals who are retarded fall into which category?
    a. mild mental retardation
    b. moderate mental retardation
    c. severe mental retardation
    d. profound mental retardation
    e. they are evenly divided among these groups

30. Pre- and post-natal factors that may affect later intellectual development include all of the following except
    a. the mother's health.
    b. mother's substance use.
    c. physical abuse.
    d. exposure to toxins.
    e. any of the above may have an impact.

31. Which of these educational strategies has been most effective for training mentally retarded children?
    a. segregating them
    b. mainstreaming them
    c. remediation
    d. both *a* and *b*
    e. none of the above

32. Down's syndrome arises because of
    a. faulty learning.
    b. metabolic abnormality.
    c. neurotransmitter insufficiency.
    d. chromosomal abnormality.
    e. childhood trauma.

33. Phenylketonuria arises because of
    a. faulty learning.
    b. metabolic abnormality.

c. neurotransmitter insufficiency.
d. chromosomal abnormality.
e. childhood trauma.

34. The difference between specific devel-
    opmental disorders and pervasive devel-
    opmental disorders involves
    a. slow development versus no devel-
        opment.
    b. early onset versus late onset.
    c. environmental causes versus biologi-
        cal causes.
    d. emotional problem versus behavioral
        problem.
    e. boys versus girls.

35. Reading difficulties are more common
    among
    a. boys than girls.
    b. children who developed language late
        than children who developed lan-
        guage early.
    c. children with family members who
        have reading difficulties than chil-
        dren with family members who do not
        have reading difficulties.
    d. *a* and *b*.
    e. all of the above.

36. Learning disorders mainly effect
    a. the development of memory skills.
    b. the development of social skills.
    c. the development of motor skills.
    d. the development of language and
        academic skills.
    e. all of the above.

37. Which is a pervasive developmental dis-
    order?
    a. autism
    b. anorexia
    c. stuttering
    d. hyperactivity
    e. depression

38. All of these are symptoms of autism ex-
    cept
    a. echolalia.
    b. failure to respond to others.
    c. clinginess.
    d. insistence on sameness.
    e. all of the above are symptoms of
        autism.

39. Autism occurs more frequently among
    a. boys than girls.

b. lower-class children than upper-class
    children.
c. whites than blacks.
d. both a and b.
e. none of the above.

40. Current ideas about the causes of autism
    are compatible with the
    a. biomedical model.
    b. psychodynamic model.
    c. behavioral model.
    d. cognitive model.
    e. existential model.

41. Evidence supporting a biological etiology
    for autism includes
    a. a genetic vulnerability to cognitive
        impairment.
    b. higher rates of obstetric and neonatal
        complications.
    c. higher rates of abnormal brain wave
        patterns.
    d. a and b.
    e. all of the above.

42. The neurotransmitter(s) thought to be in-
    volved in autism is
    a. dopamine.
    b. norepinephrine.
    c. serotonin.
    d. chlorpromazine.
    e. ritalin.

43. Current treatments of autism are derived
    from the
    a. biomedical model.
    b. psychodynamic model.
    c. behavioral model.
    d. cognitive model.
    e. existential model.

44. The prognosis for autistic children ap-
    pears
    a. excellent
    b. good.
    c. modest.
    d. bad.
    e. unknown.

45. The best prognostic indicator for child-
    hood autism is
    a. age of onset.
    b. IQ.
    c. echolalia.
    d. parental concern.
    e. early treatment.

Answer Key for Sample Exam

1.	b	(p. 599)	13.	e	(p. 612)	25.	e	(p. 621)
2.	c	(p. 601)	14.	d	(p. 612)	26.	e	(p. 621)
3.	d	(p. 601)	15.	b	(p. 613)	27.	e	(p. 623)
4.	b	(p. 601)	16.	e	(p. 616)	28.	c	(p. 625)
5.	a	(p. 600)	17.	a	(p. 618)	29.	a	(p. 626)
6.	d	(p. 601)	18.	a	(p. 618)	30.	e	(p. 630)
7.	c	(p. 603)	19.	c	(p. 618)	31.	d	(p. 631)
8.	c	(p. 606)	20.	a	(p. 619)	32.	d	(p. 628)
9.	e	(p. 608)	21.	b	(p. 619)	33.	b	(p. 629)
10.	c	(p. 610)	22.	a	(p. 620)	34.	a	(p. 633)
11.	b	(p. 610)	23.	d	(p. 620)	35.	e	(p. 632)
12.	a, b	(p. 611)	24.	d	(p. 622)			

36.	d	(p. 632)
37.	a	(p. 633)
38.	c	(p. 633)
39.	a	(p. 638)
40.	a	(p. 638)
41.	e	(p. 638)
42.	a, c	(p. 639)
43.	c	(p. 640)
44.	c	(p. 640)
45.	b	(p. 640)

SELF-TEST

1. Children's problems are more difficult to understand than those of adults because they occur in the context of _____; also, children often cannot _____ a problem directly through _____.

2. To be considered a disorder, a child's problem must _____, and it must _____ the child or others.

3. Children's disorders fall into these general categories: _____, _____, _____, and _____.

4. The disruptive behavior disorders of children are divided into _____ disorders, _____ disorders, and _____ disorders.

5. Conduct disorders are _____ likely among boys than girls.

6. Children with conduct disorders tend to come from _____ social environments.

7. Children who show conduct disturbance also have problems in maintaining _____.

8. Historically, treatment of conduct disorders has been largely _____; at the present, treatments derived from _____ seem promising.

9. Disorders of attention are often accompanied by _____.

10. Hyperactive children sometimes show improvement when treated with _____ drugs.

11. When feelings of inferiority, social withdrawal, shyness, fear, and overattachment predominate, a child may have an _____ disorder.

12. Childhood fears are surprisingly _____.

13. Habit disorders have a habitual physical component. Among these disorders are

_____, _____, _____, _____, and _____.

14. Enuresis may be successfully treated with _____ techniques.

15. Three techniques for the treatment of stuttering are _____, _____, and

_____.

16. Anorexia is characterized by substantial loss of _____ and the deliberate

_____.

17. Anorexia nervosa is _____ likely among girls than boys.

18. Bulimics _____ and then try to counteract the consequences by _____. Many

bulimics also suffer from _____.

19. Theories of eating disorders include the view that they are a variant of a _____; that

they are a consequence of _____ regarding thinness; or they are related to a history of

_____. Other views hold that bulimics may binge to _____ and purge to reduce

the _____ that the binge has caused; and, anorexics may have a malfunctioning

_____ or they may be exercising a need for _____ in a family that is

_____.

20. Mental retardation is characterized by _____ and limitations in a number of

_____. The condition must manifest before age _____.

21. The educational strategy of placing mentally retarded children in regular classrooms is

called _____.

22. Mental retardation associated with an extra chromosome is _____.

23. Mental retardation associated with an inability to metabolize phenylalanine is

_____ or _____.

24. Developmental disorders fall into three general types: _____ ; disorders, involving

developmental lags; _____ developmental disorders, such as _____,
involving developmental failures.

25. In autism, the child's ability to _____ fails to develop.

26. Autistic language is characterized by _____ and _____.

27. Autistic children insist on _____.

28. The cause of autism is _____.

29. The best predictor of prognosis for autistic children is _____.

Answer Key for Self-Test

1. development; communicate; language
2. persistent; impair
3. disruptive behavior; emotional; habit; developmental; and gender identity
4. conduct; oppositional; attention-defect hyperactivity
5. more
6. unpleasant
7. attention
8. unsuccessful; social learning theory
9. hyperactivity
10. stimulant
11. emotional
12. common
13. enuresis; stuttering; anorexia nervosa; bulimia; obesity
14. behavioral
15. delayed auditory feedback; shadowing; syllable-timed speech
16. body weight; restriction of calories
17. more
18. binge; purging; depression
19. mood disorder; cultural values; sexual abuse; escape anxiety and distress; stress; hypothalamus; autonomy; overcontrolling
20. significantly subaverage intellectual functioning; adaptive skills; 18
21. mainstreaming
22. Down's syndrome
23. phenylketonuria; PKU
24. mental retardation; learning; pervasive; autism
25. respond to others
26. echolalia; pronominal reversal
27. sameness
28. probably biological
29. IQ

MATCHING ITEMS

_____ 1. habit disorders

_____ 2. echolalia

_____ 3. attention deficit hyperactivity disorder (ADHD)

_____ 4. disruptive behavior disorder

_____ 5. stuttering

_____ 6. emotional disorder

_____ 7. autism

_____ 8. conduct disorder

_____ 9. Down's syndrome

_____ 10. Phenylketonuria (PKU)

_____ 11. anorexia

_____ 12. bulimia

A. shadowing

B. enuresis and encopresis

C. oppositional defiant disorder

D. chronic low arousal

E. develops by thirty months of age

F. antisocial personality disorder

G. bingeing and purging

H. refusal to maintain a normal weight

I. metabolic disorder

J. echolalia

K. school phobia

L. an extra chromosome

Answer Key for Matching Items

1. B	4. C	7. E	10. I
2. J	5. A	8. F	11. H
3. D	6. K	9. L	12. G

SHORT-ANSWER QUESTIONS

1. What general criteria must be met before diagnosing a child with a psychological disorder?

2. What common features do the disruptive behavior disorders share?

3. Summarize the theories explaining the origins of conduct disorders. What other disorders are often related?

4. Describe the main treatment approaches for children with ADHD.

5. How do the objects of childhood phobias change over time?

6. Describe the procedures involved in the three common techniques used to treat stuttering.

7. In what ways are anorexia and bulimia similar, and in what ways are they different?

8. What factors are considered before making a diagnosis of mental retardation.

9. What are the general symptoms of autism? Give two specific examples of each.

TYING IT TOGETHER

Childhood disorders fit uneasily with the rest of the disorders described in the textbook since they occur in the context of development. One of the truisms of developmental psychology is that little is invariant. Child development is well described by family resemblances (Chapter 1), and when its fuzzy concepts are coupled with those inherent in abnormal psychology, the result can be confusing. At the present time, psychologists concerned with childhood disorders are split on the issue of how to approach them. Should they be explained by generalizing "downward" from what is known about disorders in adults? Or does the field need its own psychology, based on a developmental model rather than on one of the prevailing adult models (Chapters 3–5)?

The answer probably is both. Some childhood disorders are profitably viewed as similar to adult disorders. Childhood fears, for instance, seem analogous to the adult phobias (Chapter 8), and childhood depression overlaps considerably with adult depression (Chapter 11). On the other hand, other childhood disorders are uniquely problems of children. The developmental disorders, for instance, must be approached in their own respect and not as variations of adult disorders. Autism seems to be a "new" disorder, and it is in particular poorly understood. Attempts to assimilate it within the psychodynamic (Chapter 4) or behavioral (Chapter 5) models have not been successful.

The adult disorders described in the other chapters frequently have their origin in childhood: emotional disorders (Chapters 8 and 9), depression (Chapter 11), paraphilias (Chapter 13), transsexuality (Chapter 13), drug abuse (Chapter 14), personality disorders (Chapter 15), and schizophrenia (Chapter 12). Increased research and theoretical attention may clarify not only disorders of childhood but also disorders that partly originate there.

The ethical and legal issues that arise when abnormality comes to the attention of the court (Chapter 18) are compounded when children are involved. Parents have traditionally been accorded "rights" that may thwart their children. On the other hand, the line between intervention and interference is fuzzy, and caution is needed when the legal system becomes concerned with children.

FURTHER READINGS

Axline, V. M. (1964). *Dibs: In search of self; Personality development in play therapy.* Boston: Houghton Mifflin.

Benton, A., & Pearl, D. (1978). *Dyslexia: An appraisal of current knowledge.* New York: Oxford University.

Bettelheim, B. (1967). *The empty fortress: Infantile autism and the birth of the self.* New York: Free Press.

Boskind-White, M., & White, W. C. (1983). *Bulimarexia: The binge/purge cycle.* New York: Norton.

Bruch, H. (1978). *The golden cage.* Cambridge, MA: Harvard University Press.

Edgerton, R. B. (1979). *Mental retardation.* Cambridge, MA: Harvard University Press.

Feingold, B. F. (1974). *Why your child is hyperactive.* New York: Random House.

Halmi, K. A. (1978). Anorexia nervosa: Recent investigations. *Annual Review of Medicine, 29,* 137–148.

Hudson, J. I., & Pope, H. G. (1990). Affective spectrum disorder: Does antidepressant response identify a family of disorders with a common pathophysiology? *American Journal of Psychiatry, 147*:5, 552–564.

Hudson, J. I., & Pope, H. G. (1984). *New hope for binge eaters.* New York: Harper & Row.

Kovacs, M., & Beck, A. T. (1977). *Depression in childhood.* New York: Raven Press.

Terr, L. (1990). *Too scared to cry: Psychic trauma in childhood.* New York: Harper & Row.

Williams, D. (1992). *Nobody nowhere: The extraordinary autobiography of an autistic.* New York: Avon books.

TERM-PAPER TOPICS

1. What is hyperactivity? Is it on the increase? If so, why? If not, then why do some think so?

2. Why are boys more apt to be retarded than girls? What does this suggest about sex differences in other disorders?

3. Compare and contrast childhood fears and adult phobias. What do your comparisons and contrasts suggest about the causes of phobias?

4. Evaluate the evidence linking childhood conduct disorder to adult antisocial personality disorder.

5. Summarize the evidence that autism is a biological phenomenon. In light of what is not known, what kinds of biological treatments might someday be possible?

EXERCISES

Exercise One—Childhood Disorders

In this exercise you will learn firsthand about common psychological disorders of children.

Arrange a classroom lecture by an elementary school teacher or counselor about common psychological disorders of childhood—hyperactivity, learning disability, depression, phobia, and so on. How are these manifest? How do they disrupt the child at school? How are they treated?

Exercise Two—Local Educational Practices

In this exercise, you will learn how your local school district approaches the education of children with intellectual, emotional, and physical difficulties.

Arrange a classroom lecture by a member of your local school board about the district's philosophies toward mainstreaming children with intellectual, emotional, and/or physical problems. What are the goals? What are the difficulties in achieving them? What changes would your lecturer like to see made?

Exercise Three—Work in a Classroom

You will gain firsthand experience in the care of children in this exercise.

Volunteer to work as a teacher's aide at a local elementary school or child-care center. Ask to be placed in a classroom with difficult children. Use this experience as an opportunity to examine your beliefs about such children and how they should be treated.

Exercise Four—Normal Development

Children develop at different rates, each with different capacities. Many children face particular developmental challenges along the way which they ultimately surmount. Poll your friends. Ask them if they had any developmental lags or behavioral conditions when they were children that they grew out of. How did they get past them?

CHAPTER 17

Disorders of the Nervous System and Psychopathology

CHAPTER OVERVIEW

This chapter describes disorders of the nervous system: so-called organic syndromes that have a clear basis in pathology of the structure or function of the nervous system. The chapter presents several basic principles describing how the brain and nervous system work, because they help explain how neurological disorders are manifested in behavior, how they can be diagnosed, and how they might be treated.

The organization of the brain can be considered in five ways: biochemical, spatial, front-back, left-right, and hierarchical. Neurological disorders can result from disruption of any of these modes of organization. Neurological function is achieved by a balance between inhibition and excitation of neurons. Again, disorders can involve problems with either process. Redundancy exists in the nervous system, allowing in many cases recovery from illness or injury. However, some areas of the brain are more vulnerable to damage than others, and these are where pathology is most likely to originate.

With these principles stated, the varieties and causes of nervous system disorders are described. Diagnosis is the strong point of neurology, and there exist techniques and devices that allow strong inferences about the exact nature of neurological dysfunction. Four disorders are described in detail: disorders of language (aphasias), disorders of reading (dyslexias), disorders of memory (amnesic syndromes), and dementia (e.g., Alzheimer's disease).

The chapter concludes with a discussion of how neurological disorders are treated, and with a caution about expecting too much—or too little—from a neurological approach to disorders.

ESSENTIAL TERMS

agnosia	disorder resulting from brain damage in which there is an inability to recognize meaningful objects (p. 654)
AIDS dementia complex	dementia caused directly by AIDS virus (p. 680)
Alzheimer's disease	common type of dementia often involving amnesia and/or language disorder (p. 677)
amnesic syndrome	disorder of memory (p. 673)

amyotrophic lateral sclerosis (ALS)	movement disorder of unknown origin; also called "Lou Gehrig's disease" (p. 649)
anomia	disorder resulting from brain damage in which there is an inability to name objects (p. 654)
anterograde amnesia	loss of memory for events since onset of amnesia (p. 674)
aphasia	general type of disorder of language resulting from brain damage (p. 666)
conduction aphasia	a type of aphasia due to damage to the nerve tract running between Broca's and Wernicke's areas; results in difficulties in repeating verbatim sentences that are heard (p. 668)
expressive aphasia	a type of aphasia due to damage to Broca's area in which speech production is disturbed; speech may be halting, labored, or ungrammatical (p. 667)
receptive aphasia	a type of aphasia due to damage to Wernicke's area in which speech perception and comprehension is disturbed; speech may appear fluent and grammatical but is incomprehensible (p. 667)
transcortical aphasia	a type of aphasia due to extensive neighboring damage which isolates the speech perception unit of the brain (made up by Broca's area, Wernicke's area, and the connection between them); patients cannot understand anything said to them (p. 668)
apraxia	a disorder resulting from brain damage in which there is an inability to execute a sequence of movements; not due to muscle weakness or specific movement inability (p. 655)
aura	unusual sensations or feelings that foreshadow an epileptic seizure (p. 660)
Babinski response	foot reflex normally shown only by infants (p. 659)
Broca's area	part of the brain involved in speech, specifically, syntax (grammar) (p. 666)
CAT scan (computer-assisted tomography)	device for taking three-dimensional X-ray pictures of the brain (p. 663)
consolidation block theory	theory of the amnesic syndrome that proposes the basic deficit to be in the formation (consolidation) of new long-term memories (p. 675)
corpus callosum	connection between the brain's hemispheres (p. 657)
dementia	progressive loss of variety of higher mental functions (p. 677)
disconnection syndrome	condition in which a nerve tract between connected brain areas is damaged (p. 668)
double dissociation	an experiment that examines which functions are preserved and which are destroyed following brain damage to specific sites (p. 653)

dyslexia	a general category of learning disability (p. 669)
acquired dyslexia	disorder in which established ability to read is lost due to injury (p. 670)
developmental dyslexia	disorder of children in which there is difficulty in reading that is not related to level of development (p. 669)
phonological dyslexia	disorder in which there is an inability to read by sound (p. 670)
surface dyslexia	disorder in which there is an inability to read words by sight (p. 670)
EEG (electroencephalogram)	assessment device for measuring electrical activity of the brain (p. 663)
epilepsy	disorder marked by excessive activity of the nervous system (seizures) (p. 660)
explicit memory	memory that requires one to consciously recollect past experiences (cf. implicit memory) (p. 675)
frontal lobes	part of the brain thought to be involved in planning and executing action (p. 680)
functional amnesia	memory loss associated with psychological disturbance rather than neurological damage (*see* Chapter 9) (p. 677)
functional MRI (fMRI)	new technique which measures oxygen levels in the blood as an indication of increased local brain activity (p. 664)
functional syndrome	abnormality caused by abnormal experience through the operation of normal brain mechanisms (cf. organic syndrome) (p. 645)
glia cells	supportive tissue in the brain (p. 648)
gray matter	areas where nerve cell bodies are concentrated (p. 652)
hemorrhage	ruptured arteries that leak blood; in the brain it can cause neurological symptoms (p. 660)
hippocampus	part of the brain thought to be involved in amnesia (p. 673)
implicit learning	skills (e.g., perceptuo-motor) which can still be learned and remembered by amnesics (p. 674)
implicit memory	memory that requires one to perform tasks, not consciously recollect events (cf. explicit memory) (p. 675)
Korsakoff's syndrome	common type of amnesia resulting from alcoholism (p. 672)
left-sided neglect	neurological syndrome caused by damage to the right parietal area of the brain and resulting in neglect of functions that involve the left side of the body (dressing, writing, reading, and so on) (p. 655)
localization of function	doctrine that particular mental functions are to be found in specific parts of the brain (p. 652)

MRI (magnetic resonance imaging)	technique for forming images of the brain by measuring spinning of hydrogen atoms (p. 664)
negative symptom	symptom characterized by loss or deficiency (cf. positive symptom) (p. 660)
neuron	basic unit of the nervous system (p. 648)
neurotransmitter	chemical released by one neuron to communicate with another neuron (p. 648)
obsessive-compulsive disorder (OCD)	mental disorder in which the individual is plagued by uncontrollable, repulsive thoughts (obsessions) and engages in seemingly senseless rituals (compulsions); symptoms can be reduced with drugs that affect neurotransmitter levels (p. 651) (See Chapter 9)
organic syndrome	abnormality caused by known pathology of the nervous system (cf. functional syndrome) (p. 645)
Parkinson's disease	movement disorder caused by degeneration of neurons leading to a depletion of dopamine in the brain (p. 651)
perseveration	difficulty in making transitions between one action and the next (p. 655)
PET scan (positron emission tomography)	device for assessing activity in different brain regions by measuring positron emission (p. 664)
Pick's disease	dementia caused by damage to frontal lobes (p. 684)
positive symptom	symptom characterized by increased behavior or nervous system activity (cf. negative symptom) (p. 660)
priming	procedure that elicits performance through cueing (p. 674)
retrieval failure theory	theory of the amnesic syndrome that suggests the basic deficit to be in retrieval of memories (p. 675)
retrograde amnesia	loss of memory for events prior to onset of amnesia (p. 674)
seizure	excessive brain activity which exaggerates expression of the function of the area involved; due to neural scarring which leaves tissue irritable (p. 660)
SPECT scan (single photon emission computerized tomography)	device for assessing activity in different brain regions by measuring photon emission (p. 664)
split-brain syndrome	result of surgical procedure that severs connections between the brain's hemispheres, resulting in what can be described as "two consciousnesses in one head" (p. 657)
left hemisphere	cerebral hemisphere that is better at language
right hemisphere	cerebral hemisphere that is better at spatial abilities
stroke	blockage of blood vessels in the brain; can result in brain damage (p. 660)
synapse	gap separating one neuron from another, into which neurotransmitters are secreted (p. 648)

Wernicke's area   part of the brain that accomplishes perception of speech (p. 667)

white matter   areas where axons are concentrated into tracts (p. 652)

CENTRAL CONCEPTUAL ISSUES

Overview.   In order to understand disorders of the nervous system, it is helpful to think in terms of what the brain does and how it does it. In the most basic terms, the nervous system mediates all experience. It receives input from the sense organs, organizes and manipulates that information, and orchestrates and executes response. This chapter is primarily concerned with disorders which interfere with normal physiological functioning in one of these areas. It is important, and humbling, to realize information does not come to us through our senses in whole form. Our eyes do not project the whole image of a tree in to our brains, nor is the printed or spoken word some indivisible entity inherent with meaning. The stimulation of the nerve receptors in our skin, our ears, our eyes, etc., are represented by electronic pulses which travel to our brain and it is only in the repackaging of these bits of information that sense and meaning are constructed as what we recognize as experience. This is achieved by the compartmentalization and specialization of different areas of the brain, each of which is responsible for particular types of information (e.g., sound, light, etc.). The signals, once received, are organized and stored, and this information is relayed to other areas which manipulate, compare, further combine and organize information, and in turn relay to yet other areas for decision making, planning, and action. A neuropsychological disorder involves a malfunctioning of the processing within an area of the brain or the communication and interaction between areas. In fact, interference with any aspect of the physical systems through which these processes take place can have an impact on perception, thought, mood, behavior, and all other physical manifestations of psychology.

Attitudes: Functional vs. organic disorders.   As with many examples of abnormal behavior, the context and interpretation of behaviors have a significant impact on the attitudes of both the actor and the observer. In addition to defining a behavior as "abnormal," context and interpretation effect our judgments of responsibility, feelings of shame or guilt, and stigma. As a rule, we hold people to be responsible for their actions, and so abnormal behavior is often seen to be the fault of the actor. However, when the behaviors are seen to result from an organic problem—a "disease"—sympathy rather than condemnation is commonly the result. This can be quite liberating to a sufferer and his family, as in the case of diagnosed schizophrenia. If a schizophrenic's problems are a result of a physical malfunction, the parents are less likely to blame themselves, or to take their child's actions personally. For the sufferer, there can be a release from self-blame if he understands that his organic processes are not subject to his control.

However, this may also be a two-edged sword. Recognizing that one has an organic disorder in which one has no control over some aspect of one's own behavior can also seem like one is not in fact in control of one's own life. The stigma here is not one of blame or judgment, but rather one of fear, or of the idea that a person is damaged. For many persons, the idea that their brain, the very thing upon which they depend for survival and knowledge of all that is real, is unreliable and has betrayed them, is terrifying. Moreover, in spite of recent improvements in some treatments, many if not most neurological disorders are at best only partially treatable and often with side-effects. Few disorders of this type can ever be made perfectly right (unlike a broken arm, or appendicitis). For these reasons, a patient who sees a neurologist or neuropsychologist dreads the idea that there is something wrong with her nervous system, and would rather discover that she had a functional disorder over which she had some control.

Because neurological disorders are so difficult to treat, there are many secondary repercussions with which the client and her social circle (including family, friends, and work associates) must contend. Much of a psychologist's work, in such cases, is involved with helping those affected to understand and deal with the stigmas, fears, depression, and practical problems of living with such a disorder.

Physical representation of mental states vs. processes.   The distinction between functional and organic disorders is often subtle and subject to much argument. One source of confusion arises from the idea that all psychological events have a physical manifestation in the brain. It would be easy, then, to jump to the conclusion that all psychopathology is organic. This confusion arises from a failure to distinguish between pathology, damage, or malfunction of the normal and basic operation of the central nervous system and its component parts, and the thoughts which are not a result of organic malfunctioning, but rather a result of learning, experience, psychological trauma, etc. It is additionally complicated by the way in which the brain and the individual develop to maturity. Learning takes place not only at the level of stored memory, but physically alters the structure and "wiring" of the brain. Early trauma, such as extended separation from primary caregivers, can have life-long organic effects in the way the brain responds to various types of stress. This may go beyond habitual and changeable reactions to certain experiences to the level of automatic physiological response. On the other hand, much of the influence of the environment in our daily lives is mitigated by our interpretation of events. The meaning we attach to a particular input can determine whether something is a threat, for example, and thereby affect whether a hard-wired response is activated. Conversely, constitutional factors such as shyness or low arousal may affect the sort of contingencies we experience in life and thus guide the lessons we learn and our interpretation of events.

Whether higher-order psychological properties reflect true free will or not is a debate which remains to be settled. It should be clear, however, that higher-order thoughts and basic organic functions are not purely independent, but rather interact in subtle and profound ways to fundamentally affect the functioning of each.

SAMPLE EXAM

1. The difference between organic and functional syndromes lies in
   a. etiology.
   b. diagnosis.
   c. prognosis.
   d. type of brain damage.
   e. none of the above.

2. The text makes which of the following analogies between brain functions and computer functions?

   a. memory/RAM; dyslexia/ROM
   b. memory/ROM; dyslexia/RAM
   c. organic/hardware; functional/ software
   d. organic/software; functional/ hardware
   e. frontal lobes/programmer

3. The gap between two neurons is the
   a. synapse.
   b. neurotransmitter.

c. interneuronal space.
d. glia.
e. corpus callosum.

4. Neurotransmitters _____ neurons.
   a. excite
   b. inhibit
   c. enhance
   d. both a and b
   e. all of the above

5. Multiple sclerosis is a disorder of
   a. synapses.
   b. glia cells.
   c. the corpus callosum.
   d. the limbic system.
   e. frontal lobes.

6. Redundancy in the brain is achieved by
   a. alternate pathways.
   b. duplication of hemispheres.
   c. excess neurons.
   d. alternative strategies.
   e. all of the above.

7. Parkinson's disease is caused by
   a. damage to Wernicke's area.
   b. selective degeneration of motor neurons.
   c. vitamin B_1 deficiency.
   d. depletion of dopamine.
   e. damage to the frontal lobes.

8. What does it mean to say that the brain is biochemically organized?
   a. higher levels of the brain build on lower levels of the brain
   b. neurons that produce the same neurotransmitters tend to be located close to one another
   c. neurons close to one another are likely to perform the same function
   d. the brain is differentiated on a left-right basis
   e. none of the above

9. All of the following are used to distinguish functional from organic syndromes except
   a. a detailed case history.
   b. consistency of symptoms/deficits with particular damage.
   c. pattern of onset of symptoms.
   d. brain imaging techniques.
   e. the presence of physical symptoms.

10. Amyotrophic lateral sclerosis (ALS) is caused by
    a. damage to Wernicke's area.
    b. selective degeneration of motor neurons.
    c. vitamin B_1 deficiency.
    d. depletion of dopamine.
    e. damage to the frontal lobes.

11. What does it mean to say that the brain is spatially organized?
    a. higher levels of the brain build on lower levels of the brain
    b. neurons that produce the same neurotransmitters tend to be located close to one another
    c. neurons close to one another are likely to perform the same function
    d. the brain is differentiated on a left-right basis
    e. none of the above

12. Pioneering research by Broca gave support to the position of
    a. empiricism.
    b. evolution.
    c. localization.
    d. psychoanalysis.
    e. rationalism.

13. Nerve cell bodies are concentrated into
    a. antimatter.
    b. gray matter.
    c. white matter.
    d. nothing matters.
    e. smatterings of ignorance.

14. Motor functions are to sensory functions as
    a. front is to back.
    b. top is to bottom.
    c. left is to right.
    d. inside is to outside.
    e. off is to on.

15. Planning is localized in the _____ of the brain.
    a. back
    b. bottom
    c. front
    d. top
    e. center

16. The qualitative difference between the functioning of the two hemispheres is evidence of the _____ organization of the brain.

a. hierarchical
b. spatial
c. front-back
d. left-right
e. biochemical

17. If an individual has an injury on the right side of the brain, the idea of contralateral projection would imply that
   a. she would show impairment on the right side of her body.
   b. she would show impairment on the left side of her body.
   c. she would show impairment on both sides of her body.
   d. she would show no impairment.
   e. none of the above.

18. Research with split brains suggests that the
   a. right hemisphere is involved in synthesis.
   b. left hemisphere is involved in synthesis.
   c. right hemisphere is involved in analysis.
   d. left hemisphere is involved in analysis.
   e. none of the above

19. Left hemisphere is to right hemisphere as
   a. old is to new.
   b. language is to spatial.
   c. spatial is to language.
   d. motor is to sensory.
   e. sensory is to motor.

20. What does it mean to say that the brain is hierarchically (vertically) organized?
   a. higher levels of the brain build on lower levels of the brain
   b. neurons that produce the same neurotransmitters tend to be located close to one another
   c. neurons close to one another are likely to perform the same function
   d. the brain is differentiated on a left-right basis
   e. none of the above

21. According to John Hughlings Jackson, higher levels of the brain
   a. appear later in evolution.
   b. appear later in development.
   c. are more vulnerable to injury or illness.

d. all of the above.
e. none of the above.

22. A disorder of language is
   a. aphasia.
   b. apraxia.
   c. dyslexia.
   d. agnosia.
   e. amnesia.

23. A disorder of movement is
   a. aphasia.
   b. apraxia.
   c. dyslexia.
   d. agnosia.
   e. amnesia.

24. A disorder of reading is
   a. aphasia.
   b. apraxia.
   c. dyslexia.
   d. agnosia.
   e. amnesia.

25. Which of these devices or techniques records the brain's electrical activity?
   a. CAT scan
   b. EEG
   c. MRI
   d. PET scan
   e. SPECT scan

26. Which of these devices or techniques takes a three-dimensional X-ray of the brain?
   a. CAT scan
   b. EEG
   c. MRI
   d. PET scan
   e. SPECT scan

27. Which of these devices or techniques measures the movement of hydrogen atoms in the brain?
   a. CAT scan
   b. EEG
   c. MRI
   d. PET scan
   e. SPECT scan

28. Which of these devices or techniques assesses the brain's blood flow?
   a. CAT scan
   b. EEG
   c. MRI
   d. PET scan
   e. SPECT scan

29. Which of these devices or techniques estimates the brain's metabolic activity?
    a. CAT scan
    b. EEG
    c. MRI
    d. PET scan
    e. SPECT scan

30. Broca's area is to Wernicke's area as
    a. expressive aphasia is to receptive aphasia.
    b. receptive aphasia is to expressive aphasia.
    c. expressive aphasia is to conduction aphasia.
    d. conduction aphasia is to expressive aphasia.
    e. transcortical aphasia is to conduction aphasia.

31. Broca's aphasia is now regarded as a problem with
    a. grammar.
    b. pronunciation.
    c. pragmatics.
    d. semantics.
    e. syntax.

32. Which of these is a common route in reading, from print to meaning?
    a. conversion to sound and then to meaning
    b. direct conversion to meaning
    c. word shape to meaning
    d. both a and b
    e. all of the above

33. In _____ dyslexia, there is a problem with reading by sound.
    a. developmental
    b. phonological
    c. surface
    d. all of the above
    e. none of the above

34. Deficits in recall of events that happen after the trauma is called _____ amnesia.
    a. short-term
    b. anterograde
    c. retrograde
    d. implicit
    e. explicit

35. Chronic alcoholism leads to
    a. Alzheimer's disease.
    b. Babinski's sign.
    c. Down's syndrome.
    d. Korsakoff's syndrome.
    e. Parkinson's disease.

36. All of the following are associated with amnesic syndrome except
    a. short-term memory loss.
    b. lack of a sense of familiarity.
    c. implicit learning.
    d. anterograde amnesia.
    e. bilateral damage.

37. The consolidation block theory of amnesia has difficulty explaining
    a. retrograde amnesia.
    b. normal skill acquisition.
    c. priming.
    d. a and b.
    e. all of the above.

38. _____ memory refers to memory that does not involve conscious recollection.
    a. Explicit
    b. Implicit
    c. Anterograde
    d. Retrograde
    e. Cued

39. Alzheimer's disease produces
    a. delirium.
    b. dementia.
    c. dissociation.
    d. retardation.
    e. none of the above.

40. Research suggests that _____ may be involved in Alzheimer's disease.
    a. biochemical deficits
    b. chromosomal abnormalities
    c. excess aluminum
    d. malformed neurons
    e. all of the above

41. Neurology is at its best when _____ disorders.
    a. diagnosing
    b. treating
    c. both
    d. neither

Answer Key for Sample Exam

1.	a	(p. 645)	12.	c	(p. 666)	22.	a	(p. 655)
2.	c	(p. 646)	13.	b	(p. 652)	23.	b	(p. 655)
3.	a	(p. 648)	14.	a	(p. 654)	24.	c	(p. 669)
4.	d	(p. 648)	15.	c	(p. 654)	25.	b	(p. 663)
5.	b	(p. 648)	16.	d	(p. 657)	26.	a	(p. 663)
6.	e	(p. 661)	17.	b	(p. 657)	27.	c	(p. 663)
7.	d	(p. 651)	18.	a, d	(p. 658)	28.	d, e	(p. 664)
8.	b	(p. 650)	19.	b	(p. 657)	29.	d, e	(p. 664)
9.	e	(p. 647)	20.	a	(p. 658)	30.	a	(p. 667)
10.	b	(p. 649)	21.	c	(p. 659)	31.	e	(p. 669)
11.	c	(p. 652)						

32.	e	(p. 670)
33.	b	(p. 670)
34.	b	(p. 674)
35.	d	(p. 672)
36.	a	(p. 674)
37.	e	(p. 675)
38.	b	(p. 675)
39.	b	(p. 677)
40.	e	(p. 679)
41.	a	(p. 686)

SELF-TEST

1. _____ syndromes are caused by known pathology of the nervous system, whereas _____ syndromes are not. The line between the two is often _____.

2. _____ and _____ work with organic syndromes, and _____ and _____ work with clinical syndromes.

3. A loss of language is called _____.

4. The basic unit of the nervous system is the _____; these units communicate with each other by means of _____.

5. Besides neurons, the nervous system is also composed of _____ cells.

6. The brain is organized in several ways. That neurons with similar biochemical properties are located together is _____ organization. That neurons close to each other perform the same function is _____ organization. And that higher levels of the brain build on lower levels is _____ organization. The brain is also organized on a _____ and a _____ basis.

7. Redundancy in the nervous system is accomplished by _____ than necessary, _____ to accomplish the same end, and the same functions in _____.

8. Neurons cannot be _____, but they can _____ if damaged.

9. Parkinson's disease is associated with a depletion of _____.

10. The left half of the brain controls the _____ of the body, and the right half of the brain control the _____ of the body.

11. Severing the connections between the two brains results in a _____.

12. The left brain appears to be involved in tasks requiring _____, and the right brain appears to be involved in tasks requiring _____.

13. Lower levels of the brain are _____ vulnerable to injury or illness.

14. People with damage to their frontal lobes often show difficulty making transitions from one action to another. This is called _____.

15. Damage to the nervous system can express itself in both _____ and _____ symptoms.

16. Epilepsy is caused by _____ of the nervous system, which leads to _____.

17. Among the devices that aid neurological diagnosis are the _____ (which records the brain's electrical activity), the _____ (which takes a three-dimensional X-ray of the brain), _____ (which detects magnetic activity of atoms in the brain), and the _____ (which measures brain metabolic activity).

18. The classical view of Broca's aphasia regards it as a disorder of language _____, but the current view sees it as a problem of _____.

19. Difficulty in reading is called _____.

20. Reading involves two pathways, _____ and _____.

21. In _____ dyslexia there is trouble in reading by sound; in _____ dyslexia there is trouble in reading by sight.

22. In _____ dyslexia there is trouble initially learning to read; in _____ dyslexia there is a loss of an established ability to read.

23. _____ results from chronic alcoholism.

24. The _____ is involved in the amnesic syndromes.

25. The full amnesic syndrome is produced by _____ damage to the hippocampus.

26. Damage to the skull can produce a transient amnesic syndrome, but usually only when _____ has been lost.

27. The _____ theory of amnesia cannot account for patients' lost sense of familiarity.

28. The progressive loss of higher mental functions is _____, and its most common cause is _____.

29. Three theories of Alzheimer's disease are currently entertained: excess _____, _____ abnormalities, and a _____ deficit.

30. AIDS dementia complex involves _____ areas initially, and then often the _____.

31. The strength of neurology is _____; its weakness is _____.

32. Psychologists should rely neither _____ nor _____ on the neurological approach in explaining and treating psychopathologies.

Answer Key for Self-Test

1. Organic; functional; fuzzy
2. Neurologists; neuropsychologists; psychiatrists; clinical psychologists
3. aphasia
4. neuron; neurotransmitter
5. glia
6. biochemical; spatial; hierarchical, right-left; front-back
7. more neurons; alternate pathways; both hemispheres
8. replaced; recover
9. dopamine
10. right; left
11. split brain
12. language; spatial abilities
13. less
14. perseveration
15. positive; negative
16. excessive activity; seizures
17. EEG; CAT scan; MRI; PET and SPECT scans
18. expression; syntax
19. dyslexia
20. sound; sight
21. phonological; surface
22. developmental; acquired
23. Korsakoff's syndrome
24. limbic system
25. bilateral
26. consciousness
27. retrieval failure
28. dementia; Alzheimer's disease
29. aluminum; chromosomal; biochemical
30. subcortical; frontal lobes
31. diagnosis; treatment
32. too much; too little

MATCHING ITEMS

_____ 1. left-sided neglect

_____ 2. confabulate

_____ 3. Parkinson's disease

_____ 4. apraxia

_____ 5. agnosia

_____ 6. anomia

_____ 7. Korsakoff's syndrome

_____ 8. perseverate

_____ 9. Amyotrophic lateral sclerosis (ALS)

_____ 10. epilepsy

_____ 11. split-brain syndrome

A. Broca

B. inability to recognize meaningful objects

C. selective degeneration of motor neurons

D. inability to name objects

E. damage to higher motor centers

F. Wernicke

G. damage to right-parietal area

H. corpus callosum

I. positive symptoms

J. "honest liars"

K. L-DOPA

_____ 12. Babinski reflex in adults

_____ 13. receptive aphasia

_____ 14. expressive aphasia

L. inability to perform a specific movement

M. try and try again

N. amnesia

Answer Key for Matching Items

1.	G	8.	M
2.	J	9.	C
3.	K	10.	I
4.	L	11.	H
5.	B	12.	E
6.	D	13.	F
7.	N	14.	A

SHORT-ANSWER QUESTIONS

1. Define what is meant when the organization of the brain is described in each of the following ways: biochemical, spatial, front-back, left-right, and hierarchical. Give examples in each case.

2. In what ways is the nervous system vulnerable to damage and in what ways is it resistant? What agents can damage the nervous system, and give examples of how each might be expressed.

3. Describe the speech perception and production "unit" in the brain and what the effects are of damage to each part.

4. How is reading accomplished (i.e., print to meaning)? What kind of damage is associated with each type of dyslexia?

5. What two theories have been proposed to explain why amnesics can't remember? Why is it important to make the distinction between "explicit" and "implicit" in memory and memory tests?

6. What is dementia? What are the similarities and differences between Alzheimer's disease and AIDS dementia complex?

7. What conditions are associated with damage to the frontal lobes?

8. What are three approaches to ameliorate some of the effects of neural damage?

TYING IT TOGETHER

This chapter describes disorders that are compatible with the biomedical model (Chapter 3), yet even the neurological disorders have fuzzy boundaries (Chapter 1) influenced by cultural values and practices. In an illiterate society, reading difficulty is not a problem at all.

Neurological diagnosis is more sophisticated than typical psychological assessment (Chapter 7), probably because it is based on well-understood neurological principles derived from many years of research (Chapter 6).

Will all the psychopathologies someday be the province of neurology? The answer here is no, because the role of experience is undeniable in many of these disorders, including fears and phobias (Chapter 8), hysteria (Chapter 9), depression (Chapter 11), and so on. Indeed, recent work in health psychology (Chapter 10) implies that even physical illness reflects psychological factors.

Nonetheless, an understanding of neurology is necessary for a full understanding of any psychopathology, because all phenomena of behavior has some basis in the nervous system. This idea is well illustrated for psychosomatic disorders (Chapter 10), schizophrenia (Chapter 12), and drug abuse (Chapter 14).

Treatment for neurological disorders is not as advanced as diagnosis. In part this reflects lack of knowledge, but also it reflects the fact that neurons cannot be replaced if destroyed.

The psychological therapies, particularly those based on the environmental model (Chapter 5), prove useful in helping patients with neuro-logical damage to overcome their problems (Chapter 19), just as eyeglasses help people cope with vision problems.

FURTHER READINGS

Allport, S. (1986). *Explorers of the black box.* New York: Norton.

Gardner, H. (1976). *The shattered mind.* New York: Vintage.

Gazzaniga, M. S. (1988). *Mind matters: How the mind and brain interact to create our conscious lives.* Boston: Houghton Mifflin.

Goldstein, K. (1939). *The organism.* New York: American Book Company.

Klawans, H. L. (1988). *Toscanini's fumble and other tales of clinical neurology.* New York: Bantam Books.

Lenneberg, E. H. (1967). *Biological founda-tions of language.* New York: Wiley.

Lezak, M. D. (1976). *Neuropsychological as-sessment.* New York: Oxford.

Luria, A. (1970). The functional organization of the brain. *Scientific American, 222,* 66–78.

Ornstein, R., & Thompson, R. F. (1984). *The amazing brain.* Boston: Houghton Mifflin.

Sacks, O. (1985). *The man who mistook his wife for a hat and other clinical tales.* New York: Summit.

Sacks, O. (1995). *An anthropologist on Mars.* New York: Alfred A. Knopf.

TERM-PAPER TOPICS

1. An understanding of brain laterality is critical for understanding neurological disorders. Some theorists believe that lateralization is also important in schizophrenia and other psy-chopathologies. Review the evidence for this claim. What is your conclusion.

2. Freud was originally trained as a neurologist. In what ways is psychoanalysis still a neu-rological approach, although phrased in psychological language?

3. Injury or illness involving the hormonal systems of the body can result in a variety of ab-normalities of thought, mood, and disorder. Survey these abnormalities. Which glands are most vulnerable to injury or illness?

4. What is the evidence pro and con for the possibility that autism is a neurological disease?

5. How does language development depend on development of the brain and nervous system? Explain this relationship, particularly in terms of its effect on disorders of language.

6. What might the future hold for the treatment of neurological disorders?

EXERCISES

Exercise One—Rehabilitation Medicine

The purpose of this exercise is to learn first-hand about rehabilitation medicine.

Volunteer to work as an aide at your local hospital. Ask to work on a rehabilitation ward, where patients have had strokes, amputations, or other occurrences that necessitate adjust-ment to some loss of function.

Above and beyond their obvious losses, what have the patients lost? How are they affected psychologically? How do the reha-bilitation counselors, nurses, and physicians attempt to help patients? How must patients help themselves?

Exercise Two—Alzheimer's Disease

In this exercise, you will learn about the char-acteristics and progression of Alzheimer's dis-ease.

Talk to individuals with family members who have Alzheimer's disease. When was their condition first apparent? What progres-sion was shown? Under what circumstances does the family member seem to do well? When does he or she do particularly poorly?

Gruetzner, H. (1988). *Alzheimer's: A care-giver's guide and sourcebook.* New York: Wiley.

Exercise Three—Neuropsychological Testing

The purpose of this exercise is to learn more about neuropsychological testing.

Arrange a classroom lecture by a neu-ropsychologist who can explain the Halsted-Reitan battery (a set of tests for determining the nature and extent of neurological damage). Ask the neuropsychologist to present several examples of the "detective work" involved in neuropsychological diagnosis. In each case, how has the diagnosis aided rehabilitation?

Golden, C. J. (1981). *Diagnosis and rehabili-tation in clinical neuropsychology* (2nd ed.). Springfield, IL: Thomas.

Exercise Four—Brain-Imaging Techniques

CAT scans, PET scans, and other high-tech marvels for glimpsing at the structure and function of the nervous system are increasingly used, but few individuals are familiar with them. In this exercise, you will gain some familiarity with these assessment devices.

Arrange a tour of a local hospital that has one or more of these devices. Ask to see them, and to have someone explain to your class how they work and the uses to which they are put.

Sochurek, H. (1987). Medicine's new vision. *National Geographic, 171*(2), 2–41.

The Law and Politics of Abnormality

CHAPTER OVERVIEW

Chapter 18 looks at abnormality from a legal and political perspective. First, what criteria are used to justify involuntary commitment? Among those described are impaired judgment, need for treatment, inability to care for oneself, grave disability, and dangerousness. It is sometimes difficult to assess these and to argue that they are valid grounds for involuntary commitment. Second, what rights are enjoyed by a mental patient? Third, what standard of proof should be required in commitment procedures: preponderance of evidence, clear and convincing proof, or beyond a reasonable doubt? Fourth, does involuntary commitment provide the right to be treated? Fifth, how has the insanity plea been used to excuse an individual from the consequences of

criminal acts? Different rules have been employed by courts in defining the grounds for an insanity plea: the M'Naghten rule, the "product of mental disease" test, and the "appreciate and conform" test. Sixth, the topic of incompetence to stand trial is briefly discussed.

The chapter discusses the legal problems involved in cases of multiple personality and the validity of repressed memories in testimony. It then goes on to discuss social and state abuse of abnormal psychology. Psychiatric hospitalization may be used to persecute an individual who does not have a disorder. Society stigmatizes ordinary people who have sought psychiatric help.

ESSENTIAL TERMS

appreciate and conform	criterion for an insanity plea: does an individual as the result of mental disturbance lack the capacity to appreciate criminality of conduct or to conform his or her conduct to requirements of law?; American Law Institute (ALI) Rule (p. 714)
civil commitment	*see* involuntary commitment
competence to stand trial	capacity to understand legal proceedings and/or to assist in one's own defense (p. 718)

criminal commitment	coerced psychiatric hospitalization of people who have acted harmfully but are not legally responsible because they lack a "guilty mind" (p. 710)
criminal insanity	psychological distress coupled with a record of past violence and expectation of future violence (p. 700)
due process of law	legal privileges afforded anyone whose liberty is threatened by state action (p. 701)
grave disability	inability to provide for one's own personal needs for food, clothing, and shelter (p. 701)
guilty but mentally ill	new verdict that has replaced "not guilty by reason of insanity" verdict in some states; results in commitment to a mental institution rather than a prison (p. 717)
insanity plea	legal defense of individuals thought not to be responsible for wrongdoing because of whole or partial irrationality when the crime took place (p. 710)
involuntary commitment	process whereby the state hospitalizes people for their own good, even over their protest; also known as civil commitment (p. 696)
mens rea	guilty mind, not present if an insanity plea is justified (p. 710)
M'Naghten rule	criterion of insanity plea: did the individual know what was done, and did the individual know it was wrong? (p. 713)
product of mental disorder	criterion of an insanity plea: was the unlawful act produced by mental disorder?; Durham rule (p. 713)
psychological disability	ill-defined precondition for involuntary commitment involving impaired judgment, need for treatment, behavioral disability, and dangerousness to self and/or others (p. 699)
right to treatment	right of an involuntarily committed individual to be treated after commitment (p. 704)
standard of proof	criteria that legal evidence must meet to be used to restrict a person's freedom, among them preponderance of evidence, beyond a reasonable doubt, and clear and convincing proof (p. 703)

SAMPLE EXAM

1. The problem in defining grounds for involuntary commitment is parallel to
   a. the nature-nurture issue.
   b. the problem in defining abnormality.
   c. the difficulty in isolating causes of abnormality.
   d. the problem in treating autism.
   e. none of the above.
2. Required in all states for involuntary commitment is
   a. psychological disability.
   b. impaired judgment.

c. need for treatment.
d. danger to self or others.
e. grave disability.

3. Incarcerating an individual because he is predicted to be dangerous in the future is at odds with
   a. common sense.
   b. Western legal tradition.
   c. research findings.
   d. the biomedical model.
   e. the behavioral model.

4. In Operation Baxstrom, what proportion of the "criminally insane" acted violently within four years of release?
   a. 3 percent
   b. 10 percent
   c. 50 percent
   d. 75 percent
   e. 97 percent

5. What is the "thank you" test?
   a. Individuals who are not grateful should be hospitalized.
   b. Individuals who are grateful should be hospitalized.
   c. Individuals who will not work for thanks alone should not be clinical psychologists.
   d. Individuals who would be grateful after recovery should be hospitalized.
   e. Individuals who thank you do not need to be hospitalized.

6. All of these are included in due process except the right to
   a. challenge witnesses.
   b. refuse psychological tests.
   c. legal counsel.
   d. trial by jury.
   e. know which laws one has violated.

7. All of these are standards of proof except
   a. statistical significance.
   b. preponderance of evidence.
   c. beyond a reasonable doubt.
   d. clear and convincing proof.
   e. all of the above.

8. The most stringent standard of proof is
   a. statistical significance.
   b. preponderance of evidence.
   c. beyond a reasonable doubt.
   d. clear and convincing proof.
   e. without a single doubt.

9. According to the Supreme Court, the minimum standard of proof for involuntary commitment should be
   a. statistical significance.
   b. preponderance of evidence.
   c. beyond a reasonable doubt.
   d. clear and convincing proof.
   e. determined by doctors.

10. Someone unable to adequately care for himself or herself has a _____ disability.
    a. behavioral
    b. grave
    c. lethal
    d. psychological
    e. spiritual

11. "Right to treatment" includes all these except
    a. individual treatment plan.
    b. suitable treatment.
    c. attempt to cure.
    d. rationale for attempt to cure.
    e. cure.

12. Patients are best off when given _____-based treatment.
    a. community
    b. home
    c. hospital
    d. institutionally
    e. no difference

13. Thomas Szasz is opposed to
    a. voluntary commitment.
    b. involuntary commitment.
    c. criminal commitment.
    d. all commitment.
    e. none of the above.

14. In what proportion of homicide cases is the insanity defense used?
    a. less than 1 percent
    b. 3 percent
    c. 10 percent
    d. 25 percent
    e. 50 percent

15. The insanity plea is based on the notion of
    a. free will.
    b. due process.
    c. overdetermined behavior.
    d. clear and convincing proof.
    e. statistical likelihood.

16. What is the "right-wrong" test?
    a. Did the individual do something wrong?
    b. Did the individual know later that what he did was wrong?
    c. Did the individual know at the time that what he was doing was wrong?
    d. Will the individual know at some time that what he did was wrong?
    e. All of the above.

17. What is the "product of mental disease" test?
    a. Did the individual do something wrong?
    b. Did the individual know at the time that what he was doing was wrong?
    c. Did the individual suffer from mental disease at the time he did something wrong?
    d. Did the individual's wrong act result from mental disease?
    e. Did the individual's wrong act produce the mental disease?

18. Why was the "product of mental disease test" withdrawn?
    a. reliance on expert testimony by psychiatrists
    b. difficulty in defining mental disease
    c. the DSM lists too many disorders
    d. both *a* and *b*
    e. neither *a* nor *b*

19. What is the "appreciate and conform" test?
    a. Did the individual do something wrong?
    b. Did the individual appreciate at the time that he did something wrong?
    c. Did the individual have the ability at the time to conform to the law?
    d. Did the individual cooperate after arrest?
    e. Did the individual's wrong act result from mental disease?

20. Which test for the insanity plea is currently used?
    a. right-wrong test
    b. appreciate and conform test
    c. product of mental disease test
    d. all of the above
    e. none of the above

21. The text calls the "guilty but mentally ill" verdict
    a. contradictory.
    b. progressive.
    c. reactionary.
    d. unnecessary.
    e. regressive.

22. A defendant found incompetent to stand trial is
    a. more common than a defendant acquitted because of the insanity plea.
    b. as common as a defendant acquitted because of the insanity plea.
    c. less common than a defendant acquitted because of the insanity plea.
    d. likely to enter an insanity plea.
    e. is automatically found not guilty by reason of insanity.

23. Incompetent to stand trial means that the defendant
    a. was mentally ill when the crime of which he was accused was committed.
    b. is mentally ill at the time of the trial.
    c. cannot understand the proceedings of the trial.
    d. cannot assist in her own defense.
    e. any of the above

24. A person who will never be competent to stand trial
    a. can be held indefinitely.
    b. cannot be held indefinitely.
    c. must be held indefinitely.
    d. is deemed to be not guilty.
    e. is deemed to be guilty.

25. Potentials for abuse in the diagnosis of mental illness arise from all these except
    a. political motives.
    b. problems in defining abnormality.
    c. changing criteria for abnormality.
    d. due process.
    e. social stigma.

26. Individuals committed involuntarily for political reasons probably have which elements of abnormality?
    a. observer discomfort
    b. unconventionality
    c. irrationality
    d. violation of ideals
    e. none of the above

27. Abuse of the mentally ill by the state and abuse of the mentally ill by society are similar in that
   a. both occur in the former Soviet Union but not in the United States.
   b. both are motivated by fear.
   c. both are rare.
   d. both are politically motivated.
   e. all of the above.

Answer Key for Sample Exam

1.	b	(p. 696)	15.	a	(p. 710)
2.	a	(p. 699)	16.	c	(p. 713)
3.	b, c	(p. 700)	17.	d	(p. 713)
4.	a	(p. 700)	18.	d	(p. 714)
5.	d	(p. 697)	19.	b, c	(p. 714)
6.	b	(p. 702)	20.	b	(p. 715)
7.	a	(p. 703)	21.	a	(p. 717)
8.	c	(p. 703)	22.	a	(p. 718)
9.	d	(p. 704)	23.	c, d	(p. 718)
10.	b	(p. 701)	24.	b	(p. 719)
11.	e	(p. 705)	25.	d	(p. 719)
12.	a	(p. 707)	26.	a, b, d	(p. 723)
13.	b	(p. 708)	27.	b	(p. 725)
14.	a	(p. 710)			

CENTRAL CONCEPTUAL ISSUES

Commitment and treatment.   The distinctions between involuntary commitment and imprisonment are highlighted by the question of right to treatment. In the U. S., if a person has been found guilty of a crime, she may be imprisoned. Her sentence must be proportionate to the crime in order to be constitutional under considerations of "cruel and unusual punishment." Once her time has been served, she is free to return to the community. However, a person who has been found not guilty under an insanity defense may be involuntarily committed for an indeterminate period of time. Without restrictions, this criminal commitment could last many times the length of the maximum term prescribed for one who is actually found guilty. If no treatment is provided, what is the difference, in terms of deprivation of liberty, between imprisonment and commitment? Similarly, in the case of civil commitment where an individual who has committed no crime is involuntarily hospitalized because he is deemed a danger to self or others, gravely disabled, or lacks insight, treatment is one of the few variables that on the face of it distinguish if from criminal incarceration. In spite of these questions, U. S. courts have not universally found that committed individuals have a bona fide right to treatment, although numerous courts have so held.

This issue is particularly acute if a person is found to be psychologically unfit to stand trial, and is remanded to the custody of a psychiatric hospital until such time as she is well enough to adequately take part in the legal proceedings. Such a person, without treatment, could in principle serve a life sentence without ever having stood trial for a crime—an apparent violation of a U. S. citizen's constitutional right to due process under the law. Other than a Supreme Court ruling that an individual who will never be competent to stand trial may not be held indefinitely, there is no set national standard limiting the amount of time she may be held awaiting competence to stand trial.

Psychology and the law.   Psychology is a square peg to the legal system's round hole. Psychologists make use of "family resemblance" criteria specifically because no single diagnostic criterion is broadly applicable. The law, however, must be specifically codified in order to promote due process and fair and consistent application. These two principles collide head-on in the cases of civil and criminal commitment. A psychologist who is 90 percent sure that he has made a correct diagnosis may be quite comfortable recommending a course of treatment. If the treatment is ineffective, something else may be tried. However, deprivation of liberty (involuntary commitment, imprisonment) based on a 90 percent certainty will unjustly deprive 10 out of every 100 persons so sentenced of their liberty. It may seem surprising then, that the minimum standard set by the Supreme Court for involuntary commitment is "clear and convincing proof"—roughly 75 percent certainty.

Predicting dangerousness.   Probably the single most pressing demand the public and legal system makes upon psychologists is the prediction of violence. This concern arises when considering both the commitment and release of mental patients. Although, psychologists look to an individual's history and their current mental state when considering this question, their success is limited indeed. In "Operation Baxstrom" (p. 700), 967 patients were released who had been held in prison beyond their sentences because they were believed to be dangerous to others as a result of their mental condition. After four years, only 2.7 percent of these individuals had behaved dangerously and were back in prison or in a hospital for the criminally insane. Even in this situation, where prior violent behavior would seem to lend weight to predictions of future violent behavior, these assessments proved markedly incorrect. If we know that 3 out of 100 persons are certain to be dangerous, but we do not know which 3 it will be, are we justified in locking up all 100?

SELF-TEST

1. The process by which the state hospitalizes people for their own good over their protest is

   _____.

2. For involuntary commitment, all states require that the individual be suffering from a

   _____, but this is poorly defined.

3. Among the incapacitating conditions required for involuntary commitment are

   _____, _____, _____, and _____.

4. It is extremely difficult to predict _____.

5. The rights and privileges accorded to citizens by the law are collectively termed

   _____. This may be violated in cases of involuntary commitment.

6. Three standards of proof, in increasing stringency, are _____, _____, and

   _____.

7. If individuals are committed involuntarily, they also have the right to _____.

8. One of the major consequences of guaranteeing greater rights to mental patients is that these patients have increasingly been _____.

9. The legal defense that claims a defendant not to have a "guilty mind" is the _____.

10. The insanity defense claims that the defendant was irrational _____.

11. The insanity defense is invoked in _____ percent of homicide cases that come to trial.

12. Historically, there have been four views of the insanity defense. First, the M'Naghten rule asks if the defendant suffered _____, understood _____ of his actions, and understood they were _____; second, the Durham rule asks if the crime was produced by _____; third, the ALI rule asks if the defendant appreciated the _____ of his or her conduct or lacked the ability to _____ to the requirements of the law; and fourth the Insanity Defense Reform Act eliminates the _____ prong of the insanity defense in federal courts.

13. Much more common than the insanity defense is the defendant's _____.

14. Until recently, there was _____ on how long people could be held until judged competent to stand trial.

15. Political abuse of abnormal psychology capitalizes on whether people possess a to abnormal people; also important are _____ conceptions of abnormality and the enormous _____ given to psychiatrists and psychologists by the state.

16. State abuse of abnormal psychology is probably underlied by _____.

17. Society _____ ordinary people who have sought mental health care.

Answer Key for Self-Test

1. involuntary commitment
2. psychological disability
3. impaired judgment; need for treatment; dangerousness; grave disability
4. dangerousness
5. due process
6. preponderance of evidence; clear and convincing proof; beyond a reasonable doubt
7. treatment
8. released
9. insanity plea
10. at the time of the crime
11. fewer than 1
12. a disease of the mind; the nature; wrong; mental disease; wrongfulness; conform; volitional
13. incompetence to stand trial
14. no limit
15. family resemblance; changing; power
16. fear
17. stigmatizes

MATCHING ITEMS

_____ 1. incompetent to stand trial

_____ 2. result of a successful insanity defense

_____ 3. civil commitment

_____ 4. beyond a reasonable doubt

A. involuntary commitment

B. the product of mental disease

C. guilty mind

D. criminal commitment

_____ 5. preponderance of evidence

_____ 6. clear and convincing proof

_____ 7. mens rea

_____ 8. ALI rule

_____ 9. Durham rule

_____ 10. M'Naghten rule

E. 75 percent standard

F. 51 percent standard

G. 90 or 99 percent standard

H. psychologically absent

I. understood actions were wrong

J. appreciate and conform

Answer Key for Matching Items

1.	H	6.	E
2.	D	7.	C
3.	A	8.	J
4.	G	9.	B
5.	F	10.	I

SHORT-ANSWER QUESTIONS

1. What requirement is necessary before involuntary commitment can be considered? What are the other "incapacitating conditions" that may be also be required?

2. Why is it necessary that due process of law be accorded in cases on involuntary commitment?

3. What is meant by standard of proof? What are the three standards generally used and when is each applied?

4. What are the arguments made against involuntary hospitalization and involuntary treatment?

5. Name and describe the four tests most widely used for the legal determination of insanity.

TYING IT TOGETHER

Central to the law is the assumption of free will and individual responsibility. As you have seen, only the existential approach addresses this notion (Chapter 4). The other models of abnormality embrace an assumption of determinism and hence are at odds with the basis of our country's legal system. Nevertheless, law and psychology come into frequent contact with each other concerning matters of involuntary commitment, competence to stand trial, the insanity plea, and so on. A more insidious interaction also occurs: the abuse of abnormal psychology by the state and by society. Witch-hunts are not necessarily phenomena of the past (Chapter 2). This chapter details the attempts by law and psychology to meld the assumptions of the respective disciplines, since their interaction is inevitable. Law, like the field of abnormal psychology, evolves. As you read this chapter, important changes in the legal procedures detailed may be occurring.

The law can deal more satisfactorily with some instances of abnormality than with others. "Willful" abnormality seems to defy both legal and psychological intervention. Lifestyles that involve psychosomatic illness (Chapter 10), suicide attempts (Chapter 11), drug abuse (Chapter 14), and antisocial activities (Chapter 15) are similar, but they are regarded differently by the law. A historical view (Chapter 2) partly explains this inconsistency, but it does not suggest how to resolve it.

Chapter 18 observes that legal, political, and social abuse may inadvertently result from the fuzzy nature of abnormality. That is, the family resemblance idea helps explain the lack of precision associated with the identification, explanation, and treatment of abnormality. It is unfortunate that most people are not accustomed to thinking in terms of family resemblances. The legal system in particular is at odds with such a formulation. Perhaps if abnormality and its fuzzy nature were better understood, both inadvertent and intentional abuses occasioned by observer discomfort (Chapter 1) would be decreased.

FURTHER READINGS

Coleman, L. (1984). *The reign of error: Psychiatry, authority, and law.* Boston: Beacon.

Fireside, H. (1979). *Soviet psychoprisons.* New York: Norton.

Goffman, E. (1961). *Asylums: Essays on the social situation of mental patients and other inmates.* Garden City, NY: Anchor.

Insanity defense: Under fire. (1981, April 20). *U.S. News & World Report,* p. 11.

Kesey, K. (1962). *One flew over the cuckoo's nest.* New York: New American Library.

Mathews, T., & Cook, W. J. (1976, March 1). Patty's defense. *Newsweek,* pp. 20–24.

Medvedev, Z. A., & Medvedev, R. A. (1979). *A question of madness.* New York: Norton.

Millet, K. (1990). *The loony bin trip.* New York: Touchstone.

Szasz, T. S. (1961). *The myth of mental illness.* New York: Harper & Row.

Szasz, T. S. (1970). *The manufacture of madness: A comparative study of the Inquisition and the Mental Health Movement.* New York: Dell.

TERM-PAPER TOPICS

1. What are current opinions within psychology and within society at large about the insanity plea? Do you think changes may be made in response to these opinions?

2. Chapter 18 describes several ways in which the legal system comes into contact with abnormality. What other ways may occur in the years to come?

3. In recent years, the rights of research subjects have been articulated, and legislation has been enacted to protect them. Describe this legislation. Describe its effect on psychological research. Has this been good or bad?

4. The federal government awards millions of dollars in research grants to psychologists. What political and ethical issues are raised by this relationship? Is there reason for alarm?

5. How frequently are individuals involuntarily committed to mental hospitals for political reasons? How can such cases be recognized?

EXERCISES

Exercise One—Beliefs about the Insanity Plea

Talk to a number of individuals of your acquaintance about the insanity plea. Ask them these questions:

1. What are the grounds for pleading insanity?
2. How are these grounds established?
3. How frequently is the insanity plea made?

4. With what success is the insanity plea made?
5. Is the insanity plea necessary?
6. Can a person be both guilty and insane?
7. What changes in the insanity plea may be made?
8. How often is it used?
9. How often is it successful?

Which beliefs are consistent with what is known about abnormality? Which are inconsistent? What is your attitude toward the insanity plea?

Bromberg, W. (1979). *The uses of psychiatry in the law: A clinical view of forensic psychiatry.* Westport, CT: Quorum Books.

Exercise Two—Commitment

The purpose of this exercise is to learn about commitment procedures in your community.

Arrange a panel discussion for your class in which a lawyer, judge, psychiatrist, and psychologist explain how individuals are involuntarily committed in your town. What safeguards are present? How frequently do commitments occur? Do you agree with local procedures?

Exercise Three—Persecution and Abnormality

In this exercise, you will learn about abuses of psychology by the state.

Arrange a classroom lecture by someone from Amnesty International. Ask this person to speak in particular about persecution in the guise of psychological treatment. What examples of such persecution are provided? What is the evidence that this persecution has occurred? In what countries is such persecution most likely? What can be done to prevent these abuses of psychology?

CHAPTER 19

A Consumer's Guide to Psychological Treatment

CHAPTER OVERVIEW

The final chapter of the textbook synthesizes much of the previous material by presenting a guide to choosing a form of psychotherapy. There are a number of factors common to all successful psychotherapy: client characteristics such as free choice, hope, and appropriate expectations, therapist characteristics such as warmth, empathy, and genuineness, and a good working relationship between the client and the therapist. There are things to be wary of in a therapist as well.

Methods of psychotherapy may be either global or specific. Prominent approaches to therapy are based on the various models of abnormality: biomedical, psychoanalytic, behavioral, cognitive, and existential. The bulk of the chapter describes which specific therapy seems best indicated for which specific disorder.

Community psychology attempts to prevent and contain disorders. As such, it is an important adjunct to traditional therapy, which is undertaken only after a problem has developed.

ESSENTIAL TERMS

Alcoholics Anonymous (AA)	group for treatment of alcoholism that stresses self-help, group support, and hope (p. 756)
aversion therapy	behavior therapy technique in which an undesired behavior is eliminated by pairing it with aversive consequences (p. 747)
behavior therapy	therapy based on the learning approach (p. 746)
biological therapy	specific therapy that attempts to resolve problems by physiological intervention; e.g., electroconvulsive shock (p. 745)
child-care	safe and healthy environment for preschool children whose parents work (p. 765)
clomipramine	drug treatment especially effective for obsessions and compulsions (see Chapter 9, "Essential Terms") (p. 754)

cognitive restructuring	specific therapy that attempts to illuminate irrational thoughts, to make clear their irrational basis, and thereby to change them (p. 747)
cognitive therapy	therapy developed by Aaron T. Beck which attempts to change thoughts and justifications of depressed or anxious patients (*see* Chapters 5 and 11, "Essential Terms") (p. 748)
common treatment factors	factors that determine the success of a therapy above and beyond the specific techniques and orientations of the therapist (p. 734)
community psychology	approach to psychological problems that attempts to prevent and contain them (p. 764)
containment service	community psychology program that attempts to limit the consequences of psychological crises (p. 766)
crises treatment	short-term psychotherapy for psychological crises in which the therapist is extremely active, helping the client focus on problems, providing support, and devising solutions (p. 768)
day hospital (or night hospital)	part-time hospital intended to serve as a transition from full-time hospitalization to discharge and as a treatment center for those who were never hospitalized (p. 771)
dereflection	existential therapy technique in which client's attention is turned from symptoms to what may be done for him- or herself and others in the absence of preoccupation with symptoms (p. 751)
dietary cycling	a cycle of weight loss and gain reflecting initiation and cessation of dieting (p. 759)
dream analysis	psychoanalytic technique in which the latent meaning of a dream's manifest content is interpreted to reveal unconscious conflicts (p. 749)
dynamic psychotherapy	therapies which assume that unconscious conflicts and impulses underlie psychopathology and insight is the goal of treatment (p. 750)
electroconvulsive shock therapy (ECT)	therapy for depression in which an electric current is passed through the brain of the patient (*see* Chapter 11, "Essential Terms") (p. 754)
empathy	characteristic of a successful therapist: the ability to understand experiences and feelings and to explain their meaning to the client during psychotherapy (p. 738)
existential therapy	global therapy based on existential psychology in which the client is encouraged to take responsibility for his or her problems (p. 751)
exposure and response prevention	behavioral technique used to treat compulsions; anxiety-producing situation while limiting possibility of avoidance results in extinction (*see* Chapter 9,1 "Essential Terms") (p. 754)

flooding

behavior therapy technique in which anxiety is extinguished by exposing the client to actual fear-producing situations (*see* Chapters 5 and 8, "Essential Terms") (p. 747)

free association

technique of psychoanalytic therapy in which the client relaxes and says whatever comes to mind (p. 749)

genuineness

characteristic of a successful therapist: the ability to avoid communicating in a phony or defensive manner (p. 738)

global therapy

therapy that attempts to resolve psychological problems by changing the underlying personality problems (cf. specific therapy) (p. 745)

halfway house

domicile with only paraprofessionals in residence, intended as a transition between hospital and community; community lodge (p. 771)

hot-line

twenty-four hour phone service for people who are undergoing deep distress (p. 767)

incompatible behavior

behavior therapy technique in which undesired behavior is eliminated by training the person to engage in behavior that makes undesired behavior difficult to perform; e.g., systematic desensitization (p. 753)

insight therapy

global therapy that encourages personal insight into sources of psychological problems (p. 745)

interpersonal therapy (IPT)

therapy used for treating depression; focuses on interpersonal difficulties (*see* Chapter 11, "Essential Terms") (p. 755)

job training and retraining

community psychology program for training the unemployed in skills necessary to find and keep jobs (p. 767)

lithium

drug used to treat bipolar depression and mania (*see* Chapter 11, "Essential Terms") (p. 755)

marriage and family counselor

therapist who treats relationship problems that arise within the family (p. 733)

methadone maintenance

biological therapy for heroin addiction in which methadone is substituted for heroin (*see* Chapter 14, "Essential Terms") (p. 758)

modeling

behavior therapy technique in which the client is exposed to desired behavior modeled by another person (*see* Chapter 8, "Essential Terms") (p. 747)

neuroleptic

a class of antipsychotic medication used in treatment of schizophrenia (*see* Chapter 12, "Essential Terms" (p. 760)

Operation Headstart

community psychology program for preschool children that intends to encourage development of cognitive and intellectual skills necessary for school (p. 767)

paradoxical intervention

existential therapy technique in which the client is encouraged to indulge and exaggerate symptoms (p. 751)

placebo effect	positive treatment outcome resulting from administration of placebo (*see* Chapter 6, "Essential Terms") (p. 737)
progressive relaxation	relaxation technique in which major muscle groups are alternately tightened and relaxed (*see* Chapter 8, "Essential Terms") (p. 753)
psychiatric attendant	paraprofessional who works exclusively in psychiatric hospitals; psychiatric aide (p. 732)
psychiatric nurse	nurse specializing in the care of hospitalized psychiatric patients (p. 730)
psychiatric social worker	social worker who has completed a two-year postgraduate program in individual and group social-work techniques, including extensive training in interviewing and treatment (p. 730)
psychiatrist	physician who has completed three-year residency in mental-health facility (p. 730)
psychoanalysis	global therapy based on psychoanalytic theory that attempts to make unconscious impulses conscious so that an acceptable means of satisfying them can be found (p. 749)
psychoanalyst	therapist, usually a psychiatrist, with training in psychoanalysis (p. 731)
psychological therapy	systematic series of interactions between a trained therapist who has been authorized by society to minister to psychological problems and one or more clients who are troubled, or troubling others, because of such problems; the goal of psychological therapy is to produce cognitive, emotional, and behavioral changes that will alleviate the problems (p. 734)
psychologist	individual with advanced graduate training in clinical, counseling, or school psychology who offers psychological assessment and therapeutic services (p. 730)
clinical psychologist	psychologist who works mainly with psychological difficulties
consulting psychologist	psychologist who works with psychological difficulties and vocational problems
school psychologist	psychologist who works with academic difficulties, mainly among children
rational-emotive therapy	therapy founded by Albert Ellis that attempts to change the irrational beliefs of an individual (*see* Chapter 5, "Essential Terms") (p. 748)
residential treatment center	approach to treatment of distressed individuals in the community or special residences, without hospitalization (p. 771)
resistance	point in therapy when client seems to be obstructing the therapeutic process by missing appointments, being late, being glib, etc.; may be seen as indicating progress in that

the client is struggling with a significant issue (*see* Chapter 4, "Essential Terms") (p. 741)

Role Induction Interview

brief interview prior to therapy in which expectations of clients about treatment are molded (p. 736)

self-help group

community of former patients who have banded together to help each other (p. 733)

skills therapist

therapist with special training in work-related, recreational, and/or artistic techniques (p. 733)

specific therapy

therapy that attempts to resolve psychological problems without changing underlying personality problems (cf. global therapy) (p. 745)

Synanon

self-help live-in community for treatment of narcotic addiction (p. 758)

systematic desensitization

behavior therapy technique in which stimuli that elicit fear are paired with relaxation or other pleasant experiences (*see* Chapters 5 and 8, "Essential Terms") (p. 747)

therapeutic alliance

relationship between client and therapist characterized by shared sense of goals of treatment and how they can best be achieved (p. 739)

TOPS (Take Off Pounds Sensibly)

group for the treatment of obesity that provides information and social support (p. 733)

transcendental meditation

relaxation technique in which thoughts are blocked through closing eyes and repeating a simple syllable or word (*see* Chapter 8, "Essential Terms") (p. 753)

transference

in psychoanalysis, transfer by clients of emotions, conflicts, and expectations from diverse sources on to their therapist (*see* Chapter 4, "Essential Terms") (p. 750)

warmth

characteristic of a successful therapist: the ability to communicate deep and genuine caring to the client (p. 738)

Weight Watchers

group for the treatment of obesity; it provides information and social support (p. 756)

YAVIS

acronym sometimes used to describe ideal psychoanalytic client (young, attractive, verbal, intelligent, successful))p. 764)

CENTRAL CONCEPTUAL ISSUES

Theory and practice.   Most areas of science have as one goal the elucidation of a comprehensive theory. This is no less true for psychology. The textbook has described many different theories that have been developed to explain the same behaviors. From these differing perspectives several therapies for abnormal behavior have been derived, and treatments from any one therapy have been found to be effective for some problems, but not for others. No single theoretical orientation has cornered the market on effective treatments for all problematic behaviors.

For the practicing therapist, whose stated goal is to relieve suffering, this can be a blessing if the therapist feels free to borrow treatments from many schools of thought—choosing the approaches that most suit a client's particular situation. On the other hand, a therapist who is bound by the long Western scientific tradition of loyalty to singular, all-encompassing theories may apply his orientation with particular expertise and insight or he may overlook potentially helpful alternative approaches. While it may be valuable for scientists to pursue the illusive goal for an all-encompassing theory, it may be equally important for the practicing therapist to think about her client's problems not as instances of a single theory, but instead to ask which theories and/or therapies would be most useful in addressing this person's needs.

Client-therapist "fit."   The outcome of therapy—even when proven techniques are appropriately applied—is heavily influenced by the "fit" between client and therapist. The therapeutic relationship goes beyond whether the two like each other or get along, although that is important. To achieve a successful outcome, the client and therapist need to agree on what outcome is being sought, what is involved in getting there, and the client must understand and agree to his own role in the process. Goals may range from changing highly specific symptomatic behaviors to very global aspects of personality. The duties of the client may be as simple and obvious as taking a drug once a day or as subtle or challenging as deep introspection or speaking freely about very intimate or frightening matters. Without both actors in the therapeutic alliance carrying out their parts, the likelihood of a successful therapy is greatly diminished.

SAMPLE EXAM

1. What percent of Americans will see a psychotherapist at some point in their lives?
   a. 1
   b. 10
   c. 20
   d. 33
   e. 50

2. Which one of the following has a Ph.D. degree?
   a. psychologist
   b. psychiatrist
   c. psychiatric social worker
   d. psychiatric nurse
   e. psychoanalyst

3. Which one of the following has medical training?
   a. psychologist
   b. psychiatrist
   c. psychiatric social worker

   d. psychiatric nurse
   e. psychoanalyst

4. Which one of the following works almost exclusively in a hospital?
   a. psychologist
   b. psychiatrist
   c. psychiatric social worker
   d. psychiatric nurse
   e. psychoanalyst

5. Common treatment factors include all of the following but
   a. choice by the client.
   b. training of the therapist.
   c. expectations of the client.
   d. personal qualities of the therapist.
   e. placebo effects.

6. The purpose of the Role Induction Interview is to

a. mold client expectations about treatment.
b. make a diagnosis.
c. ascertain a prognosis.
d. train the therapist.
e. all of the above.

7. Which of the following is(are) not characteristics of placebo effects?
a. probably shams
b. possibly mediated by endorphins
c. often powerful
d. well understood
e. None of the above are characteristics.

8. All of the following are characteristics of the successful therapist except
a. empathy.
b. warmth.
c. genuineness.
d. experience.
e. All of the above are necessary characteristics.

9. Therapeutic alliance refers to shared
a. goals.
b. personality characteristics.
c. problems.
d. rationals.
e. beliefs.

10. The traditional paradigm of psychology includes values and a world view that are all of the following except
a. male.
b. upper class.
c. white.
d. American.
e. all of the above.

11. The most effective therapies are those associated with the
a. biomedical model.
b. psychodynamic model.
c. behavioral model.
d. cognitive model.
e. none of the above.

12. All of the following are ways to assess the effectiveness of psychotherapy except
a. termination of treatment.
b. personal satisfaction.
c. personality change.
d. target behavior change.
e. All are ways to assess effectiveness.

13. It is important to shop around when looking for a therapist. All of the following should be considered when making your decision except
a. do the fees seem excessive?
b. are you comfortable with her/him?
c. is there any indication of inappropriate intimacy?
d. does he/she answer your medication questions frankly and openly?
e. All of the above should be considered.

14. Insight therapies are mainly associated with the
a. biomedical model.
b. psychodynamic model.
c. behavioral model.
d. cognitive model.
e. existential model.

15. All of these are behavioral therapies except
a. systematic desensitization.
b. flooding.
c. cognitive restructuring.
d. modeling.
e. aversion therapy.

16. Which one of the following is most similar to cognitive therapy?
a. rational-emotive therapy
b. Rolfing
c. psychoanalysis
d. Gestalt therapy
e. existential therapy

17. If you had a problem with fear, you would choose a therapy associated with the
a. biomedical model.
b. psychodynamic model.
c. behavioral model.
d. cognitive model.
e. none of the above.

18. If you had a problem with anxiety, you would choose a therapy associated with the
a. biomedical model.
b. psychodynamic model.
c. behavioral model.
d. cognitive model.
e. none of the above.

19. If you had a problem with obsessions, you would choose a therapy based on the
a. biomedical model.
b. psychodynamic model.

    c. behavioral model.
    d. cognitive model.
    e. none of the above.

20. If you had a problem with compulsions, you would choose a therapy based on the
    a. biomedical model.
    b. psychodynamic model.
    c. behavioral model.
    d. cognitive model.
    e. none of the above.

21. If you had a problem with depression, you would choose a therapy derived from the
    a. biomedical model.
    b. psychodynamic model.
    c. behavioral model.
    d. cognitive model.
    e. any of the above.

22. If you had a problem with bipolar depression, you would choose a therapist who advocated the
    a. biomedical model.
    b. psychodynamic model.
    c. behavioral model.
    d. cognitive model.
    e. none of the above.

23. Which model gives rise to a therapy for sexual dysfunction that is as successful as direct sexual therapy as used by Masters and Johnson?
    a. biomedical model
    b. psychodynamic model
    c. behavioral model
    d. cognitive model
    e. none of the above

24. For which of these problems is the least successful treatment available?
    a. phobia
    b. addiction
    c. depression
    d. sexual dysfunction
    e. schizophrenia

25. The problem with treating smoking is
    a. initial stopping.
    b. relapse.
    c. unrealistic expectations.
    d. a and b
    e. none of the above

26. About _____ of smokers who quit start again within the following year
    a. 10%
    b. 25%
    c. 50%
    d. 75%
    e. 90%

27. Treatment of heroin addiction with methadone maintenance is an example of the
    a. biomedical model.
    b. psychodynamic model.
    c. behavioral model.
    d. cognitive model.
    e. none of the above.

28. Synanon is to AA as what is to alcohol?
    a. narcotics
    b. obesity
    c. agoraphobia
    d. schizophrenia
    e. sexual dysfunction

29. The problem with obesity is
    a. losing weight.
    b. maintaining weight loss.
    c. cognitive distortions.
    d. both *a* and *b*.
    e. none of the above.

30. Anorexia appears best treated with techniques derived from the
    a. biomedical model.
    b. psychodynamic model.
    c. behavioral model.
    d. cognitive model.
    e. none of the above.

31. Bulimia appears best treated with techniques derived from the
    a. biomedical model.
    b. psychodynamic model.
    c. behavioral model.
    d. cognitive model.
    e. none of the above.

32. The quickest treatments for schizophrenia are associated with the
    a. biomedical model.
    b. psychodynamic model.
    c. behavioral model.
    d. cognitive model.
    e. none of the above.

33. The text concludes that _____ treatment is needed for schizophrenia.
    a. biological
    b. psychosocial
    c. existential

d. both a and b
e. none of the above

34. Self-exploration is best accomplished through therapy based on the
   a. psychodynamic model.
   b. behavioral model.
   c. cognitive model.
   d. existential model.
   e. none of the above.

35. Community psychology is aimed at all of the following except
   a. influencing a larger proportion of the population.
   b. prevention through intervention.
   c. containment of crises.
   d. development of alternative treatments.
   e. existential issues.

36. All of the following are examples of community psychology except
   a. child-care.
   b. Operation Headstart.
   c. Watergate.
   d. job retraining.
   e. self-help groups.

37. Hot-lines are most similar to
   a. crisis treatment.
   b. psychoanalysis.
   c. logotherapy.
   d. Gestalt therapy.
   e. Operation Headstart.

38. The first hot-line was established for
   a. child abuse.
   b. drug overdose.
   c. spouse abuse.
   d. suicide.
   e. sexual dysfunction.

39. All of these are examples of containment except
   a. hot-lines.
   b. crisis treatment.
   c. Operation Headstart.

d. shelters for battered women.
e. None of the above are examples.

40. Which one of the following does not belong?
   a. ostracism
   b. day hospital
   c. night hospital
   d. halfway house
   e. shelter

41. Which one of the following does not belong?
   a. AA
   b. CR group
   c. N.Y. Yankees
   d. TOPS
   e. SYNANON

Answer Key for Sample Exam

1. c	(p. 729)	22. a	(p. 755)
2. a	(p. 730)	23. e	(p. 755)
3. b, e	(p. 730)	24. b	(p. 756)
4. d	(p. 730)	25. b	(p. 757)
5. b	(p. 734, 737)	26. d	(p. 757)
6. a	(p. 736)	27. a	(p. 758)
7. a, d	(p. 737)	28. a	(p. 758)
8. d	(p. 737)	29. b	(p. 759)
9. a	(p. 739)	30. c, d	(p. 760)
10. b	(p. 739)	31. c, d	(p. 759)
11. e	(p. 744)	32. a	(p. 760)
12. a	(p. 742)	33. d	(p. 761)
13. e	(p. 740)	34. a, d	(p. 763)
14. b, e	(p. 745)	35. e	(p. 763)
15. c	(p. 747)	36. c	(p. 765)
16. a	(p. 748)	37. a	(p. 767)
17. c	(p. 747)	38. d	(p. 767)
18. c, d	(p. 747)	39. c	(p. 766)
19. a, c	(p. 754)	40. a	(p. 771)
20. a, c	(p. 754)	41. c	(p. 772)
21. e	(p. 754)		

SELF-TEST

1. The goal of psychological therapy is to produce _____, _____, and _____ changes that will alleviate psychological problems.

2. Clinical psychologists usually have a _____ degree, while psychiatrists have a _____ degree.

3. Successful psychotherapy depends on the establishment of a good _____.

4. Common treatment factors include the _____ of the client, his or her and _____, the _____ of the therapist, and the _____ between the client and the therapist.

5. To shape client expectations about psychotherapy, some therapists conduct a _____.

6. Positive treatment outcomes resulting from inert interventions are _____.

7. Good therapists, regardless of orientation, tend to have personal qualities of _____, _____, and _____.

8. Therapist _____ is not clearly related to effectiveness.

9. Therapists should be avoided who seem _____, _____, and _____.

10. Therapists should freely _____ and _____.

11. Among the criteria with which to assess successful psychotherapy are _____, _____, and _____.

12. At the present time, the federal government _____ regulate psychotherapies.

13. _____ therapies do not attempt to alter personality, while _____ therapies do attempt to do so, usually through _____.

14. The two classes of specific therapies are _____ therapies and _____ therapies.

15. Drugs and electroconvulsive shock are examples of _____ therapies.

16. Systematic desensitization, flooding, and modeling are _____ techniques.

17. Rational-emotive therapy is an example of _____ therapy and is similar to the therapy for depression developed by _____.

18. Global therapies are mainly those based on the _____ model or the _____ model.

19. Free association is a technique of _____.

20. Paradoxical intention and dereflection are used in _____ therapy.

21. For fears and phobias, the treatment of choice is based on the _____ model.

22. For compulsions, the exposure and response prevention treatment is based on the _____ model.

23. The treatment of choice for bipolar depression is _____; for unipolar depression, there are _____ successful treatments.

24. For sexual dysfunctions, one would probably seek out _____.

25. Treatment of the addictions seems to require a _____ approach.

26. The quickest treatment for schizophrenia is _____, but long-term treatment may entail _____ as well.

27. Global therapies are best for achieving the goals of _____ and changing the _____.

28. Community psychology attempts to _____ and _____ psychological problems. Child-care and job training are examples of _____, while "hot-lines" and crisis treatment are examples of _____.

29. Alternatives to the traditional mental hospital have recently been developed and include _____ hospitals, _____ houses, _____ treatment centers, and _____ groups.

Answer Key for Self-Test

1. cognitive; emotional; behavioral
2. Ph.D.; M.D.
3. therapeutic alliance
4. free choice; hopes; expectations; personal qualities; match
5. Role Induction Interview
6. placebo effects
7. empathy; warmth; genuineness
8. experience
9. obnoxious; sexually exploitative; expensive
10. answer questions; set treatment goals
11. personal satisfaction; personality change; impact of treatment on target behaviors
12. does not
13. Specific; global; insight
14. biological; psychological
15. biological
16. behavioral
17. cognitive; Beck
18. psychodynamic; existential
19. psychoanalysis
20. existential
21. behavioral
22. behavioral
23. lithium; several
24. direct sexual therapy
25. broad-spectrum
26. neuroleptics; milieu therapy
27. self-exploration; self
28. prevent; contain; prevention; containment
29. day (night); halfway; residential; self-help

MATCHING ITEMS

_____   1.   psychologist

_____   2.   psychiatrist

A.   cooperative spirit, shared treatment goals

B.   hot-line

_____   3.   psychoanalyst

_____   4.   therapeutic alliance

_____   5.   containment service

_____   6.   placebo effect

_____   7.   specific therapies

_____   8.   global therapies

_____   9.   Role Induction Interview

_____   10.   rehabilitation

C.   molding expectations about therapy

D.   positive expectations about therapeutic effects

E.   self-help groups

F.   undergone psychoanalysis

G.   M. D.

H.   Ph. D.

I.   personality-pattern focused

J.   problem-focused

Answer Key for Matching Items

1. H   6. D
2. G   7. J
3. F   8. I
4. A   9. C
5. B   10. E

SHORT-ANSWER QUESTIONS

1. List the distinguishing characteristics of psychologists, psychiatrists, psychiatric social workers, psychiatric nurses, psychoanalysts, psychiatric attendants/aides, skills therapists, and marriage and family counselors.

2. Describe the four general treatment factors, and their components, which contribute to the effectiveness of the therapeutic relationship.

3. List the factors that might make you wary of entering therapy with a particular therapist.

4. List the major categories of psychological dysfunction and which treatments are generally used for each.

5. What are the goals of community psychology? What are the ways in which they are realized in practice?

TYING IT TOGETHER

The textbook has described the field of psychopathology. How is abnormality defined (Chapter 1)? What has been its history (Chapter 2)? How is it explained (Chapters 3–5)? How is it investigated (Chapter 6) and assessed (Chapter 7)? What are the major types of abnormality (Chapters 8–17)? And what is the legal and political context of abnormality (Chapter 18)?

It is appropriate that the textbook ends with a discussion of how abnormality is treated. Abnormal psychology has always been concerned with how best to alleviate the suffering of individuals who have psychological problems, and the creation of effective treatment is the bottom line of the field. To this end, explanation, research, and diagnosis are undertaken. It is necessary and often useful to distinguish among types of abnormality. None of these is a pure type; rather, each is defined by a family resemblance. Abnormality involves disorders are a variety of levels—biological, emotional, behavioral, and cognitive—and any given therapy is directed at the level thought to be disordered. This last chapter presents state-of-the-art knowledge about which therapy is best for which problem. It is based on the information presented in the rest of the textbook.

FURTHER READINGS

Beitman, B. D. (1987). *The structure of individual psychotherapy.* New York: Guilford Press.

Bloch, S. (1982). *What is psychotherapy?* New York: Oxford University Press.

Carotenuto, A. (1992). *The difficult art: A critical discourse on psychotherapy.* Wilmette, IL: Chiron.

Dowling, C. (1993). *You mean I don't have to feel this way? New help for depression, anxiety, and addiction.* New York: Bantam Books.

Frank, J. D. (1974). *Persuasion and healing: A comparative study of psychotherapy.* Rev. ed. New York: Schocken.

Garfield, S. L. (1981). Psychotherapy: A 40-year appraisal. *American Psychologist, 36,* 174–183.

Garfield, S. L., & Bergin, A. E. (1986). *Handbook of psychotherapy and behavior change.* 3rd ed. New York: Wiley.

London, P. (1986). *The modes and morals of psychotherapy.* New York: Hemisphere.

Wedding, D., & Corsini, R. J. (Eds.) (1989). *Case studies in psychotherapy.* Itasca, IL: F. E. Peacock.

Weiner, I. B. (1975). *Principles of psychotherapy.* New York: Wiley.

Yalom, I. D. (1985). *The theory and practice of group psychotherapy.* New York: Basic Books.

TERM-PAPER TOPICS

1. Only recently have well-managed investigations of therapy effectiveness been conducted. What difficulties had to be solved before these investigations could be done? What difficulties remain?

2. Compare and contrast the specific training of the various mental-health professionals. What conclusions do you draw on the basis of your results about how best to choose a psychotherapist?

3. In recent years, many mental patients have been discharged into the community. What effect has this had on the former patients? What effect has this had on the community?

EXERCISES

Exercise One—Repackaging Chapter 19

The purpose of this exercise is to organize the treatment recommendations made in Chapter 19 in a different format.

Recast the text material from Chapter 19 in the form of a *Consumer Reports* article. Use tables and ratings similar to those in *Consumer Reports.* Is this a better way to present these ideas, or not?

Exercise Two—Treatment Referrals

In this exercise, you will practice making therapy referrals for different types of psychological problems.

Based on what you have learned, make an educated suggestion about the form of therapy indicated for the following individuals:

1. a six-year old girl has trouble learning how to read

2. a middle-aged man drinks a case of beer every evening
3. your mother is deathly afraid of German shepherds
4. a teenage girl has stopped eating anything except tuna fish
5. a thirty-year-old man barricades himself at home and claims that the CIA is persecuting him
6. a college student attempts suicide
7. your father is found wandering the streets, not knowing who he is
8. your elderly neighbor suddenly loses his ability to speak
9. your sister, who is twenty years old, washes her hands 250 times per day
10. your spouse reports no satisfaction from sexual intercourse

Compare your referral suggestions to those of your classmates.

Exercise Three—Different Psychotherapies

The purpose of this exercise is to compare and contrast psychotherapy as practiced by different professionals.

Arrange a panel discussion for your class by several different mental-health practitioners: clinical psychologist, counseling psychologist, psychiatrist, psychiatric social workers, and so on. Ask them to address what is common to their therapy approaches and what is different. What conclusions about therapy do your reach?